PENGUIN BOOKS

HAUNTED PLACES: THE NATIONAL DIRECTORY

Dennis William Hauck is an internationally known authority on paranormal phenomena. He is a member of the American Society for Psychical Research, California Coordinator for the Ghost Research Society, and Science Advisor to the Mutual UFO Network. The author of *The International Directory of Haunted Places* and *The Emerald Tablet: Alchemy for Personal Transformation*, he has served as contributing editor for a dozen periodicals and has consulted on several documentary films.

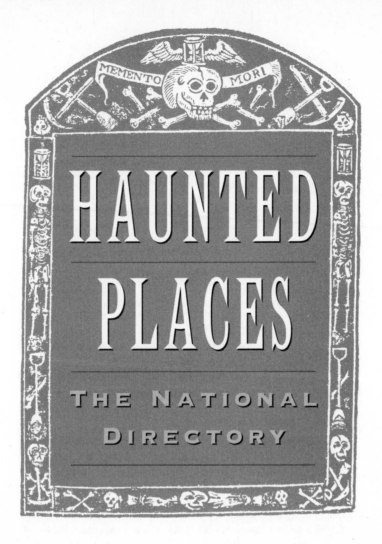

HAUNTED PLACES

THE NATIONAL DIRECTORY

Ghostly Abodes, Sacred Sites, UFO Landings,
and Other Supernatural Locations

DENNIS WILLIAM HAUCK

PENGUIN BOOKS

PENGUIN BOOKS
Published by the Penguin Group
Penguin Group (USA) Inc., 375 Hudson Street, New York, New York 10014, U.S.A.
Penguin Books Ltd, 80 Strand, London WC2R 0RL, England
Penguin Books Australia Ltd, 250 Camberwell Road, Camberwell, Victoria 3124, Australia
Penguin Books Canada Ltd, 10 Alcorn Avenue, Toronto, Ontario, Canada M4V 3B2
Penguin Books India (P) Ltd, 11 Community Centre, Panchsheel Park, New Delhi – 110 017, India
Penguin Books (N.Z.) Ltd, Cnr Rosedale and Airborne Roads, Albany, Auckland, New Zealand
Penguin Books (South Africa) (Pty) Ltd, 24 Sturdee Avenue,
Rosebank, Johannesburg 2196, South Africa

Penguin Books Ltd, Registered Offices: 80 Strand, London WC2R 0RL, England

First published in the United States of America as
The National Directory of Haunted Places by Athanor Press 1994
Updated and revised edition published as
Haunted Places: The National Directory in Penguin Books 1996
This second updated and revised edition published 2002

7   9   10   8

Copyright © Dennis William Hauck, 1994, 1996, 2002
All rights reserved

LIBRARY OF CONGRESS CATALOGING IN PUBLICATION DATA
Hauck, Dennis William.
Haunted places : the national directory : ghostly abodes, sacred sites, UFO landings,
and other supernatural locations / Dennis William Hauck.—2nd updated and rev. ed.
p.   cm
Includes bibliographical references and index.
ISBN 0 14 20.0234 8 (pbk.)
1. Haunted places—United States—Guidebooks.   2. Ghosts—
United States.   I. Title.
BF1472.U6 H378 2002
133.1'0973—dc21   2002068433

Printed in the United States of America
Set in Century Old Style
Designed by Jessica Shatan

CONTENTS

INTRODUCTION

This updated and revised edition of *Haunted Places: The National Directory* offers the most authoritative and documented study of supernatural phenomena in the United States. This directory has become an essential sourcebook for researchers, librarians, and journalists throughout the country. The general public has embraced it as a handy travel guide and entertaining collection of stories of true hauntings.

This edition of *Haunted Places* features updated investigations, expanded address information, bibliographic references to each case, an exhaustive index, and for the first time, Internet sources for further information. Every effort will be made to post the most recent information about these locations at the author's Web site (*www.Haunted-Places.com*). If you find any corrections or new information about these or other unlisted sites, please email *info@haunted-places.com* or write the author (Dennis William Hauck, P.O. Box 22201, Sacramento, CA 95822).

Over the last decade, the *Haunted Places* directories have spawned serious paranormal research in all fifty states, as well as inaugurating what has been dubbed the "haunted travel industry." The fact that this book has become so popular with travelers necessitates repeating the basic precautions stated in earlier editions. Please keep these points in mind when visiting any of the locations described in this book:

• Locations that welcome visitors are noted in the text. Secure the permission of owners or tenants of private residences before attempting to visit their property. Never trespass on private property, whether signs are posted or not. Please do not bother people unnecessarily and leave those alone who do not wish to be disturbed.

• Always confirm and update directions locally. Every effort has been made to ensure the accuracy of the information presented in this directory; however, the author assumes no responsibility for errors, misprints, or changes. Check business hours and locations of public places such as museums, libraries, and historical sites before visiting them.

• Some areas listed in this directory are in hazardous or isolated locations. Most desert locations should be avoided in the summer months. Some trails are intended for experienced hikers only. Deserted mines and caves are full of hidden dangers. A few city locations are in high crime areas. Be careful and always check locally before visiting any of the sites.

• Native Americans are understandably protective of their sacred sites located on public lands. Never desecrate holy ground by taking unauthorized souvenirs or damaging property. Remember that a disrespectful attitude at a site sacred to anyone is an act of vandalism.

I wish to thank my associate researcher Matt Muller for his tireless work in listing, updating, and confirming the information provided here. Bruce Schaffenberger, the editor for the first printing of this book, also provided invaluable assistance in researching the entries. I would also like to extend my heartfelt thanks to the following independent investigators: Richard Foster, Troy Taylor, Richard Senate, Dale Kaczmarek, L. J. Jones, Antonio Garcez, Lisa Farwell, Robert and Anne Wlodarski, Nancy Roberts, Mark Marimen, Bruce Carson, John Lamb, Judy Farncombe, Ron Beach, Heath Torstveit, Lee Holloway, Bernyce Barlow, George Eberhart, Gordon Ting, and William Uchaman.

HAUNTED PLACES

ALABAMA

AUBURN

FIRST PRESBYTERIAN CHURCH The oldest public building in Auburn is haunted by the ghost of a Confederate soldier. Built in 1851 by a Presbyterian congregation, this chapel was used as a hospital during the Civil War. In 1864, a British volunteer fighting for the South was struck in the leg by cannon shrapnel, and by the time he received aid his leg had already turned gangrenous. He bled to death during an operation to remove the leg. The Englishman, Sydney Grimlett, was buried in a graveyard not far from the chapel. Everything was quiet until a theater group, the Auburn Players, took over the old chapel in the 1960s. Some say the emotional energy expended on the premises brought back Grimlett's ghost. In any case, his restless phantom was seen by several members of the company who then used a Ouija board to discover his identity. Sydney made his presence known by moving props, whistling in the attic, tapping his one foot nervously, and producing startling, floating lights.

(Auburn is fifty miles northeast of Montgomery on I-85. Grimlett's grave is in the Pine Hill Cemetery. The building is once again a place of worship. It is on the corner of S. College and E. Thach streets at 143 E. Thach Ave., Auburn, AL 36830. Phone: 334-887-5571.) **224**

BLADON SPRINGS

BLADON SPRINGS CEMETERY The ghost of Captain Norman Staples has been reported hovering over the graves of his four children: James Alfred, Berth Jaddetta, Mable Claire, and an unnamed baby. His ghost is said to have fled his burning stern-wheeler (see *James T. Staples* Riverboat, below) and taken refuge in the cemetery here. Staples's apparition seems to be protecting the grave although the captain is sometimes seen with his hands pressed against his head, as if he is suffering from great anguish or regret.

(Bladon Springs is in Choctaw County in southwestern Alabama. Take County Road 6 south from I-84. The cemetery is located on County Road 6. Follow Highway 84 east from the town of Bladon Springs for five miles. About a half mile after the bridge, turn right onto County Road 6 and follow it for three miles.) **15**

JAMES T. STAPLES **RIVERBOAT** Some believe that this proud riverboat was destroyed by the ghost of its captain. The stern-wheeler's maiden voyage was in 1908. The most elegant vessel on Alabama's rivers, it was named after the father of the ship's designer and first captain. His son Norman, captain and owner of the ship, had a hard time making ends meet because of unfair practices by a large steamboat company that wanted to operate all the boats on the river. Finally, in December 1912, creditors seized his beloved ship and turned it over to his competition. On January 2, 1913,

Captain Staples held a shotgun against his chest and pulled the trigger. Three days after he was buried, crew members began seeing the shadowy figure of their dead captain in the hold of the ship. The entire engine room crew quit and had to be replaced with workers who had never heard of the ghost. Next, all the rats that lived on the ship scurried ashore, a frightening premonition of things to come. Staples's ghost was seen roaming around the boilers belowdecks. Finally, on January 13, 1913, the ship docked at Powe's Landing to take on wood. At the exact hour that Captain Staples took his own life, the boiler on the *James T. Staples* exploded, killing her new captain and twenty-five others. The rest of the crew and passengers, many badly injured, were able to flee the blazing ship before it broke its moorings and drifted downstream. It finally sank near the shore of the cemetery where Captain Norman Staples had been buried. See Bladon Springs Cemetery, above.

(Bladon Springs is near the river at the Coffeeville Lock. Powe's Landing is about 120 miles from Mobile on the Tombigee River.) **15, 224**

BRIDGEPORT

RUSSELL CAVE NATIONAL PARK Russell Cave is a sacred burial site that traces ten thousand years of human history. There is evidence of prehistoric burial customs which progressed from throwing bodies off cliffs, to burial mounds, to elaborate entombment. People meditating in the cave have reported an overwhelming appreciation for human struggle and evolution.

(Bridgeport is on U.S. Highway 72. The cave is eight miles west of Bridgeport on the east side of Montague Mountain. Take County Road 91 west to County Road 75 and follow the signs to Russell Cave. 3729 County Road, Bridgeport, AL 35740. Phone: 256-495-2672. www. nps.gov/ruca) **99**

CAHABA HEIGHTS

PEGUES'S GHOST A strange ball of light, which became known as Pegues's Ghost, was seen for many years in a grove of cedars behind the home of Colonel C. C. Pegues, who lived in the house from 1830 to 1860. His house had been used as a jail from 1820 to 1826, and some suggest that the phenomenon may be connected with the spirits of those who were incarcerated there. The first sighting was in 1862, when a large, brilliant ball of light was seen hovering a few feet off the

ground. The ball chased and teased visitors to the area for years, even after the Pegues' house was torn down.

(Cahaba is a suburb of Birmingham in Jefferson County. Take the Overton Road exit off Highway 280. A clump of yellow jonquils marks the spot where the ball of light was first seen. The Pegues home fronted Pine St. and the estate covered the entire block between Pine and Chestnut streets.) **225**

CARROLLTON

PICKENS COUNTY COURTHOUSE No one knew for sure who set the fire that burned down the Carrollton Courthouse on November 16, 1876. But everyone blamed Henry Wells, a rowdy black man who lived outside of town. The sheriff arrested him and held him in the attic of a building that was to become the new courthouse. One afternoon in February 1878, a lynch mob gathered in front of the new courthouse and demanded that Wells be turned over to them. As a violent thunderstorm approached the town, Wells peered out at the crowds through the garret window at the top of the building. Suddenly, a lightning bolt struck the roof, killing Wells. The flash of brilliant light etched his defiant expression into the windowpane, and no amount of scrubbing or solvents in the decades since has been able to erase it. On those days when thunderstorms roll through Pickens County, it is said that the ghost of Henry Wells stares out from the garret window again.

(Carrollton is thirty miles west of Tuscaloosa in Pickens County, at the intersection of highways 17 and 86. The face of Henry Wells can still be seen in the lower right hand pane in the garret window of the Pickens County Courthouse, 11 Courthouse SQ., Carrollton, AL 35447. www.pickens.net/~courthouse) **121, 175, 187, 225**

CLAIBORNE

McCONNICO CEMETERY The phantoms of twelve Union horsemen have been seen riding near this old graveyard. Captain and Mrs. Charles Locklin witnessed the ghostly parade in the autumn of 1865. The Locklins were in their carriage early one morning when two columns of six soldiers on gray horses passed by on each side of them. Each member of the eerie troop wore white gloves, with his hands crossed on the pommel of his saddle, and every one wore a white bandage wrapped tightly around his head. The two respected citizens were certain they had seen victims of Confederate soldier Lafayette Seigler, who ambushed Northern patrols, killed them, and then cut off their ears. Seigler's collection of Yankee ears was said to be quite impressive.

(Claiborne is in Monroe County, off I-84 on the banks of the Alabama River. The first encounter occurred on Mount Pleasant Rd. near McConnico Cemetery and sporadic sightings were reported over the next hundred years.) **223**

DECATUR

DECATUR HIGH SCHOOL White moving apparitions and the unexplainable sounds of footsteps coming from deserted corridors have been reported by students and teachers at this modern high school. No one has ever identified the source of the paranormal activity.

(Decatur is across the Tennessee River from Huntsville in Morgan County, at the junction of I-65 and U.S. Highway 72. Decatur High School, 1011 Prospect Dr. SE, Decatur, AL 35601. Phone: 205-552-3011. www.pte.dcs.edu/schools/hs/dhspage.html) **101**

HIGHWAY 11 The ghost of a young man flagging down a ride is invariably struck by drivers trying to avoid him. Lonnie Stephens was falsely accused of murdering his girlfriend in September 1934, and it was not until many years later that the real killer confessed. But it was too late for Lonnie. The innocent man managed to escape from a chain gang and was attempting to hitch a ride when he was struck and killed by a car. Lonnie's ghost is still seen standing in the middle of the road pleading for someone to stop, his arms outstretched in an imploring gesture.

(Lonnie's ghost is seen on the northbound lanes of Highway 11, an exit off Highway 565 between Decatur and Hunstville.) **166**

DEMOPOLIS

ELIZA BATTLE The ghostly outline of the *Eliza Battle* can still be seen on the Tombigee River. The palatial steamboat caught fire and sank in February 1858. The fire burned through the tiller rope and the ship drifted out of control down the river as dozens of helpless passengers jumped into the icy water. As many as fifty people died, and over a hundred were injured. Today, fishermen consider sighting the ghost ship to be an omen of impending death on the river.

(The river runs from Demopolis to Mobile. The phantom ship is most often seen in the late winter months, when the Tombigee overflows its banks. The paddlewheeler has been spotted where it sank near Naheola, thirty miles south of Demopolis, and also at Nanafalia, Tuscahoma, and Yellow Bluff.) **225**

GAINESWOOD The twelve gigantic Doric columns in front of this mansion present an imposing sight. The neoclassic showplace was built in 1842 by General Nathan Whitfield, but a restless ghost haunts the magnificent estate today. She is Evelyn Carter, sister of Whitfield's second wife. Evelyn came to live at the great house and died there of an undetermined disease. Because she died in the middle of winter, her body was stored in a sealed pine box under the cellar stairs, until the ground thawed in the following spring. The unseemly internment apparently upset Evelyn's spirit, for she began haunting the house soon after her remains were placed under the stairs. Even after she was finally buried, her soft footsteps could be heard in the hallways, and a melodious voice echoed her favorite songs from down in the cellar. Some people claim to sense her presence even today.

(Demopolis is in Sumter County at the junction of U.S. Highways 43 and 80. Gaineswood is a historic residence just outside town. www.demopolis.com/gaineswood/) **225**

EVERGREEN

INTERSTATE 65 A section of this modern thruway is haunted. Engineers built the highway over sacred Creek Indian burial grounds. The hills around Evergreen remain the Creeks' spiritual home, and many believe that their ghosts haunt the white man's highway that runs through the middle of it. The Creeks loved the land so much that they said good-bye to every tree and hill when they were forced to leave the area in the 1830s. Of fifteen thousand Creeks marched to a reservation in Oklahoma, over 3,500 died along the way. Between 1984 and 1990, there were 519 accidents, 208 injuries, and twenty-three deaths on this forty-mile stretch of highway. The road is even, straight, and well maintained, but the accident rate is well above average.

(The Haunted Highway is a forty-mile stretch of I-65 that runs between the towns of Evergreen in Conecuh County and Greenville in Butler County, in south central Alabama.) **15**

FURMAN

OLD PUREFOY HOUSE A buried well in the back-yard here is said to be haunted by the spirit of a black man who died digging it. In the early 1800s, Dr. John H. Purefoy was having a new well dug when the wooden rigging collapsed and buried a worker under tons of sandy soil. Although rescuers could hear the man screaming for help, they were unable to save him, and his body was never recovered. Today, grass will not grow over the sunken depression where the well collapsed, and people see the form of a man sitting hunched over on top of the well. His sobbing cries for help still fill the night air.

(Furman is in eastern Wilcox County in south central Alabama. Old Purefoy House is located at the junction of Highway 28 and County Road 63.) **225**

HUNTSVILLES

ATHENS STATE COLLEGE The most famous ghost of Athens State College is a young woman with golden hair who appears in a third-floor window of McCandless Hall. The phantom is always seen wearing a formal white gown, and for many years people assumed she was Abigail Lylia Burns, an operatic soprano who allegedly died in the building in 1914. Sightings continued for decades. Many expected her ghost to appear on stage at a memorial concert staged here by the Huntsville Opera Theater on May 12, 1987. Hundreds of people showed up to witness her phantom, but only three sensed anything unusual. A subsequent investigation proved that Miss Burns had never visited the area in the years from 1908 to 1922, so the identity of the ghost remains a mystery. Another ghost here whose identity is well established is Madam Childs. She was a stern proctor at one of the women's dormitories, and she still haunts this quiet campus.

(Athens State College is in Limestone County, twenty miles west of Huntsville off U.S. Highway 72. Athens State College, 300 N. Beaty St., Athens, AL 35611. Phone: 256-233-3218. www.athens.edu) **101, 148, 224**

CEDARHURST MANSION This estate was established by Stephen Ewing in 1823. The two-story house, with its fifteen-inch-thick brick walls, has survived a number of new owners and a variety of challenges over the years. During a fierce thunderstorm in the 1950s, the ghost of a tall girl with long dark hair appeared to a visitor sleeping in an upstairs bedroom. Before she disappeared he heard her say, "Help me! The terrible wind has blown my tombstone over." Thinking he had awakened from a dream, he turned over and went back to sleep. The next morning, he asked his guests if there was a graveyard on the property. He was directed to a small fenced-in plot, where he found the freshly toppled tombstone of Sally Carter, the 16-year-old sister of Mrs. Ewing. She had died in 1837.

(Huntsville is in north central Alabama, at the junction of I-65 and U.S. Highway 72. The Cedarhurst property was purchased by developers and transformed into town houses in the 1980s. The graves in the cemetery were unceremoniously removed to undisclosed locations. The mansion now serves as the Cedarhurst Club, a clubhouse for town house residents located at 2809 Whitesburg Dr., Huntsville, AL 35801.) **101, 121, 168**

KINSTON

HARRISON CEMETERY The ghost of an elderly square dancer, Grancer Harrison, still promenades in the weathered shelter built over his tomb. Grancer was a friendly cotton farmer from Virginia who built a large house in the 1840s on land bordering the Pea River. He invited his neighbors in three counties to the barbecues, horse races, and square dances held on his property. He loved dancing so much that he asked to be buried in his dancing shoes and clothes, with his body laid out on his old feather bed. He built a brick tomb large enough to accommodate the bed and then had the structure covered with a protective wood building. The sounds of lively fiddle music and Grancer's ghost kicking up the dust have been reported near the building for the last hundred years.

(Kinston is in southeastern Alabama, in Coffee County at the junction of Highways 52 and 189, The cemetery is on the opposite side of Cripple Creek, just outside Kinston.) **225**

LIMESTONE COUNTY

LOUISVILLE AND NASHVILLE RAILROAD TRACKS The ghost of a railroad bandit called "Railroad Bill" has haunted the pine woods along these railroad tracks for nearly a century. His apparition is described as a tall, broad-shouldered black man who usually has a broad smile on his face. Railroad Bill was credited with providing food and money to poor people in the area and came to be known as something of a Robin Hood. When authorities tried to capture him, he always slipped through their fingers. Some say he turned into a dog to escape.

(Limestone County is in north central Alabama. The railroad tracks run near the towns of Piney Grove, Elewy, and Nymph.) **171, 172**

LOWNDESBORO

MARENGO Marengo is an old manor house where Kathleen Powell, an invalid, committed suicide in 1961. Her spirit lingers on. Residents have reported being overcome by a sense of foreboding in the house and hearing strange, sudden laughter. A psychic helped free the confused spirit from the premises in February 1976, and no new sightings have been reported since.

(The town is located between Montgomery and Selma, off Highway 80, Marengo Plantation is managed by the Lowndesboro Landmarks Foundation. Marengo, 100 N. Broad St., Lowndesboro, AL 36752.) **224**

MARION

CARLISLE HALL The ghost of Anne Carlisle still haunts the imposing brick tower from which she leaped to her death. Her father, Edwin Kenworthy Carlisle, built the unique plantation house in 1837. His daughter was in love with a Confederate soldier, and when she heard of the young man's death she jumped from the large tower window which faces the road that leads up to the mansion.

(Marion is eighty miles southwest of Birmingham on Highway 5. Carlisle Hall is just off the main highway, about one mile west of Marion in Perry County.) **225**

JUDSON COLLEGE A phantom organist is sometimes seen playing a huge pipe organ at this Baptist women's college, which opened in 1838. Ghostly music can be heard late at night, but no one is ever found at the organ.

(Judson College, 302 Bibb St. Marion, AL 36756. Phone: 334-683-6161. www.judson.edu) **224**

MENTONE

DE SOTO FALLS The ghosts of an old mountain woman and her dog are sometimes seen walking through the woods around this rural waterfall or near the ruins of her old cabin. Some say Nancy Dollar's ghost was looking for thieves who stole the money she set aside for a proper tombstone. She was 108 years old when she died in January 1931. Friends put her old dog Buster to sleep and buried him too. However, thieves broke into the cabin and stole the money Granny had set aside for her funeral, so no tombstone was set over her grave. That did not set too well with Granny. Her ghost was seen in the area so many times that people took up a collection in 1973 and had a marker placed. That seemed to satisfy the old lady, but the phantom of Buster, her faithful dog, is still seen.

(Mentone is in eastern DeKalb County, just off I-59 on Highway 117. www.desotostatepark.com) **224**

MOBILE

BOYINGTON OAK The great oak tree that sprang up from the grave of a hanged man still proclaims his innocence. Charles Boyington was hanged for the murder of his best friend Nathaniel Frost on February 20, 1835. The two friends spent endless hours relaxing among the tombstones and witty epitaphs of the Church Street Graveyard. When Frost was found stabbed to death there, everyone assumed the two had had an argument and that Boyington had stabbed his companion in a fit of anger. Boyington steadfastly maintained his innocence. His last words on the gallows were that a great oak tree would grow from his grave as proof of his innocence. He was buried in a corner of potter's field near the wall in the Church Street Graveyard, about sixty yards from where Frost's body was found. Within a few months, a tiny oak sprouted from the center of his grave, and the living monument thrives to this day. The proud oak has survived many disasters that have claimed other trees in the area, and some hear the cries of an innocent man when the breeze rustles through its branches.

(Mobile is on the extreme southwestern tip of Alabama, at the junction of I-10 and I-65. The potter's graveyard was converted to a playground. The oak tree sits at the edge of a parking area near Bayou St. To find it, go east from the corner of Government St. and Broad St. to South Bayou St. Go south one block on Bayou St. to a gravel parking lot. The Boyington Oak is the only Live Oak tree in the area with wooden posts around it.) **15, 224**

SMALLWOOD HOUSE The ghost of a pipe-smoking sea captain haunts his old neighborhood and the house where he committed suicide. His visitations began when the William Smallwood family moved into his former residence. They were often awakened by loud bangs, sudden thuds, and the sound of someone falling down the stairs. Then the ghost started materializing in the garden behind the house. Soon he was also seen inside the house. The odor from his pipe tobacco was sometimes overpowering, and the Smallwoods were forced to move out. The house stood vacant for many years.

(The Smallwood house is a private residence on State St. The Captain's presence has also been sensed on nearby Bienville Sq.) **224**

SPRING HILL COLLEGE

SPRING HILL COLLEGE The ghost of a former mathematics professor haunts this quiet Catholic college, which was founded in 1830. The brilliant man's revenant is seen near his old office in the Mathematics Department.

(The five-hundred-acre campus is within the city. Spring Hill College, 4000 Dauphin St., Mobile, AL 36608. Phone: 251-380-4655. www.shc.edu) **224**

MONTEVALLO

MANSION HOUSE Edmund King christened this two-story brick house "Kingswood" when he built it in 1823. After he died on June 28, 1863, at the age of 82, his ghost lingered on his beloved estate for over a hundred years. His form could be seen late at night carrying a lantern through his orchards to the gravesite of his wife and son. His ghost was also seen counting silver coins in his second-floor bedroom and floating slowly across the floor. Once, during a wedding reception held in the house, a huge white-robed phantom materialized from beneath the dining-room table and drifted out an open window, in full view of all the guests.

(Montevallo is thirty-two miles south of Birmingham, at the junction of I-65 and Highway 25. Mansion House is in downtown Montevallo.) **224**

UNIVERSITY OF MONTEVALLO The ghost of a former student haunts the fourth floor of Old Main, also known as Buzzard Hall. The university was founded in 1896 and covers 160 acres of this small town.

(Montevallo University, Main St., Montevallo, AL 35115. Phone: 205-665-6000. www.montevallo.edu/ library/ghoststories.shtm) **224**

MONTGOMERY

FOURPLEX APARTMENTS When Nancy Anglin first moved into the upstairs east apartment here, she became aware of a strange presence. Then in August 1966, she heard a flute playing a "wandering, mystical pattern of notes," and looked up to see a glowing mist move from the bedroom through the living room, and into the den. Although other tenants heard strange footsteps in the halls, no other reports of ghosts were received and the identity of the musical spirit was never determined.

(Montgomery is in central Alabama at the intersection of I-65 and I-85. The building, now a private residence, is located at 710 Cloverdale Rd, Montgomery, AL 36106.) **87, 90**

HUNTINGDON COLLEGE The ghost of the Red Lady has haunted Pratt Hall on this campus for many years. She was a student from New York who was obsessed with the color red. She always dressed in red, and her room on the fourth floor of Pratt Hall was decorated in a crimson hue. The girl, never accepted by her classmates, remained aloof, alone, and homesick. One day they found her in her room dressed in her red robe, underneath a red blanket, covered with bright red blood from her slashed wrists. After she died, strange flashes of red light were seen in her former room, as the girl's red-dressed ghost roamed the fourth-floor halls and terrified students.

(Huntingdon College, 1500 East Fairview Ave., Montgomery, AL 36106. Phone: 334-833-4222. www. huntingdon.edu) **225**

LUCAS TAVERN The friendly ghost of Eliza Lucas, dressed in Victorian clothing, waves from the doorway of her old tavern. The tavern was a popular overnight rest stop in the 1820s. Soon after the building was restored in 1980, the ghost of its former owner started to appear. Eliza has also been reported in the old school-house and several other nineteenth-century buildings on the square.

(Lucas Tavern is in the Old North Hull Historic District. The address is 310 North Hull St., Montgomery, AL 36104. Phone: 205-262-0322.) **101, 168**

MOUNDVILLE

MOUND ARCHAEOLOGICAL PARK The powerful spirit of an ancient race of mound builders permeates this 317-acre archeological site. The one-thousand-year-old town is made up of twenty-four ceremonial mounds laid out in a rectangle with a seven-and-a-half-acre central plaza. Some of the mounds supported temples and homes of the nobility, while others had burial houses on top of them. The largest mound is sixty feet high and contains over four million cubic feet of earth. Symbols most commonly found on artifacts from the site are human skulls, horned rattlesnakes, and the hand and eye motif. Evidence suggests that this prehistoric culture was more complex than later Indian societies, although very little is known about their social and religious beliefs.

(Moundville is fourteen miles south of Tuscaloosa on Highway 69. It is located on the banks of the Black Warrior River. The site is operated by the Alabama Museum of Natural History. Camping is available. For information, contact the Moundville Archeological Park, P.O. Box 66, Moundville, AL 35474. Phone: 205-371-2572. www.ua. edu/mndville.htm) **15, 57, 99, 144**

MOUNTAIN BROOK

OLD BROWER RESIDENCE The ghost of a popular doctor haunts his family's Steinway piano. Dr. William Mudd Jordan always wanted to learn to play the piano that he bought for his children, but he only had time to learn two pieces. The piano was eventually passed down to his great-grandson, Dr. William Jordan Brower. The elder physician died in 1951 at the age of 78. Starting about 1970, family members and neighbors began hearing songs coming from the old piano late at night. The ghostly performances were always the same tunes: "Stars and Stripes Forever" and "Maple Leaf Rag"—the only two songs old Dr. Jordan ever learned.

(While living, Dr. Jordan played his two pieces for the Brower family in their residence at 3648 Clairmont Avenue, Birmingham, AL 35222. When the eerie music was first heard, the Browers lived at 2832 Balmoral St. in Mountain Brook, AL 35223. They later moved, with the family Steinway, to Cullman County. Dr. Jordan is buried at Oak Hill Cemetery in Birmingham.) **224**

NEWTON

CHOCTAWHATCHEE RIVER BRIDGE A shallow hole near the bank of this river is haunted. Locals say that even if the hole is filled with dirt during the day, by morning it will be empty and clean-swept. Highway workers once filled up the hole with dirt and pitched their tent directly on top of it, but the next morning the haunted hole was completely dug out again. The ghost of Bill Sketoe, former pastor of the Methodist Church, seems the likely cause. He was hanged on December 3, 1864, from an old tree that stood on the spot. A group of vigilantes accused Sketoe of being a traitor to the Confederacy. In fact, Sketoe was totally innocent. At the lynching, the tree limb holding Sketoe's body bent enough so that his toes touched the ground, and the men had to hastily dig a hole beneath his feet as the rope slowly strangled him to death. The six men soon started telling stories of meeting the innocent pastor's ghost, and eventually they all died violent deaths. For many years locals reported seeing Sketoe's vengeful phantom.

(Newton is in the southeast corner of Alabama, northwest of Dothan on Highway 123. The oak tree was located where the old bridge crossed the Choctawhatchee River on the road from Newton. The hole is still there, next to the new concrete bridge. It is about thirty inches wide and eight inches deep. Bill Sketoe's grave is in the Mount Carmel Cemetery.) **225**

PRATTVILLE

GURNEY MANUFACTURING COMPANY The ghost of a woman in black roams this old mill, looking for her son Willie Youngblood. The ten-year-old boy fell to his death in an elevator shaft nearly a hundred years ago, when he worked in the third-floor spinning room. Workers at the cotton mill, which opened in 1846, have seen his mother's shadowy form walking silently through the rows of machines. In the 1920s, she appeared to groups of night-shift workers in the spinning room or materialized in the first-floor weaving room. Dozens of operators could be seen leaning out mill windows to watch the apparition glide across the pond and disappear from sight. The site is also said to be haunted by an old dye mixer known as Moe.

(Prattville is twelve miles northwest of Montgomery in Autauga County. The mill is just south of town.) **101, 223**

ROCKY HILL

ROCKY HILL CASTLE Rocky Hill Castle was a proud mansion built by a proud man. Lawyer James Saunders built his castle in the 1840s, and Rocky Hill's first ghost was the architect who built it. Saunders refused to pay the French architect's "exorbitant" bill. Shortly after the architect died, his apparition materialized in the cellar and started hammering away at the foundation. The pounding continued as long as the house stood. During the Civil War, the house served as refuge for rebel soldiers. Two of them died there and are buried on the grounds. Later, the ghost of a beautiful Southern lady came looking for her lost lover. The Lady in Blue started appearing on the stairway and was later seen in the wine cellar. When an aggressive male ghost actually spoke to Mrs. Saunders in her bedroom, the whole family packed up and was out of the house in two hours, never to return.

(Rocky Hill is three miles east of Courtland in Lawrence County. The castle ruins are located outside of town, down a clay road lined on both sides by tall cedars.) **225**

SELMA

STURTIVANT HALL The ghost of John McGee Parkman haunts this beautiful neoclassic mansion. The white-columned house was built in 1852, but Parkman only lived there from 1864 to 1866. At the time, he was president of the First National Bank of Selma, but after only two years at his post he was arrested and sent to federal prison for speculating in cotton with bank funds. He was killed while trying to escape from prison, and his ghost began appearing at his beloved home three years later. He was seen leaning against the side portico and gazing out of the cupola at the top of the mansion. Even today, guides tell of sensing his presence in an upstairs bedroom and in the downstairs parlor. Neighbors called police when they noticed doors and windows opening and closing by themselves in the empty building, and once, the fire department was called when smoke was seen pouring out of an open upstairs window. When they arrived there was no evidence of fire and the window was tightly locked.

(Selma is on U.S. Highway 80 in south central Alabama. John Parkman is buried in Live Oak Cemetery. Sturtivant Hall is at 713 Mabry St., Selma, AL 36701. Phone: 334-872-5626. www.selmaalabama.com/strdvnt. htm) **55, 134, 225**

WINDHAM HOUSE A friendly ghost named Jeffrey haunts the home of Kathryn Tucker Windham. His footsteps can be heard clumping up and down the hall. Sometimes he slams doors, moves furniture, or rocks quietly in an antique chair in the living room. Her experiences with Jeffrey have inspired Kathryn to write a whole series of books about ghosts in the South.

(The house is a private residence in Selma. Author Kathryn Tucker Windham can be contacted through the University of Alabama Press, Box 870380, Tuscaloosa, AL 35487.) **223**

SUGGSVILLE

CLEVELAND HOUSE The sounds of a phantom horse and rider prancing up the steps and across the porch of this old wood frame house can still be heard. Stephen Cleveland finished building his unusual home in 1860. All the rooms of the L-shaped structure open onto a large front porch. The porch is so wide that Cleveland used to take his young son Walter on horse rides across it. When the boy died of an unknown illness in July 1861, his father grieved deeply. Before he would lead his cavalry company off to battle he would ride across the porch and yell good-bye to his dead son. Captain Stephen Cleveland died in 1883, but his ghost sometimes returns to take his beloved son on rides across the porch.

(Suggsville is in Clarke County, northeast of Jackson on County Road 35. The house stands in a wooded area near Suggsville. It is now used as a lodge by a private hunting club, and members still hear the phantom hooves of a horse riding up the north steps of the porch and prancing down the east steps.) **223**

TROY

OLD BARFOOT HOUSE A frightening apparition visited this house from 1932 to 1937, finally forcing the family to move out. The phantom of a man with dark hair and a high forehead, dressed in black pants and a white shirt, regularly materialized in the living room and walked through the dining room into one of the back bedrooms. Family members awoke to the penetrating stare of his deep black eyes as he stood silently at the foot of their beds. Some locals believe the ghost is Tom Johnson, hanged for the ax murder of two elderly widows who lived in rural Pike County. He was hanged on March 31, 1899, from a gallows in front of the Barfoot house.

(Troy is at the junction of U.S. Highways 29 and 231 in Pike County, which is in southeastern Alabama. The house is a private residence at 122 Orion Street, Troy, AL 36081.) **224**

TUSCALOOSA

DRISH MANSION The stubborn ghost of the original owner of this plantation house keeps returning to the tower room to light candles, which makes it seem as if the whole place were on fire. Dr. John Drish and his wife Sarah built their home in 1830. When Dr. Drish died, Sarah lit dozens of candles and burned them while he lay in state. After she put those candles safely away she asked that they be used again at her own funeral. Many years later, she became obsessed with the candle ritual and pleaded with friends and neighbors to be sure to light the candles around her coffin. When she died, her relatives were too busy to look for the candles, and Sarah was buried without the ceremony. Within months, fiery lights started appearing in the shuttered tower at the center of the house. Dozens of false alarms were called in, but no evidence of fire was ever found. Sarah's ghost materialized in the downstairs front parlor, so the residents were sure just who was responsible for the phantom candles.

(Tuscaloosa is on I-20/59, fifty miles southwest of Birmingham. Now owned by the Southside Baptist Church, the Drish mansion is located at 2300 17th St., between Greensboro Ave. and Queen City Ave. Phone: 205-758-4355.) **225**

UNIVERSITY OF ALABAMA The ghosts of Smith Hall have been making unexplainable noises for over a quarter century. A flurry of activity took place in 1955 and the early 1970s. Students and professors reported hearing the clattering of many footsteps and the disembodied voices of children on the second floor. The building was named for geology professor Dr. Eugene Allen Smith, who died in August 1927. The professor delighted in escorting tours of schoolchildren through the building. Three Yankee ghosts haunt the Little Round House. In April 1865 they were looking for whisky in the octagonal building and were shot and killed by a student. The building was eventually turned over to a senior fraternity called the Jasons, who used painful rituals to induct new members. It was then the ghosts of the Yankees returned, presumably drawn by the strong emotions. Today, the structure is known as the Jason Shrine.

(University of Alabama, 801 University Blvd. E, Tuscaloosa, AL 35487. Phone: 205-348-16010.) **224**

WINFIELD

MUSGRAVE CHAPEL CEMETERY After Robert Musgrave was killed in a train wreck in April 1904, his family consecrated his grave site with an eight-foot-tall granite obelisk. His devastated sweetheart brought fresh flowers to the grave for fifty years. Her thin silhouette could often be seen kneeling in prayer next to his marker. In 1962, six months after she died, worshippers noticed the same distinctive silhouette at his tombstone. When they investigated, they found a dark stain had leached from the stone to form her exact image. News of the image spread and hundreds of strangers descended on the quiet cemetery. The family had the image sandblasted off the side of the obelisk, but it returned as clearly as ever. Again they hired a stonemason to sandblast the image away, and again the eerie silhouette returned.

(The town of Winfield is sixty-five miles north of Birmingham on I-78. Musgrave Chapel Cemetery is near Winfield, along the Luxapaillila Creek in north Fayette County. Follow Highway 43 south out of town for six miles and turn west to the chapel.) **15, 224**

ALASKA

ANCHORAGE

EKLUTNA VILLAGE HISTORIC PARK The Native American Cemetery here is haunted by ghostly wanderers, the spirits of Eskimo ancestors searching for their belongings. The Eklutna religion is a blend of Eskimo beliefs and Russian Orthodox teachings introduced by Russian settlers in 1741. It holds that when a person dies, his spirit wanders the earth for forty days and forty nights, searching for his earthly possessions. To keep the spirits confined to the cemetery, the Eklutna build colorful miniature houses on top of the graves. Each structure is topped with the distinctive cross of the Russian Orthodox Church. The minihouses are painted with family colors and contain personal items of the deceased, such as cups, plates, spoons, a comb, a pipe, or even a rifle or camera.

(Anchorage is on the Gulf of Alaska. The park is in the town of Chugiak on Eklutna Village Rd. Phone: 907-688-6026.) **72**

DENALI PARK

DENALI NATIONAL PARK The word *Denali* means the "High One" and refers to one of the most sacred sites on the North American continent. This park is home to the 20,320-foot-tall Mount McKinley. Athabascan natives believe the mountain is home to Sa, the sun shaman, master of life itself, and legends of magic and mystery on the mountainside go back hundreds of years. Modern mystics believe the site acts as a transmitter of cosmic forces under control of the Great White Brotherhood.

(The park is 120 miles south of Fairbanks and 240 miles north of Anchorage. Follow Highway 3 into the park. Information on weather conditions at the park is available by calling 907-683-2686. Camping and lodging are available from June through August. Call Camp Denali for information at 603-675-2248. Bus tours leave from Anchorage. For information, call Denali Express at 800-327-7651. Denali National Park, P.O. Box 9, Denali Park, AK 99755. www.denalinationalpark.com) **99, 200**

GAKONA

GAKONA LODGE AND TRADING POST This lodge was built in 1900 and additions were made in the 1920s and 1940s. The older buildings are haunted by a poltergeist spirit that likes to open and close doors, lock doors from the inside, jump on beds, play with the stereo, and perform other harmless pranks. Sometimes tobacco smoke from an ethereal pipe fills the air. Unexplained voices and footsteps have also been heard. Most phenomena take place during the evening hours in the lobby and in the nine upstairs rooms of the lodge. The ghost has never been identified.

(Gakona is on the Tok Cutoff, 200 miles northeast of Anchorage on Highway 1.) **135**

ILLIAMNA LAKE

ILLIAMNA MONSTER A sixty-foot-long serpentine creature has been sighted swimming near the surface of this isolated lake. The monster was first sighted in 1929 and has been spotted sporadically ever since. Several people witnessed the monster swimming in the lake on September 7, 1975.

(Illiamna Lake is on the southwestern tip of Alaska. It is located in the Katmai National Preserve two hundred miles southwest of Anchorage. www.katmai.national-park.com) **113**

KOTZEBUE

CAPE KRUSENSTERN The rolling dunes of this remote location are considered a sacred site by Native Americans. It was here that ancient peoples crossed from the Asian continent to North America over the frozen Bering Strait. The Bering Land Bridge National Preserve is to the south, and the Arctic National Park is to the east.

(Kotzebue is on the Bering Strait in northwestern Alaska. The Cape can be reached only by boat. Inquire at the visitor center in Kotzebue, or call 907-442-3890. Cape Krusenstern National Monument, P.O. Box 1029, Kotzebue, AK 99752. www.nps.gov/cakr) **200**

CITY MUNICIPAL BUILDING Strange noises have been reported to come from the second floor here for decades. No one has ever been able to pinpoint the source. The second floor is now a museum but at one time was used as the first territorial court in Alaska. Built in 1899, the building now serves as city hall and the tourism department.

(Skagway is one hundred miles north of Juneau and is most easily accessible by boat or plane. From White-horse in the Yukon, follow Highway 2 south to the town. The Municipal Building is the only stone building in Skagway.) **134**

EAGLES HALL The second floor of this unique building is said to be haunted by several friendly ghosts. Eagles Club officers have been run out of the building by strange goings-on, and a lot of people sense an odd coldness that moves through the halls.

(The Eagles Hall was created by linking together two old hotels built in the 1890s and lies at the center of town. Fraternal Order of Eagles, P.O. Box 181, Skagway, AK 99840. Phone: 907-983-2234.) **134**

GOLDEN NORTH HOTEL Two ghosts haunt this old hotel. Employees have nicknamed one of them Mary. They believe she is the spirit of a young lady who died of pneumonia in her room while waiting for her fiancé to return from a gold-prospecting expedition. She still haunts Room 23 where ghostly images of a woman have appeared and guests have complained of choking sensations in the middle of the night. Room 14 is haunted by a strange "light form" that moves around in the room at night. Nobody knows who or what it represents.

(The three-story hotel has a corner cupola facing the street at Third and Broadway. Phone: 907-983-2294. www.alasken.com/goldenorth) **101, 134**

MULVIHILL HOUSE Built in 1904, this house is haunted by the sounds of a previous owner who lived there from 1914 to 1949. Mul Mulvihill was a dispatcher for the White Pass and Yukon Railroad, and the sounds of his heavy footsteps and the clicking of an old telegraph key are sometimes heard.

(This Victorian house is a private residence on the walking tour of the town organized by the Chamber of Commerce. For information, call 907-983-1898. www.skagwaychamber.org) **134**

RED ONION SALOON This saloon was originally built as a whorehouse in 1897 and was moved to its present location in 1914. The shadowy apparition of a female figure is seen watering nonexistent plants in the upstairs Madame's Room. Police summoned to investigate strange footsteps originating in the second-floor hallway could find no earthly explanation. The roaming scent of strong perfume is detected in the same area, and many locals believe the place is haunted by the presence of a former owner.

(The saloon is a white two-story building with dark trim and a storefront window. Red Onion Saloon, 205 Broadway, Skagway, AK 99840. Phone: 907-983-2222.) **134**

WHITE HOUSE The abandoned White House used to be a hospital, hotel, and day-care center, but now it is home only to the ghost of a woman in white. Several witnesses have reported seeing her. She is thought to be a woman who ran a day-care center in the building many years ago.

(This wood-frame building was damaged by fire in 1988 and now lies deserted at the edge of Skagway.) **134**

TONSINA

MANGY MOOSE SALOON The ghost of a tall thin man with a black mustache haunts the bar and Room 18 here. Since 1980 both employees and guests have encountered the polite apparition. The lodge was originally an officer's quarters at Fort Liscomb, but it was hauled from Valdez and set on a new foundation in Tonsina in the 1920s. In the 1950s it was run by Bill Ogden, who painted the building pink and operated a bordello and casino there. Some suspect Bill is the ghost of the Mangy Moose Saloon because he died there, but others believe the spirit is a man who committed suicide in the building many years ago.

(Tonsina is located two hundred miles east of Anchorage. Take Highway 1 northeast out of Anchorage 180 miles to Glannallen. Turn south on Highway 4 and drive fifty miles to Tonsina. The saloon is across the street from the Tonsina Lodge on Richardson Highway.) **101, 135**

ARIZONA

BISBEE

CLAWSON HOUSE INN Three murdered miners are said to haunt this quaint three-room inn. In the 1890s there was a bitter labor dispute at the Queen Mine southwest of town. Large numbers of striking workers were rounded up by authorities and shipped out of the area, and strikebreakers moved in to claim their jobs. According to some accounts, three scabs staying at the Clawson House were killed by strikers. Their spirits are said to be trapped in the house where they died, along with the much kinder presence of old Mrs. Clawson herself.

(Bisee is southeast of Tucson. From I-10 at Benson, follow Highway 80 southeast for fifty miles to the town. Clawson House Inn, 116 Clawson Ave., Bisbee, AZ 85603. Phone: 520-432-5237.) **72**

OLIVER HOUSE Five ghosts are said to haunt this bed-and-breakfast inn. Strange footsteps are heard late at night, and the sound of water running in nonexistent pipes is also reported. Most of the haunting occurs around Room 13. In 1920, a man named Nat Anderson was shot and killed in the hallway near the room. The house was built in 1909 by Edith Ann Oliver, wife of the owner of a mining company. It was used as mine offices and later became a boarding house.

(Oliver House Bed and Breakfast, 26 Sowle, Bisbee, AZ 85603. Phone: 520-432-4286.) **53 (10/95)**

The ghosts of Indians have been reported at the Casa Grande National Monument and at other sites in the region. See Casa Grande National Monument, Casa Grande, Arizona (B. A. SCHAFFENBERGER)

CASA GRANDE

CASA GRANDE NATIONAL MONUMENT The ghosts of Indians performing strange ceremonies have been seen here and at other sites in the region. Casa Grande, or Big House, is probably an ancient monastery and astronomical observatory. The unique three-story adobe building sits atop a one-story platform, and windows and holes are constructed to observe specific astronomical objects. The Hohokam Indians lived in this area from 200 B.C. to A.D. 1100 and probably built the structure to train medicine priests from many different tribes.

(The site is off I-10, forty-five miles south of Phoenix. Casa Grande National Monument, 1100 Ruins Dr., Coolidge, AZ 85228. Phone: 520-723-3172.) **32, 194**

CLIFTON

FANTASMA COLORADO The Fantasma Colorado, which is Spanish for "Red Ghost," first appeared here in 1883. The huge phantom of a red camel with a human corpse tied to its hump with tight rawhide bands terrorized prospectors and settlers for many years. The U.S. Army brought an expedition of camels into the area in 1857. Whether the red camel is real has never been determined, but its ghostly form is still reported in the area.

(Clifton is on the San Francisco River in southern Arizona, south of the Apache National Forest. Most sightings of the Red Ghost have occurred at Chase Creek, which parallels Highway 666, and at Eagle Creek, a few miles west of Clifton. The history of the U.S. Army's Camel Corps is depicted at the Sharlot Hall Museum, 415 West Gurley, Prescott, AZ 86314.) **36**

DOUGLAS

GADSDEN HOTEL The apparition of a headless man has been seen floating down hallways and in the basement here. For some reason the ghost appears most often during Lent. Some witnesses have described the ghost dressed in khaki army clothing with a cap on its headless shoulders. The five-story, 150-room hotel was built in 1907. It later burned down and was rebuilt in 1929. It was restored in 1988, which is about the time the ghost started showing up. Manager Robin Brekhus saw the ghost in a hallway in February 1991, and other employees of the hotel, including the restaurant manager and elevator operator, have also encountered Gadsden's ghastly spirit.

(Douglas is in the extreme southeast corner of Arizona at the junction of U.S. Highway 191 and Highway 80. Gadsden Hotel, 1046 G. Avenue, Douglas, AZ 85607. Phone: 520-364-4481. www.theriver.com/gadsdenhotel) **72**

DRAGOON MOUNTAINS

PHANTOM TRAIN A ghostly train has been reported chugging across the arid plains here. Many have heard the steam engine's distant whistle or seen its dim yellow headlight. Some have even gotten close enough to make out the figure of a black-sooted engineer pulling on the whistle of the locomotive. The problem is that no railroad tracks have ever been laid in the area.

(The Phantom Train of Dragoon has been seen crossing the alkali flats in southeastern Arizona, from the Dragoon Mountains to the town of Wilcox. The area is located off I-10 at Dragoon, about fifty miles northwest of Tombstone.) **5**

FLAGSTAFF

MONTE VISTA HOTEL Guests here have complained of a phantom bellboy who knocks at their door and then disappears. But the discourteous bellboy is not the only ghost that haunts this picturesque hotel. The apparition of a woman has been seen in the hall outside the Zane Grey Suite, and the ghost of a man pacing the floor been reported inside another room. Sometimes people can hear him clearing his throat or coughing.

(Flagstaff is at the junction of I-40 and I-17 in north central Arizona. Monte Vista Hotel, 100 N. San Francisco, Flagstaff, AZ 86016. Phone: 520-779-6971. www.hotelmontevista.com) **194**

RIORDAN HOUSE STATE PARK The upstairs of a magnificent log mansion at the center of this small park is haunted by the ghosts of Caroline Riordan and her daughter Anna. Caroline's ghost is seen dutifully caring for young Anna, who died of polio. The apparitions of both the mother and her ailing daughter have been seen by employees and visitors. The house was built by the Riordan brothers, who made a fortune in the lumber industry but suffered from a number of family tragedies.

(The mansion is now maintained by the State of Arizona and is open to the public. Riordan House State Park, 409 Riordan Road, Flagstaff, AZ 86016. Phone: 520-779-4395. www.pr.state.az.us/parkhtml/riordan.html) **231**

This Ceremonial Kiva in Grand Canyon National Park is a sacred site to the Hopi Indians. See Grand Canyon National Park, Grand Canyon, Arizona (B. A. SCHAFFENBERGER)

GRAND CANYON

GRAND CANYON NATIONAL PARK Where the Colorado River first meets the Grand Canyon is where the Hopi Indians emerged from another dimension, entering the Fourth World from the Third World. It is also their doorway to the next dimension, the Fifth World. The Hopis, many of whom display psychic abilities, are considered to be the most spiritual tribe by other Native Americans. They are considered to be direct descendants of the Ancient Ones, or Anasazi, and have steadfastly practiced the same religion for thousands of years. The Tusayan Ruins are a collection of religious and residential structures used by the Anasazi in the twelfth century. The Havasupai Falls at the base of the canyon have been considered sacred since pre-

historic times. The Watchtower Kiva has many reproductions of sacred symbols painted on its walls.

(The south rim of the park is seventy-three miles north of Flagstaff on U.S. Highway 180. The Arizona Office of Tourism can be reached at 800-842-8257. www.nps. gov/grca) **144, 200**

HOPI-NAVAJO RESERVATION

CANYON DE CHELLY The psychic energy in the red rock of this canyon is said to possess healing power. It was here that the Ancient Ones, the Anasazi Indians, built their homes under mountain outcroppings at what are now called White House Ruins. Another Anasazi site is Mummy Cave, where desiccated bodies dating from A.D. 300 were found. In the 1700s the Navajos, resettling from Canada, came here and sensed the power of the valley. They painted magical symbols on the canyon walls, such as those seen at Standing Cow Ruin, and in dwellings, such as depicted at Antelope House. A Navajo ceiling painting in Planetarium Cave guides dreamers to healing places in the stars. The Navajo considered the valley to be their spiritual stronghold, but white men also wanted the canyon. The Spanish killed over a hundred Indians here in 1803, and in 1863 Kit Carson killed hundreds more when he forced the Navajo to leave the canyon and resettle in New Mexico. Their sacred land was returned to the Navajo in 1868.

(The twenty-six-mile-long Canyon de Chelly is on the Navajo Reservation in northeast Arizona. Please exercise the utmost respect when visiting the Hopi-Navajo Reservation. Native Americans consider these lands sacred, not haunted. The headquarters of the Canyon de Chelly National Monument are at Chinle. Follow U.S. Highway 191 north to the town. The address is Canyon de Chelly National Monument, Box 588, Chinle, AZ 86503. Phone: 520-674-5500. www.nps.gov/cach) **15, 72**

COAL CANYON The gigantic glowing apparition of a woman has been seen floating above an outcropping here. The Eagle Woman of the Black Mesa most often appears on summer nights and has been seen by hundreds of witnesses. Scientists say that the image is formed by phosphorescent vapors from the rocks. Indians claim she comes closer as the night progresses and lures people to jump off the cliff. Hopi legend says she is a widow from the Bow Clan who lived at an ancient city founded by Hopi ancestors (see Oraibi, below). Left with no husband and three sons, she is said to have meditated all night at the cliff and then leaped to her death in an attempt to reach the moon.

(Follow Highway 264 west of Tuba City for fourteen miles toward Windo Rock. The canyon is about one mile off the highway at that point.) **15, 231**

MONUMENT VALLEY NAVAJO PARK Some people say the silence here is sacred. Indians believe the site clears the head and stimulates the imagination. Mystery Valley contains dozens of strange Anasazi petroglyphs, and the Navajo have zealously protected the valley for hundreds of years.

(The park is in the northeastern corner of the Navajo reservation, fifty miles from Four Corners. U.S. Highway 163 runs through the park. For information, contact the headquarters of the Monument Valley Navajo Park, Box 360289, Monument Valley, UT 84536. Phone: 801-727-3287. www.desertusa.com/monvalley) **144**

ORAIBI This ancient village is considered to be the longest inhabited spot in North America. It is the site of the Hopi Snake Dance, in which priests hold live rattlesnakes to their mouths and then release them to carry messages to the kachina gods. Oraibi is sacred to the Hopi, and no photography or drawing is allowed. There are no telephones in the town, and it is usually closed to white visitors.

(The town is located in Coal Canyon on the Third Mesa of the Hopi Reservation, which is in the center of Navajoland. Call the Hopi Tribal Council at 520-734-2441 for permission to visit the site. For information on observing Snake Dance ceremonies, call 520-734-6648. www.itcaonline.com/Tribes/hopi.htm) **53 (8/95), 144**

SECOND MESA Every inch of the three plateaus that make up the Hopi Reservation is considered sacred, and tourists must exercise great care when visiting the area. The Second Mesa is where most public activities take place. The town of Mishongnovi is where the one of the most important Hopi ceremonies, the Snake Dance, takes place. It is held in August of odd-numbered years. It is held in August of odd-numbered years. Corn Rock, a sacred shrine, is also located in the town. In even-numbered years, the Snake Dance is held at the village of Shungopavi. The Hopi are considered to be direct descendants of the mysterious Anasazi race.

(The Hopi Cultural Center is located on the Second Mesa and can be reached by Highway 264, or by Highway 87 from Winslow. Phone: 520-734-2901. For information about visiting the Hopi Reservation, contact the Hopi Tribal Council, P.O. Box 123, Kyakotsmovi, AZ 86039. Phone: 520-734-2441. www.psv.com/hopi.html) **144**

SPEAKING ROCK Hopi legend says that the spirit of an old woman lives here. She is a tattletale ghost who tells the giant spider on Spider Rock who among the tribe is misbehaving. See Spider Rock, below.

(Speaking Rock is a column of rock alongside Spider Rock at the juncture of Canyon de Chelly and Monument Canyon. Information can be obtained from the Navajo Tourism Office, Navajo Nation, P.O. Box 308, Window Rock, AZ 86515. Phone: 520-871-4941.) **15**

SPIDER ROCK Navajo legend says the spirit of a giant spider lives here. The white color of the peak is attributed to the bones of its victims. The Hopi and Navajo legends complement each other. See Speaking Rock, above.

(The eight-hundred-foot-tall Spider Rock is next to Speaking Rock at the juncture of Canyon de Chelly and Monument Canyon. Information can be obtained from the Navajo Tourism Office, Navajo Nation, P.O. Box 308, Window Rock, AZ 86515. Phone: 520-871-4941. www.navajocentral.org/spiderrock.html) **15**

JEROME

COMMUNITY CENTER Locals call their community center Spook Hall, because of the phantom of a prostitute seen there. The ghost moves from the front of the building to a few feet from the Little Daisy Hotel where she disappears. The area used to be the site of the "cribs," small shacks used by prostitutes to entertain their clients. One of the women, who was accidentally stabbed to death during an argument between two miners, still walks the street. Jerome was established in 1876, and a billion dollars worth of gold, silver, and copper were mined from the area in seventy-seven years. There are so many ghosts here that a monthly newspaper called the *Jerome Ghost Post* was published for a time. The town still offers such interesting diversions as the Spirit Room Bar and the Haunted Hamburger restaurant.

(Jerome is on Highway 89A, on the side of Mingus Mountain overlooking Verde Valley, at an elevation of five

thousand feet. Follow Highway 89A from either Prescott or Sedona for about twenty-five miles to the town. For information, contact the Jerome Chamber of Commerce, Box K, Jerome, AZ 86331. Phone: 520-634-2900. www.jeromechamber.com) **72, 194**

JEROME GRAND HOTEL The frightening sounds of moaning and coughing miners who used to work in the old United Verde copper mine are still heard in the halls here. An artist painting a picture of the hospital felt a zap of electric energy when he brushed against a ghostly figure floating through a corridor. The old Surgeon House, built next door to the haunted hospital in 1917, is now a hotel.

(The large three-story hospital with its distinctive arches is on Cleopatra Hill, above the Old Company Clinic. Jerome Grand Hotel, 200 Hill St., Jerome, AZ 86331. Phone: 888-817-6788. www.mebyte.com/jgrand) **194**

OLD COMPANY CLINIC Sometimes in the light of the full moon, and especially if a low-pressure weather system is entering the area, the ghosts of former patients and personnel appear at this clinic. Covered bodies litter the halls, and doctors and nurses scurry from patient to patient. The scene reenacts a terrible influenza epidemic that struck the town in 1917.

(The deserted clinic building is on the side of Cleopatra Hill, just below the present hospital.) **194**

OLD EPISCOPAL CHURCH The white, misty figure of an unidentified ghost has been seen and photographed standing in the doorways of buildings surrounding this old church. Most of the sightings have been at twilight.

(The church is halfway up Cleopatra Hill.) **194**

PHELPS DODGE MINE The ghost of a miner who was decapitated in an underground accident haunts the tunnels in this abandoned copper mine. Unexplained footprints and the ghastly figure of Headless Charlie are still reported at the mine site.

(The mine was abandoned in 1953. It is located east of Highway 89A near the Jerome State Historical Park.) **194**

The sounds of ghostly miners from a nearby copper mine are heard in the halls of the former United Verde Hospital. See Jerome Grand Hotel, Jerome, Arizona (DENNIS POOLE)

LAKE HAVASU CITY

LONDON BRIDGE When entrepreneur Thomas McCulloch bought the authentic London Bridge from the British government in 1968, he had no idea that the transfer would stir up ghosts residing in the ancient stones. At a cost of $7.5 million, the bridge was dismantled from its position over the Thames River and reassembled on the Colorado River in Arizona. It was reopened on October 10, 1971. Not long afterward, the ghosts of a woman and a British bobby were seen walking on the bridge at night.

(The city is at the California border on Highway 95. Take Exit 9 south from I-40, or Highway 95 north from I-10. Exit at McCulloch Boulevard. For more information, contact the Lake Havasu Chamber of Commerce, 314 London Bridge Rd., Lake Havasu City, AZ 86403. Phone: 520-855-4115. www.havasuchamber.com) **13**

MONTEZUMA CASTLE

MONTEZUMA CASTLE NATIONAL MONUMENT Spanish explorers called the cliff dwellers who lived here the Sinagua, or "People Without Water." The peaceful, nonthreatening presence of their spirits has been felt by a number of visitors and employees at the site. The Sinagua were the revered Anasazi, or Ancient Ones, who disappeared mysteriously before modern Indians came to the area. White settlers named the cliff dwelling after the Aztec leader Montezuma. Ghostly presences have been reported from people walking along Beaver Creek, below the cliff dwelling. Psychic impressions about at the Métaté, sets of grinding stones blessed by the Corn Maiden.

(The park is located near Camp Verde, east of Prescott and ninety miles north of Phoenix on I-17. Take the Cordes Junction turnoff. For information, contact Montezuma Castle, 2800 Montezuma Castle Highway Camp Verde, AZ 86322. Phone: 520-567-3322. www.nps.gov/moca) **99, 144, 194**

MONTEZUMA WELL The 470-foot-diameter limestone sink known as Montezuma Well is one of the most extraordinary geologic formations in America. It was formed by the collapse of a huge underground cavern, which left behind a magnificent oasis fed by natural springs at the rate of one and a half million gallons of water per day. The Yavapai Indians believe that they entered the world through this crevice in the earth and that every drop of water from the well is holy. Their spirits are said to return here, pleading with modern visitors to keep "the Greedy Ones, the Ones Without Heart" from destroying the Earth Mother.

(Montezuma Well is seven miles north of Montezuma Castle. Take the McGuireville exit off I-17. For camping information, contact the Coconino National Forest, 2323 East Greenlaw Lane, Flagstaff, AZ 86004. Phone: 520-527-3600.) **99, 144, 194**

NAVAJO MONUMENT

NAVAJO NATIONAL MONUMENT This sacred site contains the ruins of two Anasazi dwellings that date back to A.D. 950. The incredibly isolated sites remind one of lost Mayan cities. Betatakin is built beneath a massive cliff overhang at 7,300 feet elevation. Keet Seel is stuck in an eroded pocket in a red sandstone cliff. For some reason, when the Indians left this site in 1300 they sealed all the doors shut. Strenuous hiking paths lead to both locations, and guides are required.

(The Navajo National Monument is fifty miles north of Tuba City on Highway 160. Turn off onto Highway 564 and go nine miles to the site. For information, contact the Navajo National Monument, HC-71 Box 3, Tonalea, AZ 86044. Phone: 520-672-2366. www.nps.gov/nava) **144**

NOGALES

ST. ANDREW'S EPISCOPAL CHURCH This modern brick church, built in 1969, is haunted by the ghosts of Indians. One recurring spirit wearing an old blanket has been witnessed by rectors and visiting churchmen. A whole tribe of Indians materialized in the front pews during organ rehearsal one night. Priests, parishioners, police, and visitors have all witnessed strange phenomena here. During repairs on church sewer lines an Indian burial ground was discovered. Cremation urns and bones belonging to a one-thousand-year-old tribe were unearthed.

(Nogales is on the Mexican border, south of Tucson at the end of I-19. The church is located on the north side of town at 201 Country Club Road, Nogales, AZ 85621. Phone: 602-281-1523.) **134**

OATMAN

OATMAN HOTEL According to some unconfirmed reports, the spirits of Clark Gable and Carol Lombard haunt Room 15 here. They did spend the first night of their honeymoon at the hotel, and their whispering and laughter are said to haunt the room. More documented ghostly manifestations have been reported in the second-floor Theater Room Museum. Distinct outlines of sleeping bodies have been found in the dust on beds there, although the surrounding areas are undisturbed. The ghost of a former chambermaid has also been sighted on the premises. Oatman was born in 1906 as a tent camp and flourished as a gold mining town, with the area producing over forty million dollars in gold ore. Today, only about a hundred people live there year-round.

(The town is 120 miles south of Las Vegas, 30 miles from the Nevada border on old U.S. Highway 66, an exit off Highway I-40, 4 miles south of Kingman. Oatman Hotel, 181 N. Main St., Oatman AZ 86433. Phone: 520-768-4408.) **72, 136**

PAPAGO RESERVATION

VENTANA CAVE According to Papago Indian legends, this cave is the home of the whirlwind Dust Devil and the site of an eternally flowing spring. Archeologists excavating the twelve-thousand-year-old site came across a ghostly Silver-King pigeon in the deepest recesses of the cave. The mysterious bird seemed to watch over their work and stayed with them for several days.

(The reservation is in Pima County in south central Arizona. Highway 86 leads through the area between Ajo and Sells.) **131**

PHOENIX

SAN CARLOS HOTEL The white cloud of a woman's figure, accompanied by ghostly noises, has been reported by witnesses here. She is Leone Jensen, who on May 7, 1928, ended her life by jumping off the roof of the seven-story hotel. The San Carlos had been open only six weeks when the tragedy occurred. According to her friends, the twenty-two-year-old girl was heartbroken after being jilted by her lover, a bellboy at a nearby hotel. The noisy ghosts of three young boys have also been reported to run through the halls of this Italianate showplace, and the unexplainable sounds of children laughing and running are heard coming from inside some of the rooms. The hotel was built in the 1920s on the site of the first elementary school in Phoenix. One reason the hotel is haunted might be an old water well still operating in the basement. The well, dug for the school in 1874, tapped into a spring that was considered sacred for hundreds of years. Indians worshipped the God of Learning on this spot long before the school or hotel was built.

(The city is at the junction of I-10 and I-17 in central Arizona. San Carlos Hotel, 202 North Central Ave, Phoenix, AZ 85004. Phone: 520-253-4121. www.whoa. org/reunions/98phx/ghost.html) **72, 194**

PRESCOTT

HOTEL VENDOME Two ghosts occupy Room 16 at this historic hotel. One is the apparition of a woman named Abby Byr and the other is her cat Noble. Abby came to Arizona for relief from tuberculosis, and before long she married. She and her new husband bought the Hotel Vendome but eventually lost it for unpaid back taxes. The new owners allowed Abby, her husband, and her beloved cat to stay on at no charge. She died in 1921, and her ghost and that of her cat started to be seen after World War II. At a séance held in the room in 1984, four psychics discovered that Abby had died of starvation, after her husband deserted her. Her cat Noble was locked in the closet and died in the room too.

(Prescott is located in central Arizona at the junction of Highway 69 and Highway 89. Hotel Vendome, 230 South Cortez St., Prescott, AZ 86301. Phone: 520-776-0900. www.vendomehotel.com) **72, 53 (10/95)**

RAINBOW BRIDGE

RAINBOW BRIDGE NATIONAL MONUMENT The world's largest natural bridge was named by the Navajo, who considered it to be a gateway to the supernatural. The Rainbow gods on the other side of the bridge could change shape into any living form and taught the Indian shamans how to perform their shape-shifting magic.

(Boat tours to Rainbow Bridge leave from Lake Powell. For information, contact the Glen Canyon National Recreation Area, P.O. Box 9000, Window Rock, AZ 86515. Phone: 520-608-6404. There are several hiking paths for experienced backpackers. For information about hiking, contact the Navajo Parks Department, Window Rock, AZ 86515. Phone: 520-871-6647. www.nps.gov/ rabr) **99, 144**

SAN CARLOS

MOUNT GRAHAM This 10,717-foot-high mountain is considered sacred to the Apache Indians. It is a site of spiritual energy and home to the *ga'an*, mountain spirits who give their power to the Apache Crown dancers in ceremonies held there. The energy the dancers receive from the spirits is a source of medicine power, which is said to protect the Apache from illness and from their enemies. The mountain marks a boundary of the San Carlos Apache sacred lands and is also used as a burial ground. An international telescope observatory has been built on top of the mountain despite the protests of Apache leaders.

(Mount Graham is located south of the San Carlos Indian Reservation in southeast Arizona. From San Carlos, take U.S. Highway 70 southeast to Safford. Then go south on U.S. Highway 91 to Highway 366, which leads back to the mountain.) **72**

SEDONA

BELL ROCK Modern mystics use this rock as a "toning device" to balance psychic energies. People who hold on to the rock while meditating are said to be contacted by spirit guides who lead them to higher levels. Some believe the rock even attracts UFOs. Psychics say that an ethereal force exists in another dimension above Sedona and focuses spiritual energy down on the region in the form of a psychic vortex. The Southwest's most mystical city has numerous New Age centers and bookstores.

(Sedona is 120 miles north of Phoenix in central Arizona. It is twenty-seven miles southwest of Flagstaff at the junction of Highway 89A and Highway 179. Take the Highway 179 exit off I-17. For information, contact the Chamber of Commerce, Forest Road and Route 89A, Box 478, Sedona, AZ 86336. Phone: 800-288-7336. www.sedonachamber.com) **32, 144, 194**

BOYNTON CANYON This canyon is sacred to the Yavapai Indians, who believe that the First Woman was born in a cave here. Now the Great Mother is old and stooped, but she still resides in the canyon. Psychics say the area enhances creative energies.

(The canyon is south of town off of Highway 179. For more information, contact the Visitor's Guide, 431 Route 179, Sedona, AZ 86336. Phone: 520-282-9022.) **99, 144**

CATHEDRAL ROCK Another Sedona psychic vortex spot, Cathedral Rock, is one thousand feet high and seems to glow at night. The red rocks in this area have a high iron content and generate electricity when squeezed under great pressure. Nearby Airport Mesa is so charged with electricity that peoples' hair stands on end. People relaxing or meditating in this area report feeling strange forces and receiving other-worldly communications. Locals say the contrast between the area's bright red rocks and deep blue skies evokes alchemical images of uniting fire and water in the quest for spiritual perfection.

(The mesa is five miles south of town in Red Rock State Park. For more information, contact the Visitor's Guide, 431 Route 179, Sedona, AZ 86336. Phone: 520-282-9022.) **144, 194**

CHAPEL OF THE HOLY CROSS Many people have reported visionary experiences while meditating here. Some of the visions involve temples and caves from the lost Atlantean civilization.

(The Chapel of the Holy Cross is a modern trapezoid structure supporting a large cross built in the mountains near Sedona. Phone: 520-282-4069. www.sedonainfo.com/sedona/chapel.html) **194**

OAK CREEK This pristine creek is believed to cleanse people both physically and spiritually. The waters are highly oxygenated and energized.

(The creek is in Oak Creek Canyon, north of Sedona.

The Arizona State Parks Department may be reached at 520-542-4174.) **99**

SIERRA VISTA

FORT HUACHUCA The ghost of a tall lady in white has been seen many times in Carleton House on this old army post, which was founded in 1877. The house was built in 1880 and has served as a hospital, morgue, and schoolhouse. Now it serves as officers' family quarters. Brigadier General Roy Strom's family nicknamed the ghost Charlotte in the 1980s, and the name has stuck ever since. They described the apparition as wearing a light-colored gown with ruffled edges at the sleeves and hemline. The ghost is thought to be the spirit of a woman who died in the building when it was used as a hospital in the late nineteenth century.

(The 77,000-acre army post is in the town of Sierra Vista, which lies fifteen miles from the Mexican border in southeastern Arizona. Carleton House is a two-story adobe building. http://huachuca-www.army.mil) **134, 175**

SNOWFLAKE

ALIEN ABDUCTION One of the most famous UFO abduction cases took place here on November 5, 1975. At 6:30 P.M., a group of loggers was driving out of the area when they came across a brightly glowing object hovering in a clearing off the road. Travis Walton left the truck and approached the UFO. As he stood underneath, a brilliant bolt of light truck him. The other men panicked and sped away. When they returned, Travis was missing. They reported the incident to the county sheriff, who organized a search party. Travis turned up five days later, dehydrated and hysterical. He said he had been taken aboard the UFO and examined by hairless, bug-eyed extraterrestrials. The alien encounter had been witnessed by six men, all of whom passed lie detector tests. The movie *Fire in the Sky* (1993) was based on the incident.

(The town of Snowflake is in Navajo County in eastern Arizona, twenty-seven miles south of Holbrook on Highway 77. The abduction took place on a logging road along the Mogollon Rim in the Apache-Sitgreaves National Forest. Walton reappeared a quarter mile outside of Heber.) **72, 126 (7/76, 8/76, 5/81, 4/86, 2/93)**

SONOITA

LOST TRAIL HOTEL The severed head of a screaming woman was once seen floating high in the corner of a room here. The glowing head had long dark hair and bright red lipstick, and continued to scream even as it faded from view. The ghost appeared in 1976 to a couple from Sonoita, but no one has ever been able to explain it.

(Sonoita is in southeastern Arizona, in Santa Cruz County at the junction of Highways 82 and 83. The hotel is downtown.) **131**

SUNSET CRATER

SUNSET CRATER NATIONAL MONUMENT This volcanic crater was so named because it always appears to be in the setting sun no matter what the hour. The effect is due to the ring of orange cinders around the crater's rim. The Hopi consider the place sacred. It is the home of the "Kanaa" kachina gods, who perform miracles for the people. The cold wind that arises from the depth of the crater is Yaponcha, the Wind God. There is even an ice cave at the base of the crater. The mixture of heat and cold, fire and ice, makes this a powerful alchemical site. Casual visitors are reminded to treat this natural holy site with the same reverence they would show in a traditional church or cathedral.

(The park is twenty miles north of Flagstaff on Highway 89. For information, contact Sunset Crater National Monument, 2717 North Steves. Blvd. No. 3, Flagstaff, AZ 86004. Phone: 520-556-7040. www.nps.gov/sucr) **99, 144**

SUPERSTITION MOUNTAINS

LOST DUTCHMAN MINE Early Spanish explorers were convinced these mountains were the home of Cibola, the fabled seven cities of gold; the earliest Apache legends speak of the Thunder God, who lived in a cave of gold here. A fabulous den of gold was mentioned in a 1748 land grant from Ferdinand VI of Spain to Don Miguel Peralta. The Peralta family, headquartered in Mexico, inspected the mine many times over the next century. In 1864, Enrico Peralta organized a mining expedition to the site, but the party was ambushed by Apaches. Six years later, Apaches offered to take Dr. Abraham Thorne, an Arizonian on friendly

terms with the Indians, to a site where he could pick gold up off the floor. They took him blindfolded to a deep canyon about a mile from a sharp pinnacle of rock. There he was allowed to take as much gold as he could carry from a tall pile of large nuggets. When Dr. Thorne attempted to return to the spot with a group of friends, the Indians killed all of them. In 1871, German adventurers Jacob Waltz and Jacob Weiser teamed up with a Peralta family member in Mexico and organized another expedition to the secret mine. They returned with sixty thousand dollars in gold. In 1879, the two Germans returned to the mine and murdered a group of Mexicans they found there. Jacob Weiser was later killed by Apaches. In 1890, Jacob Waltz (the "Dutchman") wandered out of the mountains to a rancher's house. As he lay on his deathbed, the immigrant described the mine as a funnel-shaped pit dug into the side of a mountain. Between 1878 and 1891, an estimated ten thousand people searched for the gold. In the meantime, the Indians decided to fill in the mine with rocks and hide its location. In 1912, prospectors found gold ingots on the spot where Enrico fought Indians back in 1864. In 1931, Adolph Ruth found an old Peralta family map and headed off to rediscover the mine. His decapitated body was found three weeks later. Over seventy-five people have died searching for the treasure. The Apaches insist it is not their tribe committing the murders, but the spirit of the vengeful Thunder God. Indeed, some modern ufologists believe there is an underground alien base in these mountains. See Serpent Mound, Adams County, Ohio.

(The mine is thought to be in the area of Pinata at a point known as Weavers Needle, at the end of Peralta Road in the Superstition Mountains of Arizona. The Lost Dutchman State Park is five miles east of Apache Junction on Highway 88. Phone: 520-982-4485. www. ajnet.ci.apache-jct.az.us/museum1.htm) **1, 32, 199**

MOGOLLON RIM The Monster of Mogollon Rim is blamed for killings and missing persons in this area. He is said to be the phantom of a man captured by Indians and hanged by his hands as every bit of flesh was skinned off his body. The phantom creature is over seven feet tall and has no skin. The Navajo call him "Skinwalker."

(The Mogollon Rim mountain is just north of the Superstition Mountain Range in central Arizona. www. carizona.com/rim) **231**

MONTEZUMA'S SERPENT The spirit of Montezuma, the last Aztec ruler (from 1503 to 1520), is said to appear in these mountains in the form of a giant thirty-foot-long snake, the incarnation of the ancient god Quetzacoatl. Many Pueblo, Apache, Pima, Navajo, and Hopi Indians have reported encountering the Great Snake while on vision quests in these mountains. Legend says that whoever has the courage to kiss the serpent on the tongue will achieve supernatural power.

(The area of the Superstition Mountains where Montezuma's Serpent is encountered is near Phoenix, off Highway 70.) **194**

TOMBSTONE

AZTEC HOUSE This antique shop is the scene of many strange sights and sounds. The owners believe ghosts are drawn to authentic goods from their own era. The apparition of a woman in a white gown has been seen on the street in front of the shop. She is thought to have committed suicide after her child died of yellow fever in 1880. Her ghost sometimes blocks traffic and has been reported as far as nine miles out of town.

(Tombstone is in the southeast corner of Arizona, off U.S. Highway 80. The shop is near the Courthouse, which is now a state historic park. Phone: 520-457-3111.) **133**

BIG NOSE KATE'S The ghosts of cowboys still roam this old saloon. They have been seen standing in the doorway, seated at the bar, and knocking over beer cases in the basement. Some ghosts here have even posed for photographer James Kidd. Big Nose Kate, whose real name was Mary Katherine Harmony, was a flamboyant and promiscuous woman who owned the place in the 1880s.

(The saloon was called the Grand Hotel until the 1980s, when it became Big Nose Kate's Saloon. Doc Holiday lived in Room 201 at the hotel. Big Nose Kate's, 417 E. Allen St., Tombstone, AZ 85638 Phone: 520-457-3107.) **133**

BIRD CAGE THEATRE This 1881 burlesque hall contains a stage, bar, casino, and dance hall. Prostitutes enticed prospective clients from fourteen red velvet-draped booths. Although it closed down after only nine years, the Bird Cage is still a popular place with a bevy of spirits. Hundreds of witnesses have reported the sounds of invisible people singing and talking in the deserted rooms. The ghosts of a little boy who died here of yellow fever in 1882 and a former owner who also died in the building are thought to be responsible for a number of poltergeist effects. The apparition of a man wearing a celluloid visor and carrying a clipboard has been seen walking across the stage. In fact, encounters with ghosts wearing old-fashioned clothing have been reported by dozens of employees and tourists. In an article in 1882, *The New York Times* called this "the wildest, wickedest night spot between Basin Street and the Barbary Coast." It was the site of sixteen bloody gunfights, and 140 bullet holes riddle the walls and ceiling. Appropriately, Tombstone's original Boothill hearse, the Black Mariah, is on display on the premises.

(The theater is located at the corner of Sixth and Allen Streets in Tombstone. The mailing address is 517 E. Allen St., Tombstone, AZ 85638. www.clantongang.com/oldwest/birdcage.html. For information on Tombstone sites, contact the Tombstone Tourism Office, P.O. Box 917, Tombstone, AZ 85638. Phone: 520-457-2211.) **72, 133**

NELLIE CASHMAN'S RESTAURANT Employees and patrons at this quaint restaurant have reported the presence of spirits dating from the frontier days. The playful ghosts are blamed for moving objects and making crashing sounds.

(The restaurant is in downtown Tombstone at 117 S. 5th St. Phone: 520-457-2212.) **133**

SHIEFFELIN HALL Ghostly phenomena have been reported in this building for many years. The spirits seem to be most active during town council meetings, which are held here periodically.

(The building is on City Plaza in Tombstone.) **133**

WELLS FARGO BUILDING This old stage stop is said to be haunted by the ghosts of stagecoach drivers and cowboys. The apparition of a man wearing a black hat and frock coat is sometimes seen crossing the street here. The figure always vanishes before it reaches the other side of the street.

(The building is in Old Tombstone, near the Wells Fargo RV Park at 210 E. Fremont. Phone: 520-457-3966.) **133**

TUZIGOOT

TUZIGOOT NATIONAL MONUMENT The ancient people who built this mansionlike village could see for miles around. The spot was taken over by Sinaguan farmers, who considered it sacred. Tuzigoot was named by the Apaches and means "Crooked Water," which refers to the meandering Verde River. Psychics have reported sensing the spirits that guided the original human settlers to this vibrant area.

(The park is southwest of Sedona. It is just across the Verde River from Clarkdale, which is northeast of Prescott on Highway 279. For information, contact the Tuzigoot National Monument, P.O. Box 219, Camp Verde, AZ 86322. Phone: 520-634-5564. www.nps.gov/tuzi) **99, 144, 194**

WUPATKI

WPUPATKI NATIONAL MONUMENT This sacred site contains nearly eight hundred Anasazi ruins, including a ball court, three-story dwellings, and a large religious amphitheater. There is also an unusual geologic feature that the ancient ones may have worshipped. Called the Wupatki Blow Hole, it is an opening in the limestone that appears to breathe, inhaling and exhaling like a giant rock creature. The hole pours forth energizing, negative ions at speeds as high as thirty miles per hour. The San Francisco Peaks in this park are home to the Hopi kachinas. They are not ghosts but the spirits of animals, plants, and places that guide the tribe in their rituals. Visitors are urged to educate themselves in Hopi beliefs before traveling to this holy site.

(The park is on U.S. Highway 89, thirty-five miles north of Flagstaff. For information, contact the Wupatki National Monument, HC-33 Box 44A, Flagstaff, AZ 86001. Phone: 520-679-2365. www.nps.gov/wupa) **99, 144, 200**

ARKANSAS

ARKADELPHIA

HENDERSON STATE UNIVERSITY When this was a Methodist college, a young boy fell in love with a girl from Ouachita Baptist University. The two schools are just across the street from each other. Friends of the boy convinced him that the relationship was fruitless because of the differing schools and religions, so he stopped seeing her. When the girl found out he was taking someone else to his homecoming dance she committed suicide. Now, every year during homecoming week, her shadowy form returns to the women's dorms at Henderson State, searching for the girl who won her only love. Students here call her the "Black Lady."

(The town is seventy miles southwest of Little Rock on I-30. Henderson State University, 1100 Henderson St. Arkadelphia, AR 71999. Phone: 870-230-5000. www. hsu.edu) **121**

CROSSET

CROSSET GHOST LIGHT An eerie light has been reported near the Crosset railroad tracks for the last fifty years. The yellow ball of light, which moves about three feet above the iron rails, is said to be the ghost of a brakeman beheaded in a freak accident. See Gurdon Ghost Light, Gurdon, Arkansas.

(The town is in Ashley County, near the Louisiana border on U.S. Highway 425.) **231**

EUREKA SPRINGS

CRESCENT HOTEL A room in this seventy-eight-year-old resort hotel is haunted by the ghost of Michael, an Irish stonemason who worked on the hotel when it was being built in 1885. The man fell from the roof and died in the second-floor area which became Room 218. Now he plays tricks with the lights and TV, or pounds loudly from inside the thick walls in the room. There are also other spirits here. The ghost of a nurse dressed in white has been reported on the third floor. A gentleman in Victorian clothing haunts the lobby. He has been spotted at the bottom of the stairway and sitting at the lobby bar. Other apparitions have been sighted in Rooms 202 and 424. Built in the early 1800s, the resort hotel was used as a college in the 1920s and became a somewhat controversial hospital/ health resort in the late 1930s. The confused ghost of Doctor Baker, the charlatan who ran the hospital in the 1930s, has been seen in the old recreation room and at the foot of the first-floor stairway.

(The town of Eureka Springs is in the extreme northwest corner of Arkansas in Carroll County, near Beaver Lake at the intersection of Highway 23 and U.S. Highway 62. The building used to house the Baker Hospital. Crescent Hotel, 75 Prospect St., Eureka Springs, AR 72632. Phone: 501-253-9766. www.crescent-hotel.com) **72, 175**

FOUKE

FOUKE MONSTER This hairy, six-foot-tall humanoid creature gained national notoriety when it harassed two families living outside this town. The foul-smelling monster killed chickens, rabbits, and hogs, and mauled many dogs. A film, *The Legend of Boggy Creek* (1973), told the story of the Fouke Monster.

(The town is in southwest Arkansas, at the confluence of the Sulphur and Red Rivers in River County. Most of the sightings occurred between 1955 and 1975 along Boggy Creek, near where it crosses under U.S. Highway 71. http://home.fuse.net/rschaffner/FOUKE.HTM) **231**

GURDON

GURDON GHOST LIGHT A yellow ball of light that seems to possess a mind of its own has been spotted near here. The hovering spook light has been reported ever since a brutal murder in which a man was decapitated sixty-four years ago. Psychics say his spirit is unaware that he is deceased. The ghost light seems to travel thirty to fifty yards down the railroad tracks and then disappear. The phenomena is still going on, and thousands of people have witnessed it. See Crosset Ghost Light, Crosset, Arkansas.

(Gurden is southwest of Little Rock, twenty-one miles south of Arkadelphia on U.S. Highway 67. www.prairieghosts.com/gurdon.html) **15**

HARRISON

CROOKED CREEK This creek is haunted by the ghost of a woman who was murdered here on November 21, 1912. The body of Ella Barham was found cut into seven pieces at the entrance to an old mine shaft. A man named Odus Davidson was hanged for the murder, but that did not seem to placate Ella's restless spirit.

(Harrison is in Boone County in northern Arkansas at the junction of U.S. Highway 65 and Highway 7. The creek is eighteen miles south of Harrison near Killebrew Ford on Pleasant Ridge.) **231**

HOLLYGROVE

CAPTAIN MULLS' HOUSE This house originally stood in St. Petersburg, Florida, but was moved to Holly-

grove by a retired sea captain. He lived there with an Indian girl whom he loved very much. When she died he had her body embalmed and sealed in a glass casket, which he kept in the house. After his death in 1935, the girl was interred in a local cemetery. Sometimes the sounds of the Indian woman playing the piano can be heard coming from the deserted house, and many local residents believe that the place is haunted by her spirit.

(The house is a private residence on U.S. Highway 49, halfway between Hollygrove and Helena in east central Arkansas.) **90**

HOT SPRINGS

HOT SPRINGS NATIONAL PARK Indians considered this area sacred and declared it a neutral zone to be shared by all tribes. In 1832, the U.S. government took possession, and it became a national park in 1921. The four-thousand-year-old waters of Hot Springs bubble up from an area permeated with huge quartz crystals. In fact, the Ouachita River basin is considered to be "the crystal center of North America."

(Hot Springs National Park is located in central Arkansas off Highway 7. For information, contact the Hot Springs National Park, P.O. Box 1860, Hot Springs, AR 71902. Phone: 501-624-3383. www.hot.springs.national-park.com) **144**

LITTLE ROCK

HIGHWAY 365 Several versions of the Vanishing Hitchhiker legend originate on the highways between Little Rock and surrounding communities. Someone picks up a young girl hitchhiking, usually on a rainy night, and when the driver gets to the house where the girl wants to get out she disappears. The astounded driver knocks on the door of the residence only to be told that the ghost of the owner's daughter returns on the anniversary of her death. The girl died in a car wreck at the spot where the driver picked her up. U.S. Highway 64 north of Little Rock is the stomping ground of another highway ghost, but this one has a name. Laura Starr Latta died a month before her twentieth birthday in an accident on the old road in 1899.

(The haunted area on Highway 365 is from Little Rock to Woodson, and from Redfield to Pine Bluff. The area on U.S. Highway 64 runs from Conway to Morrilton. www.prairieghosts.com/hwy365.html) **121**

OLD STATE HOUSE The violent passions of years gone by have created a lingering ghost here. The apparition of a man dressed in a frock coat walks down the aisles of the Central Hall on the second floor. He is thought to be former Speaker of the House John Wilson. In 1837, after many heated debates with Representative Anthony, Wilson stabbed him to death in a scuffle on the floor of the august chamber. Wilson was acquitted on grounds of "excusable homicide," although his political career was ruined. There was even a coup here in 1872, when newly elected governor Elisha Baxter was physically removed from office by loser Joseph Brooks. A cannon was placed on the lawn to discourage Baxter's return, but he set up another governor's office in a storefront down the street. President Grant had to step in to reinstate the legitimate head of Arkansas.

(The Old State House Museum is located downtown, between the Robinson Convention Center and the State House Convention Center, at 300 West Markham St., Little Rock, AR 72201. Phone: 501-371-9685. www. oldstatehouse.org) **14, 101**

MONTICELLO

OLD ALLEN HOUSE This gothic Victorian house was built in 1900 by Joe Lee Allen, a prosperous Delta farmer. The ghost of one of his daughters, LaDell Allen, is said to haunt the house. In the 1940s she took her own life by drinking cyanide. The huge house was converted to apartments in the 1950s, and many tenants have reported ghostly manifestations. One couple trapped a phantom in a closet and struggled to shut the door on the giggling ghost. A doctor living in one of the rooms took a photograph of the dead girl's reflection in a mirror. Literary scholars believe that author Carolyn Wilson based her book *Scent of Lilac* on her experiences while living here. Police have been called to the apartments on several occasions to investigate reports of prowlers on the upper floors, but no living person has ever been found. The owners have denied permission to parapsychologists wanting to set up monitoring equipment in the old house.

(Monticello is in Drew County, fifty miles south of Pine Bluff on U.S. Highway 425. The house is a private residence located at 705 North Main St., Monticello, AR 71655. www.prairieghosts.com/allenh.html) **72, 101**

NEWPORT

WHITE RIVER The White River Monster was spotted here many times between 1937 and 1977. The serpentine creature has been described as gray, at least thirty feet long, with a spiny backbone visible on the surface of the water. The creature was photographed by Cloyce Warren of the White River Lumber Company on July 28, 1971. In 1973 a resolution was passed by the Arkansas legislature creating the White River Monster Refuge and making it illegal to "molest, kill, trample, or harm the White River Monster while he is in the retreat."

(Newport is ninety miles northeast of Little Rock on U.S. Highway 67. The White River Monster has been sighted along the White River near Newport, south of the town's White River Bridge. The White River Monster Refuge covers all the White River adjacent to the Jacksonport State Park. www.prairieghosts.com/whiterv.html) **34, 55, 113, 139**

SEARCY

HARDING COLLEGE The ghost of a young woman can be heard playing the piano in the music building here. She was a music student at the college in the early 1930s when she met a young man with whom she fell in love. The boy was killed in an automobile accident, and she spent her hours of grief playing a piano on the third floor of the building. She died of unknown causes before the semester was over. Soon people reported hearing the sounds of a piano coming from the third floor late at night. Years later, when the old music building was torn down and replaced with a more modern structure, people on the second floor could still hear ghostly piano music coming from above, even though there was no third floor in the new building.

(Searcy is fifty miles northeast of Little Rock on U.S. Highway 67. Harding College, 900 E. Center, Searcy, AR 72149. Phone: 501-279-4000. www.harding.edu) **231**

WARREN

MARK'S MILL In April 1864, two Civil War skirmishes occurred here, and over one thousand soldiers lost their lives. The first battle started with a Union ambush of a train loaded with Confederate gold. A Confederate soldier blinded by an artillery shell managed to set fire to the car carrying the gold. He died later in a hospital, not knowing whether the treasure was safe from Yankee hands. It is said his ghost roams the area searching for the lost gold. After another engagement near here, Yankee soldiers hastily covered their losses by throwing the bodies of their fallen comrades down a well at Mark's Mill. Sometimes, the plaintive moaning of the soldiers' spirits can be heard, pleading for a proper burial.

(Warren is in Bradley County in south central Arkansas, at the junction of Highway 4 and Highway 8. Mark's Mill is on the Saline River.) **121**

CALIFORNIA

AETNA SPRINGS

AETNA SPRINGS GOLF COURSE The ghosts of eight monks dressed in white robes are seen walking somberly across the fairway of this tranquil golf course. Witnesses say the monks' heads are clean shaven and their faces frozen in agonized expressions of pain. Some believe they are Dominican friars tortured to death by rival Franciscans in the early 1500s. The Spanish Franciscans were notorious for their cruel treatment of local Indians; the Dominicans often hid the natives to protect them. In 1963 a doctor took two photographs which showed two rows of monks who had not been visible when he snapped the pictures.

(In Napa County, take Highway 29 north from I-80 and turn off at the Angwin exit toward Pope Valley. Aetna Springs Golf Course, 1600 Aetna Springs Lane, Aetna Springs, CA 94567. Phone: 707-965-2115. www.aetnasprings.com) **15, 83**

ANZA BORREGO STATE PARK

AGUA CALIENTE SPRINGS In the Tierra Blanco canyon overlooking these hot springs, several independent witnesses have seen a Viking ship sticking out of the side of a mountain. Different legends of the Seri and Mayos Indian tribes tell of visitors who arrived in a boat "with a head like a snake." Even today, the Mayos occasionally produce offspring with blue eyes and blond hair. The Baja Gulf once flowed into this valley (see Salton Sea), connecting it to the ocean. The last sightings of the ship were in 1933 when a devastating earthquake struck the area.

(Aqua Caliente Springs is located in the Anza Borrego State Park in San Diego County. The springs are twenty-six miles north of Octillo on Highway S2. Call 760-767-5311 for park maps and guidebooks. www.desertusa. com/anza_borrego/du-abpmain.html) **72, 116**

BORREGO BADLANDS An eight-foot-tall skeleton with a glowing light in its chest has been sighted here since the gold mining days. The skeleton has been chased, shot at, and tracked, but never caught. This area is also the reputed home of the Lost Pegleg mine, which lured hundreds of prospectors in search of its fabled cache of blackened gold nuggets. A brass plaque at the site is dedicated to all those who have searched for the lost gold mine. Some locals believe that the grotesque skeleton protects a hidden entrance to the gold mine.

(The Badlands are eight miles east of Borrego Springs on Highway S22. The memorial is northeast of town at end of Pegleg Road, near the junction of Henderson Canyon Road and Highway S22. www.borrego.org/Out/index.htm) **72, 116**

BORREGO SINK In 1938 and again in 1967, campers at this site were harassed by a pack of white-furred, ape-like creatures with reddish eyes. Campers used fire

This brass plaque honors all those prospectors who have searched in vain for the fabled Lost Pegleg Mine. See Borrego Badlands, Anza Borrego State Park, California (B. A. SCHAFFENBERGER)

means "golden flame." The glowing orbs could be the legendary "money lights" that supposedly mark gold veins in quartz rock or "spirit lights," as suggested in a 1935 study of the area by the American Society for Psychical Research.

(The mountain can be seen from Highway S2, four miles west of Butterfield Ranch. Two dirt roads lead from the highway to the mountain. Butterfield Ranch Resort, 14925 Gt. S. Overland, Julian, CA 92036. Phone: 800-522-6502.) **116**

This former stagecoach stop is haunted by the "White Lady of Vallecito," a young bride-to-be who died of exhaustion on the stagecoach trip west to her wedding. See Vallecito Station, Anza Borrego State Park, California (B. A. SCHAFFENBERGER)

torches and rifle shots to keep them away. According to Indian legend, they are the Hairy Ghosts.

(This dry gulch is located four and a half miles southeast of Borrego Springs on Highway S3. Campsites can be reserved by calling 800-444-7275.) **116**

CARRIZO WASH A phantom stagecoach has been spotted several times over the last hundred years along the Old Butterfield Road. Unexplained wheel ruts in the area's dusty soil are found to this day. Descriptions of the four-mule stagecoach have been traced back to an 1860s robbery in which the driver was shot dead but the frightened team carried the stage out into the desert. Campers between Carrizo Wash and Agua Caliente have reported the sounds of a runaway stagecoach on several occasions.

(The Carrizo Wash is located off Highway S2, sixteen miles north of Ocotillo, where Sweeney Pass meets the Overland Stage Route of 1849. For information, call the park headquarters at 760-767-5311. www.desertusa.com/ mag99/oct/stories/haunted.html) **116**

ORIFLAMME MOUNTAIN From the 1880s to the present day, strange balls of light have been seen hovering over the slopes of this mountain, whose name

VALLECITO STATION This adobe lodge became an overnight stop on the Butterfield Stage Line in 1858. The ambitious stagecoach line promised to take passengers from St. Louis to San Francisco in less than twenty-four days, although it made no mention of the poor shape passengers would be in when they arrived. This stage stop was built in 1853, abandoned in 1888, and restored as a historic site in 1934. People still report seeing the ghosts of two Texans who killed each other in a gunfight, and a ghostly white horse that appears on moonlit nights. But the White Lady of Vallecito is the most famous phantom of this deserted stage stop. The harried trip west to marry a wealthy Sacramento man proved too much for Eileen O'Connor, who died of exhaustion at the station. The owners dressed her in her bridal gown and buried her in a small graveyard on the property. Sometimes in the evening twilight, she is seen rising from her grave and floating to the front of the old adobe building as if she were waiting for the next stage. One man claimed to have received an electric shock when he touched the hovering white phantom. The ghost of a laughing cowboy once materialized inside the tent of a camper here, and workers digging the foundation for the restrooms were shocked to find a woman's ghost hovering above a ditch dug for plumbing. Current custodians at the park track the mysterious movement of rocks at the site. Frequently, large rocks are found placed in tree branches or on the corners of picnic tables. No explanation has been found for the phenomenon.

(The graveyard is about one hundred feet east of the station. Vallecito County Park is four miles northwest of Aqua Caliente on Highway S2. Phone: 619-767-5311. Camping and RV hookups are available.) **72, 116, 167**

ARCADIA

LOS ANGELES COUNTY ARBORETUM This ornate house was once home to Chief Buffalo Child Long Lance, a Hollywood actor and writer. In 1932, after a reporter discovered that he was really a black man posing as an Indian, Long Lance put a gun to his head and committed suicide in the parlor. His ghost has been seen many times since. The ornate house was used as Mr. Roarke's House in the *Fantasy Island* television series, and members of the crew, actor John Anderson, and producer Aaron Spelling all reported seeing the apparition.

(Arcadia is off Highway 210, just east of Pasadena. The Arboretum is at 301 North Baldwin Aven. Arcadia, CA 91006. Phone: 626-821-3222. www.arboretum.org) **182**

ARROYO GRANDE

CRYSTAL ROSE INN Built in 1885, this ornate Victorian building is haunted by a nine-year-old girl named Alice. She has been seen at an upper window, in the turret, and even on the roof, playing with a little boy.

(The inn is located in the town of Arroyo Grande, which is located off Highway 101 in San Luis Obispo County Crystal Rose Inn, 789 Valley Road, Arroyo Grande, CA 93420. Phone: 805-481-1854. www. crystalroseinn.com) **181**

ATWATER

CASTLE AFB MUSEUM One of the planes on display at this military museum is thought to be possessed by spirits. Hatches open and close by themselves on the *Raisin' Hell*, a World War II B-29 bomber. Several guards and maintenance workers describe a "solid shadow" that moves around in the cockpit, and two master sergeants observed the plane's landing lights come on without power or bulbs in the sockets.

(The base is near Atwater in Merced County. Take the Buhach Rd. exit off Highway 99. Castle Air Force Base Museum, P.O. Box 488, Atwater, CA 95301. Phone: 209-723-2178. www.elite.net/castle-air) **116**

BAKERSFIELD

BAKERSFIELD CALIFORNIAN NEWSPAPER The ghost of a German Shepherd dog sits patiently outside this newspaper office as if waiting for someone to claim it. Inside, the apparition of an elderly watchman is seen near the first-floor elevator or in the lunchroom. The ghost of former *Californian* publisher Alfred Harrell has shown up in the building as well.

(The newspaper office is located at 1707 Eye St., Bakersfield, CA 93310. Phone: 661-395-7258.) **72**

LA LOMA On December 24, 1984, dozens of people in this old Spanish neighborhood started seeing the shimmering apparition of Our Lady of Guadalupe at various locations within the barrio. The numerous sightings went on for about six weeks.

(Bakersfield lies at the junction of Highway 99 and Highway 58 in Kern County. La Loma is a district in southeast Bakersfield.) **181**

PIONEER VILLAGE Visitors and employees say this place is haunted. One witness saw a children's birthday party replay itself in the Weill House; others have seen ghostly children play at recess in front of the 1882 Norris School building. In 1992 an investigation by a local radio station discovered a source of psychic energy in the basement storage room where Indian artifacts are kept.

(The village is operated by the Kern County Museum. For a recorded calendar of events, call 805-323-8368. The site is a quarter mile north of Garces Circle, at 3801 Chester Ave., Bakersfield, CA 93301. Phone: 661-861-2132. www.kcmuseum.org) **72**

BARSTOW

CALICO GHOST TOWN This restored 1880s silver mining town features tours through an underground mine and Iron Horse train rides to the Old Workings to the north. A ghost named Esmerelda is said to haunt the Playhouse, and some residents say the ghost of Wyatt Earp, who lived here for a short time, still strolls down the old wooden sidewalks.

(Calico is located off 1–15, about ten miles northeast of Barstow. Camping and RV hookups are available. Calico Ghost Town, 36600 Ghost Town Rd., Yermo, CA 92398. Phone: 760-254-2122. www.calicotown.com) **116**

INTERSTATE 15 Several psychics and UFO investigators claim this stretch of highway runs near an underground alien base in the desert. The intensity of the UFO energy has overpowered sensitive individuals. Other individuals have reported disorientation, time lapses, and memory loss. It has been suggested that the nearby Calico Early Man Site offers evidence that ancient astronauts arrived in this area as long as two hundred thousand years ago. Artifacts discovered at the dig are much older than the known existence of humans in the Western Hemisphere.

(The stretch of highway runs along I-15 north toward Las Vegas. It starts ten miles northeast of Barstow on I-15 and terminates thirty miles later. The region includes the Soda and Cady Mountains, and a desolate area known as the Devil's Playground. To reach the Calico Early Man Site, follow Highway 15 north out of Barstow to Mineola Rd. and turn left. Phone: 619-256-3591.) **15**

BERKELEY

FACULTY CLUB Guests in Room 219 have reported seeing the apparition of an elderly gentleman who just sits quietly in a chair. Students who walk by his window report hearing him recite poetry. The cultured ghost is thought to be Professor Henry Stephens, who died in 1919. He had lived in the room for twenty years. In 1974, a visiting Japanese scholar, Noriyuki Tokuda, reported seeing Stephens sitting in a chair in Room 219. Then, later that same evening, he saw "something like two heads floating, flying high across the room."

(The hotel is located in Alameda County on the campus of the University of California, Berkeley, CA 94720. Phone: 510-540-5678. www.berkeley.edu) **72, 116**

Sather Tower at the University of California, Berkeley, may be haunted by the ghost of a student who leaped from the tower to his death. See Sather Tower, Berkeley, California (GORDON TING)

SATHER TOWER Berkeley students consider this landmark to be haunted. A student leaped to his death from this bell tower in the 1960s. Four years later, a student reported being followed by a ghost as she crossed the lawn below the tower. Then, in the late 1960s, a photographer took a picture of a phantom hand reaching out of the same grassy area.

(The tower is at the center of the University of California campus in Berkeley. Phone: 510-642-5215.) **72, 116**

BENTON

BENTON HOT SPRINGS An abandoned group of old wooden buildings here are home to the ghosts of a man and woman wearing 1890s clothing. Sometimes, townspeople see the phantoms carrying a faint lantern at night.

(Take Highway 395 to Bishop and then follow Highway 6 north out of town for thirty-seven miles. Benton Hot Springs is about five miles west of Benton Station, which is just off Highway 6. For tourist information, call 619-873-8405.) **30, 54, 72, 140**

Benton Hot Springs is home to two nineteenth-century ghosts. See Benton Hot Springs, Benton, California (DENNIS POOLE)

BEVERLY HILLS

BARRYMORE ESTATE In the late 1970s there were frequent reports of encounters with the ghosts of John, Lionel, and Ethel Barrymore by visitors to their former mansion. One of John Barrymore's favorite possessions was an old cuckoo clock. When he died on May 29, 1942, his close friend Gene Fowler decided to set the hands on the clock, which had not worked in years, to the exact hour Barrymore had died, as a tribute. He was astonished to find the hands of the clock already stuck at 10:20, the precise time of Barrymore's passing. More recent reports describe the wandering specter of a man who was killed in an accident involving the private cable car on the property.

(Beverly Hills is off Highway 405, northwest of Los Angeles. The estate is on Summit Ridge at 6 Beverly Grove, Beverly Hills, CA 90212. For information on the city, call the Beverly Hills Visitor Center at 800-345-2210. www.bhvb.org) **81, 88, 168**

BOWMAN DRIVE Several tenants of this house have reported unexplainable events occurring in the upstairs bedrooms. Beds are messed up, pillows are cut open, and the impression of a body forms on unoccupied mattresses. The entity causing the disturbances has never been identified.

(The house is a private residence at 2320 Bowman Dr., Beverly Hills, CA 90212. For further information on Beverly Hills sites, call the Chamber of Commerce at 310-248-1000.) **168**

FALCON'S LAIR The ghost of Rudolph Valentino lingers in his former mansion. He lived there only a year before he died of peritonitis on August 24, 1926. The thirty-one-year-old actor's funeral (see Hollywood Memorial Park, Hollywood, California) was accompanied by mass hysteria and suicides. As it turned out, even Valentino could not believe he was dead. Actor Harry Carey was one of several subsequent owners who encountered the silent star's ghost. Millicent Rogers spent only one night in the house before being chased out by Valentino's specter. His apparition has appeared in darkened corridors, his old bedroom, and in the stables, where his beloved horse was kept. One stable worker promptly walked out the front gate and never returned after seeing the master's ghost petting his horse. Passersby have reported Valentino's dark silhouette looking out over the Los Angeles skyline from his favorite window on the second floor of the mansion. His ex-wife Natacha Rambova claimed to be in contact with his spirit for many years after his death. See Valentino's Place, Hollywood, California, Valentino's Beach House, Oxnard, California, and Santa Maria Inn, Santa Maria, California.

(Valentino's home, now a private residence, is located at 1436 Bella Dr., Beverly Hills, CA 90210. It is possible to drive by the stables, which are located at 10051 Cielo Drive.) **168, 182, 193**

GAYNOR HOUSE A ghostly maid dusts the chandeliers in Mitzi Gaynor's home. Mitzi and her husband Jack Bean first encountered the ghost in 1989. They call the spirit "Mrs. Walker," after a previous owner who had died in the house. Mrs. Walker is obsessed with cleaning and often dusts things that other maids have missed. The tinkling of crystal chandeliers can be heard as the ghost cleans them, and two chandeliers have fallen from the ceiling for no apparent reason. Recently a maid quit when she saw a stack of pillowcases rise up and fly around the room.

(Gaynor House is a private residence halfway up Arden Dr., between Sunset and Santa Monica boulevards.) **193**

GEFSKY HOUSE The ghost of Anne Baxter's husband, actor John Hodiak, haunts their charming hillside house. Agent Hal Gefsky, who lived in the house in the 1970s, says several of his houseguests saw Hodiak's specter hovering outside a second-floor window and walking ten feet off the ground in the backyard. Gefsky even received phone calls from the ghost, but all the departed actor could manage was a faint "hello."

(The house is a private residence near west Beverly Hills, at 8650 Pinetree Pl., Los Angeles, CA 90070.) **136, 168**

HARLOW HOUSE The ghost of actress Jean Harlow lingers in the master bedroom on the second floor of her former residence. Her husband, agent Paul Bern, beat her frequently and is said to have caused the kidney damage from which she later died. However, the actress loved him dearly, and after hearing that he had killed himself with a gun, attempted her own suicide in the upstairs bedroom. In 1966, wealthy hairstylist Jay Sebring bought the house. Sharon Tate was dating Sebring at the time, and he asked her to stay overnight in the house while he was out of town on business. In the middle of the night, Tate was awakened by the ghoulish form of Paul Bern running around in her bedroom, bumping into things and making a lot of noise. Terrified, she ran out of the room only to come upon a hideous scene at the bottom of the staircase. She saw Jay Sebring tied to the newel post with his throat slashed from ear to ear, bleeding profusely. The vision persisted, and the sounds from the bedroom grew even louder. She thought she was losing her mind, and ended up drinking herself to sleep. When Sebring returned the next morning, she told him about her strange experience. Less than two years later, her horrible vision would come true at the home of her new husband, Roman Polanski. Not far from Harlow House, Sharon Tate, Jay Sebring, and three others were slaughtered by the crazed Manson family. Tate's and Sebring's bodies were found tied together by a nylon rope that looped around an exposed roof beam in the living room.

(Harlow's home is now a private residence, off Benedict Canyon Drive, at 9820 Easton Drive. Harlow had also lived in a house farther south near Beverly Glen Blvd. at 1353 Club View Drive. The Polanski estate is on Cielo Dr. After Bern's death, Jean Harlow moved to 512 North Palm Dr., Beverly Hills, CA 90211. She died there a few years later.) **88, 168, 193**

HYAM HOUSE Actress Elke Sommer and her husband Joe Hyam witnessed supernatural phenomena in their dining room from 1964 to 1968. The apparition of a middle-aged man wearing a white shirt and tie was seen by guests on five separate occasions. Investigators from the ASPR and UCLA monitored unexplainable physical events in the house and produced a psychological profile of the ghost. The Hyams moved out after being awakened one night by mysterious knocking at their bedroom door. They opened the door to find the hallway filled with smoke from a fire in the downstairs dining room. The house was bought and resold seventeen times in the next few years, and over thirty people, including scientists and well-known Hollywood personalities, have witnessed strange events here.

(The house is now a private residence on Benedict Canyon Dr. in north Beverly Hills.) **81, 119, 136**

KEATON HOUSE This Italian villa is haunted by the ghost of Buster Keaton, who once lived here. It has been said that Keaton never knew the difference between acting life and living it, but apparently he learned how to act death, too. Television star Dick Christie is convinced he shares the house with Keaton, whose ghost likes to play mechanical tricks such as unplugging phones and turning off lights.

(Keaton House is at 1018 Pamela Dr., Beverly Hills, CA 90210.) **168**

PICKFAIR This was the home of silent-film star Mary Pickford, wife of actor Douglas Fairbanks. Mary lived in the house from 1918 until her death in 1979. She and her husband once saw the ghost of a woman carrying sheet music ascend the large staircase at Pickfair. The scene was repeated three times. Later, Mary would haunt the house, too. Her ghost, dressed in a ruffled white dress, was encountered in a den on the first floor by several subsequent owners, including comic Buddy Rogers.

(Pickfair is surrounded by a wall with two distinctive cherubs on each side of the wrought-iron gate. It is at 1143 Summit Dr., Beverly Hills, CA 90210.) **168**

REEVES HOUSE On June 16, 1959, forty-five-year-old George Reeves went into his upstairs bedroom, removed all his clothing, and shot himself in the head. Television's Superman died instantly, though some say his spirit was indestructible. Many later residents have encountered his ghost. One couple saw him materialize fully outfitted in his Superman costume and then fade slowly away. They moved out of the house that same night. Reeves's ghost has also been seen on the front lawn. There were accusations that Reeves was murdered by his girlfriend, but in 1961 his body was exhumed and cremated. That destroyed any evidence and ended the controversy.

(The house is a few doors away from where the Manson murders took place. Superman's residence is at 1579 Benedict Canyon Dr., Beverly Hills, CA 90210.) **168**

STANWYCK HOUSE Barbara Stanwyck and Robert Taylor were lovers for many years. After he died in 1969, Barbara continued to see and talk to his presence in her home. She passed away on January 20, 1990, at the age of eighty-two. Another house, which the two used as a secret love nest, has recently been the site of violent poltergeist activity. In 1976, parapsychologist Barry Taff witnessed objects tossed through the air by some unseen hand. A newscaster was chased down a hallway by a heavy flying book, and coins rained from thin air on investigators. A houseboy quit because flying cabbages had chased him through the house one day.

(The house is a private residence off Sunset Blvd. in Beverly Hills.) **193**

STRASBERG HOUSE This house was once owned by British actor Sir Cedric Hardwicke and was later purchased by Susan Strasberg and her husband Christopher Jones. All three owners reported seeing the ghost of a woman in the upstairs bedroom. Strasberg and Jones lived in the house in the 1960s and called upon a variety of priests and psychics to free the spirit, who was never identified. The actress says her experiences in the house convinced her of the reality of the spirit realm.

(The house is now a private residence in Beverly Hills.) **136**

VIRGINIA HILL HOUSE The armor-plated doors of this spacious mansion owned by his girlfriend Virginia Hill were not enough to protect gangster Bugsy Siegel. The glamour-loving mobster was gunned down in 1947 when he stepped in front of the living-room windows here. Sensitives say they can feel his panicked presence still trying duck for cover. See Flamingo Hilton, Las Vegas, Nevada.

(The house is a private residence at 810 North Linden Dr., Beverly Hills, CA 90210.) **72**

Virginia Hill House is haunted by the presence of gangster Bugsy Siegel. See Virginia Hill House, Beverly Hills, California (GORDON TING)

WEBB HOUSE Actor Clifton Webb loved this house and paid cash when he heard former owner Gene Lockhart wanted to sell it. Webb lived here for twenty years and held frequent séances in an attempt to contact his dead mother, Maybelle. Later occupants insist the persnickety ghost of the former owner still haunts the premises. Webb, who died of a heart attack in October 1966, was very forthright and outspoken—traits he is said to have taken to the grave. His ghost is not at all bashful about keeping people from smoking or sitting in his old armchair. If anyone, especially a woman, sits in the chair, it reportedly bounces and makes strange noises. Clifton Webb was a firm believer in life after death and promised never to leave his house, even after he died. Columnist Joyce Haber and producer Doug Cramer, who bought the house after Webb died, admitted to encountering his ghost on several occasions. Other owners of the house have also reported feeling the presence of Clifton Webb, and many mediums have reportedly contacted his tenacious spirit. Psychic Kenny Kingston says that Webb's influence is now extending out into the street in front of the house. Clifton Webb's ghost has also been seen standing near his crypt. See Hollywood Memorial Park, Hollywood, California.

(Clifton Webb's house is a private residence near the turnoff to Coldwater Canyon, at 1005 North Rexford Dr., Beverly Hills, CA 90210.) **81, 88, 136, 168, 182, 193**

WESTWOOD MEMORIAL CEMETERY Marilyn Monroe's apparition has been sighted near her mausoleum in this exclusive cemetery. The movie star appears as a luminescent cloud hovering near her tomb. See Monroe House, Brentwood, California.

(Westwood Memorial Cemetery, 1218 Glendon Ave., Westwood, CA 90024. Phone: 310-474-1579.) **182**

BIG SUR

FERNWOOD CAMPGROUND The ghost of an Indian wearing a corn mask has been reported by employees and campers here. The ghost is seen between 2:00 and 3:00 A.M. near the cabins. This area was sacred to the Esalen Indians, and modern New Age enthusiasts come here to meditate and rejuvenate.

(Big Sur is on the Pacific coast, thirty miles south of Monterey on Highway 1. Fernwood Campground, Big Sur, CA 93920. Phone: 408-667-2422.) **72**

BLYTHE

BLYTHE INTAGLIOS Etched out of the earth by ancient artists, these huge figures of a man, coyote, and coiled snake can best be seen from high above the mesa in an airplane. An arc that cuts across the belly of the ninety-four-foot-tall man is thought to be the mark of a ritual dance. This sacred site was discovered in 1930 and investigated by archaeologists in 1952, but no satisfactory explanation has ever been offered. The site could be as old as five hundred years.

(The Giant Desert Figures Landmark is in Riverside County, seventeen miles north of Blythe on Highway 95. Follow I-10 to Highway 95 north. For information write: 6221 Box Springs Blvd., BLM, Riverside, CA 92507. Phone: 909-697-5200. www.ca.blm.gov/caso/blythe.html) **116, 144**

BODEGA

CHARLENE'S COUNTRY TREASURES This antique shop's troubles began when owner Charlene Weber acquired a nineteenth-century doll made from the death mask of a real child: The hair, eyebrows, and lashes of the corpse had been removed and pasted onto the doll. Before long, customers started seeing the figure of a tall, bearded man bent over the crib that held the doll. When a medium identified the spirit as Captain McCuen, the original owner, further research revealed

that his brain-damaged child had been confined to a crib until her death.

(Bodega is located off Highway 1 in Sonoma County. The shop is near the Salmon Creek Bridge on Bodega Rd., Bodega, CA 94922. Phone: 707-876-3104.) **116, 119**

BODFISH

BURLANDO-APALATEA HOUSE Ghosts started to appear in this house when it was moved to its present site in the late 1960s. An old rocking chair rocked itself, windows opened by themselves, and strange cold spots moved through the house, even in 105-degree weather. Guards reported unexplained voices, laughter, and the clinking of glasses coming from the deserted house. The house was originally home to Francisco Apalatea, his wife, and their seventeen children.

(Bodfish is in Kern County, thirty-five miles northeast of Bakersfield on Highway 178. The house is in the Silver City Ghost Town in Bodfish.) **72**

The deserted town of Bodie is now home to a dozen or so ghosts. See Bodie State Historic Park, Bodie, California (DENNIS POOLE)

BODIE

BODIE STATE HISTORIC PARK In the late 1870s, Bodie had a population of ten thousand, with seventy saloons, thirty mines, three breweries, three newspapers, several whorehouses, and one school. The only residents left are a dozen or so ghosts. A former maid, a heavyset Asian woman, is said to haunt the J.S. Cain House. She likes to pin down sleeping people by sitting on their legs. A mother and her children haunt visitors to Mendocini House, and an elderly woman in a rocking chair haunts Gregory House. People have heard disembodied voices near Seiler House and the sound of a nonexistent player piano in the museum. A nosy woman's ghost can sometimes be seen peeking out of the upstairs window of Dechambeau House. Floorstomping ghosts haunt the Order of Odd Fellows building. At 4.00 P.M. in the deserted Bodie Graveyard northwest of town, the ghost of a woman is sometimes seen hovering over a man's grave. Numerous reports describe her as wearing a white dress and knitting intently. In the same graveyard, numerous people have seen the "Angel of Bodie," a little girl accidentally struck in the head with a pickax when she stood too close behind a miner.

The old mines here are haunted, too. In 1902, a runaway mine car hit a pack mule at the five-hundred-foot level of the Standard Mine. The car broke the back of the white mule. Miners shot the animal to put it out of its misery and buried it in an old depleted shaft. Within two weeks, miners started hearing the clattering of the dead mule's chains; some were overcome by the odor of fresh mule droppings. Others saw the ghost of the white mule and refused to work at the five-hundred-foot level. It is said the phantom white mule still haunts the abandoned mine site. Witnesses tossing rocks down the twelve-hundred-foot Lent Shaft have heard a ghostly voice echo back with: "Hey, you!"

The last of the gold diggings was the Lucky Boy Mine. When it shut down after World War II, there were only six people left in town. One night, in a drunken brawl, one of those remaining residents, named Ed, shot his Indian wife with a shotgun. The blast blew her right breast off, and she eventually died in a hospital in Reno. Three men in Bodie decided to take justice into their own hands. They tied up Ed and threw him into a creek that ran through the town. Then they kicked him in the head until he passed out and drowned. Two months later, the ghost of Ed appeared to each of his murderers and waved its fist in anger. Within three weeks, each of the men died mysteriously. One was found with a huge gash in his head. Another had a hemorrhage that blew up his head like a balloon. They never found the body of the third man. His skeleton

may lie in one of the many arid ravines near Bodie still haunted by Ed's ghost.

(Bodie is twenty-six miles southeast of Bridgeport. In Mono County, follow Highway 395 north and exit east on Highway 270, fifteen miles to the ghost town. A total of 168 structures remain standing in this ghost town, some dating back to 1849. Phone: 619-647-6445. www.ceres. ca.gov/sierradsp/bodie.html) **66 (6/95), 96, 116, 134, 217**

BRENTWOOD

CRAWFORD HOUSE Christina Crawford says that when she was a child she often heard other children's voices coming from inside the walls of this house and saw their wraiths moving through the halls. Her famous mother, Joan Crawford, also heard the voices and arranged for a local minister to perform an exorcism on the property, but eventually the malevolent spirit of the house seemed to possess the actress. Joan Crawford's last words to her daughter were, "Don't you dare ask God to help me!" After Joan died, the wall behind her bed kept erupting into flames for no apparent reason. Fire department investigators spent four days at the house but never determined what caused the freaky phenomenon. Comedian Donald O'Connor, who bought the house from Crawford, suffered much mental stress there. Anthony Newley, who next owned the house, had it exorcised again. Recent owners have called in yet another exorcist to work with the possessed house.

(Brentwood is a suburb of Hollywood. The Crawford home is north of San Vincente Ave., in the Mandeville Canyon area, at 426 North Bristol Ave., Brentwood, CA 90049.) **193**

GARLAND HOUSE An unidentified ghost haunts Judy Garland's former home. Later residents have described it as a cold moving shadow.

(The Garland house is a private residence at 129 South Rockingham, Brentwood, CA 90049.) **72**

MONROE HOUSE In 1973, on the eleventh anniversary of Marilyn Monroe's death, psychic Anton La Vey and Marilyn's former husband, Bob Slatzer, claim her ghost materialized in front of the house where she took a fatal overdose of sleeping pills on August 4, 1962. Although she actually died in an ambulance at 11:30

that night, her body was returned to her bedroom to give actor Peter Lawford time to clean up any traces of her affairs with the Kennedy family. Psychics who claim to have contacted her spirit all agree on the message she wants to send from the grave: her death was an accident, not a suicide. But that was not all she had to say. Just after her death, Marilyn reportedly sent a message to her psychic advisor Kenny Kingston, while he was driving his car on the Pacific Palisades. She told him she would be reborn as a boy on the Isle of Capri in December 1980. During a séance held in her former bedroom in 1982, her ghost revealed a past life in which she had lived as an Aztec maiden who had been sacrificed to the gods. See Westwood Cemetery, Beverly Hills, California.

(Marilyn's house is now owned by film director Michael Ritchie. It is located at 12305 Fifth Helena Dr., Brentwood, CA 90049. Helena is a short street west of the San Diego Freeway, between San Vincente Blvd. and Bristol Ave.) **81, 88, 136, 193**

BRIDGEPORT

ALLEN HOUSE This two-story Victorian mansion is haunted by the ghost of its original owner, A. P. Allen. He committed suicide in an upstairs bedroom in the house. Unexplainable sounds of footsteps and bedsprings creaking are heard in the one-hundred-year-old house, and the ghost is said to pull off the bedcovers of people sleeping in the bedroom where he died.

(The town is about 350 miles north of Los Angeles on U.S. Highway 395. For tourist information, call 619-932-7500. Allen House is a private residence located on Main St., Bridgeport, CA 95338.) **217**

GREEN LAKE PACK STATION The ghost of an old hermit who lived for thirty-eight years in a small cabin near here still appears to hunters and campers in the area. The man's body was found in the cabin in 1906, and he was buried in Bridgeport Cemetery. His spirit remained near the secluded cabin. "What are you doing here?" the ghost asks trespassers. "What do you want?" Many reputable witnesses have reported encountering the talking apparition over the last thirty years.

(Take U.S. Highway 395 south out of Bridgeport to the old Green Lake Rd. The Green Lake Pack Station is about fifteen miles off U.S. Highway 395 at an elevation of seven thousand feet.) **217**

MONOVILLE The town of Monoville developed after gold was discovered in 1857. Within a few years, a thousand people lived here. In 1873, two friends dug a forty-foot-deep shaft near a small stream and brought out a large sack of gold nuggets. One day the shaft collapsed, and one of the miners, named Dolar, was crushed to death. Two weeks after the accident his partner noticed that some of Dolar's belongings were scattered about. Even a bundle of personal letters, locked up the night before in a strongbox, were found strewn about the campsite the next morning. The ghost of Dolar then appeared and told his partner where to dig another placer claim. The man struck it rich and retired to Bodie. But old Dolar is said to still wander the hills east of Monoville.

(The scant ruins of Monoville are located in Mono County about ten miles from Bridgeport at an elevation of 7,800 feet.) **217**

BROOKDALE

BROOKDALE LODGE This hotel, with its indoor stream, secret tunnels, and hidden rooms, was a favorite rendezvous for Joan Crawford, Marilyn Monroe, Tyrone Power, and other movie legends. The lodge was built in 1923 on the site of a hotel that dated back to the 1880s. A string of bad luck caused the lodge to shut down in 1984. In 1972, a thirteen-year-old girl drowned in the beautiful indoor pool and the owners decided to close it. Without the pool to attract visitors, bookings dropped off. Then in 1982, Clear Creek overflowed its banks after torrential rains. The creek ran right through the middle of the lodge, in the Brook Room, and the receding flood waters deposited mud and debris throughout lodge. The lodge sat deserted until 1990, when it was purchased by LeAnn and Bill Gilbert, a lieutenant with the San Francisco Police. They completely remodeled the place and reopened the pool. Not long afterward ghostly phenomena started to occur. LeAnn and Bill had both noticed strange things happening, but it was not until their daughter Kim saw the ghost of a young girl run across the lobby and disappear through a window that they realized they had a resident ghost. They called the little lost girl Sarah and blamed her for a wide variety of effects, such as slamming doors and turning on the jukebox or television sets. Sarah's youthful spirit seems to have attracted other ghosts to the Brookdale Lodge. Sarah's mother has been seen in the Brook Room, and the ghost of a twelve-year-old boy has appeared in Room 46. The ghosts of a woman named Mary and a lumberjack named George have also been detected. In fact, psychics say that forty-nine separate entities have returned to the Brookdale Lodge—so far.

(Brookdale Lodge is located in Santa Cruz County near Boulder Creek in the San Lorenzo Valley, eleven miles northwest of Santa Cruz on Highway 9. Brookdale Lodge, 11570 Highway 9, Brookdale, CA 95007. Phone: 831-338-6433. www.brookdalelodge.com) **175, 194**

BURLINGAME

KOHL MANSION This old mansion is haunted by the ghost of its first owner, Frederick Kohl. The building now serves as a high school on the grounds of the Sisters of Mercy Convent. His apparition has been seen in the parlor and on the stairway.

(Kohl Mansion, 2750 Adeline Dr., Burlingame, CA 94010. Phone: 650-343-8463.) **72**

CALABASAS

LEONIS ADOBE Although Miguel and Espiritu Leonis died nearly a century ago, current owners of their ranch house insist that they still roam the grounds. Miguel, a Basque settler, spent much of his time shooting trespassers and suing his neighbors over property disputes. He was once called the most hated man in California. The haunting began in 1922 when the occupants, the Agoure family, began to notice strange noises and unexplainable odors throughout the house. Today, there are regular sightings of the cadaverous couple by visitors and caretakers.

(Calabasas is a suburb of Los Angeles off U.S. Highway 101 in extreme western Los Angeles County. Leonis Adobe, 23537 Calabasas Rd., Calabasas, CA 91302. Phone: 818-222-6511. www.ralphenderle.com/adobe.htm) **116**

LOS ANGELES PET CEMETERY This is where many Hollywood stars buried their pets. The Little Rascals' dog, Hopalong Cassidy's horse, and Mary Pickford's dog are interred here. The dead animal that does the most haunting is Kabar, a Great Dane that belonged to Rudolph Valentino. The animal died in 1929, but its playful phantom is still reported to pant and lick people who wander near its grave.

(The Los Angeles Pet Cemetery is at 5068 Old Scandia Lane, Calabasas, CA 91302. Phone: 818-591-7037.) **182**

CAMARILLO

CALIFORNIA STATE UNIVERSITY Many odd events have taken place in this former state mental hospital, including manifestations of ectoplasm and poltergeist effects that have been witnessed by staff and visitors. In November 1962, the entire night staff was fired, because the hospital believed they were engaged in a conspiracy to "over-turn beds, tamper with lights and televisions, and shake doors." When the effects continued, they blamed it on an unidentified ex-patient who was breaking back into the hospital, although many attributed the effects to the unconscious psychic energies of the disturbed patients there.

(The building is in Ventura County at the junction of U.S. Highway 101 and Highway 34. California State University Northridge at Channel Islands, 1 University Dr., Camarillo, CA 93012. Phone: 805-437-8500.) **10**

CANOGA PARK

SHADOW RANCH PARK This former ranch estate is now a public park. The two-story wooden ranch house at the center of the park is reputed to be haunted by its former owner, Albert Workman. Visitors and caretakers have seen his ghost floating through the upstairs halls.

(The town of Canoga Park is located in northwest Los Angeles County, at the junction of Highway 27 and Sherman Way. Shadow Ranch Park, 22633 Vanowen St., Canoga Park, CA 91303. Phone: 818-883-3637.) **116**

CAYUCOS

CAPTAIN CASS'S HOUSE Captain James Cass built this house in 1867 and later owners say he never gave it up. His specter has been encountered in the back rooms of the two-story mansion, and the sound of his harp playing can sometimes be heard coming from the empty music room.

(Cayucos is on Highway 1 between San Simeon and Morro Bay on the central California coast. The house is a

private residence located in San Luis Obispo County, at 1654 Ocean Ave. in Cayucos, CA 93430.) **181**

CHANNEL ISLANDS

SAN MIGUEL ISLAND In 1542, Spanish explorer Juan Rodriguez Cabrillo landed here at Cuyler Harbor and officially discovered California. Tragically he died from gangrene contracted while exploring the island and ended up buried in a lead coffin near Prisoner's Harbor. Soon afterward, a Spanish galleon carrying two million dollars in gold sank in the treacherous waters off Point Bennett. Neither the coffin nor the ship has ever been recovered. Self-styled monarchs, who claimed the island was outside U.S. territory, set up communes here in 1890 and again in 1928. Both men ended up committing suicide rather than surrender their kingdoms to U.S. Marines. Today their ghosts still rule over the island.

(San Miguel is northwest of Santa Cruz Island in the Channel Islands National Park in the Santa Barbara Channel. For information, contact the Park Service at 1901 Spinnaker Dr., Ventura, CA 93001. Phone: 805-658-5700. www.nps.gov/chis) **116**

SANTA CRUZ ISLAND The cadaverous form of a Chinese fisherman searches for his severed hand among the black rocks just offshore here. In the late 1800s a large Chinese colony on the island supported itself by harvesting abalone and exporting the meat to Asia, where it was thought to hold the secret of long life. One day a gatherer got his hand caught between two massive rocks while trying to dislodge one of the prized mollusks. No one heard his screams for help as the incoming tide slowly reached his chest. In desperation he took his knife and whittled at his hand until it separated from his wrist. The agonized man bled to death on the beach, although his confused spirit is seen on the island's Northeast Shore. His ghost, wearing a wide-brimmed straw hat, quietly searches through the rocks for his severed hand. Another ghost of Santa Cruz is the wife of a man who robbed and murdered hundreds of Chinese immigrants he transported to the island. The ghost of Mary Morrison Reese, wife of Daniel Reese, is seen on Christy Ranch where they once lived.

(This island is the largest of the Channel Island group off Port Hueneme in Ventura County. For information, contact the Santa Cruz Island Preserve, P.O. Box 23259, Santa Barbara, CA 93121. Phone: 805-962-9111. www. vhby.com/santacruz.htm)* **72, 116**

SANTA ROSA ISLAND The specter of a weeping lady enveloped by a glowing orb of light is seen in the deserted valleys here. Sheepherders and hikers say she has waist-long hair and wears a flimsy gown that constantly moves as if blown by an ethereal wind. Her apparition hovers a few inches above the ground and glides slowly away when anyone approaches her. She is thought to be the spirit of a lonely sheepherder's wife who hung herself from an old oak tree overlooking the ocean.

(Santa Rosa Island is just west of Santa Cruz Island in the Pacific Ocean off Ventura. For information about visiting the islands, contact Island Packers, 1867 Spinnaker Dr., Ventura, CA 93001. Phone: 805-642-7688. www.islandpackers.com) **116**

CLAYTON

TOWN HALL Mysterious poltergeist activity has occurred in this building for the last ten years. Files scatter across the room, windows open, and loud clanging sounds disturb workers.

(Clayton is located in Contra Costa County, five miles southeast of Concord. The building is on Main St., Clayton, CA 94517. Phone: 510-672-3622.) **116**

CLEAR LAKE RESERVOIR

CLEAR LAKE WILDLIFE REFUGE In an area that has come to be known as Bloody Island, witnesses have reported the wailing apparition of a woman in white. She is thought to be the lone survivor of an 1850 Indian massacre, in which Modoc Indians attacked a wagon train that had stopped near the shoreline. When the young woman returned the next night to bury her parents, the Indians captured and killed her. Her white unearthly form has frightened tourists and local sheepherders, who avoid the area at night.

(Clear Lake Wildlife Refuge is located near the Oregon border in Modoc County, sixteen miles south of Newell on Highway 139 at the Clear Lake Rd. exit. Bloody Island is located off the northern shore.) **71, 116**

COLOMA

BELL'S GENERAL STORE Built in 1849, this brick building was the center of activity for a large community of gold miners that settled around Sutter's Mill. Modern visitors have reported hearing the ringing of a nonexistent bell as the ghosts of former customers walk through the doorway.

(Coloma is eight miles north of Placerville on Highway 49 in Placer County. The remains of the store are in the Gold Discovery State Park, just north of town on Highway 49. www.windjammer.net/coloma) **18**

MARSHALL MONUMENT On June 24, 1848, James Marshall found two small gold nuggets. They were caught in the tailrace of the waterwheel at the logging mill operated by him and his partner John Sutter. It was the beginning of the California Gold Rush. Between 1847 and 1860, the population of California grew from 15,000 to 380,000, largely because of that single event. Fanatical gold seekers followed Marshall wherever he went, thinking he had a magical gift for finding gold. He died broken and destitute on August 10, 1885, and was buried here. His restless ghost has been seen as an indistinct shadow following visitors to his monument.

(The Marshall Monument is in Gold Discovery State Park in Coloma.) **18**

PIONEER CEMETERY The phantom of a lady in burgundy keeps watch over the Schieffer family plot in this old settler's graveyard. According to the markers, William Schieffer died in 1861 at the age of two years, Charles Schieffer died in 1864 at the age of forty-two, and May Schieffer died in 1890 at the age of twenty-seven. The ghost is an elderly woman whose hair is parted in the middle and pulled back tightly into a bun. She wears a long, flowing burgundy dress and can be seen from the roadside, beckoning passersby to come up to the grave site and visit with her.

(Follow Highway 49 north out of Placerville and turn left where Highway 49 meets Coldstream Rd. The cemetery is up the hill on the left, across the street from Vineyard House.) **18**

SIERRA NEVADA HOUSE A mischievous spirit inhabits this hotel, which was established in 1850. Co-owner Gail Masi says her employees named the ghost Christopher and blame him for moving pots and pans, hiding knives and forks, turning off teakettles, and other harmless pranks. A malevolent spirit named Mark formerly haunted Room 4. According to psychic Jeanne Smith, he shot and killed his girlfriend in that room. Smith was able to release his troubled spirit from the scene of the crime.

(Sierra Nevada House, P.O. Box 496, Coloma, CA 95613. The inn is on Highway 49 in downtown Coloma. Phone: 916-621-1649.) **72**

VINEYARD HOUSE In 1879, less than a year after construction was completed on his mansion, Robert Chalmers went mad. For his own protection his wife Louise chained him in the cellar, but the insane man refused to eat and starved himself to death. After he died the family's grapevines mysteriously withered away, and Louise was forced to close their winery and take on boarders to make a living. She even rented out the cellar as a jail and allowed hangings in her front yard. She died in 1913 and was buried next to her husband in the cemetery facing their home. Subsequent residents of their house were so spooked by shimmering apparitions and the sounds of rattling chains that no one would live there. Remodeled into a hotel in 1956, Vineyard House has been the scene of dozens of poltergeist events witnessed by employees and guests alike. Glasses move by themselves in the basement bar, and a few years ago a Sacramento couple ran from the hotel in the middle of the night. They insisted they heard someone being murdered in the next room, although sheriff's deputies could find nothing wrong. Recently, a guest reported seeing the phantom of a small boy being beaten in Room 5, the same room from which the Sacramento couple had heard screaming.

(Vineyard House is across the street from the Pioneer Cemetery in Coloma. The mailing address is 530 Cold Springs Rd., Coloma, CA 95613. Phone: 530-622-7050.) **18, 66 (6/92), 72, 116, 119**

WAH LEE STORE Eerie waves of murmuring voices have been reported inside this old general store, the ghostly sounds of years gone by seeming to rise and fall like ocean waves. Listeners can make out the sounds of customers chatting idly, punctuated by the sound of a meat cleaver hitting a butcher block.

(The store is now a museum in the Gold Discovery State Park in Coloma.) **18**

CONCORD

BLACK DIAMOND PRESERVE Over a hundred exorcisms performed on grave sites in this abandoned cemetery have failed to tame its unsettled spirits. Wanton looting and desecration of the old Welsh graveyard could be the cause of continuing reports of ghosts, disembodied laughter and crying, and the unexplained sound of bells tolling.

(In Contra Costa County, take Highway 4 east out of Concord to the Loveridge Road exit. Go south and turn east at Buchanan and south at Somersville. Follow the footpath to the Rose Hill Cemetery.) **116, 119**

DEATH VALLEY

WINGATE PASS Legends of an underground world inhabited by a race of fair-skinned people who speak an unknown language have circulated among the Cahroc Indians for hundreds of years, and explorers in the Wingate Pass area of Death Valley have reported finding hidden caverns illuminated by eerie green light. In 1931, Dr. F. Bruce Russell announced he had discovered a cavern near Wingate Pass filled with eight-foot-tall mummified bodies and strange artifacts. Russell later discovered thirty-two similar caves within seven miles of his original find and spent the next fifteen years exploring the caverns. In 1947 he arranged financing for archeological expeditions to bring back the artifacts and examine them scientifically. But no one from the academic community would accept Russell's invitation without seeing some of the artifacts first. When Dr. Russell returned to Death Valley to bring back proof of his discovery, he was never seen again. Mass murderer Charles Manson believes that Devil's Hole, a water-filled cavern at the entrance to Wingate Pass, is a passageway to the underground civilization. He was arrested there in 1969 before he could lead his followers through the portal. At least two people have died trying to swim through the hundreds of feet of warm salty water. Navajo legends speak of apparent flying saucers landing in Death Valley, and some ufologists believe there is an underground alien base in an eighty-square-mile cavern here.

(Death Valley National Park is in San Bernardino County. For information and maps, write the National Park Service, Highway 190, Death Valley, CA 92328, or call 760-786-2331. Campsites can be reserved by calling

800-365-2267. Lodging can be reserved by calling 760-786-2345. The entire Wingate valley was made part of the China Lake Naval Weapons Center, and permission must be secured before visiting the area. Devil's Hole is just over the state line from Death Valley Junction at Highway 127 and Highway 190. www.death.valley.national-park.com) **1, 53 (9/49), 72, 116**

RACETRACK PLAYA Rocks and boulders weighing up to 650 pounds inexplicably move about on this dry, alkaline lake bed. Although the rocks leave trails up to fifteen hundred feet long, nobody has ever seen them move. Park rangers keep careful records of the phenomenon. Geologists believe the rocks move by the natural forces of wind and water, but some investigators have suggested that the movement is caused by magnetic or gravitational forces. The Shoshoni Indians called this area Tomesha, which means "ground afire."

(Take North Highway to the Grapevine Ranger Station and turn left at Racetrack Valley Rd. Follow the dirt road for twenty-eight miles. Do not visit this area in the summer! Death Valley was named by the surviving members of a group of thirty pioneers, after twelve of them died from heat stroke crossing the valley in 1849. Since then dozens of others have perished in the heat, the last being a hiker in 1991. The man's desiccated body was found after three days; his internal organs had congealed into one indistinguishable mass. Call 760-786-2331 for information about visiting Death Valley sites in the summer months.) **56, 72, 116**

SKIDOO A cemetery, a stamp mill, several mines, and one ghost are all that remain in this once flourishing gold mining town. The ghost is supposedly that of Joe Simpson, who killed the town's only banker in a robbery attempt. That same day, a lynch mob hanged Joe from a telephone pole and buried him in the local cemetery. Several weeks later, they dug up his body and hanged him again for the benefit of news photographers who had just arrived from Los Angeles. The town itself died a decade later, when the pipeline that supplied it with water was dismantled for scrap metal during World War I.

(Look for a narrow road going southeast from Highway 190 about thirteen miles south of Stovepipe Wells in Inyo County. Follow the road seven miles into Emigrant Canyon to the ghost town. A map of the site is available at

the Furnace Creek Visitors Center, Death Valley, CA 92328. Phone: 760-786-2331.) **140**

DORRINGTON

DORRINGTON HOTEL This town was named for the Scottish bride of John Gardener, who built the hotel over 120 years ago. Rebecca Dorrington Gardner died in the hotel in 1870. It is not certain whether she fell down the back stairs or froze to death—or both. What most people here do agree on is that she still haunts the place. Her painful cries are heard coming from the second floor, and several employees and guests have reported seeing her ghost, dressed in an old calico dress, in the hallways.

(Dorrington is in Calaveras County in the Sierra Mountains, just north of the Calaveras Big Trees State Park on Highway 4. Take Highway 4 north from Angels Camp on Highway 49. Dorrington Hotel and Restaurant, 3431 Highway 4, P.O. Box 4307, Dorrington, CA 95223. Phone: 209-795-5800.) **194**

DOWNIEVILLE

DYER'S RESORT Guests and employees at this thirteen-room complex have encountered the ghost of Gertrude Peckwith, wife of the builder of the central house here. She died at the turn of the century after falling or being pushed down the shaft of her husband's gold mine. Her presence is sensed most strongly in the basement laundry room and her second-floor bedroom.

(Downieville is in Sierra County on Highway 49, forty-five miles north of Grass Valley. The resort inn is along the north fork of the Yuba River near the town. Dyer's Resort, 121 River St., Downieville, CA 95936. Phone: 530-289-3308.) **72**

JERSEY BRIDGE This bridge became a makeshift gallows for a twenty-four-year-old Spanish woman who was executed by a lynch mob on July 5, 1851. Juanita was hanged from the bridge for murdering a popular local man, whose amorous advances she had resisted. Later her skull was stolen from her grave and used in initiation ceremonies at a men's club in nearby Sierra City. Today, Juanita's ghost appears out of a fog in the southeast corner of the structure and walks toward bystanders as if trying to tell them something.

(A steel bridge has replaced the original wooden structure over the Yuba River. On a small building at the end of the bridge is a plaque dedicated to the memory of Juanita.) **18**

ESCONDIDO

ELFIN FOREST Visitors to this park have observed a friendly, smiling woman only to suddenly realize she is a ghost. The White Lady usually appears in broad daylight and even touches people on their shoulders. Then, she floats about fifteen inches off the ground and glides through solid objects, ultimately vanishing into thin air.

(The park is in San Diego County, near Escondido, at the junction of Highway 15 and Highway 78. For information, call 760-471-9354.) **53, (1/83), 116**

FALLBROOK

NORTH COUNTY TIMES NEWSPAPER Glowing white lights and the floating specter of a little girl disrupted the daily routine of this newspaper for several years. Finally, in 1989 the owners asked the Alexandra Institute, a nonprofit psychic group from San Diego, to investigate the building. They reported that four different entities were haunting the establishment. Their efforts at calming the spirits seem to have worked so far.

(Fallbrook is located in San Diego County, six miles south of Temecula on I-15. The newspaper building is on the corner of South Main Ave. and Elder St. at 232 S. Main Ave. Fallbrook, CA 92028. Phone: 760-728-6116.) **119**

FRESNO

SAINT JOHN'S RECTORY Nuns and students at St. John's Catholic School saw the ghost of Sister Irenita almost every night for five years in the building that now houses the rectory. She died in 1931 and haunted the school until a special mass was held to put her to rest. When vandals dug up her coffin and exposed her corpse, Monsignor Cullen of St. John's parish reported that she was perfectly preserved and soft to touch, although her body had been buried for over five years and a thick tree root had broken into her coffin.

(Saint John's Cathedral, 2814 Mariposa, Fresno, CA 93701. Phone: 559-485-6210.) **116**

GARDEN VALLEY

ROSECRANZ MINE Though worked sporadically from 1852 to 1939, this cement-buttressed gold mine never really struck it rich. Perhaps that is why the sounds of hammers and picks, and the voices of busy miners are heard coming from the abandoned mine-shaft. And perhaps the mysterious light seen floating to the left of the crumbling mine head points the way to an undiscovered lode.

(The deteriorating mine and crusher building are about three hundred feet off Garden Valley Rd. in the town of Garden Valley, which is about eight miles north-west of Placerville in El Dorado County.) **18**

GAVIOTA STATE PARK

LAS CRUCAS ADOBE Ghostly harlots stalk the ruins of this old hotel and gambling hall. Two prosti-tutes strangled by an insane customer, and a third who hung herself in her room, are still encountered by visi-tors to the abandoned bordello. Ironically, the adobe was built on sacred ground, blessed by priests after a savage battle between Spanish soldiers and Indians. Scores of wooden crosses which once marked the graves of fallen Indians were removed to build a stage stop here.

(The park is located in Gaviota Pass in Santa Bar-bara County. Follow U.S. Highway 101 to Highway 1, and then take Sun Julian Road exit. Go one mile to the park entrance. Phone: 805-968-1033.) **116**

GEORGETOWN

AMERICAN RIVER INN Behind a basement wall in this elegant hotel lie the bodies of an undetermined number of miners buried in the collapse of the old Woodside Mine. However, the miner that haunts the place today survived that disaster. His name is Oscar, and he was shot dead on the steps of the hotel after an argument over a prostitute. A few days later, the prosti-tute leaped to her death from the hotel's balcony. A romantic fellow, Oscar still haunts lovers and honey-mooners who check into Room 5, his former room. He likes to turn on lights in the middle of passionate scenes. Then his nebulous figure enters from the bal-cony door, walks across the room, and leaves through the door at the top of the stairs. In 1986 alone, more than a dozen guests crossed paths with Oscar.

(Georgetown is on Highway 193, fifteen miles north of Placerville in El Dorado County. The Inn's mailing address is P.O. Box 43, Georgetown, CA 95634. The Inn is located on Highway 193, Georgetown, CA 95634. Phone: 530-333-4499. www.pcweb.net/ari) **18**

GEORGETOWN HOTEL The ghost of the former owner of this frontier-style hotel harasses employees in the kitchen and wakes up guests in Room 13. He has appeared so many times that he is like part of the staff. He is a tall man, around fifty years old, with gray streaks running through his black hair. He usually materializes with a pipe in his mouth and his hands resting on his hips.

(The hotel is at 6260 Main St., Georgetown, CA 95634. Phone: 530-333-2846.) **18, 72**

PROSPECTORS ROAD This treacherous mountain road has claimed many lives in the last 150 years, but today the ghost of a gruff old prospector makes the trip even more harrowing. The parting of weeds along the side of the road is the first sign of his approach. Then he materializes and floats up the embankment, con-fronting the fearful traveler with a pointing finger. "Get off my claim," he mouths in silence.

(The seven-mile stretch of road runs between George-town and Lotus. It parallels the more modern Marshall Rd., which connects Highways 49 and 193.) **18**

GRASS VALLEY

HOLBROOKE HOTEL The ghost of a blond woman dressed in nineteenth-century clothing has been seen by employees and guests in the upstairs hallway of this 143-year-old hotel. Another ghost, a cowboy in a striped shirt with boots and spurs, was spotted leaning against a post in the Iron Door, a basement dining room. None of the colorful ghosts have been identified.

(Holbrooke Hotel, 212 West Main St., Grass Valley, CA 95945. Phone: 530-273-1353. www.holbrooke.com) **72**

GREENWOOD

GREENWOOD GRAVEYARD The apparition of a tall man with humongous hands is seen walking through this overgrown cemetery. He seems to be desperately searching for someone. Witnesses say the phantom chases people and once attacked a group of teenagers who were vandalizing headstones.

(Greenwood is in El Dorado County, between the South and Middle forks of the American River, about ten miles west of Georgetown on Highway 193.) **18**

OLD MORTUARY BUILDING This building was once a mortuary, and conveniently, the tree in front of the building was Greenwood's official "hanging" tree. That tree seems to have become a portal to the ghostly realm. The apparitions of a woman and a boy about seven years old are seen standing under the tree and entering the front door of the building. A jolly ghost likes to show off his new boots to pedestrians on the sidewalk, and motorists have reported seeing the outline of a body hanging from the tree late at night.

(The Old Mortuary is located at 300 Main St., Greenwood, CA 95635.) **18**

GRENADA HILLS

ATWOOD HOUSE Soon after Dick and Lavonne Atwood moved into their new house in 1965, they noticed a strange blue light which hovered about four inches off the floor and moved silently through the halls. They thought the weird light was some kind of reflection from the street, so they hung heavy blankets on all the windows. Again, the misty blue light appeared. Their four children and even their cat and dog saw the light, which usually moved south from the main bedroom toward the kitchen. Then, one night Lavonne woke up to find the apparition of a man in sloppy boots and baggy pants standing next to her bed. Although frightened by Lavonne's encounter with the ghost, the Atwoods decided to try to contact their uninvited guest using a Ouija board. They discovered the name of the spirit was Noel Sepulveda. The simple man had promised his mother that he would never leave the land of their inheritance, and he remains on the property to this day. Noel usually makes his presence known by turning lights off and on, or opening and closing doors. Once, Dick and Lavonne were having an argument and the ghost came to Lavonne's defense by slapping Dick hard across the face. The house has been investigated by the Southern California Society for Psychical Research and North Carolina's Duke University Parapsychology Department.

(Grenada is in Siskiyou County in extreme northern California. The town is located eleven miles southeast of Yreka on I-5. The house is a private residence located on Petit St., Grenada Hills, CA 96038.) **217**

GUADALUPE

FAR WEST TAVERN The distinctive thumping of a peg-legged phantom sometimes interrupts conversation in this friendly steak house. The ghost can be heard walking noisily about in an upstairs room, just above the dining room here. Back in the 1930s when the establishment was a hotel, a guest by the name of Mr. Franconeti died in a fire in the building. He was apparently asleep at the time the fire broke out and was unable to evacuate his room because he could not attach his artificial leg in time. The unfortunate Mr. Franconeti, who had lost his leg in World War I, burned to death. Now there is an unexplainable cold spot in the corner where his ashes were found in his room, and people still see—and hear—his ghost.

(The town is in north Santa Barbara County, ten miles south of Oceano on Highway 1. Far West Tavern, 899 Guadalupe St., Guadalupe, CA 93434. Phone: 805-343-2211.) **181**

HALF MOON BAY

MOSS BEACH DISTILLERY The gruesome ghost of a lady in a blue dress soaked in blood haunts this old speakeasy on Half Moon Bay. Waitresses, chefs, managers, and customers have seen the young woman's phantom standing near the piano, outside the ladies' room, or dancing alone in deserted rooms. Once, a boy ran screaming from the restroom, insisting that a lady covered in blood touched him. In February 1992, two waitresses saw a stool tip over and do a somersault. The woman's bloody phantom was even spotted standing in the middle of Highway 1, which runs in front of the restaurant. On average, her ghost has been sighted once or twice every year for the last fifty years. In August 1992, all the settings in the restaurant's automatic thermostat system were mysteriously changed. The complicated reprogramming would have taken most people three or four hours to perform. "The company told me that there was no way it could have been done except manually," owner John Barber related, "but I had the only access key!" Previous owners say the ghost of the Moss Beach Distillery is the spirit of a young woman stabbed to death by a jealous lover on the beach in front of this cliffside restaurant over seventy years ago.

(Moss Beach is in San Mateo County, south of San Francisco on Highway 1. The town is just north of the

Half Moon Bay Airport. The restaurant is a few blocks west of Highway 1 on the corner of Ocean and Beach streets, Moss Beach, CA 94038. Phone: 650-728-5595. www.mossbeachdistillery.com) **72, 119**

ZABALLA HOUSE Guests who spend the night in Room 6 at this inn say it is haunted and have noted their feelings in the guest book. Strange things happen in the room. Alarms go off at all hours, keys break, and windows rattle for no apparent reason. But innkeeper Simon Lowins insists there are no ghosts at Zaballa House.

(The town of Half Moon Bay is at the junction of Highway 1 and Highway 92. Zaballa House, 324 Main St., Half Moon Bay, CA 94019. Phone: 650-726-9123. www.zaballahouse.com) **72**

HILLSBOROUGH

COUNTRY CLUB DRIVE In 1988, the family living in this suburban town house witnessed terrifying poltergeist activity. Horrendous bangs issued from the walls, and dinnerware flew off the table. Investigators traced the source of the weird events to psychic energy from the fifteen-year-old boy who lived in the house with his family.

(Hillsborough is a suburb of San Francisco, off U.S. Highway 101 near Burlingame. The house is a private residence in San Mateo County at 85 Country Club D., Hillsborough, CA 94010.) **72**

HOLLYWOOD

BEACHWOOD DRIVE APARTMENTS Tenants here have reported the phantom of a very old man walking up and down the main stairway of their apartment building. His halting, deliberate footsteps can be heard during the day or late at night and seem to be centered around Apartment 4.

(Hollywood is off U.S. Highway 101, southwest of Griffith Park. The apartment building is located in the 1200 block of North Beachwood Drive, Hollywood, CA 90025. For information on Hollywood sites in general, contact the Hollywood Chamber of Commerce 7000 Hollywood Blvd., Hollywood, CA 90028. Phone: 323-469-8311. For information on haunted locations, visit www.haunted-places.com) **72**

GIVENS HOUSE Robin Givens, actress and former wife of Mike Tyson, says the ghost of John Lennon shares this bungalow with her. Lennon leased the house when the Beatles were on the West Coast. Lennon was very intuitive about choosing where he lived and was fascinated by this house, as well as his apartment building in New York where he was staying when he was gunned down by a madman on December 8, 1980. See The Dakota, New York City, New York.

(The Givens house is a private residence off Sunset Blvd. near West Hollywood.) **193**

Dozens of Hollywood stars and a handful of ghosts may be found at the Cathedral Mausoleum in Hollywood Memorial Park. See Hollywood Memorial Park, Hollywood, California (B. A. SCHAFFENBERGER)

HOLLYWOOD MEMORIAL PARK The form of a lady in black has been observed in the Abbey of the Psalms Mausoleum, kneeling in front of crypt number 1205. It was intended as a temporary resting place for Rudolph Valentino, who died of peritonitis in 1926 at the age of thirty-one. However, his own crypt was never completed, and the famous actor still lies in the temporary tomb. The ghost of actor Clifton Webb, who died in 1966, has been reported several times in the foyer of the same mausoleum. The sound of sobbing is sometimes heard near Virginia Rappe's grave site. The silent-film star allegedly died after being forced to perform sadistic sexual acts with comic Roscoe "Fatty" Arbuckle. But after three sensational trials, he was acquitted of raping and murdering the young actress.

(Dozens of Hollywood's most famous stars are buried at this cemetery, located behind Paramount Studios at 6000 Santa Monica Blvd., Hollywood, CA 90028. Phone: 323-469-1181. A map to the grave sites is available at the front gate www.seeing-stars.com/Buried2/HollywoodMemorial.shtml) **15, 116, 182, 211**

HOLLYWOOD ROOSEVELT Employees of the Hollywood Roosevelt hotel report seeing the reflections of deceased guests in mirrors in the hallways there. The ghostly reflection of Marilyn Monroe is seen in a mirror that used to belong to the star, on display in the lower elevator foyer. The ghost of Montgomery Clift has been seen pacing the ninth-floor hall of the same hotel, and sometimes he can be heard practicing his trumpet. Carole Lombard's apparition has been spotted in the topfloor suite she shared with Clark Gable.

(The Roosevelt is at 7000 Hollywood Blvd., east of U.S. Highway 101. Phone: 323-469-4169. For reservations, call 800-833-3333. A macabre sightseeing tour is available from Grave Line Tours, P.O. Box 931694, Los Angeles, CA 90093. www.hollywoodroosevelt.com) **53 (11/93), 72, 182, 193**

HOLLYWOOD SIGN The hillside around this famous sign is haunted by twenty-four-year-old Peg Entwistle, a young starlet who leaped to her death from the top of the fifty-foot-high letter *H* on September 16, 1932. Tourists and hikers on Mount Lee have reported her ghostly presence, and her apparition has been seen walking down Beachwood Drive, where she once lived. The sign was built in 1923 to advertise a housing development and was purchased by the city of Hollywood in 1949.

(Peg Entwistle's former home is now a private residence at 2428 Beachwood Dr., Hollywood, CA 90025. The sign is on the south side of Mount Lee, overlooking the city. Entwistle is buried in Hollywood Memorial Park.) **72, 182**

The ghost of Harry Houdini is said to wander through the deserted garden behind his former mansion in Hollywood (JACKI POST)

HOUDINI MANSION Harry Houdini's mansion burned down over fifty years ago, and he died on Halloween, 1926, but people report seeing his dark form standing on the scorched staircase that survived the fire or walking in a garden grotto. The great magician promised that if there were a way to return from the dead, he would find it. See Houdini House, New York City, New York.

(The ruins of Houdini's home are on private property, located near the intersection of Laurel Canyon Dr. and Lookout Mountain Ave., at 2398 Laurel Canyon Blvd., Hollywood, CA 90028.) **56, 88, 168, 182**

MANN'S CHINESE THEATER The ghost of Victor Kilian roams the sidewalk here looking for the man who murdered him. The Irish actor appeared in over 140 films, and played Grandpa in the *Mary Hartman, Mary Hartman* television series. In 1976 he befriended a man at a nearby bar and invited him back to his apartment. Kilian's bludgeoned corpse was found the next morning, and the unidentified killer was never apprehended. The movie theater was built by Sid Grauman in 1927 and is known for a backstage ghost that clutches at the mainstage curtain and harasses visitors to the dressing rooms.

(Kilian's former apartment is a private residence at 6500 Yucca St., Hollywood, CA 90028. Mann's Chinese Theater, also known as Grauman's Chinese, is at 6925 Hollywood Blvd., Hollywood, CA 90028. Phone: 323-

*464-8111. www.seeing-stars.com/Immortalized/Chinese
TheatreForecourt.shtml)* **182**

NELSON HOUSE The specter of television star
Ozzie Nelson has been seen in his old house by family
members. The once cheerful comedian is apparently
not happy in the afterlife, for his ghost is always in a
decidedly somber mood.

*(The house is a private residence located north of
Franklin at 1822 Camino Palmero Rd., Hollywood, CA
90028.)* **15**

OBAN HOTEL Many celebrities, among them Glenn
Miller, Orson Wells, and Marilyn Monroe, stayed at this
hotel in its heyday. But the place is haunted by a stunt-
man and double for actor Harry Langdon. The man's
name was Charles Love, and he is joined in his afterlife
performance by several other unidentified spirits,
including a few other male ghosts, a female ghost, and a
very sinister presence in the basement.

*(The hotel is on Yucca St., near Vine, in Hollywood.
Oban Hotel, 6364 Yucca St., Hollywood, CA 90028.
Phone: 323-464-8111.)* **72**

PALACE THEATER Formerly known as the Hollywood Playhouse, this old theater building is haunted by
several presences, including the unidentified apparitions of a man and a woman.

*(Palace Theater, 630 S. Broadway, Hollywood, CA
90028. Phone: 213-239-0959.)* **72**

PARAMOUNT STUDIOS A ghost loiters in the catwalks above Studio 5 on this massive movie lot. His
footsteps echo through the empty studio, and many witnesses have beheld the ectoplasmic presence. Actress
Robin Tapp refused to continue working in the studio
because of the disturbances. The costume department
is haunted by the ghost of Rudolph Valentino. His shimmering form has been reported among the old garments there.

*(Paramount Studios is located at 860 N. Gower St.,
Hollywood, CA 90028. Phone: 323-956-5575. www.
paramountstore.com)* **72**

RUNYON PARK "Welcome to Hell" reads the graffiti
written on the pink concrete wall behind the tennis
court at this crumbling, 148-acre estate. Built by singer
John McCormack, it was later owned by A&P heir

Huntington Hartford, and then leased by actor Errol
Flynn. In the 1960s, the abandoned estate was home to
madman Charles Manson and his "family." Today all
that is left of the mansion are a few brick foundations.
Some neighbors say the splendid old mansion reappears on some summer nights, accompanied by the
sounds of a lavish party and multicolored lights on the
second floor. In 1983, psychic investigators at the site
were confronted by a malevolent voice that told them to
"Get out!"

*(The entrance to Runyon Park, also known as the
Pines, is at the northern tip of the 1800 block of Fuller
Ave. in Hollywood. From there, it is necessary to walk up
to 2000 Fuller Ave., where the estate is located. This is
private property. For information, call 323-444-1150.)*
72, 182

**SIERRA BONITA AND HOLLYWOOD BOULE-
VARD** Pedestrians and motorists passing through this
intersection have reported a wide variety of pioneer-era
apparitions. Indians on foot and on horseback are most
frequently reported. Flying tomahawks and arrows are
also observed. One driver ran into a tree when he
swerved to avoid the specter of a covered wagon crossing the intersection.

*(The site is at the intersection of Hollywood Blvd.
and Sierra Bonita Blvd., at 1700 West Sierra Bonita.)*
72, 182

UNIVERSAL STUDIOS Two ghosts haunt Sound
Stage 28. The most frequently encountered is the dark,
caped phantom of Lon Chaney, whose ghost has been
sighted here since he died in 1930. The other presence,
which haunts the catwalks, is thought to be an electrician who fell to his death in 1925. During the filming of
Poltergeist II (1986), many cast members witnessed
strange events at the studio and had terrifying nightmares. Kevin Ryerson, consultant for the film, said that
the entire set had an eerie feeling.

*(The studios are just off U.S. Highway 101, at 100
Universal City, CA 91608. Phone: 818-508-9600. www.
universalstudios.com)* **182, 193**

VALENTINO PLACE This old apartment building
used to be an elegant speakeasy in the Roaring Twenties and was often frequented by the great lover,
Rudolph Valentino. In April 1989, a twenty-eight-year-
old actress was awakened one night when she felt the

edge of the bed sag as if someone were sitting on it. Then she saw a solid form rise from under the sheet and felt someone press against her. She could hear heavy breathing and sensed the man's excitement. Terrified, she lifted the sheet and saw the handsome face of Valentino. The woman fainted, and when she awoke there were only empty sheets strewn about the room. See Falcon's Lair, Beverly Hills, California; Valentino's Beach House, Oxnard, California; and Santa Maria Inn, Santa Maria, California.

(The building is a private residence off Sunset Boulevard in Hollywood.) **193**

WARNER PACIFIC THEATER Sam Warner started building this theater in 1927, but he died before he could see it completed. Warner suffered a cerebral hemorrhage on October 2, 1927, and died in Los Angeles on the day his first talkie, *The Jazz Singer*, premiered in New York. The Warner Pacific Theater opened in April 1928, and not long afterward, people started seeing the ghost of Sam Warner in the building. The sightings continue to this day. Employees of a security firm that guards the premises have reported encountering Sam's ghost in the offices above the theater.

(The old theater, on Hollywood Blvd., is currently being converted into a museum.) **72**

JAMESTOWN

WILLOW STEAKHOUSE The original Willow Hotel was built in 1862 on the site of a collapsed mineshaft that killed twenty-three men. When a devastating fire struck the town in 1896, residents used dynamite to blow up other buildings to save the hotel. Unfortunately there were people still in those buildings, and their ghosts seek revenge to this day. Witnesses reported nine apparitions hovering around the source of a 1975 fire in the hotel, and in 1985 a mysterious blaze burned down the hotel and several nearby stores. The bar and restaurant were rebuilt, but the hotel never reopened. Both customers and employees have reported seeing the ghost of a short man roaming through the halls, and a gambler dressed in a black suit has been glimpsed at the bar. Others have seen the redheaded figure of Elualah Sims, murdered in the bar by her husband in the 1890s.

(Jamestown is located in Tuolomne County off Highway 49 in the Sierra Foothills. The restaurant and saloon are on the corner of Main and Willow streets, 18723 Main St., Jamestown, CA 95327. Phone: 209-984-3998.) **72, 116, 119**

JOSHUA TREE

MORONGO VALLEY UFO devotees insist there is a secret alien base hidden under the floor of this valley, and certainly it has been the site of much unexplained activity. It was here that famed contactee George Adamski allegedly met with angelic Venusian visitors and rode in their spaceships in the early 1950s. More recently, there have been reports of robotlike creatures wandering over the desert and vehicles dematerializing on the highway that runs through the center of the valley. More ghostly encounters have been reported in the sacred Wind Cave near the Barker Tank at the opposite end of the valley.

(Morongo Valley runs along the Little San Bernardino Mountains in the western section of the park. Phone: 760-367-5500. Campsites in the area can be reserved by calling 800-365-2267. www.nps.gov/jotr) **50, 53 (1/79), 72, 116**

KING CITY

MISSION SAN ANTONIO DE PADUA Long before Franciscan monks built this mission in 1771, local Indians told stories of visits from flying people in long robes. Today, small multicolored clouds hover just above the buildings, and people visiting or working at the Mission San Antonio de Padua have encountered ghostlike presences. Archeologists excavating the site have reported strange robed figures who linger in doorways or under arches and then suddenly vanish from view. Military police at Fort Hunter Liggett have chased a long-cloaked figure that drifts over the nearby Gavilan Impact Area. According to legend, an enraged Spaniard murdered his unfaithful Indian wife and buried her head and body in a separate graves. Now the countryside near the mission is haunted by a headless horsewoman, sighted over twenty times. On one occasion, four military policemen in a jeep chased the white figure for miles but never caught up with it. While on an archeological dig here, author Richard Senate saw the apparition of a monk, which prompted him to devote much of his life to the study of ghosts. Robert Hoover, an archeology professor at California Polytechnic, has studied the mission for the last eight years. He says, "It has an aura of the paranormal about it. I think there is truth in the ghost stories. It's a very haunted place."

(The mission, which is part of Fort Hunter Liggett, is in the Santa Lucia Mountains in Monterey County. It is located twenty miles south of King City, off U.S. Highway 101. Follow U.S. Highway 101 to the Jolon Road exit at King City. Turn onto Mission Creek Rd., which leads to San Antonio de Padua. Phone: 408-385-4478 www. kingcity.com/ci02005.html) **66 (10/93), 72, 102, 116, 133, 194**

LAKE ELSINORE

STATE RECREATION AREA A twelve-foot-long, three-foot-thick sea serpent has been sighted here since 1884. On several occasions during the winter of 1970, state recreation officers and residents saw the shiny black creature swimming with an up-and-down undulating motion like a huge snake on the surface of the water.

(The lake is in Riverside County, near the city of Riverside, south of the junction of Highway 74 and I-15. From I-15, take Highway 74 east. The entrance to the state recreation area is off Graham Ave. on the northwest shore. Phone: 714-674-3178.) **139**

LAKE ISABELLA

CAMP BRECKENRIDGE A Chinese cook by the name of Wong was employed by a tree-cutting operation here in the early 1900s. One of the women in the camp accused Wong of raping her in the camp kitchen, and five loggers unceremoniously dragged him out of the kitchen and hanged him from the nearest tree. Then they sat down and ate the dinner he had prepared for them. The life of a Chinaman was not worth much in those days, but a powerful organization of Chinese immigrants, known as a "tong," heard of the lynching and traveled from San Francisco to seek vengeance. Using ancient Taoist techniques, the tong members contacted the spirit of Wong, who appeared to them and pointed out the five men involved in his murder. One by one, the five men disappeared, and their bodies were never found. Much later, the area was flooded in the creation of Lake Isabella, and the conjured ghost of Wong is seen hovering above the water, pointing his accusing finger into the mists.

(From Bakersfield, take Walker Pass to the town of Kernville. Follow the old logger's road up Mount Brecken-
ridge to Lake Isabella. Phone: 760-379-5646. www.lake isabella.net) **217**

The ghost of a drowned man haunts Fannette Island in Emerald Bay on Lake Tahoe. See Emerald Bay, Lake Tahoe, California (B. A. SCHAFFENBERGER)

LAKE TAHOE

EMERALD BAY The ghost of Dick Barter is said to haunt Fannette Island in the middle of Emerald Bay, on the southwestern shore of Lake Tahoe. Barter came to the lake in 1863 as caretaker for Ben Holladay, a stagecoach magnate who had bought up most of the land surrounding Emerald Bay. Though a seafaring man, Barter soon took up the life of a hermit and left Emerald Bay only to pick up whiskey and provisions over at Rowland's Station on the south shore. One January night he got caught in a squall on the lake and lashed himself to the side of his boat. It was not until the next morning that he made it home, and by then two of his toes were frozen. When they turned gangrenous, he amputated them himself and kept them pickled in a jar to show off to people. The experience changed Barter, and he dug a tomb with a crude chapel over it on Fannette Island. He let it be known that if anyone ever found him lashed to his boat, drowned, he wanted to be buried there. In 1873, three years after digging his own tomb, Dick Barter's boat smashed into the rocks at Rubicon Point. His body sunk in fourteen hundred feet of water and was never recovered, but somehow his ghost found its way back to the chapel on Fannette Island.

(Lake Tahoe is located in northern California along the California-Nevada border. To reach Emerald Bay, follow Highway 89 north out of the town of South Lake Tahoe.) **72, 233**

TAHOE TESSIE A sixty-foot-long serpentine creature has been sighted swimming in Lake Tahoe. Tourism officials downplay the sightings and even admit to suppressing film footage of the creature shot in 1985. The first reports were by the Washoe Indians in the 1800s, but a rash of sightings in the 1930s brought the legend back to life. Since then, dozens of tourists, fishermen, and even a few scientists have reported seeing the giant, dark-skinned, snakelike creature in the pristine lake.

(Most of the sightings have been along the south and east shores of the fifteen-hundred-foot-deep lake. www. tahoebest.com/101/dragonspearl.htm) **72**

The ghost of an Indian chief is often seen near Le Beck Oak Tree, where a French trapper is buried. See Fort Tejon, Lebec, California (B. A. SCHAFFENBERGER)

LEBEC

FORT TEJON More than one thousand Indians at a time were imprisoned here under inhumane conditions, and hundreds died in the years between 1854 and 1864. A whole village of Indians was driven into the heavy, mineralized water of nearby Lake Castac and drowned. The twenty-building fortress was also a stop on the Butterfield Stage run between St. Louis and San Francisco. Psychics consider the fort's orderlies' quarters, hospital, and officers' quarters to be areas of high spiritual energy, but the most haunted spot is the Le Beck Oak Tree, a great oak in the northwest corner of the parade ground. The apparition of Peter Le Beck, a French trapper, has been reported many times near the tree. The Frenchman is buried under the oak, whose bark carries the carved inscription: "Peter Le Beck, killed by a X bear, October 17, 1837." The enigmatic inscription might mean a grizzly bear, or it might mean Chief Black Bear. It is known that the chief was hanged from another oak tree about three hundred yards from where Le Beck is buried, but for some reason the Indian's ghost is seen most often near Le Beck's haunted tree.

(The five-acre Fort Tejon site is in Grapevine Canyon near the town of Lebec on I-5, thirty-six miles south of Bakersfield in Kern County. The mailing address of the site is: Fort Tejon State Park, P.O. Box 895, Lebec, CA 93243. Phone: 661-248-6692.) **15, 66 (10/85), 71, 116, 181**

GORMAN SCHOOL This Spanish-style stucco school building has been haunted since it was built, in 1938, on the site of a farm where a twelve-year-old girl named Harriet lived in the 1930s. She was accidentally crushed by her father's tractor while playing in a field and was buried on the property. Her body is said to rest under the stage in the school's auditorium, where her ghost has appeared to a number of teachers, custodians, and students over the years. In the 1940s, after a woman's club meeting in the auditorium, the child appeared to an elderly lady and warned her not to go out the front door. Ignoring what she thought was a hallucination, the woman walked out the door and slipped in freshly fallen snow. She broke her hip in two places.

(The mountain town is at 4,100 feet elevation in the northeast corner of Los Angeles County, thirty miles north of Santa Clarita on I-5. Gorman School, 49847 Gorman School Rd., Lebec, CA 93243. Phone: 661-248-6441. www.frazmtn.com/gormanschool/gorman_school_district_home.htm) **133**

LITTLE LAKE

LAVA BED INDIANS In 1948, archeologists unearthed remains of an ancient tribe of Indians who lived in this region. They lived nearly eighteen thousand years ago, when the land was a tropical paradise, and used the sharp obsidian rock of the lava beds to make cutting utensils. Their bodies were unearthed sitting upright in large vases full of oil. Some say members of the mysterious tribe still haunt these now-barren plains. In 1968, a resident of Little Lake was haunted by a force that threw kitchen utensils about and made loud crashing noises in the middle of the night. She and her neighbors were convinced that the strange activity was caused by the spirits of Indian children who played on that very spot thousands of years ago. Guests at a local motel have reported seeing the smiling ghost of a naked Indian man in their room.

(The town of Little Lake lies between U.S. Highway 395 and Highway 6, about 170 miles northwest of Los Angeles.) **217**

LOMPOC

MISSION LA PURISIMA CONCEPCION Established in 1787, this Franciscan mission has been plagued with earthquakes, fires, floods, Indian attacks, epidemics, and unsolved murders. Small wonder so many ghosts have been reported here. The wraiths of little children, buried under the church floor during a smallpox epidemic, were seen by workers who remodeled the building in the mid-1930s. A ghostly gardener still tends the beautiful flowers on the grounds, and the kitchen is haunted by the ghost of Don Vicente, who was murdered there over 150 years ago. It is not surprising that the soul of Fray Mariano Payeras has not found peace: For some strange reason, only the upper part of his body was interred in the church tomb here. The other half is buried sixty miles away at another mission. See Mission Santa Barbara, Santa Barbara, California.

(The La Purisima Mission State Historic Park is located four miles northeast of Lompoc in Santa Barbara County. Take Highway 1, Ocean Ave., to Highway 246, then drive east fifteen miles. Mission La Purisima Concepcion, 2295 Purisima Rd., Lompoc, CA 93436. Phone: 805-733-3713. Call 805-733-1303 for tour information. www.californiamissions.com/cahistory/lapurisima.html) **14, 116, 181**

RANCHO LOMPOC In 1833, soldiers digging a powder magazine at this old fort discovered a stone burial crypt that contained the remains of a twelve-foot-tall titan with double rows of teeth in his jaws. Buried with him were carved shells, stones with hieroglyphic marks on them, and several stone axes. Concerned local Indians believed that the remains were those of a member of an ancient tribe of giants, the Oh-mah, and to placate them soldiers reburied the carcass somewhere on the property. It was never found again. The Ohmahs, or "Dark Watchers," were tall, naked phantoms who lived like animals and bore a striking resemblance to our modern Bigfoot.

(The Rancho Lompoc area lies southwest of Lompoc, east of Vandenberg Air Force Base, in Santa Barbara County.) **116, 194**

LONE PINE

ALABAMA HILLS A ghost nicknamed Rescue Man roams these hills leading lost or stranded hikers to safety. He is thought to be Indian Jim, a guide and gold prospector who died here in the 1940s. Once, he appeared to a tungsten prospector and told him to head for Lone Pine immediately. The man, who recognized the ghost as Indian Jim; took his advice and made it to town just as a devastating blizzard blanketed the area. See Mountain Railroad, Owens Lake, California.

(Lone Pine is in Inyo County at the junction of U.S. Highway 395 and Highway 136. The Alabama Hills run adjacent to the town.) **217**

OLD FIREHOUSE This old building housed a hosepump wagon used to fight fires at the turn of the century. The site was also home to the ghost of an old Indian who guarded a cache of looted gold. In 1870, the Hog Back Creek tribe stole a shipment of gold coins intended for payment to soldiers at the Alabama Hills Fort and buried it about ten miles from their encampment. For the next twenty-five years the Indians guarded the treasure, until white settlers decided to construct a firehouse on the same spot. When the last Indian guard refused to budge from his appointed post, white men killed him. The tribe buried the guard not far from the firehouse, which the ghost haunted for many years. Even when the firehouse was torn down, the phantom Indian stayed at his post. In 1946, the tenacious apparition appeared to a family who parked a trailer nearby. And when the Richardson family built a house on the site, they felt an unnamed presence sharing their home.

(The old firehouse site is part of the Cain Ranch development, about three hundred yards off Portal Rd., just outside Lone Pine.) **217**

PORTAL ROAD In the late 1860s, Paiute Indians frequently attacked the Alabama Hills Army Fort that stood here. Over a century later, bands of phantom Indians are still attacking residents of the area. A black man dressed as an Indian chief leads the renegades, who have surrounded several homes and then disappeared into thin air. One resident of the area saw the ghost of a lone black rifleman lead a band of eight ghostly Indians across the freshly mowed lawn of her front yard. For fifteen minutes she heard gunshots and saw the apparitions fire on an invisible fortress located across the creek in front of her house. Her neighbors have reported similar encounters.

(Lone Pine is in Inyo County at the junction of U.S. Highway 395 and Highway 136. The incidents happen a few miles west of town on Portal Road, which leads up to Mount Whitney. For general information about the area, call 619-876-4444.) **116, 217**

LONG BEACH

RANCHO LOS CERRITOS This two-story adobe dwelling served as the hub of a large ranch. Today it is haunted by the presence of the former owners, as well as a ranch foreman whom most consider an evil presence.

(Long Beach is on the Pacific Ocean, south of Los Angeles, at the south end of Highway 710. The building is located off Long Beach Blvd. in Long Beach. Rancho Los Cerritos, 4600 Virginia Rd., Long Beach, CA 90807. Phone: 562-570-1755.) **72**

QUEEN MARY HOTEL This ocean liner, now permanently docked at the Port of Long Beach, was commissioned in 1936 and made over a thousand Atlantic crossings. Many incidents of strange rapping noises, moving objects, disembodied voices, and ghostly apparitions have been reported by staff, guests, and investigators on the drydocked ship. The first-class swimming pool is haunted by the ghosts of two women who drowned there. One is dressed in 1960s clothing

and the other wears 1930s attire. The forlorn ghost of a little boy who fell overboard near the pool has been sighted in the passageway. The old first-class lounge, now known as the Queens Salon, is haunted by the ghost of a beautiful woman in a flowing white dress. Unexplainable balls of light and the apparition of a black-haired man in a 1930s suit have been seen by tour guides in the first-class suite area.

The forward storage room, where the ship's archives are kept, is haunted by the sounds of children playing. Inexplicable pounding sounds have been recorded near the bo'sun's locker, which is the area of the hull which sliced the British light cruiser *Curacoa* in half during World War II. Because of her wartime sailing orders, the *Queen Mary* was not allowed to stop to rescue survivors, and 338 men perished in the cold ocean. The tourist-class swimming pool is haunted by the presence of a woman who drowned in it, and the third-level Cabin B340 is haunted by a murdered purser and is no longer rented out because of unexplained disturbances there.

Poltergeist activity has been reported in the kitchen, where a cook was murdered during World War II. It is said his cooking was so terrible that it caused a riot among troops being carried to the front. The violence quickly got out of hand and the cook ended up stuffed inside an oven and burned to death. His ghastly screams are sometimes heard by startled visitors.

The ghosts in the ship's morgue could have any of a number of identities. Sixteen crew members, two GIs, and thirty-one passengers have died on the ship. But the most documented sighting is the apparition of an eighteen-year-old crewman, John Pedder. Pedder was crushed to death while trying to slip through an automatically closing door in shaft alley during a routine watertight drill on July 10, 1966. It was hatchway Door No. 13. Another crewman allegedly haunting the *Queen Mary* is Senior Second Officer William Stark. He was accidentally poisoned in 1949, when he drank tetrachloride that the staff captain kept in an old gin bottle. So far, over fifty witnesses have reported paranormal happenings on this ship, and the list keeps growing.

(The Queen Mary Hotel and Museum is berthed at Pier J in the Port of Long Beach. The mailing address is: The Queen Mary, 1126 Queens Highway, Long Beach, CA 90802-6390. Phone: 562-435-3511. www.queenmary. com/QMweb/html/hotel.html.) **50, 53, (4/84, 5/91), 72, 116, 119, 135, 139, 199 (10–92)**

LOS ANGELES

ARDMORE RESIDENCE This fifty-year-old house has been the scene of recurring ghostly parties where someone apparently is murdered. Residents also hear disembodied footsteps and screaming voices warning them to run for their lives. Researchers have traced the disturbances to a young woman who was murdered by a man at a party and buried under a flower bed in the back yard.

(The house is a private residence located in the 3500 block of Ardmore Boulevard, Los Angeles, CA 90025.) **72, 116**

CITY HALL The ghost of a man wearing fancy clothing from the eighteenth century has disrupted council meetings here and harassed city managers in the restrooms.

(City Hall is located on the corner of Temple and Main streets, 200 N. Spring St., Los Angeles, CA 90012. Phone: 213-485-2121. www.parkives.com/famous_cityhall.html) **72, 116**

COMEDY STORE This old building used to house the famous Ciros Nightclub. It is thought the ghosts here date back to those days when both Hollywood celebrities and mobsters frequented the place. Apparently the ghosts really hated comedian Sam Kinison when he performed at the Comedy Store, because unexplainable problems with lighting and sound gear plagued his performances. A more sinister phantom, described as "seven feet tall and blacker than black," also haunts the premises.

(The theater is located on the Sunset Strip at La-Cienga. Comedy Store, 8433 Sunset Blvd., West, Los Angeles, CA 90069. Phone: 323-650-6268. www. thecomedystore.com) **72**

DRUM BARRACKS This old Civil War post is haunted by the ghosts of an officer and a woman named Maria, thought to be his wife. Their children are also seen, as well as a few Apache scouts. When the building was a private house at the turn of the century, residents told of encountering the bevy of departed ones. One resident even remembered being told stories by the man and woman ghosts. Sightings continue to the present day. In 1995, a couple passing by the deserted barracks reported seeing the ghosts of Civil War soldiers.

(The old outpost is located in the Wilmington district of Los Angeles. Drum Barracks, 1052 Banning Blvd., Los Angeles, CA 90744. Phone: 310-548-7509.) **72**

EL CENTRO AVENUE The ghosts of a young married couple return to the rental house where they committed suicide together. Several tenants have stated that the couples' apparitions appear in the middle of the night, standing silently at the foot of their bed.

(The Spanish-style house is in the 1200 block of North El Centro Ave., Los Angeles, CA 90005.) **72**

FOUR OAKS RESTAURANT This building was constructed in the 1880s as a way station for travelers between Los Angeles and the San Fernando Valley. Later it was used as an inn, a café, bordello, and speakeasy. All that history makes identifying the glowing figure that materializes here a formidable task. It is easier to find the identity of the headless phantom dressed in yellow who appears just down the street at the Old Roadhouse. The building was the scene of a gruesome murder in which a wealthy landowner decapitated his wife's lover when he found them in bed together at the Old Roadhouse. Her lover's favorite color was yellow.

(The Four Oaks is north of Sunset Blvd. at 2181 North Beverly Glenn Blvd. The Old Roadhouse is also on North Beverly Glen Blvd., Los Angeles, CA 90077. Phone: 310-470-2265.) **72**

GRIFFITH PARK This three-thousand-acre park has a curse on it pronounced 150 years ago by a young blind girl. "This is what I hurl on your head," Dona Petranilla shouted at her dying uncle. "Your falsity shall be your ruin. Misfortune, crime, and death shall follow all who covet these remains." She was referring to what is now the nation's largest municipal park, property that her uncle had willed to a close friend, leaving her without a home. Soon afterwards, the probate judge in the case died and the lawyer who administered the property was killed in a drunken brawl. The new owner's family was plagued by petty jealousies and ended up penniless. Later owners of the land also suffered terribly. In 1884, during a violent storm that stripped the land of nearly all vegetation, ranch hands witnessed a ghostly figure cursing the property and all who dwelt there. It is said that the last owner, Griffith J. Griffith, donated the land to the city just to get rid of it. A few years later the poor man went insane and was sent to San Quentin for trying to kill his wife.

(The huge park is located in north Los Angeles. Take I-5 to Los Feliz Blvd. and exit west to Griffith Park Dr. Phone: 213-485-5520. www.cityofla.org/RAP/grifmet/gp) **116**

JOLLY HOUSE This sixty-year-old Spanish adobe house has been the scene of amazing poltergeist activity. The trouble started when Don Jolly, the senior vice president of a respected savings and loan company, moved in. Before long, objects and furniture were moving by themselves. Books, goblets, coasters, shoes, pictures, and even cabbages levitated in front of researchers from UCLA and KTTV camera crews in 1989.

(Mr. Jolly moved out of his north Los Angeles home shortly after the events began, and later residents have reported no unusual activity.) **119**

PINK PALACE When Jayne Mansfield bought this thirteen-bathroom mansion, she had it painted a garish pink. In fact, she loved the house so much she returned to it after her death. Although she was decapitated in an automobile accident a year after joining the Church of Satan in San Francisco, she looks better than ever, according to those who have seen her lounging in her bathing suit near the heart-shaped swimming pool in the backyard. Singer Englebert Humperdinck saw her ghost walking down the stairway shortly after he bought the house.

(Jayne's three-story, six-bedroom house was built by singer Rudy Vallee. It is located at 1220 Bel Air Dr., Los Angeles, CA 90077.) **193**

POINT VICENTE LIGHTHOUSE Nothing out of the ordinary went on here until officials blacked out the landward side of the powerful beacon's glass tower. Local homeowners had complained that the bright beam disturbed them, but in attempting to alleviate the problem the coast guard accidentally summoned forth a spirit from beyond. The ghost of a tall woman with long, tangled hair is now seen walking near the lighthouse. Her flimsy gown blows slowly in the wind as she circles the tower. She is thought to be the specter of the first lighthouse keeper's wife, who fell off a nearby cliff while lost in the fog. Now, in the darkness she has returned.

(Point Vicente is near the intersection of Palos Verdes Drive and Los Verdes Blvd. in the Ranchos Palos Verdes

section of Los Angeles. It is one and a half miles west of Marineland of the Pacific at 31501 Palos Verdes Dr. Phone: 310-541-0334.) **72**

SWEET LADY JANE'S The ghost of actor Orson Welles sits at his old table in this fine restaurant. Several employees and customers have detected his cigar smoke or the aroma of his favorite brandy. His distinctive apparition, wearing a black cape, has also been seen sitting at the table.

(Sweet Lady Jane's Bakery and Restaurant, 8360 Melrose, Los Angeles, CA 90069. Phone: 323-653-7145.) **182**

TIMES-MIRROR SQUARE In 1934, mining engineer W. Warren Shufelt proposed excavating this area of Los Angeles in hopes of discovering traces of a lost civilization. According to Hopi Indian legends, the Lizard People (see Mount Shasta, California) used some sort of rock-dissolving chemical to build a subterranean city here in 3,000 B.C. Shufelt sunk a 350-foot shaft on North Hill Street and allegedly bored into secret gold-filled catacombs. Using radio waves, Shufelt produced detailed maps of the underground city and located the central treasure room four hundred feet below Times-Mirror Square. Although few people took him seriously at the time, construction workers have since unearthed miles of tunnels, which historians attribute to nineteenth-century smugglers.

(Times-Mirror Square is bounded by 1st St. and Broadway in downtown Los Angeles. According to Shufelt, the Lizard People's underground city runs under the Financial District, from Central Library to what is now Dodger Stadium. A vast network of ventilation shafts extend from the area around the Southwest Museum all the way to the Pacific Ocean.) **116**

VARIETY ARTS CENTER The ghost of a former performer is seen backstage during rehearsals at this theater. Manager Carl Fleming says the phantom of a male actor wearing a sixteenth-century costume prepares for an unscheduled performance, much to the surprise of living actors and stage crews.

(Variety Arts Center, 940 Figueroa St., Los Angeles, CA 90001. Phone: 213-362-0440.) **72, 116**

LYNWOOD

LAGO AVENUE The ghost of the original owner of this century-old European bungalow makes a point of visiting new owners and wishing them well. Within a year of the property's sale, a kind elderly lady shows up and identifies herself as a former tenant. She is interested in the changes the new owners have made and compliments them on improvements. It is not until she is gone that the owners realize she was a ghost, who has disappeared into thin air. The house has a patio and a rear garden full of unusual plants. There is also a smaller garden at the front of the house. It is in one of these two gardens that the kind old lady in the faded pink dress materializes, hinting that she would like to tour the inside of the house as well.

(Lynwood is located in Los Angeles County, fifteen miles north of Long Beach, off Highway 710. The house is a private residence on Lago Avenue, near the corner of Elm Street, Lynwood, CA 90262.) **85**

MALIBU

THELMA TODD'S GARAGE The star of 108 films died here on December 16, 1935, of carbon monoxide poisoning. The police list the case as a probable suicide, but family members say she started her car in the garage to stay warm after locking herself out of her house. To further confuse matters, an autopsy revealed that she had multiple bruises, a broken nose, and two broken ribs, suggesting foul play. Whatever the true circumstances of Thelma Todd's mysterious death, she apparently has some unfinished business. Those who work in the building which once housed her famous café repeatedly sight her ghostly figure at the top of the staircase leading from her old apartment to the courtyard.

(Malibu is eight miles west of Santa Monica on Highway 1. Thelma Todd's property is in Pacific Palisades, which is a section of Highway 1 near Malibu. Her garage is at 17531 Posetano Road. Her restaurant and residence, just down the hill at 17575 Pacific Coast Highway, Pacific Palisades, CA 90272, is now home to Paulist Productions. Phone: 310-454-0688.) **119, 182**

TRAFTON HOUSE Schoolteacher Bliss Trafton and his family say that a ghost dressed in Spanish armor walks through their home at night. In 1990, investigators from UCLA recorded unexplained pounding sounds and cold spots in the house. The disturbances continue.

(The house is a private residence in the Pacific Palisades area of Malibu.) **72**

MARIPOSA

HORNITAS One of the best preserved gold rush ghost towns also has its share of well-preserved ghosts. In the 1850s the streets of Hornitas were crowded with robbers, gunslingers, gamblers, and prostitutes. The town was so tough that outlaws who killed each other were simply dumped into a deep gully called Dead Man's Gulch. The ghost of Joaquin Murrieta is said to wander these parts, searching for his missing head and deformed hand, which were cut off by bounty hunters to prove they had killed the notorious bandit.

(Mariposa is at the junction of Highway 49 and Highway 140 in the Sierra foothills. Inquire at the County Mariposa Museum, 5119 Jessie St., Mariposa, CA 95338.) **140**

MARKLEEVILLE

GROVER HOT SPRINGS STATE PARK For many years the specter of a Civil War soldier dressed in full Union battle gear has been encountered along the back roads in this area. When confronted by witnesses, he walks slowly away and fades from view. The soldier ghost was first seen in the early 1870s by stagecoach drivers coming up from Genoa, Nevada. An intrepid driver drove his horses right through the apparition.

(Markleeville is on Highway 89 in Alpine County at an elevation of 6,500 feet. The park is west of town. Grover Hot Springs State Park, Hot Springs Road, Markleeville, CA 96120. Phone: 530-694-2248.) **116, 217**

MARYSVILLE

LANEY HOUSE Anita and Francis Laney believe their old Victorian house is haunted by the original owners, the Norman Abbott Rideout family. The Laneys have seen a little boy and girl playing in the upstairs halls while the children's fashionably dressed parents stood by the front window. Visitors to the house have reported that dinnerware and vases have a way of falling to the floor for no apparent reason.

(Marysville is in Yuba County, fifty miles north of Sacramento, off Highway 99. The house is a private residence at 710 D St. Marysville, CA 95901.) **119**

MENDOCINO

MENDOCINO HOTEL Built in 1878, this beautifully renovated hotel is haunted by a variety of unidentified spirits. Some of the ghosts appear to be fishermen who lost their lives at sea, but others are beautiful young women. One female specter, dressed in a Victorian gown, haunts tables 6 and 8 in the restaurant and is seen in a mirror there. An invisible presence haunts Room 10 but leaves visible impressions of its body on the bed. In Room 307, the image of a man's face has appeared mysteriously in the bathroom mirror.

(Mendocino Hotel, 45080 Main St., Mendocino, CA 95460. Phone: 707-937-0511. www.mendocinohotel. com) **72**

A shimmering green apparition has materialized at the Peninsula School. See Peninsula School, Menlo Park, California (GORDON TING)

MENLO PARK

PENINSULA SCHOOL Carmelita Coleman did not move into her beautiful house until after she died. The house was finished in 1880, but while Carmelita and her husband were packing to move in, she accidentally shot herself with her husband's gun. Afterward, her husband refused to set foot in the mansion, and eventually it became a private school. Since then, Carmelita's restless spirit has returned frequently, appearing as a shimmering green apparition to scores of witnesses. Once, it materialized before a class of twenty students and a

teacher for over five minutes. Another time, instructor Joe Starr encountered the green lady face-to-face in a hallway. The amazed man watched her slowly vaporize before his eyes.

(Menlo Park is in San Mateo County, thirty miles southeast of San Francisco on Highway 82. Peninsula School, 920 Peninsula Way, Menlo Park, CA 94025. Phone: 650-325-1584.) **72, 119**

MOJAVE

KELSO VALLEY For the past sixty years, hunters in this isolated valley have tried to bag a magnificent deer that always eludes them. The phantom deer, seven feet tall with a huge rack of antlers, never leaves tracks or trampled brush. Parties of hunters have had the animal surrounded, only to see it disappear before their eyes.

(Mojave is in San Bernardino County. Take Highway 14 north out of Mojave and turn left onto Jawbone Canyon Rd. at the Cantil Post Office. Go 18.5 miles to Kelso Valley Rd. The valley begins here and runs twenty-five miles to Highway 178. Most of the sightings have been near Sheep Springs.) **116, 217**

This photograph depicts George Leger, the founder of the century-old Hotel Leger. His specter is still seen in the halls. See Hotel Leger, Mokelumne Hill, California (S.A. SCHAFFENBERGER)

MOKELUMNE HILL

HOTEL LEGER Before you take a room at Hotel Leger, be sure to take a good look at the portrait on the north wall of the dining room, a photograph of the founder of the century-old hotel, George Leger. He was an aristocratic French immigrant who lived and died in Room 7 of the hotel. George was known for his amorous adventures with the wives of the local gold miners and for the meticulous way he ran his hotel. Many witnesses can attest to the fact that George never really left. Startled guests have confronted his well-attired specter gliding silently through the halls. Some people have complained of rowdy laughter and ladies' giggling behind the door of an otherwise empty Room 7. The hotel's personnel accept George's presence as a normal part of their jobs, and manager Ronald Miller remembers to pay his respects. Not long ago, while patrolling the halls, he noticed the shadow of a man following him. Miller turned around, and though he could see nobody there, the shadow remained on the wall. "Good night, George," he said, and the shadow disappeared.

(The Leger Hotel is just off Highway 49 in Calaveras County. Leger Hotel, 8304 Main Str., Mokelumne Hill, CA 95245. Phone: 209-286-1401.) **18, 66 (6/92), 72, 217**

MONTECITO

ORTEGA ROAD The ghosts of three nuns allegedly tortured and killed by Indians have haunted this roadway for over a century. Las Tres Hermanas, as they have come to be called, stand on the roadside with their arms folded, wearing black and white habits.

(Ortega Road is in Montecito, which is on Highway 192 in Santa Barbara County.) **181**

MONTEREY

CUSTOM HOUSE Although this is the oldest government building in California, at one time it was a boarding house with at least one resident ghost. He was an elderly gentleman, whose form was regularly sighted near the storehouse tower. Even today, the sounds of his coughing are sometimes heard echoing through the south halls of this building.

(The 1827 building is on Custom House Plaza in the Monterey State Historic Park. Phone: 831-649-7118.) **116, 153**

LA CASA BODEGA LIQUOR STORE The phantom of a young male clerk murdered during a robbery at this liquor store returns to warn customers of trouble. He appears to employees and customers, usually between the hours of 7:30 and 9:30 P.M.

(The store is at Del Monte St., Monterey, CA 500 93940. Phone: 831-649-6660.) **116**

MISSION SAN CARLOS The phantom of a man on horseback has been seen riding past this mission heading toward Monterey. He is dressed in a cape in the style of a Spanish officer. Legend says he is the ghost of a Spaniard killed by Indians as he tried to deliver an important dispatch.

(The mission, founded by Fray Junipero Serra in June 1770, is just south of Carmel off Highway 1. Mission San Carlos Borromeo del Rio Carmelo, 3080 Rio Rd. Carmel, CA 93921. Phone: 408-624-3600.) **66 (10/93)**

SAN CARLOS CATHEDRAL A ghostly candle held by an invisible hand has been seen by dozens of witnesses here. The church was founded in 1770 and became the chapel for the Monterey Presidio in 1795, but has only become haunted in the twentieth century. Parishioners see the candle floating in midair and some have come face-to-face with the ghost of a priest who served there in the 1920s. The tower bells sometimes ring unexplainedly in the middle of the night as well. The otherworldly encounters have taken place both in the church and the rectory next door.

(San Carlos Cathedral, also known as the Presidio Chapel, is at 500 Church St., Monterey, CA 93940. Phone: 831-373-2628.) **116, 151, 152, 153**

STEVENSON HOUSE Robert Louis Stevenson lived in this apartment house in 1879, but it is the ghost of his landlady, Mrs. Girardin, who haunts the place. When Stevenson boarded there, his landlady's two grandchildren caught the dreaded typhoid disease. While trying to nurse them back to health Mrs. Girardin also contracted the illness and died on December 21, 1879. Today, the grandmother's apparition, dressed in black clothing, hovers over a small bed in the nursery and is seen by caretakers, guides, and tourists. Toys on display in the nursery are said to move mysteriously, and an unoccupied rocking chair in the Stevenson bedroom moves serenely back and forth for hours.

(Stevenson House is a few blocks from San Carlos Cathedral. Stevenson House, 536 Houston St., Monterey,

CA 93940. Call 831-649-2836 for information on tours, which are held irregularly.) **116, 151, 152, 153, 156**

STOKE'S ADOBE RESTAURANT This quaint Victorian house, built in 1838, was the scene of so many unexplained disturbances that a restaurant operating there was forced to close down. Manager Paul Johnson said that an unseen entity tugged at guests' clothing and trashed the kitchen almost daily.

(The restaurant formerly Gallatin's is at 500 Hartnell St., Monterey, CA 93940. Phone: 831-373-1110.) **116**

U.S. NAVAL POSTGRADUATE SCHOOL The ghost of a man in gray has been spotted numerous times in this building, which at one time was one of the grandest hotels on the west coast. Some investigators have suggested that the gray specter is Charles Crocker, a wealthy businessman who helped finance the Hotel Del Monte's construction in the late 1870s. Many other strange and unexplainable events occur regularly in this unique and beautiful building.

(The U.S. Naval Postgraduate School is now housed in the old Hotel Del Monte, University Cirole, Monetery, CA 93943. Phone: 831-656-2441.) **152, 154, 155**

MOORPARK

MOORPARK MELODRAMA AND VAUDEVILLE THEATER An unidentified male ghost haunts this old building. Employees and actors report that his presence is most often felt in the overhead light booth.

(Moorpark is at the junction of highways 118 and 23, northeast of Oxnard in Ventura County. The theater was built in 1928 and used to be known as the El Rancho. The theater is on High Street in downtown Moorpark at 45 E. High St., Moorpark, CA 93021. Phone: 805-529-1212.) **182**

MOUNT DIABLO PARK

DEVIL'S MOUNTAIN The Bolgones Indians believed that inside this mountain lived a devil, whom their medicine men could summon and control. Called Puy, the demon was seen fighting next to Indians in battles with Spanish armies and was spotted again after the Civil War by white settlers in the area. Some believe the chimera has taken the form of a huge black panther, reported many times stalking through the dark forests of this mountainside.

(Mount Diablo Regional Park is in Contra Costa County. Take Highway 680 to the Diablo Road exit and go five miles to the entrance. Phone: 510-635-0138.) **116**

This Victorian mansion, known as Rengstorff House, stood empty for many years because of reports of spooky activity. See Rengstorff House, Mountain View, California (GORDON TING)

MOUNTAIN VIEW

RENGSTORFF HOUSE Built in 1887 by German immigrant Henry Rengstorff, this Victorian mansion stood empty for many years because of spooky occurrences. Unexplained thumps and cries and the faint image of a young lady staring out the upstairs window dissuaded anyone from taking up permanent residence. Eventually the beautiful house was boarded up and deteriorated. The house was later restored and is now open for tours.

(The town of Mountain View is northwest of San Jose, near the junction of U.S. Highway 101 and Highway 85. The original Rengstorff House, located at 1737 Stierlin Road, has been restored and moved to Shoreline Park, Mountain View, CA 94043. 3070 N. Shoreline Rd., Phone: 650-903-6088.) **219**

MOUNT SHASTA

UNDERGROUND CITY Legends of an underground city beneath the majestic Mount Shasta go back two thousand years. Hopi legends say the mountain is one of the thirteen homes of the Lizard People (see Times Mirror Plaza, Los Angeles, California), and California tribes considered the isolated fourteen-thousand-foot-high mountain taboo, the dwelling place of an invisible

For two thousand years, people have believed in the existence of an underground city beneath Mount Shasta. See Underground City, Mount Shasta, California
(B. A. SCHAFFENBERGER)

race of men. Later accounts describe Mount Shasta as an inlet to the Lemurian world, a fifteen-thousand-year-old civilization said to survive in the tunnels of dead volcanoes. Some authors have suggested the mountain is a meeting place for the Lothinian Brotherhood, who use a strange force called "Vis Mortuss" to carve caverns out of solid rock.

In 1904, J. C. Brown, an explorer for a British mining company, reported that he had discovered a caved-in hollow in the side of the mountain that contained giant skeletons and hieroglyphic writing on the walls. Brown later quit his job and settled in Stockton, where he lived out his life selling gold trinkets that he had found in the cave. In 1932, Edward Lanser reported that a clan of people dressed in white robes, and possessing a huge supply of pure gold, was living at Shasta's higher elevations. In 1934, Abraham Mansfield said he encountered a tribe of Lemurians, who had dug tunnels connecting Mount Shasta and the Bluff Creek area (see Bluff Creek). In 1930, G. W. Ballard told of meeting a mysterious young man on the mountainside. Supposedly, the angelic being gave Ballard a creamy potion to drink, which imbued him with the ability to understand the laws of life. By 1955, Ballard had accumulated nearly five thousand devoted followers, most of whom attended annual meetings at the Quail Hill Amphitheater at Mount Shasta. In 1972, a San Jose man hiking on the southern slope came across what he called "a reptilian humanoid." Other visitors to the mountain have reported seeing dwarfs, ape-men, and white-robed giants.

On August 16, 1987, thousands of New Age enthusiasts gathered at the mountain as part of an international "Harmonic Convergence," designed to bring peace to the whole world. Mount Shasta was designated one of the seven major planetary chakras or spiritual "tuning forks." Because of its location at the foot of the mountain, the tiny town of Shasta is now headquarters for a wide variety of New Age groups. In addition, some modern ufologists have suggested that an underground base of "good" extraterrestrials exists inside the mountain.

(Mount Shasta is located in Siskiyou County, near the junction of I-5 and Highway 89. Follow the Essential exit to the Shasta Ranger Station. For information write: Mount Shasta Ranger District, 204 West Alma, Mount Shasta, CA 96067. Phone: 916-926-4511. Information about the city of Shasta can be obtained from the Chamber of Commerce, 300 Pine St., Mount Shasta, CA 96067. Phone: 916-926-4865. Information on esoteric activity is available from the Mount Shasta Transformational Network, P.O. Box 1656, Mt. Shasta, CA 96067. Phone: 916-926-2365. www.mtshasta.com) **1, 32, 53 (8/83, 12/92), 56, 116, 144**

MURPHYS

MURPHYS HOTEL Murphys is the second oldest continuously operated hotel in America. First opened in 1856, the hotel's register includes such names as Daniel Webster, Mark Twain, Horatio Alger, Ulysses S. Grant, J. P. Morgan, and Charles Bolton (also known as Black Bart, the Gentleman Bandit). Bullet holes in the thick iron shutters on the hotel's windows bring back memories of lawless times and the famous ghosts that roam its corridors. Black Bart's specter has been observed roaming the second-floor corridor.

(Take Highway 26 east from Stockton to Highway 49. Go eleven miles southeast to Altaville and turn northeast. Follow the Highway 4 for seven miles to the town of Murphys. Murphys Hotel, 459 Main St. P.O. Box 329, Murphys, CA 95247. Phone: 209-728-3444. For reservations, call 800-532-7684. www.murphyshotel.com) **72, 119**

NEVADA CITY

FIREHOUSE MUSEUM Built in 1861, this ornate Victorian structure served as a fire station for seventy-seven years, but not until it was turned into a museum in 1948 did bizzare events start to occur. Many trace the recurring reports of ghosts and poltergeists to a thousand-year-old Taoist shrine taken from a Chinese church in Grass Valley. An old piano taken from a frontier whorehouse could also be the source of paranormal energy. A priest and two graduate students once witnessed a redheaded female phantom playing a song on the antique upright.

(Nevada City is in the Sierra Foothills northeast of Sacramento, at the junction of Highways 49 and 20. The museum is at 214 Main St. Nevada City, CA 95959. Phone: 530-265-5468.) **18, 119**

RED CASTLE INN Built in 1860, this picturesque Gothic mansion is home to the apparition of a lady in gray. Owners Conley and Mary Louise Weaver say the ghost is so real that guests believe her to be a living person until she passes through a door without opening it. The lady in gray is thought to have been the governess for the John Williams family, the original owners. Most encounters have taken place in the Gold Room, in the halls, and in the fourth-floor bedrooms.

(Red Castle Inn, 109 Prospect St., Nevada City, CA 95959. Phone: 916-265-5135.) **18, 72**

NEWCASTLE

NEWCASTLE INN RESTAURANT The ghost of a young man in his twenties haunts this old saloon. Employees have nicknamed him Gary, and he is blamed for wine bottles and glasses that fly off the shelves behind the bar. The glasses never break when they fall to the floor. Gary also likes to roam the basement and switch lights on and off.

(Newcastle is twenty miles northeast of Sacramento on I-80. Soracco's, 525 Main St., Newcastle, CA 95658. **72**

NEWPORT

WILD GOOSE This luxury yacht is thought to be haunted by its previous owner, actor John Wayne. The rugged movie star owned the 140-foot converted minesweeper for twenty-five years. It was his favorite possession. He personally supervised its sale, just a month before his death, to ensure that the boat found a good home. In August 1979, shortly after Wayne's death, new owner Lynn Hutchins reported seeing a tall, smiling apparition in the doorway to the master bath and in the main salon. Appearances have continued at random times, day and night.

(Newport is south of Long Beach on Highway 1. For information, contact Lynn Hutchins, 2412 Wilshire Boulevard No. 208, Santa Monica, CA 90403.) **41, 135**

Ghosts and poltergeist activity have been reported at this site since the Firehouse Museum opened in 1948. See Firehouse Museum, Nevada City, California (B. A SCHAFFENBERGER)

NORTHRIDGE

MEYERS HOUSE Immediately after receiving two antique children's rocking chairs from the home of his grandmother, Jack Meyers started noticing some strange things. A "moving fog or mist" appeared in his bedroom one night, and dainty footsteps could be heard throughout the house. One night the fog appeared to his wife Barbara and identified itself as the spirit of a little girl named Carmen. The Meyers's eight-year-old daughter Kelley, seventeen-year-old son Kevin, and nineteen-year-old daughter Tina all had run-ins with the ghost, which seemed to hang around the two rocking chairs. As it turned out, the chairs belonged to an eleven-year-old girl named Carmen who died in the 1940s of epilepsy. Occasionally the ghost touched someone's hair or shoulder. At other times, Carmen sang "A tisket, a tasket, a green and yellow basket." Sometimes she could be plainly seen: a little girl with long, dark, curly hair, wearing a long dark dress with white ruffles. The haunting continued for over five years and was investigated by Dr. Freda Morris of the UCLA Neuropsychiatric Institute. She believed that the Meyers were not hallucinating, and described the ghost as an energy source that science has not yet discovered.

(Northridge is northwest Los Angeles County off U.S. Highway 101. The house is a private residence in Northridge.) **217**

OAKLAND

WHEELER & HALLFORD BUILDING This modern office building became the center of national attention in 1964, when employees witnessed violent poltergeist activity. Astonished workers saw heavy cabinets tip over and pictures fly off the walls for no apparent reason. Telephones would ring with no one on the line, and then ring again as soon as they were hung up. Other freaky electrical phenomena plagued workers almost daily for over eight months. Frustrated Pacific Bell technicians replaced every phone in the building, and city building inspectors and repairmen wasted weeks trying to find some rational cause for the problems. Then, on June 16, the effects became so violent that owners summoned police. Eventually, Dr. Arthur Hastings of the University of California was asked to investigate the case. The parapsychologist's studies traced the source of the bewildering activity to a twenty-year-old man, employed with a court reporting firm since January. The man worked as a typist and was the subject of much teasing in the office because of his effeminate behavior. Dr. Hastings believed the man was unconsciously evoking psychokinetic events, which stopped as soon as the young man left the company.

(Taylor Wheeler Court Reporting Company, 2030 Franklin St., Oakland, CA 94601. Phone: 510-893-2507.) **119**

OCEANO

BLACK LAKE The ghost of a faceless Spanish lady wearing a frilly black dress has been encountered walking over the sandy beach here. A diffuse white light shines from where her face should be. Dubbed Agnes by locals, her apparition appears most often around 12:30 at night. No one has ever discovered the reason for her lonely vigil.

(Oceano is on Highway 1 in San Luis Obispo County. Black Lake is one of several small lakes in the dunes, south of Pismo Beach.) **181**

OJAI

CAMP COMFORT COUNTY PARK This small county park is host to a number of ghoulish inhabitants. A peculiar stone vault at a crossroads here is said to hold the remains of a vampire. The vampire allegedly moved from Spain at the turn of the last century and settled on the Pacific coast. A huge black phantom dog guards the sarcophagus and shares his master's taste for blood from humans or cattle. The spirit of a woman on horseback has also been observed riding through the park, as well as a headless biker riding an old Harley-Davidson. Another ghost, a lady in a wedding dress, has been seen hitchhiking through the haunted park.

(Ojai is fifteen miles north of Ventura on Highway 33. The word means "the Nest" and refers to a geologic formation overlooking the ocean at 3,500 feet elevation. Camp Comfort Park is in Ventura County, 1.5 miles south of Ojai at 11969 Creek Rd. Phone: 805-646-2314.) **116**

CREEK ROAD BRIDGE "Charman" is the name given to a hideous phantom who lurks around this modern bridge. Witnesses describe him as wearing burned, tattered clothing, with pieces of seared skin hanging loosely from his skull. His charred phantom smells of burned flesh and clothing. He is said to be the ghost of a man caught in a automobile fire on Shelf Road in the 1950s. Engulfed in flames, the man ran away from the scene and was never found.

(Creek Road runs from Highway 33 to Ojai. The two-lane concrete bridge is just south of Ojai on Creek Road.) **181, 182**

WHEELER CANYON The ghost of a Basque sheepherder murdered by cattlemen over a century ago is seen wandering through these hills. The humble ghost is most often seen tending a herd of phantom sheep.

(Wheeler Canyon is just north of Ojai in Ventura County.) **181**

OWENS LAKE

CERRO GORDO This ghost town was the center of a silver discovery in 1865 that brought thousands of hopeful miners to the area. The lawless town also attracted prostitutes and criminals, and it became known as a shooting gallery. Some locals report the ghostly images of those lost souls still moving about in the old wooden buildings, which include the American Hotel, built in 1871, and the general store. Remains of old mines and smelters cover the area. See Alabama Hills, Lone Pine, California.

(Owens Lake is off U.S. Highway 395 in Inyo County. Follow the dirt road from the town of Keeler, on Highway 136 on the east shore of Owens Lake. Continue for eight miles through the Inyo Mountains to the ghost town of Cerro Gordo. www.totalescape.com/destin/all_towns/ cerrogordo.html) **140**

OXNARD

BANK BUILDING One would never expect this modern commercial building to be haunted, but employees here encounter a shimmering apparition with astonishing regularity. The nine-foot-tall human form appears before closing in the late afternoon and glides slowly across the bank lobby or through the upstairs offices. At other times, heavy footsteps and loud thumps are heard.

(Oxnard is on the Pacific Ocean in Ventura County. It is located about five miles southeast of Ventura on Highway 1. More information can be obtained by writing directly to investigator Richard Senate at 458 Dorothy Ave., Ventura, CA 93003.) **181**

VALENTINO'S BEACH HOUSE The dark phantom seen pacing the veranda here is thought to be the ghost of Rudolph Valentino, who stayed at the house during the filming of *The Sheik* (1921). See Falcon's Lair, Beverly Hills, California; Valentino's Place, Hollywood, California; and Santa Maria Inn, Santa Maria, California.

(Valentino's Beach House is now a private residence, at 224 Cahuenga St., Oxnard, CA 93030.) **182**

PACHECO PASS

HIGHWAY 152 Psychics insist this harmless-looking mountain pass is cursed, or in New Age parlance, "invested with negative energy." The Pacheco Valley area does have an unusual history of violence which dates back to bloody battles between Indians and settlers. Today, the California Highway Patrol recognizes the pass as one of the most dangerous stretches of highway in the state. There are numerous reports of drivers trying to run each other off the road, as well as frequent roadside fistfights, which lend credence to the violent emotions felt by psychic individuals here.

(Highway 152 runs between I-5 and U.S. Highway 101 in central California. The cursed section of the pass is on a five-mile stretch of Highway 152, which begins a few miles west of the Santa Clara County line.) **116, 119**

PALMDALE

ELIZABETH LAKE Indian legends say that the devil created this lake for one of his demons, and Spanish missionaries christened it Laguna del Diablo. Settlers arriving there in the 1830s found the old superstitions to be justified. Reports of their confrontations with a fifty-foot-long dragon with huge batlike wings and a head that resembled a bulldog can be found in several newspapers of the period. In 1886, a hunting party claimed to have fired at the monster but only wounded it. They said it left a horrendous stench that lingered for months. After the turn of the century no more sightings of the beast were reported, but some current residents still feel an eerie presence in the lake.

(Palmdale is thirty-five miles north of Los Angeles at the junction of Highways 14 and 138. The lake has public access on its western shoreline. It lies off Elizabeth Lake Rd., seventeen miles west of Palmdale in Los Angeles County.) **116**

PLACERVILLE

CHAMBER OF COMMERCE BUILDING The ghost of a bearded man wearing a black top hat has been spotted on the mezzanine of this old landmark. Employees summoned police many times over the last fifteen years in attempts to rid the building of his presence. They say he resembles descriptions of the town's official hangman, seen in old pictures taken nearly 150 years ago when the town was known as Hangtown. Most of the hangings took place on the property where the chamber of commerce is now located.

(Placerville is east of Sacramento, on U.S. Highway 50 in El Dorado County. The Chamber of Commerce Build-

ing is at 542 Main St., Placerville, CA 95667. Phone: 530-621-5885. www.eldoradocounty.org) **18, 140**

HANGMAN TREE CAFE The ghosts of claim jumpers and outlaws, many sentenced to hang from an old oak tree here, are said to harass patrons and employees of this small restaurant. Several drivers have reported seeing the apparitions while passing by in their automobiles.

(Hangman Tree Cafe, 305 Main St., Placerville, CA 95667. Phone: 530-622-3878.) **140**

POMONA

CASA ALVARADO This adobe house was built by Spanish settler Ygnacio Alvarado and his wife Luisa Avila in 1840. What was originally a large barn on the property was turned into another residence, and gradually the city of Pomona grew up around the site. The adobe house still stands and is thought to be haunted by the ghost of Ygnacio. Starting in 1967, Mrs. Jo Ann Leimbach, her husband, and their teenage daughters Denise and Dana all encountered the figure of a large dark man roaming through the house, and their housekeeper saw the ghost standing in the doorway to the former barn and horse stable. Heavy footsteps were heard in the upstairs bedrooms, accompanied by the sounds of drawers and closet doors opening and closing. On two occasions, the Leimbach children woke in the middle of the night to the figure of a man with hostile, glaring eyes standing next to their beds.

(The town of Pomona is located about thirty miles east of Los Angeles on Highway 10/60. The historic house is a private residence in the city.) **72**

PORT HUENEME

MUGU ROCK This town took its name from the ghost of a Chumash Indian maiden. Beautiful Hueneme fought hard to keep the love of her husband, who was mesmerized by another woman. Hueneme and her husband realized that although they loved one another, they could not break the spell of the other woman. One evening they strolled hand in hand into the tidewater near Mugu Rock and drowned. For years, Indians brought offerings of food to the spot where the two lovers sacrificed their lives. Hueneme's alluring form is still seen clinging to the giant pointed rock just beyond the surf. The landmark became even more haunted in

August 1994, when a sixty-five-year-old man committed suicide by crashing his car into Mugu Rock. The man was despondent after confessing to the molestation of a young relative.

(Port Hueneme is west of Highway 1 at Oxnard. The landmark is on the Pacific Coast Highway, just off Point Mugu near Port Hueneme in Ventura County.) **72, 181**

PORTERVILLE

TOWNHOUSE This single-story stucco house, built in 1979, was haunted by a persistent poltergeist for several weeks in 1984. The confrontations took place in the hall and a bedroom closet of the eight-room house, and consisted mostly of strange intonations and rapping sounds. The poltergeist activity seemed to coincide with the visit of the resident couple's granddaughter. Investigators have suggested that the childish poltergeist was the spirit of the granddaughter's twin, who died of a virulent cancer at the age of five months.

(The town of Porterville is about 140 miles north of Los Angeles in Tulare County, near the junction of Highway 65 and Highway 190. The house is a private residence at 2020 Tomah Ave., Porterville, CA 93257.) **134**

SACRAMENTO

AMERICAN RIVER One of Sacramento's most famous ghosts is the phantom of a young man sighted on a public beach along this river. The ghost's age is estimated at about twenty years, and his apparition has been reported numerous times over the last fifty years. His identity has never been established, but he is thought to be the spirit of a man who drowned in the swift currents here.

(Sacramento is in the San Joaquin Valley in central California, at the junction of I-5 and I-8. The sandy area is called the American River Sailor's Bar and is located in Fair Oaks, where Sunrise Blvd. crosses the American River.) **72**

CALIFORNIA STATE UNIVERSITY The CSUS Theater on this 288-acre campus is haunted by the ghost of a young man who died in an accident during construction of the building. He fell from the second floor and was impaled on the steel girders of the unfinished site. His presence has been felt near the elevator that runs between the scene shop and the costume shop, on the catwalks, and in the light booth.

(The elevator is behind the main stage in the scene shop and runs up to the costume shop on the second floor. California State University, 6000 J St., Sacramento, CA 95819. Phone: 916-278-6011.) **72**

CITRUS HEIGHTS Houses built on the site of a holding facility for the Tulelake Japanese Internment Camp have been plagued by the ghosts of people who were held there during World War II. The forlorn ghosts of Japanese couples have appeared in the bedrooms, living rooms, garages, and even in the front yards of homes in the area. Parapsychologist Robyn Street has helped many residents rid their houses of the unwanted guests.

(The area is near Antelope and Roseville roads in Citrus Heights, which is a suburb northeast of Sacramento. Robyn Street can be reached at 916-978-0100.) **72**

FOLSOM STATE PRISON Opened in 1880, this high-security prison now houses nearly four thousand inmates. Designed to hold incorrigible prisoners serving long sentences, Folsom Prison has a violent and bloody history. Today the place is so haunted that officials have called in Roman Catholic priests to exorcize the grounds. The ghost of a guard killed in a 1927 riot, now known as the Folsom Phantom, walks the catwalk at the front gate on foggy days. Discarnate voices are heard in the old Prison Morgue and in the thirteen cells of the old Death Row, where ninety-three men were hanged between 1895 and 1937. Four ghosts hang out in Building 5, the oldest cellblock. The three-story Guard Tower 13 is haunted by an unseen presence that walks the building at night, opening and closing security doors.

(Folsom State Prison, 300 Prison Rd., Represa, CA 95671. Phone: 916-985-2561.) **72**

J STREET A family's terrifying encounter with a ghost took place in the basement of a Victorian apartment building here. Roland Johnston and his wife were led to the basement by their four-year-old daughter, who told them a man named Sam had asked her to dig up something there. When Roland picked up a shovel lying on the dirt floor, the giant specter of a white-haired man appeared before them. The ghost, dressed in black with a long white beard, pointed to a spot on the ground. When Roland refused to dig there, the ghoul's eyes turned fiery red, and the family fled from the cellar. They boarded up the basement and moved to Tehachapi, where Roland later became chief of police.

(The house was torn down in 1954. Workers installing a new foundation found a small cache of gold coins buried in the cellar.) **66 (2/93), 72**

NEW GOVERNOR'S MANSION Maybe the reason no California governor has ever taken up residence in this 25,000-square-foot, ranch-style mansion is because it was built on top of an Indian burial ground. In 1937, 117 Indians buried around 1,000 B.C. were unearthed here and stacked haphazardly in a Quonset hut. When the hut was destroyed by a mysterious fire, the bodies were lost forever. In 1972 the state sponsored an archeological dig and uncovered eleven more bodies, which they left buried. Workers estimated that several hundred more bodies could be lying beneath the building. Governor Jerry Brown refused to live there, and Governor George Deukmejian never had a chance. The California legislature voted to sell the property rather than deal with all the problems.

(The modern mansion is a private residence in Sacramento County, at 2300 California Ave., Carmichael, CA 95609.) **72**

OLD CITY CEMETERY Of the thirty-six thousand people buried in this historic graveyard, several are thought to walk the earth again. One alleged ghost is railroad engineer William Brown, who died on September 26, 1880, after saving hundreds of lives. Because someone had thrown the wrong switch, his train headed onto a ferry wharf that led directly into the San Francisco Bay. He was able to unhitch the passenger cars from his locomotive just before it plunged into the water. When they dredged the engine out of the bay, they found Brown still grasping the controls in a last-minute bid to brake the machine. Another ghost is that of May Woolsey who contacted her parents and told them she was not yet dead but waiting for them on the other side. The twelve-year-old girl died from encephalitis in 1879. In 1979, a trunk of her toys and other secret things was found behind a wall in her home. Finally, Old City Cemetery officials are still marveling at the bodies of John Wesley Reeves and his daughter Ella. When they were exhumed from their ninety-year-old iron coffins, caretakers were amazed to find them in perfect condition. Their smooth skin had its natural color and their clothing was like new.

(The cemetery is at 10th and Broadway, Sacramento, CA 95810. Pick up a map to the grave sites at the front gate or call 916-448-5665 for tour information. The ghost of May Woolsey is said to haunt her former home on E St. The contents of May's trunk are on display at the Sacramento History Museum, 101 I Street, Sacramento, CA 95814. Phone: 916-264-7057. www.sacmuseums.org/cemetery) **72**

OLD SACRAMENTO Frightening phantoms have been reported in the maze of tunnels that run underneath this section of Sacramento. The tunnels date from the period of 1864 to 1877, when buildings and streets were raised an entire story to protect them from flooding. Between the retaining walls an underground maze of tunnels resulted, enclosed from above by wooden sidewalks. Before long the tunnels were being used as opium dens and hideouts for criminals. The owners of nine of the restored buildings got together and hired a professional parapsychologist to free them of one troublesome demon. See Records below.

(The underground area is bounded by H and L streets, and Front and 12th streets near the Sacramento River. The most haunted section is between Front St. and 8th St. The former level of the city is discernible at several "sunken" restaurants and plazas in Old Town, which is the riverfront section of downtown Sacramento.) **72**

POCKET AREA Some homes in this section of Sacramento are built on top of an old Portuguese cemetery; others border an earthen levy built over Indian burial grounds. Houses located on the north edge of the area are said to be haunted by an old Indian chief. Tara Pierce reports that family members and guests at her home have encountered the apparition ascending a staircase. Sometimes the plodding sounds of his footsteps can be heard late at night.

(The Pocket Area is in southwest Sacramento along the Sacramento River. Take Pocket Rd. west from I-5.) **62 (2/93), 72**

RECORDS This used record store is haunted by the ghost of a very old woman dressed in a black Victorian dress with a white ruffled collar. In 1993, she appeared to a customer and told him to get out of the store because he was making too much noise. The owners

have named the ghost Gertrude. She shows up only in the basement sales area, which was once at street level. In 1998, the ghost of a young man in his twenties started being sighted in the basement. In the 1860s, the entire downtown section of Sacramento was raised one story to protect from flooding. See Old Sacramento, above.

(The store is on the K-Street Mall at 710 K St., Sacramento, CA 95814. Phone: 916-446-3973.) **72**

SACRAMENTO THEATRE COMPANY This fifty-year-old building is full of ghosts. A male ghost is encountered here so frequently that employees nicknamed him Pinky. In 1991, three clairvoyants uncovered five more spirits. Two phantasms have appeared in the upstairs, stage-left dressing room—a very sad Hungarian woman who wanted to be a famous actress but never succeeded, and a tall, thin man with a mustache, who wears a beret and an ascot. He has been identified as a man named Joe, who used to help around the building and was always impeccably dressed. In 1994, investigators recorded unexplainable footsteps crossing the McClatchy mainstage and photographed numerous infrared anomalies in the Stage Two area.

(The theater is at 1419 H St., Sacramento, CA 95814. Phone: 916-443-6722. www.haunted-places.com/current.htm) **53 (12/95), 66 (2/93), 72**

A woman ghost haunts Snowball Mansion. See Snowball Mansion, Sacramento, California (MATT MULLER)

SNOWBALL MANSION This two-story brick mansion was built by Englishman John Wells Snowball in 1877 and remained in his family until 1944. The ghost of his wife Lucy Knight Snowball now walks the halls after dark. She is blamed for footsteps heard late at night and doorbells that ring at odd hours. Once, her mournful specter walked through a bedroom door and sat on the bed of a flabbergasted boarder.

(The mansion is at Knights Landing, thirty miles northwest of Sacramento on the Sacramento River. The small community is in Yolo County, at the junction of Highways 45, 113, and E10.) **72**

Leland Stanford, the governor of California, was moved to found Stanford University after his dead son appeared to him in a vision here at the mansion now called Stanford House. See Stanford House, Sacramento, California
(B. A. SCHAFFENBERGER)

STANFORD HOUSE This nineteen-thousand-square-foot Italianate mansion is named for Leland Stanford, inaugurated governor of California in 1862. The governor's son, Leland Jr., died of typhoid fever when he was fifteen years old. His father was devastated and overcome with grief. Then, one night, his son appeared to

him and asked him to rededicate his life to founding a university to educate young men. After visiting and evaluating several famous colleges, Leland Stanford completed his task in 1891 with the opening of the university that bears his son's name today.

(The Stanford-Lathrop Memorial Home is on the corner of 8th and N streets at 802 N St., Sacramento, CA 95810. For tour information, call 916-323-0575.) **72**

WOODLAND OPERA HOUSE A shy ghost haunts this nineteenth-century building. His presence is presaged by the odor of cigar smoke, and he is most often detected in the upper balcony. The graffiti on the walls in the dressing rooms and on the bricks by the side stage door dates back to the 1870s.

(Woodland is twenty-three miles northwest of Sacramento on I-5. Woodland Opera House, 340 Second St., Woodland, CA 95695. Phone: 530-666-9617. www. wohtheatre.org) **72**

SAN BERNARDINO

KUNZE APARTMENTS The ghost of a man dressed in 1900s clothing, with high, stiff collars, shirt-sleeve garters, and a straw hat, has been seen walking out of a bedroom closet here. Former owner Verna Kunze says the man appeared on several occasions but dematerializes when he realizes he is being observed.

(The city is at the junction of Highway 215 and 1-10 in San Bernardino County. The apartment building is in the 900 block of G St., San Bernardino, CA 92402.) **72**

SAN DIEGO

ARROYO ABDUCTION On June 19, 1991, Laura Arroyo was abducted from her home and murdered. The nine-year-old's body was found in an industrial area of Chula Vista, about four miles from her home. In early July, Laura's image started appearing on a blank billboard at night. Her face seemed to be looking up into the sky. The image appeared after sunset, when the sign's lights were turned on. Some said her killer's face was also visible on the billboard, to the right and behind Laura's face. Luis Arroyo and his two sons identified the image as that of his daughter. On July 18, an estimated crowd of twenty thousand people showed up at the billboard and caused a huge traffic jam. On July 25, the billboard company turned off the lights to the sign, but local residents quickly reconnected them.

(The billboard is two miles from Laura Arroyo's home in San Diego and two miles from the spot where her body was found in Chula Vista.) **148**

EL CAMPO SANTO CEMETERY Many early citizens of San Diego are buried in this Catholic cemetery, which was founded in 1849. The name means "the holy field," and it once covered much of the present commercial district. Numerous ghosts have been reported along the brick wall in the graveyard, but no one has been able to pinpoint the source responsible for the poltergeist phenomena reported by businesses bordering the cemetery. One adjacent house is plagued with a multitude of inexplicable problems with lighting, electrical power, appliances, and the alarm system. Neighbors have organized to have the area exorcised.

(The remaining graveyard is at the center of the commercial district in Old Town San Diego in the 2400 block of San Diego Ave. It once extended all the way to Old Town Ave.) **194**

EL FANDANGO RESTAURANT The misty form of a woman in white has appeared in the main dining room here. The phantom materializes in a darkened corner and seems repulsed by light. She sits at a corner table near a front window when the shade is drawn. The restaurant was built on top of home of the Machado family, an early San Diego family who became very prominent and built two other mansions that bore their name. In 1992, investigators researching the history of the site suggested that one of the Machado women is the Lady in White.

(The restaurant is at 2734 Calhoun St., San Diego, CA 92110. Phone: 619-298-2860.) **194**

HORTON GRAND HOTEL One of the rooms in this magnificent Victorian hotel is haunted by the ghost of Roger Whittacker, who was shot to death in 1843 by the father of his would-be bride. Owner Dan Pearson is unsure why the ghost haunts the area around Room 309 but says the man's specter has appeared to dozens of employees and guests. One lady guest asked the real-looking apparition where the ice machine was, only to see him vanish before her eyes. The hotel was constructed in 1986 from two other hotels that were built in 1886. Whittacker was killed before any of the hotels were built, but some suspect his body was dumped in a swamp that used to be on the property. All of the brick facade, bay windows, and main stairway of the 110-room hotel were taken from the two hotels. Hotel guest Shelly Deegan once saw a whole group of twenty ghosts dressed in 1890s clothing walking up the spiral staircase to the third-floor ballroom.

(Horton Grand Hotel, 311 Island Ave. San Diego, CA 92101. Phone: 619-544-1886. www.hortongrand.com) **134, 194**

HOTEL DEL CORONADO At the end of November 1892, Kate Morgan checked into Room 302 of this posh hotel. Born in 1868 in Dubuque, Iowa, she had married a gambler named Tom Morgan and followed him out west. In October 1892, Tom wrote to Kate at their home in Visalia, California, and told her that he could no longer live with her. Kate was pregnant and sure her husband would settle down if he knew he was going to be a father, so she traveled to the Hotel Coronado, where she registered as Mrs. Lottie Anderson Barnard. She found her husband in the card room, in the arms of another woman. According to legend, instead of confronting him, she left the hotel and purchased a gun. Alone in her room on Thanksgiving Day, she put the gun to her right temple and pulled the trigger. However, a 1989 investigation turned up evidence that Tom Morgan murdered his young wife. In any case, her restless ghost, wearing a black lace dress, has haunted the hotel ever since. At one time, the room was sealed off because so many guests reported unusual disturbances there. Now known as Room 3502, it is the scene of unexplained cold spots, gurgling sounds, and footsteps. Both guests and employees have encountered frightful apparitions there, nearby in Room 3505, and in Room 3312. In a recent investigation using infrared cameras and computer monitoring equipment, thirty-seven abnormalities were found in temperature, humidity, and magnetic and electronic emissions coming from Room 3502. The 106-year-old hotel was featured in the movie *Some Like It Hot* (1959).

(Exit I-5 at Highway 75 to Coronado in San Diego County. Follow the road over the bridge until Orange Avenue, then make a left. Hotel del Coronado, 1500 Orange Ave., Coronado, CA 92118. Phone: 619-435-6611. For reservations, call 800-HOTEL-DEL.) **14, 119, 168, 211**

JULIAN HOTEL This inn was built by freed slaves Albert and Margaret Robinson in 1897. Their spirits most often manifest in the upstairs rooms, where lace doilies and furniture are mysteriously rearranged.

Recently, a maid caught a glimpse of Albert, with a pipe in his mouth, in a mirror in one of the rooms.

(The town of Julian is in San Diego County. Julian Hotel, 2032 Main St., Julian, CA 92036. Phone: 800-734-5854. www.julianhotel.com) **72**

KELLNER HOUSE When Peggy Kellner bought this bungalow in 1964, she had no idea she was going to have a ghost for a housemate. The fifty-eight-year-old house was already occupied by the spirit of a former owner, Victoria Magee. The ghost communicates her decorating tastes by smashing statues or turning pictures that she does not like to the wall. Nor is she shy about letting guests know what she thinks. She bangs cabinet doors and throws objects across the room if a man stays overnight in her house or if guests play Monopoly. Her apparition once appeared to a visiting accountant, who was idly strumming an antique harp while waiting to see Peggy. The ghost spoke to her. "Don't do that, just go sit down!" The accountant left so quickly, she left her purse behind.

(The house is a private residence at 3342 Albatross St., San Diego, CA 92103.) **72**

LA CASA DE ESTUDILLO Built in 1829, this Spanish estate has served as a fort, government office, orphanage, hotel, church, and museum. The building was restored in 1908 and became the backdrop for Helen Hunt Jackson's famous romance novel, *Ramona*. In addition to these claims to glory, the place, according to members of the museum's staff, is haunted. They see unknown faces appear in mirrors, hear music from nowhere, and watch in astonishment as ghostly figures dance across the floor. In 1988, a team organized by the *Riverside Press* to investigate the phenomena were forced out of the house by the violent effects they encountered. They were confronted by brilliant red flashes of light, and a photographer was attacked by an unseen force that smashed his camera lens. Finally, they recorded an angry voice demanding them to "Get out!"

(The town of Hemet puts on a Ramona Pageant every year. It is located north of San Diego in San Bernadino County at the junction of Highways 74 and 79. For information, call 909-658-3111. La Casa de Estudillo is in the Old Town Historical Park, 4002 Wallace Ave., San Diego, CA 92110. Phone: 619-220-5422.) **119**

POINT LOMA LIGHT HOUSE Ghostly footsteps and strange moaning sounds echo through this restored lighthouse. The spirit responsible has never been identified, though some suspect he is Juan Rodriguez Cabrillo, a Portuguese explorer who claimed this coast for Spain in 1542. The lighthouse was built on his claim in 1851, but low-lying clouds obscured the beacon so often that the site was abandoned in 1891.

(The old lighthouse is now part of the Cabrillo National Monument, at the end of Highway 209 on Point Loma. For information, write Cabrillo National Monument, P.O. Box 6670, San Diego, CA 92106. Phone: 619-557-5450.) **72**

RANCHO JAMUL Ever since this ranch was established in 1829, it has been the scene of fierce Indian attacks, bloody family feuds, and grisly murders. Small wonder that over the last 110 years, ranch hands and visitors have reported ghostly forms, unexplained lights, and disembodied cries and screams. Today, the owners, Lawrence and Bertha Daley, say the place is still haunted, but they have learned to live with their freaky guests.

(Rancho Jamul is nine miles southeast of San Diego, on Highway 188. The ranch is in San Diego County at 14726 Campo Rd., Jamul, CA 92035. Phone: 619-697-3424.) **119**

ROBINSON-ROSE HOUSE The Robinson family built this house in 1853. They used the downstairs as a store, making the building the first commercial structure in San Diego. Tourists and park employees have reported several different ghosts. Some apparitions appear as cloudlike vapors, while others are dressed in old-fashioned clothing.

(The Robinson-Rose house is now the visitor center for the Old Town Park. The office is at San Diego and Mason Streets. Old Town San Diego State Historic Park, 2645 San Diego Ave., San Diego, CA 92110. Phone: 619-220-5422.) **194**

VILLA MONTEZUMA This Victorian mansion was built in 1887 by famed opera singer Jesse Shepard. In a special room at the heart of the house, Shepard held musical séances in which he summoned spirits by using his voice to simulate an entire orchestra. His behavior caused him to be ostracized by San Diego's society elite, and he moved back to Europe. Yet, some people can still feel his presence in the old séance room; some have reported a mournful figure peering out of the cupola. Records indicate that one of Shep-

A mournful figure has been seen peering out of the cupola here at Villa Montezuma. See Villa Montezuma, San Diego, California (GORDON TING)

ard's servants hung himself in the tower shortly after the death of his wife.

(The house is now a museum run by the San Diego Historical Society. Villa Montezuma, 1925 K St., San Diego, CA 92102. Phone: 619-232-6203.) **116**

WHALEY HOUSE This two-story brick house is recognized by the State of California as an official haunted house. It was built in 1857 by Thomas Whaley, who also rented out part of the house as a county courtroom and records depository. But the sixty-five-dollar-per-month rent never made up for all the grief he received because of it. His beautiful home became the center of a power struggle between people in Old Town, where the mansion was located, and the New Towners, who wanted the county records kept in their section of the growing city. One day while Thomas was out of town, a gang of New Towners broke into his house, terrorized his wife and daughter, and stole all the records. For nearly twenty years Thomas tried to collect damages from the county for his ransacked house, but he died without ever receiving a dime.

Almost a century later, when the county bought the house and started restoration, strange things began to happen. Workers told of ghosts walking on the second floor, windows that opened by themselves, and alarms that went off for no reason. Throughout the house are odd cold spots, strange lights, and unexplainable noises. Visitors have reported seeing the ghosts of Thomas and his wife Anna Eloise in the hallways and descending the staircase, as well as the ghosts of his dog, little girl, and baby son (who died at seventeen

months old). One of the most active ghosts is Annabelle Washburn, a neighbor child who ran into a clothesline and died of a crushed trachea in the Whaley kitchen. Others have seen the ghost of a woman in the old courtroom and the figure of a man dressed in pantaloons and a frock coat on the landing at the top of the stairs.

Several people have reported seeing a man hanging in a doorway in the house. He is thought to be the ghost of "Yankee Jim" Robinson, who was caught stealing a pilot boat in 1852 and sentenced to death. When Yankee Jim was hanged on a gallows built on the Whaley property, the noose failed to snap his neck. The poor man hung flailing in the air for over fifteen minutes, cursing and screaming, before he finally strangled to death.

The last of the Whaley children, Lillian, lived in the house until 1959, when she died at the age of eighty-nine. Although scheduled for demolition several times, the house was saved and reopened as a historic site. Many recordings of disembodied voices have been made by investigators here.

(The Whaley House museum is in Old Town, on the corners of San Diego Ave. and Harney St. Take exit I-5 at Old Towne Ave. and continue to San Diego Ave. The address is 2482 San Diego Ave., San Diego, CA 92110. Phone: 619-298-2482. www.thewhaleyhouse.com) **14, 68, 86, 89, 116, 134, 148, 168, 188, 194**

SAN FERNANDO

MISSION SAN FERNANDO The long archway in the 247-foot-long Convento Building is haunted by a phantom figure, seen walking under the archway on moonlit nights. The mission was founded in 1797, and the Convento is one of the few buildings that dates back to the days of the padres and has not been reconstructed. The building's long archway is made up of nineteen smaller arches.

(San Fernando is in northwest Los Angeles County, six miles southeast of Santa Clarita off I-5. The mission is 1.5 miles west of the city. Mission San Fernando Rey de Espana, 15151 San Fernando Mission Blvd., San Fernando, CA 91341. Phone: 818-361-0186. www.californiamissions.com/cahistory/sanfernando.html) **66 (10/93)**

PICO ADOBE The brother of Pio Pico, the Mexican governor of California, still walks the courtyard of this adobe mansion. Andre Pico's ghost has been seen many times over the last thirty years by custodians and visitors.

(The Adobe is at 10940 Sepulveda Blvd. in Mission Hills. Phone: 818-365-7810.) **72**

SAN FRANCISCO

ALCATRAZ The Miwok Indians thought evil spirits inhabited this island and never set foot there until 1859, when they arrived in shackles as the island's first prisoners. By 1912, the army had built the largest reinforced concrete structure in the world: a huge fortress that would later house the nation's most dangerous criminals. In 1963, the island was taken over by the National Park Service; only the ghosts of its tormented inmates remain. Clanging sounds, screams, and crying can sometimes be heard in Cell Block B and the dungeon area near Cell Block A. Disturbances in Cell Block C became so frequent that the park service called in psychic Sylvia Brown to try to figure out what was happening. She made contact with the spirit of a man called Butcher, who resisted all her efforts to calm his violent soul. Prison records confirmed that Abie Maldowitz, a mob hit man with the nickname of Butcher, was killed by another prisoner in the laundry room of the cell block. In Cell Block D, four cells are thought to be haunted. Strange voices have emanated from Cells 11, 12, and 13 there. Even in the summer months, Cell 14-D feels ice-cold, and some visitors have been overcome by emotion in one corner of the cell. This was the tiny cell where killer Rufe McCain was kept in solitary confinement for over three years. Sometimes the sounds of banjo playing are reported coming from the deserted shower room, where Al Capone frequently played the instrument.

(Boats to Alcatraz island leave every few hours from Pier 41 in San Francisco. Call 415-705-5555 for tour information. For information on visiting San Francisco, call the San Francisco Visitor's Bureau at 415-391-2000. www.nps.gov/alcatraz) **68, 72, 116, 119**

ATHERTON MANSION Dominga Atherton built this magnificent landmark in 1881, with money from her dead husband's estate. The huge house became the residence of Dominga, her daughter Gertrude, and son-in-law George, whom the two ladies totally dominated. In 1887, in an attempt to get away from his female oppressors, George accepted an invitation to visit friends in Chile. Many weeks later a cask of rum was delivered to the mansion, and when the butler opened it he found George's pickled body. His master had died of kidney failure aboard the ship to Chile, and the captain preserved the remains as best he could. The ladies started feeling that there were more spirits in that barrel than just rum. They heard him knocking on their bedroom doors at night, trying to alert them to his arrival home. Frightened of George's lingering presence, Dominga sold the mansion. The house changed hands many times, but in 1923 it became a boarding house. Former tenants have told of roaming cold spots and unexplained knocking at their doors, and one boarder moved out after seeing a bevy of apparitions in the tower apartment. A séance conducted by researcher Antoinette May and medium Sylvia Brown revealed four presences. One was the frail spirit of George. The others were the nagging ghosts of Dominga, Gertrude, and the lady who ran the boarding house.

(The Atherton mansion is a private residence at 1990 California St., San Francisco, CA 94104.) **72, 119**

BANK OF AMERICA This modern office building, the headquarters of one of the nation's largest banks, was haunted for nearly five years. The well-documented poltergeist activity started in the early 1970s and included such startling phenomena as files flying across offices, moving cold spots, and telephones lifting off receivers by themselves.

(The building is at 555 California St., San Francisco, CA 94104. Phone: 415-622-3456.) **72**

EMBARCADERO The *Squando*, a Norwegian sailing vessel, was the scene of a brutal murder while docked here in 1890. The captain's wife had been having an affair with the first mate. After her husband discovered their improprieties, she agreed to get the sailor drunk and hold his arms while her husband cut off his head with an ax. The two murderers fled when the man's headless body was found floating in the bay. Strange things started happening on the ship as soon as it left port. The new captain was killed by the crew in a mutiny, and the vessel became known as haunted. The next two captains were found murdered in their cabin. Finally, in 1893 the entire crew deserted the ship when it docked in Bathurst, New Brunswick. The ship's reputation made it impossible to find a new crew. The Norwegian Consul hired two watchmen to guard the ship, but they abandoned the vessel on their first night, after encountering a grotesque headless apparition in the passageway leading to the captain's cabin. The same thing happened to six more night watchmen over the ensuing weeks, until the ship gained such notoriety that no one would set foot on her. The owners were forced to demolish the ship for salvage, but before long the ghostly outline of the barque sailing vessel would be sighted again in the dense fog off the Embarcadero.

(The Embarcadero is a waterfront boulevard that runs from the Oakland Bay Bridge to Fisherman's Wharf on the northeast edge of San Francisco.) **142**

GOLDEN GATE BRIDGE Over one thousand people have leaped to their death from this suspension bridge. A psychologist who studied the phenomenon said, "There is an indecipherable aspect of this bridge that draws people, something we may never understand." Another thing we may never understand is sightings of a phantom sailing vessel under the bridge. The two-masted clipper ship *Tennessee* has been seen in dense fog near the bridge, where it sank nearly a century ago. The ship stays visible for less than a minute before vanishing, and its decks are always deserted. The most spectacular sighting occurred in November 1942, when crewmen aboard the *USS Kennison* saw the tattered vessel pass alongside their ship and leave behind a visible wake. However, the destroyer's radar detected no floating objects for miles around.

(The Golden Gate Bridge connects Highway 101 between San Francisco and Marin County. The best vista point is northbound on the Morin County side. Information is available from the Junior Chamber of Commerce at 415-337-2593.) **53 (9/95), 116**

GOLDEN GATE PARK According to modern esoteric tradition, this park is home to an ancient Atlantean city called Tlamco. It was a sacred city of seven hills, laid out to conform to the orbits of the first seven planets. The Temple of Neptune was located on Strawberry Hill in the present park. Other temples were spread throughout the peninsula. The Temple of the Sun was at the intersection of Haight and Shrader streets. The Temple of Venus was located at Alamo park. Mystics believe the hidden history and special energies of San Francisco explain why it is a center of love and expanded consciousness. In 1988, a crane uncovered an unusual egg-shaped rock in the park. Members of the Ashram Art Studio recognized the four-foot-tall granite rock as a Shiva linga, a powerful reservoir of psychic

energy. Soon, hundreds of New Age devotees started coming from all over the country to behold the phallic stone. Many people claimed the sacred rock cured them of diseases. But the influx of New Agers was too much for park officials, who threatened to remove and destroy the rock. The Ashram filed a federal lawsuit to prevent the sacrilege, and the city finally agreed to donate the rock to the Ashram, where it now resides.

(The Golden State Park Recreation Office is on the corner of Fell and Stanyan streets. Phone: 415-558-3706. For information on the sacred Shiva linga, call 415-560-4002. www.nps.gov/goga) **72, 99**

GRACE CATHEDRAL This Gothic-style Episcopal church is the scene of an eight-hundred-year-old ritual designed to develop the spiritual powers of the participants. Parishioners set up a forty-foot duplicate of the octagonal labyrinth at Chartres Cathedral in France, and receptive path walkers experience feelings of purgation, illumination, and finally union with God. The mystical experiences occur while passing through specific areas of the convoluted path. Reverend Lauren Artress says members are building a permanent stone version of the seven-hundred-foot-long maze. The octagon symbolizes a kind of Christian alchemy that can transform one's soul. In the 1960s, Grace Cathedral was home to Bishop James Pike, who was relieved of his duties for not following church doctrine. Pike attended a number of séances to contact his dead son Jimmy, whose ghost he believed left many curious messages related to the exact time of his suicide in New York. The message Jimmy wanted to convey, according to medium Arthur Ford, was that he was sorry for what he had done and his death had nothing to do with his father, whom he loved dearly. See Christ Church, Poughkeepsie, New York.

(Grace Cathedral is at the top of Nob Hill on the corner of California and Taylor streets at 1051 Taylor St., San Francisco, CA 94108. Phone: 415-749-6300. www.gracecom.org) **72**

HASKELL HOUSE The two-story, white frame house known as Quarters Three by Fort Mason personnel is haunted. U.S. Senator David Broderick died from a gunshot wound here in a duel with State Supreme Court Justice David Terry in 1859. Terry was a powerful Southerner who wanted California to become a slave state. Broderick was a vociferous critic of a new California law that allowed any white person to bring a freed slave to authorities and claim him as his own property. When the smoke cleared, Broderick lay on the ground bleeding from a chest wound, and Terry stood over him. Broderick was taken to the home of his close friend Leonides Haskell and died there three days later. The senator had spent the evening before the duel at his friend's house, where he paced about anxiously all night long. Haskell's home was confiscated by the Union Army in 1863 and remains military quarters to this day. Many of the officers and family members who lived there have reported seeing the ghost of Senator Broderick pacing back and forth, reliving his anguish the night before the duel. Recently, Captain James Lunn's family reported disembodied shadows moving back and forth in the parlor. Colonel Cecil Puckett felt someone following him around the house, even watching him in the shower. Captain Everett Jones and his family experienced a variety of frightening poltergeist activity—until they stopped joking about the ghost. According to Captain James Knight, "There's no doubt the house was haunted."

(Haskell House is now Quarters Three, near Franklin St. and McDowell Ave., Fort Mason, San Francisco, CA 94123. For information, call 415-656-4600.) **72, 119**

MAMMIE PLEASANT'S GHOST The evil spirit of a voodoo priestess is said to linger in a clump of old eucalyptus trees on a San Francisco street corner. Mary "Mammie" Pleasant arrived in the city in 1848 and immediately became a celebrity among the black population. She performed voodoo rituals in exchange for information about the rich white households, where many of the blacks worked as servants. Her knowledge of the skeletons in white folk's closets paid off well, and before long she was holding wild voodoo parties, inviting both her black informants and white clients to the drunken orgies. Mammie's front man was Thomas Bell, an investment banker over whom Mammie had complete control. She put her entire fortune in his name and even arranged his marriage with one of her blackmail victims. All three lived together in a thirty-room mansion and amassed a fortune practicing voodoo among the city's richest people. It all came to an end on October 16, 1892, when Mammie murdered Thomas after a heated argument over money. Mammie was eighty-six years old at the time and was not prosecuted, but Thomas's wife inherited all the money and property. Mammie became a penniless street person, hiding in the eucalyptus trees in front of her old mansion, curs-

ing and spitting angrily, trying to make the magic work one more time.

(In the 1920s, Mammie Pleasant's former house was destroyed by fire. A hospital now occupies the site, located on the southwest corner of Octavia and Bush streets in San Francisco. The eucalyptus trees are still there.) **116**

MANSIONS HOTEL When you check into the Mansions Hotel, be sure to tell the desk clerk if you want a nonhaunting room. The unique hotel consists of two magnificent mansions. The newer one is free of ghosts. The older one is haunted. The hotel documents its uncanny history in a display that includes affidavits of witnesses, transcripts of séances, and photographs of ghosts. For years guests have complained about strange noises, cold shadows moving about, and even toilet seats flying across the room. Actor Vincent Schiavelli, who portrayed the disturbed subway spirit in the movie *Ghost* (1990), encountered a female ghost as he entered his room at the hotel late one night. In 1991, an apparition materialized in front of several witnesses during a séance in a third-floor suite. That ghost's photograph is now part of the hotel's haunted gallery. In July 1992, a scientific study conducted by the Office of Paranormal Investigation of JFK University discovered powerful electromagnetic forces in the old section of the hotel. The results confirmed the impressions of psychic Sylvia Brown, who sensed numerous spirits in the hotel. In August 1992, a man and his wife checked into a room in the old mansion. Ten minutes later, the man returned to the front desk in a state of shock. His face was ashen. His whole body was shaking. Something had frightened him badly, but he refused to talk about it. Since he had already checked in, the clerk was forced to charge him. "I don't care," the man said. "I just can't be here anymore!" Owner Bob Pritikin commented, "The man just didn't know there were ghosts in the hotel. We get all kinds of weird things happening in this place."

(Mansions Hotel, 2220 Sacramento St., San Francisco, CA 94115. Phone: 415-929-9444.) **72**

MONTANDON HOUSE Pat Montandon was a popular San Francisco television personality in the late 1960s, when her home became a living hell. Suddenly the whole house was overcome with a bone-biting chill that no amount of heating could dissipate. Locked windows would open by themselves, and small fires started for no reason. Two of her closest friends, who shared the home with her, committed suicide. Then her secretary Mary Louise Ward died during a fire in the house while Pat was out of town on business. An extensive autopsy revealed Mary was already dead before the fire started. Before moving out of the house, Pat had an exorcism performed and the disturbances suddenly ended. Investigators could not come up with any reasonable explanation for the fiendish events.

(The Montandon town house is now a private residence on Lombard St., San Francisco, 94109.) **66 (10/95), 119, 123**

NOB HILL The ghost of a lost teenage girl has been reported on the streets of this fashionable San Francisco district. Several witnesses have claimed to have seen the girl in the last twenty years. She is most often seen wearing a white Victorian-era dress and seems to wander aimlessly along the sidewalk. The pathetic ghost is thought to be Flora Sommerton, who disappeared in 1876. A $250,000 reward for her return went unclaimed for forty years. She was finally found in 1926 at a flophouse in Butte, Montana. Flora's lifeless body was found dressed in a nineteenth-century ballroom gown that was covered with thousands of tiny crystal beads. Apparently, Flora's mind snapped at the thought of marrying an older man her family had picked for her, and she lived the rest of her life in poverty rather than return to San Francisco. Ultimately her spirit did return to the city by the bay. Her physical body was also brought back to San Francisco and buried in a family plot.

(Most reports of her ghost take place on California St., between Jones and Powell.) **87, 88, 119, 158**

SAN FRANCISCO ART INSTITUTE More hauntings are reported in the Russian Hill area than any other section of San Francisco. An old cemetery now buried under tons of concrete construction might be the source of the manifestations, and at least a few of those lost souls seem to have found a home in the tower of the San Francisco Art Institute. The monastic tower, which is adjacent to the cemetery site, has been considered haunted for fifty years. Unexplainable footsteps are heard climbing the stairway to the observation platform, lights turn off and on again for no reason, and doors open and shut by themselves. One former student was taking a break on the tower's third level when he heard footsteps coming up the stairs. He watched in disbelief as the door opened and closed, and listened as invisible footsteps went past him to the observation

The San Francisco Art Institute is built on the site of an old cemetery. Center Tower, adjacent to the cemetery site, has been considered to be haunted for fifty years. See San Francisco Art Institute, San Francisco, California (B. A. SCHAFFENBERGER)

deck. Other students, a watchman, and a janitor have also witnessed apparitions climbing the stairs of the tower. During remodeling of the tower, workers reported an evil presence that caused "breaking sounds," and three near-fatal accidents occurred. A group of psychics attempted to contact the ghost during a seance, but they only succeeded in verifying the presence of many "frustrated" spirits.

(The Art Institute is on Russian Hill at 800 Chestnut St., San Francisco, CA 94132. Phone: 415-771-7020. www.sfai-art.com) **119**

WHITTIER MANSION William Franklin Whittier's residence was completed in 1896, and something in the basement of his mansion keeps bringing him back. Over the years, several people have encountered a shadowy outline in the basement or felt an ice-cold presence there. One of the founders of the Fuller O'Brien Paint Company, Whittier was an active member of the business community until his death in 1917, at the age of eighty-five. His family sold his mansion in 1938 to the Deutsche Reich, and it became the city's German Consulate. After the war, Mortimer Adler's Philosophical Institute used the building as a retreat for scholars. In 1956, the California Historical Society acquired the house for its headquarters, but the group recently vacated the building. For other San Francisco haunted locations, visit www.Haunted-Places.com/californ.htm) **14**

(The Whittier Mansion is a red sandstone building on the corner of Jackson and Laguna at 2090 Jackson St., San Francisco, CA 94109.) **14**

SAN GABRIEL

SAN GABRIEL VALLEY A male Indian ghost is a regular phenomenon here. The ghost has appeared in the backyards, bedrooms, and living rooms of dozens of residents. He only stays a few seconds, then disappears. The apparition can appear at any time, day or night. Wanda Sue Parrott, a former reporter for the *Los Angeles Herald Examiner*, has tracked the reports for several years.

(San Gabriel is a Los Angeles suburb, just east of Alhambra on I-10.) **193**

SAN JOSE

GANGELHOFF HOUSE The ghost of a woman dressed as a maid has disrupted this household for five years. Owner Joel Gangelhoff says her floating form has been observed cleaning the oak banister on the staircase and making beds on the second floor. No one has ever seen her doing windows, however.

(The house is a private residence on Pickford Ave., East San Jose, CA 95103.) **72**

WINCHESTER HOUSE Sarah Winchester started building this house in 1884 and never stopped. She was living in New Haven, Connecticut, when her husband and only child died within months of each other. In an attempt to contact her lost loved ones, she went to Boston medium Adam Coons. He contacted her husband, who asked Sarah to build a house for all of the spirits of people killed by the rifle that bears the Winchester name. She traveled west and came upon an eight-room farmhouse being built in the Santa Clara

Sarah Winchester built this house as a home for the spirits of all people killed by the rifle that bears the Winchester name. See Winchester House, San Jose, California (B. A. SCHAFFENBERGER)

Valley in California. Immediately she knew it was the right place and bought the entire forty-acre farm. Work continued on the house around the clock for the next thirty-eight years. She eventually spent six million dollars and ended up with a house of 700 rooms, 950 doors, and 10,000 windows. She had a special room for séances, called the Blue Room, where she received building plans direct from the spirit world. Every night at midnight, 1:00 A.M., and 2:00 A.M., a large bell in the bell tower rang out to summon spirits. To discourage evil spirits from entering her home; she built many blind passageways and based much of the construction on the number thirteen. She even slept in a different bedroom every night to keep one step ahead of them. She was convinced that evil spirits had found her when the 1906 earthquake leveled the upper stories of her mansion. Only 160 rooms remained, and she boarded up the bedroom where she had slept that night. On the other hand, Sarah treated good spirits royally. She held regular banquets in her lavish dining room, where servants set out five-course meals on thirteen solid-gold plates and cutlery. The only guests were herself and twelve invisible ghosts. Real people rarely set foot in her home, and she even turned away such notables as Theodore Roosevelt and Mary Baker Eddy. One of her few guests was Harry Houdini, who never spoke of his single visit to Winchester House. Sarah died in September 1922 and bequeathed her estate to a niece with the instructions that "the ghosts continue to be welcomed and provided for." Guided tours of the house have been offered since 1923. Several famous psychics have contacted ghosts here, and staff members have seen moving balls of light and a gray-haired female apparition floating through the halls. Visitors have heard organ music, whispering voices, and slamming noises. The management of Winchester House maintains a file of affidavits by witnesses of unusual events.

(Follow Highway 17 into San Jose and turn onto Stevens Creek, then go west to Winchester Blvd. Winchester House is at 525 South Winchester Blvd., San Jose, CA 95129. Phone: 408-247-2000. www. winchestermysteryhouse.com) **5, 14, 36, 42, 53 (7/ 94), 56, 68, 116, 119, 131, 135, 139, 188, 211**

WYNDHAM HOTEL A single room in this prestigious hotel is said to be haunted by the ghost of a businessman who dressed in a dark suit. Manager Ralph Malter believes him to be the spirit of a salesman who committed suicide in Room 538.

(The hotel is at 1350 North First St. San Jose, CA 95112. It was formerly the Le Baron Hotel.) **72**

SAN JUAN CAPISTRANO

LOS RIOS STREET For over ninety years, the ghost of a black-haired woman wearing a white dress has terrorized this neighborhood. Witnesses say a white fog forms from out of nowhere, then the phantom lady steps out of the mist. Sometimes she is seen with a big black dog at her side. A house on Los Rios was the scene of destructive poltergeist activity in December 1978, and recently a stewardess witnessed the lady in white enveloped by a white fog in a hallway in another one of the homes. Many encounters with the presence have taken place in front of the large pepper tree in front of Rios Adobe on Los Rios Street.

(San Juan Capistrano is in Orange County at the junction of I-5 and Highway 74. Take the Ortega Highway exit from I-5. Los Rios St. is the main commercial street south of the Mission.) **116**

MISSION SAN JUAN CAPISTRANO It is not only the swallows that return here, but a host of ghosts as well. Invisible bell ringers haunt the tower, and a headless soldier is seen riding through the outer courtyard.

A headless ghost, a faceless monk, and a pensive young lady haunt the Mission San Juan Capistrano. See Mission San Juan Capistrano, San Juan Capistrano, California (B. A. SCHAFFENBERGER)

The apparition of a dark-shrouded woman is seen standing under the last archway of the northern corner of the mission. The inner courtyard is the haunt of a faceless monk, and the face of a pensive young lady lit by candlelight is seen near the great stone church restoration. She is Magdalana, caught by the holy friars in a romantic tryst and forced to do penance by carrying a lit candle around the mission for one entire day. The day was December 8, 1812, the date of a great earthquake in southern California. Magdalana dutifully held the lit candle in her hand as the magnificent church collapsed around her, and she was crushed to death along with thirty-nine other people.

(The Mission, founded in 1776 by the Franciscan priest Junipero Serra, is south of Los Rios St. Mission San Juan Capistrano, 31882 Camino Capistrano No.

107, P.O. Box 697, San Juan Capistrano, CA 92693. Phone: 949-248-2048. www.missionsjc.com. The swallows arrive on March 19 and leave on October 23.) **66 (10/93), 116**

SAN LUCAS

SANTA LUCIA MOUNTAINS "Dark Watchers," ghoulish creatures in black capes and hats, have been sighted staring out into the sky from the tops of these mountains many times over the last century. Their black silhouettes were described in a story by John Steinbeck and a poem by Robinson Jeffers. A local school principal recently encountered one of the mysterious figures on a peak looking out over a canyon near San Lucas.

(The town is located in Monterey County, nine miles south of King City, at the junction of U.S. Highway 101 and Highway 198. The mountain range runs southeast from Monterey to San Luis Obispo.) **116**

SAN LUIS REY

MISSION SAN LUIS REY DE FRANCO This mission, founded in 1798, was confiscated by Spanish soldiers in 1835 who forced the padres to leave. Some believe the spirits of the displaced padres still return to claim their lost home. The monastery and church have been restored, and there are barracks standing from 1846, when the U.S. Mormon Battalion took over the fort. Thorton Wilder's novel *The Bridge of San Luis Rey* caught the peaceful spirit of this place.

(San Luis Rey is part of Oceanside, which is on 1-5 on the Pacific coast between San Clemente and San Diego. The Mission is in San Diego County, 3.5 miles east of Oceanside at Peyri Rd. and Mission Rd., which is Highway 76. Mission San Luis Rey, 4050 Mission Avenue, Oceanside, CA 92054. Phone: 760-757-3250. www.sanluisrey.org) **71**

SAN MIGUEL

MISSION SAN MIGUEL The victims of a brutal massacre are believed to haunt this otherwise peaceful mission. John Reed and his family purchased the adobe compound from the Mexican government, then turned it into an inn. Their enterprise prospered, and Reed used to brag about a treasure in gold he had stashed on the property. Rumors were enough for a gang of English pirates, who raided the compound one moonlit night in 1848. They didn't find treasure but left behind the thirteen bodies of Reed, his family, and guests strewn throughout the courtyard. The bodies were so badly mutilated that they were buried in a common grave behind the church. Their ghastly phantasms are still seen wandering the grounds.

(San Miguel is thirty-seven miles north of San Luis Obispo on U.S. Highway 101. The Mission is in San Luis Obispo County, at San Miguel, which is eight miles north of Paso Robles. Mission San Miguel, 775 Mission St., San Miguel, CA 93451. Phone: 805-467-2131.) **66 (10/93), 116, 181**

This photograph by Rex Heflin is one of the most intriguing UFO pictures ever taken. See Heflin Sighting, Santa Ana, California (IUFOR)

SANTA ANA

HEFLIN SIGHTING On August 3, 1965, county traffic investigator Rex Heflin encountered a round metallic object hovering about 150 feet above the road in front of him. It appeared to be about thirty feet in diameter and eight feet thick. He took four Polaroid photographs of the object, which turned out to be some of the most intriguing UFO pictures ever taken. The pictures clearly show dust trails stirred up by the rotating disc, as well as atmospheric disturbance when it departed rapidly upward. Although a local newspaper published the photos, government officials confiscated the originals and never returned them.

(Santa Ana is southeast of Los Angeles in Orange County, south of Anaheim on I-5. The incident occurred

in Orange County on Myford Rd. about a half mile from the Santa Ana Freeway underpass. The unidentified object maneuvered over Myford Rd. between Roberts and Bryan streets.) **72, 126 (2/77)**

WESTMINSTER A house in a subdivision here is haunted by the ghost of a little boy and his mother. The pitter-patter of a child and the deliberate footsteps of an adult are heard in the second-floor halls when no one is there. Sometimes the invisible child is heard falling down the stairs. Once, the child's apparition was seen in a second-floor closet. The small boy wears a striped shirt and gray pants. Meanwhile, the ghost of a woman wearing a flimsy negligee is seen in the house next door. The hauntings started simultaneously in two neighboring homes, one owned by the Trausch family and the other owned by the Swansons. An investigation by Hans Holzer discovered that a barn stood on the property in the 1920s. Medium Sybil Leek contacted the spirit of a nine-year-old boy named Peter Fairley, who was murdered in the loft of the barn by two brothers in 1925. His confused spirit lingers in the area, while the ghost of his mother, who lost her mind when her son's brutalized body was found, still searches for her lost child.

(Westminster is a small suburb of Santa Ana. The development borders Chestnut St. The address of the original farmhouse and barn was 14611 Golden West St., Westminster, CA 92711.) **80**

SANTA BARBARA

COMMUNITY COLLEGE The ghost of a woman in a white shawl has been seen near an ocean bluff on the campus here. Several students have seen the image glide over the lawn about six inches off the ground. When the phantom reaches the edge of the cliff, she disappears in a blue flash of light.

(The college is in south Santa Barbara, about forty miles west of Ventura on Highway 101 5BCC, 365 Loma Alta Dr., Santa Barbara CA 93109. Phone: 805-963-4091. www.sbcc.cc.ca.us) **181**

HOPE RANCH For about three weeks in 1986, a family here experienced startling poltergeist effects. Small figurines floated from a bookcase to the floor, pictures would not stay hung, and loud tapping noises came from inside the walls. Investigators traced the cause to

a psychokinetic adolescent girl who had just broken up with her boyfriend.

(The house is a private residence in the exclusive Hope Ranch area of Santa Barbara.) **181**

MISSION SANTA BARBARA This twin-towered adobe mission was founded in 1786. Its fascinating history is chronicled in a museum on the grounds, but the walled cemetery next to the church is where the ghosts are seen. The graveyard contains the remains of five thousand pioneers and Indians. See Mission La Purisima, Lompoc, California.

(Mission Santa Barbara is in northwest Santa Barbara at the junction of Los Olivos and Laguna streets. Mission Santa Barbara, 2201 Laguna St., Santa Barbara, CA 93101. Phone: 805-682-4149. www.sbmission.org) **66 (10/93), 181**

SANTA CLARITA

WILLIAM HART PARK AND MUSEUM The ghost of cowboy actor William Hart has been seen reading a newspaper in the living room and sitting in his former bedroom here. The shimmering specter of his wife. Mary Ellen has been observed near her bed. Hart's last film was *Tumbleweeds* (1926). Mary Ellen died in 1943, and he followed her three years later, at the age of seventy-six.

(Santa Clarita is on I-5, about eight miles north of San Fernando. William Hart's mansion, in the Newhall section of Santa Clarita, is now the William S. Hart Park and Museum, 24151 San Fernando Road, Newhall, CA 91321. Phone: 805-254-4584. www.hartmuseum.org) **182**

SANTA CRUZ

RED, WHITE, AND BLUE BEACH A wood house and campground area on this popular nudist beach is the haunting ground of an old sea captain. The sea captain, unlike many of the swimmers here, is usually dressed, in a raincoat and cap. The old salt strolls out the back door of the clapboard house and quietly makes his rounds through the campground. When he gets angry, pictures and knickknacks fly through the house, which was built by a retired sailor in 1857. In November 1975, a skeptical visitor was nearly hit by a heavy flowerpot, flung toward him by an invisible hand.

Every year, an average of ten people encounter this stubborn apparition.

(Santa Cruz is on north Monterey Bay. The haunted beach is located six miles north of Santa Cruz on Highway 1. Turn toward the ocean at the red, white, and blue mailbox.) **119**

SANTA MARIA

SANTA MARIA INN The ghost of Rudolph Valentino is believed to return to his former suite here. Guests staying in Room 210 feel a heavy presence on the bed and hear eerie knocking sounds in the walls. Valentino often journeyed here to escape from the hectic Hollywood scene. See Falcon's Lair, Beverly Hills, California; Valentino's Place, Hollywood, California; and Valentino's Beach House, Oxnard, California.

(Santa Maria is thirty miles south of San Luis Obispo on Highway 101. Santa Maria Inn, 801 South Broadway, Santa Maria, CA 93454. Phone: 800-462-4276. www. santamariainn.com) **72, 182**

SANTA PAULA

ALISO CANYON This canyon is home to the infamous Billiwack Monster. The beast was first sighted at the abandoned Billiwack Dairy, which closed down when its owner mysteriously disappeared in 1943. Shortly afterward, people reported seeing a tall, muscular creature covered in gray hair, with long claws on its fingertips. The apelike creature stood upright, and ramlike horns grew out of its head. In 1964, the abhorrent beast made headlines all over the state when it terrorized a group of young hikers for hours.

(Santa Paula is at the junction of Highway 126 and Highway 150, about eighteen miles northeast of Ventura. Follow Highway 126 from U.S. Highway 101. Aliso Canyon is in Ventura County. The canyon area begins six miles west of Santa Paula, south of the Los Padres National Forest.) **116, 181**

OLD GLEN TAVERN INN A ghost's photograph taken in 1987 was on display in the lobby of this Tudor-style hotel. The picture was taken in Room 307, which has been haunted for many years by a man with long white hair and a beard. The elderly apparition is usually seen dressed in a cowboy suit, wearing a leather string tie. Less frequently, the apparition of a woman is seen in Room 218, and an eight-year-old boy's ghost plays in the first-floor lobby. Dozens of customers and employees have witnessed apparitions at the former; which was built in 1911. The building is now deserted.

(From Highway 126 take the Tenth Street exit north in Santa Paula. The building is at 134 North Mill St. Santa Paula, CA 93060.) **14, 72**

SANTA SUSANA

PISGAH GRANDE This ghost town was a Pentecostal Christian commune from 1914 to 1921. The faithful held twenty-four-hour prayer vigils in a brick tower overlooking the community. Now the area is haunted by a floating, square-shaped white light, which moves slowly through the trees and deserted buildings. Some have suggested that it is the spirit of Dr. Finis Yoakum, founder of the commune.

(Santa Susana is on Highway 118 in western Ventura County. Pisgah Grande is in the Las Llajas Canyon near the town. The site is now on private property, and permission must be obtained to visit it.) **181**

SANTA SUSANNA MOUNTAINS In January 1984, two men crashed their all-terrain vehicle after seeing an eight-foot-tall, hairy creature standing in the middle of the road. One month later, three hunters came across a similar beast near their campsite.

(The mountains run along the Santa Susanna Pass near Highway 118, between Ventura and Los Angeles Counties.) **181**

SANTA YNEZ

SOLVANG ROAD A phantom stagecoach drawn by four black horses with a driver in a tall black hat is described in old legends told by Indians and settlers in this area. In the late 1980s, the ghostly vehicle was reported by drivers along local roads. Most said the fast-moving coach emerged from a dark cloud and rushed silently past them. One couple reported seeing lanterns on the sides of the coach, which illuminated an old woman sitting inside.

(Santa Ynez is northeast of Santa Barbara, at the junction of Highways 154 and 246. The sightings take place in Santa Barbara County outside the town of Santa Ynez, on the narrow roads that head west toward Solvang.) **181**

SONOMA

JACK LONDON STATE PARK Writer Jack London employed nearly two dozen men to build a castle in these woods, but before it was completed his dream home was destroyed by fire. The ruins of London's Castle are said to be haunted by not only the author but also some of the characters from his fertile imagination.

(Sonoma is located in northern California, next to Napa on Highway 128, about fifteen miles north of Vallejo. The park is located in the Sonoma Valley, two miles north of Sonoma on Highway 12. For information, call the park office at 707-938-5216.) **72, 98**

VALLEY OF THE MOON SALOON The ghost that inhabits this century-old saloon likes things a certain way. Pantry doors must remain closed or they close by themselves. Furniture gets rearranged by itself. Lights go off for no reason. Certain records pop out of their slots in the jukebox. A tenant in an upstairs apartment said a bar of soap floated into his hand while he was taking a shower. No one has identified the spirit witnessed by employees, customers, and owner Carolina Ceelen.

(Valley of the Moon Saloon, 17154 Sonoma Highway, Sonoma, CA 95476. Phone: 707-996-4003.) **119**

STINSON BEACH

EASKOOT HOUSE Captain Alfred Easkoot had a way of turning adversity into good fortune. He was only thirteen years old when a fire at sea left his face disfigured and turned one of his hands into a useless stump. Yet the stubborn lad overcame his handicap to become captain of a merchant ship and eventually bought his own lumber schooner. When his ship went aground on Duxbury Reef, he used the lumber that drifted ashore to build a house. Soon he became a respected businessman and in 1861 married into a wealthy family. The old captain became obsessed with his beach property and constantly patrolled it looking for trespassers, whom he frightened away with the glistening gold hook attached to his withered hand. During his funeral, his coffin was dropped, spilling his corpse out onto the sand. Somehow, his gold hook fell off and was carried away by the tide. Now every night at 2:00 A.M. (the hour of his death), he comes stomping out of his house to search for the golden hook. Residents of Easkoot house verify

the tales, and the house has been resold many times because of the haunting.

(Stinson Beach is just west of Highway 1 in Marin County, north of San Francisco. Easkoot House is a private residence, at 3548 Shoreline Highway, Stinson Beach, CA 94970.) **119**

SUMMERLAND

BIG YELLOW HOUSE RESTAURANT The town of Summerland was founded as a spiritual center by H. L. Williams in 1883. Seances were held regularly in this house which was converted into a restaurant in 1973. It still has at least one visiting spirit. The employees call him Hector, and he likes to smash dishes, rattle doorknobs, tug at waitresses' skirts, and play other harmless pranks. The dirty old ghost seems especially attentive to young women.

(The town is on U.S. Highway 101 east of Santa Barbara. Big Yellow House Restaurant, 108 Pierpont Ave., Summerland, CA 93067. Phone: 805-969-4140.) **66 (6/93), 181**

TIDEPOOL REFLECTIONS GIFT SHOP This old house was haunted for many years by moving objects, odd noises, and "misty figures." After the gift-shop owners asked a spiritualist to bless the place, the activity lessened greatly.

(The town is named for the first of the seven heavens of spiritualism. Tidepool Reflections Gift Shop, Lillie Ave., Summerland, CA 93067.) **66 (6/93)**

SUNNYVALE

TOYS 'Я' US This modern toy store was built in 1970 and has been haunted ever since. Employees first thought someone was scattering roller skates and books throughout the aisles as a practical joke, but when they started hearing voices and being touched by phantom hands, they asked manager Judy Jackson for help. She discovered that customers had also been reporting strange things: faucets that turned themselves on after being turned off, and invisible hands tapping their shoulders or stroking their hair. Assistant Store Director Jeff Linden was having a hard time with employees who were frightened to go in some areas of the store alone. According to some workers, objects were flying twenty feet through the air and hitting them. Finally, psychic Silvia Brown was called in to investigate. The medium contacted a presence by the name of Johnny Johnson, who worked on a ranch that had existed on the site of the store. She discovered that Johnny was mentally impaired and came to be known as Crazy Johnny by ranch hands. In 1884, he hit his leg with an ax while cutting wood and bled to death near a well on the property. Records showed that a well did exist beneath the store at the spot indicated by Johnny's ghost.

(Sunnyvale is west of San Jose, near the junction of U.S. Highway 101 and Highway 237. The Toys 'Я' Us store is at 130 East El Camino, Sunnyvale, CA 94087. Phone: 408-732-0331.) **119, 135**

SUTTER CREEK

SUTTER CREEK INN Although this house was already over a century old when Jane Way bought it in 1966, she had no idea it came with its own ghost. Two weeks after she moved in an apparition appeared in her doorway. She later identified the spirit as State Senator Edward Voorhies, who had lived there with his wife and family in the 1880s. There were also other ghosts in the old house. The senator's daughter once materialized in front of several guests who were sitting in the lounge. She curtsied politely and disappeared. Less polite was the spectral flasher, who appeared in broad daylight in the lobby and promptly dropped his pants in front of a group of elderly ladies.

(Sutter Creek is in Amador County, thirty-two miles south of Placerville on Highway 49. Sutter Creek Inn, 75 Main St., Sutter Creek, CA 95685. Phone: 209-267-5606. www.suttercreekinn.com) **18, 72, 116, 119**

TARZANA

MAGUIRE HOUSE Fred and Sharon Maguire and their two young sons Davy and Daniel shared this house with a poltergeist for many years in the 1970s. They first heard crying and disembodied footsteps, then doors and windows started opening and closing by themselves. Appliances operated and unplugged themselves when no one was around, and pots and pans vanished. It was impossible to keep drugs or pills in the house, and once a vitamin tablet levitated in mid-air. Psychometrist Peter Hurkos investigated the case and declared the phenomena were caused by the ghosts of

the former owners, who had committed suicide in the house. Research showed that an alcoholic man killed himself in the house, followed within several months by his wife, who was addicted to various types of pills.

(Tarzania is in northwestern Los Angles County at U.S. Highway 101 and Reseda Blvd. The house is on Hatteras St. in Tarzana, CA 91356.) **217**

THOUSAND OAKS

CONEJO PLAYERS A ghostly critic named Alfred lets actors at this community theater know when they have put on a poor performance. His displeasure takes the form of banging footsteps in the aisles or props moving by themselves. He is even known to take personal items from actors, although he always returns them to the rightful owner. Some believe the ghost accompanied the theater company when it moved from its original home. See Missionary Baptist Church, below.

(Thousand Oaks is off U.S. Highway 101, halfway between Los Angeles and Oxnard. The theater is now at 351 South Moorpark Rd, Thousand Oaks, CA 91362. Phone: 805-495-3715. www.conejoplayers.org) **181**

STAGECOACH INN A tall female ghost haunts this old stagecoach stop, now a museum, on the Butterfield Mail route. She is only seen for a few seconds, but the pungent smell of her perfume lingers afterward. The nineteen-room museum is a replica of the Grand Union Hotel, built here in 1876. Oddly enough, the ghost of a man murdered in his sleep at the original hotel has turned up in one of the rooms of the restored inn. Weird disturbances in that room prompted the museum's director, Dr. Cyril Anderson, to call in parapsychologists. A séance was held in the room and medium Sybil Leek contacted the spirit of Pierre Duvon, a bearded mountain man who was killed in the hotel in 1885. Just a month after the seance, a gun holster and chaps, purported to belong to Duvon, were donated to the museum. The eerie voice of a child heard in the building is thought to be that of a little boy who stayed at the inn in the 1890s. He wandered away and got lost in the nearby hills, and was never seen again. Perhaps he has finally found his way home.

(The museum is in Newbury Park, which is twelve miles west of Thousand Oaks. Stagecoach Inn Museum, 51 South Ventu Park Rd., Newbury Park, CA 91320. Phone: 805-498-9441.) **89, 91, 181**

TRACY

BANTA INN This inn is haunted by a former owner who died of a heart attack behind the bar in 1968. While the apparition of Tony Gukan has been seen only a few times, his playful spirit likes to move glasses, ashtrays, coins, chandeliers, and other objects at the inn.

(Tracy is forty-five miles east of Oakland off I-580. The town of Banta is five miles east of Tracy. Banta Inn, 22565 South 7th Ave., Banta, CA 95304. Phone: 209-835-1311.) **53 (10/92, 9/95)**

TULELAKE

CAPTAIN JACK'S STRONGHOLD The Modoc War began here in what is now Lava Beds National Monument Park in 1872, when a band of fifty Indians, under the leadership of Chief "Captain Jack," held out for six months against a thousand U.S. Army troops. When they finally surrendered, the tribe was banished to a reservation in Oklahoma, and Captain Jack was hanged. But before the Indians departed, they left a curse on the Lava Beds that to this day keeps the white man away. Many of those brave enough to visit are stranded, after their automobile engines stop running for no apparent reason.

(Tulelake is in northeast Siskiyou County near the Oregon border in extreme northern California. Follow I-5 to U.S. Highway 97 at Weed. Go fifty-five miles to the Highway 161 turnoff to Tulelake. The Lava Beds National Monument Park is south of town. Phone: 530-667-2282. www.nps.gov/labe) **116**

VENTURA

BELLA MAGGIORE INN This picturesque Italianate inn is haunted by the ghost of Sylvia Michaels, who committed suicide here in 1947. The despondent prostitute hanged herself in a closet in her room. After numerous poltergeist disturbances, the management called in a group of ghost hunters led by researcher Richard Senate. Their efforts seemed to have lessened the spectral presence. A séance held in 1994 was unsuccessful at contacting Sylvia's spirit.

(Ventura is on U.S. Highway 101, thirty-two miles southeast of Santa Barbara on the Pacific coast. Bella Maggiore Inn, 67 South California St., Ventura, CA 93001. Phone: 805-652-0277.) **72, 182**

CASITAS RESERVOIR Some evidence suggests that there is an underwater extraterrestrial base here. In 1964, Air Force pilot Frank Kinsey and his brother-in-law were standing on shore when they saw a glowing oval object rise out of the lake. While it hovered about thirty feet above the water, Frank got his binoculars and was able to see a humanoid figure inside the vessel. The UFO suddenly sped out over the Sierra Madre Mountains. As it increased speed, the object changed color from lavender to bright orange. Before it was out of sight, Kinsey was able to take an infrared photograph of the unidentified object.

(The reservoir is eight miles northwest of Ventura. Take Highway 33 to Foster Park and follow the Casitas Vista Rd.) **72**

CITY HALL The superior court room in this 1912 building is haunted by a spirit that enjoys harassing police officers. The persistent presence is felt near the judge's bench and its activity keeps a special emergency telephone line in the chamber constantly busy. Some investigators have suggested that she is "Ma" Duncan, who was convicted of murdering her daughter-in-law in 1958. The third floor west is haunted by another spirit. Elevators are often called to the deserted third floor for no reason. In 1990, a visitor reported encountering a ghostly lady in blue, wearing 1940s clothing, standing near the third-floor elevator doors.

(Ventura City Hall is at the top of California St. at 501 Poli St., Ventura, CA 93001. Phone: 805-654-7800. The city holds ghost tours year round. For information, call 805-641-3844. www.ghost-stalker.com) **182**

MISSION SAN BUENAVENTURA The ghost of an old monk has been seen strolling through the garden of this Moorish adobe, which is the original structure built in 1782. The friar has even been seen wandering out onto the city's main street or sitting on the banks of the Ventura River. The description is always the same: he has gray hair and wears a loose gray robe, not the brown garment of the present-day Franciscan order.

(The mission, the ninth and last founded by the zealous Franciscan priest Father Junipero Serro, is just off U.S. Highway 101 at the Mission Boulevard exit. Mission San Buenaventura, 211 East Main St., Ventura, CA 93001. Phone: 805-643-4318. www.californiamissions.com/cahistory/sanbuenaventura.html) **181, 182**

OLIVAS ADOBE The original owner of this hacienda is thought to have returned as the ghostly Dark Lady, who is seen in the kitchen and living room or standing on the balcony. Perhaps Teodora Olivas is looking for one of her twenty-two children or searching for her husband's lost fortune. Bandits raided their ranch in 1855 and made off with $75,000 in gold, which has never been recovered. The thieves ripped her pierced earrings from her ears, then mercilessly killed her.

(The Olivas State Historical Monument is at 4200 Olivas Park Dr., Ventura, CA 93005. Phone: 805-644-4346.) **66 (10/84, 10/95), 116, 119, 181, 182**

SANTA CLARA HOUSE The ghost of a young woman who hung herself in the attic of this stately Victorian home, now a pleasant family restaurant, has been seen in the upstairs ladies' restroom and peering out a round window in front of the house. In the late nineteenth century this young married Italian woman named Rosa became pregnant in an adulterous love affair with a salesman from San Francisco. The strict social morals of the time left her with no choice but to take her own life. Today, she peers from the second-floor window as if waiting for her lover's return to face their sins together.

(The restaurant is on Santa Clara St., Ventura, CA 93005.) **181**

VENTURA THEATER This concert hall is haunted by the spirit of a young lady killed in a backstage accident. The ghost's luminescent form has been seen dancing happily at the center of the stage, but her final, soul-wrenching scream also lingers here. She was crushed to death by falling lighting equipment.

(Ventura Theater, 26 South Chestnut St. Ventura, CA 93001. Phone: 805-653-0721. www.venturatheater.net) **182**

ZANDER BUILDING The spirit of an unknown man haunts this building. Employees at the Cat's Meow Shop have seen the tall ghost of a male figure on several occasions. The apparition is usually seen wearing an unbuttoned gray suit. The benign spirit also makes himself known in Eddie's Treasure room, and his presence is also sensed on the rear stairway that leads to the parking lot of the Zander Building.

(The commercial building is at 427E Main St., Ventura, CA 93001. Eddie's Treasure Room is at the front of the building. Phone: 805-648-3456. www.rockcitynews. com/clubs/ventura) **182**

WARNER SPRINGS

DEADMAN'S HOLE A family of Sasquatch creatures has inhabited this peaceful hollow for over a century. The area takes its name from the unusual number of violent deaths that have occurred here, mostly blamed on the mysterious creatures. In 1858 an unknown man was found beaten to death here, and in 1870 a Frenchman was attacked in his cabin near Deadman's Hole. In 1888 the mutilated bodies of a prospector and a young woman were found in separate locations in the area. That same year, two hunters came across a cave littered with human bones. While exploring the darkened cavern, they were attacked by a ferocious apelike creature. They described the beast as having a human face with coarse black hair covering its body. The hunters shot at the monster with their rifles and were able to escape. In 1922 a man was found at Deadman's Hole. He had his neck crushed by "someone with tremendous strength." Not long afterward, an Indian girl was found strangled in the same savage manner. A few months later, two other hunters encountered the hairy beast and fired shots at it.

(Warner Springs is near San Marcus in north San Diego County. The area is northwest of town. Follow Highway 79 out of town for about seven miles to the Deadman's Hole turnoff.) **116, 194**

WESTLAKE VILLAGE

U.S. HIGHWAY 101 ON-RAMP On four separate occasions in 1980, drivers reported a phantom hitchhiker at the Westlake on-ramp to U.S. Highway 101. The specter was that of an elderly, disoriented man, who cried out "Christ is coming, Christ is coming!" and then vanished before their eyes. One hysterical lady reported that he disappeared from the front seat of her car while she was driving fifty miles per hour down the freeway. All the cases were reported to the California Highway Patrol.

(Westlake Village is in Los Angeles County, east of Thousand Oaks on U.S. Highway 101.) **181**

WILLOW CREEK

SIX RIVERS NATIONAL FOREST Road crews working here started encountering a hairy creature with sixteen-inch footprints in August 1958. A few weeks later, two doctors reported seeing a similar beast crossing Highway 299. The reports became so frequent that the press started referring to the apelike creature as "Bigfoot," and over the next two decades, scores of sightings were reported near Bluff Creek and Laird Meadow. Willow Creek is at the heart of Bigfoot Country, and many of its residents can recall instances of finding huge footprints in their lawns or hearing unrecognizable screams coming from the surrounding woods. Some have caught glimpses of the hairy beasts in their headlights at night. Since 1958 there have been over a hundred reports of Bigfoot sightings near this town. A hiker who encountered a Bigfoot near Willow Creek in November 1989 gave a typical description: He described it as a human-faced ape over seven feet tall, weighing four hundred pounds, and smelling like rotten garbage. See Mount Shasta, California.

(Willow Creek is in Humboldt County, forty-two miles east of Eureka at the junction of Highways 96 and 299. At the center of town, there is a full-sized wooden sculpture of one of the creatures, and a Bigfoot Days celebration is held there every year. The first sighting occurred at a logging operation in the Klamath River country, seventy-five miles north of Willow Creek and slightly east of Weitchpec. The Bluff Creek watershed is northeast of Eureka in Humboldt County and can be accessed by following Fish Lake Rd. A campground is located four miles north of the junction of Highways 96 and 169 near Weitchpec. Phone: 707-442-1721. To report a sighting, call 800-BIGFOOT.) **72, 116, 139**

YORBA LINDA

OLD YORBA LINDA CEMETERY The ghost of the Pink Lady is said to appear here on June 15 of every even-numbered year. Her specter sometimes pauses to weep near an unmarked grave. She is thought to be Alvina de Los Reyes, daughter of Bernardo Yorba, who died at the turn of the century. She was killed in a carriage accident while returning from a formal ball.

(Yorba Linda is in Orange County, northeast of Anaheim on Highway 91. The cemetery is at the center of town.) **72**

RICHARD NIXON LIBRARY The ghost of former president Richard Nixon has returned to haunt us. His ghost has been seen entering the front door of the Nixon birthplace house, and a luminous green mist sometimes floats over the Nixon grave. A night watchman has heard strange tapping sounds coming from

the Watergate Display Room, and the machines that play the Watergate tapes over and over have mysteriously malfunctioned.

(Richard Nixon Library and Birthplace, 18001 Yorba Linda Blvd., Yorba Linda, CA 92686. Phone: 714-993-3393.) **72**

YUCAIPA

FAIRVIEW ROAD A modern ranch house here is haunted by the energetic ghost of a teenage boy with a tendency to throw books and dinnerware across the room. The temperamental ghost's activities have disrupted the lives of several owners, but his identity has never been determined.

(Yucaipa is in San Bernardino County, near the junction of I-10 and Highway 38. The house is a private residence, at 33843 Fairview Rd., Yucaipa, CA 92399.) **72**

The Integraton is a giant domed device built in the belief that it could reverse aging and allow time travel. It is located at Giant Rock Airport, which is believed by a nationwide UFO cult to be a landing zone for space aliens. See Giant Rock Airport, Yucca Valley, California (AFSCA)

YUCCA VALLEY

GIANT ROCK AIRPORT According to members of a nationwide UFO cult, this is a landing zone for space aliens. From 1954 to his death in 1978, alien contactee George Van Tassel held meetings at this site to tap into the wisdom of the alien Space Brothers. He built an electronics laboratory under the landmark seven-story Giant Rock and, following the instructions of the Space Brothers, built a giant domed device that allegedly would reverse aging and allow travel through time. Called the Integratron, the entire upper dome of the structure was designed to rotate at high speed. The strange hemisphere still stands today, behind a barbed wire fence, guarded by the few remaining believers in Van Tassel's twenty-four-year cosmic connection. A sign at the site described the Integratron as a "time machine for basic research on rejuvenation, antigravity, and time travel." Today, another sign reads: Available for Weddings, Parties, Bar Mitzvahs, etc.

(The airport is located in San Bernardino County about fifteen miles from Yucca Valley. Follow Highway 247 north out of town for 10.5 miles, then turn east onto Reches Rd., Continue about two miles to Belfield Rd. and turn left. The Integratron is at 2477 Belfield Rd., Giant Rock Airport, Yucca Valley, CA 92284. www. integratron.com) **72, 116**

COLORADO

ALAMOSA

LUTHER BEAN MUSEUM In one of the strangest cases of unexplainable animal mutilation, Mr. and Mrs. Berle Lewis's three-year-old gelding was found on September 9, 1967, with all the flesh on its neck and shoulders carefully removed. Nothing remained of the head but a glistening white skull. All the internal organs were missing, yet the rest of the carcass was intact. UFO sightings in the area led some to suggest extraterrestrial beings were responsible. Bushes near Snippy's body were flattened, several unexplained dark spots stained the grass, and unusual holes were found punched into the ground. The hoofprints of two other horses turned away from Snippy's tracks and headed back toward the ranch house, but no prints of any kind could be found in a hundred-foot radius from the body.

(Alamosa is in south central Colorado, at the intersection of U.S. Highways 160 and 285. Snippy's skeleton was put on display at the Luther Bean Museum of Adams State College, Richardson Hall, Room 256, Alamosa, CO 81101. Phone: 719-587-7151.) **139, 149**

BROWN'S PARK

BROWN'S HOLE This isolated area was named for fur trapper Baptiste Brown, but it gained fame as the hideout for some of the country's worst outlaws. The ruins of Butch's Cabin, used by Butch Cassidy and the Wild Bunch, are nearby. Many locals and visitors experience eerie sensations of being drawn back in time by the powerful emotions of the colorful individualists who once rode through this valley. People report being overcome and even possessed by the powerful personalities that linger here.

(Brown's Park is in the extreme northwest corner of Colorado in Moffat County. Follow Highway 318 northwest for sixty-five miles from U.S. Highway 40 at Maybell. The area is on the old Outlaw Trail on the Green River in the Brown's Park National Wildlife Refuge, 1318 Highway 318, Maybell, CO 81640. Phone: 970-365-3613.) **131**

CENTRAL CITY

MASONIC CEMETERY The ghost of a lady in a black satin dress has been seen placing blue columbine flowers on the grave of John Edward Cameron. Cameron died of "heart paralysis" on November 1, 1887, at the age of twenty-eight. A beautiful woman in black attended the funeral and reappears every April 5 and November 1 to put flowers on his grave. Nobody knew who she was. Rumors spread that the elusive lady was the ghost of a former lover who committed suicide after Cameron wed another woman. Perhaps, they said, the jealous lover had even poisoned the young man. By 1899 people were convinced the lady in black was a phantom. On November 1, over a dozen people gathered at the grave hoping to catch a glimpse of the ghost. Then, at sundown, she appeared. As she lay the flowers on the grave two men tried to grab her, but she vanished over the top of the hill. Ever since, people have been trying to catch the faithful wraith of Cameron monument.

(Central City is in Gilpin County, twenty miles west of Golden on Highway 119. The hilltop cemetery is north of the city.) **118**

CHIVINGTON

SAND CREEK After fierce fighting here on November 29, 1864, the phantom of a gray wolf appeared to Cheyenne women and children to lead them to safety. Colonel John Chivington led the Third Colorado Regiment in the bloody attack on Chief Black Kettle's camp at Sand Creek. The mysterious animal escorted the few survivors all the way to another Cheyenne camp, near the forks of the Smoky Hill and Republican Rivers.

(Chivington is twenty-eight miles north of Lamar in Kiowa County. A marker commemorating the Sand Creek Massacre is located three quarters of a mile east of Chivington on Highway 96. Just west of the marker, follow the dirt road east for a half mile to the battlefield. The Sand Creek bluffs are a short distance along the north road. There are historical markers designating the battlefield and the bluffs area.) **36**

COLORADO SPRINGS

BLACK FOREST HAUNTING Although previous owners felt this two-story log cabin was haunted, the paranormal activity began in earnest when the Steve Lee family purchased it in 1992. "One day we came home," said Beth Lee, "and it was like the Fourth of July in our living room and in our bedroom. We had all kinds of lights flashing through, and it sounded like people stomping across the roof. We would lie in bed at night and hear chains rattling. One night we woke up and heard orchestra music. Strange things started happening every day." Their two boys complained of weird lights and shadows in their rooms, lights and appliances started turning on and off by themselves, and pungent odors burned family members' eyes and throats. After the sheriff stopped responding to their pleas for help, the Lees hired private investigators to try to figure out what was going on. About that time, Steve noticed that photographs and videotape taken in certain locations on the property had strange light streaks running through them, and sometimes trans-

lucent faces even appeared on the film. Determined to document the activity, Steve photographed eerie phenomena that included brilliant beams, floating balls of light, and glowing outlines of humans and animals. Sometimes the mysterious lights could be seen with the naked eye, though most often, they lasted just a split second and showed up only on film. To this day, red, yellow, and white lightforms are seen and recorded, as well as apparitions of an old lady, a little girl, a burly man dressed in 1800s clothing, and a "flying dog," not to mention the hundreds of forlorn faces seen floating in mirrors in the house. Dozens of psychics, paranormal specialists, government investigators, and scientists from around the world have recorded unexplainable phenomena at the site. Psychics have suggested everything from portals to the Other Side to "alien ghosts" as the possible cause, while Hopi shamans believe the site is located over a "Rainbow Vortex" of psychic energy. The Lees have so far has invested over $70,000 in security equipment trying to capture the "presence" responsible for the activity. So far, there are over four thousand photographs and four hundred videotapes supporting the validity of this case.

(The Black Forest area is directly east of the Air Force Academy. The haunted property is in El Paso County, fifteen miles northeast of Colorado Springs. Take I-25 North to Route 83 North for seven miles to the Black Forest exit. www.haunted-places.com/current.htm)

DEAD MAN'S CANYON This canyon is haunted by the ghoulish phantom of a man with an ax in his forehead. The ghost of William Harkins has haunted the area since 1863, when he was murdered by a gang of Mexican religious fanatics. Over the years, dozens of people have reported being chased by the angry phantom near his cabin on Little Fountain Creek. Some have fired bullets at his ghastly shade, and one mother struck him in the ear for scaring her son. It took a few seconds before she realized the man with the ax in his head was a ghost.

(Colorado Springs is in central Colorado at the junction of I-25 and U.S. Highway 24. Dead Man's Canyon is ten miles south of Colorado Springs. Follow Highway 115 through the canyon toward Canon City.) **118**

CRIPPLE CREEK

DUNN BUILDING This building used to be a funeral parlor, but when her mortician husband died, Mrs. T. F.

Dunn turned it into a boarding house. Her presence is still felt in the eleven original rental rooms, and her footsteps are often heard scurrying about as she attempts to clean up the rooms. But psychics have reported sensing a much more disturbed presence in the building. Legend says it is the restless spirit of a miner killed in an explosion (see Mamie R Mine, below). Late one night, while the undertaker was preparing the body, the "dead" miner began to moan in pain. Not wanting to delay his job or cancel preparations, the mortician injected morphine to quiet the man and continued his work.

(Cripple Creek is southwest of Colorado Springs. Follow Highway 24 west for twenty-six miles to Divide, then take the Cripple Creek Road south nineteen miles to the town. The Dunn Building is about five miles southeast of Cripple Creek, at 213 Victor Ave., Victor, CO 80860.) **35**

FAIRLEY BROS. AND LAMPMAN BUILDING This block-square building is home to a ghost locals call Maggie. She wears a white shirtwaist with a long brown dress and high-heeled boots. Witnesses say Maggie appears to be in her late twenties and keeps her shoulder-length brunet hair pinned up. Sometimes she appears as an amorphous blue light that wanders through the top two floors. Contractors, employees, and visitors have all detected Maggie's ghost walking in the second-floor corridor or dancing in the third-floor ballroom.

(The red-brick Fairley Bros. and Lampman Building is on the corner of Third St. and Bennett Ave. in Victor. The bottom floor is now occupied by the Sarsaparilla Saloon Ice Cream Parlor.) **35, 53, (10/83), 101**

MAMIE R MINE The ghosts of three miners haunted the depths of this gold mine for several years. The men all died in separate accidents at the Mamie R Mine in 1894. Miners reported encountering their phantoms in the main shaft, at the 375-foot level, and in isolated drifts in the deeper recesses of mine. One ghost carried his severed arm over his shoulder, and another liked to ride in the ore buckets. It was said that the Mamie R was possessed by mischievous sprites called Tommyknockers. The earth spirits caused beams to give way and explosives to go off prematurely. See Dunn Building, above.

(After several unexplained accidents and ghost sightings, the mine shut down in 1895. It is located on Raven Hill at Cripple Creek.) **49, 118**

PALACE HOTEL This old hotel is haunted by the presence of one of the original owners. Mrs. Kitty Chambers's ghost likes to keep candles lit and placed in certain spots, just as they were when the Palace Hotel first opened. Mrs. Chambers died in Room 3 of the hotel in 1908. Her ghost is said to haunt the room, but that does not stop her from turning up all over the hotel. She may be responsible for turning down beds in the other rooms and for stealing all the keys to Room 9 as well.

(The Palace Hotel and Casino is located at 172 Bennett Ave, Cripple Creek, CO 80813. Phone: 719-689-2992. www.palacehotelcasino.com/hotel.htm) **35, 53 (10/83), 231**

DENVER

BELLE WORDEN'S HOUSE The ghost of John Fitzgerald haunts the whorehouse where he was murdered. On March 19, 1884, he was stabbed to death as he lay sleeping in the bed of a prostitute. His lifeless body was thrown into Cherry Creek and found by a group of boys two months later. Madame Belle Worden and two of her employees were sent to jail for the murder-robbery, and the ghastly phantom of Fitzgerald returned to the scene to make sure it would never again become a house of ill repute.

(The house is now a private residence, at 578 Holladay St., Denver, CO 80207.) **118**

BOMBAY CLUB Owner Greg McAllister says he serves cowboy ghosts as well as living guests in this 1895 tavern. The spirits seem to be quite content to be treated as equals with the living.

(Bombay Club, 1128 Grant St., Denver, CO 80203. Phone: 303-322-5409.) **101**

BRADMAR The haunting of this Tudor mansion began when an exposed ceiling beam was split by a ghost. The thirty-three-room mansion was built in 1920 by department store owner George Gano. When he died, Hubert Work bought the house and married Gano's widow Ethyl. For many years before her death, Ethyl told friends and relatives that when she died she wanted to lie in state in front of the fireplace. She promised that on that night she would split a certain exposed cross-beam on the ceiling above her coffin. The beam split just as she predicted. After the Works died, no one lived in the house until 1962, when it was purchased by Dr. Robert Bradley, a nationally respected obstetrician. Soon after moving in, the Bradleys experienced ghostly presences, levitating objects, overwhelming odors, unexplained footsteps, and moaning sounds. Heavy chandeliers in the house jumped around "like cork bobbers in water." Jewelry mysteriously disappeared and turned up later at a different location. Dr. Bradley consulted the nation's foremost psychic at the time, Arthur Ford. The medium visited Bradmar and identified the spirits as Hubert and Ethyl Work. Their experiences convinced the Bradleys of the reality of spiritual forces, and Dr. Bradley wrote a book, *Psychic Phenomena: Revelations and Experiences*, detailing his personal theories. Bradley sold the house in 1980. The people who bought it could not tolerate the paranormal activity and moved out after only a few months.

(Bradmar is a private residence, at 4100 South University Blvd., Denver, CO 80210.) **101, 135, 175, 186**

CHEESMAN PARK This innocent-looking city park is built on top of a graveyard. The Mount Prospect graveyard, which came to be known as Boot Hill, was created in 1858. In 1873 officials renamed the place City Cemetery but buried only criminals, transients, and epidemic victims there. In 1893 the city gave notice that all bodies had to be removed within ninety days. Needless to say, most of the graves remained untouched. The city hired an undertaker to dig up the six to ten thousand remaining bodies, put them in one-foot by three-and-a-half-foot pine boxes, and deliver them for burial at Riverside Cemetery. It was a horrifying sight. Workers broke corpses into pieces to get them to fit into the minicaskets. Body parts littered the ground and got mixed together in the process. Many of the graves were looted by the men digging them up. During the work, psychics warned workers the dead would return unless a short prayer was uttered for each casket, but no one listened to them. One worker, removing valuable brass from the coffins, ran hysterically from the graveyard saying a ghost jumped on his back. People in neighboring houses reported confused spirits wandering through their homes or appearing in mirrors. A huge scandal erupted, and Mayor Platt Rogers ordered all work halted while an investigation was conducted. No one was able to sort out the mess the workers left behind. The remaining bodies were plowed under, and grass and trees planted. Today, psychics detect an undertone of sadness and confusion at the site, and some say they can hear a low moaning sound coming from the restless ground.

(The Catholic section of the original cemetery was removed in an orderly fashion by church members and is now occupied by the Botanical Gardens. The Jewish section was also completely cleared and is now called Congress Park. Cheesman Park, named for a prominent citizen, is in central Denver, in the Civic Center area. The park is bounded by 8th and 13th avenues, near University Blvd.) **15, 118**

CROKE-PATTERSON-CAMPBELL MANSION The haunting here started in 1970, shortly after the previous tenant's offices were remodeled. The new owners often heard the sounds of someone typing in the deserted building. When they bought two Doberman pinschers to guard the premises, they found the dogs lying dead on the sidewalk the next morning. The frightened animals had leaped through a third-floor window, and whatever scared them might still be in the building. In the 1970s, a baby died in the third-floor nursery and the distraught mother committed suicide. The mansion was then turned into a museum.

(The mansion/museum is in the Capitol Hill area of Denver, at 428 East 11th St., Denver, CO 80203.) **72, 101**

DENVER COURTHOUSE The doors of Hell opened on the second floor here in 1900. At 3:00 A.M. every night for nearly a week, the ghosts of departed souls walked the halls, always accompanied by the overpowering stench of brimstone. Not just one, but dozens of apparitions were reported by night watchmen and janitors. Many were identified as deceased persons. One of the ghosts was a courthouse elevator operator who had fallen to his death down the elevator shaft. The sulfurous scenes drove two men to quit their jobs and move out of the city.

(The courthouse is on the corner of 16th St. and Tremont Ave., Denver, CO 80202.) **118**

DENVER INTERNATIONAL AIRPORT This high-tech showplace was a humbling experience for many engineers. Over a year late opening owing to technical problems, the new Denver airport was built on land considered sacred by Native Americans. This was confirmed by experts in Feng Shui, the Chinese art of placing human structures in harmony with nature. When they surveyed the airport, they said the site was "full of images of death and grief." In spring 1995, Colorado Indians held a ceremony to put their ancestors' spirits to rest.

(Denver International Airport, Denver, CO 80295. Phone: 303-342-2000.) **72**

DUNNING MANSION Former tenants of this triplex residence tell of objects moving by themselves and strange sounds, but the ghostly presence has never been identified.

(The mansion is now an apartment complex on the corner of Pennsylvania St. and East 12th Ave., Denver, CO 80203.) **72**

GRANT-HUMPHREYS MANSION This old house is said to be haunted by five different ghosts. One is A. E. Humphreys, a former owner of the mansion. Known as an excellent marksman, Humphreys died on May 8, 1927, from a suspicious gun accident that took place on the third floor. A séance sponsored by radio station KNUS contacted several of the departed spirits. The house was built by Governor James Grant in 1902 and was sold to the Humphreys family in 1917.

(The Grant-Humphreys Mansion is in the Cheesman Park area in central Denver, four blocks from the Dunning Mansion, and is now the home of the Colorado Council on the Arts. Ghost lectures are held at the mansion in October. For information, call 303-830-1651. The address is 750 Pennsylvania St., Denver, CO 80203. Phone: 303-894-2617.) **15, 72**

LITTLETON TOWN HALL ARTS CENTER Ghostly laughter and music have been heard coming from this community theater building late at night. Whoever the entertaining spirit is, it likes to mess up workers' desks and move their personal belongings. The building was constructed in 1919 as combined firehouse, town hall, and ballroom.

(Littleton is a southern suburb of Denver on U.S. Highway 85. Town Hall Arts Center, Littleton, CO 80120. Phone: 303-794-2787.) **198 (6–90)**

MOLLY BROWN HOUSE The ghost of Molly Brown wanders through her former home, which was built in 1889 and bought by Molly and her husband James Joseph Brown in 1894. Molly survived the sinking of

the *Titanic* in 1912 and became a national heroine. She died in 1932, but the "unsinkable Molly Brown" might also be imperishable. Her ghost and that of her husband have been detected in their gray brick mansion.

(Molly died at the Barbizon Hotel in New York City and is buried in the Holy Rood Cemetery on Long Island. Ghost Lectures are held at Molly Brown House in October. It is located on Capitol Hill near the corner of Pennsylvania and 13th streets. Molly Brown House Museum, 1340 Pennsylvania St., Denver, CO 80203. Phone: 303-832-4092. www.mollybrown.com) **72**

PEABODY MANSION This house was built by Colorado Governor James Peabody at the turn of the century and is haunted by later residents. It is rumored that a woman was brutally raped in the basement and that someone committed suicide in the bathroom. Whatever the source of the disturbances, many people have felt bad vibes here. In the early 1980s, a nightclub opened in the old mansion. In deference to the unseen occupants, it was called Spirits.

(The mansion is four blocks from the state capitol, at 1010 Pennsylvania St., Denver, CO 80203.) **72**

PECCORA HOUSE On October 21, 1875, police discovered the mutilated bodies of Guiseppe Peccora and three young Italian boys in the cellar of this house. Peccora was an old scissors grinder who abducted the boys and made them earn money for him by playing music in the streets of Denver. Three acquaintances of Peccora had broken into his house to rob him and ended up cutting the throats of everyone they found there. Soon afterward, horrified neighbors reported hearing sounds of screaming, mixed with chaotic harp music, coming from the abandoned structure. Families moved out of the neighborhood after seeing dark forms roaming about in the house of death. Then, one night someone set fire to the house and burned it to the ground.

(The Peccora residence was located at 2334 Lawrence St., Denver, CO 80205.) **8**

REYNOLDS COTTAGE This historic house is haunted by Madge Reynolds, who had an adulterous love affair with *Denver Post* owner Fred Bonfils. She collapsed and died in her bedroom after returning from a horseback ride with Bonfils. Ever since, her white ghost is seen in the rooms on the north side of the house.

(The house is a private residence on Logan St. in the Capitol Hill area of Denver, CO 80202.) **72**

UNION DEPOT The ghost of a man called the Soldier by employees haunts this once-grand railroad station. No apparition has been seen, but people sense the unmistakable presence of a military officer in the great hall. In the 1930s a shadowy apparition was reported several times in the station, but the confused ghost, which seemed to be seeking a way out of the building, eventually found its escape. The Union Depot replaced the original Denver Depot in 1880. It is said the first station was torn down because of the dozens of apparitions reported by telegraph operators and agents who worked there. Among the ghosts at the Denver Depot was a three-fingered hobo who harassed agents by tapping on the glass partitions at ticket counters. The translucent tramp was seen scores of times over a ten-year period. At around 2:00 A.M. he would appear on train platforms, in the lobby, and inside the offices of Denver Depot. Several agents quit rather than work with a ghost.

(The Union Depot is on 22nd St. in downtown Denver.) **118**

ESTES PARK

BALDPATE INN This twelve-room, log-cabin lodge is haunted by the couple who built it in 1917. The ghosts of Ethel and Gordon Mace walk the hallways of their quaint inn and have been seen by several employees and guests. Ethyl is especially active in her old bedroom and in a small storeroom called the Key Room, which houses "the largest collection of keys in the world." The collection was started in 1923, when lawyer Clarence Darrow donated one of his keys. Now the collection of celebrity keys has grown to over twelve thousand. They include Edgar Allan Poe's dorm room key (No. 13), and Stephen King's key to the hotel room where he wrote *The Shining*.

(Estes Park is seventy miles northwest of Denver on Highway 36. The inn is seven miles south of the city on Highway 7. Baldpate Inn, 4900 S. Highway 7, Estes Park, CO 80517. Phone: 970-586-6151. www.baldpateinn. com) **134**

FAIRPLAY

BUCKSKIN CEMETERY A restless spirit inhabits the bones of J. Dawson Hidgepath. The man came to Fair-

play to find gold and a wife, but found only tragedy. In July 1865, Dawson's broken, lifeless body was found at the bottom of the west side of Mount Boss, where he had apparently fallen several hundred feet while trying to prospect on the mountainside. Soon after his burial, Dawson's bones were discovered on the bed of a dance-hall girl in the town of Alma. Believing some tasteless prank had taken place, townspeople reburied the bones in Buckskin Cemetery. But time and time again, the bones would show up at the house of some fair lady. By 1872, Dawson's bones were the talk of the state, and people were throwing them down outhouses to get rid of them. What really went on is almost impossible to determine today, but whatever force kept Dawson's bones from staying buried is said to still reside in the old cemetery.

(Fairplay is in Park County at the junction of U.S. Highway 285 and Highway 9. Alma is two miles east of Buckskin, but not much is left of the ghost town. Buckskin Cemetery is in the town of Laurette in the Higginbottom district, eight miles northwest of Fairplay. Mount Boss is west of Fairplay in the Pike National Forest.) **118**

GEORGETOWN

BAINBRIDGE'S CURSE Edward Bainbridge had a nasty temper. The Scotsman was lynched in 1867 for killing a man in a card game at John Mickle's Saloon. Just before he was hanged, he promised to haunt this town for all eternity. Bainbridge's ghost was first reported in August 1868 in the building in which he had been incarcerated. For over two years his spirit haunted the place. He was blamed for knocking furniture over, banging cupboards, blowing out lanterns, and making hideous laughing sounds. Several people encountered his grinning apparition, and the building was abandoned and eventually torn down. People came from throughout Colorado to witness the angry ghost's antics. Bainbridge's ghost emerged again exactly twenty years after he was hanged. He appeared near Point of Rocks, his ghostly form still carrying a noose around his neck, and is said to return regularly every twenty years.

(Georgetown is located on U.S. Highway 6, about thirty-five miles west of Golden. John Mickle's Saloon was on the corner of Fourth and Rose streets in Georgetown. Point of Rocks can be seen to the west of town.) **118**

GOLDEN

HIGHWAY 93 The remnant of a fading ghost haunts this modern highway. On July 20, 1881, a Colorado Central locomotive struck a man walking on the Ralston-to-Golden tracks near Van Bibber Creek. The violent impact knocked the man far into the bushes. Despite extensive searching, his body was never found. Only a derby hat was discovered laying near the railroad tracks where he was struck. Within a month, the man's apparition began appearing at the scene of the accident. Wearing a derby hat and stinking of rotting flesh, the macabre phantom showed itself inside of trains, along the tracks, and to people passing through the area. The tenacious ghoul continued to haunt the spot, but with time he started to fade away. Today the tracks have been supplanted by a modern highway, but the man's presence is still felt. He appears now as a vaporous shape, cloud of dust, or a lingering sense of uneasiness.

(Golden is five miles west of Denver, just off I-70. The presence has been reported north of Golden, along Highway 93 near Van Bibber Creek.) **118**

GRAND JUNCTION

DENVER AND RIO GRANDE RAILROAD The phantom of an old steam locomotive, Engine 107, haunts the Denver and Rio Grande Railroad tracks outside Grand Junction. At the turn of the century, engineers avoided the unlucky locomotive, which they dubbed Dread 107. The steam engine was the instrument of death for scores of people. On one of its first runs the train went off a trestle, killing several trainmen and many passengers. The rebuilt engine then struck a massive boulder, tossing passengers from their seats like dolls. Dozens of people were killed or injured. Repaired once again, Locomotive Number 107 hit a snowslide in the Black Canyon and claimed more victims. The railroad finally scrapped the cursed locomotive in 1909, but the phantom train, or its ghostly whistle, are still seen and heard along these tracks.

(Grand Junction is in west central Colorado, twenty miles from the Utah border on I-70. The phantom train is seen along the old Denver and Rio Grande railroad tracks that ran between Grand Junction and Gunnison. The train, or its ghostly whistle, is most often encountered near the Gunnison River and Crystal Creek.) **118**

MANITOU

MANITOU SPRINGS The word *Manitou* is Algonquin for "Great Spirit." The name refers to the magical power the Indians believed resided in these waters. They worshipped the site and left offerings of blankets, beads, weapons, food, and carvings. Modern psychics make pilgrimages here to partake of the spiritual energy, which is said to rejuvenate both body and mind.

(The springs are at the foot of Pikes Peak. Follow I-25 to Exit 141. Take Highway 24 west for four miles to Manitou. Phone: 800-642-2567. www.manitousprings.com) **99**

MESA VERDE

MESA VERDE NATIONAL PARK The ghosts of Anasazi Indians, the mysterious "ancient ones" who suddenly disappeared around A.D. 1500, are still seen among the ruins of their 220-room dwelling, called Cliff Palace. Their apparitions are encountered most frequently near the twenty-three pit houses, or kivas, on the floor of the canyon. Each of these ceremonial buildings has a hole in the floor that serves as a spirit gateway, or "Earth Navel." Inside one building, the Sun Temple, there is a great sunflower carved in stone. Called the Sun Shrine, the two-foot-diameter stone flower is mounted on an altar. Geologists say that it was not carved by human hands but was formed by the natural erosion of a sandstone boulder. The sacred symbol is painted on the walls of pueblos throughout the Southwest. In their architecture, the Anasazi expressed their belief in the spiritual linkages of all things. Tunnels and secret passages connected many sacred chambers. Perfectly straight roads link Mesa Verde with its sister city Chaco. See Chaco, New Mexico.

(Mesa Verde National Park is in southwest Colorado. It is located west of Durango on U.S. Highway 160, between Mancos and Cortez. For information, contact Mesa Verde National Park, P.O. Box 8 Mesa Verde, CO 81330. Phone: 303-529-4465. For a visitor's guide, contact the Mesa Verde Visitor Bureau, P.O. Box HH, Cortez, CO 81321. Phone: 800-253-1616. www.nps.gov/meve) **15, 144, 200**

PENROSE

OLD GLENDALE STATION This stage stop on the Granite-Colorado City line is a two-story stone building constructed in 1861. Waiting on the front porch is the ghost of a woman in a white satin wedding dress. The ghost bride only appears to witnesses on horseback, as if the sounds of pounding hooves somehow bring her back. She is Kathleen Cooper, who still waits for her beloved fiancé to appear on his horse along the South Park Road. The gold miner was killed in a holdup on his way to join her on their wedding night in May 1878.

(Penrose is just east of Canon City, at the junction of U.S. Highway 50 and Highway 115. The ruins of Glendale Station stand on a bluff on the eastern bank of Beaver Creek in Fremont County. The site is just east of Penrose, where Red Creek meets Beaver Creek.) **49, 118**

SILVER CLIFF

SILVER CLIFF CEMETERY The ghosts of deceased pioneers take the form of shimmering blue lights that hover above the graves in this old cemetery. The haunting lights were first reported by silver miners in 1882 and continue to be seen to this day. Some believe the lights are the "dancing blue spirits" of sacred hilltops spoken of in Indian legends. A 1967 article in *The New York Times* made the site a tourist attraction, and hundreds of people reported seeing the strange floating lights. Edward Linehan of *National Geographic* investigated the site in 1969 and observed "dim round spots of blue-white light" glowing over the graves, but when he approached one it disappeared and then slowly reappeared. The lights are not reflections of car, train, or airplane headlights, and a Geiger counter survey revealed no radioactivity in the area.

(Silver Cliff is at the junction of Highway 69 and Highway 96 in Custer County in south-central Colorado. The cemetery is in Silver Cliff, near Rosita in the foothills of Wet Mountain. The elevation is 8,011 feet.) **20, 37, 56, 96, 115, 118, 194, 231**

CONNECTICUT

CORNWALL

DUDLEYVILLE This abandoned settlement is known for its overwhelmingly negative psychic energy. The land here was first settled in 1738 by the William Dudley family, but conditions proved too harsh for farming. The production of charcoal from pine trees was the only profitable industry, although it lasted only a few decades. Residents of the settlement were viewed with great suspicion. Odd accidents, suicide, and insanity seemed to plague the people of Dudleyville. The town quickly gained a reputation for being cursed, and no one wanted to live there. Today, sensitive individuals still feel the dark forces, and modern witches hold annual ceremonies here. The area is technically a dead zone, where birds and other animals rarely tread. Recently, a film producer and a group of friends encountered a black shape rising out of an old stone foundation. As they got closer they all experienced trouble breathing, as if the life force were being sucked out of them. Dudleyville is considered one of the most haunted locations in the United States. So far, there have been over a hundred reports of paranormal activity at the site.

(Dudleyville is in Litchfield County in northwestern Connecticut. Dudleyville is now a private nature preserve occupying eight hundred acres overlooking the Housatonic River on Coltsfoot Mountain. Follow U.S. Highway 7 to Cornwall Bridge and go east for two miles to Cornwall. Then take Dark Entry Road from Cornwall, past Witch's Dam, up to Dudleyville.) **72, 133**

Huguenot House, built in 1761, may be home to several eighteenth-century ghosts. See Huguenot House, East Hartford, Connecticut (TRISTRAM DEROMA)

EAST HARTFORD

HUGUENOT HOUSE When this restored house was moved to a new location in a city park, the ghost of a lady in a blue dress appeared. Workers at the site reported unexplainable crashing and knocking noises in the basement and living room. The sounds of some-one hammering echoed through the building even when it was empty. Security officers at the scene were mystified. After a while, the men nicknamed the presence Benny, and the project foreman started issuing a work list for the ghost who seemed so eager to assist them. In 1982, police were called to the scene when a faceless phantom frightened a little girl playing in the park. Some believe the ghosts are the original builders of the house. The woodframe structure was built in 1761 by a family of Huguenots, a French Protestant sect. They were practical men and women, who loved carpentry and woodworking.

(Take the Robert Street exit from I-84 and turn right. Turn left at Hillside Street and left again at Burnside Avenue. Huguenot House is in Martin Park, at 307 Burnside Ave., East Hartford, CT 06108. Phone: 860-528-0716. Further information is available from the East Hartford Tourism Office, at 860-289-0239. www.ehcoc. com) **14, 101**

"Lepkes"—apparitions that seem exactly like real people, until they vanish from sight—appear in Union Cemetery. See Union Cemetery, Easton, Connecticut
(TRISTRAM DEROMA)

EASTON

UNION CEMETERY For many years, visitors to this cemetery reported having conversations with lifelike apparitions who walk among the tombstones and then disappear into thin air. This type of ghost, known as a "lepke," seems as real as any other person until it vanishes from sight. Acquaintances of people buried here say the apparitions talk and behave exactly as they did when alive. This is also the haunt of the infamous White Lady, observed many times over the last fifty years. See Our Lady of Holy Rosary Cemetery, Monroe, Connecticut.

(Easton is in southwest Connecticut near the junction of Highway 136 and Highway 59. The cemetery is on Highway 59, near the Easton Baptist Church.) **15, 72, 215**

HADDAM

MOUNT TOM Strange booming sounds, the Moodus Noises, have been studied here since 1765, when a team from England excavated the area. They found huge calcium "pearls" in the Rocky Moodus Cave, which they believed were causing the rumbling sounds. Indian legend says the noises are caused by an evil spirit; colonists believed they were the sounds of underground warfare between the witches of West Haddock and the witches of East Haddock. In 1791, the sounds became so loud that they could be felt as far away as New York and Boston.

(Haddam is southeast of Hartford. Take Highway 9 south for twenty-five miles to the Highway 154 split, then go five miles to Haddam. Mount Tom is near the confluence of the Moodus and Salmon Rivers, just before they flow into the Connecticut River.) **49**

HAMDEN

SLEEPING GIANT PARK This site has been considered sacred since prehistoric times. The Sleeping Giant is a two-mile-long, 740-foot-tall basalt mountain that looks just like a man lying down on his back. Indians believed the mountain was a living presence, and even today people speak of the mountain as if it were a person. Legend says the mountain is really an evil giant by the name of Hobbomock, who was put to sleep to prevent him from doing any more damage to the area.

(Take Exit 38 off I-95 and follow it to the town of Hamden. The park is located outside of town at 200 Mt. Carmel Ave. The telephone number of the ranger station on the mountain is 203-789-7498. www.kelseypub.com/ct-guide/stparks/slpgiant.shtml) **99**

MERIDEN

WEST PEAK STATE PARK Since the 1800s, the mysterious phantom of a large black dog has greeted hikers near the Hanging Hills. The dog silently follows people to the summit of West Peak but never leaves behind footprints. According to legend, the first time a person sees the dog it brings him happiness. A second sighting is a warning. The third time the dog is seen means imminent death. Even today, an average of three people a year fall to their deaths from West Peak.

(Meriden is seventeen miles south of Hartford on U.S. Highway 5. The Hanging Hills are high cliffs above the Quinnipiac River. In Hubbard Park, follow Reservoir Ave. north. Turn west onto Percival Park Rd. and follow the road up to the hill to the West Peak State Park.) **36**

A white lady ghost, possibly the specter of a murdered woman, is seen near this cemetery. See Our Lady of the Rosary Chapel Cemetery, Monroe, Connecticut (TRISTRAM DEROMA)

MONROE

OUR LADY OF THE ROSARY CHAPEL CEMETERY The same White Lady ghost is seen near this cemetery and at another nearby (see Union Cemetery, Easton, Connecticut). She wears a white nightgown with a bonnet. In 1993, a local fireman "ran over" the ghost in his pickup truck. Sometimes witnesses observe dark, shadowy figures attempting to grab the White Lady. Investigator Ed Warren believes she is Mrs. Knot, whose husband was murdered near Easton in the 1940s. The woman may have been murdered, too, shortly after her husband's funeral.

(Monroe is north of Bridgeport in Fairfield County. Take Highway 25 northwest to Highway 111 and go north three miles to Monroe. The cemetery is near the Stepney Green in Monroe at 15 Pepper St. Phone: 203-261-8290. The White Lady appears in the cemetery and on Pepper Street.) **72, 215**

NEW HAVEN

NEW HAVEN HARBOR A phantom sailing vessel disappeared in front of hundreds of spectators in the harbor here. The mysterious event took place in June 1648. The broken ship drifted into the harbor after a violent thunderstorm and then "vanished into a smoky cloud, which in some time dissipated, leaving, as everywhere else, a clear air." The colonists assumed it was the ghost of a ship that had sailed from New Haven a year previously and was feared lost at sea.

(New Haven is on the southeastern shore of Connecticut on at the junction of I-91 and I-95. The harbor stretches from Bradley Point to Morgan Point.) **68**

A ghostly organist is heard by students in Woolsey Hall on the Yale campus. See Yale University, New Haven, Connecticut (TRISTRAM DEROMA)

YALE UNIVERSITY The unexplainable sounds of organ playing have been heard by students and custodians at Woolsey Hall on this prestigious campus. The identity of the ghostly organist is unknown.

(Yale University, 149 Elm St., New Haven, CT 06520. Phone: 203-432-2300.) **101**

The eighty-five-year-old Ledge Lighthouse is haunted by the spirit of a former lighthouse keeper. See Ledge Lighthouse, New London, Connecticut (TRISTRAM DEROMA)

NEW LONDON

LEDGE LIGHTHOUSE This eighty-five-year-old structure is haunted by the spirit of a former lighthouse keeper who cut his own throat and then jumped off the upper level. He was despondent over his wife's running off with another man. Known as Ernie, the ghost is a tall, bearded man who wears a slicker and round rain hat. Sometimes the mischievous ghost unties skiffs docked here, moves objects such as coffee cups and radios, or slams refrigerator doors. A séance was conducted in December 1981, in the presence of coast guard personnel, to try to free the spirit from the premises.

(New London is on I-95 in the southeastern corner of Connecticut. The Ledge Lighthouse is atop a sixty-five-foot-high, three-story square building in the water at the convergence of the Thames River, Fisher's Island Sound, and Long Island Sound in New London Harbor. Phone: 860-442-2222.) **101, 135**

MONTE CRISTO COTTAGE This charming cottage, now a museum, is haunted by Ella Quinlan O'Neill, mother of the Nobel Prize-winning author Eugene

O'Neill. Ella was addicted to morphine and once attempted suicide when she could not get a fix. Her frantic pacing is still heard coming from an upstairs bedroom, and sudden drops in temperature in the room are attributed to her. Eugene spent his summers here when he was a boy and wrote about his experiences in *Long Day's Journey into Night.*

(The cottage museum is on Pequot Ave., between Plant St. and Thames St. The address is 325 Pequot Avenue, New London, CT 06320. Phone: 860-443-0051. www.newlondongazette.com/Monte.html) **14, 101, 102**

SAYBROOK WOODS The ghost of a young girl appears here only in the winter months. She is the spirit of Lottie, daughter of Elihu Enken. She lived here in the early 1700s at her father's tavern, the Wild Goose, a coach stop on the Williamantic-Saybrook run. An old crony, whom locals called Old Dreary, took a fancy to the young girl. Some say Old Dreary "witched her away," but whatever happened, Lottie disappeared one evening. That winter, people started seeing the blue-caped girl romping in the woods. Wherever she went she left a trail of blood-soaked footprints in the snow. Finally, two hunters came across her decomposed body hidden away in a cave. She still wore her blue cape, but both her arms had been broken. Scraps of food littered the cave floor and a tattered old shawl was found in a corner. Lottie's ghost continues to be seen during the winter here, and wherever her faint form dances over the white snow, tiny crimson footprints are left behind.

(Saybrook Woods are near New London, on the west shore of the Thames River.) **158**

NORTH WOODSTOCK

LYONS TAVERN This sixteen-room farmhouse was known as Lyons Tavern before the Revolutionary War. By the time the Viner family took possession in 1951, the historic building was in sad shape. Mr. and Mrs. Charles Viner and their eleven-year-old daughter Sandra decided to take on the awesome task of restoring the house to its original splendor. Apparently the remodeling stirred up some slumbering spirits, because soon after the Viners moved in a number of unusual events occurred. The family and visitors started hearing panicked footsteps, running around upstairs, always followed by two loud thumps on the floor. The pattern kept repeating itself, although no prowlers or visible disturbances were ever found. The phenomenon escalated into reverberating explosions of violent sounds and sudden freezing temperatures in the upstairs rooms. The Viners called police on numerous occasions, but officers never found any intruders. Then, one day in 1959, Mrs. Viner removed the wallpaper in one of the upstairs rooms to prepare for painting. To her horror, the wallboard underneath was covered with blood stains. She decided to research the history of the house and came upon the tragic tale of one of the servant girls at Lyons Tavern. She was a beautiful young lady who sparked a jealous argument between two guests at the inn. The two men retired to one of the upstairs rooms and ended up killing each other in a bloody sword fight. Mrs. Viner realized that the sounds her family had been hearing were the ghostly replay of that violent night. As the effects grew in intensity, the Viners could no longer tolerate the disruptions and moved out of the house in 1961. The new owners would never live in the house, and the abandoned dwelling became the target of vandals and thieves.

(North Woodstock is near the Massachusetts border in northeastern Connecticut, at the junction of Highways 169 and 197. The house is on private property, on Brickyard Rd., North Woodstock, CT 06280.) **5**

Unexplained events are ascribed to ghostly visitors at this quaint eighteenth-century inn. See Red Brook Inn, Old Mystic, Connecticut (TRANSTRAM DEROMA)

OLD MYSTIC

RED BROOK INN Verne Sasek and Ruth Keyes have put up with the ghosts of their quaint old inn for many years. Both guests and employees experience moving

cold spots and hear inexplicable voices in this building, which was constructed in 1756.

(Red Brook Inn, routes 184 and 27, Box 237, Old Mystic, CT 06372. Phone: 860-572-0349. www.virtualcities. com/ons/ct/z/ctz4501.htm) **101**

POMFRET

BARA-HECK SETTLEMENT This isolated colony was founded by two Welsh families in 1780. Although it was abandoned in 1890, the sounds of the former inhabitants remain. Children's laughter, singing, mothers calling their husbands and children, barking dogs, mooing cows, and the rumble of wagon wheels can still be heard here. The sounds emerge as if from a portal in time and float over the ruins of the stone cellars and old cemetery. Investigations carried out in 1971 and 1972 failed to record the sounds, but researchers did encounter the apparition of a bearded man at the cemetery's west wall and the wraith of a small child in an elm tree near the north wall.

(Bara-Heck can be reached from the intersection of U.S. Highway 44 and Highway 97 in Pomfret Township in northeastern Connecticut. Take Highway 97 north to a side road just north and to the left of Mashomoquet Brook. Follow the dirt road about a quarter mile to the settlement.) **53 (11/85), 135**

SIMSBURY

CHARTHOUSE RESTAURANT This old colonial building features ornate wood carvings, massive fireplaces, and an uppity female ghost who likes to poke customers in the ribs while they are eating. The spirit has gotten even more active since the place was modernized, and it is thought she is upset with the latest changes to her environment.

(Simsbury is northwest of Hartford, at the junction of U.S. Highway 202 and Highway 309. Charthouse Restaurant, 4 Hartford Rd., Weatogue, CT 06070. Phone: 860-658-1118.) **72**

OLD GLOWACKI HOUSE This house was haunted from 1977 to 1980, when the Glowacki family lived here. Apparitions included a shadowy figure in the bedrooms, a bemused elderly woman, and a one-armed man wearing suspenders. An unseen hand turned children's dolls and crucifixes to face the wall, turned lights on and off, and choked a family member sleeping in an upstairs bedroom. A Catholic priest blessed the house and a Mass was said, but the hauntings continued. A six-month investigation by Hartford parapsychologist Boyce Batey confirmed the presence of the confused spirits, whom Batey believed "had lost their way and were trying to communicate with people on the physical plane."

(The former Glowacki residence is occupied by new tenants. It is a yellow duplex house at 85B Woodland St., Simsbury, CT 06070.) **50, 53 (12/79), 72**

SOUTHINGTON

SNEDECKER HOUSE Allen and Carmen Snedecker moved into their new home in 1986. They had no idea their new house was haunted until their fourteen-year-old son Phillip began seeing monklike apparitions in the house. The entire family started hearing strange scratching sounds and frightful whispering coming from the walls. Several ghosts were encountered in the basement, including an old man in a blue suit with his eyes rolled back in his head, a young man with long black hair, and a little boy wearing Superman pajamas. Then, an evil presence started molesting Tammy, their eighteen-year-old daughter. Several nights in a row, Tammy awoke screaming, saying something had sexually assaulted her. After a grueling exorcism that lasted many hours, a Vatican-trained demonologist priest declared the house clean of spirits. Ed and Lorraine Warren investigated the case and discovered that the seventy-five-year-old house was once a funeral home, and the embalming room was located in the basement. They suspected that necrophilia had taken place there.

(Southington is eight miles southwest of Hartford, at the junction of Highway 10 and Highway 364. The white, two-story wood-frame house is in central Southington.) **72, 216**

STAMFORD

1780 HOUSE This house was named for the year it was built. The ancient house was in the Weed family until 1927, when the Clayton Rich family bought the property. In 1955, the house was purchased by Robert and Dorothy Cowan. Strange moving shadows have been seen in the parlor, and unaccountable music is heard in an upstairs bedroom. The translucent figure of an Indian has been encountered in the kitchen. A local historian revealed that the house was originally built by Augustus Weed on the private hunting ground of an Indian named Chief Ponus. During an investigation by Hans Holzer in March 1964, several spirits were contacted, including a Revolutionary War soldier by the name of Benjamin Harmon.

(Stamford is on I-95 in Fairfield County, in the extreme southwestern tip of Connecticut. The house is on Woodpecker Ridge, Stamford Hill, CT 06902. For information, contact the Stamford Historical Society, 1508 High Ridge Rd., Stamford Hill, CT 06901. Phone: 203-329-1183. www.stamfordhistory.org) **82, 86**

STRATFORD

PHELPS MANSION Dr. Eliakim Phelps was a Presbyterian minister who liked to dabble in spiritualism. He held a number of séances and experimented with other ways of contacting the dead. Whatever it was he conjured up terrorized his family for nearly six months. It all started on March 10, 1850, when the Phelps family returned from church. They found the front door of their home wide open and draped with black cloth. In the parlor, they saw the apparition of a shrouded corpse laid out on the table. Within a few minutes, the ghostly vision vanished. They later discovered the apparition was Goody Bassett, a woman hanged as a witch in 1661. That afternoon they discovered their clothes arranged on the beds like the bodies of dead persons, with the arms folded across the chest. A week later they found eleven lifelike, life-size effigies meticulously made of stuffed clothing. In the next few weeks, they found nineteen more. Objects seemed to move by themselves and odd noises thundered through the house. Dr. Phelps invited another clergyman to stay with them and witness the phenomena. The man stayed for three weeks and saw chairs and tables levitate, objects materialize in midair, and a heavy candlestick holder move from the mantel and beat against the floor until it broke. The events seem to center around two of the Phelps children: twelve-year-old Harry and four-year-old Anna. A three-year-old boy and a sixteen-year-old girl were rarely bothered by the spirit.

As news spread of the Stratford Knockings, reporters, scientists, and psychics from around the country came to the Phelps' house to witness the phenomena. Dozens of reputable witnesses heard the odd knocking sounds and saw heavy objects float through the air. Some objects "danced" across the floor and "jumped" through windows. Finally, after Harry and his sister were sent off to boarding schools, the activity stopped. Then in 1971, police investigating reports of vandalism in the abandoned house chased the ghost of a little girl up the stairs into a third-floor bedroom. Ghost hunters Ed and Lorraine Warren investigated the case.

(Stratford is next to Bridgeport, off I-95 in southwestern Connecticut. The mansion is not far from the famous Stratford Shakespearean Theater. Phelps Mansion, 1738 Elm St., Stratford, CT 06497. www.prsne.com/phelps. htm) **101, 109, 189, 204, 214, 222**

TOLLAND

DANIEL BENTON HOMESTEAD Daniel Benton started building this brick and wood-frame house in 1720. He died in 1776, but the families of his three sons continued to live in the house for many years. Today, the place is haunted by two ghosts from the Revolutionary War period. One is a Hessian soldier, possibly one of two dozen Hessian mercenaries imprisoned in the cellar. The other is the revenant of Elisha Benton, returning to search for his eighteen-year-old sweetheart Jemina Barrows. Both young people died of smallpox in the house, and they are buried in the family graveyard on the west lawn. Unfortunately, their graves are on opposite sides of the carriage road, and they remain separated forever. Mysterious sounds such as weeping, rapping noises, and voices still echo through the house.

(Tolland is twenty miles northeast of Hartford at I-84 exit 68. Follow Grant Hill Rd. to Metcalf Rd. The site is at 160 Metcalf Rd., Tolland, CT 06084. Phone: 860-870-9599. The Benton Homestead is operated by the Tolland Historical Society. Phone: 860-875-4693. Additional information is available from the East Hartford Tourism Office, 20 Hartford Rd., Manchester, CT 06040. Phone: 860-646-2223.) **14, 101, 168**

DELAWARE

BETHANY BEACH

ADDY-SEA INN A copper bathtub in Room 1 of this inn sometimes shakes violently, as if it were a magnet for the ethereal energy in the building. Ghostly organ music is heard in Room 6. Unexplainable footsteps are heard on the roof and in the second-floor hall. The ghosts here date back to the John Addy family, who built the house ninety years ago. The footsteps are thought to belong to Kurtz Addy, their rambunctious son, who fell to his death from the roof. Room 11 is said to be haunted by Paul Dulaney, a famous swimmer who worked as a handyman for the Addys.

(Bethany Beach is in southeast Delaware, below Rehoboth Bay at the junction of Highway 1 and Highway 26. The eleven-room bed-and-breakfast inn is at 99 Ocean View Parkway N. Atlanta. Bethany Beach, DE 19930. Phone: 302-539-3707. www.addysea.com) **179**

BEACH AT BETHANY The confused and tattered ghost of Eddie Rickenbacker has been seen along this stretch of beach. No one has determined why the naval hero haunts this beach, or why he looks so bedraggled.

(The Atlantic beach is in the town of Bethany.) **179**

BOWERS BEACH

BOWERS BEACH BOOGIES Three ghosts haunt the area around this resort town. One is a depressed-looking man dressed in high-fashioned clothes. His cel-luloid collar is said to glow in the dark as he walks through the downtown area late at night. Another apparition haunts Lover's Lane outside of town, and was also recently spotted by motorists driving on a sharply curved road near an old oyster factory at the outskirts of town. Finally, the ghost of a man who committed suicide by walking into the ocean haunts the beach at Bowers.

(Bowers Beach is at the end of Highway 1 southeast of Dover. The town is near the Harvey Conservation Area on Delaware Bay.) **179**

BRANDYWINE CREEK

BRANDYWINE CREEK STATE PARK A werewolf, or werefox as the case may be, has been seen slinking through the underbrush along this creek bed. Locals call the phantom Red Dog Fox. Sometimes the large fox turns into a coon-skinned form of Gil Thoreau, a teenage guide whose father worked for General Lafayette. The scout lived mostly in the wild and still looked like a teenager when he died at the age of forty-five, back in the 1830s.

(Brandywine Creek is on the Pennsylvania border, three miles north of central Wilmington on I-202. The park is one mile south of town. The sightings have occurred from Brandywine Creek State Park to as far north as Manoir Le Ray, near Watertown, New York. Phone: 302-577-3534.) **158**

CAPE HENLOPEN

CAPE HENLOPEN STATE PARK A cylindrical shaft of ruff stone rises out of the mist here and shines a flickering beacon at ships approaching the coast. Some locals call it the Corpse Light; others have dubbed it the Bad Weather Witch. The phenomenon is often mistaken for a lighthouse and has been responsible for many deaths. The first disaster was on December 25, 1655, when the captain of the *Devonshireman* steered his vessel toward the "lighthouse" during a storm. Nearly two hundred people died when the ship crashed against the rocks.

Over the years, hundreds more also died in wrecks here. Legend says that the phantom lighthouse is an old Delaware Indian curse of a "drum of stone signaling death" to all white men. The curse punished British soldiers who massacred a group of Indians celebrating a marriage ceremony. On May 25, 1798, the British sloop *DeBraak* was lured too close to shore and broke apart in the bay. Sometimes the phantom ship returns to reenact the disaster. The ghost of a lone Indian atop a mysterious rock was sighted by multiple witnesses in 1800, just before an excursion barge smashed against the rocks, killing many people. In 1980, the *USS Poet*, a twelve-thousand-ton grain carrier, vanished without a trace near the coast here.

(Cape Henlopen is at the entrance to Delaware Bay. The park is seventeen miles northeast of Georgetown at the end of Highway 404 at 42 Cape Henlopen DC, Lewes, DE 19958. Phone: 302-645-8983.) **158, 179**

CYPRESS SWAMP

CYPRESS SWAMP CONSERVATION AREA Locals call this Burnt Swamp because of a fire caused by an illegal alcohol still in the 1930s. The fires burned for twelve months. The area has always been considered out-of-bounds and home to mysteries best left unspoken. The ghost of an old shingle maker is said to still ply his trade at the edge of the swamp. The most fearsome phantom here is the Swamp Creature. The hairy, apelike animal has been reported by several witnesses and is believed responsible for half-eaten carcasses of dogs found in the swamp.

(The swampland lies between the towns of Gumboro and Selbyville, along the south Delaware-Maryland border. Highway 54 goes through the middle of the swamp.) **72**

DOVER

DICKINSON MANSION The ghost of lawyer John Dickinson haunts his former home. Called "the penman of the Revolutionary War," Dickinson wrote many essays supporting the American colonies. Today, his ghost is still busy writing. Tape recordings made in the den have reportedly captured the scratching sounds of a quill pen on parchment, as well as other unexplainable noises. Dickinson's ghost still takes afternoon naps in his old bedroom, where the bedsheets are sometimes found rumpled for no discernible reason.

(Dover is in Kent County in central Delaware, at the junction of U.S. Highways 13 and 113. The Dickinson Mansion is seven miles southeast of Dover, near the Kitts Hummock Road. For information, contact the Delaware Travel Development Bureau, 630 State College Rd. Dover, DE 19901. Phone: 302-678-4254.) **78, 179**

DOVER PUBLIC LIBRARY Although there have been a few reports of supernatural manifestations surrounding a human skull stored in a hatbox here, the library officially denies any ghostly activity. The skull belongs to a notorious female outlaw named Patty Cannon, who was arrested in April 1829. She was involved in illegal slave trading and confessed to at least one murder and to being an accomplice in a dozen more. But before she could be executed, Patty took a fatal dose of poison in her cell at the Sussex County Jail. A law clerk severed her head from her body "for posterity," and in the early 1960s, the skull ended up at the Dover Public Library.

(Patty's skull is kept in a hatbox in the library's technical services area. Dover Public Library, 45 S. State St., Dover, DE 19901. Phone: 302-736-7030. www.cityofdover.com/library.html) **179**

WOODBURN Four ghosts haunt Delaware's Governor's Mansion. The great house was built in 1790 by a Revolutionary War colonel, Charles Hillyard, on land given to his family by William Penn. When a Quaker by the name of Daniel Cowgill owned the house during the Civil War, a tunnel was dug from the cellar to the St. Jones River, and escaped slaves used the mansion as a stop on the Underground Railway. The house was haunted for over 160 years before it became the official home of the governor of Delaware in 1966. The first ghost at Woodburn appeared in 1805 to Lorenzo Dow, a Methodist evangelist staying there. He described the elderly "stranger upstairs" to the wife of the owner of the house one day. She told him no one else lived in the house, but later she saw the same apparition. In the 1870s, another houseguest had to be revived from a fainting spell when he saw the ghost of an elderly man sitting by the fireplace. The phantom could be the original owner, Charles Hillyard, who died in the house. Another ghost is a man in a powdered wig, who has a predilection for fine wine. Governor Charles Terry, Jr., accused the ghost of draining off some of the vintage wines in the cellar of the mansion, and one of his servants saw the ghost help himself from a decanter in the dining room. Earlier residents placated the dry spirit by setting out wine decanters, which mysteriously drained overnight. The ghost of a slave kidnapper seems to stay near an old poplar tree in the yard. It is the tree from which he was hanged, although he was not strung up with a rope. He climbed the tree hoping to kidnap runaway slaves, when the house was owned by abolitionist Daniel Cowgill. But as fate would have it the man slipped, and his head was caught between two branches. On moonlit nights his struggling ghost can be seen dangling from the gnarled old tree. His awful moans and chain rattling sometimes fill the inside of the house as well. The fourth ghost is a little girl in a red-checked gingham dress. She was seen playing by the pool in the garden during the 1940s but has never been identified. At the January 1985 inauguration party for Governor Michael Castle, guests complained of an invisible presence tugging at their clothing, and one woman saw the apparition of a little girl in a corner of the reception room. The governor himself reported a few ghostly encounters and even allowed a teacher and three of her students to bring their tape recorders and Ouija boards to Woodburn. After spending the night, the children were genuinely spooked, insisting that a portrait of a woman in one of the rooms kept smiling at them.

(Go south on State Street in downtown Dover until King's Highway. The Governor's Mansion is at 151 King's Highway, Dover, DE 19901. Phone: 302-739-5656. www.state.de.us/woodburn) **5, 14, 66 (10/86), 101, 135, 168, 175, 186, 187**

FREDERICA

HIGHWAY 12 A huge dog with glowing red eyes haunts this stretch of highway. Called Fence Rail Dog because of its size, the ghoul has been reported here since the turn of the century. Some say it is the spirit of

A huge dog with glowing eyes has haunted this stretch of Highway 12 since the turn of the century. See Highway 12, Frederica, Delaware (TRACEY JOHNSON)

a murderer who lived in a farmhouse that once stood near the road. The man disposed of the body of his landlord by grinding it up and mixing it with cornmeal, which he fed to his dog.

(Frederica is thirteen miles south of Dover, off Highway 113 in central Delaware. The phantom is seen along the stretch of Highway 12 between Frederica and Felton.) **179**

MORDINGTON This old mansion is haunted by a beautiful slave girl known only as Tom's Daughter. The young woman was confined to the attic when she resisted the amorous intentions of her owner. Out of desperation she leaped from the window. Her screams as she fell to her death are still heard.

(The house is a private residence on McColley Pond, just outside Frederica.) **179**

FORT DELAWARE

FORT DELAWARE This pentagonal fortress housed Confederate prisoners during the Civil War and was used in the coastal defense networks of World Wars I and II. In 1951, it was restored and opened to the public. Visitors have reported the sounds of chains and fearful moaning issuing from the old dungeon, and some have seen the fleeting ghosts of rebel soldiers under the ramparts and on the parade ground. In 1985, a tourist took a picture of a translucent Confederate officer standing in an archway.

(The fort is located on 178-acre Pea Patch Island, located in the bay fifteen miles south of Wilmington, near the junction of U.S. Highway 301 and Highway 7 near Delaware City. Phone: 302-834-7941. www.destateparks. com/fdsp/fdsp.htm) **179**

INDIAN RIVER BAY

DELAWARE SEASHORE STATE PARK The ghost of a young woman wearing an old-fashioned bathing suit has been reported walking over the sand dunes here. Her translucent form has been known to ask for help from passersby on the beach. No record has been found of any drownings in the area, and the identity of the panicked ghost remains a mystery.

(Indian River Bay is just south of Rehoboth Bay in southeastern Delaware. The Delaware Seashore State Park is a peninsula fronting both bays along Highway 1 and the Atlantic Ocean. Phone: 302-227-2800. www.destateparks.com/dssp/dssp.htm) **179**

LEWES

CANNONBALL HOUSE This house is named for a cannonball imbedded in the front wall. It commemorates April 6, 1813, when the building was hit with cannon fire from a British frigate in the War of 1812. Part of the house dates back to 1743, and a new addition was built in 1790. The place is thought to be haunted by the ghost of a former owner who burned to death in the building. The victim got too close to the fireplace and her dress caught fire.

(Lewes is near Cape Henlopen at the junction of U.S. Highway 9 and Highway 404. The house has an antique cannon in the front yard. It is a private residence at 118 Front St. SE; Lewes, DE 19958. www.lewes.com/tour23. html) **179**

FIDDLER'S HILL Back in the late 1800s, two young men were courting the same woman. Late one night, one of the men decided to frighten the other away from the lady's house. The man hid in a tree and made scary sounds with his violin when the other man crossed a nearby path. The prank worked, but the fiddler fell from the tree and broke his neck. Ever since, the sounds of his wild fiddling have haunted the site.

(Fiddler's Hill is a bluff along Highway 277 at Rabbit's Ferry. The site is just southwest of Lewes in Sussex County. A gravel path crosses through Love Creek near Goslee Mill Pond.) **179**

MILFORD NECK

MILFORD NECK WILDLIFE AREA Tales of Indian ghosts haunting this area go back two centuries. The Island Field site here contains a hundred exposed graves thought to be twelve hundred years old, the ancestors of the Lenni Lenape Indians. In 1972, the site was exorcised by an Indian princess, but the continuing display of the open graves is said to have angered the spirits even more since then.

(Milford Neck is north of Milford, between Highway 113 and Big Stone Beach, twenty miles south of Dover. A museum at the site explains the diggings.) **179**

NEW CASTLE

AMSTEL HOUSE This house, built in the seventeenth century by Dr. John Finney, is haunted by the same mysterious presence which haunts his son's residence, just down the street. The two homes were connected by a secret tunnel at one time. See David Finney Inn, below.

(New Castle is on the Delaware River, five miles south of Wilmington on Highway 273. The house is a private residence on Delaware St. in the New Castle Historical District. www.ohwy.com/de/a/amstehou.htm) **179**

DAVID FINNEY INN Built in 1683, this inn was once the home of lawyer-soldier David Finney. The identity of the ghost haunting the third floor, however, is unknown. Windows open and objects move by themselves, and dogs refuse to step onto that floor, as if they sense some discarnate presence. See Amstel House, above.

(The bed-and-breakfast inn is located at 216 Delaware St. New Castle, DE 19720. Phone: 302-322-6367.) **179**

KENSEY JOHN HOMESTEAD The ghost of a woman in a white silk gown appeared in front of many reputable witnesses at a dinner party here in the late 1800s. One of the visitors had left a crying baby in a crib while she joined the other guests. Then, someone noticed the baby had stopped crying and checked on the child. They found a pale-looking woman rocking the crib and comforting the baby. The woman wore a white silk dress, with a pearl comb in her hair and soft-leather slippers on her feet. Although she never spoke a word, the revenant joined the guests at the dinner table, and disappeared without a trace later that night.

(The farmhouse is now a private residence on Dupont Highway, New Castle, DE 19720.) **49**

OLD WOODEN DOCKS The ghosts of Dutch soldiers have been seen near the deserted remains of old wooden boat docks here. One headless Dutchman marches up and down the shoreline in front of the docks. The ghosts are most often seen in the autumn months, after nightfall.

(The ruins are south of town, in the New Castle harbor area.) **179**

REDDEN

ELLENDALE STATE FOREST The phantom of a headless figure walks along the highway that runs through this forest. No one has identified the gruesome ogre, but police report an unusual number of accidents along Haunted Highway 113.

(Redden is three miles north of Georgetown on U.S. Highway 113. The Ellendale State Forest is just north of the town of Redden. The phantom is seen along the section of U.S. Highway 113 within the park.) **179**

REDDEN STATE FOREST The ranger's house in a barren section of this forest is haunted by the ghost of a woman who died there. Built at the turn of the century, the house was taken over by the state when the land became a park in the 1930s. Electrical equipment goes off and on by itself, disembodied voices drift through the hallways, and unexplainable sounds emanate from empty rooms upstairs. The strange occurrences are attributed to a young woman who died here under mysterious circumstances in the early 1900s.

(The area is east of Redden, along the Broadkill River, between U.S. Highway 113 and Highway 30.) **179**

ST. GEORGES

OLD SCOTT RUN BRIDGE Anyone who throws a few coins into Scott Run stream, just south of the St. Georges Bridge, might be able to call up the spirit of an old black man named Jacob. In the days before the Civil War, he used to sit on the railing of the wood bridge

here and play his homemade fiddle to travelers. But after being beaten senseless by his overseer, Jacob lost both his musical ability and his reason. No longer useful as a slave, Jacob built a shack next to the old bridge and played screeching, incoherent sounds on his fiddle. One day, when he was in his seventies, he was sitting on the bridge playing his violin, when he fell into the swollen, raging waters. His battered body was found face down on a boulder along the riverbank. Children started hearing the sounds first, then adults began walking out to the bridge to hear the mysterious violin music from nowhere. Before long, the whole countryside knew of the haunted bridge. Today the ghostly music can still be heard, just below the roar of traffic on the new bridge.

(Take U.S. Highway 301 south from Wilmington for fifteen miles to St. Georges. The old bridge crossed Scott Run stream two miles south of the present St. Georges Bridge, which is part of the Dupont Highway, U.S. Highway 301/13.) **15, 179**

SLAUGHTER BEACH

FORT SAULSBURY This deserted army fort was built in 1917 as a defense against German invasion during World War I. In World War II, it was used as a POW camp. The site was abandoned in 1946, but the ghosts of former prisoners are still felt in the old cell blocks.

(Slaughter Beach is at the end of Highway 36, seven miles east of Milford. The fort ruins are on private property near Slaughter Beach in Sussex County. www.state.de.us/facts/history/fortsals.htm) **179**

SLAUGHTER NECK The ghost of a man who shot himself in a ditch here still haunts the area. Several hikers have come across his malevolent spirit. Another ghost, said to wander the Boardwalk Trail between Slaughter Neck and Broadkill Beach, is thought to be Johnathan Morris, whose farmhouse stood near the trail. His presence is most often felt near his tombstone in the old Morris Family Graveyard.

(Slaughter Neck is part of the Prime Hook National Wildlife Refuge, which extends from Slaughter Beach to Broadkill Beach, along Delaware Bay.) **179**

WILMINGTON

ROCKWOOD MUSEUM Strange moving balls of light and eerie sounds haunt this forty-five-room Victorian mansion. Investigators have been unable to explain the phenomena.

(Wilmington borders Philadelphia in northern Delaware. It is at the junction of I-95 and U.S. Highway 202. The mansion is at 61 Shipley Rd., north of the Wash- *ington Street Extension in Wilmington. Rockwood Mansion, Shipley Rd., Wilmington, DE 19801. For tour information, call 302-761-4340. www.brandywinevalleyonline. com/attractions/rockwood.html)* **72**

DISTRICT OF COLUMBIA

CAPITOL BUILDING

HOUSE OF REPRESENTATIVES The ghost of John Quincy Adams, who was elected to nine terms as congressman after serving as president of the United States, still returns to his old seat on the House floor to make speeches. On February 23, 1848, at the age of eighty-one, he suffered a stroke at his chair and died two days later. He was delivering an impassioned speech on what he considered to be the unjust war with Mexico. The specter of Civil War General John Alexander Logan has been seen in the old Committee on Military Affairs room and in the House basement corridors, where his stuffed horse is stored. The ghosts of President James Garfield and his assassin, Charles Guiteau, were also seen in the basement area. The ghost of Kentucky Congressman William Taulbee haunts the stairs leading to the House gallery. The stains on the white marble steps are said to be the Taulbee's blood, dating back to a winter day in 1890 when he was shot and killed by newspaper reporter Charles Kincaid. The spirits of two former speakers of the House, Champ Clark and Joe Cannon, still return late at night to continue their emotional series of debates begun in 1910. The ghost of Republican leader Boise Penrose has been spotted in his old office, where he spent so many late hours in the 1920s.

(U.S. Capitol Building, Washington, DC 20006. Phone: 202-224-3121. www.senate.gov/vtour/index.html)
4, 101

ROTUNDA The ghost of a worker who fell from scaffolding during construction of the Capitol Building's Rotunda in the 1860s is seen floating through a hallway carrying his wooden tool tray. Another ghost in the Rotunda, that of a cleaning man who died while scrubbing the marble floor, is said to return after all the maintenance staff has gone home. A male librarian haunts the rooms west of the Rotunda, where the original Library of Congress was housed. The man died before he could fetch the money he had hidden there. When the library was moved, workers discovered nearly six thousand dollars stashed between the pages of books. The apparition of a doughboy, thought to be the spirit of the World War I soldier sealed in the Tomb of the Unknown Soldier at Arlington Cemetery, appears briefly whenever a fallen military man is laid in state at the Rotunda. He gives a quick salute and disappears.

(For general information on Washington, contact the Washington Visitors Association, 1212 New York Ave. Northwest, Suite 600, Washington, DC 20005. Phone: 202-789-7000.) **4**

SENATE The ghost of a stonemason sealed behind a wall during construction of the Senate building in 1790s has been seen passing through a wall in the Senate basement. Legend says he was sealed in the chamber after being hit in the head with a brick during an argument with another mason. The ghost of a Revolutionary War soldier, outfitted in a splendid Continental uniform, walk's near the Washington Crypt, the empty tomb where our first president was supposed to have been buried.

The whole Capitol Building was cursed by engineer John Lenthall as he lay dying under a collapsed archway. Lenthall was crushed to death by falling bricks in September 1808, when he pulled out a support arch to demonstrate to the supervising architect that the support was unnecessary. Today, Lenthall is said to have his revenge in the crumbling walls, cracked columns, and shifting foundation of the building that killed him.

The ghost of another engineer roams the basement area. He is Pierre Charles L'Enfant, George Washington's original designer for Federal City. He is seen carrying a parchment, perhaps a bill for money due. The French engineer was never paid for his work.

The basement was also a favorite spot of former Vice President Henry Wilson. He spent almost as much time in the bathtubs there as he did in his office. In November 1875, he caught a chill that proved his ultimate undoing, but that did not stop his spirit from returning to his favorite pastime. His lathered ghost and the sounds of wheezing and sneezing have been reported in the corridor outside the Vice President's Office.

The singing of a deceased barber, Bishop Simms, has been heard coming from the Senate barbershop, where the haircutter (and part-time preacher) used to sing to his clients.

The caterwauling of Demon Cat, said to stalk the basement near the Catafalque Storage Room, can sometimes be heard echoing through the damp corridors. In 1862 and again in 1898, guards shot at a black cat that had swelled to the size of an elephant. In the 1950s, a guard came across the demon cat and watched in astonishment as it swelled to the size of a tiger, then vanished. Over the years, such encounters with the ferocious feline (nicknamed "D.C.") have portended unpleasant events for the nation.

(The Senate offices are at 1st Street and Constitution Ave. Northeast, Washington, DC 20006. Phone: 202-484-0200.) **4, 106**

STATUARY HALL Witnesses describe seeing the "illuminated transparency" of John Quincy Adams when Statuary Hall is darkened for the night. In 1890, a guard reported seeing the entire 1840 House of Representatives convened in this room, which used to be the House Chamber. Another guard insisted he saw all the statues in the room come to life at the stroke of midnight on New Year's Eve. They supposedly climbed down from their pedestals and danced in celebration that the Republic had survived yet another year. Although the guard was promptly dismissed, similar events were reported in following years.

(Statuary Hall leads into the Rotunda in the Capitol Building.) **4**

CAPITOL HILL

FIRST STREET The ghost of Judge Advocate General Joseph Holt is seen late at night here. He wears a blue Union suit with a dark cape thrown over his shoulders. The judge presided over the trial of Mary Surratt and three other conspirators sentenced to hang for the assassination of President Lincoln. Legend says he is on one of his agonized midnight walks trying to figure out the innocence or guilt of the four alleged conspirators.

(Judge Holt lived just a few blocks from the Old Brick Capitol Prison on Capitol Hill.) **4**

UNITED STATES SUPREME COURT The ghosts that haunt this building are from the Old Brick Capitol, which used to stand here. The building served as the nation's capitol for seven years, after the British burned Congress during the War of 1812. It was later used as apartment housing and then as a prison during the Civil War. While famed southern orator John C. Calhoun was living there, he was visited by the spirit of George Washington, who warned the South Carolinian about the consequences of secession. Calhoun heeded the Founding Father and passed his warning on to Congress. After he died in 1850, Calhoun's ghost was seen frequently in his old residence, and he still seemed worried about the dissolution of the Union. In the 1920s, a congressman came across the phantom of a Union guard with a long rifle over his shoulder, pacing in front of the former jail. In 1922, the National Woman's Party took over the building and made the upstairs rooms into women's apartments. The suffragettes' presence seemed to encourage the materialization of the spirits of women who had been imprisoned there. Confederate spy Belle Boyd, who used her charms to seduce Yankee officers, returned to her spartan chamber in the Union prison. Her bitter laughter could be heard echoing through the building late at night. On the anniversary of Mary Surratt's death, her ghostly figure would appear in the window of her former jail cell. See Fort Lesley McNair, Lafayette Square, White House all in the District of Columbia; and Clinton, Maryland.

(The Old Brick Capitol was located on Jenkins Hill, where the Supreme Court building now stands, directly behind the Capital building on the corner of 1st Street and East Capitol Street.) **4**

GEORGETOWN

BRITCHES OF GEORGETOWN This building has served as a theater, restaurant, tavern, and most recently, a clothing store. Over the years, five suicides have taken place here. So many weird things happened in the late 1960s that the people who lived in the house started meeting in the basement to try to contact the resident spirits. Dozens of strange shadows seemed to roam the old structure, and the ghosts gathered regularly on the third floor to throw noisy parties.

(The building is the former home of Mr. Henry's Pub. It is located at 1247 Wisconsin Ave. Northwest, Washington, DC 20007. 202-338-333. www.britchesusa.com) **84**

FOXALL A strange ritual was performed regularly by a ghostly presence here. The mansion was built by Henry Foxall, who enjoyed relaxing in the evening by playing violin music with his good friend Thomas Jefferson. The haunting started in the 1890s, when the ghost of Foxall's elderly housekeeper started appearing in the third-floor hall. Whenever her floating apparition was seen, always just before 10:00 P.M., all the lights in the house would suddenly be extinguished. The phenomenon continued until the 1950s and included candles, gaslights, and electric lights.

(Foxall is a private residence near Dumbarton Ave., a block off Wisconsin Ave., in Georgetown. The address is 2908 N St. Northwest, Washington, DC 20006.) **4, 67, 101**

GENERAL BRADDOCK'S TROOPS The sounds of British troops marching off to their death during the French and Indian War are still heard on the streets of Georgetown. In 1755, General Edward Braddock was killed along with seven hundred of his men, when a small group of French and Indian troops ambushed them at the fork of the Ohio River. The rattling of sabers, barked orders, and the clatter of horses and men's boots are heard coming from nowhere. During the Civil War, a Union patrol heard the ghostly sounds of Braddock's troops and mistook them for invading Confederate forces.

(The sounds are heard on the bluffs above the Potomac, where the general assembled his troops, and near Long Bridge in Georgetown.) **4**

HALCYON HOUSE The spirit of the first secretary of the Navy, Benjamin Stoddard, has been encountered in his old house. The founder of the Marines died in 1813, spending his last years as a pauper and invalid, alone in the house, waiting patiently for death to come. Stoddard named the house for the mythical ocean bird said to have the power to calm the seas. But his beloved home is anything but calm. Constant rapping noises, distant moaning, unintelligible whispers, and the appearance of a ghostly figure have been reported in the building for over a century. During the Civil War, the house served as a stop on the Underground Railroad, although many exhausted slaves died in the cellar or in the tunnel leading to the Potomac. In the 1930s, the house was acquired by Albert Adsit Clemons. His own instability or something about the house caused him to encase the north side in a brick facade and turn the attic into a religious shrine. He undertook a program of constant construction and filled the house with doors that open into walls, rooms framed without walls, and a stairway going nowhere. Clemons made the coach house into a crypt, buried mummies in the garden, and fastened pie tins on the heads of stone angels that adorned the house. He also refused to have electricity in the house, even for tenants who rented out tiny apartments sandwiched between the facade and the original house. Clemons said his efforts would allow him to live forever, so his death on March 17, 1938, was certainly premature. His final wish was to be buried with a silver instrument pierced through his heart, though no one had the nerve to do it. Ghostly events plagued owners of the house in the 1940s and 1950s, and unexplainable electrical problems became everyday nuisances. Between 1963 and 1972, three separate cases of levitation happened to persons sleeping in the second-floor bedroom. The ghost of a woman was sighted several times in the 1970s, and strange events continue to this day. Tenants in Apartment 1214 have reported that every Thursday between 1:00 and 2:00 A.M., ghostly footsteps can be heard in the attic above their room.

(The ghosts appear on the stairway, near an old upholstered chair in the south drawing room, and in darkened rooms at the center of the house. Stoddard's ghost is dressed in tan, whereas Clemons's prefers black. Halcyon

House is now a women's dormitory for Georgetown University, overhanging M St. in Georgetown, at 3400 Prospect St. Northwest, Washington, DC 20007. Phone: 202-338-3295.) **4, 67, 68, 82, 139, 187**

KEY HOUSE The angry ghost of Francis Scott Key, author of "The Star Spangled Banner," haunted his beloved home. He built it in 1802 and lived there for over thirty years. The haunting started in the late 1800s, when owners remodeled his house into a more modern style. Horrifying moans and sighs, creaking floors caused by unseen footsteps, and unexplained bloodstains on the attic ceiling were a few of the manifestations. The phenomena spread and increased in intensity as the once proud house deteriorated. By the 1920s no one would live in the house. The haunting stopped when the house was finally restored to its former likeness. But that was not the end of the story. Key's ghost is said to have returned to the spot when the house was torn down to make way for a freeway ramp.

(The Key House stood on M St. in Georgetown. The northeast ramp of the Key Bridge goes right over his former house. The access ramp serves both the bridge and the Whitehurst Freeway.) **4**

K STREET For many years around the turn of the century, a headless ghost terrified people walking along K Street on the riverbank and near the K Street Bridge. Newspapers were full of accounts of encounters with the specter, thought to be a man beheaded by vigilantes for some unknown crime.

(The K Street Bridge was one of the most used bridges across the Potomac in the early 1900s.) **4**

OLD STONE HOUSE Built in 1795 by Christopher Layman, this old farmhouse is haunted by eleven ghosts. The most active has been dubbed George. He haunts the third-floor bedroom and has a violent hatred of women. George has been accused of shoving, strangling, knifing, and even raping women who venture into his room. Residents and visitors to the house, which is now a museum, have reported encountering his malevolent presence several times. Another ghost here is a lady wearing a brown, 1700s-style dress, seen near the fireplace. The phantom of a young woman with tight ringlets in her hair has been seen running up and down the staircase. The apparition of a stout woman in an antebellum gown is seen on the staircase and in the

kitchen. Also seen in the kitchen area is the ghost of a man wearing short pants with long stockings. A man with long, dark blond hair, wearing a blue jacket, once materialized near a front-room window. The wraith of a small boy named Joey has been seen running up and down the third-floor hallway, and a little black boy has also appeared there. A German carpenter thought to be the ghost of Christopher Layman has been reported in the house. Many people observed a colonial gentleman who partially materialized in the master bedroom. Another unidentified colonial man has been seen on the second floor. The upper floors of this house were used by families living on the property, while the lower floors were rented out to travelers. In the 1930s, the house became a bordello, and then it was used as an auto shop. The National Park Service acquired the property in 1950 and restored most of the building.

(The three-story, L-shaped Old Stone House has been restored and is now a museum operated by the National Park Service. Old Stone House Museum, 3545 Williamsburg Lane, Washington, DC 20008. Phone: 202-426-6851. www.nps.gov/rocr/oldstonehouse) **55, 134, 101**

THREE SISTERS ROCKS An old Indian curse has plagued this section of the Potomac for over four hundred years. In 1607, three daughters of a Powhatan chief tried to cross the river to avenge the deaths of three young braves killed by the Susquehannock tribe. Because all their canoes were destroyed in the raid, the Powhatans were forced to hold on to logs as they crossed the river. The current was too swift, and the three sisters were swept away. Just before they went under, they grasped hands and proclaimed the curse. If the three daughters of the chief of the most powerful tribe on earth could not cross the river at this spot, then no one would cross it there. Legend says three granite rocks, called Three Sisters Rocks appeared in the middle of the river the next morning. Over the years, hundreds have died crossing the river at this point in the river. Even today, the Metropolitan Harbor Police record five or six new deaths each year at the spot. In 1972 the city tried to build a bridge over the Three Sisters, but delays and controversy persuaded them to give up the project.

(The three tiny granite islands are in the middle of the Potomac, between the Chain Bridge and the Key Bridge. They can be seen from the George Washington Parkway.) **4, 38, 67**

WILSON HOUSE President Woodrow Wilson suffered a debilitating stroke in 1919, and it was kept secret until after he left office in 1921. Woodrow spent the remainder of his days with his wife Edith at this distinguished house. His ghost still roams the premises. President Wilson's slow steps, aided by a cane, can be heard climbing the steps to his former bedroom. The sounds of a man's sobbing can sometimes be heard coming from the same room. A caretaker quit in 1969, no longer able to put up with the unexplained "slow shuffle" that moved through the house.

(Wilson House is now maintained by the National Trust for Historic Preservation. The Wilson House Museum is located at 2340 S St. Northwest, Washington, DC 20008. Phone: 202-387-4062. www.woodrowwilsonhouse.org) **4, 67, 84, 101**

JUDICIARY SQUARE

PENSION BUILDING This brick monstrosity was once dubbed Meigs Old Red Barn, after U.S. Quartermaster General Montgomery Meigs, who conceived it. Built in 1885 on the site of a former jail and insane asylum, the fifteen-million-dollar building was the first centralized office of veteran affairs. President Grover Cleveland used it for his inaugural ball, attended by such notables as Buffalo Bill Cody and General Sherman. The first supernatural phenomenon was reported in 1917, when a guard saw the design on one of the simulated onyx columns change into an Indian head with a wild buffalo. The next day, the news spread that Buffalo Bill Cody had died. More unexplainable swirls appeared in the form of "a malevolent, grinning skull" a few months later.

Over the next few years dozens of faces appeared, including those of George and Martha Washington. The columns were designed by General Meigs, who wanted them to be solid onyx. To save money, his superiors forced him to use hollow columns with a simulated onyx veneer. The general was very upset with the compromise and is said to have stuffed the eight hollow columns with the priceless papers of our founding fathers. Included are said to be papers given to Meigs by Secretary of War Robert Lincoln. Abraham Lincoln's son never believed the whole story had been told of his father's death and initiated his own investigation. It is said that what he discovered would have torn the country apart, so he gave the evidence to Meigs to seal in the hollow columns, which Meigs promised "would

stand for centuries." Many thought the spirit of Meigs was behind the strange series of faces that appeared in the swirling onyx pattern. The situation became so notorious by the late 1920s that officials ordered the columns painted to hide the weird faces, and the building was turned over to the District of Columbia Superior Court. But the ghosts stayed and before long, "wandering shades" were detected in the halls. One night a guard went screaming from the building after being chased by the phantom of a soldier on horseback.

Numerous ghosts were encountered over the years, but the most interesting cases involve the ghoulish figure of James Tanner. Tanner was the court recorder who transcribed the testimony of witnesses to Lincoln's assassination. He later became an authority on the subject and believed further information would someday be revealed. Oddly enough, Tanner became one of the first pension commissioners, heading veteran's affairs at Meigs Old Red Barn in 1889. Most of Tanner's income came from his public lectures on the Lincoln assassination. They say his ghost returns to the Old Pension Building, still seeking the truth about Lincoln's death. In 1972, a guard encountered Tanner's ghost on the third floor. He followed the figure of a man in a light suit with a peculiar angling gait. (Tanner lost both feet from a Civil War injury.) When he came up behind the intruder to ask him what his business was, the man turned and looked into his face. The guard let out a frightened scream and ran from the building. When police found him walking down the middle of Pennsylvania Avenue, the guard told them he had gazed into the fires of hell in a man with no eyes who "smelled of the stench of the dead." The guard never fully recovered from his frightful encounter. Today, the Smithsonian Institution, the nation's archivist, has taken over the building.

(The eight Corinthian columns stand inside a great hall at the center of the building. The Old Pension Building covers the block bounded by F and G streets, and 4th and 5th streets. It is now the National Building Museum. The address is 440 G St. Northwest, Washington, DC 20006. For information, call 202-272-2448. The Smithsonian Visitors Center is at 1000 Jefferson Dr. Southwest, Washington, DC 20007. Phone: 202-357-2700.) **4, 67, 102, 136, 101**

LAFAYETTE SQUARE

ADAMS HOUSE Harvard historian Henry Adams lived here with his frail wife Marian Hooper Adams in the 1880s. Henry found her dead body collapsed in front of the fireplace when he returned home one wintry evening. He refused to talk further about the circumstances of her death. That caused a lot of rumors about her demise, and many people accused Adams of neglecting his wife. Adams ordered that the marker over her grave list no name, dates, or inscription. Instead, he commissioned sculptor Augustus Saint-Gaudons to create a mysterious statue that no one would ever be able to fathom. (See Marian Adams Gravesite, Rock Creek Cemetery, Washington, D.C.) When Henry Adams wrote his autobiography, he made not a single reference to his wife. He spent less and less time in the house, which neighbors insisted was haunted by the presence of Marian. At dusk, they heard the sounds of a weeping woman coming from the darkened house. Later residents reported a persistent cold spot in front of the fireplace, even when it was piled with blazing logs. The phantom of Marian, sitting in an wooden rocking chair in her bedroom, appeared to several people at different times. Always she stared directly into their eyes until they were overcome by a feeling of loneliness, or until someone let out a scream. Then the apparition slowly faded away.

(To reach Lafayette Square, travel east on M St. to Pennsylvania Ave. The Square is located on Pennsylvania Ave., seven blocks past Washington Circle. Adams House sat on H St. Northwest, across from St. John's Church in Lafayette Square. Today, the site is occupied by the Hay-Adams Hotel at 800 16th St. Northwest. Phone: 202-638-6600. www.hayadams.com) **4**

DECATUR HOUSE Despite attempts to keep it away, the ghost of Commodore Stephen Decatur has returned to his former residence. Just before the War of 1812, Decatur pushed for the conviction of Commander James Barron for not resisting a British patrol looking for American deserters on his frigate, the *Chesapeake* Barron was convicted and suspended from the navy, and Decatur took over his post on the *Chesapeake*. Barron hated Decatur for ruining his career and eventually challenged him to a duel. Decatur kept the duel a secret from his wife Susan, and spent the night before staring blankly out of his first-floor bedroom window. The next morning, March 14, 1820, Decatur sneaked out the back door and rode to a field in Maryland to meet Barron in a duel. (See Bladensburg, Maryland.) Decatur was shot in the liver and mortally wounded. He died at

his home in his first-floor bedroom. His hysterical wife was not fit to be at his side. Since 1821, passersby have seen his morose figure staring from the downstairs bedroom window. To prevent his reappearance, the window on H Street was ordered walled up, and a fixed shutter now hides the wall. Recently his apparition has been seen in the early morning hours, slipping out the back door with a small box under his arm. It is the black velvet box that carries his dueling pistols. The haunting sounds of a sobbing woman, assumed to be his wife Susan, have also been reported in the house.

(Decatur House is a three-story brick structure on the corner of Jefferson Place and H St. in Lafayette Square. It is now occupied by the National Trust for Historic Preservation. The address is 748 Jackson Place Northwest, Washington, DC 20006. Phone: 202-842-0920. www.decaturhouse.org) **4, 39, 68, 139, 101**

DOLLEY MADISON HOUSE Dolley Madison, the wife of the fourth president, spent her last days at this house. On moonlit nights her ghost is seen rocking on the porch. At one time, her ghost was so famous that gentlemen leaving a nearby men's club (see Washington Club, below) late at night would habitually tip their hats to Mrs. Madison's specter. See Octagon, the Rose Garden, and the White House, Washington, DC; and Scotchtown, Hanover County, Virginia.

(Madison House is on the corner of Madison St. and H St. Northwest, Washington, DC 20007.) **4**

HICKMAN'S GHOST The specter of notorious Washington gambler Colonel Beau Hickman has been seen standing on the corner where his hotel once stood. He came to Washington from Virginia in 1833 and stayed at the same address for forty years. He died penniless in 1873 and was buried in a pauper's field, but friends got together and decided to move his body to the prestigious Congressional Cemetery. After getting drunk one night, they headed for Hickman's grave and came upon grave robbers, who had the colonel's half-exposed body sticking out of the ground. They frightened away the grave robbers and tossed the gambler's tattered body into the back of a wagon. The wagon raced down G Street into the gates of the Congressional Cemetery, where the motley crew dug a hole and plopped in the remains of Hickman. The unceremonious transplant seems to have awakened the spirit of Beau Hickman, who is said to roam the corner near his old hotel to this day.

(The hotel was torn down in 1892, and the spot was occupied by the headquarters of the Atlantic Coastline Railroad. Colonel Hickman haunts the corner of 6th St. and Pennsylvania Ave.) **4**

PHILIP KEY'S GHOST Philip Barton Key, son of Francis Scott Key, fell in love with the beautiful wife of Congressman Daniel Sickles. Key signaled their adulterous meetings by walking in front of the Sickles home on Lafayette Square and waving a white handkerchief. That was exactly what Key was doing the day Daniel Sickles confronted him with a pistol and shot him to death. Key died leaning against a tree, gazing up into the window of his paramour. Sickles was arrested, but a jury found him innocent by "temporary aberration of mind," the first time the insanity defense was used in this country.

Sickles went on to command a contingent of volunteers at the Battle of Gettysburg, where he lost a leg. His amputated limb was put on display at a military museum, and after his death some years later, Sickles's ghost was seen visiting his leg, enshrined in a glass case at the museum. In 1865, Key's ghost is said to have warned Secretary of State William Seward of an impending assassination attempt.

(The apparition of Key has been reported in front of his former house on 15th St. where a monument now marks the spot, and between 15th and 16th streets, across from the Washington Club, on the spot where he was shot. Sickles's ghost appeared at the Medical Museum of the Armed Forces Institute of Pathology, which is now the Hirshhorn Museum at Independence and 7th St. Southwest. http://hirshhorn.si.edu) **4**

RATHBONE HOUSE Major Henry Rathbone and his lovely fiancée Clara Harris shared a box with President and Mrs. Lincoln at the Ford Theater on the night John Wilkes Booth shot the President. Rathbone was stabbed in the head and neck by Booth as the assassin made his escape. Rathbone recovered from his life-threatening wounds, but the event changed his life. He resigned his commission and moved to Hanover, Germany, with his new wife. Several years later, Rathbone lost his mind completely. He shot his wife to death, tried to murder his children, and then shot himself. Rathbone survived and spent the rest of his life in a lunatic asylum. Strange crying sounds started to echo from his former house in Washington, and people crossed the street to avoid the haunted ground. Eventually, the house had to be demolished because of the haunting. See Loudon Cottage, Loudonville, New York.

(Rathbone House stood at 8 Jackson Place on Lafayette Square.) **4**

ST. JOHN'S CHURCH Whenever a great American leader dies, the ghosts of six great Washingtonians appear at midnight in the Pew of the Presidents here. They sit with their arms folded, looking straight ahead as if paying final respects, then disappear after a few moments. The unique church, built in 1821, with six columns in front and a three-tiered steeple, has served as a place of worship for many presidents.

(St. John's is a brick church on Lafayette Square, at the corner of 16th St. and H St. St. John's Church, 1525 H St. Northwest, Washington, DC 20006. Phone: 202-347-8766.) **4, 67, 101**

SURRATT'S BOARDING HOUSE The ghost of Mary Surratt, accused conspirator in the Lincoln assassination, is thought to be responsible for the unexplainable noises and cries heard in her former boarding house. Her daughter Annie sold the three-story house for a meager amount after her mother was executed. The new owners only lived in the house a short while before moving out. They reported strange moaning and howling sounds and disembodied voices coming from the second floor. See Capitol Hill, Fort Lesley McNair, and the White House, Washington, DC; and Clinton, Maryland.

(The house is at 604 H St. Northwest, Washington, DC 20001.) **4**

TRACY HOUSE Navy Secretary Benjamin Tracy ignored tales of a haunting and took up residence in this house in the 1890s. The stories went back to the 1870s and told of the grisly murder of a tailor's new bride. After her death, the ghostly figure of a woman in white was seen stalking from room to room, mumbling a name as if she were searching for someone. The ghost appeared with astonishing regularity and the house was very difficult to keep rented. Finally, not long after Secretary Tracy moved in, a mysterious fire erupted and consumed the house with frightening speed. The fire killed both Tracy and his wife, and some say, freed an earthbound spirit from the endless search for her murderer.

(The house was just off Connecticut Ave., near Lafayette Square, at 1634 I St. Northwest, Washington, DC 20006.) **4**

WASHINGTON CLUB This two-story brick building was home to the city's most prominent men's club for many years (see Dolley Madison House, above) and then home to the families of Henry Clay and John C. Calhoun, whose ghosts are said to walk its corridors. When Secretary of State William Seward moved his family into the house in the early 1860s, he suffered many tragedies, including an assassination attempt and the deaths of his wife and daughter. After he moved out in 1869, tales of a Mephisto spirit in the house spread throughout the city, and no one wanted to live there. The YMCA, which occupied the building in the 1880s, was also forced to move out after numerous unexplained disturbances. The house was finally torn down in 1895, because the owners could find no new tenants.

(The Washington Club was located on Lafayette Square, between 15th and 16th streets. The present club is at 15 Dupont. Circle Northwest, Washington, DC 20036. Phone: (202) 483-9200.) **4**

WIRT HOUSE This house was the scene of heated arguments about slavery in the years before the Civil War. Attorney General William Wirt, Justice John Marshall, Henry Clay, Andrew Jackson, and other political leaders sat up until the early morning hours arguing about the emotional issue of state's rights. When Postmaster Aaron Brown moved into the house, he had heard stories of disturbances there, but considered it an honor to live at such a prestigious Washington address. Soon after moving in, Brown's personality started to change. He became moody and morose, complaining of constant voices and noises in the house. Even his servants complained of the sounds and began sleeping elsewhere. Brown was unable to concentrate, and his health rapidly deteriorated. There were rumors that he had lost his mind. On March 8, 1859, he died after "a painful illness of some ten days duration." A subsequent owner committed suicide in the house, which continued to be haunted until it was demolished.

(The Wirt house was just northwest of Lafayette Square.) **4**

FATHER BOYLE'S EXORCISM In September 1907, Father Boyle of St. Patrick's Church was asked to perform exorcism rites at a deserted home here. When he and an assistant entered the house and began igniting the gas lights, poltergeist activity swept through the building. A heavy iron bar lifted across the front door, wailing and moaning sounds moved from room to room, and a "maniacal whirlwind blew furniture around like cardboard." The priest left without finishing the exorcism, and the owner of the house decided to have the house torn down rather than take any more chances with the evil presence there.

(The house stood at 11th St. and D St. in northwest Washington.) **4**

NORTHWEST WASHINGTON

FORD THEATER Actors standing near a line at left-center stage in the Ford Theater feel an icy cold presence. Many become nauseated and nervous, forgetting their lines and trembling involuntarily. Hal Holbrook in his Mark Twain recital, and Jack Aronson in his evening with Herman Melville, are just two actors who admitted to the odd sensations. The effect is said to be caused by psychic impressions left by John Wilkes Booth, as he zigzagged across left center stage with a broken leg, after assassinating Abraham Lincoln on April 14, 1865. A photo taken by respected photographer Matthew Brady showed Booth's transparent figure standing in Box 7, where the Lincoln party sat the fateful night. The theater was then closed and used for storage. In 1893, twenty-two federal employees died in Ford Theater, when a ceiling collapsed on top of them. The theater was reopened in 1968, and since then Booth's ghost has been reported by actors, stagehands, and theatergoers. The ghost of Lincoln has been reported at the nearby Parker House, where he died.

(The theater was renovated in 1968 and opened as a playhouse and museum. Ford Theater, 511 10th St. Northwest, Washington, DC 20006. Phone: 202-426-6927. The Parker House is a private residence at 516 10th St. Northwest, Washington, DC 20006. Phone: 202-426-6924. www.fordstheater.org) **69, 94, 101**

KALORAMA The Kalorama was a parcel of land that occupied nearly all of northwest Washington. A house was built on the property in 1807 by Joel Barlow. Later, the estate became the property of General John Bomford, a close friend of Stephen Decatur. When Decatur died in a duel, his body was entombed at Kalorama. One day, blood started to appear on the outside of his tomb. The phenomenon happened so frequently that Susan Decatur ordered her husband's body removed and buried with his parents in Philadelphia. (See Decatur House, Lafayette Square, Washington, DC; and Blandensburg, Maryland.) During the Civil War, the house at Kalorama was used as a hospital. A fire on Christmas Eve, 1865, gutted the east wing of the house and several patients were burned to death. Their agonizing screams haunt the site to the present day. Disembodied howls and cries, and "sinister shadows" seen walking the grounds give Kalorama a well-deserved reputation for being haunted.

(The manor house at Kalorama stood in the 2300 block of S St. Northwest, Washington, DC 20008.) **4**

McLean Mansion The apparition of a beautiful nude woman is sometimes seen descending the palatial stairway here. She is Evalyn Walsh McLean, former owner of this mansion, whose life was ruined by the curse of the Hope Diamond. She acquired the magnificent piece in 1922 from a dethroned sultan and continued to flaunt the huge stone even after being warned by former owners of its disastrous power. The Hope Diamond was originally a piece of the 112-carat diamond eye of a Hindu idol. The sapphire blue diamond was stolen and everyone who handled it over the next two hundred years suffered some horrible calamity. Just a few examples make the curse abundantly clear. The Frenchman who took it from India was torn apart by a pack of wild dogs. When it passed into the hands of Louis XIV, it devastated his family and court. In an attempt to defeat the curse, the diamond was split apart. In 1830, English banker Henry Thomas Hope acquired a forty-five-carat piece. The Hope Diamond caused more family problems and was later purchased by a Turkish merchant. He and his family were killed in a fiery crash down a mountainside, just after he sold the Hope to a sultan. The sultan bought it for his favorite wife, who died soon after she began wearing the diamond. Then the sultan was dethroned. Evalyn's life also took a turn for the worse when she bought the Hope Diamond, which she would end up calling "a talisman of evil." Her nine-year-old son was struck by a swerving automobile and died. Her husband tried to divorce her after having a series of affairs, but Evalyn had him committed to an insane asylum. Her only daughter died from an overdose of sleeping pills. Finally, Evalyn broke her hip, then caught a "wasting" disease, and died in April 1947. The Hope became the property of a New York diamond merchant, who promptly put the piece on permanent loan to the Smithsonian Institution. Even the mail carrier who delivered the stone to the Smithsonian suffered from its curse. Within nine months, his leg was crushed under a mail truck, his wife died, his dog hung itself by its leash, and his house burned to the ground. Since the Hope Diamond went on display at the Smithsonian, some have suggested that the country has not fared much better. Today, the Indonesian Embassy occupies the former McLean Mansion.

(Indonesian Embassy, 2020 Massachusetts Ave. Northwest in Washington, DC 20036. Phone: 202-775-5200.) **4**

National Theatre Not long after this theater was built in the 1830s, a handsome young actor was slain by a jealous fellow thespian. The man buried the youth's body in the basement beneath the stage. During renovations to modernize the theater, the slain youth's spirit arose from his grave. Members of the theater company admit the presence of a ghost but are very protective of him. One night watchman did confess to encountering the ghost in the old basement.

(The theater is on E St., between 13th and 14th streets Northwest. National Theatre, 1321 Pennsylvania Ave. Northwest, Washington, DC 20006. Phone: 202-628-6161. The National Theatre Archive can be reached at 202-347-0365. www.nationaltheatre.org) **4, 67**

Oak Hill Cemetery John Peter Van Ness built the beautiful Van Ness Mausoleum for his wife Ann, who died in childbirth in 1822. He spent half as much on the mausoleum as he spent for his entire mansion (see Van Ness Mansion, Washington, DC). John joined his wife in 1846, and his six cherished white horses pulled his funeral carriage through the streets of Washington. The horses' phantoms are sometimes reported circling the mausoleum here. Once, a driver on the nearby Rock Creek Parkway was forced off the road by the misty outlines of six headless white horses galloping across the road.

(The mausoleum sits on top of the highest hill in the cemetery, overlooking Rock Creek. The Oak Hill Cemetery is off Rock Creek Parkway, at 30th St. and R St. Northwest. Phone: 202-337-2835.) **4, 67**

Octagon Museum This unusual building, known as the Octagon, was constructed in 1800 by Colonel John Tayloe (see Mount Airy, Essex County, Virginia). Ghostly manifestations have been reported

The Octagon building has a colorful and tragic history. Ghosts have been reported here for 150 years. See Octagon Museum, Northwest Washington, Washington, D.C. (PHOTRI)

near the spiral staircase, near the banister on the second floor landing, and on the third floor. A screaming female voice, the sounds of male and female footsteps, doors opening and closing, and a carpet at the bottom landing that keeps flipping up are a few of the many phenomena reported here over the last 150 years. One of Colonel Tayloe's eight daughters leaped to her death from the second-floor landing because her father refused his permission for her to wed a British officer. In the early 1800s, a young servant girl also leaped to her death from the third-floor landing, after being forcefully propositioned by a British soldier. The Madisons lived here in 1814, while the White House was being rebuilt after being set on fire by the British. Dolley Madison liked the mansion so much that her busy ghost sometimes returns, standing near the fireplace in the drawing room. Her apparition is always accompanied by the scent of lilacs. (See Dolley Madison House, Lafayette Square, and the Rose Garden, White House, Washington, DC; and Scotchtown, Hanover County, Virginia.) Another strange story involves the skeleton of a young girl found buried in a wall in the house by workmen. After she was removed, a century of mysterious thumping sounds heard near the wall suddenly stopped.

The Tayloes lived in the building until 1855. When they left, the apparitions of footmen, hailing carriages for the many famous guests who visited the house, appeared near the front entrance. A gambler who lived in the house after the Tayloes was shot in his upstairs bedroom by a farmer he had cheated. The gambler's ghost is still seen reaching for the bellpull near his bed.

During the Civil War, the tunnels that led to the Potomac River from the basement were used by slaves escaping from southern plantations. Their suffering cries and hushed murmuring were heard coming from the tunnels many years after they were sealed. In 1891, the Sisters of Charity moved into the house. Despite purifying the entire premises with holy water, the ghosts remained and eventually drove the Catholic order from the house. In 1900, the American Institute of Architects acquired the building. During the 1950s, a caretaker reported encountering the ghost of a military man dressed in the uniform of the early 1800s. In the 1960s, Superintendent Alric Clay battled an unseen presence that kept turning on the lights in the empty building. Visitors, curators, and employees in the building continue to report encounters with restless spirits in the house. Over the past thirty years, ghosts have been seen on the central staircase, in the upstairs bedrooms, and at the rear of the house, near the garden. It is now a museum of the American Architectural Foundation.

(The three-story brick Octagon is two blocks from the White House, on the corner of New York Ave. and 18th St. Northwest, at 1799 New York Ave. Northwest, Washington, DC 20006. Phone: 202-638-3221.) **4, 68, 78, 82, 84, 86, 89, 135, 139, 101, 114, 175**

ROCK CREEK CEMETERY The grave of Marian Hooper Adams has no inscription and no date. Marking the grave site is an unusual statue commissioned by her husband Henry Adams. He asked sculptor Augustus Saint-Gaudens to make a bronze monument that would never be "intelligible to the average mind." The result was a mysterious statue of a woman shrouded in a full-length veil. At first, officials at Washington's oldest cemetery refused to allow the marker to be placed, but Adams persisted and they reluctantly agreed. The statue was nicknamed "Grief," and visitors to the site have been overwhelmed by feelings of despair and sorrow. Sometimes at dusk, the delicate wraith of Marian is seen next to the statue. See Adams House, Lafayette Square, Washington, DC.

(The cemetery is off North Capitol St. in northwest Washington, at Rock Creek Parish and Webster St.

Northwest, Washington, DC 20009. Phone: 202-726-2080.) **4, 38**

VAN NESS MANSION John Peter Van Ness built this White House-styled mansion in 1816. After his wife passed away in 1822, the man became eccentric and despondent. Some believe his weird moods brought back the spirit of his wife. The sounds of "footsteps unattached to bodies" forced servants to leave and never come back, and the apparition of his wife wearing an old-time bonnet was seen in the upstairs hallway. Van Ness had kept six beautiful white horses on his property for many years, and they led his funeral procession when he died in 1846. Soon, reports started circulating of six headless white horses that galloped around the mansion during the twilight hours. Even after the mansion was torn down in 1907, the sightings continued. Today, the horses are sometimes seen circling the Pan American Union building constructed on the site of the Van Ness Mansion.

(The mansion stood where the Pan American Union, or Association of American States stands today. The building is on the corner of 17th St. and Constitution Ave. Northwest, Washington, DC 20007. Phone 202-458-3000.) **4**

SOUTH WASHINGTON

FORT LESLEY MCNAIR The ghost of Mary Surratt has been seen floating across the courtyard here. Surratt and three other accused conspirators in the assassination of Lincoln were hanged in the nearby Arsenal Penitentiary July 1865. Their bodies were first buried under the gallows but were later removed to permanent graves. A boxwood tree grew up from Mary's original grave. Some say it proclaims the innocence of Mary Surratt, who seems doomed to roam the environs of Washington until her name is cleared (See Capitol Hill, Lafayette Square, and White House, Washington, DC; and Clinton, Maryland). The bespectacled ghost of Walter Reed is also seen by soldiers walking across the court yard. The former professor at the Army Medical School strolls slowly along with his hands folded behind him.

(Fort Lesley McNair is in the vicinity of Capitol Hill, opposite Hains Point in East Potomac Park. The military post is situated on P St. between 3rd and 4th streets southwest. The main gate is at 3rd St. Southwest. The gallows

was erected at the northern end of the courtyard. For information, call 202-545-6700.)* **4, 67, 101**

HOWARD HOUSE This two-story frame house is the home of "Old Howard," the ghost of a tough marine who died in 1871. His ghost continued to abuse his wife and child, and they were forced to move out just two months after he died. Howard's luminous apparition appeared to the new tenants, whom he tormented with loud rapping sounds at all hours of the day and night. On two nights in a row, the poltergeist pulled the bed of a sleeping couple into the middle of their bedroom and made grotesque groaning sounds. Police investigated but could find no reason for the phenomena, and the couple moved out immediately. In the early 1900s, a young girl sleeping in the same room was attacked by a phantom who lifted the covers and started panting next to her. She screamed and lit a gaslight but could see no one. The family moved out the next day. Old Howard must have found another outlet for his energies, because reports of his libidinous spirit have become rare in recent years.

(The house is behind the Marine Corps Barracks on 9th St., between G and H streets southeast.) **4**

MARINE CORPS BARRACKS The sparsely furnished building at the end of the parade grounds here is haunted by the ghost of the Marine Corps' first commandant, Captain Samuel Nicholas. His barely distinguishable figure returns periodically to his old quarters, the Commandant's home, as if to update himself about marine activities. The rustling of papers and the sounds of deliberate pacing are sometimes heard coming from empty rooms.

(The old Marine Corps barracks and parade grounds is on 8th St., between G and I streets, in southeast Washington, DC.) **4**

WASHINGTON NAVY YARD This quaint two-story house with a framed-in glass porch is haunted by Captain Thomas Tingey, who set fire to the naval yard in 1814 to prevent it falling into the hands of the British, and supervised its reconstruction after the war. He lived in Quarters A for nearly a quarter century and tried to will it to his wife, but the navy fought and won possession of the house. Tingey's ghost has been seen looking out the upper windows, and his presence is felt by many occupants of the house.

(The Washington Navy Yard is between M St. Southeast and the Anacostia River. For information, call 202-433-2651. www.history.navy.mil/faqs/faq52-1.htm) **4, 67**

WHITE HOUSE

ATTIC The ghost of William Henry Harrison can sometimes be heard rummaging about in the White House attic. During the Truman administration, a guard heard the voice of David Burns, who owned the White House property in 1790, coming from the attic area above the Oval Room.

(The White House is at 1600 Pennsylvania Ave. NW, Washington, DC 20500. White House tours can be arranged by contacting the White House Visitor Center, 1450 Pennsylvania Ave. NW, Washington, DC 20004. Phone: 202-208-1631. For a twenty-four-hour recording of tour information, call 202-456-7041.) **4, 5, 67**

EAST ROOM White House staffers have reported the ghost of Abigail Adams hanging laundry in this airy room. Heading toward the East Room, her apparition passes through closed doors with her arms outstretched. Sometimes the faint smell of damp clothes and soap is detected.

(The East Room is on the first floor of the White House and is part of the White House tours. For general information on the White House, write the National Capitol Region, 1100 Ohio Dr. SW, Washington, DC 20242.) **4, 5, 86, 14, 175**

LINCOLN BEDROOM President Lincoln was perhaps the nation's most mystical leader, and he generated tremendous psychic energy. While living in the White House, he and his wife held several séances in an attempt to contact the spirit of their son Willie, who died there. One medium who visited the White House regularly gave Lincoln advice from great leaders of history. At one of those séances, the spirit of Daniel Webster pleaded with Lincoln to follow through with his efforts to free the slaves. Medium J.B. Conklin conveyed a message to Lincoln from his close friend Edward Baker, who had been killed at the battle of Ball's Bluff. The cryptic message said, "Gone elsewhere. Elsewhere is everywhere." In 1863, medium Charles Shockle visited the White House and performed a levitation. At another levitation, Lincoln allegedly ordered a Maine congress-

man to sit on top of a piano that was floating in midair. In November 1860, Lincoln told his wife he knew he would be elected for a second term but would die in office, and he saw his own assassination in a series of dreams ten days before that fateful day of April 14, 1865. Afterward, many people reported seeing his ghost in the White House. Franklin D. Roosevelt's personal valet ran screaming from the White House one day, after seeing Lincoln's ghost. Eleanor Roosevelt's maid Mary Eben saw the ghost sitting on his bed pulling off his boots. Even the Roosevelt's dog Fala was said to have sensed Lincoln's presence. Grace Coolidge, Theodore Roosevelt, Eleanor Roosevelt, Winston Churchill, Harry Truman, Margaret Truman Dwight Eisenhower, James Haggerty, Jacqueline Kennedy, Ladybird Johnson, Susan Ford, and Maureen Reagan have all admitted sensing the presence of the Civil War president in the White House. The wife of Lyndon Johnson witnessed Lincoln's mysterious presence while she watched a television program about his assassination. She felt compelled to read a plaque above the fireplace, which explained the dead president's connection to the room. Gerald Ford's daughter Susan saw Lincoln's ghost in the room in the 1980s. In 1987, Ronald Reagan's daughter Maureen and her husband Dennis Revell both saw Lincoln's translucent form next to the bedroom's fireplace.

(This room was actually Lincoln's Cabinet Room. He signed the Emancipation Proclamation here. It was named the Lincoln Bedroom when his nine-foot-long bed was moved here. The room is on the second floor, between the Treaty Room and the Yellow Oval Room.) **4, 5, 37, 42, 68, 81, 86, 87, 96, 115, 136, 139, 14, 1, 175, 176, 187, 188, 211, 212, 148**

NORTH PORTICO The ghost of Anne Surratt has been seen pounding on the doors of the White House, pleading for the release of her mother. Mary Surratt was executed in 1865 for her part in the conspiracy to assassinate President Lincoln. Her daughter is said to appear on the steps of the White House on July 7, the anniversary of her mother's trip to the scaffolds. The tenants of the H Street apartment house where Mary lived reported eerie moaning and sobbing sounds for many years. See the Capitol, Fort Lesley McNair, Lafayette Square, Washington, DC; and Clinton, Maryland.

(The North Portico is the front entrance to the White House.) **4, 84**

ROSE BEDROOM The ghost of Andrew Jackson is said to haunt his canopy bed here. White House personnel have reported an inexplicable cold spot and the sound of hearty laughter coming from the empty bed. In 1865, Mary Todd Lincoln reported encountering Jackson's ghost, and in the 1950s, White House seamstress Lilian Parks felt Jackson's presence lean over her while she sat hemming a bedspread in a chair next to his bed. An aide to Lyndon Johnson heard the cussing, hollering ghost of Jackson in this room in 1964. The Rose Room is also known as the Queen's Suite, because visiting queens have often stayed there. Queen Wilhelmina of The Netherlands was sleeping in this room, when she answered a knock at the door. Standing in the hallway was the ghost of Abraham Lincoln, whose bedroom was right across the hall.

(The Rose Bedroom is located on the second floor of the White House.) **4, 5, 14, 175**

ROSE GARDEN The ghost of Dolley Madison appeared in the Rose Garden during the administration of Woodrow Wilson. Dolley had planted the garden a hundred years earlier, but Mrs. Wilson gave orders to have it dug up. Workmen reported that Dolley's ghost appeared in the garden and kept them from carrying out their job. After that, no one dared harm the famous White House Rose Garden. See Dolley Madison House, Lafayette Square, Washington, DC; the Octagon, Washington, DC; and Scotchtown, Hanover County, Virginia.

(The Rose Garden is on the White House grounds.) **42**

SECOND-FLOOR BEDROOMS Members of Ulysses S. Grant's household are said to have conversed with the ghost of young Willie Lincoln here. President Johnson's daughter Lynda Johnson Robb sensed the child's spirit in his former bedroom. The cries of Mrs. Grover Cleveland have also been reported coming from this area of the White House. She was the first president's wife to give birth in the building. In another bedroom, in 1953 the ghost of a British soldier appeared to a visiting couple. Husband and wife reported that the ghost was carrying a torch and tried to burn their bed. The ghost, seen on other occasions in the White House, is thought to be the spirit of a soldier involved in setting fire to the structure on August 24, 1814.

(The bedrooms on the second floor are used by the presidential family and are not open to the general public.) **4, 5**

SECOND-FLOOR HALLS During William Taft's presidency, the ghost of John Adam's wife Abigail was first reported passing through doors on the second floor of the White House. More recently, she has been reported roaming through the secondfloor hallways. The footsteps of Abraham Lincoln have also been reported in this corridor by several White House residents, including Eleanor Roosevelt. Harry Truman once wrote to his wife, "I sit here in this old house, all the while listening to the ghosts walk up and down the hallway. At 4 o'clock I was awakened by three distinct knocks on my bedroom door. No one there. Damned place is haunted, sure as shootin'!" See Truman Home, Independence, Missouri.

(The entire second floor of the White House is the private residence of the presidential family.) **5, 42, 72**

YELLOW OVAL ROOM The first person to see Lincoln's ghost was the wife of Calvin Coolidge, Grace, who said she saw him in a window in the Oval Room. When Lincoln was alive, he used the room as a library and spent a lot of time meditating, gazing out the windows. White House employees have seen his figure standing in front of those same windows. Army Chaplain E. C. Bowles remembers Lincoln's sad look as his ghost stared out a window here. The sixteenth president's biographer, Carl Sandburg, said he felt Lincoln come stand beside him at that window. Mary Todd Lincoln encountered the ghosts of Thomas Jefferson and John Tyler in this room.

(The Yellow Oval Room is next to the Lincoln Bedroom on the second floor. The window is above the front entrance to the White House.) **4, 5, 42, 14, 183, 187**

FLORIDA

ARCHER

KOSICKI HOUSE When Linda and Bob Kosicki bought this old house in 1993, they had no idea that it was haunted. That is, not until the apparition of a woman in a white nightgown with a lacy hood started to appear. They researched the history of the house and discovered that it was built in 1893 by Charles and Cora Wood. The Kosickis believe Cora, whose two babies died in the house, has returned to search for their spirits.

(Archer is twelve miles southwest of Gainesville on Highway 24. The house is a private residence, at 300 West Main St., Archer, FL 32618.) **72**

CASSADAGA

SPIRITUALIST SETTLEMENT This entire town is made up of mediums engaged in the business of contacting dead spirits. The town was founded in 1895 by George Colby, who said three spirits led him to the spot. He willed the land to the Spiritualist Church, and the town of Cassadaga grew up around it. The narrow streets and moss-covered oak trees give the town a somewhat Gothic look, appropriate, perhaps, since its four hundred residents are always ready to talk to the dead.

(Cassadaga is twenty-three miles north of Orlando on Highway 4 in central Florida. The Spiritualist Church is on Highway 17/92, just outside of town. For information, contact the Cassadaga Spiritualist Church, Cassadaga, FL 32706.) **53 (3/82), 196**

CLEARWATER

INDIAN ROCKS BEACH A hideous sea creature emerged from the ocean and turned over a lifeguard platform on the beach here. The slimy beast left behind deep gouges in the wood from its claws. The first incident took place near the Everingham Pavilion, but the Clearwater creature was seen elsewhere on many occasions in the 1940s and 1950s. The creature, with a crocodile-like head, a short jaw, and razor-sharp teeth, left behind three-toed footprints and walked on its hind legs with an eight-foot-long stride. The creature terrified guests at the Indian Rocks Hotel and was also spotted on beaches at Dan's Island, Honeymoon Island, and Tarpon Springs. Police and coast guard investigations failed to provide an explanation for the numerous sightings.

(The town of Clearwater is located on the Gulf of Mexico, on the west central coast of Florida, just west of Tampa on Highway 275.) **57**

CORAL GABLES

BALTIMORE HOTEL This Victorian-style hotel was built in 1925 but was closed for most of the 1970s and 1980s. During that time, ghosts took up residence. Townspeople congregated on the golf course to observe the strange lights and eerie sounds coming from the empty building at night.

(The town of Coral Gables is just south of Miami on U.S. Highway 1. Biltmore Hotel, 1500 Anastasia Ave., Coral Gables, FL 33134. Phone: 305-445-1926. www. biltmorehotel.com) **66 (7/86), 72, 101**

CRYSTAL RIVER

CRYSTAL RIVER STATE ARCHEOLOGICAL SITE This sacred site dates back to 200 B.C. and was home to several different cultures of mound builders. Some of the first pyramid earthworks in North America were constructed here, and two magnificent stone stellae from the site are startlingly Mayan in appearance. There are two temple mounds intended for worship and two burial mounds, which contained almost five hundred skeletons. This was a flourishing center of trade in prehistoric times, when religion was based on worship of the sun.

(The site is located seventy-five miles north of Tampa. Follow I-75 to Highway 44 west. Turn north onto U.S. Highway 19 at Crystal River. For information, contact the Crystal River Archeological Site, 3400 North Museum Point, Crystal River, FL 32629. Phone: 352-795-3817.) **99, 144**

EVERGLADES

FAKAHATCHEE STRAND This sacred area in the Everglades is thought by the Seminole Indians to be the home of God, the Great Breathmaker. They believe all life is intertwined, like the gigantic cypress trees and the strangler fig vines that grow over them in this primeval swamp.

(The Everglades National Park is west of Highway 27 in the southern tip of Florida. The Fakahatchee Strand is at 137 Coastline Dr. Copeland, FL 33926. For tour information, contact Swampland Tours, Copeland, FL 33926. Phone: 941-695-2740.) **72**

L-1011 CRASH On December 29, 1972, an Eastern Airlines L-1011 Tristar jumbo jet crashed in the Florida Everglades. Captain Robert Loft died in the cockpit about an hour after the crash. Second Officer Don Repo died thirty hours later in a hospital. The crash occurred when the two men, preoccupied with a landing gear warning light, failed to notice the plane's descent. Afterward, their ghosts were observed by reputable airline employees more than twenty times. An Eastern Airlines vice president reported striking up a conversation with a uniformed pilot on board a flight to San Francisco. As soon as he realized he was talking to Captain Loft, the figure vanished before his eyes. Other airline employees reported seeing the ghosts of the two men on several other flights, mostly on another L-1011 with the number 318. Once, a flight was canceled when the ghost of Captain Loft appeared in the first-class cabin. In February 1974, the ghost of Don Repo warned a stewardess on a flight to Mexico City that the airliner would catch fire. On the return leg of the flight, an engine burst into flames and had to be extinguished in midair. Many similar potentially life-saving encounters were reported by dozens of witnesses, and an investigation showed that all the planes on which the strange events took place had spare parts from the wreckage of Flight 401. An embarrassed Eastern Airlines finally removed all of the parts of Flight 401 from its planes, to keep its logbooks free from ghost sightings. Many investigators believe this case could have provided definitive evidence for the reality of ghosts had the phenomena been allowed to continue.

(Flight 401 crashed in the Everglades, a few miles from Miami International Airport. Seventy people survived the accident; 101 died. For further information on the area, contact the Everglades Chamber of Commerce, 32016 Tamiami Trail East, Everglades City, FL 33929. Phone: 941-695-3941.) **20, 37, 41, 60, 68, 69, 96, 108, 139, 149**

FORT LAUDERDALE

BERMUDA TRIANGLE Awareness of this region grew with the mysterious disappearance of the five Avenger torpedo bombers on December 5, 1945. Flight 19 took off from Fort Lauderdale and was never seen again. A flying boat sent out to search for the bombers also disappeared. A five-day search of 250,000 square miles failed to turn up any trace of the missing planes. A few years later, a DC-3 with thirty-six people on board disappeared only fifty miles south of Miami. The story was the same for dozens of other aircraft and ships. The Bermuda Triangle is not just a modern phenomenon. Strange lights have been observed in the region as far back as Christopher Columbus. Some researchers believe the Bermuda Triangle is growing steadily westward and now encompasses much of southern Florida. See Gulf Breeze, Florida.

(The Bermuda Triangle stretches from Bermuda in the northeast to Puerto Rico in the southeast, to the Gulf of Mexico in the west. The city of Fort Lauderdale is North America's launching point into the mysterious area and is now considered a part of the triangle.) **34, 56, 139**

HOMESTEAD

CORAL CASTLE In 1918, Ed Leedskalnin began carving stone blocks for his castle, intended to be a monument to a mysterious figure he called "Sweet Sixteen." The house, furniture, and lawn decorations are all carved from huge pieces of limestone, which the five-foot tall, one-hundred-pound man moved about with ease. He claimed to have learned the secrets of the ancient builders of the Egyptian pyramids. No one has been able to discover how Leedskalnin created the ten-acre site, but many believe he somehow harnessed the powers of psychokinesis.

(Homestead is near the junction of U.S. Highway 1 and Highway 27 in the southern tip of Florida. The Coral Castle is located at 28655 South Dixie Highway, Homestead, FL 33030. Phone: 305-248-6344. www.coralcastle.com) **13, 196**

JACKSONVILLE

CARRIAGE HOUSE APARTMENTS There were so many reports of ghostly activity in Apartment 40 here that the management stopped renting out the unit and turned it into a storage room. The spirits in Apartment 40 are thought to be an elderly couple who lived there from the late 1960s until 1985, when their family had them admitted to a nursing home. Several tenants and visitors have described feeling uneasy when they pass by Apartment 40, and some have heard whispering sounds and other strange noises emanating from the vacant unit. However, the apartment was considered haunted long before either of the couple died, and some of the activity might be due to other ghosts on the premises. Investigator Lee Holloway believes the spirit haunting the front office is Mrs. Billie Boyd, who managed the Carriage House for more than twenty years. After she died in February 1987, her presence was detected by a new manager. A phantom cat has been sighted in the courtyard, as well. The unearthly feline looks like an ordinary white cat, until it vanishes into thin air.

(Jacksonville is in the northeast corner of Florida, at the junction of I-10 and I-95. Carriage House Apartments, 2260 University Blvd. North, Jacksonville, FL 32211. Phone: 904-743-2260.) **72**

GREENBRIAR LIGHT This mysterious ball of concentrated light seems to be attracted to moving objects. Cars moving slowly down the road in either direction bring out the light, which follows twenty-five to three hundred feet behind. Occasionally the light moves over the cars, but it never passes them. In 1987, the St. John's County Sheriff's Department asked several scientists to investigate the phenomenon, but no definite conclusion as to the source of the light could be reached. According to legend, the light is the headlight of a phantom motorcycle. A young man was supposedly pushing his new motorcycle to maximum speed on the road when he lost control and hit the support cable of a telephone pole. His decapitated body was found the next day.

(The site is in St. John's County, south of Mandarin, between the towns of Switzerland and Orangevale. The three-mile dirt road is known as Greenbriar Rd. or Light Rd. It runs east off Highway 13, approximately seven miles south of the Duval County line.) **72**

HOMESTEAD RESTAURANT This restaurant is located in a two-story log cabin built in 1934. The ghost here, seen and heard by the bartender and several other employees, has been identified as Mrs. Alpha Paynter. She once operated a boarding house in the cabin and is buried in the yard behind the building. Alpha's apparition has appeared near the huge limestone fireplace in the center of the main dining room and in other parts of the restaurant.

(Homestead Restaurant, 1712 Beach Blvd, Jacksonville Beach, FL 32250. Phone: 904-249-5240.) **72**

KINGSLEY PLANTATION This old plantation is haunted by a sinister presence known as Red Eyes. According to legend, Red Eyes is the ghost of a former slave who tortured, raped, and murdered two or three very young female slaves. When his deeds were discovered, he was taken down the narrow drive leading to the plantation and hanged from the limb of an old oak tree. But death could not extinguish the black man's wickedness. People driving along the one-lane road through the woods here report seeing two glowing red eyes in the rearview mirror. Miss Tes Rais of Jacksonville reported seeing Red Eyes in October 1993,

A sinister presence known as "Red Eyes" haunts the old Kingsley Plantation. "Red Eyes" is the ghost of a former slave turned murderer, who was hanged from a tree along the driveway. See Kingsley Plantation, Jacksonville, Florida (LEE HOLLOWAY)

when she and some friends were driving down the road. A former tour guide at Kingsley also reported hearing the ghostly cries of a child coming from a well on the property. The child is thought to have fallen into the well and drowned. The manor house was built by Zephaniah Kingsley, who lived there from 1813 until his death in 1889.

(Kingsley Plantation is located on Fort George Island within the city limits of Jacksonville. The site is operated by the National Park Service. Phone: 904-251-3537. www.cr.nps.gov/nr/travel/geo-flor/21.htm) **72**

KEY WEST

ARTIST HOUSE A life-size doll named Robert inhabits the upstairs cupola of this inn. The effigy is a likeness of artist Gene Otto when he was five years old. Made in 1904, the doll is said to have acquired a malevolent personality all its own. Witnesses have heard it giggle and even seen it move. Sometimes the doll turns up in spots where no one has placed it. Gene Otto died in 1974, and his wife Ann passed away three years later. Since then, her benevolent presence has been felt in the second-floor back bedroom, while the ghost of an unidentified little girl has been detected on the back stairs. What force or spirit possesses the doll in the cupola is anyone's guess.

A life-sized doll kept at Artist House is believed to be possessed by evil spirits. See Artist House, Key West, Florida (TRISTRAM DEROMA)

(Key West is at the end of U.S. Highway 1 in the large group of islands off the southernmost Florida Gulf Coast. The bed-and-breakfast inn is in the old town section. Artist House, 534 Eaton Street, Key West, FL 33040. Phone: 305-296-3977. www.artisthousekeywest. com) **133**

AUDUBON HOUSE The apparition of naturalist artist John James Audubon has been seen in broad daylight on the porch of this house. Some speculate that his tall ghost, dressed in a ruffled shirt and long jacket, has returned to reveal his true identity. Recent evidence and confessions by family members unveiled a startling fact about Audubon. He is said to be the son of King Louis XVI and Mary Antoinette of France. During the French Revolution, just after his mother was beheaded, the nine-year-old boy was smuggled out of

The apparition of naturalist John James Audubon has been seen in broad daylight on the porch of this house, now a museum. See Audubon House, Key West, Florida (JAGDISH CHAVDA/SOUTHERN STOCK PHOTO)

prison and legally adopted by a woman named Jean Audubon, who brought the heir to the French throne to America. John James Audubon renounced all claims to the throne on instructions from his adopted father, who feared for the dauphin's safety.

(Audubon House is a museum operated by the Florida Audubon Society. Follow U.S. Highway 1 through the Florida Keys to Whitehead Street in Key West and turn right. Audubon House is on the corner of White-head and Greene streets, 205 Whitehead St. Key West, FL 33040. Phone: 877-281-2473. www.audubonhouse.com) **14, 186**

HEMINGWAY HOUSE Ernest Hemingway lived all over the world, but he spent his happiest times here between 1928 and 1940. Former caretakers claim the author's ghost appeared soon after he died of a self-inflicted gunshot wound in 1961. Witnesses have seen Papa's pale form moving about the house and hear the clacking of his typewriter. A neighbor says his specter appears most often around midnight and can some-times be observed staring out a second-story window. His ghost has even been known to wave at passersby.

(The house is open to the public. Hemingway House, 907 Whitehead St., Key West, FL 33040. Phone: 305-294-1575. www.hemingwayhome.com) **72**

INN AT CABBAGE KEY The ghost of an Indian is seen in two rooms here, and the kitchen is home to two

other Indian spirits, who are heard arguing late into the night. The inn was built in the 1920s on top of an Indian burial ground.

(The inn is located at #60 Pineland on Cabbage Key, which is off Fort Meyers. The island can be reached by a twice-daily boat. Phone: 941-283-2278.) **72**

LITTLE WHITE HOUSE This house is so named because President Harry Truman stayed here when he visited the area. Caretakers have noticed unexplainable dark shadows moving about the house. Several employ-ees quit their jobs because of the ghost. Psychics visit-ing the old dwelling maintain that the restless spirit is that of a former maid who is angry because the building was allowed to fall into disrepair.

(The Little White House Museum is located at 171 Front St. Key West, FL 33040. Phone: 305-294-9911.) **72**

LAKE CITY

COLUMBIA COUNTY BOARD OF EDUCATION In 1978, this building housed the Lake City Middle School. On February 9 of that year, twelve-year-old Kimberly Diane Leach was abducted from school by serial killer Ted Bundy and taken to a wooded area where she was murdered. Kimberly had just been voted runner-up in the Valentine Queen contest and was looking forward to shopping for a party dress. The following year around Valentine's Day, students reported seeing the ghost of a young girl resembling Kimberly wearing a red party dress. It is said that each year around Valentine's Day, the ghost can be seen wandering the halls of her former school. See Chi Omega Sorority and Phi Delta Theta Fraternity, Talla-hassee, Florida.

(Lake City is in Columbia County, sixty-five miles west of Jacksonville at the junction of U.S. Highway 41 and U.S. Highway 90. Columbia County Board of Education Administrative Complex, U.S. Highway 90, Lake City, FL 32056.) **72**

LAKELAND

HIGHWAY 98 A phantom semitrailer truck haunts a stretch of highway near Lakeland. Since 1985, the ghost truck has followed drivers hauling produce from the East Coast to Texas. The ghost truck has been wit-nessed by at least two truckers.

(Lakeland is in central Florida, twelve miles east of Tampa on U.S. Highway 4. The phantom rig has appeared northbound on Highway 98 between Highway 471 and Highway 50. It also appeared fifty miles from Brooksville on a thirty-mile stretch of Highway 471.) **148**

MIAMI

CLUB ALHAMBRA APARTMENTS Tenants of Apartment 5-110 of this modern apartment building were harassed by an unusual phantom in 1977 and 1978. A disembodied arm jiggled doorknobs, waved a white cloth, and even painted pictures on the living-room wall.

(Miami is on I-95 at the southeastern tip of Florida. The apartments are in south Miami on Alhambra Boulevard.) **53(8/89)**

HIRSCHFIELD THEATER This dinner theater is haunted by an unseen presence whose footsteps are heard in the stage area. Owner Abe Hirschfield says a number of other strange effects, such as lights that turn on and off by themselves, are associated with the ghost.

(The old Hirschfield Theater in central Miami was recently turned into condominiums.) **101**

TROPICATION ARTS, INC. This wholesale novelty warehouse was the scene of 224 documented manifestations of poltergeist activity. The troubles started on December 15, 1966, when a number of amber glass steins were discovered broken. Then mugs, combs, plastic hand fans, and other merchandise started rolling off the shelves by themselves. Within a month, workers in the warehouse were starting to panic, and the owners of the firm, Alvin Laubheim and Glen Lewis, decided to call the police. Patrolman William Killiam witnessed so many strange events in his first hour at the scene that he called for a team of police officers as backup. The American Society for Psychical Research was contacted, and investigators William Roll and J. G. Pratt began a comprehensive study of the site on January 21, 1967. Their ten-day survey documented 150 events and concluded that they could not have been faked. They also discovered that most of the poltergeist activity centered around a nineteen-year-old Cuban worker by the name of Julio Vasquez. Julio was burdened with personal problems, which may have culminated in subconscious bursts of psychic energy. On January 30, Julio broke into the warehouse and stole some petty cash. He was fired, but no charges were filed. That same day, the poltergeist activity ceased. A few days later, he was arrested for stealing an engagement ring, intended for his fiancé, from a local jewelry store. He was sentenced to a short term in jail. After he was released, ASPR researchers tested him and found that he showed a marked ability to produce psychokinetic effects. Julio married Maria Santos in June 1968, and the couple had a baby girl in February 1969. Then, in March 1969, while working at a service station in Miami, Julio was shot three times by a teenage robber. The bullets entered his intestines and severed his aorta, but the remarkable man survived, although he can no longer engage in any strenuous activity. The Psychical Research Foundation offered the destitute man a financial grant if he would attend the Durham Technical Institute in North Carolina, but Julio refused. He said he did not want to become a guinea pig for scientists.

(Tropication Arts, 117 Northeast 54th St., Miami, FL 33137. www.haunted-places.com/florida.htm) **68, 105, 107, 186, 188**

VILLA PAULA In 1989, *The Miami Herald* labeled this mansion the most haunted house in the city. Residents were plagued with poltergeist activity, and several sighted the apparition of a woman. Several cats were found strangled to death near the iron gate at the entrance to the building. The mansion was built in 1925 and became Miami's first Cuban embassy.

(Villa Paula, 5811 North Miami Ave., Miami, FL 33122.) **102**

WITHERSPOON HOUSE During the 1960s, this house was haunted by the vengeful presence of a man whose wife shot him to death after he beat their teenage son with a chair. The murder of Carrington Harvey Witherspoon occurred on February 25, 1962. At the trial, witnesses told of how he had beat his wife and children, smashing furniture over their bodies and firing his shotgun at them. Mrs. Witherspoon was acquitted of the homicide. Only a few months later her sixteen-year-old son was killed in a motorcycle accident in front of the house. Later tenants reported hearing crashing sounds coming from the living room in the middle of the night, and during the day an unseen presence moved furniture around in the sun room. Feelings of intense discomfort and a horrible stench often overpowered people in the house. In May 1967, medium Harry Levy contacted the spirit of Witherspoon and reported that the violent man had promised with his dying breath to come back to get even with his wife.

(The former Witherspoon home is now a private residence. The terra-cotta house is on Northwest 25th Ave., Miami, FL 33125.) **186**

NEW PORT RICHEY

LEVEROCK'S RESTAURANT During the digging of a foundation for this modern restaurant, a prehistoric altar was found. Haunting faces are carved on the eight-foot-long, four-foot-wide altar stone, which was used by Timucuan priests as far back as A.D. 1 to make offerings of precious items to the gods. The artifact is on display at the entrance to the restaurant. Some psychically sensitive individuals have reported feeling a mysterious, cohesive force when touching the stone.

(The town is located near the intersection of Highway 54 and U.S. Highway 19, north of Clearwater on the west-central coast. Follow I-75 to Highway 54 and go west twenty-two miles to Highway 19. The restaurant is at 4927 U.S. Highway 19 South, New Port Richey, FL 34667. Phone: 727-849-8000.) **99**

OKLAWAHA

OLD BRADFORD HOUSE Strange footsteps on the stairway, the sounds of card playing in the parlor, and the apparition of a woman combing her long dark hair in the Green Bedroom have haunted residents of this two-story summer home for many years. On January 16, 1935, the house was the site of a bloody shoot-out between the FBI and members of the notorious Ma Barker gang. Barker was gunned down in the Green Bedroom, and her son Freddie was killed on the stairs. The woodwork and plaster have been repaired and repainted, but evidence of the bullet holes remain to this day.

(Oklawaha is Marion County in north central Florida, eight miles southeast of Ocala. The house is a private residence on the north bank of Lake Weir.) **11, 72**

ORLANDO

DEADMAN'S OAK A headless horseman roams the vicinity of this old oak tree south of Kissimmee. Legend says that a man riding a white horse through the wilderness was captured by Spaniards for some crime he committed, and his abductors beheaded him beneath a nearby tree. Around midnight, the man's headless ghost is said to retrace the same route astride his white horse.

(Kissimmee is five miles south of Orlando on U.S. Highway 441. The tree known as Deadman's Oak is approximately eighteen miles south of Kissimmee and two miles north of Canoe Creek.) **72**

PENSACOLA

PENSACOLA NAVAL AIR STATION Two structures on this military base are thought to be haunted. The Chief of Naval Education and Training Building was built in 1826 and was used as a hospital until 1985, when it was turned into offices. Workers at the hospital reported hearing the sounds of someone operating a buffing machine in the hallway when no one was there and detecting the untraceable odor of pipe tobacco. After the building was converted to offices, staffers started reporting objects flying across the room, doors slamming, and office machines turning on and off by themselves. They have also seen wraithlike figures on the stairs and discovered strange writing on the walls, such as "Death Awaits!" and "Help, Let Me Out!" The other haunted building on the base is the Pensacola Lighthouse. A former lighthouse keeper had many unusual experiences there and declares the place is very definitely haunted. Phantom footsteps and other noises are thought to belong to a lighthouse keeper who died on the job.

(Pensacola is in the extreme western panhandle of Florida at the junction of I-10 and U.S. Highway 98. The Naval Air Station is directly south of the city.) **72**

UFO VIEWING AREA Multiple UFO sightings started here on November 11, 1987, and continue to this day. The bluish-gray crafts have been seen and photographed by hundreds of people. In the six-month period from November 1987 to May 1988, sixty-eight sightings were made by a total of 135 witnesses. In addition, six blue beams were seen coming from the crafts, four alien beings were sighted, and over sixty photographs were taken. There were also nine cases of missing time suggesting abductions. On May 1, 1988, Ed Walters, the man who first reported the strange objects, was rendered unconscious by a beam from a

UFO while he was attempting to take stereoscopic photos of the craft. On June 20, 1991, a group of fourteen observers photographed two bright UFOs that turned red and disappeared. Donald Ware, MUFON Florida State director, has said that he believes the sightings are proof of alien visitation. See Fort Lauderdale, Florida.

(The sightings are concentrated in the Pensacola Bay area, between Santa Rosa Island and Pensacola. The town of Gulf Breeze is located on a peninsula that connects with Pensacola by Highway 98 over the Pensacola Bay Bridge. The town is looped by Highway 30A, which intersects with Highway 98. Viewing areas include Towne Point, Tiger Point, Fair Point, and Deer Point, although sightings have occurred in Villa Venyce, Heron Cove, Whisper Bay, and along the Santa Rosa Park Road. But the best spot to look for UFOs is from the southern end of the Pensacola Bridge, which offers an unobstructed view of the whole area. On almost any night, a group of UFO watchers can be found there.) **53 (2/90), 126 (2/90, 4/90, 2/91, 7/92, 1/93, 2–/94, 6/94, 11/94), 150, 213**

ROCKLEDGE

ASHLEY'S RESTAURANT The ghost of a young girl dressed in Roaring Twenties clothing haunts the ladies' room here. Her likeness emerges from one of the stalls or appears in the mirrors. Several women have reported feeling a choking sensation when passing through the corridor to the ladies room. The ghost ventures to other places in the Tudor-style building—to break dinnerware in the kitchen, turn lights on and off in the bar, or shove customers from behind in the dining room. She is thought to be either the spirit of Ethyl Allen, brutally murdered in a storage room here in the 1920s, or the ghost of a young woman who died in a car accident on Highway 1 in front of the restaurant. Dozens of employees and customers have reported apparitions over the years, and sightings have increased since 1979. A 1993 investigation documented a variety of phenomena, including a swirling mass of ghostlike energy recorded on a thermographic camera.

(Rockledge is on the east central coast, twelve miles north of Melbourne on U.S. Highway 1. Ethyl Allen's burned and mutilated body was found at Eau Gallie, on the banks of the Indian River. Ashley's Restaurant is at 1609 South U.S. Highway 1, Rockledge, FL 32955.

Phone: 321-636-6430. www.mindreader.com/fate/articles/ Fate0794.txt) **53 (7/94), 101, 135, 148**

ST. AUGUSTINE

ABBOTT MANSION This three-story manor house is now an apartment building, and tenants have been relating their encounters with two apparitions here for nearly five decades. One is a plump woman in an old-fashioned dress called Miss Lucy, who is thought to be a member of the original Abbott family who built the house in the 1870s. The other is a man dressed in a sea captain's garb, dubbed simply the Captain by residents.

(St. Augustine is twenty-six miles south of Jacksonville on U.S. Highway 1 on the northeastern coast of Florida. Abbott Mansion, now called Old Mansion, is a private residence, at 14 Joiner St., St. Augustine, FL 32084.) **53 (10/84), 72**

CASABLANCA INN ON THE BAY This waterfront house has a prominent widow's walk on the roof. The building was once a boarding house run by a vivacious lady who rented out rooms to revenue agents during the Prohibition. The agents were puzzled that they were so unsuccessful at seizing rum-running boats that regularly came into St. Augustine Harbor. Finally, they discovered that their landlady was going up the widow's walk at midnight and hanging out a lantern to warn the bootleggers of their presence. Today, shrimp and pleasure boats entering the harbor close to the midnight hour sometimes still see a strange light on the widow's walk slowly swinging back and forth.

(Casablanca Inn on the Bay, 24 Avenida Menendez St., St. Augustine, FL 32084. Phone: 800-826-2626. www.casablancainn.com) **72**

CASTILLO DE SAN MARCOS NATIONAL MONUMENT An eerie glow accompanied by the faint odor of a woman's perfume is sometimes detected near a wall in the dungeon of this 1672 Spanish fort. The wall was the ghastly tomb of Señora Dolores Mari and Captain Manuel Abela. Señora Dolores was the wife of Colonel Garcia Marti, assigned to the Spanish garrison in 1784. When Colonel Marti found out his wife was having an affair with Abela, he chained them to a wall in the dungeon and mortared a new wall of coquina stone in front of them. Human bones were discovered in a hidden room in the gunpowder storage area in 1938,

An eerie glow and the scent of woman's perfume are detected near a wall in the dungeon of this 1672 Spanish fort. See Castillo de San Marcos National Monument, St. Augustine, Florida (LEE HOLLAWAY)

when Lt. Stephen Tuttle and his men were cleaning the area. Another story says the bones were discovered in 1833, when an engineer broke into the hollow section. In any case, visitors have reported seeing eerie, floating lights and discerning the unexplainable odor of a woman's perfume at certain spots in the old fort.

(The Castillo de San Marcos is on a peninsula just east of St. Augustine. Castillo de San Marcos National Monument, 1 Castillo Dr., St. Augustine, FL 32084. Phone: 904-829-6506. www.nps.gov/casa) **72, 223**

HARRY'S SEAFOOD BAR & GRILL

This restaurant was not considered haunted until a few years ago when the former owners reported that a basket of freshly laundered uniforms had caught fire for no apparent reason. They later learned that two previous buildings on the site had burned down and were rebuilt on the original foundation. When they started seeing wispy shadows moving about the place, they decided it was time to sell.

(The restaurant was previously known as the Chart House Restaurant and Catalina's Gardens. Harry's Seafood Bar & Grill, 46 Avenida Menendez, St. Augustine, FL 32084. Phone: 904-824-7765.) **72**

CINCINNATI AVENUE HOUSE

This turn-of-the-century house is said to be haunted by an elderly lady who once occupied a second-floor bedroom. When she became an invalid and could no longer climb the stairs, she spent the remainder of her life in a room on the lower level. After she died, neighbors reported seeing a strange light in her old upstairs bedroom. One tenant felt the woman's invisible skirt brush past him while he was sitting on the front porch. The present owners have not yet encountered any ghosts, but admit they never go into the old lady's room on the second floor.

(The house is a private residence at 24 Cincinnati Ave., St. Augustine, FL 32084.) **72**

DON PEDRO HORRUYTINER HOUSE

The apparitions at the Governor Don Pedro Horruytiner House go back 150 years. Brigita Gomez, lady of the house in 1821, encountered two spectral women while tending her rose garden. The amazed Gomez presented her uninvited guests with some of her cherished yellow roses, which she later discovered lying near the entrance to the house. The building is also said to be haunted by two other woman, a seventeenth-century Spanish soldier, and possibly by the governor himself. A coffin left in the attic by a physician who once lived here is said to move back and forth, making odd scraping sounds. The house is plagued with strange electrical problems, and neighbors have reported eerie lights flitting through the house at night. In March 1995, another round of spook lights were seen in the house.

(The house is a private residence, at 214 St. George St., St. Augustine, FL 32084.) **72**

THE HOUSE

June Moore Ferrell wrote a book about this old dwelling entitled, simply, *The House*. In the book, Ferrell states that a small child, the result of an incestuous relationship between a mother and her son, is buried in the backyard. Neighbors and passersby have seen the ghostly figure of a woman in a flowing black cape standing on the long balcony in front or walking in the backyard. During renovation of the balcony, workers reported several unusual incidents, such as boards moving or falling for no apparent reason.

(The house is a private residence, at 8 Ardenta St., St. Augustine, FL 32095.) **72**

HUGUENOT CEMETERY

One of the oldest cemeteries in the United States is haunted by a headless apparition. In the early 1800s, when the caretaker arrived for work one day, he discovered one of the aboveground tombs vandalized and the body on the ground beside the sepulcher. The corpse's head was missing and never found. The body was reinterred, but sometimes, during the evening twilight, the phantom body wanders through the cemetery searching for its head. The latest sighting was in March 1995.

(The Huguenot Cemetery is on San Marco Ave., just outside the old city gates of St. Augustine.) **72**

OLDEST HOUSE MUSEUM The oldest house in America's oldest city is haunted. Strange lights have been observed moving in the rooms late at night, even though the house does not have electricity. Two children's dresses and other objects in Maria's Room are sometimes discovered in different positions from the ones they were in the day before. Recently a tour guide reported that a woman's poodle became unduly disturbed and began shaking as if it were terrified of something, but once outside the dog was fine. The house was constructed shortly after the British burned the town in 1702.

(Oldest House Museum, 14 St. Francis St., St. Augustine, FL 32084. Phone: 904-824-2872. www.oldcity.com/oldhouse) **72**

OLD FIRESTONE HOUSE This house has such a reputation for being haunted that passing children often walk on the other side of the street. Although there have been accounts of tables rocking and tipping over, lights going on and off by themselves, objects disappearing and then reappearing in unusual locations, doors opening and closing, and beds shaking, there has been only one reported sighting of a ghost. A former occupant saw and conversed with a woman in white who appeared one night at the foot of the bed. The ghost is thought to be Helen Firestone, a former owner who killed herself in the garage.

(The house is a private residence, at 272 St. George St., St. Augustine, FL 32084.) **72**

ST. AUGUSTINE LIGHTHOUSE This lighthouse was built in 1874, and a few years later a man hanged himself in the keeper's house. A later lighthouse keeper said he often heard phantom footsteps following him from the house to the tower. When the lighthouse and surrounding buildings were being restored, several inexplicable accidents caused workmen to become apprehensive about finishing the job. Eerie lights have also been observed in the area.

(The St. Augustine Lighthouse is located on Anastasia Island, just off Highway A1A at 81 Lighthouse Ave. Phone: 904-829-0745. www.stauglight.com) **72**

SCARLETT O'HARA'S RESTAURANT An old-fashioned bathtub on display in this restaurant is haunted. One side of the tub has been cut away and upholstered to form a very unusual sofa, but it was not such a comfortable place for the man who died in the tub many years ago. The house occupied by the restaurant used to belong to a lighthouse keeper who died while taking a bath. Late at night, the sounds of splashing water and the low moan of the old man taking his last breath are heard.

(Scarlett O'Hara's Restaurant, 70 Hypolita St., St. Augustine, FL 32084. Phone: 904-824-6535.) **72**

SEA CAPTAIN'S HOUSE On certain nights a ghostly melody drifts from the third story of this lovely old Victorian mansion. The house was built in 1892 by a sea captain and featured a ballroom where receptions and dances were held. When the man was at sea, his wife used to go up to the ballroom and sit for hours playing his favorite tunes on the harpsichord. One night, she did not come down to dinner and the servants discovered her lifeless body slumped over the keyboard. Eventually, the place was turned into an apartment house and tenants sometimes reported hearing music coming from the third floor. In the summer of 1979, a young lady named Bobbie Bay, who rented an apartment on the second floor, followed the music to the old ballroom. There, she encountered the apparition of an auburn-haired lady in a vintage yellow satin gown. She observed the apparition several other times—always preceded by the tinkle of the nonexistent harpsichord.

(The house is a private residence, at 268 St. George St., St. Augustine, FL 32084.) **72**

WILDWOOD BAPTIST CHURCH Sometimes when this congregation sings the hymn "Zion's Hill," the ghost of their former preacher enters the room and sits in the minister's chair. His apparition has also been seen at the front door greeting parishioners. The graveyard next to the church is also said to be haunted. The statuesque phantom of an angel was seen over one grave, and while a census of the cemetery was being taken a voice from nowhere called out to a worker that she had missed the grave of Henry O'Barnum. Sure enough, the moss-covered tombstone had been overlooked.

(The church is just south of St. Augustine. Follow U.S. Highway 1 to Wildwood Dr. The church and cemetery are on the right.) **72**

ST. PETERSBURG

DON CESAR RESORT During restoration here in 1972, construction workers and staff began seeing the apparition of Thomas Rowe, the man who built the original hotel in 1928. The sightings were very frequent until one evening, when the new owner came face-to-face with the ghost in the hotel kitchen. The owner, who felt the ghost was disrupting business, offered him a deal: He would redecorate four rooms with antique furnishings from the 1920s and 1930s if the ghost would confine himself to those rooms when they were empty. Thereafter, public appearances of the ghost became less frequent. But recently another ghost seems to have brought Thomas out of hiding. After renovations in 1987, the apparition of Thomas's one true love, an opera singer named Lucinda, started to appear. Now she is seen walking at Thomas's side in the courtyard.

(St. Petersburg is on the west-central Florida coast on Tampa Bay. Don CeSar Beach Resort, 3400 Gulf Blvd., St. Petersburg, FL 33706. Phone: 727-360-1881. www.doncesar.com) **73**

MADIRA BICKEL MOUND This sacred site was used for mystical ceremonies from 200 B.C. to A.D. 1500. The large temple mound, made mostly of seashells, is a trapezoidal structure 20 feet tall and 100 by 170 feet at its base. A smaller white sand mound, ten feet across and eighteen inches high, is thirty yards north of the temple. The mounds were built by the ancient Timucuan people to worship the spirits of the sun and rain.

(Take I-275 south five miles from St. Petersburg and take the Highway 19 exit to Terra Ceia Island. Follow Terra Ceia Road to Center Road. Turn left toward Bayshore Road, which leads to the site. For information, contact Madira Mound Site, Gamble Plantation, 3708 Patten Ave., Ellenton, FL 33532. Phone: 913-722-1017.) **99**

SKYWAY BRIDGE The ghost of a blond-haired girl in a tight T-shirt has been seen at the top of this bridge by dozens of motorists. She has also been seen hitchhiking on the approach to the bridge. She has not been identified, but is thought to have committed suicide here.

(The Skyway Bridge crosses Tampa Bay between St. Petersburg and Sarasota on Highway 41.) **49**

SILVER SPRINGS

BRIDAL CHAMBER A section of this group of crystal-clear springs is the final resting place for two lovers. Claire Douglas was the classic rich boy in love with a poor girl, Bernice Mayo. The boy met her secretly at an old black woman's hut near the swamp. Then, one day in a boat near Boiling Spring, he presented Bernice with an antique bracelet his estranged mother had given him, and asked her to marry him. The girl was never happier, but Claire's tyrannical father found out and shipped his son off to Europe under the watchful eye of an aunt. The father intercepted all the letters the boy wrote to Bernice, and soon the fragile girl grew depressed and sickly. Before she died she asked the black woman to lower her corpse into Boiling Spring, where she had pledged her love to Claire. The boy returned not long after her death. His father had evicted the Mayo family from their sharecropper farm, and no one knew their whereabouts. The forlorn boy rowed out to Boiling Spring and gazed despondently into the clear water. In the crystal-clear water, he saw the glistening gold bracelet he had given Bernice, whose body was wedged in a crevice directly below him. He dove into the water, and unable to free her, drowned in her embrace. People named the spot the Bridal Chamber in memory of their love, and some people still report seeing the two lovers locked in an eternal embrace in the turbulent waters of Boiling Spring.

(Silver Springs is in north-central Florida, just northeast of Ocala on Highway 40. Camping and glass-bottom boat tours to the Bridal Chamber are available.) **223**

TALLAHASSEE

CHI OMEGA SORORITY HOUSE This sorority house was the scene of a murderous assault by serial killer Ted Bundy during the early morning hours of January 15, 1978. Four young women were attacked and bludgeoned; two, Margaret Bowman and Lisa Levy, were killed; two others were severely beaten. Bundy also attacked a fifth woman in her apartment a few blocks away, who also survived. One sorority girl confided to crime writer Ann Rule that on the night of the murders she got out of bed to go for a drink of water, but for some reason could not bring herself to open the door. She had a strange feeling there was some horrible evil outside her door, so she locked it and returned to bed. Following the murders, many sorority sisters admitted they felt uneasy, and over the years it came to be accepted that the two murdered women were haunting the house. One coed asserted that while she did not believe in ghosts, when she was in the house she often experienced a peculiar feeling that she had never felt anyplace else. See Phi Delta Theta Fraternity, below; and Columbia County Board of Education, Lake City, Florida.

(Tallahassee is in northern Florida at the junction of I-10 and U.S. Highway 319. The sorority is near the Florida State University campus. Chi Omega Sorority, 661 Jefferson St., Tallahassee, FL 32304.) **72**

OAKLAWN CEMETERY People often report having weird feelings around the Phillips Mausoleum in this cemetery. The unusual tomb was erected in the early 1900s by Calvin C. Phillips, one of the city's most eccentric characters. His was the first sepulcher in the cemetery, a twenty-foot-high structure topped with a minaret. Once his mausoleum was completed, Phillips had a cherry wood coffin taken inside, and literally crept into his crypt and died. He left a key with a friend so the vault could be locked after Phillips's death.

(Oaklawn Cemetery is on Bronough Street, between Brevard St. and Fourth Ave., in Tallahassee.) **72**

OLD CITY CEMETERY The most-visited grave in this cemetery is a towering obelisk monument known as the Witch's Grave. Here rests Elizabeth Budd "Bessie" Graham, who died in 1889 at the age of twenty-three. Bessie was a good or "white" witch, although she reportedly concocted a spell to ensnare a very rich man into marrying her. The two were indeed married and had a child, but Bessie became ill and died after only two years of wedlock. Her elaborate monument and its enigmatic epitaph have been subjects of conversation for more than a century. The inscription reads, in part: "Come let the burial rite be read/The funeral song be

sung/A dirge for her, the doubly dead/In that she died so young." Contrary to custom, Bessie's is the only grave in the cemetery facing west. Today, members of witches' covens visit the site regularly to meditate over flowers and white candles they have placed on the grave. They claim the grave site has a mysterious magnetic quality and a "presence" conducive to meditation.

(The Old City Cemetery is on King Blvd., between Park Ave. and Call St. in Tallahassee.) **72**

OLD LEON COUNTY JAIL This old jail was considered to be haunted even before its use as a place of incarceration was discontinued in the 1960s. People reported supernatural occurrences, such as being pushed, feeling invisible entities pass them on the stairs, hearing pounding in the walls, and the unexplained opening and closing of heavy cell doors.

(The Old Leon County Jail is on Calhoun St. near its intersection with Pensacola St. in Tallahassee.) **72**

PHI DELTA THETA FRATERNITY HOUSE Before it was bought and renovated by the Phi Delta Theta fraternity, this old building was a rooming house called "The Oak"—in honor of the thousand-year-old, moss-draped oak tree in the front yard. On December 31, 1977, Ted Bundy, awaiting trial for murder in Colorado, escaped from jail and made his way to Tallahassee, where he rented a room at The Oak. He planned to assume a new identity, find a job, and make a new life for himself. Bundy believed the two years he had spent in jail had conquered the evil force within him that he later came to call the "Entity." Unfortunately, he was wrong. During the early morning hours of January 15, 1978, Bundy took a short walk. When he returned, two young women were dead and three others severely injured by his hand. Bundy was apprehended and sentenced to death for those and another murder in Lake City and died in Florida's electric chair on January 24, 1989. A few weeks following his execution, two women walking past The Oak saw a man standing on the porch, and one of them remarked how much the man resembled a young Ted Bundy. When they looked again, the figure had vanished. Perhaps the ghost of Ted Bundy is nothing more than a fraternity ploy to scare female visitors. Then again, perhaps Bundy's spirit really haunts the one place he tried to start over, the one place where he was happy for a few days before the Entity emerged again. See Chi Omega Sorority, above; and Columbia County Board of Education, Lake City, Florida.

(The fraternity house is near the Florida State University campus. The old oak tree is still standing in front of the house. Phi Delta Theta Fraternity, 409 College Ave., Tallahassee, FL 32301.) **72**

TAMPA

TAMPA THEATRE This building is haunted by Foster Finley, a projectionist who worked here for thirty-five years, until he died of a heart attack suffered in his booth over the balcony. The Mediterranean-style movie palace opened in 1926 and was restored in the 1970s by the Arts Council of Tampa-Hillsborough Counties. It was after renovations that Finley's ghost started showing up. Maintenance workers, ushers, and patrons have all had run-ins with his spirit. His invisible presence is most often encountered in the projection booth, but sometimes he just taps people on the shoulder or manifests as chilling cold spots on the staircase. Sometimes strange sounds, such as heavy chains rattling, are heard coming from the lobby. A séance held in 1984 was able to conjure up a presence that appeared in mirrors and in front of the stage.

(Tampa is on the western coast of Florida at the junction of I-4 and I-75. The theater is used for special events, and the Tampa Film Club shows movies there. Tampa Theatre, 711 Franklin St., Tampa, FL 33602. Phone: 813-274-8981. www.tampatheatre.org) **175**

USEPPA ISLAND

USEPPA ISLAND CLUB This island is named for a kidnapped Cuban girl who chose death over defilement. Beautiful Useppa was kidnapped in Havana by pirate Jose Gaspar and imprisoned on this island. When she refused to submit to sex, he slashed off her head with his cutlass. Her headless ghost has been reported roaming the coastline, scanning the horizon for her rescuers. The ghosts of naked Indians have also been observed on the island, which archeologists say was inhabited as far back as 3500 B.C.

(Useppa Island is off Flamingo Bay, west of Fort Myers on the southwestern coast of Florida. Useppa Island Club is on Useppa Island. Phone: 813-283-1061. Day trips to this private resort leave from South Seas

Plantation on Captiva Island. Take Highway 869 from Fort Myers Beach over Sanibel Island to the plantation. Phone: 941-283-5255. www.useppa.com) **15**

WEST PALM BEACH

BURGER KING The ghost of a young man has appeared to several employees here. Janitor Herman Herrera chased the phantom through the restaurant, only to see it disappear before his eyes. When he saw the ghost a second time, he quit his job. A night manager encountered the apparition on his shift in 1993. Two assistant managers have also seen the apparition.

(West Palm Beach is on U.S. Highway 1 on the southeastern coast of Florida. The Burger King is located in Royal Palm Beach, which is directly west of West Palm Beach on Highway 704.) **72**

HENRY MORRISON FLAGLER MUSEUM The ghosts of the former owners of this marble mansion walk its cold corridors. Built in 1902 by millionaire Henry Morrison Flagler, Whitehall Mansion was judged "one of the six most imposing private houses ever built in the United States." After Flagler's first wife died, he married her nurse, who later lost her mind. He then decided he wanted to marry a beautiful southerner by the name of Mary Lily Kenan. It took a special act of the Florida legislature to allow him to divorce the nurse and marry Kenan. He built Whitehall for his new wife, who was thirty-seven years younger than he was. Two factions developed in the family: those who approved of Mary Lily and those who did not. Apparently the feud has lasted beyond the grave. When the mansion became a museum in the 1970s, possessions of former family members who belonged to opposing factions could not be placed in the same display case. The objects would mysteriously move to other locations, and sometimes plates and other breakable objects would simply explode inside protective covers. Mary Lily's ghost has been sighted in the museum's ladies' room and upstairs hall.

(The museum is in Palm Beach, which is just north of West Palm Beach. Henry Morrison Flagler Museum, Coconut Row at 1 Whitehall Way, Palm Beach, FL 33480. Phone: 561-655-2833.) **136**

LAKE WORTH PLAYHOUSE This theater was opened in 1925 by two brothers, Lucian and Clarence

Oakley. Lucian committed suicide, and ever since, his spirit has haunted the theater. Witnesses have seen the impression of a giant hand imprint on a wall and have encountered unexplainable blasts of cold air. There are accounts of heavy objects being moved by unseen hands, and one private investigator experienced a choking sensation after which he concluded that Lucian must have hanged himself.

(Lake Worth Playhouse is a National Historical Landmark located in Lake Worth, five miles south of West Palm Beach at 713 Lake Ave. Phone: 561-586-6410.) **72**

GEORGIA

ADAIRSVILLE

BARNSLEY GARDENS The ruins of this Gothic mansion testify to the curse that followed the Barnsley family for over a hundred years. The mansion was built by Godfrey Barnsley in 1844 on a knoll that Cherokee Indian legends said would bring tragedy to anyone who lived there. Despite the warnings of local townsfolk, the family moved onto the magnificent estate, which they called Woodlands. Within months, Godfrey's wife Julia died from a lung infection. Not long afterward, their infant son followed her to the grave. In 1858, one of Godfrey's daughters died at Woodland, and in 1862 one of his sons was killed by pirates during a trip to China. The house was ransacked by Union soldiers in 1864, and several of Godfrey's friends and relatives ended up buried on his property during the Civil War. One was Colonel Robert Earle, who was killed on the property when he tried to warn the Barnsley family that the Yankees were coming. Godfrey Barnsley deserted the cursed land and moved to New Orleans, but one of his daughters, Julia Baltzelle, stayed on with her husband. In 1868, he was killed by a falling tree on the property. Godfrey died in 1873 and his body was buried at Woodland, but vandals dug up his grave and cut off his hand for use in voodoo rites. Julia's daughter Adelaide was living in the mansion in 1906 when a tornado tore off the roof and did extensive damage. One of Adelaide's sons went insane and was confined to the state hospital.

In 1935 he broke out and returned to Woodland, where he shot his brother in the chest. The mortally wounded man died in his mother's arms in the living room.

Now deserted and overgrown with weeds and vines, Woodlands is said to be haunted by its unfortunate inhabitants. The ghost of Julia Barnsley has been seen among the boxwoods at the front entrance, and Godfrey Barnsley's movements have been heard coming from the old library. The ghost of a Confederate soldier thought to be Colonel Robert Earle has been seen drinking from a spring in back of the house. The property is now known as Barnsley Gardens.

(Adairsville is located in the northwest corner of Georgia, twenty-six miles northwest of Atlanta on I-75. The grounds are a historical site just outside Adairsville in Bartow County. Barnsley Gardens Inn, 597 Barnsley Gardens Rd., Adairsville, GA 30103. Phone: 770-773-7480.) **58, 226**

ALTAMAHA SWAMP

ROCK OVEN The caves in this area are said to be haunted by the spirits of Indians who performed sacred rituals in them. Strange voices echo, mysterious green lights move slowly over the landscape, and the ghosts of Indians are seen dancing at the entrances to the caves. Evidence suggests Indians lived here as long as four thousand years ago. Local Native Americans call the area Tama.

(The Altamaha River Swamp is in southeast Georgia, near the town of Jesup. Rock Oven is a limestone ridge overlooking a small lagoon formed off the river. It is a few miles downstream of the Edwin Hatch Nuclear Power Plant.) **57**

AMERICUS

COLONEL FISH'S HOUSE The ghost of Colonel George Fish moved with this quaint house when it was transported in 1969 from Oglethorpe to Americus by Mr. and Mrs. Donald Nelson. The colonel's ghost resisted the move. Strange occurrences and unexpected setbacks plagued workers at the job site. Two crews of carpenters walked off the job and refused to return. The ghost of the colonel was even seen in the house on the day of the move, just hours before the building slid off its carriage into a ditch. But once the house was set on its new foundation, the colonel appeared to Mr. Nelson and apologized for the trouble he had caused. Mr. Nelson cordially invited the displaced spirit to stay. After that, the colonel's presence was often felt near one particular stuffed chair in the parlor. See Oglethorpe, Georgia.

(The white wooden house has a double stairway in front and a lower bricked level. It is a private residence, on Main St., Americus, GA 31709.) **226**

ANDERSONVILLE

ANDERSONVILLE NATIONAL CEMETERY The ghost of Captain Henry Wirz is said to roam this cemetery, which contains the remains of prisoners who died in the stockade he commanded. Over thirteen thousand Federal prisoners died from starvation and disease at Camp Sumter, and Captain Wirz became the only Confederate officer to be tried for war crimes. Wirz made an honest effort to secure food and medicine for the prisoners but refused to implicate others in the criminal conditions that existed at the camp. He was hanged in Washington on November 10, 1865. His ghost has been seen along Highway 49 near the cemetery, wearing an old military overcoat and a Union cap. The latest sighting was in July 1990. In addition, the ghosts of six Southerners buried here, part of a violent prison gang known as the "Raiders," are said to return on the anniversary of their hanging, July 11. Confederate prisoners eagerly built the gallows for their fellow inmates, who preyed on other prisoners.

(The Andersonville National Cemetery is located nine miles northeast of Americus in Sumter County. From I-185, follow U.S. Highway 280 west to Highway 26. Take Highway 26 west to Highway 228, then follow Highway 228 west to Highway 49. Go south on Highway 49 for one mile to the cemetery entrance. Andersonville National Cemetery, Andersonville, GA 31711.) **15, 163, 226**

ATLANTA

DONALDSON HOUSE Residents David and Linda Chestnut have reported a ghostly presence in their old house. A moving cold spot and the sounds of invisible footsteps are thought to be manifestations of a former owner.

(The house is a private residence, at 4831 Chamblee-Dunwoody Rd., Atlanta, GA 30338.) **72, 101**

MILAM HOUSE The ghost of Dr. Bob Mabry returns to the home of his adopted mother Mrs. Frances Milam. His presence is felt in the master bedroom and a nearby office. Sometimes the spirit writes personal messages to relatives through Mrs. Milam's hand. Much of her automatic writing contains warnings to youth about the dangers of suicide. "Suicide is not an ending," he says. "We still have the same problems, for the soul is eternal." Dr. Mabry should know. In 1983, he put a gun to his head and pulled the trigger.

(This modern Mediterranean-style house is a private residence in the College Park suburb of Atlanta. The address is 4065 Pierce Rd., College Park, GA 30349.) **135**

AUGUSTA

EZEKIAL HARRIS HOUSE Considered one of America's most haunted houses, the former MacKay Trading House is where thirteen American patriots (one for each of the colonies) were executed by British Colonel Thomas Browne on September 18, 1780. They were hanged from an open-air stairwell built into the back of the building. Another sixteen prisoners were given over to Indians to be brutally tortured to death in front of the trading house. Today, the spirits of the martyrs linger there. Visitors who stand in the stairwell and count to thirteen are said to be able to hear the ghastly twang of the tightening nooses. Dozens have reported hearing the moans of the tortured victims from the thirteenth step on the stairway. On the third floor, the ghost of a thin woman glides silently around the room. She is thought to be Mrs. Glass, the mother of two teenage boys hanged by Colonel Browne, who watched the activities from a third-floor bedroom.

(Augusta is at the intersection of I-20 and U.S. Highway 25 on the South Carolina border. The three-story, wooden house is now a state historic monument. It is located at 1840 Broad St., Augusta, GA 30904. Phone: 706-724-0436.) **225**

BAINBRIDGE

NEW ENTERPRISE FREEWILL BAPTIST CHURCH CEMETERY For many years, people who lived across from this church would occasionally see a ball of fire hovering over the graveyard. The phenomenon came to be recognized as a portent of death, because whenever they observed the fireball, a new grave would need to be dug in the cemetery within a few days. The area around the graveyard is also said to be haunted by a demon dog, a huge black canine that leaves no tracks and has a bloodcurdling howl. Family members at the nearby John Askew farm saw the large creature trot across a freshly plowed wet field, but when they investigated they could not find any tracks.

(Bainbridge is in southwestern Georgia at the junction of U.S. Highway 27 and U.S. Highway 84. The church is west of Bainbridge in Seminole County. Take Highway 27 west from Bainbridge, then turn left onto Highway 285 after crossing Spring Creek. The church and cemetery are about 1.5 miles on the right) **72**

CALHOUN

WORCESTER HOUSE A two-story farmhouse has been haunted for over a century. Newspaper articles from as far back as 1889 tell of ghostly manifestations traced to the murder of a Cherokee Indian in an upstairs room in the 1830s. The house was built in 1828 by missionary Samuel Worcester, who came to the New Echota settlement to work with Indians. In 1825, the Cherokee Nation officially established the site as their capital and set up a government patterned after that of the United States. But the State of Georgia considered the establishment of New Echota to be an act of insurrection. Worcester and two other missionaries were beaten, loaded with chains, and forced to walk behind a wagon for thirty-five miles because they signed a proclamation of rights for the Cherokees. They were sentenced to four years at hard labor, and Worcester lost all his land and belongings. By 1838, seventeen thousand Cherokees had been forced out of their Georgia homeland to a remote location eight hundred miles west. Over four thousand Indians died on what came to be known as the Trail of Tears. As soon as the Indians were gone, whites looted the Cherokee burial grounds and took over New Echota and Worcester House. Then, in the 1900s, two men playing cards got into an argument and killed each other in the downstairs area of the house. The strong emotions of those violent times are impregnated in these walls. The sounds of dragging chains, disembodied footsteps, and slamming doors, the apparition of a thin man of short stature, and a heavy feeling of uneasiness still haunt Worcester House.

(Worcester House is located at the New Echota State Historic Site on Highway 225, one mile east of I-75 exit 131. The address is 1211 Chatsworth Highway, Calhoun, GA 30701. Phone: 706-624-1321. www.northga.net/ gordon/echota.html) **14, 101**

CHATSWORTH

FORT MOUNTAIN STATE PARK The sounds of distant drums, flickering lights, and the images of men wearing bearskins are encountered along a collapsed wall of stones that was once a prehistoric fort. Bronze markers on the trail leading up to the stone fortress relate Cherokee legends that the builders were mysterious "moon-eyed, white-skinned" people. The only thing known for sure is that the Indians lacked the engineering skills to build the fortress. The 855-foot-long wall of the fort winds back and forth on the mountain top. It is up to twelve feet thick and three feet high, although at one time it probably stood as high as seven feet. Archeologists have no idea who built it or why. Speculation centers on the Lost Tribes of Israel and a Welsh explorer named Prince Madoc, who is said to have landed on the East Coast in 1170.

(Chatsworth is in the extreme northwest corner of Georgia, thirty-five miles southeast of Chattanooga, Tennessee. Old Stone Fort is on Fort Mountain, east of Chatsworth off County Rd. 2/52 at 181 Fort Mountain Park Rd. Chatsworth, GA 30705. Phone: 706-695-2621.) **57, 166**

COLUMBUS

SPRINGER OPERA HOUSE This 1871 theater house is haunted by the ghost of Edwin Booth, brother of John Wilkes Booth, the man who assassinated President Lincoln. Edwin appeared at the theater in the role of Hamlet in 1876 to thunderous applause. The reception finally freed the great actor from the stigma of being John Booth's brother. When the theater was renovated in 1963, strange things started happening. Keys disappeared, doors opened by themselves, costumes closets were rearranged for no apparent reason, and eerie music could be heard coming from the building when it was empty. Workers at the playhouse believe Edwin is upset because the theater has deserted its classical repertoire and will never again perform his favorite play, *Hamlet.*

(Columbus is in Muscogee County, at the south end of Highway 185 on the Alabama border. The opera house is downtown. Springer Opera House, 103 10th St., Columbus, GA 31901. Phone: 706-324-1100.) **226**

CONYERS

FOWLER FARMHOUSE On the thirteenth day of each month, the Virgin Mary is said to visit a simple farmhouse just outside Conyers. Nancy Fowler first saw visions of Mary and Jesus in 1988, and today she announces the visitations to thousands of faithful pilgrims who come to her farm. Sometimes the crowds swell to nearly sixty thousand people, many of whom share in the miraculous visions.

(The town of Conyers is twenty miles southeast of Atlanta on Highway 138. The Fowler Farmhouse is just outside of town.) **72**

EASTMAN

KIGHT HOUSE Residents of this house got tired of sharing the premises with a ghost, so they built a new house two hundred yards from the old one. But the ghost moved with them. Bob and Betty Kight bought the house and surrounding land in 1962. Before long, they discovered they shared the house with the ghost of Mrs. Sammy King, who died in the 1920s, struck by lightning while shutting an upstairs window. Many reports describe the ghost as an elderly woman in a brown dress with bushy sleeves, wearing an oversize

bonnet. The apparition is most often seen in the garden or sitting on the front porch. When the Kights moved in, Mrs. King's ghost first appeared in the garden, near a group of canna lilies. When Betty Kight cut down the flowers, hoping to dispel the spirit, Mrs. King started to appear inside the kitchen, then all over the house. The Kight children grew more and more frightened of the apparition. In 1973, the Kights decided to turn over the house to the ghost and build a new home nearby. Slowly the ghost of Mrs. King made its presence felt in the new house too. Though not as strong as in her own house, Mrs. King managed to fade in and out at various locations around the new house. Now, over twenty years later, the lonely ghost of Mrs. King is an accepted member of the Kight household.

(Eastman is fifty miles southeast of Macon on U.S. Highway 29. The Kight house is a private residence near Eastman in Dodge County.) **58**

EATONTON

PANOLA HALL The ghost of Sylvia, a young woman who once lived in the upstairs bedroom at Panola Hall, has haunted this plantation-style brick mansion since the 1870s. She appeared on numerous occasions to Dr. Benjamin Hunt and his wife, poetess Louise Reid Pruden, who wrote poems about their uninvited houseguest. The ghost also appeared to a male visitor to the Hunt residence in the early 1900s. During the 1920s, the shy ghost showed herself again to the town librarian, and later to a friend visiting Mrs. Hunt. The silent apparition has dark hair and wears a white, full-skirted dress. She has been seen in the second-floor hallway and bedroom, on the stairway, and staring out the living-room window.

(Eatonton is in north central Georgia near the Oconee National Forest, at the junction of U.S. Highway 441 and Highway 16. Panola Hall is a private residence outside Eatonton in Putnam County.) **223**

ROCK EAGLE EFFIGY This site has been considered sacred for six thousand years. Prehistoric shamans created a flying eagle out of white quartz stones on a plateau here. The giant bird has a wingspan of 130 feet and is thought to have been used in religious ceremonies. The eagle is symbolic of the shaman's journey to the spirit world. A tower has been built to view the entire effigy.

(The site is seven miles north of Eatonton off U.S. Highway 441. For information, contact the Rock Eagle State 4-H Club Center 350 Rock Eagle Rd., Eatonton, GA 31024. Phone: 706-485-2831. www.griffin.peachnet.edu/ ga/ga4hmain/RockEagle/effigy.html) **50, 53 (12/81), 122, 144**

ELBERTON

GEORGIA GUIDESTONES The construction of this modern Stonehenge was funded by an anonymous donor using the name R. C. Christian, which might be an acronym for Christian Rosencrantz, the nineteenth-century alchemist. The configuration of megalithic stones is said to be on top of an energy vortex. In older times, the hill was the site of ritualistic dancing, occult ceremonies, and witches' Sabbaths. The Cherokee Indians called it "the center of the world." During construction, workers at the site complained of hearing strange noises and feeling dizzy while placing the huge granite slabs. Four major, pyramid-shaped monoliths, each over nineteen feet tall and weighing twenty-eight tons, tower above the hill. At the center is a narrower slab, with another granite beam capping the top of the structure, which is aligned astronomically with the summer and winter solstices. On the major columns are inscribed Ten Commandment-like messages in twelve languages: 1) Maintain humanity under five hundred million, in balance with nature. 2) Guide reproduction wisely— improving diversity. 3) Unite humanity with a new language. 4) Rule passion, faith, and tradition with tempered wisdom. 5) Protect people with fair laws. 6) Let all nations rule internally, resolving disputes in a world court. 7) Avoid petty laws and useless officials. 8) Balance personal rights with social duties. 9) Prize truth and seek harmony with the infinite. 10) Be not a cancer on earth. Leave room for nature—leave room for nature.

(Elberton is a small town in northeast Georgia, thirty-two miles northeast of Athens on Highway 72. The Guidestones are on a grassy knoll along Highway 77, about seven miles north of Elberton. For further information, contact the Elberton Granite Association, P.O. Box 640, Elberton, GA 30635. Phone: 706-283-2551. www.elbertga. com/attractions/guidestones.html) **13, 58**

ETOWAH MOUNDS

ETOWAH MOUNDS STATE HISTORIC SITE This site was considered sacred by several ancient cultures and was inhabited for nearly one thousand years. The central temple mound is almost six stories high. The ceremonial plaza is paved with red clay. Two strange statues carved from marble have also been discovered at the site and are on display, although no one knows for what ceremonies they were used. See Mounds Complex, Macon, Georgia.

(Etowah Mounds is nineteen miles northwest of Atlanta off Highway 113/61 on Etowah Mounds Road, which is just south of Cartersville. For information, contact the Etowah Mounds State Historic Park, 813 Indian Mounds Road SW, Cartersville, GA 30120. Phone: 770-387-3747.) **144**

GREENSBORO

DUCARO HALL This mansion was built in 1837, and its ghost is thought to be one of the original residents. Untraceable footsteps are heard late at night, and a presence is felt in the upstairs halls.

(Greensboro is fifty-five miles east of Atlanta on I-20. Ducaro Hall is a private residence on Lick Skillet Road, not far from the Early Hill Inn in Greensboro.) **101, 168**

EARLY HILL INN Built by Joel Early in 1840, Early Hill Inn has acquired two ghostly occupants over the years. One is a man dressed in a frontiersmen outfit who likes to relax in a rocking chair on the front porch. The other is the wraith of a little girl who roams the upstairs bedroom and backyard. The child died from a broken neck when the chain on her tree swing broke, and she plummeted to the ground. But ever since Leonard Shockley turned the mansion into a bed-and-breakfast inn, the two ghosts of Early Hill have been no-shows.

(Early Hill is a three-floor, wood frame house with a balcony on the second floor. It is now a bed-and-breakfast inn about three miles from downtown. Early Hill Inn, Lick Skillet Road, Greensboro, GA 30642. Phone: 706-453-7876.) **101, 168**

JEKYLL ISLAND

JEKYLL ISLAND CLUB HOTEL A spacious apartment at this exclusive hunt club is haunted. Known as Spencer's Suite, the rooms are haunted by the ghost of Samuel Spencer, a president of the Southern Railroad Company. Guests report finding their coffee sipped and morning newspaper disturbed by the invisible presence. For years it was his daily ritual to drink a cup of coffee while scanning the paper, and old habits die hard. In 1909, while riding one of his own trains, he was killed instantly when it collided with another train he owned. The 134-room hotel was opened in 1887 as an exclusive resort for America's richest families. Today, it is owned by the Radisson hotel chain.

(Island is off the southern coast of Georgia. Take the Brunswick exit off I-95 and follow Highway 520 to the island. Island Club Hotel, 371 Riverview Dr., Jekyll Island, GA 31527. Phone: 912-635-2600. For reservations, call (800) 535-9547. www.jekyllclub.com) **73**

LEARY

LIONS CLUB This is the site of President Jimmy Carter's UFO sighting on January 6, 1969. At the time, he was governor of Georgia and about to give a speech at the Lion's Club. Carter and about twenty other witnesses observed a gigantic, glowing, oval object the size of the full moon pause in the sky and slowly change color from blue to red. The object varied in brightness and was estimated to be between three hundred and one thousand yards above the Lions Club. The crowd observed it for ten minutes, watching it move closer then back away and finally disappear into the night sky.

(Leary is in southwestern Georgia in Calhoun County, at the junction of Highways 62 and 37. Carter became president in 1977.) **57, 139**

MACON

MOUNDS COMPLEX When the first colonists arrived on the East Coast, they found a vast network of over one hundred thousand mysterious mounds in what is now several southeastern states. They attributed the work to the devil and stayed away, but today the earthworks are considered sacred sites. The site in Macon dates back many thousands of years. The area is dominated by a group of larger mounds surrounded by many hillocks. There are underground chambers that were used for secret ceremonies, and bones and artifacts have been found inside the mounds. See Etowah Mounds, Georgia.

(Macon is at the center of Georgia, at the intersection of I-75 and U.S. Highway 16. The Macon Mounds Complex is along the banks of the Ocmulgee River. A similar mound complex exists near Cartersville, along the banks of the Etowah River.) **57**

MARIETTA

DOBBINS AIR FORCE BASE A three-story wood building on this base is haunted by a young blond-haired woman and an elderly couple. Over twenty witnesses have encountered the ghosts or their manifestations. The building was built in the 1800s and used as a private home and officer's club for many years. General Sherman spared the building during the Civil War because it flew the British flag; the Englishman who lived there committed suicide in 1880.

(Marietta is just northwest of Atlanta. The, haunted building is now used by the Lockheed Corporation for corporate offices. It is located on the Dobbins Air Force Base, Marietta, GA 30060.) **135**

KOLB RIDGE COURT Residents of this housing development have reported the apparitions of Civil War soldiers walking through their homes. The land was the site of the Battle of Kolb Farm, a Civil War skirmish in which several soldiers died. According to homeowners Katherine and James Tatum, who moved to Kolb Ridge Court in 1986, the figure of a man wearing a hat and dark overcoat started appearing in the upstairs rooms. The sightings continue to this day, and the Tatums have traced a number of mischievous, unexplainable events to their ghost.

(The housing project was built on the former Kolb Creek Farm outside Marietta. The original Kolb Creek farmhouse is still standing.) **175**

SEWELL'S WOODS These woods became known as "the haunted hunting grounds" in the 1920s because of the unexplained disappearance of many hound dogs. Packs of dogs would take off on the scent of a possum or fox and never be seen again. Finally hunters discovered that their dogs were heading for an old family cemetery hidden under blackberry bushes on a secluded hilltop deep in the woods. Witnesses said the dogs converged on a certain grave, as if they had treed a possum, then were thrown through the air by some invisible force. All the dogs would take off running and never be seen again.

(The mysterious woods are located about fifteen miles from the town of Marietta, not far from the Etowah Mounds State Historic Site.) **223**

MILLEDGEVILLE

OLD WALKER HOUSE People in central Georgia used to say that Sam Walker was the wickedest man in the state. He was known for cheating local cotton farmers and being a leader in the Ku Klux Klan, and it was widely believed that he conspired with the Yankees during the Civil War to save his house from Sherman's troops. But he was cruelest to his own family. Rumors had it that he murdered his first wife. Then, when his only son, Josiah, became deathly ill, he refused to call a doctor, saying that the boy was lying in bed because he was plain lazy. One night Josiah came to the top of the stairs and pleaded for help, then collapsed and toppled down the stairs, dead. The child's ghost started appearing in the house soon afterward. Usually, the apparition materialized at the foot of his father's bed and just stared silently. Before long, the ghost was following Walker wherever he went, and the tortured man finally died of a stroke. But later residents said Josiah's ghost remained in the house. Sometimes light footsteps are heard at the top of the stairway, followed by a sickening thud on the landing below.

(Milledgeville is in Baldwin County in central Georgia, at the junction of U.S. Highway 441 and Highway 49. The two-story wooden house, a private residence, sits on the corner of Jefferson and McIntosh streets.) **226**

OGLETHORPE

COLONEL FISH'S HOUSE The ghost of Colonel George Fish started haunting this house in 1871, soon after he was found murdered. The former judge was gunned down outside the courthouse by two men with whom he had crossed paths. The colonel's tenacious ghost stayed with the house, even after it was moved to its new location in Americus. See Americus, Georgia.

(Oglethorpe is in Macon County at the junction of Highways 26 and 128. The courthouse used to be in the building now occupied by Taylor's Pharmacy. The house in Oglethorpe was on Randolph St.) **226**

OKEFENOKEE SWAMP

LOST ISLAND According to Creek Indian legend, in the middle of this huge and foreboding swamp there is an island populated by a race of dark-eyed women known as the "Daughters of the Sun." With a language musical in nature, the women were said to move about the island slowly and gracefully, with the countenance of angels. In the 1500s, Spanish explorers risked their lives to find the island paradise, but none succeeded. Later European settlers also searched the swamps, and tales of the angelic race, called the "Fatchaskia," grew. Many claimed to have sighted the strange women, and others entered the swamp and never returned. Today, hunters and fishermen tell of seeing the shimmering forms of beautiful women dashing through the twilight mists.

(The Okefenokee Swamp covers the extreme southeastern corner of Georgia. Highway 177 from Edith leads to the Stephen Foster State Park at the center of the swamp.) **55, 58**

OXFORD

ORNA VILLA The sounds of pacing footsteps, a squeaky rocker moving back and forth, and sudden crashing noises have plagued this elegant house for over a century. Some believe the sounds are caused by the spirit of Dr. Alexander Means, a distinguished scholar who bought the house in the 1830s. Dr. Means loved books and liked to sit in his rocking chair reading until the early morning hours. Others believe the sounds come from Tobe, one of the doctor's nine sons. A restless child with no patience for book learning. Tobe wanted to travel and learn by experience. He often quarreled with his father and would throw things around the room. He further vented his anger by pacing back and forth on the back porch. One night, he slammed the front door and rode off on his horse, never to be seen again. Many residents have reported strange sounds in the house. The Rheberg family, who owned the house in the 1940s, often thought there was someone on the back porch, when in fact no one was there. The current owners, Mr. and Mrs. John Watterson, hear odd sounds in the house. Sometimes doors slam shut for no reason, and hanging pictures and even their bird cage have flown off their hooks and crashed to the floor.

(Oxford is twenty miles east of Atlanta on I-20. Orna Villa is a private residence in Oxford. It is a two-story white house with four square columns across the front.) **226**

RABUN COUNTY

RABUN BALD MOUNTAIN Indian legends say that fire-breathing demon people inhabit this mountain.

Strange sounds that locals call the "Music of the Bald" have been heard here for over a century. Sometimes the music echoes like a cannon; other times it sounds like babies crying. Hikers and campers in the area have reported encountering the presence of "something evil and strange."

(Rabun County is in northeastern Georgia. The mountain is near Highway 441. It is the highest peak in the southern Appalachia Range.) **57**

ST. CATHERINES ISLAND

LEBANON Spanish friars came to this sea island off Georgia in the 1570s and quickly converted the local Indians to Catholicism. The ghostly antiphonal chanting of the Franciscan friars and their Guale Indian converts has been heard near the Lebanon marshes.

(St. Catherines Island is thirty miles south of Savannah, off South Newport. Lebanon is a small settlement near the marshes on the South Island.) **226**

ST. SIMONS ISLAND

CHRIST CHURCH CEMETERY The flickering candlelight over the grave of an island resident who died many years ago is not real. During her lifetime, the woman was intensely afraid of the dark and was known to hoard candles and have one burning constantly. When the woman died of blood poisoning from an infected wound, her husband lit a candle on top of her grave every night. In the years since he died and was buried next to his wife, hundreds of people have reported seeing a candle flame over the woman's grave.

(St. Simons Island is fifty-five miles south of Savannah. Take the Brunswick toll bridge, thirty miles north of the Florida border on I-95. The cemetery is located in Frederica.) **226**

DUNBAR CREEK The chanting of a group of African Ibo tribesmen can still be heard at the mouth of this creek. When unloaded from a ship here, they ceremoniously marched into the water and drowned, rather than live their lives as slaves.

(The creek is near Sea Island on the southeast coast of St. Simons Island.) **58, 226**

FORT ST. SIMONS The ruins of this old fort are haunted by a polyglot ghost, who is heard speaking in the Cherokee, German, Spanish, and Latin languages.

He is Dr. Christian Priber, who proclaimed himself prime minister of the Republic of Paradise and demanded that all colonists leave America. Priber arrived on the East Coast in 1736 and promptly joined a tribe of Cherokee Indians. He was arrested for insurgency in 1743 and taken to St. Simons, where he died many years later.

(The Barracks Prison was part of Fort St. Simons. The ruins are located at the Fort Frederica National Monument at 286 C St., St. Simons Island, GA 31522. Phone: 912-638-3639. www.nps.gov/fofr) **171**

KELVIN GROVE PLANTATION The spirit of the former owner of this cotton plantation walks the grounds searching for his murderer. A phenomenon called "Flora de Cookpot," the delicious odors from the stove of a long-dead chef, can also be detected here.

(The plantation is on the southwestern section of St. Simons Island.) **226**

MARY DE WANDA This ghost, also known as Mary the Wanderer, roams the coastal roads of St. Simons Island. She is said to be searching for her drowned husband.

(Mary de Wanda has been sighted on the outlying County Roads at the south end of the island and on the primitive coastal roads that circle its perimeter.) **226**

ST. SIMONS LIGHTHOUSE The ghost of a former lightkeeper haunts his old workplace. His heavy footsteps are heard on the spiral stairway that leads up to the beacon chamber. The footsteps are so loud they can sometimes be heard from the neighboring cottages.

(The white lighthouse tower has an iron walkway that rings the top of the tower. It is located on the eastern tip of the island. Phone: 912-638-4666. www.schoonerman.com/stsim.htm) **226**

SAVANNAH

BONAVENTURE CEMETERY This moss-covered cemetery was once the site of one of Savannah's most beautiful estates. Built entirely of imported English brick by Colonel Mulryne in the 1750s, the house called Bonaventure was landscaped with beautiful hanging terraces and surrounded by hundreds of Live Oaks. The colonel's daughter Mary married Josiah Tattnall, and they soon had two sons, John and Josiah Junior. The Mulrynes and Tattnalls were loyal to King

George III and returned to England when the Revolutionary War began, but Josiah Junior returned to Georgia to fight with the Colonies. He became very prominent in the new state of Georgia and would eventually be elected governor. Years later, during a lavish dinner party at Bonaventure, with many socially elite guests in attendance, the old mansion caught fire. Josiah Junior insisted his guests finish dinner and had his servants take the massive dining table into the yard. As the guests watched the great house burn out of control, they politely reminisced about Bonaventure's proud history. Perhaps that timeless moment of poise and sadness lives on today. Cemetery visitors sometimes complain to caretakers about the clatter of tableware and the laughter from a nearby dinner party, when there is in fact no one around.

(Savannah is on the Atlantic coast of Georgia. The cemetery edges the Wilmington River. Take Bonaventure Road from Savannah to the cemetery at 330 Bonaventure Rd. Phone: 912-651-6843. For information on the area, contact the Savannah Area Visitors Bureau, 101 East Bay St., Savannah, GA 31402. Phone: 877-SAVANNAH.) **15, 164, 171, 226**

ELBA ISLAND A striking bronze statue was erected on a Savannah plaza in memory of the city's favorite ghost. For forty-four years, Florence Martus greeted every ship arriving in Savannah Harbor by flapping her apron or waving a lantern from the front lawn of her home near the lighthouse on this island. Florence had made a solemn vow to her fiancé that she would greet every ship until he returned to her. Unfortunately he never came home again. The Waving Girl of Savannah, "the Sweetheart of Mankind," lived on the island with her brother, the lighthouse keeper from 1887 to 1931. She is said to appear there still, waving her apron, waiting patiently for her lover's return. Many ships still sound a salute to her memory upon entering the harbor.

(Elba Island and the harbor lighthouse are 7.5 miles south of Savannah in Savannah Harbor. In 1971, a statue was erected to Florence Martus on River Street. For information, contact the Savannah Visitor Center, 301 Martin Luther King Jr. Blvd. Savannah, GA 31401. Phone: 912-944-0460.) **49, 159**

HAMPTON-LILLIBRIDGE HOUSE Ghostly manifestations began when this house was moved a few blocks in 1963. Construction workers reported the sounds of heavy footsteps when there was no one walk-

This statue was raised in memory of Florence Martus, the Waving Girl of Savannah, who once greeted ships in Savannah Harbor hoping for her lost fiancé's return. Her apparition was seen there after her death. See Elba Island, Savannah, Georgia (CONVENTIONS AND VISITORS BUREAU)

ing around. The owner felt a disturbing presence in the bedrooms and sometimes heard music coming from nowhere. Neighbors saw the ghost of a tall, dark-haired man wearing a white shirt and bow tie standing in front of a third-floor window. The five-story wooden house was built in 1796, and no one has been able to determine the identity of the ghost jarred loose during the move.

(The house, a private residence, is also known as the James Arthur Williams House. It used to sit at 312 Bryan St., but is now located at 507 East St. Julian St., Savannah, GA 31401. At the end of December, the city conducts a Ghostly Christmas Spectacular, which tells the history of Savannah's ghosts. For information, call 912-233-9800.) **90, 101, 102, 198 (11–93)**

HASLAM HOUSE The ghost of a tall man in a cloak emerges and disappears back into corners in the rooms of this Italianate town house built in 1872. The dark spirit is also blamed for poltergeist activity in the kitchen and dining room.

(The inn is adjacent to Troup Square. Haslam House, 417 East Charlton St., Savannah, GA 31401. Phone: 912-233-6380.) **72**

JULIETTE GORDON LOW GIRL SCOUT CENTER On Halloween 1860, Juliette Gordon Low, the founder of the Girl Scouts of America, was born here, and her parents still haunt the house. Her father Willie commissioned a general in the Spanish American War, died in Savannah in 1912. On February 22, 1917, her mother Ellie died in the front bedroom. At the moment of Ellie's death, witnesses saw the ghost of General Gordon emerge from his former bedroom and walk down the front stairs and out the front door. Ellie Gordon's ghost has been reported upstairs, in the north parlor, and at the dining-room table.

(The pink stucco building is downtown on the corner of Bull Street and Oglethorpe Street at 142 Bull St. Savannah, GA 31405. Phone: 912-233-4501.) **49**

OLDE PINK HOUSE RESTAURANT AND TAVERN James Habersham only haunts his former home from October to March. What he does the remainder of the year is not known. Built in 1771, the pink stone building is visited regularly by Habersham's ghost during the autumn and winter months. Nearly all of the employees of the restaurant that now occupies his home have encountered his ghost. When the place is empty he has been known to burn candles.

(The Pink House Restaurant is located in Reynolds Square at 23 Abercom St. Savannah, GA 31401. Phone: 912-232-4286.) **159**

PIRATE'S HOUSE RESTAURANT Although this house was once the home of famous pirate Jean Laffite, it is the ghost of another notorious pirate known as Captain Flint, who haunts the place. It is said that as he lay on his deathbed, Flint kept calling to his first mate, Darby McGraw, to bring him more rum. Today, his cries are still heard by visitors to the restaurant that now occupies the house. His scar-faced phantom has also been seen roaming in the basement tunnel. The tunnel, big enough to drive a bus through, was discovered during renovations. It leads to the river and proba-

bly served as an escape route for pirates trying to make it back to the sea.

(Pirate's House is at the corner of East Broad and Bay Streets. The address is 20 East Broad St., Savannah, GA 31401. Phone: 912-233-5757. www.thepirateshouse.com) **101, 159, 164, 198 (11–93)**

17-HUNDRED-90 INN The ghost of a girl who leaped to her death from the top floor haunts this charming old building. Ann Powell committed suicide at the turn of the century. It is said that she fell hopelessly in love with a German sailor who did not return her affections. Her ghost has even been spotted at the home of the inn's owner, Chris Jurgenson.

(The restaurant and fourteen-room inn are in the Historic District, near the corner of Lincoln St. and Bay St. 17-Hundred-90 Inn, 307 East President Street, Savannah, GA 31401. Phone: 912-236-7122. For reservations, call 800-487-1790.) **159**

TELFAIR ARTS MUSEUM This unique building, which features curved walls and doors, was constructed as a "little palace" by the famous nineteenth-century architect William Jay. Now a museum, it is also a haunted house. Doors open by themselves, invisible footsteps echo through the hallways, and the sound of a harp playing is heard. Sometimes the unexplained paranormal disturbances are so powerful they set off the security alarms.

(Telfair Arts Museum, 121 Barnard St., Savannah, GA 31412. Phone: 912-232-1177. www.telfair.org) **198 (11–93)**

STATESBORO

HOLLINGSWORTH HOUSE Members of the Stothard Hollingsworth family started seeing the ghost of a woman with long hair in the early 1970s. The apparition, wearing a white nineteenth-century gown, appears most often in the living room or the master bedroom of the house, which was not built until the 1930s. The identity of the seemingly misplaced spirit remains a mystery.

(This house is now a private residence at 9 Cetterower St., Statesboro, GA 30458.) **135**

SURRENCY

SURRENCY TERROR A ghost put this town on the map. In 1872, Mrs. Welthier Surrency told her two boys to sit and talk with a visiting minister in the parlor of their large home. But the minister cut his visit short when a heavy, blazing log flew out of the fireplace and across the room. Later, the Surrency's daughter was pelted with a shower of hot bricks as she walked up the front steps. Once, Mrs. Surrency was sewing in the parlor when her stitching was jerked from her hands and started circling the room. Her thimble, scissors, and spools of thread joined the amazing aerial procession. Eventually the ghost broke every piece of glass and pottery in the house. The family had to live on cheese and crackers, because the poltergeist would not allow food to be prepared in the kitchen. Pots turned over and spilled their contents onto the stove. Pans of biscuits floated out of the oven and through the back door. The case became famous, and thousands of people come to the Surrency house to see the moving furniture, broken dishes, and missing windowpanes. Sometimes, the ghost hurled logs or irons at the visitors. The Surrency house became so popular that the railroads ran special excursion trains from Macon, Atlanta, and Brunswick. The strange haunting continued for five years, with most of the activity centering around the daughter Clementine. When the Surrency family moved to a small house on a plantation five miles from their mansion, the ghost followed them and the terrifying events started all over again. The beleaguered family moved back to town and lived with the poltergeist until the summer of 1877, when it suddenly stopped tormenting them. But the house was still considered to be possessed of evil and was burned down in 1925.

(The town is about 125 miles from Macon, near Jesup on Highway 82. A pecan orchard grows along the tracks where the Surrency Mansion once stood. Allen and Welthier Surrency are buried in the Overstreet Cemetery, three miles out of town on Highway 121.) **57, 172, 223**

TALBOT COUNTY

O'NEIL'S DISTRICT Georgia's only reported werewolf is said to be buried in this small town. At one time a two-hundred-dollar reward was offered for the werewolf, which was observed attacking sheep and other animals. The monster never took any flesh for food; it seemed to kill only for the pure joy of killing. Locals suspected a strange-acting spinster, a member of the Burton family, of being the werewolf. When she went to Europe for several months the killings stopped. When she returned they started up again. When hunters wounded the werewolf, Burton wore bandages at the same locations on her body. Finally, when they shot off the left foot of werewolf using silver bullets, old Miss Burton lost her left hand and wrist "in an accident." That was when the strange attacks finally stopped.

(Talbot County is between Macon and Columbus in west-central Georgia. O'Neil's District is five miles off U.S. Highway 19.) **49**

TIFTON

OMEGA ROAD OVERPASS A student at Abraham Baldwin Agricultural College was returning home to Florida one weekend when she lost control of her car and died in a car wreck under this overpass. The sounds of her squealing tires, in varying degrees of loudness and pitch, are reported by travelers here.

(Tifton is in south-central Georgia at the junction of I-75 and U.S. Highway 82. The Omega Road Overpass is on I-75, about five miles south of Tifton. The sounds have been reported by drivers going south toward Valdosta.) **121**

TUCKER

CHEROKEE HOUSE The original Cherokee House was built of chestnut logs in the early 1800s by Cherokee Indians, who used it as a shelter for their sick. White settlers moved into the structure in 1854. An addition was made in 1910, and another in the late 1940s. When remodeling started in 1960, the gray apparition of a man began appearing to the occupants. The ghost was most often seen crossing the front porch, in the bedrooms, or in the 1910 section of the house. In 1968, a hand materialized alongside the bed of one of the owners.

(Tucker is a northeast suburb of Atlanta, on Highway 29. The building is a private residence just outside Tucker. It is located four miles from the Stone Mountain Park and one mile off the High Tower Trail.) **90, 101**

WASHINGTON

ABRAM SIMON'S TAVERN The ghostly sounds of a galloping horse and rider are heard on the dirt roads near the site of this old tavern: It is the spirit of Captain Abram Simon on his steed Babylon, trying to outrun the devil. Captain Simon's tavern was always a high-energy place with plenty of drink, women, and song. He even had a racetrack built so his patrons could wager on horses. But one day a circuit-riding preacher told him that he had better close down his tavern and repent, or the devil would catch up with him no matter how fast he rode. The preacher's words troubled Abram, and he became obsessed with outrunning the devil. He rode his horse at breakneck speeds around the racetrack in the woods here. He chose the place he wanted to be buried, on a knoll with a good view of the surrounding area. He built a thick stone wall around the grave site and requested to be buried standing up with a musket at his side—"so I can shoot the devil," he said. When he died in 1824, his instructions were followed to the letter.

(Washington is in northeast Georgia, thirty-seven miles southeast of Athens on U.S. Highway 78. The ruins of the tavern are not far from the old Smyrna Church on a dirt road. The iron gate and stone wall around Simon's tombstone are behind the tavern site.) **226**

HAWAII

HAWAII ISLAND

CITY OF REFUGE NATIONAL PARK Huna, the old Hawaiian religion, was very hard on sinners. Anyone breaking the laws, called *kapu*, was put to death. However, if the sinner could reach a temple before being killed, he could work off his sins there. This park is called Pu'uhonua O Honaunau or "City of Refuge," because the largest of Huna temples was here. It is said that the ghosts of some poor souls are still trying to reach the gates of the sanctuary. The kapu laws were abolished in 1819.

There is also a heiau, a stone temple built to house the bones of deceased leaders, at this site known as Hale O Keawe, which contains the bones of at least twenty-three island chiefs. The Hawaiians believed the mana, or life force, of a person remained in his bones after death, and they built heiaus to house the bones, to save the mana. It was not uncommon to try to steal the mana from heiaus, so the greatest rulers had their bones hid in jungle caves so their power would not be misused. Over the years, many ancient heiaus became known as haunted sites.

(The City of Refuge National Historic Park is located off Highway 11 between the towns of Honaunau and Hookena on the southwestern coast of Hawaii. Pu'uhonua National Historic Park, Route 160 and Hale O Keawe Rd., Honaunau, HI 96726. Phone: 808-328-2326. www.nps.gov/puho. For general information on Hawaii, contact the Hawaii Visitor's Bureau, 2270 Kalakaua Ave., Honolulu, HI 96815. Phone: 808-923-1811.) **9, 15, 197, 200**

KAENA POINT This sacred outcropping is considered a jumping-off point into an area outside of time. It is a gateway to Po, the eternal dwelling place of the gods, where land, sea, and sky are merged into one fabric of space and time. It is a combination of heaven and hell, known and unknown, light and darkness. At Kaena Point and near the heiau at Pokai Bay, witnesses have reported hearing thousands of interdimensional voices.

(Kaena Point is near Waianae, on the western coast of Hawaii. Another jumping-off spot is at South Point.) **197**

KONA Visitors touring the Hulihee Palace here have reported seeing the apparition of a little Hawaiian boy. Built out of lava rock and coral in 1838, Hulihee was used as a vacation retreat by Hawaiian kings and their families. King Kalakaua's family was the last royalty to use the facility (see Everett, Washington).

(The city of Kona is on Kailua Bay on the west coast of Hawaii, at the junction of Highway 19 and Highway 190. The Hulihee Palace State Monument is south of town on the shore.) **66 (2/94)**

MAUNA LOA VOLCANO The Kilauea Crater on the eastern slope of this 13,680-foot-tall mountain is home to the Huna volcano goddess Madame Pele. Rumblings within the volcanoes on the islands are said to drive her out to warn people of impending eruptions. Her ghost appears along forest roads or in public places (see Hilton Hotel, Honolulu, Hawaii). Although her age varies, she is always seen wearing a red muumuu and is usually accompanied by a small white dog. She has been reported by natives and visitors for over two centuries. Her home was originally the island of Kauai, but she moved to the island of Hawaii when Mauna Loa erupted to form the Kilauea Crater. (See Lihue, Kauai Island, Hawaii.) Two ruined heiau platforms, one at Uwekahuna and the other on Waldron Ledge, are said to contain spiritual imprints dating back to the times when human sacrifices were made to Pele. It is said that Pele spares Volcano House at the rim of Mauna Loa only because the owner regularly pours gin into the crater to keep her happy. Hawaiians kneel in reverence to the goddess and sometimes lay chickens on the rim of Kilauea to seek her favor. Park rangers, tourists, newspaper reporters, and even scientists studying the volcano have reported encountering Pele's ghostly figure. Her actual home, called Halemáumáu, is a 280-foot-deep pit within the crater. Incidentally, all the volcanic rock on the islands is considered possessed by kupua spirits, which are demigods inhabiting specific locations. There are numerous tales of bad luck befalling anyone trying to take pieces home for souvenirs. It is also forbidden to eat the sacred ohelo berry, which grows on the island.

(Follow Highway 11 into the park and on to Crater Rim Road. The Kilauea Crater is at 4,090 feet elevation. Uwekahuna, the "place of priestly weeping," is located on Uwekahuna Bluff where the observatory now stands. Waldron Ledge is the high wall above Byron Ledge. For information, contact the Hawaii Volcanoes Visitor Center, P.O. Box 52, Hawaii National Park, HI 96718. Phone: 808-967-7311. Call the Eruption Update Line at 808-985-6000 to check on Pele's current mood. www.nps.gov/havo) **5, 9, 188, 197, 200**

PU'UKOHOLA HEIAU Pu'ukohola means "Hill of the Whale," and this sacred site is said to receive its spiritual power from a natural spring at the base of the hill. The prophet Kapoukahi told chieftain Kamehameh that if he wanted to conquer all the islands of Hawaii, he must build a temple to honor Ku, the god of war. The temple was completed in 1791, and the prescribed ceremonies and human sacrifices were performed. Within three years, Kamehameh had conquered Maui, Lanai,

and Molokai. In 1795, he took Oahu. By 1820, Kauai and Hawaii had joined the empire.

(Pu'ukohola Heiau is off Highway 270 overlooking Kawaihae Bay at the northwest tip of Hawaii. The temple is in poor condition, and it is requested that tourists not visit the site. However, its power can be appreciated by parking at Spencer Beach or the information center and walking to the base of the Hill of the Whale. Pu'ukohola National Historic Site, P.O. Box 44340, Kawaihae, HI 96743. Phone: 808-882-7218. www.nps.gov/puhe)

HONOLULU

ALAKEA STREET For nearly a century, Hawaiians have considered this area haunted by Wai-lua, or the Night Marchers, ghosts that come out at night to take over the streets and play games. The sporting specters have terrified generations of natives here, but few *haole,* or Caucasians, have witnessed the phenomenon.

(Honolulu is on the southern coast of Oahu. The Wailua are said to gather nightly on the corner of Alakea Street and Merchant Street in downtown Honolulu.) **15, 175, 188**

FORT STREET The heads of human sacrifices decorated a famous Huna temple here. Called Pakaka, it was the most important of over a hundred heiaus that have been discovered on the island of Oahu. The heiaus are stone platforms used for worship and ceremonies by ancient Kahuna priests. A school for priests was located in Pakaka, and their spirits are said to assemble there still.

(The temple stood on the west side of Fort Street.) **15**

HILTON HOTEL The ghost of a beautiful woman in a red dress has been seen wandering the halls here. In 1959, an employee saw her vanish before his eyes as he was escorting her to a room. Some say she is the ghost of a woman murdered in a tower room; others say she is none other than Madame Pele herself. See Mauna Loa Volcano, Hawaii Island, Hawaii.

(The hotel is at 2005 Kalia Rd., Honolulu, HI 96815. Phone: 808-949-4321.) **188**

HOTEL STREET The ghosts of residents of an ancient Hawaiian village go searching for their former homes among the offices and buildings that now populate the area. The village of Kou existed where the business district is now, and the heart of the village was on Hotel Street.

(The Kou chief's lodge was between Alakea St. and Nuuanu Ave. on Hotel St. Specters of the Kouans have been seen in the buildings at the corner of Nuuanu Ave. and King St. Alakea Street, Merchant St., and Nuuanu Ave. all branch off north King St., which runs north and south through downtown.) **15**

IOLANI PALACE On summer nights, the glowing ghost of a young native girl wearing a white dress is seen near the fountain here. See Punchbowl Hill, Oahu, Hawaii.

(The palace is on King St. in central Honolulu. Phone: 808-522-0832. www.iolanipalace.org) **15**.

KEWALO Hundreds of lower-class natives known as Kauwa were put to death here. They were forced into the sea, where they drowned. The ceremony was called *ke-kai-he-hee*, or "sliding the servants under the waves of the sea." Whether the bizarre ritual was intended for sacrifice or punishment is not known. The ghosts of the Kauwa are said to march out of the ocean late at night, which is why native Hawaiians avoid the harbor after dark.

(Kewalo is an outcropping near the inlet to Honolulu Harbor, across from Sand Island.) **15**

STATE CAPITOL BUILDING The ghost of Queen Liluokalani haunts the legislative heart of Hawaii. Her ghost, carrying leis, has been reported on the stairway in front of the building. A statue of her likeness was erected on the building's west side.

(The State Capitol Building is on King St. in central Honolulu. For information, call 800-468-4644.) **15**

KAHO'OLAWE ISLAND

SACRED SHRINES Kaho'olawe Island is sacred to Hawaiian natives. Their ancestors held magic ceremonies at the site and built shrines to their gods. Unfortunately, the U.S. Navy now uses the island for bombing practice, although Hawaiians are allowed on the property to rebuild the battered shrines.

(Kaho'olawe is off the southwest coast of Maui. Trips to the island are allowed only on special days. Permission must be obtained from the U.S. Naval Operations Center in Honolulu. Phone: 808-471-7110.) **200**

KAUAI ISLAND

LIHUE The area around this modern, commercialized city is considered sacred to native Hawaiians. There are many temples along the Wailua River. Another spot that has been sacred to islanders for centuries is an intriguing rock formation now called Kalalau Cathedral. Kauai Island was the first home of the goddess Pele, who later moved to Oahu, then Molokai, then Maui, and finally Hawaii. She seems to follow the earth's magma as it bubbles up from the ocean floor to form the Hawaiian archipelago.

(Kauai is the northernmost island in the chain. Lihue is on the southeast coast, off Highway 56. The Wailua River State Park is three miles northeast of Lihue. For information about Kauai, contact the Hui Ho'okipa, 4505 Kauai Str., Suite 16, New Pacific House, Kauai, HI 96746. Phone: 808-821-2267. For a recording of events on the island, call 800-262-1400.) **9, 53 (7/89)**

WAIMEA A powerful vortex of mysterious energy is said to exist around the Waimea Canyon Falls. The entire Waimea River is said to be spiritually charged, and the heavens certainly do favor the area. The source of the river, on the northern slope of Kawaikini Mountain, is the wettest spot on earth. To take advantage of all the water, the industrious "Little People" are said to have built the Menehune Ditch and the Menehune Fishpond on the island. The Little People are said to be a race of dwarves responsible for inexplicable geological formations throughout the western hemisphere.

A more traditional ghost, that of a seven-foot-tall headless man is said to haunt the Waimea Firehouse.

(The city of Waimea is at the junction of Highway 50 and Highway 550 on the southwest coast. The Menehune Ditch is just off Menehune Rd., outside Waimea. The Menehune Fishpond can be viewed from Niumalu Bluff, off Highway 56, on the northeast coast.) **9, 102**

LANAI ISLAND

TOMB OF PUUPEHE The Tomb of Puupehe is a sea cave in a giant slab of lava rock here. Puupehe, the daughter of a Maui chieftain, was in love with Makakehau, a chief of Lanai, but before they could be married she was swept into the sea cave during a squall and drowned. When the devastated Makakehau found her body, he leaped to his death from the top of the jagged rock. The imprint of their love is still strong at this site.

(Lanai Island is due west of Maui and south of Molokai. Lanai City is at the center of the island on Highway 440. The Tomb of Puupehe faces the Auau Channel on the east side of the island.) **9**

MAUI ISLAND

HALEAKALA NATIONAL PARK The Haleakala volcano crater is considered sacred by Kahuna priests. The name means "House of the Sun." It is where the god Maui captured the sun and brought it to earth. Also in the park, Hosmer's Grove is known for its life-giving energy, and the "Specter of the Brocken" is sometimes visible from Leleiwi Overlook. The effect occurs when the late afternoon sun projects the shadowy images of visitors on low-lying clouds, often surrounded by a spectacular rainbow. There are ancient burial sites still hidden in the park, but bad luck awaits anyone who disturbs them.

(Take Highway 37 south to Highway 377/378, which leads into the park. Follow the Haleakala Mountain Road to the park headquarters, which is at 9,745 feet elevation. The Leleiwi Overlook is six miles further up the mountain. For information, contact the Haleakala National Park, P.O. Box 369, Makawao, Maui, HI 96768. Phone: 808-572-4400. www.nps.gov/hale) **99, 144**

KULA O KA MAOMAO Many people have experienced strange ghostly images on the Kula o Ka Maomao isthmus. According to legend, it is the "plain of spirits and mirages."

(Kula o La Maomao is the isthmus that joins the east and west portions of Maui Island. Highway 380 traverses the isthmus between Maalaea and Puunene.) **102**

MOLOKAI ISLAND

HALAWA VALLEY The abandoned stone ruins that lie along a trail through the center of this valley are considered sacred. The ruins are of the Iliiliopae Temple, and are said to be frequented by the poison-war goddess Kalaipahoa, a powerful and fiercely independent deity whose story is thought to be told at the petroglyphs of Kawela.

(Molokai is located between Oahu and Maui. The Halawa Valley extends inland from Cape Halawa on the eastern tip of the island.) **9**

KAUNAKAKAI The fish ponds at the sacred coconut grove here are said to be charged with the power of Moaalii, the Molokain shark god. According to researcher Bernyce Barlow, every one of the sacred sites on this island is charged with its own powerful spirit of place.

(The city of Kaunakakai is located on Highway 450 on the south-central coast of Molokai.) **9**

MAUNALOA The ghosts of Hawaiian warriors killed in fierce battles here are seen on the plains east of this town. Scores of misty apparitions have been reported here in the last fifty years.

(Maunaloa is near Leau Point in western Molokai at the western terminus of Highway 460.) **102**

OAHU ISLAND

KAAAWA Hidden burial caves in the cliffs above this site are said to contain the spirits of Kahuna priests. Hawaiians believed a person's spirit, or *unihipili*, resided in his bones. They were careful to hide burial locations and sometimes assigned a person, known as a *kahu*, to guard the grave. The kahu could use the mana residing in bones for good or evil purposes, and sometimes exorcism rituals had to be performed to dispel the unihipili spirits. Kaaawa is said to be home to the bones and spirit of Kamehameha the Great, a powerful and revered Hawaiian king. His son King Liholiho abolished the old kapu laws and brought Hawaii into the modern world.

(Kaaawa is on the northeast shore of Oahu, on Highway 83 at Puumahie Point. The burial caves are known as Pohukaina.) **205**

KAIWAINUI MARSH This lush, sacred site is said to be a reservoir of magic power. It is home to Haumea, the earth goddess. Much of the area can be seen from the volcanic-stone Heiau Platform behind the YMCA building. The heiau, which are scattered throughout the island, are said to have been built by the Menehune elves. Krider's Rock is thought to be the focal point of Haumea's magical energy. The marsh is guarded by the Mo'o, the daughters of Haumea, who can turn into lizards.

(The marsh is on the north island, near Kailua.

Krider's Rock is a large boulder at the center of Kaiwainui Marsh.) **9, 53 (7/89), 200**

KUHIO BEACH Four large boulders on this popular beach are known for possessing great spiritual power. Long ago, four mysterious wizards appeared on the island and performed many miracles and healings. Their names were Kapaemahu, Kahaloa, Kapuni, and Kinohi. Before they left Oahu, they requested that four large stones be brought to the beach, and each of them transferred his powers into a rock. The wizard stones were worshipped for hundreds of years but were hidden away when white men came to the island. Finally, in 1958 they were rediscovered and eventually placed back on the beach for all to share in their power.

(Kuhio Beach is at Waikiki. Take Kalakaua Avenue to the beach. It is directly across from Hyatt Hotel, which is at 2424 Kalakaua Ave. The stones are sitting next to the police station on the beach. A plaque on one of the stones tells their history.) **99**

MOUNT TANTALUS The ghost of Madame Pele made an appearance two days before the eruption of Mauna Loa that destroyed the village of Kapoho. She appeared as a young, beautiful woman in a red muumuu. She was seen walking with a white dog along the edge of the road here.

(Madame Pele has been seen walking along the side of the Tantalus Mountain Rod.) **5**

NUUANU VALLEY A group of gnomes known as the E'epa are said to populate this lush valley. This tribe of Little People are active only at night, when they complete unbelievable tasks before daybreak. They are also blamed for gremlin activity at E'epa gathering sites now given over to more modern activities.

(The valley is inland from Honolulu, southwest of the Nuuanu Pali Pass. Follow Highway 61 northeast from Honolulu into the valley. The two-mile-long Puu Ohia Trail starts from Tantalus Drive. According to legend, the original home of the E'epa was where the Oahu Country Club now stands.) **15**

PUNCHBOWL HILL Tiny, mischievous dwarfs of the early morning hours, called Menehunes, have been reported on the beaches and in the secluded valleys near here. The spectral night marchers are seen bathed in a dim, unearthly light while parading on the beaches of Oahu. Their home is said to be in a volcanic crater at the top of this hill. The Menehunes are industrious workers who once built several guest houses for a queen "like the motion of an eye." Some theorists postulate that the Menehunes were an actual race of advanced people who populated the islands before the first Hawaiians came.

(Punchbowl Hill is now the site of the National Memorial Cemetery of the Pacific, where over twenty thousand servicemen are buried. The cemetery is located near the center of Honolulu, northeast of the junction of Highway H1 and Highway 61. The three Menehune valleys are visible from the Puu Ohia Trail, off Tantalus Dr. at the top of Round Top Hill. Follow Ward Avenue, which begins at Ala Moana Blvd. in Honolulu, to Round Top Hill. The hill is just above Honolulu in the Manoa Valley.) **15, 53 (7/89), 85, 205**

IDAHO

BAKER CREEK

WOOD RIVER CAMP The ghost of a big immigrant miner, Russian John, started haunting this creek bed in the 1920s. His apparition steps from behind bushes and has frightened several campers.

(Baker Creek is about six miles south of the Wood River in central Idaho. There is a ranger station named after Russian John there. The primitive campsite is just below the ranger station on the banks of Wood River.) **49**

BAYHORSE

YANKEE FORK Bulgarian Monk was named for his clothing, not his religious proclivities. He wore hooded burlap robes tied at the waist with rope. The young recluse was rarely seen, except when he chased adventurous boys away from his cabin. It was a sport he is said to have enjoyed, as did the children. However, one day while chasing them, he slipped off a boulder, fell into the Salmon River, and drowned. In the early 1900s, his ghost was reported chasing young boys throughout the Sawtooth Range.

(Bayhorse is a tiny settlement in the Payette National Forest in central Idaho. The Bulgarian Monk has been seen at Yankee Fork on the Salmon River, near Bayhorse. He was also reported near an old mining camp called Bonanza, twenty-five miles away, and in the Five Points area.) **49**

BOISE

LOON CREEK The ghost of Manuel Sato haunted the deserted hills along this creek for years after his death in 1870. He was cooking breakfast when a robber sneaked up to his campsite and knifed him to death. The outlaw had recently robbed a bank and is said to have buried his plunder nearby. Soldiers from Fort Boise, hunting for the lost loot, encountered the ghost of Manuel Sato, who seemed to be directing a pack-string of invisible mules.

(Boise is in southwestern Idaho on I-84. Manuel's ghost haunted the gulches of the Boise Basin, just north of the city.) **49**

CHESTERFIELD

BIGFOOT SIGHTING An eight-foot-tall, apelike creature harassed a party of skaters here in 1902. The Bigfoot wielded a club and chased the group for some distance. Its four-toed footprints measured twenty-two inches long and seven inches wide.

(Chesterfield is a small town near Arco in Butte County, which is in east-central Idaho.) **139**

COEUR D'ALENE

LAKE CITY HIGH SCHOOL This high school is haunted by an unidentified apparition that paces back and forth behind the last row of seats in the auditorium. He is most likely to appear just before the lights are turned off before a play begins. He is also seen after a production during cleanup or just before the cast leaves for the night. The strange presence is blamed for scattering items and opening doors in the backstage and storage areas.

(Lake City High School, 406 North 10th St., Couer d'Alene, ID 83814. Phone: 208-765-4327.) **72**

LAKE COEUR D'ALENE What the Indians called "water mysteries" are said to inhabit this lake. Unexplainable noises and the figure of a fish-woman have been reported near a large pointed rock here. A mysterious wind sometimes churns up the lake, and a huge horned creature is said to lift boats out of the water.

(The lake is in northern Idaho near the junction of I-90 and U.S. Highway 95. The fish-woman was seen near a large rock off Conklin Park. A tree near Harrison was used to hang offerings to the water mysteries. The horned creature, sometimes called the water buffalo, was said to have roamed the area near the mouth of the Coeur d'Alene River.) **33**

CRATERS OF THE MOON

CRATERS OF THE MOON NATIONAL MONUMENT According to Shoshoni and Bannock legends, a race of warrior Indians came into this valley from the north. They lived in stone huts and pushed the native tribes from the streams and hunting areas. A great Shoshoni medicine man is said to have brought the fury of the earth upon the intruders and wiped them from the face of the valley. Evidence has been discovered that an ancient village here was destroyed by a volcanic eruption. Modern Indians considered the present Craters of the Moon area to be possessed by the devil, and avoided it.

(The lava beds of the buried tribe are just southwest of the Craters of the Moon, off Highway 26 in central Blaine County. For information, contact Craters of the Moon National Monument, P.O. Box 29, Arco, ID 83213. Phone: 208-527-3257. www.nps.gov/crmo) **13, 33**

EMMETT

EMMETT MIDDLE SCHOOL A deceased music teacher still returns to his former school. The man has manifested several times in the halls, music room, auditorium, and various other parts of the school.

(Emmett Middle School, 301 East 4th St., Emmett, ID 83617. Phone: 208-365-2921.) **72**

FREMONT COUNTY

MESA FALLS The spirit of a Shoshoni Indian haunts the Lower Mesa Falls. Her form, dressed in white, is seen within the mists of the cascading water. She seems to warn people of the dangerous currents beneath the falls and is said to be the spirit of a girl who died trying to rescue a loved one caught in the rushing river.

(Mesa Falls are on the Snake River, a few miles west of Yellowstone National Park in Fremont County. The Lower Mesa Falls are about one mile southwest of the Upper Mesa Falls.) **33**

GENESEE

JOYCE BUILDING This single-story brick building was built in 1880 and used for a variety of commercial purposes, including a museum that housed many rock crystals and Indian artifacts. Sara Joyce purchased the property in 1974 and moved there with her daughter Heidi and her granddaughter Solara. Almost immediately the family noticed weird happenings and unexplainable sounds. One night the ghost of a tall, thin, elderly man bathed in an eerie blue light appeared in the doorway of Sara's bedroom and asked, "Do you see me? Do you see me?" Not long afterward, the phantom of a huge silver-gray rat appeared in the kitchen. Sara's son Bill later discovered the mummified corpse of a large rat under the floorboards when he remodeled the kitchen. In fact, whenever Bill visited to help renovate the building, he would be plagued by spirits interfering with his work. Once a visiting ballet dancer from Australia was awakened by a female ghost with long black hair, who tried to get into a sleeping bag with her.

(Genesee is fifteen miles south of Moscow on U.S. Highway 95 in northern Idaho. The Joyce Building is at 206 Walnut St., Genesee, ID 83832. The property is presently owned by Sara's daughter, Ms. Heidi Linehan, at Route No. 1, Genesee, ID 83832.) **135**

IDAHO CITY

BOOT HILL CEMETERY This once-booming gold rush city is now a small town of only about three hundred people. Of course, that does not count the ghosts that linger from Idaho City's violent past. Many are said to wander through the Boot Hill Cemetery after dark.

(Idaho City is in western Idaho, forty-five miles northeast of Boise on Highway 21. The Boise Basin Museum is south of town, and the infamous Boot Hill Cemetery is just northeast of town. For information, call the Idaho Tourist Office at 800-635-7820.) **102**

LEWISTON

WAHA LAKE The apparition of an Indian maiden wearing buckskin has been seen sitting beside the water here. If approached, she walks into the water and disappears, leaving behind a whirlpool of white foam. Adult Nez Perce Indians stay away from the lake, although teenage boys are sent there for their guardian spirit quest.

(Lewiston is at the junction of U.S. Highway 95 and U.S. Highway 12, near the Washington border, in northern Idaho. Waha Lake is north of Lewiston.) **33**

OWYHEE COUNTY

OWYHEE MOUNTAINS Some caves in the Owyhee Mountains are said to be inhabited by naked, cannibalistic dwarves. The two-foot-high creatures are exceedingly strong, and one of them can carry a dead elk on his back. According to legends of the Shoshoni and Bannock Indians, the dwarves can be identified by their long tails, which they sometimes hide by wrapping them around their bodies. The dwarves have been accused of kidnaping little children and eating them.

(Owyhee County is in the southwest corner of Idaho.) **33**

WHITE STALLION A ghostly white stallion, leading a pack of phantom horses, is reputed to save cowboys and farmers who find themselves in trouble in the wilderness of Owyhee County. The wild herd is said to appear from a rift in the clouds and lead lost souls in the direction of safety.

(Highway 51 runs through the center of the desolate country. It crosses I-84 at Mountain Home, forty-three miles southeast of Boise.) **49**

PRESTON

DESERET THRIFT SHOP This popular thrift store is haunted by the spirit of an unidentified man, who is also thought to roam other stores along State Street. He is blamed for eerie electrical problems with phones, the time clock, intercoms, alarms, lights, and other appliances. Some believe the man might be an electrician who used to work in the older buildings downtown.

(Deseret Thrift Shop, 36 South State St., Preston, ID 83263. Phone: 208-852-1286.) **72**

SPIRIT LAKE

KANISKEE Kaniskee is the name given this lake by Coeur d'Alênes Indians. It means "Lake of the Spirit," and refers to the ghost of a young girl who rides over the water in a phantom canoe. She is always dressed in white and has long black hair down to her waist. Legend says she is the spirit of an Indian maiden who committed suicide after learning the young warrior she loved had died in a tribal skirmish. The girl rowed her canoe to the center of the lake one moonlit night, jumped into the dark water, and drowned herself.

(Spirit Lake is the northern Idaho panhandle, near the Montana border.) **33**

WIND RIVER RESERVATION

BULL LAKE This lake is haunted by a great white buffalo. Shoshoni Indians call the body of water the "Lake that Roars." One winter long ago, Indians chased a herd of buffalo onto the ice here. As the ice started to crack and the herd fell into the middle of the lake, their leader, a great white bull, let out a horrendous roar that can sometimes still be heard.

(Bull Lake is in a deep canyon on the Wind River Reservation, north of Pocatello in southeast Idaho.) **33**

ILLINOIS

BARRINGTON

WHITE CEMETERY Eerie glowing globes have been seen hovering in this 1820s cemetery. The lights float near the fence and sometimes over the road surface. A phantom black car has also been reported in the cemetery and near an old house that stood a block away. Although the house burned down years ago, it sometimes reappears, only to vanish from view within a few seconds.

(Barrington is a northwest suburb of Chicago at the intersection of U.S. Highway 14 and Highway 59. The cemetery is on Cuba Rd., just east of Old Barrington Road. www.barringtonarealibrary.org/local_information/ Cemeteries/white.htm) **72**

BELLEVILLE

OLD MEYER HOUSE This old brick house was built nearly 150 years ago by a German coal miner named Jakob Meyer. On June 26, 1923, in the parlor of his beloved house, seventy-seven-year-old Jakob, despondent about his deteriorating health, fired a 32-caliber bullet into his head. Forty years later, he returned to haunt the house, in the company of another ghost.

Judy and Dollie Walta opened a music school in Meyer's house in 1956. No one lived in the house, and it was deserted on evenings and weekends. Then, on August 28, 1962, a sailor friend of the two sisters drowned in an accident at sea. Within two days of his death, they started feeling the man's presence in the house. They heard the back door open and close by itself, followed by the sailor's soft footsteps going down the hallway to his favorite chair. The strange ritual continued for months, until one day the footsteps were those of someone else. Now the footsteps were much heavier and seemed to lead into the parlor, where the faint outline of a large man dressed in gray clothes could be seen standing in the middle of the room. Sometimes they detected the distinct odor of cigar smoke. Next, objects such as chairs and umbrellas started to move for no apparent reason. The Waltas' students were terrified. The sisters researched the history of the house and discovered Meyer's suicide. The poltergeist activity halted for the most part, but every once in a while, students at the music school smell cigar smoke or hear the sound of a chair moving with no one around, and at times a muffled gunshot is heard in the parlor.

(Belleville is in St. Claire County, southeast of East St. Louis at the junction of Highways 159 and 161. The house is on Main Street, near the corner of 17th St., in Belleville, IL 62223.) **5, 87**

BERWYN

MOLINE HOUSE This house is haunted by a shadowy figure who moves objects and hides personal belongings. The ghost's identity is not known.

(Berwyn is west of Cicero in the western suburbs of Chicago. The town is located at Exit 21B of I-290. Moline House is a private residence, at 3101 Wesley Ave., Berwyn, IL 60402.) **72, 101**

CAHOKIA MOUNDS

CAHOKIA MOUNDS STATE HISTORIC SITE This sacred site dates back to A.D. 700 and was a city of over twenty thousand residents by A.D. 1200. But today no one knows who they were. Archeologists call them simply the Temple Mound Builders, as they built 120 mounds at this site. Monk's Mound is the largest earthwork at the site and, for that matter, in the Western Hemisphere. The hundred-foot-tall, fourteen-acre mound was home to the principal ruler and is said to be a source of powerful psychic energy even today. In August 1987, it was the meeting place of a thousand people who took part in the worldwide Harmonic Convergence, designed to bring peace to the planet through meditation. Mound 72 is the grave of nearly three hundred young women. It is thought they were sacrificed to accompany a deceased god king on his journey to the Other Side. The king himself was laid out on a blanket made of twenty thousand shells and surrounded by eight hundred arrowheads, along with the bodies of his servants. Woodhenge is made up of forty-eight wooden posts set at exactly 7.5 degrees apart in a 410-foot-diameter circle. By lining up central observation posts with specific perimeter posts at sunrise, the exact date of all four equinoxes can be determined. It is believed Woodhenge was built long before the Temple Mound Builders identified the area as sacred. Some of the Cahokians left this colony and moved to Indiana around A.D. 1100. See Angel Mounds, Indiana, and Gorham Petroglyphs, Gorham, Illinois.

(The town of Cahokia is thirty miles southeast of East St. Louis, but the site is actually in Collinsville, which northeast of the city. Take Exit 6 from I-55/70 to Highway 111 south. At U.S. Highway 40, go east into the park. For further information, contact the Cahokia Mounds Museum Society, P.O. Box 382, Collinsville, IL 62234. Phone: 618-344-9221. Or contact the Cahokia Mounds State Historic Site, 30 Ramey St., Collinsville, IL 62234. Phone: 618-346-5160.) **32, 53 (10/82), 99, 144, 194**

CHARLESTON

EASTERN ILLINOIS UNIVERSITY A ghost named Mary haunts the Pemberton Hall female dormitory here. Her spirit moves silently from room to room, making sure doors are locked, turning stereos and TVs off and on, and generally behaving like a housemother from the Other Side. In 1981, one of the girls left her door slightly open late one night, and the apparition drifted into the room as if it were checking on her. According to legend, Mary is the spirit of a counselor bludgeoned to death by a crazed custodian on the third floor of Pemberton Hall in the 1920s.

(Charleston is fifty-five miles south of Champaign/Urbana. Take I-57 to Highway 16 east. Eastern Illinois University, 600 Lincoln Ave., Charleston, IL 61920. Phone 217-581-5000. www.eiu.edu) **175, 210**

The ghost of a young woman and mysterious flickering lights are seen at the Beverly Unitarian Church. See Beverly Unitarian Church, Chicago, Illinois
(B. A. SCHAFFENBERGER)

CHICAGO

BACHELOR'S GROVE CEMETERY No one has been buried in this small cemetery since 1989, and the ghosts seem to have taken over. Over a hundred instances of paranormal activity have been reported on this acre of land. The property was set aside as a cemetery in 1864, though some of the plots date back to the 1830s. Bachelor's Grove is named for the large number of single men resting in its graves, yet one of the most prominent ghosts is a woman known variously as the White Lady, the Madonna of Bachelor's Grove, or affectionately as Mrs. Rogers. She appears only during the full moon and is thought to be a woman who was buried in a grave next to her young son. Other ghosts congregate at the lagoon, a favorite spot for animal sacrifices and voodoo rituals. Apparitions seen near the lagoon include a two-headed man and a farmer with a horse and plow. The farmer died in the 1870s, when his horse suddenly bolted into the water, taking the man and the plow with it. Nobody has yet suggested an identity for the two-headed ghost, but during the late 1920s, the site was a favorite dumping ground for victims of Chicago mobsters. In the 1950s, a ghostly farmhouse, complete with a white picket fence, appeared on several occasions. Strange blue lights are sometimes seen dancing from tombstone to tombstone here, and in December 1971, a woman said she put her hand right through the ghost of a figure walking down a path in the cemetery. In 1984, a skeptical investigator encountered the yellow glowing apparition of a man. The image only lasted for a few seconds but was followed by a display of darting red lights. Additionally, phantom cars have materialized on the roads surrounding the cemetery (see Midlothian Turnpike, below).

(Bachelor's Grove is located west of Midlothian, which is a suburb south of Chicago. Follow I-294 south to Cicero Ave. and take the Midlothian Turnpike. The graveyard is at 143rd and Ridgeland. www.graveyards.com/ bachelors) **4, 53 (11/90), 62, 66 (11/82, 1/84), 68, 176, 211**

BEVERLY UNITARIAN CHURCH The ghost of a young woman in a long dress has been seen in the living room and descending the stairway here. Sometimes she appears as a flickering light, like someone holding a candle, which moves from window to window within the empty building. The house was built in 1886 by Robert Givens, who modeled it after a castle he visited on a trip to Ireland. The building soon came to be known as the Irish Castle, although a church has used Givens's former residence as a meeting place since 1942.

(Follow Highway 57 Memphis and exit at Halsted St. Go south to 103rd St. and turn west. The Beverly Unitarian Church, also known as the Irish Castle, is at 103rd and Longwood Drive, at 10244 South Longwood Dr., Chicago, IL 60643. Phone: 773-233-7080. Dale Kaczmarek hosts Excursions into the Unknown tours of haunted Chicagoland. For information, call 708-425-5163. www.ghostresearch.org/tours) **14, 53 (11/90), 66, 101**

BIOGRAPH THEATER The ghost of a man has been seen racing down the alley next to this movie theater. It is the ghost of John Dillinger, who died in a hail of police gunfire here in 1934. At least, the FBI identified the man as the infamous John Dillinger; some claim the body was really that of a small-time hood by the name of Jimmy Lawrence. The FBI explained the discrepancies in the appearance of the body by claiming that Dillinger had undergone extensive plastic surgery.

(The Biograph theater is in north Chicago, St. at 2433 North Lincoln. Phone: 773-348-4123.) **53 (11/90), 72**

CLARK STREET The anguished cries of passengers from the ill-fated *Eastland* can still be heard near the Clark Street Bridge. The boat capsized in 1915, and 812 people died under the bridge. Further north on Clark Street, unexplainable sights and sounds still haunt the site of the St. Valentine's Day Massacre. On February 14, 1929, the Bugs Moran gang was wiped out by rival gangsters dressed as Chicago police. See Mt. Carmel Cemetery, Hillside, Illinois.

(The Clark Street Bridge is across the Chicago River in the Loop. The St. Valentine's Day Massacre took place at 2122 North Clark St. The building is gone, but the parking lot that took its place is still considered to be haunted.) **53 (11/90)**

EVERGREEN CEMETERY The ghost of a brunette girl thought to be buried in this cemetery likes to see the sights of Chicago. In the 1980s, the child's phantom was reported hitchhiking rides in the west Chicago area. Once, she even got on a CTA bus. When the driver walked back to tell her she had not paid, the girl vanished in front of him.

The cries of dying passengers from the capsized *Eastland* can still be heard coming from underneath the Clark Street Bridge where it sank. Eight hundred and twelve people died (GINGER HAUCK)

(The cemetery is located at 87th St. and Kedzie Ave. in Evergreen Park. Phone: 708-422-9051.) **66 (4/84)**

FIREHOUSE ENGINE COMPANY NO. 107 The strange legacy of a dead fireman haunted this firehouse for twenty years—exactly. While Frank Leavy was washing a window during spring cleaning at the station on April 18, 1924, he paused with his left hand resting on the window and told a fellow firefighter that he thought he was going to die that day. At that moment, the station received an alarm, and the firefighters headed for a fire at Curran Hall, an old office building in central Chicago. While fighting the blaze, a brick wall collapsed and killed eight firefighters. Leavy was one of them. The next day, firefighters noticed an unusual stain on one of the windows. It was the imprint of Frank's hand, made as he was cleaning the window on that fateful day. Try as they might, the firemen could not erase the handprint. The stain seemed to be etched into the glass. For the next twenty years, the handprint was a grim reminder to firefighters of the danger of their profession. Then, on April 18, 1944, a careless newspaper boy tossed a paper through the window and broke it to pieces.

(Engine Company 107 and Truck Company 12 share the same fire station at 13th and Oakley, Chicago, IL 60622. For information, contact the Chicago Firefighters Association, 1800 South Halsted, Chicago, 60608. Phone: 312-226-6310.) **176**

FORT DEARBORN During road work near the site of the original Fort Dearborn, workers unearthed bodies dating from the early 1800s. Ever since, people have reported the apparitions of settlers floating over this parcel of land.

(The site of Fort Dearborn is a vacant field at 16th St. and Indiana Ave. in Chicago. www.ci.chi.il.us/Landmarks/S/SiteFtDearborn.html) **66, 72**

GLESSNER HOUSE The John Glessner family have reported an invisible, cold presence moving through their house, which was built in 1886. They have also encountered a white apparition on the stairs and in the bedroom.

(The house is a private residence, at 1800 South Prairie St., Chicago, IL 60616. Phone: 312-326-1393.) **72, 101**

GRACELAND CEMETERY This cemetery, opened in 1860, is haunted by a variety of spirits. The lifelike statue above the grave of a seven-year-old girl reportedly sheds tears and moves around the grounds. The statue marking the grave of Inez Clarke is covered by a glass case, which does not stop it from disappearing frequently, especially during violent thunderstorms. Guards have reported it gone on several occasions, only to find the statue in place the next morning. Inez died in 1880, and her ghostly figure is still seen walking among the tombstones. Another eerie statue marks the grave of Dexter Graves, who died in 1844 at the age of fifty-five. The statue, a menacing, hooded figure of death, is said to give those who look into its face a taste of what is to come. Graceland's most lavish monument is the thirty-foot-long, twelve-foot-high tomb of Ludwig Wolff. The area around the stone building is the stomping ground of a green-eyed ghoul who likes to howl at the full moon.

(From the downtown Loop area, follow Lake Shore Drive north and exit at Irving Park Rd. The cemetery is at the corner of Irving Park Rd. and Clark St. at 4001 North Clark St., Chicago, IL 60613. Phone: 773-525-1105. www.graveyards.com/graceland) **4**

HEPHZIBAH CHILDREN'S HOME A variety of poltergeist effects have been reported by visitors and employees at this children's home. The paranormal activity was linked to an emotionally troubled child, who had unconsciously released some sort of psychokinetic energy.

(Hephzibah Children's Association, 946 North Blvd., Chicago, IL 60614. Phone: 708-386-8417) **101**

HOLY FAMILY CHURCH A unidentified white apparition has appeared to parishioners and clergy at this Protestant church.

(Holy Family Church, 1019 South May St., Chicago, IL 60607. Phone: 312-492-8442.) **101**

HULL HOUSE This landmark building, constructed in 1856 by Charles Hull, was the alleged refuge of an infamous "devil baby." The child, born to a devout Italian woman and her atheist husband, was said to have hooves and cloven feet, pointed ears and horns, scale-covered skin, and a long tail. In 1913, the father brought the miniature Satan to Hull House, a welfare organization run by Jane Addams, and asked them to take in the unruly creature. Rumors spread quickly, and in just six weeks hundreds of people traveled to Hull House to see the devil child. Addams steadfastly denied its existence, although some said she was only trying to protect the infant. Reports continue to this day of a wild creature that looks out the upstairs-left attic window and of manifestations of luminous ectoplasm that ascend the attic stairway. Several photographs have been taken of the mysterious ectoplasmic mist. Also caught on film were four monklike figures that appeared on the stairway to the second floor.

(Jane Addams received a Nobel Prize for her efforts for charitable causes and the woman's movement. Hull House moved to larger quarters in 1963, and the original structure was turned into a museum. It is on the corner of Halsted and Polk streets. Take the Roosevelt Rd. West exit off the Dan Ryan Expressway. Hull House Museum, 800 South Halsted St., Chicago, IL 60607. Phone: 312-413-5353.) **14, 53 (11/90), 66 (7/85), 68, 82, 176**

JEWISH WALDHEIM CEMETERY The ghost of a 1920s flapper girl has been reported near this cemetery. There were numerous sightings in 1933 and 1973.

(Jewish Waldheim Cemetery is in North Riverside, across from Woodlawn Cemetery. The ghost is seen at the cemetery gates and on Des Plaines Avenue, between the Melody Mill Ballroom and the cemetery. Jewish Waldheim Cemetery, 1800 S. Harlem Forest Park, IL 60130. Phone: 708-366-4541.) **66 (4/84)**

LOURDES HIGH SCHOOL Custodians, students, and teachers at this Catholic high school have reported hearing the sounds of disembodied footsteps and untraceable music echoing through the halls.

(Lourdes High School, 4034 West 56th St., Chicago, IL 60629. Phone: 773-581-2555.) **72, 101**

MIDLOTHIAN TURNPIKE Phantom automobiles and trucks have caused drivers along this section of highway to swerve to avoid hitting them. Sometimes collisions occur, but when drivers pull over to the shoulder to inspect damage, there isn't any, and the phantom vehicle is nowhere in sight. Some mystified drivers even report hearing the ripping of metal and the shattering of glass. No historical accidents or events cast light on the phenomenon, although a section of the freeway runs past a local cemetery that is known to be haunted. See Bachelor's Grove Cemetery, above.

(The section of the Midlothian Turnpike is between Ridgeland Ave. and Central Ave.) **68**

The ghost of gangster Al Capone appears when his grave site is treated with disrespect. See Mount Carmel Cemetery, Hillside, Illinois (LINDA MATLOW/PIX INT'L)

MOUNT CARMEL CEMETERY The gravesite of Al Capone is haunted by the mobster's ghost, which is said to appear to disrespectful people visiting his family plot. Capone himself was haunted by the ghost of James Clark, brother-in-law of Bugs Moran and one of the victims of the St. Valentine's Day Massacre (see Clark Street, Chicago, Illinois). The life-size statue of Julia Buccola Petta, who died in childbirth in 1921, is haunted by her ghost, which is seen in a white dress near the grave. Her casket was opened in 1927, and her body was still in perfect condition. A photograph of the corpse taken then is displayed on her tombstone.

(The cemetery is on Harrison St., west of Roosevelt Street, in Hillside, which is a western suburb of Chicago at Exit 16 of I-290. Phone: 630-449-8300. www. graveyards.com/mtcarmel) **11, 66 (10/84), 72**

RED LION PUB A doorway to the unknown was opened in this 1882 building when John Cordwell decided to turn the three-story brick structure into a quaint English pub. As part of his renovation, Cordwell installed a stained-glass window over the stairway and added a brass plaque honoring his father, who had been buried in England without a tombstone. Before long, people passing the window were overcome with unexplainable dizziness, and John sensed the presence of his father's spirit on the second-floor. A half-dozen other ghosts seem to have accompanied his father. The strong smell of lavender signals the presence of a twenty-year-old retarded girl who died in the building. The upstairs ladies' room is haunted by a strange force that traps women inside. The apparition of a man sometimes walks through the downstairs bar and up the stairs, and the ghost of an unshaven young man wearing cowboy clothes is seen in the upstairs bar. A woman in a 1920s outfit, a blond-haired man with a broad face, and a bearded man wearing a black hat also haunt the tavern.

(Red Lion Pub, 2446 North Lincoln Ave., Chicago, IL 60614. Phone: 312-348-2695.) **101, 134**

RESURRECTION CEMETERY The ghost of a blond, blue-eyed girl has haunted the district around this graveyard since 1939, five years after a young Polish girl was buried here. Mary Bregavy, or Resurrection Mary, as she has come to be called, died in a car accident after an evening of dancing at the old O'Henry Ballroom (now the Willowbrook Ballroom). Sometimes her glowing, faceless ghost is seen walking along the shoulder of the road, but most often her white appari-

tion is seen hitchhiking. Sometimes her aloof ghost will dance with a few young men at the ballroom and ask for a ride home. During renovations at the cemetery in the 1970s, sightings of her ghost reached a peak. In December 1977, a passing motorist saw Mary holding on to the bars of the cemetery gate. He called police, thinking a girl was trapped in the cemetery. Investigators found no one in the cemetery, but two bars in the gate were bent apart. Etched into the iron were two small handprints. Supervisors had the sections cut out to keep curiosity seekers away, but embarrassed officials welded the pieces back in place a year later. Dozens of witnesses, including many taxi drivers, have seen Mary's ghost along the road. In 1989, a cab driver picked up a girl fitting Mary's description in front of the Old Willow Shopping Center. As they passed Resurrection Cemetery, the girl vanished from the front seat.

(Resurrection Mary's ghost appears along Archer Avenue in south Chicago. Take I-294 to 95th Street. Follow 95th St. west to Roberts Rd. Take Roberts Rd. north to Archer Ave. Resurrection Cemetery, 7201 Archer Rd., Justice, IL 60458. Phone: 708-458-4770. www. graveyards.com/resurrection) **11, 15, 53 (11/90), 66, (10/83), 66 (4/84), 68, 139, 176**

ROBINSON WOODS Strange faces have been reported staring from the behind the foliage here, and the spectral sounds of tom-toms and wood chopping have been recorded. Several passing motorists have also observed eerie lights moving through the woods. The occurrences may be linked to the nearby graves of an anglicized Indian family. A granite boulder marks the burial plots of Alexander Robinson, his wife, and other members of their family. The Robinsons were granted the land in 1829 in gratitude for saving a white family during the Fort Dearborn massacre. It is said they were killed by jealous tribe members.

(The woods are on East River Rd. and Lawrence Ave., near O'Hara Airport, west of Norridge. Most of the voice phenomena have been recorded on the left side of the monument. www.ghostresearch.org/sites/robinson) **72**

ST. ANDREW'S PUB Employees and patrons here report being touched by an unseen presence and encountering eerie cold spots in the building. Owner Jane McDougall says that glasses, ashtrays, and other objects move by themselves in the bar area. Investigators blame former owner Frank Giff, who died when he fell off a bar stool here.

(St. Andrew's Pub, 5938 North Broadway, Chicago, IL 60660. Phone: 312-784-5540.) **53 (11/90), 101**

ST. TURBIUS CHURCH Parishioners have reported an unidentified apparition near the altar of this old church.

(The church is on the corner of 56th St. and Karlov Ave., Chicago, IL 60646. Phone: 773-581-2730.) **101**

THAT STEAK JOYNT Customers and employees of this restaurant have reported hearing strange footsteps and being touched by invisible presences, as well as encountering moving apparitions.

(That Steak Joynt, 1610 North Wells, Chicago, IL 60614. Phone: 312-943-5091.) **101**

VICTORIAN HOUSE ANTIQUES Mysterious cold spots and doors that open and close by themselves are reported by customers who approach the attic area of this antique shop. The house was built in 1879. A woman was murdered in the house in the 1880s, and four people later died in a fire in the attic rooms.

(Victorian House Antiques, 906 West Belmont, Chicago, IL 60657. Phone: 773-472-0400.) **66, 72, 101**

WATER TOWER The ghost of a man has been reported staring out of the windows of Chicago's Water Tower. The man was hanged from the garish structure in the late 1800s. The historic building survived the Chicago Fire and marks an area of the city known as Streeterville, named for explorer John Streeter. Streeter laid claim to the area, and when it was taken from him by the state of Illinois, cursed the property. Indeed, Streeterville was the source of the Great Chicago Fire of October 1871.

(Chicago's Water Tower is on the corner of Michigan Ave. and Chicago Ave. Streeterville extends from the Water Tower to just beyond the John Hancock Building.) **66, 72**

CICERO

MORTON COLLEGE Custodians and students at this college have reported hearing footsteps in empty corridors and seeing a cloudlike apparition drift through classrooms. The phenomena occur most frequently in the late fall.

(Morton College, 3801 South Central Ave., Cicero; IL 60650. Phone: 708-656-8000. www.morton.cc.il.us) **101**

ST. GEORGE ORTHODOX CHURCH An icon of the Virgin Mary on a panel behind the altar in this church began weeping on April 22, 1994. The day marked the end of the Orthodox Christian Lent and the beginning of Holy Week. Two streams of dampness began issuing from each eye as the Reverend Nicholas Dahdal was preparing for the Liturgy of Lazarus services at 6:00 P.M. Eight bishops inspected the icon before it was officially declared a miracle. Thousands of people have since witnessed the phenomenon.

(Cicero is in Cook County, just west of and adjacent to Chicago. St. George Orthodox Church, 1220 South 60th Court, Cicero, IL 60650. Phone: 708-656-2917.) **72**

CLARENDON HILLS

COUNTRY HOUSE RESTAURANT The ghost of a former customer haunts the bar at this two-story roadhouse. Her presence has been detected by both employees and customers near the bar, in a storeroom, and in an upstairs bedroom. Once, the apparition of a young blond woman beckoned a male customer to join her in the upstairs bedroom.

(Clarendon Hills is twenty miles west of Chicago. Take the Ogden Avenue west exit from I-294 and turn south at Highway 83. The restaurant is at 241 West 55th St., Clarendon Hills, IL 60514. Phone: 630-986-5444.) **101; 135**

CRYSTAL LAKE

STICKNEY MANSION This mansion, built by George Stickney in 1849, is still haunted by his ghost. His presence has been detected by several subsequent owners.

(Crystal Lake is northwest of Chicago in McHenry County, eleven miles northwest of Barrington on U.S. Highway 14. Stickney Mansion, 1904 Cherry Valley Rd., Crystal Lake, IL 60014.) **101**

DECATUR

GREENWOOD CEMETERY This cemetery has a troubled history, and is haunted by a number of strange apparitions. The phantom of a man with black holes for eyes was first seen in 1977, and the ghost of a lady in a black dress has been seen numerous times. Ever since the Sangamon River overflowed its banks and flooded the cemetery, dislodging a number of coffins from the loose soil, flickering ghost lights have been reported in the cemetery. Some say that the lights are the lost souls of those whose coffins were disturbed. Other lost souls are said to roam an area of the graveyard known as Hell Hollow, where eight unsolved murders took place in the 1930s, and where grave robbers have used the cover of the hollow to mask their gruesome work. The area also contains a number of unmarked graves that were part of a hill that collapsed in a huge mudslide. Coffins and bodies littered the ground afterward. The site was rebuilt with concrete terraces, but many of the remains got lost or wrongly marked. Many of the tombstones labeled "Unknown Union Soldier" are actually Confederate soldiers who died of yellow fever on a prison train that stopped at Decatur in the middle of the Civil War. Greenwood Cemetery was founded in 1857, but got an unofficial start in 1828, when a group of moonshiners massacred a band of Indians, dumped the bodies in a shallow ravine, and covered them over with stones.

(Decatur is in central Illinois, thirty-two miles east of Springfield on I-72. The entrance to Greenwood Cemetery is at the dead end of South Church St. Hell Hollow is located in the far southwest corner of the cemetery. The ghost lights are seen in the southern part of the cemetery, along Lincoln Park Dr. The Indian burial pit is on the side of a hill in the south end of the oldest section. www.prairieghosts.com/greenwd1.html) **210**

LINCOLN SQUARE THEATER A ghost called One-Armed Red has haunted this old theater for the last seventy years. He is thought to be a stagehand who worked here back in the vaudeville days. Red was working on a steel beam above the stage when he lost his balance and fell. On the way down, his arm caught in the angle between two supports and was ripped off. He later died from his wounds. His footsteps and voice are sometimes heard from the stage below, and his dark figure is said to appear near the spiral staircase in the rear right corner of the stage.

(Lincoln Square Theater, 141 North Main St., Decatur, IL 62521. Phone: 217-422-1711.) **210**

MILIKIN UNIVERSITY The ghost of an employee who fell down the elevator shaft at the Gorin Library haunts the basement area where he died; and the apparition of an unidentified woman has been seen at Blackburn Hall. The Old School Gym, built in 1911 but now used by the theater department, is haunted by a mis-

chievous presence who takes items and returns them the next day. The sounds of voices and ghostly applause have been heard coming from the deserted building. Milikin is a Presbyterian university founded in 1901.

(Milikin University, 1184 West Main St., Decatur, IL 62522. Phone: 217-424-6210.) **210**

OLD NEHI PLANT A dilapidated brick tower at this abandoned bottling company is haunted by a malevolent presence. The factory is located in a part of town known as the Levee, which was once the center of bawdy saloons and whorehouses. A boy nearly died in an unexplained attack in the old Nehi tower.

(The abandoned tower is on private property, near the corner of Sangamon and Morgan streets at the edge of town.) **210**

VOORHIES CASTLE This fourteen-room manor house is haunted by the ghosts of the Nels Larson family. Larson built the house on his 540 acres in the 1870s. It is rumored that the Larsons kept a severely retarded child chained in a tiny room. When in 1914, Nels' wife Johanna was found lying dead on the central stairs, Nels gathered the rest of his family and left the mansion on the same day. All their clothing still hung in the closets, and all the furniture was left behind. The table was still set for dinner. No one lived in the house for the next fifty-eight years. For many years after her sudden death, the glowing ghost of Johanna Larson was seen in the upper window of the west tower. The sounds of rattling chains and animal-like noises haunt the upper floors of the house to this day. The house has changed hands many times over the last twenty years and was put up for sale once again in 1994.

(The farmhouse is on private property in Voorhies, a tiny settlement northeast of Decatur on Highway 105 between Bement and Monticello. www.prairieghosts.com/voorhies.html) **210**

FOREST PARK

OLD LOBSTEIN HOUSE This Painted Lady Victorian house has been considered to be haunted for over fifty years. Residents have reported loud banging noises, eerie cold spots, the sounds of a child running in the upstairs hall, and someone pacing back and forth in the attic. Neighbors have seen a ghostly figure standing at the attic window, and the attic area seems to explode with strange noises every November 6. One of the ghosts is a little girl named Addie, daughter of John Lobstein, who built the house in 1897. The other is probably her half-brother Charlie, who committed suicide in the attic.

(Forest Park is a western suburb of Chicago. Take Highway 43 south from I-290. The fourteen-room house is a private residence owned by Kathy and Richard Bertucci.) **72**

GLEN ELLYN

MARYKNOLL COLLEGE This Roman Catholic seminary was haunted by the ghost of a former priest for many years in the 1970s. The ghostly father materialized in front of students, gently touched their cheeks, and then disappeared before their eyes. The dead priest's presence was often detected in the photography lab, where unexplainable cold spots suddenly appeared and moved about in the cramped quarters.

(Glen Ellyn is west of Chicago in Dupage County, at the junction of Highways 83 and 38. The seminary, which closed in 1972, was located on Maryknoll Boulevard, Glen Ellyn, IL 60137.) **80**

GODFREY

LEWIS AND CLARK COMMUNITY COLLEGE The ghost of former headmistress Harriet Haskell has been reported on this campus for the last twenty years. She is blamed for elevators that operate themselves, inexplicable footsteps, and a ghostly perfume that sometimes fills the halls.

(Godfrey is two miles west of Alton on Highway 3 in Madison County, which is opposite St. Louis in south western Illinois. The college is at 5800 Godfrey Rd., Godfrey, IL 62035. Phone: 618-467-2270.) **72**

GORHAM

GORHAM PETROGLYPHS The two-hundred-foot tall bluff that rises up from nowhere in the middle of the Shawnee National Forest originated as a molten mass pushed up by tremendous forces deep within the earth. Ancient people considered the bluff sacred. They covered many of its flat surfaces with mysterious symbols, which still perplex archeologists. Shamanistic initiations took place here, but no evidence for human sacrifice has been found (see Cahokia Mounds State Park, Illinois.) The White Hand petroglyph at the site is generally recognized as representing the hand of God, reaching out from the Other Side.

(Follow I-57 to Highway 13 west. Take the road that becomes Highway 149 and turn south on Highway 3 at Grimsby. Turn west onto the unmarked road just before the Gorham bridge. Follow it east to the petroglyphs.) **72**

GRAND TOWER

DEVIL'S BACKBONE AND DEVIL'S BAKE OVEN These two landmarks were used by rivermen since the 1670s to signal a shallow spot in the Mississippi River. Before the river was dammed, keelboats and barges were towed over the sandbar using mules. The bottleneck became a natural hijacking area for river pirates. In the late 1800s, an iron foundry was built on the hillside on Devil's Backbone. The two-story house of the superintendent of furnaces stood nearby. The house is gone today, but the superintendent's daughter haunts the site. When the stubborn man refused to allow her to marry the man she loved, she lost all will to live. Her ghostly figure has been seen floating up the path to the site and disappearing behind bushes. The sounds of her mournful crying are said to pull at the heartstrings of even the hardest man.

(Grand Tower is on Highway 3 in Jackson County, in the southwest corner of Illinois. The Devil's Backbone is a rock ledge promontory over the Mississippi River, a few miles north of Grand Tower. The Devil's Bake Oven, another outcropping of rock, is a few yards south of Devil's Backbone. A natural gas pipe bridge on the Illinois side of the river marks the area. The bridge starts near the south edge of Devil's Bake Oven. Ruins of the foundry house can be found on the eastern side of the hill below Devil's Bake Oven.) **176**

GURNEE

GOLD PYRAMID HOUSE This house is a one-hundredth-scale reproduction of the Great Pyramid at Giza, Egypt. There is a full-size, gold-covered recreation of Tutankhamen's chariot and a solid gold sarcophagus lid, in which the face of the boy king is carved. The sarcophagus is in the Chariot Room, which is full of ancient artifacts and models of Egyptian gods and goddesses. Strange occurrences began at the pyramid house during construction when a bulldozer uncovered a huge outcropping of high-grade gold ore, which became the only gold strike ever recorded in the state of Illinois. Then, an underground spring bubbled up out of nowhere at the center of the pyramid. The water from the spring formed a natural moat around the structure and was so pure that owner James Onan was allowed to bottle and sell it. In 1986, hordes of black birds started attacking anyone using the north entrance to the Chariot Room. According to legend, such birds protected the north entrance to the real tomb of Tutankhamen. Some believers in the ancient powers of pyramidology have felt powerful energy at the north wall, and also in the middle of the meeting room, which is directly over the source of the spring.

(Gurnee is in the northeast corner of Illinois. Take I-94 north from Chicago and exit at Highway 132 east. The Gold Pyramid House is located at 37921 N. Dilleys Rd., Wadsworth, IL 60083. For tour information, call 800-525-3669. In Illinois, call 847-662-7777.) **99**

HARRISBURG

HICKORY HILL The first two floors of this mansion, containing six rooms each, were where the John Hart Crenshaw family lived after they moved into their new home in 1838. Behind the thickened walls of the third floor attic are twelve tiny rooms and a large, open hall with two whipping posts. This was where Mr. Crenshaw bred slaves for sale. These children, along with kidnapped blacks, were quickly sold to southern buyers, who sent boats up the Ohio River to pick them up. While unspeakable cruelty took place just above their heads, Mr. and Mrs. Crenshaw and their five children led the lives of a privileged family, earnestly attending church and school. Many years later, the attic can't shake its demons. In the 1920s, exorcist Hickman Whittington took on the job. After only a brief time alone in the attic, he ran from the house and died a few hours later. In 1966, two marines decided to tackle the spirits on the third floor. After a few hours, they, too, were driven from the house by "a cacophony of voices," as ghostly figures danced all around them. A total of 150 people tried to spend a night alone in the attic, and none succeeded. Finally in 1978, David Rodgers, a reporter for WSIL-TV, became the first man to make it through the night at Hickory Hill. Still, the attic of this old house is one of the scariest spots in the country.

(Harrisburg is in the southernmost tip of Illinois, at the junction of U.S. Highway 45 and Highway 13. Hick-

ory Hill overlooks the Saline River in Gallatin County, fourteen miles east of Harrisburg, near the town of Equality. The house is at the top of the hill, on Highway 13. Old Slave House Museum, Highway 13, Junction, IL 62954. Phone: 618-276-4410.) **14, 101, 176, 210**

JOLIET

RIALTO THEATRE This beautifully renovated theater building is haunted by the ghost of a woman. The unknown spirit is most active after hours and has been encountered by a number of employees and visitors. The granite theater was built in the 1920s and restored during the 1980s.

(Joliet is southwest of Chicago, at the junction of I-80 and U.S. Highway 52 on the Des Plaines River. Rialto Square Theatre and Office, Joliet, IL 60431. Phone: 815-726-7171.) **72**

VLASEK HOUSE A strange poltergeist followed a terrified family from house to house in August 1957. For over a week, the James Mikulecky family was frightened by loud, unexplainable noises and objects flying through their Wilmington home. Mrs. Mae Vlasek invited the distraught family to move into her house, but the scary activity just started up all over again.

(Wilmington is eighteen miles south of Joliet, on Highway 53.) **72**

JONESBORO

DUG HILL ROAD This road has been haunted since the Civil War days. Reports include apparitions of a person lying in a pool of blood in the middle of the road and a phantom wagon with sideboards that is pulled by two ghostly black horses. A provost marshal named Welch was killed by two Union Army deserters on this road in 1865, and many believe it is Welch's ghost that has returned.

(Jonesboro is at the junction of Highways 146 and 127 in the southern tip of Illinois. Dug Hill Road is a section of Highway 146 that cuts through a hill five miles west of Jonesboro.) **176, 210**

LAKE FOREST

SCHWEPPE MANSION This twenty-bedroom, eighteen-bathroom stone mansion lay abandoned for nearly fifty years after its owner committed suicide. Ghostly servants were said to walk the halls and dining room, and apparitions of the former owners roamed the bedrooms. The strangest mystery is a window overlooking the driveway in the master bedroom which never needs cleaning, even when the other windows are smudged and covered with grime. The Tudor mansion was built in 1913 as a wedding gift for Laura Shedd and Charles Schweppe. Laura died in 1937, and Charles put a pistol to his forehead in 1941. His suicide note read simply, "I've been awake all night. It is terrible."

(Lake Forest is a northern suburb of Chicago on Lake Michigan. Schweppe Mansion, Lake Forest, IL 60045.) **72, 101**

LEMONT

ST. JAMES SAG CHURCH Reports of ghosts in the cemetery here, founded in 1817, started in 1847. The phantoms of monks chanting Latin liturgies have been seen by numerous witnesses on the surrounding grounds, although no monks are known to have lived in the area. Late one night in November 1977, a policeman chased eight ghostly monks who floated out of the woods and moved toward the rectory.

(Lemont is southwest of Chicago in Cook County, ten miles southwest of Justice on the Chicago Ship Canal. Take Exit 271, Lemont Ave. South, off I-55. St. James, 10600 Archer Ave., Lemont, IL 60439. Phone: 630-257-7000.) **66 (1/83)**

MACOMB

WESTERN ILLINOIS UNIVERSITY Poltergeist effects that occur only at night have plagued the top floor of Simpkins Hall for many years. Doors and windows open and or close by themselves, lights go on and off for no reason, and typewriters operate with no one at the keyboard. Students and teaching assistants working in the building have christened their invisible night visitor Harold.

(Macomb is at the junction of U.S. Highways 136 and 67 in western Illinois. Western Illinois University, 1 University Circle, Macomb, IL 61455. Phone: 309-298-1955. www.wiu.edu) **72**

WILLEY FARM In a case that has become known as the Macomb Poltergeist, an emotionally disturbed teenaged girl was apparently responsible for causing fires to erupt simultaneously in different parts of a farmhouse. Custody of Wanet Willey was awarded to her father after bitter divorce proceedings, but the sensitive young girl wanted to live with her mother. She hated her uncle's farm where her father had taken her to live. Somehow, her anger expressed itself psychokinetically. For nearly a week in 1948, she is thought to have caused scores of smoldering fires to appear in the wallpaper, curtains, furniture, bedsheets, and clothing in the house. Brown spots, caused by heat in excess of 400 degrees, appeared throughout the house in front of dozens of startled witnesses. A fire brigade stood by outside the house, and they would wet down the hot spots to keep the house from catching fire. Investigations by the fire and police departments, the air force, and numerous freelance investigators failed to identify a physical cause for the phenomenon.

(The Willey farm is private property on Three Mile Line Road east of Macomb.) **176, 210**

MCLEANSBORO

LAKEY'S CREEK The ghost of a headless horseman appears along this stream just after sundown to observers walking along the east side of the creek. The apparition rides a black horse that gallops down the west, downstream side of Lakey's Creek. The stream was named for a settler who built a cabin nearby. Just before his home was complete, his headless torso was found propped up against a tree stump on his property, and his severed head was found in the leaves a few feet away. Lakey was buried nearby, and his killers were never discovered. His headless phantom has been encountered sporadically over the last 150 years.

(McLeansboro at the junction of Highway 142 and Highway 14 in Hamilton County, in southern Illinois. The creek runs through the town of McLeansboro. The cabin stood on the west side of Lakey Creek, where a concrete bridge marks the trail from Mount Vernon to Carmi.) **176, 210**

MOLINE

19TH AVENUE A strange apparition, which can be seen only by children, has been reported on this street for the last fifty years. The descriptions are always the same: a silent, unmoving, shrouded figure, dressed in black. The unidentified phantom usually appears under a large tree, near the curb.

(The haunted street is in East Moline on the Mississippi River in northwest Illinois. Follow I-80 to the Highway 88/92 West exit. Most reports of the phantom are along 19th Ave., near Butterworth Park in East Moline.) **26, 72**

23RD AVENUE A peculiar ghost has haunted this street for over sixty years. The apparition is known as the Pointing Ghost, because she is always seen pointing her finger with her arm outstretched. Dressed in 1920s clothing, the pointing ghost has appeared in houses and yards, and in the middle of the road.

(Moline is across the Mississippi River from Davenport. Take I-80 west to I-74 north. The ghost is seen on 23rd Ave. in west Moline.) **26**

MURPHYSBORO

MUD MONSTER A filthy, apelike creature has been sighted near this riverside town on several occasions. The eight-foot-tall beast has light brown fur matted with mud, and smells like dead fish and river slime. In June 1973, a couple parked in a car heard wild growls and saw the creature cross in front of them. A police investigation discovered a trail of thick black slime. Workers at a carnival saw the mud monster loitering near a pony pen.

(Murphysboro is seven miles west of Carbondale on Highway 13 in southern Illinois. The creature has been sighted along the banks of the Big Muddy River.) **199**

PRAIRIE DU ROCHER

OLD FORT DE CHARTRES A ghostly funeral procession forms here between 11:00 P.M. and midnight on every July 4th that falls on a Friday. The phantoms of about forty wagons with thirteen pairs of soldiers on horseback escort a casket lying on a flat wagon. The body is believed to be that of a prominent man murdered at the fort and buried with full honors by the light of the moon. Fort De Chartres was built in 1756 for King Louis XV. The phantom funeral entourage was first seen in 1889 and was last reported in 1989. July 4th falls on a Friday next in 1997, then again in 2003 and 2014.

(Prairie du Rocher is near the Mississippi River, fifteen miles south of East St. Louis, Illinois. The strange procession travels from the site of the old fort north of town to a nearby cemetery, Old Fort De Chartres, RR2 Prairie du Rocher, IL 62277. Phone: 618-284-7230.) **176**

QUINCY

BURTON CAVE A ghostly celebration of death took place here in the 1880s. A group of picnickers saw a dark-robed figure at the mouth of the cave. The ghostly figure wore a hood over its head and a full-length robe, with long sleeves covering its hands. Deeper inside the cavern they found the body of a woman in white, lying prone on a funeral bier with candles at her feet and head. They ran to get the sheriff, but no evidence of their strange encounter could be found.

(Quincy is on the Mississippi River at the extreme western edge of Illinois. Burton Cave is in Adams County, four miles east of Quincy. The meadow in front of the cave entrance is a popular picnic ground.) **176**

MADISON GRAMMAR SCHOOL A woman was brutally stabbed to death in a house that once stood here, and her killers were never found. Later residents were unable to remove bloodstains from the oak flooring. They also reported many unexplainable noises in the house, such as an invisible dog running up and down the stairs, doors opening, and a body being dragged down from the second floor. The dead woman owned a bulldog who followed her everywhere; her body was taken from the second floor and stuffed in a closet under the staircase. Ultimately, the house was torn down. The school that was built on the site is also believed to be haunted.

(Madison School is located at 26th Street and Madison St., Quincy, IL 62301.) **176**

OLD REBEL HOUSE This old house, where Southern soldiers hid out during the Civil War, was once visited by the devil himself. In the 1880s, a family living in a second-floor apartment here reported that the ghastly figure of the devil, complete with horns and red eyes, walked through a locked door and stood staring at three children. It leaped over a porch banister and escaped over a verandah, leaving a trail of sulfurous smoke behind.

(The Old Rebel House stood at 2nd St. and Vermont St. in Quincy.) **176**

ROCK ISLAND

SHOVELING GHOST Rock Island's famous Shoveling Ghost first made its appearance in April 1916, when residents of a row house reported the apparition of a skeleton digging a hole in their backyard. The hardworking ghost left behind shallow holes with dirt neatly piled nearby. In 1917, a group of neighbors dug up the yard to look for buried treasure, but all they found was a few worthless trinkets. The ghost, however, is still digging.

(Rock Island is in the Mississippi River, between Davenport, Iowa, and Moline, Illinois. The house is a private residence between Mann Park and Mel Hodge Park on Rock Island.) **26**

SPRINGFIELD

BREWHOUSE The ghost of a former bartender haunts this dance bar. Albert "Rudy" Cranor's spirit has not left the place since he committed suicide by shooting himself in the head on June 27, 1968. Not long afterward, a bone-chilling cold spot started moving around the building, which had no air conditioning. An invisible hand touched people on the shoulder or threw glasses across the room. Once a waitress saw a disembodied head floating in midair. Employees and customers were so bothered by the persistent presence that the owners asked the church to perform an official exorcism. Rudy was a devout Catholic, and his friends believed he wanted to be forgiven for his desperate deed. In August 1979, two priests from the Catholic Diocese of Springfield performed an exorcism ritual, and Rudy has not been heard from since.

(The Brewhouse, formerly the Sober Duck Disco, is in south Springfield.) **176**

LINCOLN'S TOMB The ghost of the Civil War president has been reported hovering near his grave site here. It has been suggested that Lincoln is not really buried there, and that Honest Abe does not want to deceive the good people of Illinois.

(The Lincoln Tomb State Historic Site is in Oak Ridge Cemetery in Springfield. For information, contact the State Historical Sites Division, 313 6th St. North, Springfield, IL 62701. Phone: 217-785-1584. www.state.il.us/HPA/Sites/LincolnTomb.htm) **5, 42**

OLD COURTHOUSE Lincoln's ghost is said to walk the streets surrounding the old courthouse, where the sixteenth president pleaded many cases as a young lawyer. Vachel Lindsay's famous poem describes Lincoln's mournful ghost pacing up and down the sidewalk near the courthouse.

(Springfield is in central Illinois at the junction of I-55 and I-72. The courthouse is at the center of the city plaza. Phone: 217-782-2424.) **5**

WATSEKA

VENNUM HOUSE The Watseka Wonder first appeared here on July 11, 1877. That was the day that thirteen-year-old Lurancy Vennum first fell into a strange catatonic sleep, during which she "traveled to heaven and spoke with spirits." The attacks continued to occur three to twelve times per day and sometimes lasted eight hours. During her trancelike state, Lurancy would speak in dozens of different voices and reported conversations with discarnate souls. When she awoke she remembered nothing. News of the girl who conversed with spirits quickly spread throughout the state. Doctors diagnosed the young girl as mentally ill and recommended committing her to the State Insane Asylum at Peoria. Finally, on January 31, 1878, a man named Asa Roff, also from Watseka, visited the Vennums and told them that his daughter had been afflicted with the same condition. The man was convinced that his own daughter, Mary, had actually communicated with spirits. Mary died in 1865, after being committed to the Peoria asylum. Roff wanted to spare Lurancy a similar fate and brought along Dr. E. Winchester Stevens, a physician who believed in spiritualism. The Vennums agreed to allow Dr. Stevens to examine their daughter. During his examination, two spirits spoke through the girl for over an hour, until she fell to the floor, rigid as a board. Dr. Stevens proceeded to "mesmerize" the girl, who responded to the treatment and finally relaxed. While still in her trance, the voice of another young girl started talking through Lurancy. It was Mary Roff, Asa's daughter. The spirit had sensed the presence of her father and wanted to go home with him. To everyone's amazement, the spirit described intimate details of the Roff family life. Mary possessed Lurancy's body throughout the night and into the next day. Roff sent for his wife, who brought along a married daughter. As they approached the Vennum house,

Lurancy shouted out their nicknames, known only to family members. Mary refused to leave Lurancy's body and pleaded to be allowed to return home.

On February 11, the Vennums agreed to allow their daughter to be taken home with the Roffs. They hoped the act would in some way speed Lurancy's recovery. Lurancy-as-Mary stayed with the Roffs for three months. During that period, she recognized visitors, told of family outings, identified her favorite possessions and clothing, and related incidents and facts that were only known to the family. Then, on May 21, Lurancy surfaced and announced that she wanted to go home. She was completely cured of the alarming condition which had afflicted her for over ten months. As a way of thanking Mary for her help, Lurancy periodically returned to the Roff house and allowed their daughter to enter her body. At such times, they visited with their dead daughter as if she were alive.

(Watseka is in eastern Illinois, fifty miles south of Chicago on Highway 1. In 1896, Lurancy Vennum married and moved to Rollins County, Kansas. She was never again visited by Mary's spirit. The house is now a private residence in Watseka.) **143, 176, 222**

A mysterious red-yellow ball of light appears over Maple Lake and in the nearby woods. See Maple Lake, Willow Springs, Illinois (LINDA MALLOW/PIX INT'L.)

WILLOW SPRINGS

MAPLE LAKE A mysterious red-yellow ball of light appears over this man-made lake and sometimes travels into the nearby woods. It has been observed many times over the years but only lasts about a minute.

Investigators have not been able to come up with a plausible explanation, but some reports associate it with an accident in which a man was decapitated.

(Willow Springs is southwest of Chicago. Take I-294 to Justice and exit southwest on Archer Ave. The lake is located between Archer Ave. and 104th Ave. in an open preserve bounded by the Chicago Ship Canal and the Calumet Sag Channel.) **15, 72**

WOODSTOCK

WOODSTOCK OPERA HOUSE A ghost called Elvira is said to haunt the balcony here and even has her own seat, No. DD-113. She has been known to voice her criticism at dress rehearsals by booing or banging the seats. Shelley Berman encountered the ghost when he played here in the 1940s, as did a number of other stars. Elvira has haunted the building since the 1890s. She is described as a tall, very attractive young lady with waist-length blond hair, and is thought to be a frustrated actress who flung herself from the bell tower a few years after the theater opened. Honda once did a TV commercial centered around the ghost of Woodstock, but the theater's management denies supernatural activity.

(Woodstock is in northern Illinois. Follow U.S. Highway 90 to Route 47 North, which runs through the town. Turn east on Calhoun St. and go eight blocks to Dean St. where the entrance to the theater's parking lot lies. The 450-seat opera house is at 121 Van Buren St. Woodstock, IL 60098. Phone: 815-338-4212. www.prairieghosts.com/woodst.html) **14, 176, 210**

WORTH

HOLY SEPULCHRE CEMETERY The grave of a girl believed to have healing powers gives off the odor of fresh roses. Mary Alice Quinn died in 1935 at the age of fourteen. A gentle, pious child, she reportedly healed several people before she died. Hundreds have made a pilgrimage to her grave in hopes of finding relief from their ills.

(Worth is a southwest suburb of Chicago, at the junction of 111th Street and Highway 43. Holy Sepulchre Cemetery is located west of Cicero Avenue, between 111th and 115th streets. Mary is buried in the Reilly plot 6001 West 111th St. Worth, IL 60482. Phone: 708-422-3020. www.graveyards.com/holysepulchre) **66 (11/93), 176**

INDIANA

ANDERSON

MOUNDS STATE PARK Prehistoric people believed this site was too sacred for human habitation. Instead, they created eleven mysterious earthworks and held rituals and public ceremonies here. The people treated the land with great respect and never visited the site unless they were in large groups. The 9-foot-high, 384-foot-diameter Great Circle Mound is the central feature, although there were other mounds in various geometric shapes, such as figure eights and rectangles. Young men were sacrificed here and their bodies laid at the entrance to the Circle Mound. It was believed that the innocent victims would be resurrected and reborn into another, better world. Many of the features of this two-thousand-year-old site have eroded away, but the ground remains sacred. Some people have reported encountering blue-gowned dwarves in the park and nearby along the White River at Noblesville. According to Delaware Indian legend, they are the Puk-wud-ies, a tribe of little people that still inhabit the forests.

(Anderson is northeast of Indianapolis. Take I-69 to Exit 28 and follow Highway 9 north to Highway 232. Exit at Mounds Road. For information, contact the Mounds State Park, 4306 Mounds Rd., Anderson, IN 46017. Phone. 765-642-6627.) **53 (3/95), 99**

ANGEL MOUNDS

ANGEL MOUNDS STATE MEMORIAL PARK This site was inhabited for over seven hundred years by an ancient people who worshiped the sun. Archeologists believe the Angel Mounds people originated from a larger settlement in Illinois (see Cahokia, Illinois). They suddenly abandoned their Indiana home in 1310 for unknown reasons. There were two hundred dwellings here and eleven earthen platforms, on top of which sat large religious temples. A reconstruction of one of the great temples stands in the park. A number of unusual graves have been found at Angel Mounds, such as the circular earthen pots used as burial urns for children. The religious leaders, or shamans, were accorded special burials. The tooth of a mastodon was found in the grave of one of them here.

(Angel Mounds State Memorial Park is near Evansville, which is located in the southwestern tip of Indiana. Take Highway 64 to Highway 164 south, then follow South Green River Rd. to Pollack Ave. Turn east to the park. Angel Mounds State Memorial Park, 8215 Pollack Ave., Evansville, IN 47715. Phone: 812-853-3956. www.angelmounds.org) **99**

BLOOMINGTON

BLOOMINGTON INDIANA UNIVERSITY The ghost of a murdered coed haunts the halls of Read Hall dormitory. The girl was killed in an argument with her medical student boyfriend late one night. He stabbed her in the throat with a scalpel, and she bled to death almost instantly. The young man hid the blood-soaked body in one of the deserted tunnels in the basement, but ended up confessing the whole thing when police questioned him. Now the ghost of a girl with long black hair and a yellow nightgown haunts her boyfriend's third-floor room and other areas of the X-shaped building.

(Read Hall used to be a men's dorm but is now a women's residence. Indiana University, Bloomington, IN 47405. Phone: 812-855-0661. www.iub.edu) **37, 41, 72**

STEPP CEMETERY A deformed stump in the shape of a chair at the center of this graveyard is the seat of a woman ghost, believed to be the mother of the child in a nearby grave. The child was struck and killed by a car. It is considered very bad luck for anyone but the ghost to sit in the chairlike tree trunk. Indiana University folklorists have collected dozens of other legends about Stepp Cemetery.

(Stepp Cemetery is outside Bloomington. The entrance is at a curved stone wall at the side Old State Highway 37 in the Morgan-Monroe State Forest. Follow the dirt path to the cemetery. There are about twenty-five tombstones still standing. www.prairieghosts.com/stepp.html) **175**

CICERO

ECK HOUSE Ghostly manifestations began in this house when the kitchen was remodeled in 1982. Contractors reported a troublesome presence that interfered with their work. A psychic detected the ghost of Leonard Eck, who built the house in the 1930s. He was seen near the fireplace smoking an old-fashioned bulldog pipe.

(Cicero is in Hamilton County in central Indiana, sixteen miles north of Indianapolis at the junction of Highways 19 and 47. The old Eck House is a private residence in Cicero.) **53(9/89)**

CROWN POINT

LAKE COUNTY COURTHOUSE The original courthouse in Crown Point was haunted for over fifty years, but the ghosts disappeared when the building was remodeled. However, strange voices and unexplained sounds are still heard in the old jailhouse in the building, where John Dillinger once spent time.

(Crown Point is in Lake County in northwest Indiana. Take U.S. Highway 41 to U.S. Highway 231 east. Courthouse, 2293 N. Main St., Crown Point, IN 46307. Phone: 219-756-0502.) **72, 101**

This bridge replaces an earlier trestle where an Irish laborer was tragically killed. His ghost haunted the earlier bridge and is still seen roaming the area. See White Lick Creek, Danville, Indiana (JAMES E. RAINBOLT)

DANVILLE

WHITE LICK CREEK The ghost of an itinerant Irishman haunts this creek bed. He was one of many Irish laborers who helped build a railroad trestle across the creek in the 1850s. The man fell from the trestle framework into a huge concrete vat and unintentionally became part of the bridge support. For many years, the Irishman's ghost haunted the bridge and was seen flagging down trains. After the trestle was torn down, his pathetic form was still seen roaming the area near a later bridge.

(Danville is fifteen miles west of Indianapolis on U.S. Highway 36 in Hendricks County. The haunted area is marked by a concrete bridge built in 1906. It crosses White Lick Creek and a blacktop road. The stone foundations of the original trestle can be found not far from the concrete bridge.) **72, 176**

DUBLIN

HEACOCK ROAD The ghost of a sobbing woman who died in an automobile accident here has been seen looking for her lost baby. The woman drowned when her car went off an old bridge into a rain-swollen creek. Searchers found her body in the car, along with a pink blanket and pacifier, but they could not locate the baby.

The woman's pitiful, moaning apparition was seen by several witnesses and the bridge came to be known as Cry-Woman Bridge.

(Dublin is between Indianapolis and Richmond on U.S. Highway 40 in east central Indiana. Heacock Road parallels Highway 40 outside of town.) **176**

EVANSVILLE

REYNOLDS HOUSE The ghost of a lonely nineteen-year-old boy attached himself to a family who lived in his old house. He became such a part of their family that he even moved with them to a new residence. Warren and Gladys Reynolds believe the friendly spirit of Oscar, a boy who died in 1922, has lived with them since 1942, when they first moved into the house. They discovered his spirit during a violent thunderstorm when an unseen presence ran up the stairs and shut all the windows on the second floor. The Reynolds' twelve-year-old daughter also felt his presence on the stairway. Later, the boy's shadowy figure was seen in the bedroom where he had died of unknown causes. When the Reynolds family moved out in 1965, Oscar accompanied them to their new home. They still hear his soft footsteps and watch Oscar's cane-bottomed rocker move slowly back and forth with nobody sitting in it.

(Evansville is in the southwest corner of Indiana, about one hundred miles west of Louisville on Highway 64. Oscar's original home is now the site of Doctor's Plaza, a medical clinic in downtown Evansville.) **176**

WILLARD LIBRARY This Gothic library building was not considered to be haunted until 1936, when a custodian quit after repeatedly encountering the apparition of a lady in gray in the basement. Since then, janitors, employees, and patrons of the Willard Library have all reported sensing the elusive ghost, sometimes only as a cold spot or the odor of perfume. The Lady in Gray has been encountered near the restrooms, near the elevator, and in the Children's Room, which was moved to the basement in the 1940s. Margaret Maier, who served as children's librarian until her death in 1989, saw the ghost repeatedly in the 1950s. When the Children's Room was remodeled in 1985, Maier insisted that the Lady in Gray came home to live with her until the remodeling was completed. Maier's sister and nephew both reported seeing the apparition in her home. The Lady in Gray was later caught on a security camera placed near the restrooms at the library. The

Willard Library first opened in 1885, and the female apparition is always dressed in the fashion of that time. In 1992, a child reported seeing two ghosts in the Children's Room. She described Margaret Maier sitting in a peacock chair. Standing behind her was the figure of the Lady in Gray.

(Willard Library, 21 First Ave., Evansville, IN 47710. Phone: 812-425-4309. www.knoxstudio.com/ghostcam/ ghost) **72, 133**

FAIRMOUNT

PARK CEMETERY Every year hundreds of people make the pilgrimage to James Dean's simple grave in this small cemetery. Many take home a handful of dirt from the site. Visitors have felt Dean's spirit here, and several of his loyal fans say they have been in contact with him. Near Cholame, California, the ghostly sounds of screeching tires are still reported by truckers passing the tree on Highway 46 where the star lost control of his Porsche and died on September 30, 1955.

(Fairmont is in central Indiana. Take Exit 55 west from I-69. There is a memorial to Dean in the Jack Ranch Café parking lot at Cholame, California. Park Cemetery is at 102 East First, Fairmount, IN 46928. Phone: 765-948-4040.) **72, 196**

GARY

DUNES STATE PARK The naked ghost of Diana of the Dunes has been reported many times here. The apparition is of a real person, Alice Mable Gray, who lived on the rugged Lake Michigan shoreline from 1915 to 1925. Alice was the daughter of a prominent physician, and she graduated with honors from the University of Chicago. But failing eyesight and family problems made her take refuge at the Indiana dunes, where she had spent many happy days as a child. In 1920, she met a penniless drifter by the name of Paul Wilson. Together, they lived in a shack near the beach. She died on February 11, 1926, of uremic poisoning caused by massive blows to her abdomen. It is believed she was beaten by Wilson, who was a suspect in several violent crimes that occurred in the beach area. He ended up in a California prison and was later killed trying to steal a car.

(Gary is in the northwest corner of Indiana at the junction of I-80 and I-65. Diana of the Dunes haunts the beaches east of Gary, between Miller and Michigan City. Alice Gray is buried with other unidentified bodies in a

potter's plot at Oak Lawn Cemetery in Gary. For information on the Indiana dunes lakeshore, call the National Park Service at 219-926-1952.) **72, 176**

LA LLORONA The phantom of a Mexican woman with long black hair and pointed fingernails is said to roam the streets of the Calumet Region. It is believed the Mexican woman, known as La Llorona, drowned her illegitimate children in the Calumet River and has returned to search for them. La Llorona might also be responsible for other ghost sightings in this area. Many reports describe a lady in white flagging down taxis or hitching rides to Calumet Harbor. She always disappears from the car while en route, or simply appears in the car and then vanishes seconds later. See Billings, Montana; El Paso, Texas; Guadalupita, New Mexico.

(La Llorona has been reported in Cudahey, a Mexican community of steelworkers in the Indiana Harbor area. She is most often encountered near the intersection of Cline Ave. and Fifth Ave. The Lady in White has been spotted hitchhiking along Indianapolis Boulevard near the Cline Avenue overpass and north of Chicago Avenue, in East Chicago, Indiana. www.prairieghosts.com/lalloron.html) **68, 72, 176**

GREENCASTLE

DEPAUW UNIVERSITY The buildings on this picturesque campus are free of ghosts, but the books are haunted. The ghost of James Whitcomb, governor of Indiana from 1843 to 1848, protects a collection of rare books he donated to the university library over 150 years ago. He left instructions in his will that the Whitcomb Collection should never leave the library building, and it became accepted that anyone who dared to remove part of the collection could be assured of a visit by his ghost. One student, who took a copy of *The Poems of Ossian* (the legendary Gaelic warrior) to his room, found himself awakened by Whitcomb's figure standing at the foot of his bed. The specter pointed its finger at the terrified student and chanted "Ossian! Ossian! Who stole the Ossian?" After the figure faded, the student stayed awake all night and returned the book to the library first thing the next morning. The collection was later moved to a new building, and rumors of the ghost continue, although now it is virtually impossible for anyone to take any of the Whitcomb Collection out the building. The books are kept in the noncirculating Special Collections Division.

(Greencastle is thirty-seven miles west of Indianapolis. The collection is now housed in the Roy O. West Library, 400 S. College St., Greencastle, IN 46135. Phone: 765-658-4434.) **5, 72, 176**

HAMMOND

INDIANA BOTANIC GARDENS A stone mansion that once served as the headquarters of a nationally known herbal supply company is haunted by the presence of a female ghost, whose white form has been observed in the 1920s building. She is thought to be a former owner.

(Hammond is on the Illinois border in extreme northwestern Indiana. The company has since moved to Hobart, Indiana. The deserted building is at 626 177th St., Hammond, IN 46325. A Haunted House show is held at the location in October. For information, contact Hluska Enterprises at 219-853-0518.) **72**

The smell of rotting flesh, mysterious cold spots, and unexplained movements beset this Italianate mansion, known as Hannah House. See Hannah House, Indianapolis, Indiana (JAMES E. RAMBOLT)

INDIANAPOLIS

HANNAH HOUSE The sickening smell of rotting flesh drifts from a second-floor bedroom here, and mysterious cold spots move about, seemingly of their own volition. Sometimes, the apparition of a bearded man in a black frock coat can be seen. This Italianate mansion was built in 1858 by state legislator Alexander M. Hannah, but it was not until 1967, after the house had sat vacant for five years, that strange things started happening. The overpowering stench of death on the second-floor may be the ghostly manifestation of the Hannah's stillborn child. The apparition of Alexander Hannah was last reported in 1972, standing on the second-floor near the stairway arch. The ghost of an unidentified woman was reported near a window on the same floor, and phantom slaves have been seen hiding in the basement. Other strange activities, such as moving chandeliers and picture frames, and unaccountable sounds, have been witnessed by television crews investigating the grand but spooky old house.

(Indianapolis is at the center of the state, at the intersection of I-65, I-70, and I-74. The graves of Alexander and Elizabeth Hannah are in the Crown Hill Cemetery at 700 W. 38th St., in Indianapolis. Next to them is a small, unmarked tombstone with only a single date. Take I-465 to U.S. Highway 31 north. The Hannah mansion is on the corner of National Ave. and Madison Ave. Hannah House, 3801 Madison Ave., Indianapolis, IN 46225. Phone: 317-787-8486.) **72, 176**

TUCKAWAY HOUSE Mary Pickford, Carole Lombard, Joan Crawford, Walt Disney, Rudy Vallee, Douglas Fairbanks, Helen Hayes, and dozens of other movie stars and celebrities came to this simple house to have their palms read. The house was built in 1907 and purchased three years later by George and Nellie Meier. Nellie Meier was one of the world's most famous palm readers. When she died in 1944 the house went to her niece Ruth Austin. The ghosts of Nellie, George, and Ruth all have appeared in their former home. Their peaceful presences are frequently encountered on the balcony and in the forty-foot-long dining room. The current residents, the Kenneth Keene family, believe the strong spirits of the colorful people who used to live there influence the style of furnishings and activities in their home.

(The two-story bungalow is located in a residential section in north Indianapolis.) **53 (9/85), 134**

LAPORTE

TENTH AND I STREETS A corner at the intersection of these two streets is haunted by the spirit of a Potawatomi Indian maiden who died there nearly 150 years ago. She died in 1848, during a forced march westward, at a small pond that sat on the site. The Indians called the pond Came and Went, because it filled with water during storms and then dried up. The pond was on land owned by Dr. George Andrew, who built a three-story mansion in 1845. The house was considered haunted for many years. Later owners told of old coins materializing out of thin air, mysterious footsteps, and moving shadows. Eventually, no one wanted to live in Andrew's mansion, and it was torn down in the 1970s. Today, employees and visitors to the medical/dental center built on the spot continue to report strange events, such as doors opening and closing by themselves.

(La Porte is between Gary and South Bend in northwest Indiana, at the junction of U.S. Highway 35 and Highway 2. The dental center is located on the corner of Tenth and I streets, LaPorte, IN 46350.) **72, 101, 176**

NEW HARMONY

NEW HARMONY STATE HISTORIC SITE Walking through a shrub maze here symbolizes man's search for the source of eternal life. Some people have experienced a change of consciousness in which they realize there is no death, only rebirth and renewal. The labyrinth was built in 1814 by a religious commune known as the Harmonists. They believed man could prosper by living in harmony with nature. The group was attracted to a site used by the ancient Temple Mound Builders, who believed essentially the same thing. An outdoor roofless church at the site expresses the Harmonist idea that only the roof of the open sky should enclose the worshipers of God.

(The New Harmony State Historic Site is on the Wabash River in the southwestern tip of Indiana. Take I-64 to Highway 165 South, and follow it to Highway 66. Go west eight miles to New Harmony. The labyrinth is on the corner of Main St. and Tavern St. For information, contact the Historic New Harmony Promotion Co-ordinator, 410 Main St., New Harmony, IN 47631. Phone: 812-682-3276. www.newharmony.org) **99**

ODON

OLD HACKLER FARM A peculiar fire-causing poltergeist attacked the William Hackler farm in April 1941. The family was doing chores one day when they detected a smoldering fire coming from inside the walls of a second-floor bedroom. Later, a mattress in another bedroom started to burn from the inside. Between 8:00 and 11:00 A.M., nine mysterious fires erupted. Firefighters from two communities stayed on the scene all day to put out the fires. They witnessed fires starting inside closed books, in the middle of calendars, and in other household items. By the time the day was over, they had extinguished twenty-eight fires, although the house itself never burned. The house had no electricity and no open flame of any kind, and the children were carefully monitored. The official cause of the fires was recorded as "a most baffling mystery." Nonetheless, Traveler's Insurance Company paid for the damages and took out a full-page ad in *Collier's Magazine* proclaiming that they even covered fires of supernatural origin.

(Odon is forty-five miles southwest of Bloomington. Take Highway, 45/54 to U.S. Highway 231 South and turn west on Highway 58 to Odon. Rather than continue to fight the poltergeist, William Hackler destroyed his farmhouse and moved a few miles away.) **176**

PLYMOUTH

HAYLOFT RESTAURANT Employees and guests of this rustic restaurant report encountering the ghost of an old farmer. The man was killed in a barn fire at the same location and has returned to the scene of his painful demise. The odor of burned wet wood is detected just before the apparition makes an appearance.

(Plymouth is in northern Indiana at the junction of U.S. Highways 30 and 31. The restaurant is on the edge of town. Hayloft Restaurant, Plymouth, 15147 Lincoln Highway, IN 46563. Phone: 219-936-6680.) **72**

PORTAGE

WOLANIN HOUSE The ghost of a little girl haunts this 150-year-old house. Robert Wolanin, his wife Emma, and daughter Holly have all encountered the five-year-old girl, whom they call Lisa. The girl wears modern clothing and appears sporadically in all areas of the house.

(Portage is in northwest Indiana, just east of Gary on I-80. The house is a private residence in south Portage.) **72**

ROACHDALE

BIGFOOT SIGHTING In August 1972, several farmers here tracked a large creature covered with black hair that smelled like garbage. The first encounter was connected with a UFO sighting near a mobile home owned by the Rogers family. They saw a luminous object hovering over an adjacent cornfield and later observed the creature walking through their cornstalks. Other farmers in the area also witnessed the beast, which broke into a hen house and mutilated dozens of chickens. The Bigfoot was seen standing in the doorway of a farm building and completely covered the eight-foot-wide opening. The creature was in the area for several days, and a group of farmers chased and shot at it but were never able to down the beast.

(Roachdale is thirty miles west of Indianapolis. Take I-74 to Highway 75 South and go east on Highway 236 to Roachdale.) **139**

A ghost dog near the Heinl Mausoleum is just one of the spirits to frequent Highland Lawn Cemetery. See Highland Lawn Cemetery. Terre Haute, Indiana (JAMES E. RAINBOLT)

TERRE HAUTE

HIGHLAND LAWN CEMETERY When John Heinl died in 1920 there was an unexpected complication at his grave site. His constant companion, a bulldog named Stiffy Green, could not be pulled away from his master's tomb. The green-eyed dog took up a post outside his master's mausoleum and refused to let anyone near it. The few times the pugnacious Stiffy was captured and taken back to the Heinl residence, the dog escaped and found his way back to the his master's graveside. For many weeks, exposed to all types of weather, the animal stood his ground. But the trauma proved too much, and one morning Stiffy Green was found dead next to a pillar at the entrance to the Heinl Mausoleum. Today, if you peer through the bronze grill of the mausoleum, you will see Stiffy sitting next to the crypt. Heinl's wife had the dog stuffed and placed him next to her husband for all eternity. When vandals shot at the stuffed animal, she had a statue made to replace it. Sometimes, just after dark, people see the figure of John Heinl and his bulldog strolling through the grounds. They even hear his low voice, hushing his faithful companion.

At the opposite end of the cemetery, flowers appear mysteriously at the Sheets Mausoleum. Martin Sheets was an eccentric businessman who had a chandelier and telephone installed in his mausoleum. It is even rumored he hid whisky bottles in the tomb pillars.

(Terre Haute is in western Indiana at the junction of I-70 and U.S. Highway 41. John Heinl founded the Heinl Flower Shop. The cemetery is east of town at 4520 Wabash Ave., Terre Haute, IN 47808. Phone: 812-877-2531. www.prairieghosts.com/h_lawn.html) **72, 176**

TIPPECANOE

PROPHET'S TOWN A remarkable Shawnee prophet known as Elskatawa ("the Open Door") made some of the most amazing predictions ever recorded. Elskatawa had a vision one night that pointed the way toward a new Indian Nation that relied on the old Indian ways with a curious mixture of Christian ethics. His brother Tecumseh, one of the nation's most respected Indian leaders, joined Elskatawa to make his dream reality. In June 1808, they set up an idealized Indian community known as Prophet's Town. Nothing intoxicating was allowed in the self-sufficient town, which relied totally on crops planted on the surrounding land. Elskatawa was known for his accurate predictions. He had successfully predicted an eclipse of the sun and other natural phenomena. However, in 1807 he presaged a remarkable event. He said there would be two days of darkness in December 1811. The animals would come out of the earth and the Great Spirit would shake down every house in Tuckhabatchee, an area that extended from Detroit to Tennessee. In the first weeks of December 1811, hordes of squirrels suddenly left Indiana and tried to swim across the Ohio River. Thousands drowned. No one could explain their mysterious behavior. Then, on December 16, the strongest earthquake in modern American history struck the area. The Madrid Fault Quake affected three hundred thousand square miles, causing the Mississippi and Ohio Rivers to flow backward, creating and emptying whole lakes in less than an hour (see Reelfoot Lake, Tennessee). An area of thirty thousand square miles sank up to twenty-five feet; other areas rose by an equal amount. The sky was dark for two days from the dust of collapsing trees, huts, and cabins.

Elskatawa's most famous prophecy was his presidential curse. He was moved to proclaim it by General William Henry Harrison's irreverent 1840 campaign slogan: "Tippecanoe and Tyler Too!" which referred to the Indian defeat at the Battle of Tippecanoe. Elskatawa pronounced that every president elected in a twenty-year cycle beginning in 1840 would die in office. Harrison died a month after his inauguration. Lincoln, elected in 1860, was assassinated. Garfield, elected in 1880, was assassinated. McKinley, reelected in 1900, was assassinated. Harding, elected in 1920, died in office. Franklin Roosevelt, elected in 1940, died in office. Kennedy, elected in 1960, was assassinated. By surviving an attempted assassination, Ronald Reagan was the first president to break the 120-year-old curse.

(Tippecanoe River State Park is in Pulaski County in northwest Indiana 4200 N. US Highway 35, Winamac, IN 46996. Phone: 219-946-3213. The park is just south of town. The heart of the Shawnee territory was between the White River and the Wabash River in the southern third of Indiana. Prophet's Town was on the west bank of the Wabash River near the mouth of the Tippecanoe at Oswego in Kosciusko County. www.prophetstown.org) **53 (6/95), 62**

VINCENNES

SIGMA PI FRATERNITY EXECUTIVE OFFICES This fraternity headquarters is said to be haunted by Colonel Eugene Wharf, the original owner of the building. The thirteen-acre estate was once known as Rebel Hill, because it was a meeting place for Southern sympathizers before the Civil War. The Wharf family left it to Vincennes University in the 1950s, and in 1962 it was given to Sigma Pi. The colonel's presence is manifested by roaming cold spots, lights that go on and off by themselves, moving objects, and a discarnate male voice. The ghost has a nasty habit of turning cups of hot coffee into cold muck with a gust of icy cold wind.

However, the fraternity's executive director insists the building is not haunted.

(Vincennes is in southwestern Indiana at the junction of U.S. Highways 41 and 50. The offices are in a 1916 Georgian-style mansion at 705 Mound St., Vincennes, IN 47591. Phone: 219-462-9138.) **135**

IOWA

AMANA

AMANA COLONIES The Amana Colonies were formed in 1854, when a group of mystical Lutherans called the "Community of True Inspiration" moved from New York to Iowa. The devout Germanic settlers moved away from the temptations of the East Coast to take up the simple life of the Iowa prairie. But their lives were complicated by ghosts. Geiste Ecke, or "Ghost Corner," was believed haunted by a variety of spirits whose white apparitions have been reported by many witnesses over the years. The Indian Dam site was built three hundred years ago by Sauk Indians and is still haunted by their spirits. During a full moon, the sounds of drums are sometimes heard there. After a while, the members of the colony avoided the area altogether. The ghosts of children buried in the Main Amana Cemetery are said to rise up on Christmas to claim pine boughs left on their graves by living children. A blue aura is seen above Mary Wright's grave at the Sprague Cemetery. The miasmic light is said to appear during the last minute of every year. Mary died of an infection in 1854 at the age of six.

(The seven Amana Colonies are in Iowa County off I-80 at Highway 6 and Highway 151. Geiste Ecke is a sharp bend in the road near a ravine between Middle and High Amana. Indian Dam is north of Homestead on the Iowa River. Mary Wright's is the only grave left in the old Sprague Cemetery, just west of Homestead on Highway 6.

The marker is on the north side of the road. For information, call 319-622-7622. www.jeonet.com/amanas) **52**

AMES

IOWA STATE UNIVERSITY No one has been able to figure out where the low moaning sounds coming from the Tribute Hall in the Memorial Union. The hall pays tribute to graduates of Iowa State University who have died in wars. The eerie moans are frequently reported in this hall, and many believe it is coming from the only female ISU graduate to have died in war (World War I). No one has yet figured out any conventional explanation for the otherworldly sounds.

(Iowa State University, 117 Beardshear Hall, Ames, IA 50011. Phone: 515-294-4111.) **72**

BETTENDORF

CENTRAL AVENUE The ghost of a chubby, middle-aged washwoman walks into houses here and starts doing the laundry. She has been reported since the late 1800s but has apparently kept up with the times. She was first seen with a wooden wash tub. Then, she started to appear with a double-wringer machine.

(Bettendorf is along the Mississippi River in Scott County, opposite Moline in Illinois. The ghost has appeared along Central Ave., although some reports place her on Oak St. also.) **27**

BURLINGTON

HIGHWAY 34 The apparition of a black man carrying a leather bag is seen along this highway. The phantom is always walking westward along the north side of the road, and he is always seen between 1:00 and 2:00 A.M. He is thought to be the ghost of an escaped slave who died of diphtheria in the 1860s and was buried in the basement of a Burlington home.

(Burlington is in the southeast corner of Iowa at the junction of U.S. Highways 34 and 61. The apparition is seen on old U.S. Highway 34, between Burlington and Danville.) **22**

CEDAR RAPIDS

BRUCEMORE A strange groaning presence has been detected in the library of this 1886 mansion. Objects move by themselves and sometimes untraceable laughter is heard. At the turn of the century, a University of Chicago professor was called in to investigate. He confirmed the presence and wanted to remain in the house for several months to study it. Fearing news of the poltergeist would leak out, the owners refused.

(Cedar Rapids is in Linn County in east central Iowa, at the junction of I-380 and U.S. Highway 30. Brucemore is a private residence that is open for tours. Brucemore, 2160 Linden Dr. SE, Cedar Rapids, IA 52403. Phone: 319-362-7375. www.brucemore.org) **29**

CEDAR RAPIDS ART MUSEUM Prior to 1985, this building housed the Cedar Rapids Public Library. One morning in the late 1960s, reference librarian Elizabeth Schoenfelder noticed one of her regular patrons, named Hazel, walking down from the balcony where current newspapers were kept. Hazel passed within fifteen feet of her and was also seen by two other employees of the library. When the afternoon paper arrived, Schoenfelder was shocked to learn that Hazel had suffocated in a fire in her apartment building at 4:00 that same morning. The library staff had witnessed a "crisis apparition," one-time apparitions who appear shortly before or after a person dies.

(Cedar Rapids Museum of Art, 410 3rd Ave. SE, Cedar Rapids, IA 52401. Phone: 319-366-7503.) **29, 72**

COE COLLEGE A ghost called Helen haunts this campus. The young coed died of influenza in 1918 and her spirit is said to have taken up residence in an old grandfather clock in Voorhees Hall, her former dorm. The clock had been donated to the school by Helen's parents. At night, her ghost left the clock and played the piano in the parlor or walked the stairs to her old room on the second floor. Late at night, the white apparition would appear at the foot of students' beds. Sometimes it would slam doors or pull off the bedcovers. When the grandfather clock was moved to Stuart Hall in the early 1970s, the ghostly manifestations started to take place there.

(Coe College, 1220 First Ave. NE; Cedar Rapids, IA 52402. Phone: 319-399-8000. www.coe.edu) **29**

OAK HILL CEMETERY The ghost of a Czech girl named Tillie walks the graveyard here, carrying a flickering candle. Sometimes she tries to pull people into one of the mausoleums. Tillie is buried in the potter's field section.

(Oak Hill Cemetery, Mt. Vernon Rd., Cedar Rapids, IA 52403.) **29**

CHEROKEE

AMERICAN THEATRE This old movie house is haunted by its former owner, "Mr. Goldie." The staff at the theater all have stories about their encounters with the friendly spirit. One manager said one afternoon as he was walking across the stage, he looked out into the auditorium. About four rows in front of him, two seats were rocking slowly, as if two people were having a leisurely conversation with one another. But there was no one else in the theater at the time.

(American Theatre, 108 East Main St., Cherokee, IA 51012. Phone: 712-225-2345.) **72**

CLINTON

CAMANCHE ROAD The phantom of a man in a top hat has haunted this road for nearly a century. If anyone stops to give him a ride, he rewards them with a small gift. In the early 1950s, the ghost gave a man a pair of tickets to a dinner theater.

(Clinton is on the Mississippi River in east central Iowa, at the junction of U.S. Highways 30 and 67. Camanche Road runs east of U.S. Highway 67, between Clinton and the town of Camanche.) **24**

COUNCIL BLUFFS

OLD POTTAWATTAMIE COUNTY JAIL This jail-house is also known as the Squirrel Cage Jail because of its unique three-story rotary jail. Prisoners were housed in pie-shaped cells, which were accessed by turning a hand crank until the cells lined up with a single door on each floor. But the jail, which closed down in 1969, has another claim to fame. The building is haunted by the first superintendent, J.M. Carter, who oversaw construction of the jail in 1884. He lived in the apartment on the fourth floor, and by all accounts stayed on in the old jail longer than any of his prisoners. His presence has been sensed over the years by jailers and prisoners alike, and his restless spirit is blamed for paranormal activity that occurs in the building to this day.

(Council Bluffs is on I-80, across the Missouri River from Omaha in southwestern Iowa. Squirrel Cage Historic Jail, 226 Pearl St., Council Bluffs, IA 51501. Phone: 712-323-2509. www.prairieghosts.com/oldpot.html) **53 (10/94)**

DAVENPORT

PALMER COLLEGE OF CHIROPRACTIC This respected college of chiropractic medicine is haunted by flying ghosts. The oldest lecture hall, built in the 1850s, is home to several airy ghosts that fly up near the ceiling. Their presence is sometimes evidenced only by swaying lamps hanging from the ceiling. There are no air vents or fans to account for the eerie movements.

(Palmer College, 1000 Brady St., Davenport, IA 528033. Phone: 563-884-5741.) **72**

PHI KAPPA CHI FRATERNITY The ghost of a large man has been seen entering the front door of this old house, walking up the stairs, and entering the upstairs front bedroom. No matter what the season, the man wears a winter overcoat with the collar pulled up. The apparition is said to be a homeless man brought in from the cold in 1922, when the house was a private residence. The man died that night in the upstairs front bedroom.

(Davenport is on the Mississippi River in east central Iowa, at the junction of I-80 and U.S. Highway 61. Phi Kappa Chi Fraternity, 723 Main St., Davenport, IA 52801.) **27**

DECORAH

LUTHER COLLEGE The ghostly footsteps of a woman in high heels are heard in the corridors of Larsen Hall. They are most often reported in the section of the building used as the college health service. The third floor of the same building is haunted by another ghost nicknamed Gertrude. Her mischievous presence is blamed for rifled drawers, false fire alarms, and missing items. People have reported missing articles of clothing, only to find them replaced with old-fashioned items. Gertrude is said to be a Decorah High School student graduate who longed to attend the college before it was coeducational. She was killed in 1918, after being struck by a car as she rode her bicycle down West Broadway.

(Decorah is in the northeast corner of Iowa, at the junction of U.S. Highway 52 and Highway 9. Luther College, 700 College Dr., Decorah, IA 52101. Phone: 319-387-2000. www.luther.edu) **75, 76**

PORTER HOUSE MUSEUM Playful spirits haunt this 125-year-old house. Their presence is detected on the main stairway, in the tower, and in the basement. The house was built by the Porter family, but the ghosts are thought to be the children of Dighton Ellsworth, who lived in the house in the late 1870s.

(The museum is at 410 West Broadway, Decorah, IA 52101. Phone: 319-382-8465.) **76**

DEEP RIVER

PAWNEE BRAVE The ghost of a young Pawnee brave leading a scrawny mustang was seen in the 1800s here. The hair on the horse was singed as if it had been caught in grass fire, and the boy was sometimes heard singing a high-pitched Pawnee chant.

(Deep River is in southeastern Poweshiek County, off Highway 21.) **158**

DES MOINES

DRAKE UNIVERSITY OBSERVATORY The astronomical observatory on this campus is haunted by the spirit of a former professor. Dr. Robert Morehouse was the first Chairman of the Astronomy and Physics Department and is credited with discovering a comet in the 1920s. The cremated remains of Dr. Morehouse and his wife were interred in the wall of the entryway to his beloved observatory. Witnesses have reported strange feelings of being watched or brushing against an invisible presence, especially in the basement work area. Some students insist that an unknown force sometimes corrects mistakes in calculations in their observation logs.

(Drake University, 2507 University Ave., Des Moines, IA 50311. Phone: 515-271-2011.) **72**

UNIVERSITY AVENUE The ghost of University Avenue is a moving, cloudlike presence that smells like kerosene. Sometimes the form of a man is discerned; at other times, small flickering lights are seen within the fog. Researchers discovered that in 1881, a Des Moines man died when his kerosene-soaked clothes accidentally caught fire. The ghost was reported in 1891, 1892, 1893, 1894, 1909, 1910, 1911, 1920, 1921, 1922, 1944, and 1945.

(Des Moines is in Polk County in central Iowa, at the junction of I-80 and I-35. The ghost was often seen downtown, along University Ave.) **219**

WEAVER HOUSE When Mr. and Mrs. James Weaver bought a small table from a friend in 1937, they had no idea it carried a ghost. Shortly after they brought it home, the table began to make rapping noises. The strange noises began occurring once or twice per week and soon escalated to six times a week. The spooky table was quieted only when the minister's wife read from the Bible while holding on to it. The Weavers consulted a spiritualist, who believed the table was once used in a séance and was now possessed by a confused spirit.

(The Weaver house is now a private residence, at 1942 Francis Ave., Des Moines, IA 50314.) **176**

DUBUQUE

GRAND OPERA HOUSE The opera house was opened in 1890 and became a movie house in 1928. In 1986, the building was renovated and turned into a community theater. About that time, people started hearing weird voices and shuffling footsteps in the deserted building. Employees blamed the unseen spirits for hiding objects, changing lighting, and playing pranks. Then in 1991, apparitions started appearing in the back of the theater. Investigators later discovered that years

before, when the opera house became a movie theater, cleaning women called police several times complaining of strange voices in the building at night.

(Dubuque is on the Mississippi River at the Iowa-Illinois-Wisconsin border. The old opera house is now the home of the Barn Community Theatre Company, 135 Eighth St., Dubuque, IA 52001. Phone: 319-588-4356.) **175**

An invisible presence has been detected in this Gothic mansion, the Mathias Ham House. See Mathias Ham House, Dubuque, Iowa
(DUBUQUE COUNTY HISTORICAL SOCIETY)

MATHIAS HAM HOUSE Ghostly manifestations have been reported in this limestone Gothic mansion since 1964. A window in the upstairs hall opens by itself, and footsteps are heard racing from the second floor to a tunnel in the basement. An invisible presence has been detected by custodians and tour guides. Electricians have been unable to locate the source of a problem which turns lights turn off and on and causes organ music to pour out of fuse sockets. The mansion began as a stone cottage built by shipping tycoon Mathias Ham in 1840. He lived there with his wife and five children. His first wife died in 1856; he remarried in 1860 and had two more children. That was when he expanded the cottage and built a twenty-three-room mansion. The only violence reported to have taken place here was in the 1890s. One of the Ham daughters was living in the house alone, when she shot and killed a burglar who broke into the house two nights in a row.

(Follow Kerper Blvd. to Hawthorne St., and go one block to Rhomberg. Turn left and follow the signs to the Mathias Ham House, which is at 2241 Lincoln St., Dubuque, IA 52001. Phone: 319-583-2812. For further information, call the Riverboat Historical Society at 319-557-9545.) **14, 101, 176**

EARLING

CONVENT OF THE FRANCISCAN SISTERS A twenty-three-day exorcism here finally freed Emma Schmidt of the demon that had terrorized her for twenty-six years. Emma spoke and understood languages which she had never been taught, blasphemed when religious relics were brought near her, levitated to the ceiling in front of several witnesses, was able to detect and reject blessed food, and foamed at the mouth in uncontrollable rage. When doctors gave up on her, her parents appealed to the Catholic Church for an exorcism. The rites took place in September 1928 and were conducted by Father Theophilus Riesinger, a Capuchin monk and experienced exorcist. The exhausting ritual required the attendance of a dozen nuns, who were kept busy removing buckets of foul-smelling excrement and vomit. Although Emma hardly ate, she spewed forth a greenish vomit as often as thirty times a day during the exorcism. Many strange voices and the howling of a variety of animals seemed to originate from her chest, and a strange, pea-sized lump moved all over her body just under her skin. Her body was completely distorted, swollen so badly that the nuns feared she would burst. Emma's head swelled and turned red, her eyes bulged from their sockets, and her gray lips protruded to twice their normal size. Sometimes she seemed to float above the bed; other times, her weight became so great that it bent the bed's iron frame. Curious people from miles around lined up outside the brick convent building to hear the horrible sounds coming from the frail woman's body. Finally, on September 23, 1928, Father Riesinger expelled the last of several demons who inhabited the body of Emma Schmidt. She cried "My Jesus Mercy!" and slept soundly for the first time in twenty-six years. The nauseating odor in the room immediately dissipated.

(Earling is in Shelby County, north of Harlan in western Iowa. Follow U.S. Highway 59 to Highway 37. Go west five miles to the town. The convent is north of town.) **176**

ELDRIDGE

NELSON FARM An old barn here is haunted by the ghost of a man in work clothes, wearing a straw hat. He was first seen in the 1880s, usually in the autumn months. In the 1980s, he was spotted standing in the hayloft and was visible from outside the barn.

(Eldridge is seven miles north of Davenport on U.S. Highway 61. The Nelson farm is on private property east of Eldridge.) **27**

ELKADER

LOVER'S LEAP The spirit of a young Indian maiden named White Cloud is said to haunt this clifftop. She leaped to her death from the spot when she was told her tribe had murdered her white lover. But the man survived and returned to bury her body at the top of the cliff.

(Elkader is in Clayton County in northeast Iowa, at the junction of Highways 13 and 56. Lover's Leap is a cliff overlooking the Turkey River, behind the County Office Building.) **76**

FORT MADISON

OLD VOGEL HOUSE Emil and Anna Vogel bought this house in March 1897 and soon realized it was haunted. Every night at 2:00 A.M., the cellar door opened and heavy footsteps plodded up the stairs into the kitchen. They could not see anybody there, until one night when they encountered the ghost of a heavy-set man with a beard ascending the stairway from the cellar. They moved out the next day, but curious people from all over the county started camping out in the front yard, in the hopes of catching a glimpse of the Vogel's punctual ghost.

(Fort Madison is eighteen miles south of Burlington on U.S. Highway 61. The Vogel house burned down on August 16, 1899. It was located at 2426 Des Moines St., Fort Madison, IA 52627.) **176**

INDIANOLA

SIMPSON COLLEGE A 125-year-old building on this campus, known as Old Chapel, is haunted by the ghosts of students who died there. A male student committed suicide in the old tower, and a woman is said to have hanged herself from the ceiling beams in 1924. Another woman is said to have hanged herself from the chandelier, which is visible through the second-floor Palladian window. At least two female students have fallen to their deaths in the open stairwell inside the chapel. Over the years, dozens of students and a security guard have reported encountering apparitions on the wooden staircase in the building.

(Indianola is seventeen miles south of Des Moines on U.S. Highway 65/69. Old Chapel has been used as a church, library, and conservatory. It was declared unsafe for occupancy in 1980. Simpson College, 701 North C St., Indianola, IA 50125. Phone: 515-961-1606. www.simpson.edu) **176**

IOWA CITY

MERCY HOSPITAL An exorcism ritual dispelled a pesky ghost here in 1979. After an elderly man died of cancer, nurse Victoria Meyer noticed that his former bed was always messed up. Just after the bed was freshly made, something pulled out the sheets and rumpled the covers. Finally, the nurse called in a priest to bless the bed and pray for the departed man's soul. The problems with the unkempt bed ended immediately.

(Iowa City is near the junction of I-80 and I-380 in southeast Iowa. The hospital is at 500 East Market St., Iowa City, IA 52245. Phone: 319-339-0300.) **28**

OAKLAND CEMETERY The ghost of a dead woman rose from a grave to comfort a troubled man. Recently, David Lenier was going through a divorce and often went for long walks in the cemetery. He was strangely attracted to the tombstone of Annie Oliver (1889–1921) and spent many hours sitting on her grave deep in thought. Then one day, according to Lenier, the ghost of Annie rose from her grave and danced with him to ease his mind. The experience so relaxed him that he slept on the grave overnight. But the most famous presence in Oakland Cemetery is not so friendly. The Feldevert Monument, better known as the Black Angel, is said to kill anyone who touches it, with the exception of virgins. Vandals who try to deface the monument come down with odd ailments that are sometimes fatal. The nine-foot-tall bronze statue of an angel with outstretched wings turned black shortly after being erected, and legend says it turns a shade darker every Halloween. The cold stare from the angel's eyes has unnerved many visitors, although it has been the site of a few moonlight weddings. The statue was commissioned in 1911 by Teresa Feldevert as a monument for both her teenage son Eddie and her husband Nicholas.

(The cemetery is at 1000 Brown St., Iowa City, IA 52240. Phone: 319-356-5105.) **28**

UNIVERSITY OF IOWA The ghosts of three coeds haunt Currier Hall. The dormitory was the scene of a triple suicide, when the roommates found out they were all in love with the same man. Ever since, students feel their presence as if voices are telling them never to keep secrets from one another. People living at Married Student Housing have to contend with more active ghosts. Strange tapping sounds move through the walls, dishes flies out of sinks, silverware flies out of drawers, and residents suffer from unexplainable nightmares of being suffocated. The source of the poltergeist energy is unknown.

(Currier Hall is four blocks north of the Old Capitol Building downtown. The Married Student Housing Building is located on Hawkeye Dr. University of Iowa, Iowa City, IA 52242. Phone: 319-335-3500.) **28**

KEOKUK

CONCERT STREET A strange presence showed up at the Harnes family home every October 11, from 1934 to 1936. The periodic poltergeist would wreak havoc in the house by moving furniture and objects. Each time, the apparition of a young man appeared. Usually only his lower torso could be seen, although he once rode a phantom bicycle through the house. The date coincided with the birthday of one of the Harnes boys.

(Keokuk is in Lee County, on the Mississippi River at the extreme southeast tip of Iowa. The house is a private residence on Concert St., Keokuk, IA 52632.) **25**

MANCHESTER

STAGECOACH HOUSE This old house and former stables are haunted by members of the Baker family, who ran a stagecoach stop on the property in the nineteenth century. The Bakers are buried in the family graveyard nearby and are said to believe they still run the establishment.

(The Stagecoach House Inn and Museum is near Coffins Grove Park at 1363 Candle Rd., Manchester, IA 52057. Phone: 563-927-3639.) **72**

MARQUETTE

EFFIGY MOUNDS NATIONAL MONUMENT No one knows the significance of the 191 geometric burial mounds at this 2,500-year-old sacred site. The twenty-nine animal effigies include the Marching Bears, a remarkable procession of ten earthen bears led by two eagles and trailed by yet another soaring eagle. Another effigy, the Great Bear Mound is nearly four feet high and 137 feet long. The effigies symbolize the various types of animal energies in the spirit world. "The visitor," says the park's guidebook, "can visualize prehistoric man carefully forming each effigy to receive the body of the departed, selecting by ritual the most fitting bird or animal form for this solemn purpose." Spook Cave, eight miles to the southwest, is thought to be haunted by the spirits of those who built these mounds.

(Marquette is in the northeastern corner of Iowa, across the Mississippi River from Prairie du Chien, Illinois. Effigy Mounds National Park is located three miles north of Marquette on Highway 76. Spook Cave is three quarters of a mile north of Froelich off U.S. Highway 18/52. Effigy Mounds National Monument, 151 Highway 76, Harpers Ferry, IA 52146. Phone: 319-873-3491 www.nps.gov/efmo) **102, 144**

MILFORD

LUTHERAN CEMETERY In the early 1900s, workers here encountered a strange force that prevented them from building a fence along a cemetery border. Augers and other tools twisted, broke, and moved by themselves while a certain posthole was being dug. The frustrated men dug up the area and discovered an unrecorded coffin at the fenceline.

(Milford is in Dickinson County. The Lutheran church cemetery is outside of town, overlooking the Little Sioux River. The present west fence takes a jog at the fourth post to avoid the haunted ground.) **23**

MILLVILLE

MEYER FARM On Thanksgiving evening 1959, William Meyer, his wife, and their teenage grandson Gene were resting in their darkened living room after dinner. Suddenly, there was a loud bang above them and Gene's face was covered with a "wet and gray soot." The black substance had settled all over the living room. Nothing strange happened again until December 16, when Gene was once again sitting in the dark with his grandparents. They heard a loud thud and turned on the lights to find that a large wooden flower stand had moved across the room. All three witnessed a glass of water levitate from a table and spill over Mrs. Meyer's head. The next day the poltergeist activity became so violent that the Meyers were forced to stay with relatives in nearby Guttenberg. They reported the events to authorities, who formed a team of investigators under the direction of Sheriff Forrest Fischer. The team witnessed a bottle fly out of a case and crash to the floor, and a photographer touring the empty home saw a brick dislodge from a wall in the basement and smash a ten-gallon crock. On January 6, 1960, a group of people decided to spend the night in the house. One member of the group was thrown out of bed by an unseen force and saw a chair move across the room. Teams of professors and students from Northwestern University set up twenty-four-hour surveillance inside the house. Electromagnetic field detectors and radiation monitors were set up throughout the building but failed to detect anything unusual.

(Millville is in Clayton County, thirty-three miles north of Dubuque on U.S. Highway 52. After the Meyers moved out, curiosity seekers and vandals ransacked the premises. The deserted house, which was located northeast of town, was deliberately burned by the Colesburg Fire Department in October 1986.) **76, 107, 176**

PALO

PLEASANT RIDGE CEMETERY This 1800s graveyard is more commonly known as "13 Stairs," because there are thirteen stairs leading up the hill into the graveyard. Many of the graves belong to the Lewis and Blackburn families, local farmers. In January and February 1997, investigators reported a "ghost dog" running past them and were also able to take a photo of a disappearing house that is sometimes seen over a square patch of faded grass. Photos of balls of light have been taken over the Lewis family gravestone. Discarnate voices have also been recorded, and people have reported being touched by "unseen things." Witnesses have also reported seeing ghostly figures walking among the tombstones that appear suddenly and disappear just as fast.

(The private graveyard is just outside Cedar Rapids about three miles from the town of Palo on Covington Rd. in Linn County. www.haunted-places.com/current.htm) **72**

STRAWBERRY POINT

MOSSY GLEN Something about a certain section of this peaceful valley attracts spirits. Several ghosts are said to walk the moss-covered paths. The ghost of a traveling peddler robbed and killed as he traversed the valley in 1858 wanders here. Another likely ghost of this area is a man who committed suicide by jumping into a muddy sinkhole in the glen. However, the best known ghost of Mossy Glen is a woman named Pearl Shine. In 1936, she and a hired hand conspired to murder her husband. After they killed him, the two tried to make it look as if he had committed suicide. Pearl was convicted of first-degree murder and sent to prison, where she died. Yet the cold, calculating presence of Pearl Shine is still felt in the valley she called home.

(Strawberry Point is on Highway 3 in Clayton County, which is in northeast Iowa. Haunted Mossy Glen is located eight miles east of Strawberry Point in Lodomillo Township.) **76**

WASHTA

WASHTA GRAVEYARD The face of their murderer mysteriously appeared on the tombstone marking the grave of Heinrich and Olga Schultz. Farmhand Will Florence split their heads open with an ax and stole their cash. When police were unable to come up with enough evidence to convict Will, the likeness of his face started to appear in the white marble marker over the German couple's grave. The mysterious image caused police to

dig deeper and come up with new evidence, but by that time, Will Florence had disappeared.

(Washta is on Highway 31, along the Little Sioux River, in northwest Iowa. The hillside burial ground is located in Cherokee County, near Washta.) **176**

WATERLOO

WAL-MART STORE This modern department store is haunted by the ghost of a small boy. He appears to be about twelve years old and has been nicknamed Jeremiah. One Wal-Mart employee described him as "small, very pale and thin, wearing black trousers with suspenders, a white shirt, and an Amish looking straw hat." Jeremiah apparently likes to play pranks like moving or hiding merchandise, tugging on employees' smocks, turning on and off appliances, tapping on customers' shoulders, and other such mischief. It is thought that Jeremiah lived on the property long before the shopping center was built.

(The haunted Wal-Mart is located in the Crossroads Shopping Center at 1334 Flammang Dr., Waterloo, IA 50702. Phone: 319-232-3661.) **72**

WAVERLY

CAMP INGAWANIS This Boy Scout camp is haunted by the friendly spirit of a twelve-year-old boy, who died in an accident on the property in the 1990s. The unfortunate lad was swinging when he jumped and hit his head on a rock. He was killed instantly and apparently relives the moment over and over. The swing is often seen moving at the same height—never higher, never lower. There is never a breeze or other factor to account for the eerie movement. Witnesses have also reported hearing the giggling sounds of a young boy near the swings.

(Camp Ingawanis, 2482 Grand Ave., Waverly, IA 50677. Phone: 319-352-5880.) **72**

WEST BEND

GROTTO OF THE REDEMPTION This site is sacred because of the "sacred will and spiritual intention" that went into its construction. The grotto was constructed with hundreds of thousands of precious and semiprecious stones from every state in America and every region of the world. Stones include quartz, blood-stone, amethyst, and lapis lazuli. There is a three-hundred-pound amethyst in the Christmas Chapel, and Bethlehem Cave is constructed from sixty-five tons of petrified wood. There are scores of beautiful statues. The value of the Grotto has been estimated at $2.5 million, and it weighs so much that its foundation reaches twenty feet underground. Although Oriental in appearance, the Grotto portrays redemption according to Christian principles. It was built by two men, Father Louis Greving and Paul Dobblestein, who labored for forty years beginning in 1912.

(West Bend is on Highway 15 in northwest Iowa, fifty miles northwest of Fort Dodge. The grotto is located near the St. Peter and Paul's Church at 300 N. Broadway, West Bend, IA 50597. Phone: 515-887-2371. www. nw-cybermall.com/grotto.htm) **72, 196**

KANSAS

COLUMBUS

SPOOKSVILLE TRIANGLE This twenty-mile-sided triangle of strange, multicolored light phenomena borders Joplin, Missouri; Columbus, Kansas; and Miami, Oklahoma. The area is traversed by Highway 66 and the Spring River. The lights have been observed regularly for over 110 years and are most often seen hovering over deserted roads and fields. See Joplin, Missouri; and Miami, Oklahoma.

(Columbus is at the junction of U.S. Highways 69 and 96 in the southeast corner of Kansas. www.prairieghosts. com/spooksville.html) **20**

DELPHOS

UFO LANDING On November 2, 1971, a "mushroom-shaped UFO with multicolored lights" hovered just two feet off the ground behind the sheep pen on the Johnson farm. The nine-foot-diameter saucer emitted an intense white light that temporarily blinded Ronald Johnson. His parents saw the object fly away into the night sky, and observed a glowing ring in the dirt, left behind by the UFO. The ring was totally dehydrated to a depth of twelve inches. The soil was crystallized and had a slick crust. Investigators who touched the white dust inside the ring reported numbness in their fingers. Nothing would grow in the ring and snow that fell on the area remained long after surrounding snow had melted. See Siler City, North Carolina.

(Delphos is in Ottawa County, forty miles north of Salina off U.S. Highway 81.) **126 (9/85, 1/86), 139, 190**

A "mushroom-shaped UFO with multicolored lights" landed here in 1971. See UFO Landing, Delphos, Kansas (IUFOR)

ELLIS COUNTY

SALINE RIVER The ghost of an old Indian by the name of Takaluma is said to roam the banks of the Saline River. The ghost appeared to a cowboy camping on the riverbank on January 23, 1879. Takaluma was condemned to wander the riverbanks until he found the skull of his father, an Indian chief murdered by white men in the 1840s. The skull had been exhumed from his resting place by a farmer digging up a field. The ghost emerged from its burial mound and warned of more powerful spirits who might join in the search. But the skull was never found.

(Ellis County is in central Kansas. The ghost was seen in northern Ellis County, on the Saline River, several miles south of Oak Canyon.) **49**

GREAT BEND

KOMAREK HOME This four-story, sixteen-room, Victorian house is haunted by a force that moves chairs around the kitchen table, rearranges objects, and materializes old coins and antique jewelry, among other things. The phenomena seem to be connected with members of the Moses family, who lived in the house for generations. The younger family members seem to possess unconscious psychokinetic powers.

(Great Bend is located in central Kansas at the junction of Highways 56, 96, and 281 in Barton County. The house is a private residence, at 1407 Washington St. Great Bend, KS 67530.) **14, 101**

GREELEY COUNTY

WHITE WOMAN CREEK This creek is named for the ghost of a white woman who married a Cherokee chief and bore him a son. She sings an Indian death dirge while wandering the stream bed. The woman originally was part of a group of settlers who stole meat and horses from the Cherokees. In an Indian ambush many of the white men died and the rest were taken prisoner. One of the white women, whom the Indians called Anna-Wee, fell in love with Chief Tee-Wah-Nee. Years later, a white man escaped and brought soldiers from Fort Wallace. In the first skirmish, Anna-Wee's husband and son were killed. She died the following day while defending the tribal village she had come to think of as home.

(White Woman Creek runs eastward from Greeley County in west central Kansas, all the way through Wichita and Scott Counties.) **176**

HANOVER

HOLLENBERG STATION The ghosts of young Pony Express riders are seen galloping along their old routes which converge at Hollenberg Station. This is the only surviving Pony Express stop still standing in its original location. The station was built on the Great Hollenberg ranch, 123 miles from St. Joseph, Missouri, which was the starting point of the two-thousand-mile run. A Pony Express advertisement of 1860 described the kind of men it was looking for: "WANTED—Young, skinny, wiry fellows not over 18. Must be expert riders, willing to risk death daily. Orphans preferred."

(Hanover is forty-five miles north of Manhattan in northeastern Kansas. The Pony Express Station is at the intersection of Highways 148 and 243. The Pony Express Barn is ten miles farther east. Hollenberg Station, 2889 23rd Rd. Hanover, KS 66945. Phone: 785-337-2635.) **176, 231**

HAYS

OLD FORT HAYS A ghost walked into a room in the old officer's quarters here and sat on the edge of a bed, as a startled witness watched the bed sag under the weight of the invisible presence. The incident happened in the 1960s, when the building was used as a student apartment house for a local college. Since the structure was moved back to the fort in 1987 no similar incidents have been reported.

(Hays is at the junction of I-70 and U.S. Highway 183 in central Kansas. Fort Hays is a state historic site southwest of the city. Old Fort Hays, 1472 Highway 183 Alt, Hays, KS 67601. Phone: 785-625-6812. www.prairie ghosts.com/sentinel.html) **101, 131**

SENTINEL HILL The Blue Light Lady haunts the bluffs and farmland surrounding this hill. At the top of the hill is a monument to Elizabeth Polly, who died at old Fort Hays in 1867. Elizabeth was a selfless woman who became known as the Angel of Fort Hays during a cholera epidemic, when she worked tirelessly to comfort the ill and dying. She contracted the deadly disease herself, and on her deathbed asked to be buried on top of Sentinel Hill overlooking the fort. The summit of the hill was her favorite place, but because it was so rocky she was allegedly buried in the side of the hill. Her ghost was first seen in 1917, and since then, the radiant ghost of a woman in a long blue dress and wearing a bonnet has been seen by dozens of farmers, policemen, and other witnesses near Sentinel Hill.

(A limestone statue of Elizabeth Polly has been erected in the Elizabeth Polly Park in Hays. Both the statue and

her monument were created by artist Peter Felton.) **112, 131, 176, 231**

KANSAS CITY

MORNINGSIDE PARK Houses built on a lot in this section of Kansas City have been plagued by a variety of poltergeist effects, including unaccounted-for-smoke, moving furniture, and odd noises. The land was known as Hinkle's Grove in the early 1900s but dates back to the mid-1800s, when it was a rest stop on the Santa Fe Trail. A house built on the site burned to the ground in 1876 and was rebuilt. No other source for the phenomena has been suggested.

(Kansas City is at the junction of I-35 and I-70 in eastern Kansas. The site is Lot No. 189 of the Morningside Park development in Kansas City.) **66 (2/90)**

SAUER CASTLE This stone mansion, built in 1871, is said to be haunted by a former resident. Later occupants of the building reported a variety of ghostly manifestations.

(The house is a private residence. Sauer Castle, 935 Shawnee Rd., Kansas City, KS 66103.) **101**

STULL CEMETERY Legend says this cemetery is the resting place of a devil child. Locals have nicknamed the place the Gates to Hell. A seventeen-year-old boy who died of typhoid in the 1890s is said to materialize as a werewolf and hide in trees in the old cemetery. Satanists conduct rituals in the graveyard, and evil presences are said to materialize during the spring and autumn equinoxes.

(The tiny town of Stull is in northeastern Kansas, west of Kansas City near Lawrence in Wyandotte County. The cemetery is east of town off Highway 5.) **66 (10/89)**

LEAVENWORTH

FORT LEAVENWORTH A bevy of ghosts haunt this base, the oldest continuously operated military post west of the Mississippi. Many people have witnessed the ghost of Catherine Sutter walking among the tombstones of the national cemetery and on the grounds of the present golf course. Bound for Oregon, she stopped over at the fort in 1880 with her husband and two children. One day, her husband sent the children out to collect firewood, but they never returned. The Sutters stayed on through the winter, hoping against hope that their loved ones would be found, and Catherine spent many lonely hours walking through the snow calling out to her children. That same year, the distraught woman caught pneumonia and died. Her apparition, wearing an old calico dress and black shawl, is seen desperately searching for her lost children. Sometimes she is observed carrying a lantern, while other times her voice can be heard calling out in the darkness. Another ghost reported in the cemetery is Chief Joseph, a proud Nez Perce Indian leader, who was incarcerated at the fort in 1877.

Several ghosts populate the rookery, the oldest house on the base. The apparitions of a busybody old woman, a bushy-haired old man in a white robe, and an angry young girl disturb residents trying to sleep in the 162-year-old house. Sheridan House is haunted by the vengeful spirit of Mrs. Sheridan, wife of General Philip H. Sheridan. In 1869, he deserted his wife on her deathbed to go to Chicago on business. A few doors down, at the chief of staff's quarters, the sounds of a tea party can be heard coming from the empty parlor. The presence of a man with a mustache and goatee is occasionally felt at the McClellan Officer's Quarters. His apparition has appeared in the fireplace, and his loud footsteps are heard late at night, stumbling through the house. The former site of St. Ignatius Chapel is haunted by the ghost of the priest who burned to death in an 1875 fire that destroyed the building. Father Fred has turned up at the fireplace, in the kitchen, near a sewing machine, and other places in the new house that was built on the site. Houses along Sumner Place are haunted by the presence of a lady in black, who is sometimes seen trying to calm crying children or attempting to help with the dishes. The ghost of General George Custer has been seen roaming the first floor of the General's Residence. While still a colonel, Custer was court-martialed in 1867 for shooting soldiers who disobeyed him. The hearing was held in the commanding general's quarters, where Custer was found guilty and given a year's suspension without pay. The men Custer sacrificed at Little Big Horn, some of whom are buried here, have also returned. Their ghostly figures have been reported marching on the main parade.

(Fort Leavenworth is two miles north of the city of Leavenworth on Highway 73 in the northeastern corner of Kansas. The rookery is at 14 Sumner Place. Sheridan House is at 611 Scott Ave. The chief of staff's quarters are

at 624 Scott Ave. The haunted officer's quarters are at 605 McClellan Ave. The house built over St. Ignatius Chapel is at 632 Thomas Ave. The Lady in Black has been seen at 18 and 20 Sumner Place. The General's Residence is at 1 Scott Ave. Fort Leavenworth, Leavenworth, KS 66027. Phone: 913-684-5604. www.prairieghosts. com/leavenworth.html.) **15, 72**

MANHATTAN

DELTA SIGMA PHI The two ghosts that walk the halls of this fraternity house have nothing to do with college life. They are leftover spirits from St. Mary's Hospital, which owned the building at one time. The specter of a nurse was observed making its rounds for several years in the 1960s, but the more active ghost is George, a patient who died in a freakish accident when the hospital was moving to a new location. The elderly gentleman rolled off his bed in a third-floor room and was wedged against the wall, where he suffocated. The room looked empty, and his body was not discovered until the following day. His noisy ghost is still heard on the third floor, and students blame him for a variety of poltergeist effects. For instance, it is known that George loved to watch *Star Trek*. In 1973, during an ice storm that knocked out power for several days, the electricity at Delta Sigma Phi mysteriously came on just long enough to watch *Star Trek* on TV.

(Manhattan is eight miles north of I-70 on Highway 177. The fraternity is at 1100 Fremont St., Manhattan, KS 66502. Phone: 785-776-9191.) **176**

KANSAS STATE UNIVERSITY The Purple Masque Theater here is haunted by a mischievous ghost named Nick. The spirit's voice has been recorded on tape, though his apparition has never been seen. He is thought to be an ex-football player, who died in the building in the 1950s when it was used as an athletic dormitory. The injured player was carried into the ground-level cafeteria and laid on a table, where he died. His playful spirit has since been heard clomping through the hallways, on stairways, and near the stage. He also moves chairs in the auditorium and plays music late at night, but his most spectacular pranks involve levitating objects. Wooden boxes stacked in the dressing room have jumped to the floor and then restacked themselves, and a fire extinguisher once spun around in midair, while discharging its contents.

(The theater is on the main floor of East Stadium on the campus. Kansas State University, Manhattan, KS 66506. Phone: 785-532-6250. www.ksu.edu) **176**

KAPPA SIGMA The ghost of a sophomore student who hanged himself in a file room here still haunts his fraternity brothers. His specter takes the shape of a moving white haze and has been detected on the stairway, on the second floor, and on the roof.

(The fraternity is at 1930 College Heights Rd., Manhattan, KS 65502. Phone: 785-776-0113.) **176**

PHI GAMMA DELTA This fraternity house is haunted by a ghost named Duncan. This former student died during an initiation ceremony for the Theta Xi fraternity, which used to occupy the building. He was accidentally hit on the head with an initiation paddle and died from a brain concussion. The haunting started in 1965, when Phi Gamma Delta moved into the house and threw away several Theta Xi paddles hanging in the library. Students have encountered Duncan's lifeless presence and blankly staring face ever since.

(The fraternity is at 1919 Hunting Ave., Manhattan, KS 66502. Phone: 785-539-6644.) **176**

OLATHE

JOHNSON COUNTY INDUSTRIAL AIRPORT Unexplainable noises, whistling sounds, footsteps, and moving objects have been reported in Hangar 43 over the last fifty-two years. Employees have dubbed the restless spirit the Commander, although he could be any one of thirty-four fatalities that occurred at the navy flight training base, which was commissioned in 1942.

(Olathe is a suburb southwest of Kansas City. The airport is eight miles southwest of Olathe at 153355 Pflumm Rd., Olathe, KS 66062. Phone: 913-782-1245.) **133**

PAOLA

PAOLA HIGH SCHOOL The ghost of a former band member haunts this building. He is said to be the spirit of an ambitious teenage boy who wanted to play first chair in the band with his trumpet. He practiced constantly but was never good enough to make first chair. One evening, while the band was practicing on the football field, the director asked him to fetch some sheet music from a storage room above the stage. As the boy climbed back down the steep metal stairway from the room, he slipped and fell. A blow to the head killed him. Today, students and visitors report hearing the lonesome playing of a trumpet, even when the band is no longer practicing.

(Paola is Miami County, thirty miles southwest of Kansas City on U.S. Highway 169. Paola High School, 401 Angela Dr., Paola, KS 66071. Phone: 913-294-4367.) **37**

SALINA

INDIAN BURIAL GROUND The troubled spirits of long-dead Indians are said to haunt this town. Approximately 150 skeletons were removed from a prehistoric burial grounds four miles east of Salina.

(Salina is in central Kansas at the junction of I-70 and I-135. The burial ground is on Highway 140, four miles northeast of Salina. There is a Prehistoric Indian Burial Grounds Museum at the site. For more information, call the Kansas Tourism Office at 800-252-6727.) **102**

TOPEKA

GARDNER HOUSE Retired General J.E. Gardner and his wife Dorothy share their home with a poltergeist spirit, whom they believe to be a former owner. Mysterious events began in 1972, when the Gardners were remodeling the house. Loud banging sounds, as if someone were hitting the floor with a wood plank, started coming from an unoccupied guest room and continued intermittently for over a year. Next, they detected a strange presence in their own bedroom. They heard loud, heavy breathing at night, as some invisible presence sat on the edge of the bed. One night something tried to pull Dorothy's legs off the bed. Afterward, objects started moving by themselves. The house was built in 1888, and the Gardners have yet to identify their uninvited houseguest.

(Topeka is in eastern Kansas at the junction of I-70 and I-335. The house is a private residence in the Potwin Place area of Topeka. The address is 424 Greenwood Ave., Topeka, KS 66606.) **72, 101, 176**

ROCHESTER CEMETERY The ghost of an albino woman retraces the route from her home to the cemetery where she is buried. The woman had few friends because of her affliction, which gave her pink eyes and white hair and skin. Her glowing white phantom was first reported shortly after she died in 1963. The ghost seems to pulsate and emits a low moaning sound. She was especially active from 1966 to 1969, when dozens of reliable witnesses saw her gliding down the road and in the cemetery. The ghost is attracted to young people and has been known to approach them.

(Sightings have occurred on Lower Silver Lake Rd. and Rochester Rd., from the Seaman district to Rochester Cemetery. The area is bounded by Soldier Creek, the Goodyear Tire Factory, the Boys Industrial School, and Lower Silver Lake Road. Highway 24 goes right through the middle of the area. Rochester Cemetery, 1200 Northwest Menninger Rd., Topeka, KS 66618. Phone: 785-286-0291.) **176**

WACONDA LAKE

WACONDA SPRING Indians considered the cavernous sea-green spring that feeds this lake sacred. They called it Wahkandah, the Spirit Spring. Arapaho, Pottawatomies, and every tribe passing through the area paid homage to the spirit of the spring, and even after white men discovered it in 1806, the Indians held ceremonies here. The spirit of Waconda is one of self-sacrifice. A legend tells of an Indian maiden who jumped into the bottomless spring with the body of her lover, a brave from another tribe killed in a nearby skirmish.

(Cawker City is the largest city on Waconda Lake, which lies in Mitchel County in north central Kansas. Take U.S. Highway 281 north from I-70 and turn east on U.S. Highway 24 to the town. Waconda Spring was forty feet above the Solomon River on a hill. The area was flooded in 1965 to create Waconda Lake.) **49**

KENTUCKY

This tombstone, which marks John Rowan's resting place, is believed to be haunted by his spirit. See Bardstown Cemetery, Kentucky (JAMES E. RAINBOLT)

BARDSTOWN

BARDSTOWN CEMETERY One of America's most prominent men expressly forbade that any monument or stone be placed over his grave. John Rowan was a state judge, served seven terms in the legislature, and was elected to the United States Senate. He also became Kentucky's secretary of state and chief justice of the court of appeals. His beautiful mansion was visited by many dignitaries, and his cousin Stephen Collins Foster wrote "My Old Kentucky Home" there. But when he died on July 13, 1843, his relatives and friends decided to ignore his wishes and erected a fit-

ting monument over his final resting place. Within a few months, the tall marker started tumbling from its base for no apparent reason. At one point, frightened stonemasons repairing the marker refused to return to the cemetery. Ever since, workmen have struggled to keep the monument in place.

(Bardstown is thirty-five miles southeast of Louisville on U.S. Highway 31E/150. Bardstown Cemetery is at the center of town, and the monument is a tall obelisk with a stone wreath and a carved listing of Rowan's many achievements. His former mansion, called Federal Hill, is a popular tourist attraction www.prairieghosts.com/ bardst.html) **223**

CAMPBELLSVILLE

HIESTAND HOUSE An abandoned stone house here is haunted by the ghosts of the Hiestand family, who built the structure in the late 1800s. Their ghosts have been reported in the building and in the family graveyard many times over the last fifty years. A destitute family allowed to live there in the 1930s reported a number of ghostly phenomena, including oil lanterns that would light by themselves.

(Campbellsville is in central Kentucky, nineteen miles south of Lebanon on U.S. Highway 68. The two-story house is at 1075 Campbellsville By-Pass, Campbellsville, KY 42719) **124**

HIGHWAY 55 The phantom of a teenage girl haunts this stretch of road. Several independent witnesses have reported encountering the ghost in the last two decades. She hitchhikes in rainy, dismal weather and is usually seen wearing a wet cotton dress. The ghost is a typical "vanishing hitchhiker," who usually disappears as the driver approaches the spot where she has asked to be dropped off.

(The hitchhiking phantom has been seen on Highway 55 south, along Green River Lake and in the Cane Valley area.) **166**

SMITH RIDGE A large, hairy creature terrorized this area in the 1890s. Dozens of people reported seeing it, and horses refused to enter the woods where the monster was sighted.

(The woods are in South Campbellsville in the Smith Ridge-Carthelidge area.) **124**

COVINGTON

MARY WHEELDON The ghost of Mary Wheeldon and her thoroughbred stallion Hussar's Gold roam the countryside near here. In the 1890s, she owned a breeding farm called Corbett Acres, but family problems caused her to lose her farm and all she owned. She escaped to the thick woods and lived there with her beloved horse. After twelve years of living in the woods, Mary was discovered by two men from Lexington, who spread the word of her meager existence and the glorious horse that lived with her. People started visiting her, including her relatives, but she wanted nothing to do with them. She lived the rest of her life in the forest with Hussar's Gold. Her ghost and that of the horse have been spotted by dozens of people over the years. She appears wearing a calico dress, walking slowly next to her beloved stallion.

(Covington is on the Ohio River in the northern tip of Kentucky. The phantoms walk the berry-bush country about thirty miles northwest of Covington.) **87**

FRANKFORT

LIBERTY HALL The ghost of the Gray Lady stalks the corridors of this elegant, three-story brick mansion. The house was built in 1796 and, until 1937 was in the family of John Brown, a prominent Kentucky senator. The Gray Lady is thought to be an aunt, Mrs. Margaret Varick, who died in the house shortly after arriving

from New York in the early 1800s. She was buried in the garden, although her remains were later moved to a cemetery. Sightings of her small gray ghost gazing out a window or doing chores were reported for over 150 years. Two other ghosts have also been seen. One is an opera singer who stayed here in 1805. She was kidnapped by Indians from the garden behind the house. The other is a soldier from the War of 1812 who comes to one of the ground-floor windows and peers into the living room.

(Frankfort is twenty-five miles northwest of Lexington off I-64. Liberty Hall is now a museum run by the Society of Colonial Dames of America at 218 Wilkinson St., Frankfort, KY 40501. Phone: 502-227-2560. www. libertyhall.org) **101, 135**

GLASGOW

RIDGE CEMETERY The ghosts of two brothers who killed each other in an argument that took place in this graveyard in the 1880s still haunt the place. Locals say they make their presence known by a tinkling sound, like a tiny bell ringing.

(Glasgow is thirty miles east of Bowling Green on the Cumberland Tollway. The cemetery is north of Glasgow in Barren County.) **124**

GREENSBURG

HAPPY HOLLOW The strange apparitions of four men carrying a black coffin have been seen in the kitchen of a house here. On top of the coffin is a small white lamb. The disconcerting display was first seen by the Ragland family in 1932, as they entered the kitchen for breakfast one morning. Sheriff J. W. Thomas could find no evidence of pranksters, nor could he explain the incident to the distraught family.

(Greensburg is thirty miles south of Lebanon on U.S. Highway 68. Happy Hollow is one mile southeast of Greensburg on Highway 61. The house is a private residence located on Highway 61 in the community of Happy Hollow.) **124**

HARRODSBURG

HARRODSBURG SPRINGS PARK The ethereal figure of a young girl dressed in a white gown has been seen in the park where she is buried. Her ghost is observed wandering through the park and disappears into a springhouse behind her grave. Using a fictitious name, the girl checked into the Harrodsburg Springs Hotel over 125 years ago. On her first night at the hotel, she danced on the ballroom floor until the early morning hours. Eager young men lined up to ask her to dance. But at the end of the night, one of her partners realized she had died in his arms. She was given a funeral and buried on hotel property, and when the hotel burned down fifty years ago, the city took over caring for her grave. The metal marker over her grave says: "UNKNOWN—Hallowed and Hushed Be the Place of the Dead. Step Softly. Bow Head."

(The town of Harrodsburg is twenty-five miles southwest of Lexington on U.S. Highway 68. Harrodsburg Springs Park is at the center of town. www.prairieghosts. com/h_spring.html) **124**

LEXINGTON

ASHLAND This mansion was the home of American patriot Henry Clay. His white-haired ghost, dressed in a black frock coat, has been seen leaning against the mantel on the fireplace in the parlor. Clay ran unsuccessfully for president three times before he died in 1852. Known as "the Great Compromiser," the statesman seems to have kept one foot in both worlds. See Oakland Manor, Franklin, Louisiana.

(Lexington is in central Kentucky, at the junction of I-64 and I-75. Ashland is now a public museum on the corner of Richmond and Sycamore roads, 1.5 miles east of downtown Lexington. Ashland, 120 Sycamore Road, Lexington, KY 40502. Phone: 606-266-8581. www.henryclay. org) **86**

HUNT-MORGAN HOUSE The ghosts of former residents Mam Bet and Mr. Hunt still walk the halls of this old mansion.

(The Hunt-Morgan House is managed by the Blue Grass Trust Association. The address is 201 North Mill St., Lexington, KY 40508. Phone: 606-233-3290. www. uky.edu/LCC/HIS/sites/hopemont.html) **72**

LIBERTY

ALIEN ABDUCTION In January 1976, three women were driving to their homes near Liberty after having dinner together. Suddenly a gigantic UFO glided over the highway in front of them. The gray object was one hundred yards in diameter with a white dome on top.

The middle of the UFO was encircled in red lights, and four red and yellow lights were visible underneath the craft. The next thing the women could remember was approaching the lights of Hustonville at 1:25 A.M., nearly two hours after seeing the object. Mrs. Louise Smith, Elaine Thomas, and Mona Stafford were examined by doctors, who found unusual red burns on their necks. All three were exhausted and suffered from dehydration. When the women were placed under hypnosis, they all recalled being taken aboard the alien vessel and physically examined.

(Liberty is in central Kentucky twenty-five miles south of Danville on U.S. Highway 127. The group was leaving Stanford, and the UFO was sighted eight miles south of Hustonville on Highway 78. The abduction occurred next to the entrance to a cow pasture flanked by a fieldstone wall.) **7, 126 (1/77)**

MAMMOTH CAVE

MAMMOTH CAVE NATIONAL PARK The largest cave in the world has attracted a number of ghosts. One is a black slave guide named Stephen Bishop, who loved the cave so much he refused to leave it, even when offered his freedom. Another spirit of the cave is a Southern lady named Melissa, who brought her Yankee lover to the cave in 1843. She took the man deep within the cave to Purgatory Point and left him there as a prank. The man was never seen again, and Melissa's ghost still searches the area known as Echo River. The ghost of Floyd Collins, who died after being trapped for sixteen days in nearby Crystal Cave, is also said to wander the grounds. The case became so popular that in 1926, Collins's body was removed from his family plot and displayed in a glass coffin at the entrance to Crystal Cave. The grisly tourist attraction proved very profitable, until someone stole the corpse. It was finally returned to the cave; however, for some reason the body was missing its left leg. In recent years, tourists have reported the unidentified ghost of a man dressed in an old-fashioned cummerbund. Others have witnessed a disembodied pair of legs running down the hill near the main visitors' center. The legs were wearing denim overalls and work shoes. With over 150 sightings of ghosts reported, Mamouth Cave is one of the nation's most haunted locations.

(Floyd Collins now rests in the Flint Ridge Baptist Cemetery on the park grounds. Mammoth Cave is twenty miles northeast of Bowling Green on I-65. Mammoth

Cave National Park, P.O. Box 7, KY 42259. Phone: 270-773-2111. www.prairieghosts.com/mammoth.html) **133**

RUSSELLVILLE

RUSSELLVILLE GIRL The legend of the Russellville Girl is told throughout the state of Kentucky. In the 1920s, a teenage girl was waiting for her boyfriend to pick her up to go to a dance. When it started raining hard, she feared the boy would not be able to make it through the storm, and she did not want to miss the big dance. As she stood watching for him near an open window in the house, a bolt of lightning struck her. It killed her instantly. Afterward, whenever it rained her image would reappear in the glass of the window where she died. No amount of cleaning would erase the image, and later owners of the house resorted to painting it over.

(Russellville is in Logan County in southwestern Kentucky, at the junction of U.S. Highways 68 and 79. The house is now a private residence on Clarksville Rd., near the Maple Grove Cemetery. www.prairieghosts.com/russell.html) **124**

TOMPKINSVILLE

MESHACK ROAD Since the 1950s, locals here have reported encountering an invisible presence that jumps on their horses or motorcycles as they pass a particular sycamore tree. The strange phantom holds tightly on to the rider's waist for about a mile before it vanishes. No explanation for the odd phenomenon has ever been suggested.

(Tompkinsville is in Monroe County in south central Kentucky, twenty-five miles southeast of Glasgow on Highway 63. Meshack Rd, runs along a small creek outside of town. www.prairieghosts.com/meshack.html) **124**

STRODE HOMEPLACE The four-room shack that used to be the residence of the Strode family now lies abandoned. At the turn of the century, the family was plagued by a number of unidentifiable apparitions and cold, moving shadows that eventually forced them to move. The site was considered to be haunted for the next seventy-five years.

(The abandoned Strode house is in the Forkton community near Tompkinsville.) **124**

WICKLIFFE MOUNDS

WICKLIFFE MOUNDS PARK This sacred site consisted of a huge wood and grass temple constructed on top of a massive pyramid mound. It was built around A.D. 900 by a nature-worshiping people who disappeared without a trace four hundred years later. The Lifeways Museum and Cemetery Building on the premises displays artifacts found during excavation.

(The park is in the southwestern tip of Kentucky. Take I-57 or I-24 to the Highway 62 exit and follow it toward the Kentucky side of the Mississippi River. For information, contact the Wickliffe Mounds Research Center, 94 Green St., Wickliffe, KY 42087. Phone: 270-335-3681.) **99**

WILDER

BOBBY MACKEY'S MUSIC WORLD Malevolent spirits roam this 1850s building, now a popular nightclub. At one time, the structure was a slaughterhouse, and a deep well was dug in the basement to collect animal blood and body fluids. When the slaughterhouse closed, Satanists used the well of blood for rituals. In 1896, two devil worshippers beheaded a woman named Pearl Bryan and used her head in their ceremonies. Before they were hanged, the men were offered life sentences in exchange for disclosing the whereabouts of the missing head, but both refused, claiming that to do so would bring down the wrath of the devil himself. The cursed building was a speakeasy in the 1920s, and several unsolved mob murders added more violence to the already diabolic ambiance. So far, twenty-nine witnesses have signed affidavits testifying to ghostly phenomena at the nightclub, and a recent exorcism on the premises has failed to halt the harrowing activity. In September 1994, a customer was assaulted in the men's restroom by a ghost wearing a cowboy hat. The injured customer is suing Bobby Mackey for not getting rid of the ghosts in his establishment. Douglas Hensley investigated the case and published his account in a 1994 book entitled *Hell's Gate*.

(Wilder is in Campbell County, across the Ohio River from Cincinnati. It is 1.5 miles south of Covington on Highway 9. Bobby Mackey's Music World, 44 Licking Pike, Wilder, KY 41076. Phone: 606-431-5588. www.haunted-places.com/current.html) **66 (2/95), 72**

LOUISIANA

BATON ROUGE

PARLANGE PLANTATION The ghost of a young girl is seen running between two rows of oak trees that line the path to the old manor house here. She wears a veil and a flowing wedding gown. In the middle of ceremonies for her prearranged marriage to a French nobleman, Julie de Ternant ran from the house and flung herself head-on against one of the oaks. She killed herself because she could not have the man she really loved. The plantation was built in 1754 by Marquis Vincent de Ternant and remains in the possession of his descendants.

(The plantation is a private residence located thirty-five miles north of Baton Rouge at False River, New Roads. Follow I-90 west to Highway 1 north for five miles to the plantation. Parlange Plantation, 8211 False River Rd., New Roads, LA 70760. Phone: 225-638-8410.) **15, 78, 101**

BAYOU GRAND SARA

MOONRISE PLANTATION The ghost of Dominique de Laboutre still haunts her old home. The hardy woman survived a machete attack that nearly severed her head, a poisoning by her ex-husband, malaria, pneumonia, and other diseases, as well as several near-fatal accidents, and lived to be 107 years old. Her ghost, as tenacious as she was, has been sensed by dozens of people over the last century.

(Bayou Grand Sara is a private residence in Terrebonne Parish in southeastern Louisiana.) **158**

CHURCH POINT

ST. EDWARDS CHURCH Visitors to the grave of a twelve-year-old girl, buried in a cemetery behind this Catholic church, claim that the child's spirit has curative powers. Charlene Richard was a little Cajun girl who died over thirty-five years ago, and is now considered an angel of mercy. Charlene was always full of life, and as she lay dying, displayed implacable grace despite excruciating pain. Testimonies of her cures come from all corners of the world. A box on top of her gravestone allows the faithful to drop their petitions at all hours of the day and night. On August 11, 1989, the anniversary of her birth, four thousand people gathered at her grave. Charlene is now a candidate for sainthood in the Catholic church.

(Church Point is in Acadia Parish, at the junction of Highway 35 and Highway 178. St. Edwards Church, 1463 Charlene Highway, Church Point, LA 70525. Phone: 318-684-5816.) **58**

DESTREHAN

DESTREHAN MANOR Ghosts started to appear in this 1790 manor house after restoration in the 1980s. A white figure appeared, sitting in a phantom chair, crossing a driveway, and peering out a second-floor window.

The ghost, as well as spectral lights and disembodied faces, has been reported by visitors, museum workers, and deliverymen. The spirit is thought to be Stephen Henderson, who lived at the manor with his wife Elenore in the 1850s. Elenore died at age nineteen and Stephen, overcome by grief, died a few years later. Others propose former resident Jean Lafitte, who owned ten pirate ships in the early 1800s. Vandals searched for his lost treasure here in the 1960s.

(Destrehan is about thirteen miles north of New Orleans. The private manor house faces the Mississippi River at 13034 River Rd., Destrehan, LA 70047. Phone: 504-524-5522.) **66 (10/85), 135**

FRANKLIN

OAKLAWN MANOR The ghost of patriot Henry Clay returns to this beautiful house, which he often visited while alive. The white-pillared mansion with marble floors is filled with fine European antiques. See Ashland, Lexington, Kentucky.

(Franklin is in St. Mary Parish, thirty miles southeast of New Iberis on Highway 182. Oaklawn Manor, 3296 East Oaklawn Dr., Franklin, LA 70538. Phone: 318-828-0434.) **78, 101**

HAHNVILLE

VIE FORTUNE PLANTATION An old white oak near the bayou road here is considered to be haunted. Known as the moaning oak, the tree starts creaking and making odd noises at midnight, then abruptly stops an hour later. The tree is on the estate of the old Vie Fortune Plantation, built by Alexander Gailbraith in the 1700s. In 1790, an eighteen-year-old girl named Josephine Darrel came to live at the plantation. She had escaped from Olantho Plantation, where her penniless father had tried to sell her to a man in need of a wife. After she discovered that the man she really loved, whose baby she carried, was already married, she decided to kill herself. Late one night she walked down the lonely road, tied a rope around her neck, and hanged herself from the great oak.

(Hahnville is twenty-five miles west of New Orleans on Highway 3127. Vie Fortune Plantation, Hahnville, LA 70057.) **158**

NEW ORLEANS

BEAUREGARD HOUSE A legion of ghosts haunts this house, which was built in 1812. General Pierre Gustave Toutant de Beauregard lived in the house until 1869. He commanded Southern soldiers at the disastrous Battle of Shiloh, where thousands of Americans lost their lives. Sometimes, around 2:00 A.M., the ghosts of Beauregard and his troops stage the Battle of Shiloh right in the hallway outside the ballroom. Beauregard and his troops first appear in full Confederate dress, then slowly turn tattered and bloody, as if reliving the course of the doomed fight.

(New Orleans is on I-10 at the toe of Louisiana. General Beauregard's House, also known as LeCarpentier House, is across the street from the Convent of Ursula in the French Quarter, at 1113 Chartres St., New Orleans, LA 70116. Phone: 504-523-7257. For general information on New Orleans, contact the Visitors Bureau at 800-672-6124. www.neworleanscvb.com) **42, 78, 175, 187, 188**

GARDETTE-LEPRETRE HOUSE This lavish house was leased by a Turkish Sultan and his family in the late 1790s. One stormy night, assassins from a fanatical Arabian sect searching for the sultan's brother traced him to the house. They brutally murdered everyone they found, including the sultan's wives and servants. The killers buried the sultan's brother under a date tree in the courtyard and left behind an inscription: "The justice of heaven is satisfied, and the date tree shall grow on the traitor's tomb." The date tree is known as the Death Tree. Ghostly forms accompanied by the sounds of Oriental music were seen there for many years, but after the house was turned into apartments, the visitations stopped.

(The 2½-story Sultan's House was divided up into apartments. It is located in the French Quarter on the corner of Dauphine St. and Orlean St.) **42, 175, 188**

GRIFFIN HOUSE This French-style house, built in 1852, is home to an unidentified presence that is blamed for a variety of eerie phenomena, including invisible footsteps and other sounds.

(The house is a private residence, at 1447 Constance St., New Orleans, LA 70130.) **101**

HERMANN-GRIMA HOUSE The ghosts here are very considerate. They are said to scatter fragrant rose and lavender about the parlor to freshen the room. On cold mornings they light the fireplaces to keep things cozy.

(Hermann-Grima Historical House, 820 St. Louis St., New Orleans, LA 70116. 504-525-5661. www.gnofn. org/~hggh) **72**

LALAURIE HOUSE Delphine Lalaurie was a rich and beautiful New Orleans matriarch who built this house in 1832. But the seemingly charming woman harbored an intense hatred for black people and kept slaves chained in the attic, where she maimed and tortured them. In 1833, one young girl slave freed herself from her chains but was cornered on the roof by Dame Lalaurie. Witnesses saw the crazed woman beat the black girl with a whip, until the slave leaped to her death to escape. Dame Lalaurie hid the body in a well, but police discovered it after a neighbor told them what had happened. Lalaurie was fined and forced to sell her slaves; however, friends purchased the slaves at public auctions and returned them to her. On April 10, 1834, a black cook set the kitchen on fire because she could not stand the living conditions anymore. Firefighters who put out the fire found the cook chained to the floor and discovered seven slaves fastened to various torture devices in the attic. An angry crowd formed and forced Lalaurie to leave town. She settled in southern France and died on a hunting expedition a few years later. (She was gored to death by a wild boar.) At the turn of the century, the house was turned into apartments. Tenants reported many different ghostly figures on the premises, including Madame Lalaurie, a tall black man on the staircase, and strange shrouded forms moving about. Strange sounds were also heard: an invisible chain being dragged down the staircase; the pitiful cries of the slave girl near the cherub fountain in the courtyard; and tortured screams coming from the attic. Even today, passersby whisper, "La maison est hantée" ("The house is haunted").

(Delphine Lalaurie's house is at 1140 Royal St., New Orleans, LA 70116. www.prairieghosts.com/lalaurie. html) **42, 58, 175, 188, 223**

LAVEAU HOUSE An illegitimate mulatto born in 1794, Marie Laveau was the Voodoo Queen of New Orleans. She led voodoo dances in Congo Square and sold charms and potions from her home in the 1830s. Sixty years later she was still holding ceremonies and looked as young as she did when she started. Her rites at St. John's Bayou on the banks of Lake Ponchartrain resembled a scene from hell, with bonfires, naked dancing, orgies, and animal sacrifices. She had a strange power over police and judges and succeeded in saving several criminals from hanging. Her perpetual youth led some historians to speculate that there were actually two Laveaus, perhaps a mother and daughter. In fact, two tombs are said to belong to Laveau in an old cemetery in the French Quarter (see St. Louis Cemetery, below.) In any case, by 1895 Marie Laveaus I and II had disappeared. Her ghost and those of her followers are said to practice wild voodoo rituals in her old house, where one can still buy voodoo potions and gris-gris bags of spells. Laveau has also been seen walking down St. Ann Street wearing a long white dress. The phantom is that of the original Marie, because it wears her unique tignon, a seven-knotted handkerchief, around her neck. On St. John's Eve, her spirit can be heard singing at St. John's Bayou. See Voodoo Museum, below.

(Marie Laveau lived in the 1900 block of North Rampart St. from 1819 to 1855, before she moved to St. Ann St. Laveau's House is in the French Quarter at 1020 St. Ann St., New Orleans, LA 70116. Phone: 504-581-3751.) **5, 13, 37, 42, 57, 58, 68, 175, 188, 231**

PHARMACIE FRANCAISE This museum displays ancient cures and methods, including a collection of voodoo hexes and magical gris-gris potions. It is listed by the U.S. Department of Commerce as an official haunted site. Most of the instruments, furniture, and glassware date from the nineteenth century. An apothecary was opened on the first floor of this town house in 1823 by Louis Dufilho, the nation's first licensed pharmacist. It became a museum in 1950.

(The museum is located in the Vieux Carre section of the city. New Orleans Pharmacy Museum, 514 Chartres St., New Orleans, LA 70130. Phone: 504-565-8027. www.pharmacymuseum.org) **78, 101**

ST. LOUIS CEMETERY Two unmarked, graffiti-covered tombs here are thought to contain the remains of the two Marie Laveaus (see Laveau House, above). Even today, people leave voodoo offerings, mark an *X* for good luck, or knock three times to summon her spirit. Many believe Laveau's spirit can be seen as a large black crow that flies over the tombs. One man claimed that the ghost of Marie slapped him

The Pharmacie Francaise displays ancient cures, voodoo hexes, and gris-gris magic potions. See Pharmacie Francaise, New Orleans, Louisiana (PHARMACIE FRANCAISE)

across the face and then floated to the ceiling, when he failed to acknowledge her presence in a drugstore in the French Quarter. The scene was witnessed by the owner of the store. Others claim she takes the form of a large black dog that roams through the cemetery.

(The grave of the first Marie Laveau is twenty-five feet to the left of the entrance to St. Louis Cemetery No. 1. The second Marie is in St. Louis Cemetery No. 2. St. Louis Cemetery, 400 Basin St., New Orleans, LA 70116. Phone 504-482-5065. www.yatcom.com/neworl/lifestyle/cemstlouis.html) **5, 42, 196**

VOODOO MUSEUM This museum traces the history of the voodoo cult in New Orleans and contains many items relating to voodoo spirits and spells. See Laveau House, above.

(Voodoo Museum, 724 Rue Dumaine St., New Orleans, LA 70116. Phone: 504-523-7685. www. voodoomuseum.com) **78**

OPELOUSAS

CHRETIENNE POINT This beautiful antebellum mansion is haunted by a killing that took place there. After the death of pirate Jean Laffite (see Laporte, Texas), his men returned to Louisiana to rob Madame Chretienne, a rich recluse and close friend of Laffite. The woman heard them breaking into her home and tried to escape, but she was cornered by one of the pirates. Taking a Derringer pistol she had hid in her clothing, the aristocratic dame shot the pirate right between the eyes. The other robbers fled the scene when they heard the gunshot. Madame Chretienne stuffed the body in a closet, where it remained for three days until authorities could arrive at the remote site. The bloodstains in the closet have never been washed away, and the ghost of Madame Chretienne has never left her mansion. She walks the halls at night.

(Opelousas is in south central Louisiana, twenty-five miles north of Layfeyette on I-49. Chretienne Point is a private residence in St. Landry Parish.) **231**

PLEASANT HILL

OLD HENDERSON HOUSE A house built around 1825 became the scene of a strange haunting just after the Civil War. The family that lived there found a set of white teeth while crossing a field where a battle was fought in April 1864. They were real, not false, teeth, and the family took them home and put them in a jar. That same night, the bloodied face of a man with strawberry blond hair appeared at their window. The face appeared every night, but the family could not find footprints near the house the next morning. They decided to bury the teeth back where they found them. The face stopped appearing, but within a few months they awoke to find that the entire front porch had moved several yards from the rest of the house. Again, they could find no footprints. They abandoned the house that same day.

(Pleasant Hill is in western Louisiana, on Highway 175 in Sabine Parish. The house is now a private residence south of town.) **121**

POVERTY POINT

POVERTY POINT STATE COMMEMORATIVE AREA This is one of the most sacred sites in North America, and one of the oldest cities ever founded in the United States. It is a place of deep reverence and worship of nature. A female effigy found here strongly resembles prehistoric statues of the Great Mother from Europe, although evidence suggests that the site is of Mayan origin. Some of the mounds are arranged in six concentric semioctagons that line up with the spring and autumn equinox sunrises. The octagon shape, of uncertain significance, is found throughout the Mound Builder sites. The spaces between the remaining mounds line up with the summer and winter solstices. The huge Bird Mound effigy has a wingspan of 640 feet and stands seven stories high. The site is named for a cotton plantation that once stood here.

(The site is in West Carroll Parish, which is in the northeast corner of Louisiana. Follow Highway 134 east to Highway 577 north. The park is five miles northeast of the town of Epps. For information, contact the Poverty Point State Commemorative Area, P.O. Box 276, Epps LA 71237. Phone: 318-926-5492.) **99, 144**

ST. FRANCISVILLE

COTTAGE PLANTATION This twenty-two-room mansion was built in 1824 by Abner Duncan as a wedding gift to his new son-in-law Frederick Conrad. Frederick and his wife Frances lived in the house until the beginning of the Civil War, when it was taken over by the Union Army. Frederick and his faithful personal secretary Mr. Holt were held prisoners in the house until after the war. Frederick died soon after being released, but his loyal servant stayed on. Mr. Holt lived another twenty years at the disintegrating plantation, and, after his death, his white-bearded ghost, wearing a nightshirt, was spotted and even photographed on the grounds. After the mansion burned down in 1960, Holt's ghost and the apparitions of former slaves were seen wandering through the ruins.

(The town of St. Francisville is approximately seventy miles north of New Orleans, or about twenty-five miles north of Baton Rouge, on U.S. Highway 61. Cottage Plantation, 10528 Cottage Lane, St. Francisville, LA 70775. Phone: 225-635-3674. www.virtualcities.com/ons/la/p/lap8601.htm) **15, 78, 101**

MYRTLES PLANTATION Many ghosts roam the halls of this picturesque home, built in 1796 by General David Bradford. There have been ten murders in the house, plus at least one suicide. A frequent visitor is the ghost of Cleo, a former slave hung for murdering two little girls. General Bradford's son-in-law Clarke

Woodruff cut off the black woman's ear for eavesdropping, and she took her revenge by mixing oleander into the children's birthday cake. Another ghostly guest is attorney William Winter, who lived here from 1860 to 1871. He was shot by a stranger on his front porch. The lawyer staggered into the house and made it up seventeen steps of the stairway before he collapsed and died. His ghost still plods up those seventeen stairs. Ghosts from the slave graveyard on the property report for chores, and the ghosts of the two children poisoned by Cleo play on the verandah. One ghost, dressed in khaki pants, is said to meet visitors at the gate and tell them the plantation is closed. Jane Roberts, a psychic who investigated the house, said that walking into the parlor was like walking into a crowded cocktail party full of departed spirits. Frances Kerman, who now runs the former plantation as a bed-and-breakfast inn, says the ghosts have proved to her the reality of life after death.

(The two-story wood-frame bed-and-breakfast inn is three miles north of St. Francisville on Highway 61. Myrtles Plantation 7747 U.S. Highway 61, St. Francisville, LA 70775. Phone: 800-809-0565. www.praireghosts.com/myrtles.html) **66 (10/91), 78, 101, 168**

ST. JOSEPH

MISSISSIPPI RIVER A strange phenomenon occurs along the Mississippi River here. On numerous occasions since the mid-1870s, witnesses have reported hearing the screams of a woman coming from the middle of the river. Sometimes they can hear her say in French, "Aidez-moi au nom de Dieu. Les hommes me blessent!" ("Help me, in the name of God. The men are hurting me!"). The ghostly voice is thought to be connected with the disappearance of a steamboat nearly 125 years ago. The *Iron Mountain* was among the largest boats on the Mississippi. It was over 180 feet long and thirty-five feet wide, and was powered by five huge boilers. Besides passengers, the ship usually hauled several barges of freight. In June 1872, the ship disappeared without a trace. The barges had been cut loose, but none of the fifty-four people aboard were seen again. No wreckage or debris was ever found. The ship had left port at Natchez and was last seen at Vicksburg, Mississippi. People could only speculate that river pirates had hijacked the ship, stripped it bare, and killed all the passengers and crew.

(The town is on the Mississippi River, thirty-eight

miles south of Tallulah on U.S. Highway 65. Take Highway 128 east to St. Joseph. The mysterious cry is heard most often by fishermen and boaters on the Mississippi river just north of St. Joseph.) **15**

ST. MAURICE

ST. MAURICE PLANTATION A child's ghost rises from the family cemetery here and walks through locked doors into the halls of this massive manor home. The mischievous presence likes to startle people by rushing past them or making sudden noises. He also has a penchant for turning calendar pages to the wrong date. Some say the ghost started the fire that burned this mansion to the ground on January 6, 1980.

(St. Maurice is in central Louisiana, off U.S. Highway 165. The ruins of St. Maurice Plantation are just outside of town.) **78, 101**

THIBODAUX

LAUREL VALLEY VILLAGE Ghosts abound in this abandoned plantation village. Over sixty-five original structures are still standing, including the manor house, school, slave cabins, and barns. The remains of an old sugar mill are also on the property. The creepy scenes from the motion picture *Angel Heart* (1987) were filmed on location here.

(Thibodaux is fifteen miles west of Raceland on Highway 1. The site is off Highway 308 near Thibodaux, just north of Houma.) **72**

VACHERIE

OAK ALLEY PLANTATION The ghost of a lady in black has been seen combing her shoulder-length hair in the master bedroom, pacing the window's walk, and riding a phantom horse around the grounds. In 1987, the image of the ghost appeared on a photograph taken in the master bedroom by a tourist. The mysterious Lady in Black is thought to be the spirit of Louise Roman, daughter of Jacques Roman, who built the mansion in the 1830s. While fleeing from a drunken suitor, Louise fell and gashed her leg on a wire hoop in her dress. Gangrene set in and her leg had to be amputated. Her family saved the leg so it could be buried with her later. She entered a Carmelite convent in St. Louis to recover from the traumatic experience but returned to her southern home in her later years.

(Vacherie is on the Mississippi River in the southeast section of Louisiana on Highway 18. Take I-10 southeast across the Sunshine Bridge. At the end of the bridge turn left onto Highway 18 and follow it sixteen miles to the plantation in St. James Parish. The address of the Oak Alley Plantation is 3645 Highway 18, Vacherie, LA 70090. Guest rooms are available. Phone: 225-265-2151. www.oakalleyplantation.com) **14, 101**

VALCOUR AIME PLANTATION GARDENS The "Versailles of Louisiana" now lies in ruins. It was built by wealthy planter Valcour Aime, whose ghost still haunts the grounds.

(The gardens are located in St. James Parish. For information, contact the Louisiana State Tourism Division, 1051 N. 3rd St., Baton Rouge, LA 70804. Phone: 800-633-6970.) **78, 101**

MAINE

APPLEDORE ISLAND

GOLDEN GIRL POINT The ghost of a beautiful young woman with waist-length golden hair haunts this rugged island. She appears to be looking out to sea for someone. Sometimes she can be heard to murmur, "He will come again." She most often appears on a low-lying outcrop on the dawn of a clear day. Locals say she is the ghost of one of Blackbeard's lovers, whom he put on shore to guard buried treasure. Before her pirate lover could return, he was captured off the coast of North Carolina and beheaded.

(Appledore Island is one of the seven islands that make up the Isles of Shoals. It is located about ten miles off the southernmost coast of Maine.) **5**

BAXTER STATE PARK

MOUNT KATAHDIN The Abenaki Indians call this the Greatest Mountain, and believe it to be haunted by a spirit named Pomola. The strange being has the head of a bull moose, wings of an eagle, and the body of a human. His spirit helpers are small birds, who can foretell the weather. The 5,268-foot-high peak is the highest point in the state.

(The mountain park is located in north central Maine, twenty miles northwest of Millinocket.) **200**

BELFAST

HIGH POINT The ghost of a woman condemned as a witch has roamed this overlook for hundreds of years. Barbara Houndsworth was sentenced to be hanged after an unlucky series of events struck this village. An outbreak of distemper struck cats and dogs, a black plague struck the cows, Barbara's neighbor came down with an unknown disease, and the town church caught fire for no apparent reason. Barbara, a maker of aromatic potions and remedies, was blamed for all the sudden calamities. Some locals say she was also accused of murdering her baby or poisoning her husband. In any case, Barbara was manacled and led to the town square where she was sentenced to be executed. But a stone intended for Barbara hit the forehead of the town clerk, who dropped to the ground. In the ensuing commotion, Barbara broke away from the crowd and ran down a forest path. With her tormentors in hot pursuit, she headed for the coastline. A torrential rain came out of nowhere, and gusty winds forced the townspeople to give up their chase. Barbara reached the rocky path along the coast that led to freedom, but slipped on the wet rocks and fell to her death into the raging sea. Witnesses on land and in boats off High Point have seen her thin shackled ghost on the rocks. Others have reported her apparition wandering through flocks of seagulls, their plaintive cries mixing with her own.

(Belfast is on U.S. Highway 1 on the central coast in Penobscot Bay. Barbara's ghost has been sighted along the Maine coastline from Rockland to Searsport. High Point is a cliff overlooking the ocean off Highway 1 near Belfast.) **158**

BOOTHBAY HARBOR

BOOTHBAY OPERA HOUSE A second-floor room in this old theater is haunted by an unknown presence. The building was constructed in 1894, and the upstairs room housed the headquarters of the Knights of Pythias, a men's religious fraternity. Since 1949, people have sensed a strange presence in the room, and sometimes a player piano in the corner turns on by itself. The spirit may be that of Earl Cliff, who played the piano for programs at the opera house in the early 1900s. Sierra Abbey and her husband bought the building in 1988 and experienced a number of odd manifestations. But they did not know its haunted history until they happened to read about it in this book!

(Boothbay Harbor is east of Brunswick on the southwestern coast. The town is ten miles south of U.S. Highway 1 on Highway 27. Old Boothbay Opera House, Boothbay Harbor, ME 04538. www.prairieghosts.com/boothbay.html) **174**

BUCKSPORT

BUCKSPORT CEMETERY The spirit of a woman executed as a witch returns to this cemetery to leave her mark on the tombstone of the man who condemned her to death. Ida Black was a victim of the witch hysteria that swept the colonies. Before she was hanged, she swore to come back and dance on the grave of her accuser, Colonel Jonathan Buck. The superstitious man took the curse very seriously. As the founder of this community, he was provided with a magnificent gravestone when he died in 1795, but on the anniversary of Ida's death, the blood-red image of a woman's dancing leg appeared on the front of the marker. The stone was sanded and cleaned over a dozen times, but the horrific blemish would always return. The family had the tombstone replaced twice, but both times the dancing foot reappeared on the white stone. Buck's descendants gave up trying to fight the curse in 1852. Today, the fifteen-foot-tall monument dominates the graveyard.

(The town of Bucksport is on the central Maine coast, twenty miles south of Bangor on Highway 15. The Bucksport Cemetery is located on Highway 1 just outside Bucksport, about eighteen miles south of Bangor. www.prairieghosts.com/bucksport.html) **66 (2/94), 72, 175**

SILVER LAKE A female ghost has stalked this lake for over sixty years. She is thought to be Sally Weir, whose mutilated body was found in the brush outside Bucksport in September 1898. She had been sexually assaulted, and her jaw and cheekbone were missing. Her lips and left ear were found nearby, and what remained of her body was buried in a nearby cemetery. That cemetery was dug up in 1930 to make way for a reservoir, but Sally's grave was never found.

(Sally's head is kept in a safe at the Ellsworth Courthouse. The old cemetery is at the bottom of Silver Lake, about fifty feet offshore.) **174**

CAPE ELIZABETH

BECKETT'S CASTLE This stone house with its three-story tower was built in 1871 by publisher Sylvester Beckett, who is said to have haunted his home since he died in 1882. His presence is manifested by a billowy blue form, cold spots, yanking on bedsheets, and a door between a bedroom and the tower that refuses to remain closed even when nailed shut.

(Cape Elizabeth is on the coast, eight miles south of Portland. Beckett's Castle is now a private residence, at 1 Singles Rd., Cape Elizabeth, ME 04107.) **101, 135**

BLAIDSELL HOUSE One of the most witnessed ghosts in history haunted the home of Captain Paul Blaidsell and his wife Lydia. In 1793, the apparition of a woman appeared to the family and asked them to fetch her father, Mr. David Hooper. Hooper identified the spirit as his daughter after it answered a number of personal questions about their family affairs. As word of the haunting spread, Reverend Abraham Cummings decided to expose what he believed to be trickery. But outside the home, he saw a rock levitate and turn into a mass of light, which changed into a woman's shape. Soon dozens of people witnessed the talkative specter. Once, fifty people assembled in Blaidsell's cellar to hear the phantom, which passed right through the crowd. The ghost preached to the crowds about proper moral behavior and successfully predicted the death of Blaidsell's wife and father.

(The house is now a private residence on the coast of Cumberland County, near Cape Elizabeth.) **8**

DARK HARBOR

STONER HOUSE No matter how many times the carpet is replaced in the parlor of this wood frame house, it lumps up in the center of the room and bloodstains appear. The phenomenon has plagued several families since 1900, when Salathiel Stoner owned the house. Stoner met Amanda Carter in Falls Church, Virginia, and brought her back to Maine as his wife. Amanda hated her husband's austere house and begged him for a carpet to lay down over the cold parlor floor. After months of nagging and violent arguments, Salathiel sailed to Bangor and brought back a beautiful red-rose carpet. But as he laid it in the parlor and started to nail it down, his wife said she hated the carpet as much as she hated him. In a blind fury, Salathiel raised his hammer and beat Amanda bloody. Then he proceeded to nail down the carpet, right over her body. Bleeding profusely, Amanda spent two days under the carpet, until she finally expired. Salathiel ignored the hump in his parlor carpet, even when friends came to visit. He was committed to an insane asylum in Portland, but his house has never forgotten the deed.

(Dark Harbor is a small town on Muscongus Bay, fifty miles east of Brunswick. The house is a private residence on the white knoll overlooking Dark Harbor.) **157**

GARDNER

SWAIN HOUSE Mary Swain bought this house in 1959 and suspected it was haunted from the day her family moved in. Their Siamese cat sensed some invisible presence, and painters were spooked by windows and doors opening and closing by themselves. Finally, Mary and her sister contacted the spirit with a Ouija board. They discovered the ghost was an Indian girl, whom they named Beatrice. Beatrice had died many years ago and her spirit was trapped in an old maple tree on the property. Later, they found out that the Indian had fallen in love with a white man named Gordon, who met with immediate disapproval from the tribe's elders. They captured the man and burned him to death near the maple tree, in front of a horrified and transfixed Beatrice.

(Litchfield is at the junction of Highways 3 and 11, about eighteen miles northeast of Lewiston. The white wood frame house is near Gardner on Highway 197, Litchfield, ME 04350.) **135**

HARPSWELL

HARPSWELL HARBOR The phantom schooner *Sarah* has been seen in the late afternoon mists of this harbor. The ship was built in 1812 at the Soule Boatyard in South Freeport. During construction, George Leverett met and fell in love with Sarah Soule. They married, and he named the ship for her. But Charles Jose, a jealous Portuguese man who also loved Sarah, took command of the *Don Pedro* and hunted Leverett's ship as it left on its maiden voyage. In the battle that ensued, all of the men on the *Sarah* were killed except Captain Leverett, who was tied to the mainmast as the ship was turned out to open sea. Then, most amazingly, the ghosts of the dead seamen rose to take control of the drifting ship. In November the tattered ship sailed down the unmarked channel and landed at Harpswell Harbor. The townspeople unlashed George Leverett from the mast and took his unconscious body ashore. George was reunited with Sarah, as the ghost ship that bore her name sailed back out to sea. The *Sarah* returned several times to the harbor. The final sighting was in the late 1880s, when many guests at the Harpswell House saw the phantom ship enter the harbor for the last time.

(Harpswell is on Casco Bay, just northeast of Portland. It is south of I-95 on Highway 123.) **49**

KENNEBUNK

KENNEBUNK INN The original building here was built in 1791 by Phineas Cole and later expanded to twenty-two rooms. It became the Kennebunk Inn in the 1940s. After renovations in 1980, ghostly activity began to manifest. Moving and flying crystal goblets, exploding wineglasses behind the bar, disarrayed silverware, and moving chairs are commonplace events here. Owners believe their uninvited guest is Silas Perkins, a former owner who died in the eighteenth century.

(Kennebunk is eleven miles south of Biddeford on U.S. Highway 1, in the southwest corner of Maine. The three-story yellow inn is at 45 Main St., Kennebunk, ME

04043. Phone: 207-985-3351. For reservations, call 800-743-1799.) **72, 101, 135, 175**

KENNEBUNKPORT

CAPTAIN FAIRFIELD INN This Federal-style mansion is haunted by the ghost of Captain James Fairfield, who was captured and imprisoned by the British during the War of 1812. After he was released in 1815, he settled in Kennebunkport with his wife Lois and built this house. He died of pneumonia just five years later, at the age of thirty-eight. During restoration of this bed-and-breakfast inn, Fairfield's ghost was seen hovering in a dark corner of the basement, and guests have reported sensing Fairfield's affable presence in their rooms.

(The captain's portrait may be viewed at the Brick Store Museum, 117 Main St., Kennebunk, ME 04043. Captain Fairfield Inn, 8 Pleasant St., Kennbunkport, ME 04046. Phone: 800-322-1928. www.captainfairfield. com) **53 (8/95)**

The ghost of a nineteenth-century woman has been spied by guests to the Captain Lord Mansion, now a bed-and-breakfast inn. See Captain Lord Mansion, Kennebunkport, Maine (CAPTAIN LORD INN)

CAPTAIN LORD MANSION The Lincoln Room in this picturesque three-story inn is haunted. The ghost of a woman in 1800s clothing floats across the room and vanishes into thin air. She has been seen on several sep-

arate occasions by guests staying in the room, originally called the Wisteria Room, which means "remembrance of the dead." The ghost has also been encountered on the spiral staircase that leads to an eight-sided cupola on the roof. Many believe the ghost to be the wife of Captain Lord. Nathaniel Lord had workers from his shipyards build the mansion in 1812, but he died before he could move in. The house stayed in the Lord family until 1972, when it became a boarding house for elderly ladies. In 1978, it was remodeled into a bed-and-breakfast inn. Not long after it opened, a young bride's honeymoon was spoiled when the ghost of a woman wearing a nightgown drifted through her bedroom and vanished into a wall.

(Highway 35 leads from Kennebunk to Kennebunkport, which is on the Atlantic. Take Route 9 in the town to Ocean Ave. Follow it to Pleasant St., where the mansion is located. Captain Lord Mansion, Pleasant St., Kennebunkport, ME 04046. Phone: 207-967-3141. www. captainlord.com) **14, 72, 101, 175**

SHAWMUT INN This quaint old inn is haunted by a friendly presence that likes to play tricks on employees and guests. The spirit is blamed for moving keys at the front desk and hiding personal belongings of guests.

(Shawmut Inn, Turbats Creek Rd., Kennebunkport, ME 04046. Phone: 207-967-3931.) **72, 101**

MACHIASPORT

OLD BLAISDEL HOUSE In one of the longest continuous hauntings on record, a ghost named Nelly Butler returned to this house for nearly 200 years. A disembodied voice announced the coming of the ghost to the Blaisdel family in 1799, and four weeks later, the apparition of Nelly Butler started to appear. Dozens of residents of the town witnessed the glowing, haloed figure of the young woman. The ghost has not been reported since 1970, so she may feel she is wearing out her welcome.

(Machiasport is located off Highway 1, on Machias Bay on the northern coast of Maine. The house is now a private residence in the center of town.) **69, 186, 188**

MOUNT MEGUNTICOOK

MAIDEN'S CLIFF The ghost of a thirteen-year-old girl who fell to her death from this cliff still haunts the trails here. Sarah Whitesell was attending a family picnic on May 6, 1865, when a gust of wind pushed her off the edge of the cliff. Family members erected a white wooden cross on the spot, and the area was named Maiden's Cliff. Sarah's spirit is said to return during the spring and summer months. Sometimes she is enveloped in a warm wind or seen hovering over flower beds. Dozens witnessed her apparition in the 1930s and 1940s, and she was last seen in 1976.

(The mountain is in Knox County near Lincolnville, on the coast north of Rockland.) **174**

NEWFIELD

OLD STRAW HOUSE This house is named for Gideon Straw, who built it in 1787, and it is haunted by his daughter who is buried inside. Hannah Straw died at the age of thirty in March 1826 when the cemetery ground was too frozen to dig up. She is therefore buried under a flat tombstone in the kitchen. Later residents of the house reported encountering Hannah's apparition on numerous occasions for the next 150 years. For many years in the 1960s, her image appeared almost nightly in a window in a storage room off the kitchen, and poltergeist activity accompanied the sightings.

(Newfield is in York County in the southwestern corner of Maine, about thirty miles west of Portland. Take Highway 25 west from Portland to Highway 11 South. The house is a private residence in Newfield, ME 04056.) **188**

NORTHPORT

COSGROVE HOUSE A phantom house materializes in an abandoned lot off a narrow road here. The white mansion with two chimneys appears just as it once stood, before it was destroyed by fire in December 1954. The fire killed two elderly babysitters and all three of the Cosgrove boys, aged five, seven, and nine. The cries of the children were heard by residents for many years afterward. Recently, a family on vacation took a picture of the tall chimney still standing at the ruins. When they had the film developed, the photograph showed a large white mansion with two chimneys. Since 1990, several other people have taken pictures of the "house that wasn't there."

(Northport is in Knox County, off U.S. Highway 1 near Rockport. The lot is on an unnamed one-lane road west of town.) **174**

PEMAQUID

FORT WILLIAM HENRY The spirit of an Indian chief haunts the fort where he was murdered by English soldiers. Legend says that in July 1696, as Taukolexis was about to be hanged, he poured out his spirit into the tree that was the instrument of his death. Ever since, the Tarratine chief has manifested as a misty white light. Today, tourists and employees report a strange luminescence that comes from the front gate of the fort and moves toward a large tree across the grounds.

(Pemaquid is on the coast south of Brunswick in southwestern, Maine. The restored fort is near the Makooshan Tribe 4. Taukolexis is buried on Tappan Island.) **174**

PENOBSCOT

PENOBSCOT INDIAN RESERVATION This Indian reservation is haunted by an evil white man who married an Indian woman in the 1890s. He treated his wife cruelly and tried to intimidate local Indians in an effort to rule the area and control everyone around him. His form is still seen on the forested island at the center of the reservation.

(The Penobscot Indian Reservation is northeast of Bangor, on the Penobscot River in Penobscot County, four miles north of Milford on U.S. Highway 2.) **214**

PORTLAND

CLAPP HOUSE This Greek revival-style house was built by Charles Clapp in the mid-1800s, but the place is haunted by his father Captain Asa Clapp. He was the most powerful ship and house builder in Maine when he died in October 1848. Oddly, when his wife died in 1920, she left instructions that their beautiful mansion be torn down and a marker placed on the land. She also requested that their huge, four-poster bed be destroyed, as well as their Pierce-Arrow automobile. Some suggest she did it to prevent her own ghost from returning. Instead, her action might have forced her husband's ghost to come back just to guard the family's remaining assets. Captain Clapp's ghost also haunts the house next door, which once belonged to him. See McLellan-Sweat House, below.

(Portland is on the southwestern coast of Maine. Clapp House is on the corner of Elm and Congress streets.

It is now the Maine College of Art, 97 Spring St., Portland, ME 04101. Phone: 800-639-4808. www.meca.edu) **14, 101**

McLELLAN-SWEAT HOUSE The ghost of a pushy neighbor haunts this house, built by merchant Hugh McLellan in 1800. Captain Asa Clapp bought the house in 1817, but never lived in it. Another sea captain, Joshua Wingate, bought the house in 1825. Wingate's daughter married Charles Clapp, son of Asa, and the newlywed Clapps built the house next door (see Clapp House, above.). Now Asa Clapp is said to haunt both houses—one he never lived in, and one where he was never more than a guest. In 1880, Mr. and Mrs. Lorenzo Sweat bought the old mansion, which later became the original building of the Portland Art museum.

(McLellan-Sweat House is next door to the Clapp House in south Portland. The mansion is part of the Portland Museum of Art on the corner of Congress and High streets at 7 Congress Square, Portland, ME 04101. Phone: 800-639-4067. www.portlandmusuem.org) **14, 101**

ROCKPORT

GOOSE RIVER BRIDGE A phantom known as Pitcher Man haunts this bridge. He does not carry a pitchfork or brandish any other weapon, but offers a pitcher of beer to terrified witnesses. William Richardson was killed by three Tory soldiers on the bridge in 1783. They had taken it as an insult when he offered them beer in celebration of the Treaty of Paris, which ended the Revolutionary War. After the bridge was replaced in the 1920s, people began reporting the ghostly figure of a man holding out something in front of him, crossing the bridge. In 1953, two terrified observers saw the ghost offer them a pitcher and then vanish in front of them.

(Rockport is seven miles north of Rockland on U.S. Highway 1, on the central coast.) **174**

SKOWHEGAN

SKOWHEGAN CINEMA This ornate movie house, built in 1929, is home to a hostile ghost. The presence started playing dirty tricks when an apartment was added to the building in 1978. The ghost vandal threw tools, splattered stains on freshly painted walls, and gave workers electric shocks even when the power was not connected. The shadowy presence was once seen in the auditorium and was blamed for a hurling a piece of the ceiling from the balcony into the seats below.

(Skowhegan is seventeen miles north of Waterville on U.S. Highway 201 in southern Maine. The redbrick cinema theater is at 15 Court St., Skowhegan, ME 04976. Phone: 207-474-3451.) **101, 135**

SWANS ISLAND

SWANS ISLAND This island has been considered to be haunted for nearly two hundred years. Mysterious balls of fire, some with distinct faces, have been reported floating over the dark beaches surrounding the island. Several witnesses have reported encountering the ghost of a woman. She carries a baby in her arms and walks slowly over the mudflats. Her footprints have been found in conjunction with the sightings.

(Swans Island is in the Atlantic along the central coast, thirty miles directly south of Ellsworth. It lies just off Blue Hill Bay.) **72**

TENANTS HARBOR

EAST WIND INN The third floor of this white wood-frame inn is haunted by an unknown presence. Guests in Rooms 12 and 14 have reported being held down in their beds by unseen hands. Other guests on the same floor have heard eerie crying sounds or sensed strange cold spots moving around in their rooms. The gray figure has also been seen climbing the main stairway and looking out a window facing the ocean. The house was built in 1860. The third floor was used by a Masonic lodge for secret ceremonies from 1860 to 1894. The building was deserted from 1954 to 1974, when it was renovated for the East Wind Inn. The strange ghost was last reported by a woman doctor and her husband staying in a third-floor room in 1987.

(From Brunswick, go east on U.S. Highway 1 to Thomaston, then go south nine miles on Highway 131 to Tenants Harbor. The restaurant is on the waterfront at Tenants Harbor. East Wind Inn, P.O. Box 149, Tenants Harbor, ME 04860. Phone: 207-372-6366. www.eastwindinn.com) **133, 174**

KEAG STORE This old house, built in 1854, is haunted by a shadowy apparition seen on the second floor. Manager Tom Kierstead says both employees and guests have sensed the presence.

(Keag Store, Highway 73, South Thomaston, ME 04858. Phone: 207-596-6810.) **72, 101**

WISCASSET

CANFIELD'S RESTAURANT The poltergeist who haunts this quaint restaurant has been known to turn teapots upside down, move chairs, unlatch doors, and smack people on the back. The house was built in 1800 by Charles and Lydia Dana. The ghost of Canfield's Restaurant is thought to be Mrs. Dana, an owner of the original house who took in boarders. Locals call her ghost Mother Dana.

(Wiscasset is on the Sheepscot River, fifty miles north of Portland on Route 1. Formerly East Wind Restaurant, Canfield's Restaurant is located downtown on Main Street, Wiscasset, ME 04578. Phone: 207-882-5238.) **187**

MARINE ANTIQUE SHOP When this building housed a restaurant, customers and employees had to deal with a poltergeist who moved tables, chairs, and dinnerware. When it became an antique shop the ghostly activity slowed down, as if the spirit were more satisfied with the older furnishings.

(The Marine Antique Shop is at 14 High St., Wiscasset, ME 04578. Phone: 207-882-7208.) **78, 174, 187**

MUSICAL WONDER HOUSE This mechanical music-box museum is said to be haunted by the shadowy form of a young man in his early twenties. He has been seen on a couch in the sitting room, in the kitchen, and in the upstairs hallway. No one has been able to identify the serene young man, but he is thought to be a former resident of the house, which was built by a sea captain in 1852.

(Musical Wonder House, 18 High St., P.O. Box 604, Wiscasset, ME 04578. Phone: 207-882-7163. www. musicalwonderhouse.com) **78, 174, 187**

SMITH HOUSE The ghost of an elderly lady is sometimes seen rocking by the window here, and the sounds of children echo from the deserted attic. The twenty-three room mansion was built in 1852 and has been considered haunted for the last seventy-five years. The lady ghost is thought to be Lee Payson Smith, a descendent of Governor Samuel Smith.

(Smith House is on High St., Wiscasset, ME 04578. For information on Wiscasset locations, contact the Chamber of Commerce, P.O. Box 150, Wiscasset, ME 04578.) **187, 188**

YORK VILLAGE

OLD YORK CEMETERY The grave of a witch in this cemetery is said to be haunted by her spirit. Mary Miller Jason was a "white" witch, who never meant to harm anyone. When alive, she prescribed herbs and exorcised evil demons from her neighbors' homes. Locals have been encountering her spirit since she died in 1774, and no one has ever gotten scared. In fact, her unseen presence is said to have pushed children on swings in a playground across the street from the cemetery.

(York Village is in the extreme southwestern tip of Maine, just south of I-95 on Highway 91. The cemetery is east of town.) **174**

MARYLAND

ANNAPOLIS

U.S. NAVAL ACADEMY A group of naval officers testified that at 1:30 A.M. on the morning of October 13, 1907, Lt. James Sutton suddenly went berserk, put a gun to his head, and pulled the trigger in front of several witnesses. That same day, the ghost of James Sutton began appearing to his mother and sister in Portland, Oregon. The young man told them that he did not kill himself but was beaten to death by one of the officers. The Sutton family launched an investigation, which culminated in the exhumation of his body from Arlington Cemetery. An autopsy revealed he had been badly beaten before being shot, but no charges were ever filed.

(Annapolis is at the junction of I-97 and U.S. Highway 50/301 on Chesapeake Bay. U.S. Naval Academy, Annapolis, MD 21402. Phone: 410-267-6100.) **37, 41**

BALTIMORE

CANTONSVILLE On the first full moon in September, the ghost of a pirate walks through the garden in the back of a house in this neighborhood. When the phantom reaches the house, he turns into a ball of fire and disappears into the ground. Many suspect the fiery apparition is returning to look for buried treasure, probably discovered long ago by construction crews in the area.

(The house is a private residence in the Cantonsville section just northwest of central Baltimore.) **8**

FELLS POINT The Fells Point area is haunted by at least two ghosts. The ghost of a man wearing eighteenth-century clothing walks Shakespeare Street late at night. He is believed to be one of the Fell brothers, Edward or William, who founded the town. The Whistling Oyster seafood restaurant is haunted by an unidentified presence, detected by both employees and guests.

(Fells Point is a southeastern suburb of Baltimore. Shakespeare St. is off Broadway. A marker on the street tells the history of the Fell Brothers. The Whistling Oyster is at 807 South Broadway, Fells Point, MD 20670. Phone: 410-342-7282.) **66 (10/87), 101**

GRIDIRON CLUB The ghost of an elderly lady and the slaves she kept walk these grounds. Just before the Civil War, Mrs. Hillen became infirm and required the attendance of a nurse twenty-four hours a day. One night, her slaves sneaked through a secret passage in the house and kidnapped her from her third-floor bedroom. Their plan was to force her into granting them their freedom, but the old lady could not take the stress, and died. Later residents of the house reported seeing her ghost and the apparitions of slaves in chains.

(The colonial house was originally known as the Hillen House. The old slave quarters stood where the

swimming pool is now. For further information about historic sites in Baltimore, contact the Maryland Historical Society, 201 West Monument St., Baltimore, MD 21202. Phone: 410-685-3750. www.mdhs.org) **90**

JONES HOUSE One of the most important cases of modern poltergeist phenomena took place here between January 14 and February 8, 1960. Edgar Jones was a retired fireman who lived in the house with his wife and their daughter and son-in-law, Mr. and Mrs. Theodore Pauls. The Pauls had a seventeen-year-old son, Ted, who was very intelligent but had dropped out of high school to edit his own science-fiction newsletter. The unexplained activity began when fifteen miniature pots on a dining-room shelf suddenly exploded. That was followed by three weeks of moving objects, falling pictures, broken windows, leaping plants, and bursting soda bottles. A small table moved from the living room and threw itself down a flight of stairs, and a pile of logs exploded. Things got so bad that the family moved all breakable objects into a pile in the backyard, so they could get some sleep. Nandor Fodor investigated the case and concluded it was caused by the unconscious mental powers of the teenage boy. After the boy received counseling, the poltergeist departed.

(The case is known in paranormal literature as the Baltimore Poltergeist. Jones House is now a private residence, at 1448 Meridene Dr., Baltimore, MD 21239.) **49, 72**

LOCUST POINT An old house here has been haunted by the ghost of an Englishwoman since before the Civil War. The woman was destitute, but she was too proud to ask anyone for help. One day, neighbors found her sitting in a rocking chair with her two small children snuggled in her lap. They were all dead from starvation. For decades afterward, the woman's ghost appeared to tenants of the house. The form of a woman in a rocking chair could be seen by the front window in the early evening hours, and the area around the third step on the staircase to the second floor was always unusually cold. No one could carry a lit lantern past the third step without the light extinguishing. Sometimes an unseen hand slapped unsuspecting residents hard across the face, and other times the quiet weeping of a woman could be heard.

(Locust Point is near old Fort Henry, between Fort Avenue and Clement St. The private wood-frame house has been covered in a stucco facade.) **8**

O'DONNELL HEIGHTS A whole neighborhood chased a fiendish ghost back into his grave here. The black-capped phantom was first seen hiding under cars, enticing little girls to "Come closer, my dear." The specter emerged from a nearby graveyard, leaping six-foot walls and jumping from twenty-foot heights but leaving no footprints behind. The neighborhood formed a vigilante team, armed with shotguns and butcher knives, to hunt the ghoul. One night, they chased him back to the graveyard, where he jumped into a sarcophagus. The Phantom of O'Donnell Heights appeared for those two weeks in August 1951, and that was the last anyone ever saw of him.

(O'Donnell Heights is in west Baltimore.) **49**

POE HOUSE Edgar Allan Poe's former home is haunted by an unidentified female spirit. She is described as a heavyset woman with gray hair dressed in clothing of the early 1800s. Poe lived here with his grandmother, aunt, and cousin from 1832 to 1835. He later married his cousin Virginia Clemm. His grandmother Elizabeth Poe died in the house in 1835. The house sat vacant from 1922 to 1949, when it became a historical site and private museum. Since the 1960s, the sounds of hushed voices, windows and doors opening by themselves, and a phantom finger touching visitors on their shoulders have been reported. Most of the activity is in Poe's attic room and the grandmother's bedroom. During rioting after Martin Luther King's assassination in April 1968, neighbors called police to report strange flickering lights in Poe House, even though all the power in the district was out. It is said that the premises are protected from local street gangs by Poe's ghost, whom gang members call Mr. Eddie. Poe died in 1849, after a debauch of drinking that lasted several days. He is buried in a small graveyard a few blocks from his house. See Westminster Churchyard, below; and Poe House, New York City, New York.

(The two-and-a-half-story, four-and-a-half-room brick house is now a museum at 203 North Amity St., Baltimore, MD 21202.) **66 (6/94), 68, 72, 101, 135**

USF *CONSTELLATION* This proud frigate is haunted by three ghosts from the early 1800s. One is a sailor in an old naval uniform who is sighted on the forecastle deck. His appearances are so regular that Navy Commander Brougham was able to take a photograph of him in December 1955. The second ghost is sailor Neil Harvey, sometimes seen on the orlop deck, below the

USF *Constellation*, the first ship of the U.S. Navy, is haunted by three separate ghosts. See USF *Constellation*, Baltimore, Maryland USF *CONSTELLATION* FOUNDATION)

main deck. He was strapped to a ship's gun and blown to pieces for falling asleep on watch in 1799. His uniformed apparition appeared to a Catholic priest touring the ship in 1964. The third ghost is the captain who ordered Harvey's grisly execution, Captain Thomas Truxtum. The *Constellation* is the first ship of the U.S. Navy, and the oldest commissioned warship in the world. It was built as a frigate in 1797 and rebuilt as a sloop of war in 1853. The current vessel is an exact reproduction made with parts and antiques from the original.

(The ship and Constellation *Center museum are located on Pier 1, near the corner of Pratt St. and Holiday St. in Baltimore Harbor. USF* Constellation, *Pier 1, Pratt St., Constellation Dock, Baltimore, MD 21202. Phone: 301-539-1797.)* **49, 66 (10/87), 78, 79, 89, 101, 175**

WESTMINSTER CHURCHYARD Since 1944, a mysterious dark figure has swept down on the grave site of Edgar Allan Poe to leave behind three red roses and a bottle of cognac. The man is dressed in a black frock with a black fedora and a scarf pulled up over his face. The nocturnal phantom has appeared every January 19 for the last fifty years. Despite crowds of people waiting at the site, the elusive presence has never been identified. In 1990, a *Life* magazine photographer armed with expensive night-vision photographic equipment captured the image of a man kneeling at the grave site. The man wore a wide-brimmed hat, but the camera was unable to distinguish any facial features. Since then, cemetery officials have refused to allow anyone else to take pictures. Whether it is the ghost of Poe or one of his ardent admirers is open to speculation.

(The graveyard is in West Baltimore at the corner of Fayette St. and Greene St. Information on the Edgar Allan Poe grave site can be obtained by calling 410-382-7228.) **66 (6/94), 101, 175**

BLADENSBURG

DUELING GROUNDS More than fifty bloody pistol duels were fought here, and a number of corpselike ghosts are said to walk the grounds. The ghosts appear as "dark but not transparent" forms that disappear at the slightest sound. One specter is that of Colonel John McCarty, who killed his cousin General Armistand Mason in February 1819. McCarty survived the twelve-pace musket duel but lost his mind because of it. The scene haunted him for many years, and now he haunts the place where it happened. Stephen Decatur, who was gunned down here in 1820, also haunts the grounds, as he eternally repeats the day he died. (See Lafayette Square, District of Columbia.) The ghost of one of the sons of Francis Scott Key, Daniel Key, roams here too. He was killed at the age of twenty in a senseless duel with a fellow Annapolis student, John Sherbourne. The duel took place in June 1836. The two young men had argued over which of two steamboats was fastest. A reluctant participant in another duel was Maine Representative Jonathan Cilley. In February 1838, he was killed by Congressman William Graves of Kentucky. Graves was a stand-in for New York newspaper editor James Webb, whom Cilley had called corrupt. Cilley was inexperienced with guns, and Graves was allowed to use a much more powerful rifle. Cilley was hit in an artery in his leg and bled to death in ninety seconds.

(Bladensburg is northeast of Washington, on Highway 202 in Prince Georges County. A creek that ran through the dueling grounds was called Blood Run, but it has been renamed Eastern Branch. The former dueling area is just across the District of Columbia border, near Fort Lincoln Cemetery. A historical marker is located in front of the grounds on Highway 450.) **4**

CHESAPEAKE BAY

CHESSIE Since this sea monster first appeared in Chesapeake Bay in the 1970s, there have been over three hundred sightings. About thirty-five percent of the sightings describe Chessie having a long neck about twelve inches in girth, which protrudes from the water. Her black-green body, estimated at fifty feet long, undulates through the water in classic sea-monster fashion, with several humps showing above the waves. Some evidence suggests that Chessie swims with large populations of bluefish, although she has never been observed attacking the fish. After viewing a videotape of Chessie taken in 1982, scientists at the Smithsonian Museum of Natural History concluded that she was probably not any type of known marine creature.

(Chessie is most often seen in the Chesapeake Bay at the mouth of the Potomac River. At Leonardtown, take Highway 5 to Point Lookout, which overlooks the Potomac and Chesapeake Bay.) **15, 53 (1/95), 198 (5–90, 3–88)**

CLINTON

SURRATT HOUSE AND TAVERN This two-story wooden tavern is where John Wilkes Booth and David Herold stopped on their flight from Washington after the assassination of President Lincoln. The murder was actually the culmination of a kidnap plot gone awry, and the men had hidden weapons and supplies at the tavern as part of the kidnapping scheme. Since the 1940s, the restless ghost of owner Mary Surratt has been seen on the wide porch here, as well as on the stairway between the first and second floors. The voices of several men talking together are heard near the back of the tavern, and the ghost of an unidentified man has been sighted more recently. Mary lived here for many years with her husband, and after his death, moved to Washington. She rented the building to John Lloyd. It was Lloyd's testimony, accusing Mary of being a conspirator in the Lincoln assassination, that sent her to the gallows. See the Capitol, Fort Lesley McNair, Lafayette Square, and the White House, District of Columbia.

(The town of Clinton used to be called Surrattsville, but the name was changed after the assassination of President Lincoln. The town is in Prince Georges County, thirteen miles south of Washington. Take the Branch Ave. South, Highway 5, exit from I-95. Turn right onto Highway 223W and then left onto Brandywine Rd. The house, now a museum, is operated by the Maryland National Capital Park Commission. Surratt House Museum, 9118 Brandywine Rd., P.O. Box 427, Clinton, MD 20735. 301-868-1121. www.surratt.org) **4, 63, 86, 89**

DRAWBRIDGE

GYPSY GHOST Every year in August, a ghostly white stallion is said to gallop over the roads here. The horse carries a gypsy man and his beautiful lover reunited in death. The gypsy was murdered in the late nineteenth century by the woman's seven brothers, who disapproved of their pending marriage. But a powerful gypsy curse was at work. Every year for seven years one of the brothers died mysteriously. In the eighth year, the woman fell into an unexplainable trance and also died. Then, in the early 1900s, her ghost began to be seen with that of her gypsy lover, both of them riding on the back of a great white horse.

(The town of Drawbridge is in south Dorchester County, at the edge of the Greenbriar Swamp. The phantoms are seen riding north toward Drawbridge.) **49**

EASTON

FAIRVIEW Visitors to the garden at Fairview report hearing strange voices among the boxwoods. The voices may or may not be related to the ghost of a headless man seen on the wide lawn in back of the yellow-brick mansion. The ghost is thought to be a British sympathizer caught guiding British war vessels in an attack on St. Michaels.

(Easton is in Talbot County on U.S. Highway 50. The Fairview estate is a private residence along the Miles River near Easton. The mansion is included in the annual Maryland House and Garden Pilgrimage.) **63**

GROSS' COATE The ghost of Aunt Molly Tilghman, who lived in this house at the turn of the century, has been observed late at night, floating down the stairway to unlock the front door. It was a ritual she performed almost nightly, when she lived in the house with her young nephew. The rebellious youth often stayed out late, but stubborn Aunt Molly never gave him his own key. The English-style country home was in the Tilghman family from 1760 until 1983.

(The sixty-three-acre estate is just outside Easton at 1658-11300 Gross Coate Rd., Easton, MD 21601. Phone: 410-819-0802.) **63**

ELKRIDGE

THE LAWN A long-term poltergeist terrorizes people who move into this house. Since the 1950s, owners have reported strange scratching sounds, doors that unlock themselves, and flying objects. Once, a head of lettuce shot straight up into the air in front of several witnesses. One family held a Ouija board séance to contact the presence and discovered several ghosts in residence. Their six-year-old son started holding regular conversations with the spirits. The two-story mansion was built in the 1830s by Judge George Dobbin, and remained in his family until 1951.

(Elkridge is in northeast Howard County, just east of Ellicott City. The Lawn is in a wooded residential area known as Lawyers' Hill.) **63**

ELLICOTT CITY

JUDGES' BENCH SALOON A noisy spirit, who flushes toilets when no one is around, has haunted this old tavern for several years. This colorful place has so many candidates for ghosts, that no one knows whom to elect as the saloon's raucous presence.

(Ellicott City is located just southwest of Baltimore on Highway 144. Judges' Bench Saloon, 8385 Main St., Ellicott City, MD 21043. Phone: 410-465-3497. www. thespiritrealm.com/MD.htm) **101**

LILBURN This Gothic mansion is haunted by several ghosts. A small child is heard crying in an upstairs bedroom, footsteps lumber up the tower staircase, and unaccountable cigar smoke drifts through the library. Reports of supernatural activity began in the 1920s, when owner John McGinnis remodeled the tower. The shape of a man once materialized in a doorway, and a housekeeper reported seeing the ghost of a little girl in a chiffon dress. The twenty-room mansion was built in 1857 by entrepreneur Henry Richard Hazelhurst, who died in 1900 at the age of eighty-five.

(Lilburn is located off the Rogers Avenue exit of Highway 40 West outside Baltimore. Lilburn is now a private residence on College Ave. www.prairieghosts.com/lilburn. html) **63, 101, 168**

OAK LAWN The Cooking Ghost is what people call the spirit who resides in this old house. Oak Lawn mansion is now an office building owned by the Howard County District Court, but employees often smell bacon and eggs frying or the aroma of fresh soup in their offices, despite the absence of cooking appliances in the building. In the 1970s, a rocking chair in one man's

The Cooking Ghost is smelled, not heard, in the Oak Lawn mansion. See Oak Lawn, Elliott City, Maryland (TRACEY JOHNSON)

office became notorious for rocking by itself, and once, a dense white fog materialized on the stairway.

(Oak Lawn housed the parole office in the 1970s. Now, the building is in the middle of the Ellicott City Courthouse complex and houses the Howard County Law Library. 8360 Court Ave., Ellicott City, MD 21043. Phone: 410-313-2135. www.prairieghosts.com/cooking. html) **63, 101, 168**

EMMITSBURG

MOUNT SAINT MARY'S COLLEGE AND SEMINARY The apparition of Reverend Simon Bruté has been seen following groups of students along the campus sidewalks here. The former college president died in 1839. A frightening poltergeist haunts Room 252 in the residence hall. Several boys and priests have reported an unseen presence that throws furniture and personal items about the room. It is impossible to keep furniture in place in one corner of the room. Unusual electrical problems also plague occupants, but an electromagnetic survey of the room revealed nothing out of the ordinary. The college was founded in 1808 and is the oldest independent Catholic college in America.

(The college maintains files on ghost legends and folklore. Mount St. Mary's College, 1630 Old Emmitsburg Rd., Emmitsburg, MD 21727. Phone: 301-447-6122. www.msmary.edu) **125, 218**

ST. JOSEPH'S COLLEGE The apparition of Mother Seton glides through the corridors here. She is often accompanied by the phantom of a man carrying a doctor's leather bag. The former women's college was used as a hospital during the Civil War. Mother Seton's tomb is on the campus. The selfless woman was sainted in 1975.

(The town of Emmitsburg is at the junction of U.S. Highway 50 and Highway 140, near the Pennsylvania border north of Frederick. The college is at the center of town. Vincentian Fathers, 47 Depaul St., Emmitsburg, MD 21727.) **218**

FREDERICK

AUBURN The ghost of Edward McPherson haunted his home for many years, until the door to the stairway up to his room was locked. McPherson was killed in 1848 in the Mexican War. His loud, stumbling footsteps were heard regularly until the outside access to the stairs was sealed.

(Frederick is at the intersection of I-70 and I-270, forty-five miles from either Washington or Baltimore. Auburn House is on a private estate near Frederick, on the west side of U.S. Highway 15, one mile south of Catoctin Furnace, in Thurmont. McPherson is buried in Mount Olivet Cemetery.) **101, 218**

FREDERICK HISTORICAL SOCIETY Volunteers here have reported seeing the ghost of a woman wearing a long-sleeved, floor-length dress. She has been observed sitting on a velvet rocking chair in a storage room. Old trunks seem to move by themselves and music is sometimes heard coming from a broken Grafanola machine. The unusual house was built in 1834 by Dr. John Baltzell. A hanging spiral staircase rises from the ground floor to the roof of the Federal-style building.

(Frederick Historical Society, 24 East Church St., Frederick, MD 21701. Phone: 301-663-1188. www. prairieghosts.com/histsociety.html) **218**

HOOD COLLEGE The oldest building on the campus of this women's college is haunted by foot-stomping ghosts. The sounds of raucous laughter and animated conversation are most often heard on the top floor of the structure. The college was established in 1893, but Brodbeck Hall was built in 1868 as a biergarten tavern.

(Brodbeck Hall is next to the Administration Building. Hood College, 401 Rosemont Ave., Frederick, MD 21701. Phone: 301-663-3131. www.hood.edu) **218**

SCHIFFERSTADT Frederick's oldest house is haunted by Joseph and Elias Brunner, who built the place in 1750. The distinctive voices and footsteps of the two German immigrants are still heard in their eighteenth-century home.

(Schifferstadt House is maintained by the Landmarks Foundation and is open for tours at 1110 Rosemont Ave., Frederick, MD 21701. Phone: 301-663-3885.) **218**

TYLER HOUSE A woman living in the second-floor rear apartment in this boarding house has reported regularly encountering the ghostly figure of a man with stringy hair. The white-robed figure is said to walk down the steps from the attic every night at 2:30 A.M.

(The house is a private residence, at 112 West Church St., Frederick, MD 21701.) **218**

HAGERSTOWN

STANFORD HALL A lady in silk, enveloped in a ghostly mist, appears in a first-floor room here, and the apparition of an old moonshiner is said to roll a barrel of whisky down the front steps late at night. There is also talk of a secret room which brings disaster to anyone who finds it. The thirty-six-room brick mansion was built in 1734 by the Mason family. Maryland Governor William Hamilton owned it for nearly fifty years. In 1920, it was bought by the Leo Cohill family. A local magistrate, who found the room in 1924, and one of the Cohill daughters, nine-year-old Margaret, who found the room in 1926, are both said to have died because of it.

(Hagerstown is at the intersection of I-70 and I-81 on the Pennsylvania border. Stanford Hall is a private mansion ten miles from Hagerstown, on a hilltop overlooking Clear Spring.) **49**

HEBRON

HEBRON GHOST LIGHT A dull yellow ball of light chases people and vehicles down Ghost Light Road near Hebron. In 1952, two Maryland State Troopers were harassed by the light, which hovered about twenty feet from their patrol car. No matter how the driver varied the speed of the car, the ball of light remained at the same distance. Legend says the light is the lantern of a man killed in an accident on the railroad that ran through the area. Some families living on the road reported poltergeist effects in the 1960s, and an abandoned house with a family graveyard in the yard was considered to be haunted for many years. Hundreds of people saw the spook light from the mid-1950s to the mid-1970s, but the phenomena became very rare after the road was blacktopped in 1974.

(Hebron is on Highway 347 in Wicomico County in eastern Maryland, six miles northwest of Salisbury off U.S. Highway 50. Ghost Light Road, also known as Old Railroad Rd., was officially renamed Church St. in 1974.) **53 (6/94), 66 (10/88)**

HOLLYWOOD

ST. ANDREW'S CHURCH ROAD BRIDGE The ghosts of two women haunt this bridge. One is thought to be a young white girl who was killed by a car speeding around the curve entering the bridge. She was run over by her own husband, anxious to get home just after World War II ended. The girl had the man's baby boy in her arms, and when she was struck the child was hurled over the bridge and into the cold waters below. The baby was never found, but its cries can still be heard from the stream, which is now called Cry Baby Creek. The other ghost on this bridge causes accidents by jumping out in front of cars. She is a young black girl whose slave quarters stood near the bridge. After she murdered her white owner, who had been sexually abusing her, she was followed by a posse and killed in the nearby swamp.

(From the south Baltimore area, go south thirty-eight miles on Highway 5 to Highway 4, which is St. Andrew's Church Rd. Take the road east for three miles to the bridge.) **15**

LAUREL

MONTPELIER MANSION The ghosts of our Founding Fathers are said to walk the grounds of this beautiful estate. The house was often visited by George Washington, Thomas Jefferson, and John Adams, and their ghosts have been seen many times over the years.

(Montpelier Mansion, Maryland National Park, 9401 Montpelier Rd., Laurel, MD 20708. Phone: 301-953-1376. www.pgparks.com/places/historic.html) **101**

OAKLANDS This Georgian mansion was built in the 1700s by Richard Snowden and has had plenty of time to accumulate ghosts. For many years, the sounds of an invisible horse could be heard galloping up the drive-

way around 10:00 P.M. The front door would then be heard to open and close when no one was there. The wraith of a small boy has been seen sitting on the edge of a bed, and a young female ghost was once seen crossing the front yard. The apparition of a big black woman has startled witnesses over the years, and the image of a black male slave has also been reported. The frightening sounds of dragging footsteps and a woman's uncontrollable sobbing are heard throughout the house.

(Laurel is in north Prince Georges County, northeast of Washington on U.S. Highway 1. Oaklands is at the edge of town www.prairieghosts.com/oaklands.html) **63**

LEITERSBURG

OLD LEITER HOUSE Residents of this nineteenth-century house have reported eerie, moving vibrations, which they attribute to ghosts of the Leiter family. James Van Leiter was a Dutch Calvinist who settled in the area in the 1760s. The house was built by his descendants around 1850. Most of the odd sounds come from the basement area, although more recently, a man's apparition was photographed sitting in the front seat of an old-time car parked in the driveway.

(The town is in north Washington County, near the Pennsylvania state line. The house is a private residence on Main St., Leitersburg, MD 21740.) **63**

LEONARDTOWN

ST. MARY'S HISTORICAL SOCIETY The spirit of a suspected witch, whose one-room hut was burned by fearful townsfolk in the late 1700s, still plagues this seaside town. Moll Dyer was an eccentric hermit. She was driven from her meager home in the middle of winter by townspeople, who blamed her for all their troubles. A few days later, her body was found frozen in a kneeling position on a boulder near the sea. When they removed the body, they found the impression of her knee and hand etched into the stone. To this day, the area where her hut stood is barren, and her ghost is seen hovering over the desolate land. In 1975, the 875-pound boulder on which she died was moved in front of the St. Mary's Historical Society building in Leonardtown. Ever since then, people have reported feeling ill at ease near the rock. Tourists' cameras often malfunction, and some people suffer such agonizing aches and pains that they cannot stand near the haunted boulder.

But things have not really changed much in two hundred years. Moll Dyer is still blamed when a calamity strikes this quiet community.

(Take Highway 5 in southern Maryland to Leonardtown, in St. Mary's County. Moll's hut was on a stream that is now called Moll Dyer's Run. St. Mary's Historical Society, 41625 Court House Dr., Leonardtown, MD 20650. Phone: 301-475-2467.) **15**

MADISON

BLACKWATER NATIONAL WILDLIFE REFUGE A devil mule haunted this swampy area for many years. Sighting the green-eyed, white-furred phantom meant that some sort of disaster would befall the observer within three days. When it was alive, the stubborn, biting mule was thought to be possessed by the devil. He was deliberately led into quicksand by a group of tobacco wagon drivers in the early 1800s. After its murder, the devil mule returned to prophesy havoc for the men and their families.

(The town of Madison is located in Dorchester County on Taylor Island Road. Follow the road east to Church Creek, then go south on Golden Hill Road four miles to the wildlife refuge at 2145 Key Wallace Dr., Cambridge, MD 21613. 410-228-2692.) **36**

MOUNT RAINIER

DEEN POLTERGEIST Douglas Deen was almost fourteen years old in January 1949, when strange noises began coming from his bedroom walls. His mother called an exterminator, but nothing was found. Then the boy's bed trembled, furniture started moving, and objects fell to the floor for no reason. The events became more violent and were witnessed by neighbors and other family members. Finally, the Deens contacted their minister, Reverend Winston. He spent the entire night of February 18 with the boy. The reverend heard unexplainable scratching sounds in the walls, saw the bed move, and watched as a chair heaved the boy to the floor. Douglas was taken to Georgetown Hospital for complete physical and mental testing, but no problems could be found. He was later sent to St. Louis Hospital in Missouri for further testing. In desperation, the family decided to have exorcism ceremonies performed. A team of Jesuit, Lutheran, and Episcopal priests performed over twenty exorcisms in thirty-five days. Another priest stayed with the boy for two months and performed over thirty exorcism rituals. By May 1949, the demon seemed to have left the boy, and the poltergeist manifestations stopped. The case was the basis for William Peter Blatty's novel and film, *The Exorcist* (1973).

(The Deen family house is now a private residence in Mount Rainier, which is a suburb of Washington, just northeast of the city on U.S. Highway 1.) **37, 50, 53 (1/75), 68**

PIKESVILLE

DRUID RIDGE CEMETERY The eyes of a black angel statue perched on top of a tombstone here are said to glow with eerie light at midnight. The sculpture marks the grave of General Felix Angus, a newspaper publisher who died in the 1920s. Dubbed Black Aggie by locals, the tombstone is believed to be the meeting place of ghosts who inhabit the graveyard. It is said that anyone who gazes into the glowing eyes will be blinded and pregnant women who pass in the stone's shadow will suffer miscarriages. Allegedly, a member of a college fraternity died of fright after a midnight initiation ceremony at the foot of the grave. In 1962, a man was arrested for sawing an arm off the angel, although he insisted the statue had sawed off her own arm. Before long, Black Aggie was so famous that tourists were crowding the cemetery at midnight, hoping to glimpse the glowing eyes. Finally, in 1967 the tombstone was removed from the grave and donated to the Smithsonian Institution.

(Pikesville is a northwestern suburb of Baltimore on the I-695 ring. The cemetery is located in Pikesville at 7900 Park Heights Ave. Phone: 410-486-5300. www. prairieghosts.com/druidridge.html) **37**

POINT LOOKOUT STATE PARK

FORT LINCOLN Hundreds of paranormal events have been recorded in this Civil War prison camp, which was the sight of unspeakable horror. Prisoners lived in small tents in wet, filthy conditions. In just two years, over four thousand Confederate soldiers died of disease or abuse. In the 1970s, a park manager sighted the ghostly figure of a young man with dark hair and eyes outside the kitchen of the lighthouse residence, and another employee saw the apparition of a woman standing on top of the outside stairway. The sounds of unexplainable footsteps, slamming doors, and even snoring have been heard in the duplex dwelling, which was converted from a functioning lighthouse in 1965. Inexplicable voices have been reported (and recorded) in the area around the Confederate monument. The voices say such things as "Let us not take objections," "Fire if they get too close," and "Going home." Ghosts have also been reported by fishermen and tourists on the roads and paths within the park. In fact, park rangers keep track of unusual phenomena here and conduct a ghost tour in October.

(Fort Lincoln was originally called Camp Hoffman. Point Lookout State Park is on the extreme southern tip of Maryland, at the end of Highway 5. The mailing address of Point Lookout State Park is Star Route Box 48, Scotland, MD 20687. Phone: 301-872-5688. www. prairieghosts.com/ftlincoln.html) **14, 39, 63, 101**

POOLESVILLE

ANNINGTON MANOR The ghost of an Oregon senator haunts these grounds, along with twenty-five other soldiers who died here. Colonel E. D. Baker was killed in the Battle of Ball's Bluff in 1861. Sightings of ghosts in the old battlefield along the C&O canal caused the place to be nicknamed Haunted House Bend. Baker and the others are buried in a small national cemetery at the battlefield.

(Poolesville is in southern Montgomery County, at the junction of Highways 107 and 109. Annington Manor is a private residence five miles west of town at White's Ferry. Ball's Bluff Battleground and Cemetery is at the end of a dead-end road off U.S. Highway 15.) **218**

PORT TOBACCO

PEDDLER'S ROCK This boulder is named for a peddler who was robbed and murdered here in the eighteenth century. Today, the ghost of Blue Dog, the peddler's faithful pet, still guards the spot where the man was killed. Legend says the spectral hound guards a buried sack of gold taken from his master. Ghostly howling and the misty blue shape of a dog are most often encountered in February.

(Port Tobacco is in western Charles County, at the junction of Highway 6 and the Port Tobacco River. Follow Highway 6 east out of town for two miles and turn north on Rose Hill Rd. The bloodstained rock is one mile down the road on the west side. Further north is the Rose Hill Mansion, many of whose residents encountered Blue Dog.

For information about tours of the mansion, contact Charles County Chamber of Commerce, 6360 Crain Highway, La Pata, MD 20646. Phone: 301-932-6500.) **36**

POTOMAC

HARKER PREPARATORY SCHOOL An unidentified shadow moves through the upper floors at this prestigious school. Disembodied footsteps are heard and a dark form has been seen by students and administrators. The place was built by Henry Clagett and has been used as both a trading post and a tavern.

(Potomac is in Montgomery County, northwest of Washington at the junction of Highway 189 and Highway 190. Harker Preparatory School, Potomac, MD 20851. Phone: 301-299-5555.) **198 (10–92)**

ROCKVILLE

COUNSELMAN FARMHOUSE This century-old farmhouse is said to be haunted by two recently departed souls. One is Rosie Counselman, who committed suicide here on April 29, 1969. The other is Jack Peyton, who died in the master bedroom in 1976. The current owner, Ned Williams, says many spooky things happen in the house. His dogs sense the presence of the ghosts, and once, a housesitter ran from the premises when he encountered one of the apparitions.

(Rockville is in Montgomery County, northwest of Washington, just off I-270. The old farmhouse is on Bradley Boulevard. The house is part of the October Ghost Tours operated by the Montgomery County Historical Society. For information, call 301-762-1492.) **198 (10–92)**

SNOW HILL

FURNACE TOWN The ghost of a black slave stands guard over the remains of a blast furnace in this abandoned foundry town. The Maryland Iron Company opened the Nassawango Iron Works in 1832, and the operation was shut down several times and closed for good in 1847. Sampson Hat was a slave who stoked the huge coal furnace. He came to think of Furnace Town as his only home and refused to leave the settlement, even when everyone else had abandoned it. Sampson lived there alone until he died at the age of 107. His last wish was to be buried at Furnace Town, but the local almshouse would not honor his request. It is believed that until Sampson Hat finds eternal rest in his beloved town, his ghost will return to the place where he passed so many years alone.

(Furnace Town is in Worcester County near Snow Hill, which is fifteen miles south of Salisbury on Highway 12. Furnace Town is three miles beyond Snow Hill on the Old Furnace Town Rd. Furnace Town has been restored and has a museum. Furnace Town, P.O. Box 207, Snow Hill, MD 21863. Phone: 301-632-2032. www. prairieghosts.com/furnace.html) **14, 101**

ST. MARY'S COUNTY

BECKWITH MANOR The ghosts of a gentleman and his lady, both dressed in courtly garments, have been seen standing beneath an old elm tree here. Both apparitions look toward the sea, as if expecting someone. They are the 325-year-old ghosts of George and Frances Beckwith. Frances died in 1676, several months after her husband had sailed to England on business. Her shadowy form was soon spotted under the elm tree looking seaward for her husband's ship. One day, a large sailing vessel entered the harbor and a lone man climbed into a rowboat and made for shore. Local residents headed for the wharf to greet the man, whom many believed to be George Beckwith returning home. As the crowd neared the dock, the rowboat and the mysterious ship suddenly disappeared from sight. The astounded populace learned months later that George Beckwith had died in London.

(Beckwith Manor is a private estate located on the south shore of the Patuxent River in St. Mary's County.) **49**

SUSQUEHANNA RIVER

PEDDLER'S RUN This area was haunted by a headless ghost for eighty years. In 1763, the decapitated body of a peddler was found near a grist mill operated by John Bryarley. The headless man's ghost was frequently seen along the riverbanks. In 1843, a farmer digging a drainage ditch found a human skull buried four feet underground at the site of Bryarley's Mill. The peddler's body was disinterred and the head laid to rest with the body. After that, the ghost was never seen again.

(Peddler's Run is in Hartford County near Castleman. It is a tributary of the Susquehanna River just north of the Conowingo Dam and was previously known as Rocky Run.) **49**

SYKESVILLE

HOWARD LODGE This three-story brick house was built in 1774 by Edward Dorsey, and was named for Governor Howard, the first governor of the state of Maryland, who lived there for many years. Governor Howard's ghost is thought to be the strange presence that people sense standing at the second-floor landing. The governor's elusive shadow has also been encountered in other areas of the great house.

(The town of Sykesville is west of Baltimore, at the junction of Highway 32 and Highway 125. The Howard Lodge is now a private residence in Sykesville.) **84, 91**

RELIANCE

PATTY CANNON'S HOUSE The ghost of Patty Cannon has returned to the place where she made a living kidnapping freed slaves and selling them back to southern plantation owners. She kept slaves hidden in her house and in her son-in-law's tavern next door, where she beat and tortured them in the an attic room. In 1829, after several skeletons turned up on the property, Patty was arrested for murder. But the woman killed herself by taking poison hidden in the hem of her dress. Today, people sense her evil presence, and the sounds of her heavy footsteps are still heard in both the house and the tavern. Patty Cannon's life was the basis for George Alfred Townsend's novel, *The Entailed Hat.*

(Reliance is at the junction of Highway 392 and Highway 577 in extreme eastern Maryland. The site borders Caroline and Dorchester counties, near the Delaware state line. Cannon House is located two hundred yards from Joe Johnson's Tavern, at Johnson's Crossroads on Highway 392. A marker in front of the tavern details its history. www.prairieghosts.com/patty.html) **63**

TOWSON

HAMPTON MANSION The chandeliers in this old mansion are said to predict the death of family members. Built between 1783 and 1790, the palatial estate at one time included seven thousand acres and was the home of the Ridgely family for 158 years. According to the legend, whenever the sounds of a crashing chandelier echo through the house, a family matriarch dies within hours. Many times, servants and family members have heard the shattering sound of one of the huge crystal chandeliers crashing to the floor, only to find nothing amiss. Then, the lady of the house soon dies. Although reports of ghosts in Hampton House are numerous, the National Park Service, which oversees the site, insists it is not haunted.

(The mansion is now a national historic site in Baltimore County, about ten miles north of Baltimore. From I-95, go west on U.S. Route 695. Take Exit 28 North onto Providence Rd. Hampton House is at 535 Hampton Ln., Towson, MD 21204. Phone: 410-823-1309. www.nps. gov/hamp) **8, 14, 101**

UPPER MARLBORO

MOUNT AIRY PLANTATION In the 1930s, this house was investigated by the London Society for Psychical Research, which detected the spirit of Elizabeth Bresco Calvert. The ghost was searching through the house for jewels she hid away while living there. The plantation was built by Charles Calvert in 1725 and remained in the family until 1903. Other ghosts in the Calvert home include a forlorn young woman in white who pines for her forbidden lover, and the phantom of an elderly lady who wanders the house late at night waking up people. A horseman in riding gear haunts the entrance, and the apparition of a man in a red shirt was seen suspended in midair outside a second-story window. The ghost of Eleanor Calvert does not like the parlor to be used and keeps it locked. The eighty-one-year-old woman fell down the stairs and died in the house in 1902.

(The town of Upper Marlboro is in central Prince Georges County at the junction of U.S. Highway 301 and Highway 4. The plantation restaurant is part of the Rosaryville State Park. 8714 Rosaryville Rd., Upper Marlboro, MD 20772. Phone: 301-856-8987. www. prairieghosts.com/mtairy.html) **63**

WESTMINSTER

AVONDALE Legh Master constructed an iron smelter here in the early 1700s. Today he is known as the Ghost of Furnace Hills. His phantom has been reported walking alone or riding a black horse through the woods near his former home. After nearly two hundred years of roaming his property, his spirit is still not at rest, though perhaps his dark secret has been discovered. In the 1930s, the skeletons of a woman and child were found hidden behind a fireplace wall at Avondale.

(Westminster is in Carroll County, twenty miles northwest of Baltimore on I-795/Highway 140. Tours of the town's haunted sites are conducted by the Westminster Public Library. Avondale is a private residence five miles west of downtown Westminster.) **63**

COCKY'S TAVERN The ghost of a Civil War soldier walks the center staircase here. The unseen presence even helps himself to a drink from the bar on occasion. The sounds of his heavy boots and the clanging of invisible glasses are heard by both employees and patrons. Sometimes the ghost signals his displeasure with a topic of conversation by moving pictures on the walls.

(The historic tavern is on East Main St., Westminster, MD 21157. For further information, call 410-848-9050.) **63**

OPERA HOUSE PRINTING COMPANY The headless phantom of Alabama, comedian Marshall Buell, is seen on the outside backstairs of this former theater building. He was stabbed to death there over a hundred years ago, after making anti-Union jokes during his performance.

(The old theater is now the Opera House Printing Company, 140 East Main St., Westminster, MD 21157. Phone: 410-848-2844.) **63**

MASSACHUSETTS

ASHLAND

JOHN STONE'S INN The sign over the entrance to this 164-year-old pub offers "spirits, food, and lodging," but it is not until you see Captain John Stone's picture staring down from above the bar that you know about which kind of spirits they are talking. Daniel Webster gave speeches here, and there are secret rooms that served as hiding places for runaway slaves, but the inn's greatest claim to fame are the ghosts walking its halls. The apparition of a ten-year-old girl is often reported staring out a window in a storage room near the kitchen, and an invisible intruder puts his hands around the necks of customers in the dining room. Near an ice machine in the cellar, several employees have felt an unseen presence tap them on the shoulder or hold their hands under the ice when they try to fill buckets. Other manifestations include glasses flying across the dining room, cups falling off shelves for no reason, and mysterious ten-dollar bills materializing in a tip jar. In 1984, investigators held two televised séances in an upstairs lounge in front of 150 witnesses. They claimed to have contacted the spirits of a little girl, a woman innkeeper, and yes, old Captain Stone himself.

(In Middlesex County, take the Framingham exit off Highway 90 and follow Highway 135 for five miles west to the town. John Stone's Inn, 179 Main St., Ashland, MA, 01721. Phone: 508-881-1778.) **101, 135**

BOSTON

BOSTON PUBLIC GARDENS The friendly ghosts of two elderly women have been encountered in this popular city park. They emerge from the Ritz Carlton Hotel and stroll arm in arm through the park. The apparitions wear 1930s-style clothing and sometimes smile at witnesses.

(The park is in the center of Boston, along the Boston Common.) **133**

CHARLESGATE HALL Charlesgate Hall is an 1890s hotel that was converted into a dormitory by Boston University, and purchased by Emerson College in 1980. Legend says a student hung himself in a stairwell in the building, and many students who lived here were involved in satanic cults in the 1970s. A séance held in 1988 contacted several spirits in the building, including a girl who was crushed to death by a malfunctioning elevator in 1985. The college sold the building in 1996.

(Charlesgate Hall is now a private residence in the Back Bay section of Boston.) **53 (2/90)**

FORT WARREN The ghost of a lady in black has haunted the old barracks and prison at Fort Warren since the Civil War. The young wife of Lt. Andrew Lanier was not about to let her new husband rot in a dungeon at Fort Warren. Shortly after he and six hundred other Confederate soldiers were imprisoned there, she began planning their escape. Dressed in a man's dark suit, she managed to break into the prison and contact her husband. She had brought along a shovel, a pickax, and a pistol. The prisoners began digging a tunnel to the parade ground, where they planned to enter the armory and take over the fort. Just as they reached their target, the tunnel was discovered and the prisoners surrendered. Among them was Lanier's wife, who drew the pistol and fired at a colonel leading the Union soldiers. The damp gun misfired, and the fragmented bullet mortally wounded her husband. On February 2, 1862, Mrs. Lanier took her turn on the gallows, asking only that she be allowed to wear a dress. Soldiers found a black theatrical gown and gave it to her to wear. Seven weeks after her execution, a night sentry felt two hands tightening around his throat. He turned to see the Lady in Black, bathed in a mysterious light, trying to choke him to death. One by one, she appeared to the soldiers and has continued to haunt other guards over the years. Her ghostly footprints have been found in the snow, and sometimes a rock rolls from nowhere across the floor in the old ordnance storeroom. During World War II, an army sentry was so frightened by the Lady in Black that he subsequently spent over twenty years in a mental institution.

(The Fort Warren Historic Site is located on a rocky point on George's Island, about seven miles from Boston in Boston Harbor. Ferries to the island leave from Long Wharf and Rowes Wharf. Information, including a brochure describing the haunting, is available from the Metropolitan District Commission, 20 Somerset St., Boston, MA 02108. Phone: 617-727-5114.) **5, 14, 38, 101**

HAMPSHIRE HOUSE RESTAURANT
This restaurant and hotel is home to the bar featured in the television series *Cheers*. The original mansion was built by Judge Thayer, who lived there with his wife and children. Rumors are that the judge had an improper relationship with his twin daughters, one of whom committed suicide at the age of twelve by hanging herself from the top of the spiral staircase. Since then, her ghost has been seen peering over the banisters and out of first floor windows.

(Hampshire House, 84 Beacon St., Boston, MA 02108. Phone: 617-227-9600. www.hampshirehouse. com)

MIDDLE STREET
The ghost of a former resident is said to return to a house on this street looking for his wife. Peter Rugg lived on Middle Street in 1730. One day, he and his daughter departed on a horse and buggy trip to Concord. They disappeared during a violent storm that hit the area, and no trace of them was ever found. Then in 1826 a strange carriage began to appear on the road to Concord. It was an open carriage driven by a man accompanied by a young girl. The appearance of the carriage was always followed by an instant storm that only lasted a few seconds. The ghostly carriage was sighted so often that it was nicknamed "Storm Breeder." Sometimes the driver even stopped to ask for directions to Boston. Once, he appeared at the old Rugg house on Middle Street in Boston and asked for "Mrs. Rugg," but when he was told she never lived there, the man became agitated and mumbled about how much the city had changed. Before he climbed into his wooden wagon, he was heard to mutter: "No home tonight."

(Rugg's phantom carriage haunts the main connecting link between Boston and Hartford, Connecticut, along the Massachusetts Turnpike and Wilbur Cross Parkway.) **37, 68**

OMNI PARKER HOUSE HOTEL
This hotel is the oldest continuously run hotel in the United States. Founded by Harvey Parker in 1855, the hotel became famous for its great food and outstanding service. Mr. Parker may even be responsible for the continuing good reputation of his hotel, because his ghost is still seen inspecting the hallways and rooms. During recent reconstruction work, his apparition was seen wearing a hardhat, as if he were supervising the workers. The furniture in some of the better rooms, such as the Dickens Room, has a way of rearranging itself, and many employees suspect it is the original owner keeping things up to his high standards.

(Omni Parker House Hotel, 60 School St., Boston, MA 02108. Phone: 617-227-8600.)

SHIP'S CHANDLERY MUSEUM
When this museum was moved to a position closer to the Boston highway, a few old spirits were shaken free. Built in the late 1700s by Samuel Bates, the wood-frame house suddenly became haunted. Workers at the museum started hearing the inexplicable sounds of chains being dragged and heavy footsteps from upstairs. Sometimes the eerie

sounds interrupted lectures. Employees believe their unseen presence is John Bates, flamboyant son of Samuel. The large-framed man kept a closet full of ladies clothes tailored in his own size.

(The museum is located in Cohasset, which is about forty miles southeast of Boston, off Highway 3A. Ship's Chandlery Museum, 14 Summer St., Cohasset, MA 20814. Phone: 781-383-1434.) **91**

BOXFORD

WITCH HOLLOW FARM This Colonial farmhouse was built in 1666 and is haunted by the ghost of a woman who lived there and was condemned as a witch in 1693. Mary Tyler confessed her witchcraft and was thus spared hanging, but her ghost lingers at her former home, known as Witch Hollow Farm. She has been seen walking from the carriage house toward the main house and in an upstairs bedroom. Her presence has been felt by a number of residents, workers, and visitors in the attic, kitchen, and near the fireplace in the living room.

(Boxford is in the northeast corner of the state, ten miles southeast of Methuen. The farmhouse is now a private residence, at 474 Ipswich Rd., Boxford, MA 01921.) **101, 135**

CAMBRIDGE

HARVARD COLLEGE A 175-year-old building on this Ivy League campus is haunted by a half-dozen ghosts trying to get in from the outside. Thayer Hall used to be a textile mill, and it is the spirits of former workers who are trying to get inside. Their apparitions, clad in period clothing, are seen late at night at the entrances. They are even seen at places where there are no doorways now but perhaps were at one time. Reports were most frequent during the winter months but have lessened since outdoor artificial lighting was installed.

(Harvard College, 8 Garden St., Cambridge, MA 02138. Phone: 617-495-1555. www.college.harvard. edu.) **72**

LESLEY COLLEGE Students and professors at this women's college have reported experiencing ghostly activity in a classroom building on Avon Hill. Phenomena include disembodied footsteps and objects that move by themselves. The college was founded in 1909 on a five-acre campus in north Cambridge.

(Lesley College, 29 Everett St., Cambridge, MA 02138. Phone: 617-868-9600. www.lesley.edu) **102**

YMCA The Men's Health Club in the basement of this five-story redbrick building is haunted by the ghost of a man who died of a heart attack there in the 1930s. His glowing green apparition is most easily seen when the room is completely dark, although he has been witnessed in broad daylight.

(Cambridge is a western suburb of Boston. The Young Men's Christian Association building is at 820 Massachusetts Ave., Cambridge, MA 02138. Phone: 617-661-9622.) **133**

CAPE COD

BEECHWOOD INN The ghost of a young woman has been spotted walking the halls here. The house was built in 1716 on an old stone foundation that had been used as a fortification against attacks by Indians. For many years, the house was owned by a sea captain who had been a slave trader. Later owners and guests at the inn that opened on the property reported a variety of paranormal phenomena, including sightings of the ghost, strange footsteps, moving objects, and eerie feelings of an unseen presence.

(Cape Cod is located at the southeastern tip of the state. Take U.S. Highway 6 to the Barnstable exit and follow Highway 6A into town. Formerly Cap'n Grey's Smorgasbord Inn. Beechwood Inn, 2879 Main St., Barnstable, MA 02630. Phone: 508-362-6618. www.beechwoodinn. com) **91**

CAPE COD BAY The phantom of a drifting dory has been seen on numerous occasions off the coast here. It was first spotted in 1880, when a steamer, the *Nantuckett*, tried to effect a rescue. But the boat disappeared. The dory is described as a black boat like those used for short-distance trawling. Sometimes it is surrounded by an eerie phosphorescence; other times the bloodied body of a white man is seen in the bottom of the boat, while a black man stands at the bow. One holiday party from Martha's Vineyard told of detecting the odors of spices mixed with decomposing flesh coming from the phantom boat. Always, the shout is heard: "Helloo-o-o."

(The dory has been spotted by people in sailing boats, trawlers, and rowboats in Cape Cod Bay at the extreme eastern tip of Massachusetts.) **158**

PLAZA GUEST HOUSE At least two of the thirteen rooms in this pre-1830s inn are haunted. Dogs and cats refuse to cross the threshold into Room 6, noted for its frequent spooks. An eerie, luminescent form haunts Room 7, where suspicious bloodstains were found under the linoleum. One male guest in yet another room awoke one night to find himself floating two feet above his mattress! The only spirit identified here is Zeke Cabal, who was the town drunk in the 1920s. Now his confused ghost cowers behind a large corner desk in the living room.

(The inn is located in Provincetown, which is on the Cape Cod National Seashore, at the end of U.S. Highway 6 on the northernmost peninsula of Cape Cod. Plaza Guest House, 11 Pearl St., Provincetown, MA 02657: Phone: 508-487-1818.) **101, 135**

A grayish, shadowy figure haunts Room 24 of the Colonial Inn. See Colonial Inn, Concord, Massachusetts
(COLONIAL INN)

CONCORD

COLONIAL INN A grayish figure haunts Room 24, on the second floor here. The ghost is thought to be a guest who stayed at the inn in the late 1800s. The haunted room is in the oldest section of the inn. Built in 1716 by physician Captain Joseph Minot, the house later became part of an inn that enveloped two other houses. A conventional brick building was added to the rear of the inn in the 1960s. The first sighting of the ghost was on June 14, 1966, when a woman on her honeymoon at the inn was awakened by a shadowy figure four feet from the edge of her bed. The apparition floated to the foot of the bed and vanished. Recently, a businesswoman from Virginia also encountered the ghost of Room 24.

(Concord is eighteen miles northwest of Boston, north of Highway 2 on Highway 126. Colonial Inn, 48 Monument Square, Concord, MA 01742. Phone: 978-369-9200. For reservations, call 800-370-9200. www.concordscolonialinn.com) **53 (3/83), 101, 135**

ORCHARD HOUSE The house where Louisa May Alcott wrote *Little Women* in 1868 is haunted. The ghost is thought to be Alcott's sister, Mary.

(Orchard House Museum, P.O. Box 343 Concord, MA 01742. Phone: 978-369-4118. www.louisamayalcott.org) **102**

DEERFIELD VALLEY

HOOSAC TUNNEL This five-mile-long tunnel through the center of Hoosac Mountain completed on Thanksgiving Day, 1873, was quite an engineering feat. By the time it was done, the tunnel had cost the lives of 195 workers. At least two of those workers still haunt the spot where they lost their lives. On March 20, 1865, explosives experts Ned Brinkman and Billy Nash had just set a huge nitro charge when a co-worker, Ringo Kelley, ignited it prematurely. Both men were crushed by tons of rocks, but Kelley walked away unscathed. Yet Kelley did not get away so easily. The ghosts of Brinkman and Nash stalked him for exactly one year. Then, on March 20, 1866, the lifeless body of Kelley was found strangled to death at the exact spot where the other two men had died. In 1868, reports of strange voices and moaning in the tunnel prompted an investigation, which concluded that the disembodied voice of a groaning man was indeed issuing from a spot about two miles inside the tunnel. In 1872, two engineers not only confirmed the eerie moaning sounds but also came across a headless ghost enveloped in blue light at the same location. In 1874, a hunter from North Adams, lured into the tunnel by the voices, was assaulted by ghostly figures. The young man was found three days later in a state of shock on the banks of the Deerfield River. In 1875, a railroad fire tender disappeared in the tunnel and was never found.

(The Deerfield Valley follows the Deerfield River through Franklin County in northwest Massachusetts. The Hoosac Tunnel is twenty-two miles west of Greenfield off Highway 2. It is just northeast of the town of Florida. www.intac.com/~jsumberg/hoosac.htm) **72**

JOHN WILLIAMS HOUSE On February 29, 1704, a band of fifty Frenchmen and two hundred Abenaki and Caughnawaga Indians attacked Deerfield. The war party slaughtered 49 settlers and captured 111, of whom 20 died on a two-hundred-mile forced march into Canada. John Williams was the town minister and one of those taken prisoner. Two years later he found his way back to his parish, although his daughter chose to stay with the Caughnawagas. His house is haunted by the presence of a woman who did not survive the massacre. The pregnant woman was scalped and killed by the Indians as she tried to make it through a hidden tunnel that ran from the John Williams House to the river. Her presence has been detected in the house, and every leap year on February 29, the sounds of her mournful wailing are said to emanate from Old Deerfield Cemetery where she is buried.

(Historic Deerfield is in Franklin County, two miles south of Greenfield on U.S. Highway 5. The John Williams House served as a dormitory at Deerfield Academy for many years and is now a museum. For further information, call the Deerfield Historical Society at 413-774-5581.) **72**

FALL RIVER

LIZZIE BORDEN BED AND BREAKFAST INN The home where Lizzie Borden is said to have killed her parents with an ax has been haunted since renovations were made in 1996. Most of the activity takes place in the John Morse Room, the room in which Abby Borden was murdered on August 4, 1892. A month after renovations were complete, a housekeeper claimed she saw an imprint of a body on the bed in the room. She ran out of the house and never returned. Others have experienced unnerving effects such as invisible presences rubbing against them. There are also reports of disembodied voices, invisible children playing marbles, slamming screen doors that do not exist, poignant crying sounds, and the rumbling of furniture being moved around upstairs when no one is there. The apparition of an elderly woman with gray hair and wearing Victorian clothing is seen doing chores around the house. Most believe this is Bridget Sullivan, the Bordens' maid.

(Borden Bed & Breakfast and Museum, 92 Second St., Fall River, MA 02721. Phone: 508-675-7333. www. lizzie-borden.com)

FALMOUTH

VILLAGE GREEN INN Built in 1804, this large house is haunted by the original owners, the Dimmick family. A teenage daughter named Sarah died in the house in 1823, and her apparition, dressed in a white old-fashioned nightgown, is sometimes seen in one of the rooms. She also is seen hovering above people sleeping in the bed and looks at them with a quizzical look on her face, as if asking "What are you doing in my bed?" Apparitions of a man and woman dressed in old-fashioned clothing have been seen standing at the top of the stairs. The specter of an older man with wearing a flannel shirt has been identified as Dr. Tripp, who owned the house after the Dimmick family moved out.

(Village Green Inn, 40 W. Main St., Falmouth, MA 02540. Phone: 508-548-5621. www.villagegreeninn.com)

WILDFLOWER INN Built in 1898, recent renovations have spurred paranormal activity in this mansion. Workmen reported being tapped on the shoulder and on the hips, and their tools were in mysterious disarray when they arrived for work in the morning. Today, the pool balls in the Billiard Room are rearranged every night by unseen hands, and the apparition of a young girl in a long dress has been spotted in the Forget-Me-Not Room. The ghost has appeared several times at exactly 4:15 A.M., and it is thought that this is when the girl died in the room.

(Wildflower Inn, 167 Palmer Ave., Falmouth, MA 02540. Phone: 508-548-9524. www.wildflower-inn.com)

FORT DEVENS

MILITARY INTELLIGENCE SCHOOL The top floors of Hale Hall at this military training center are haunted by a presence nicknamed George. Guards report the ghost slams doors, turns on lights, and makes unearthly noises.

(The fort is in Worcester and Middlesex counties. Fort Devens, MA 01433. Phone: 508-772-6976.) **72**

GLOUCESTER

GLOUCESTER HARBOR During a fierce gale in Gloucester Harbor in 1869, the fishing schooner *John Haskell* started dragging anchor and rammed another schooner, the *Andrew Johnson* from Salem. The *Andrew Johnson* was taking water fast, but the captain of the *John Haskell* ordered his ship to make for the harbor. The cries of help from the drowning crew of the wrecked schooner followed the *John Haskell* all the way back to dock. That very night, people reported seeing eerie blue lights moving aboard the deserted *John Haskell*. Every night for several months, people gathered on the wharf to watch the glowing specters move about the battered ship. The ghosts, presumably the dead souls of the crew from the *Andrew Johnson*, pulled up unseen fishing nets and worked at various mundane jobs on the deck. Then the ghostly crew boarded invisible rowboats and rowed out to sea, only to repeat their strange performance each night until the *John Haskell* put out to sea. After months in port, the *John Haskell* was sold to a Nova Scotian, because nobody else would sail on her.

(Gloucester Harbor is at the end of Highway 128 in extreme northeast Massachusetts.) **139, 187**

HADLEY

BISHOP HUNTINGTON HOUSE This hip-roofed house has been haunted for so long by a ghost named Elizabeth that people have forgotten who she was in life. At least three women named Elizabeth have lived in the house since it was built in 1752. Residents over the years learned to live with the friendly ghost, who tucks the children in at night, keeps things dusted, and looks after things in her own unique way.

(Hadley is in Hampshire County in west central Massachusetts, two miles north of Northhampton on I-91.

Bishop Huntington House museum is open to the public. Bishop Huntington House, Highway 47, Hadley, MA 01035.) **188**

LENOX

THE MOUNT The Mount is a country retreat completed in 1902 by Edward Wharton and his wife, author Edith Wharton. The Whartons sold the house in 1912, and many tenants have leased the large house over the years, including a girls' boarding school known as Foxhollow. An actors' playhouse group, Shakespeare & Company, purchased the building in 1978. Persistent haunting has been reported in the old house through the years. Incidents include sightings of a shadowy man with a ponytail in the Henry James Room, the ghost of Edith Wharton in a second-floor hallway and on the terrace, and a hooded, mean-spirited figure who sits on people's chests while they are sleeping. In 1979, voice teacher Andrea Haring was resting on a mattress stored in the old writing room, when she was awakened by an extreme drop in the temperature of the room. She saw three people in the previously empty quarters, which was now full of antique furniture. Haring recognized the ghosts of Edith Wharton and her husband Edward. Another man, possibly Edith's male secretary, sat at a desk taking dictation. All three apparitions turned and acknowledged Miss Haring's presence. She immediately ran from the room but returned sometime later to find it once again warm and empty of spirits. The dozens of witnesses to strange phenomena at The Mount include visitors, actors with the Shakespearean theater group, and alumnae of the Foxhollow School.

(Lenox is in western Massachusetts, seven miles south of Pittsfield on U.S. Highway 7/20. The front entrance to The Mount mansion is on the corner of Highway 20 and Plunkett St., Lenox, MA 01240.) **68, 101, 135**

MELROSE

APARTMENT HOUSE Tenants of a third-floor apartment here witnessed an explosion of poltergeist activity in January 1987. Doors would slam shut, then reopen. Electric lightbulbs burst in their sockets. Drawers opened and closed by themselves. The apartment, in a house built in 1894, was briefly hit by an unseen psychic tornado that spread havoc everywhere.

(The town of Melrose is a northern suburb of Boston, at Main Street and Wyoming Avenue. The three-story, brown clapboard apartment building is at 39 Linden Rd., Melrose, MA 02176.) **134**

METHUEN

OLD MARTIN HOUSE The residence of the Francis Martin family was visited by one of the most peculiar poltergeists ever recorded. While the family was watching television one evening, they noticed a damp spot in a wall. Suddenly a spout of clear water shot from the wall. The phenomena repeated itself throughout the house. The water spouts lasted about twenty seconds and happened about every fifteen minutes. They were usually accompanied by a popping sound. Plumbers, building inspectors, and police could find no reason for the odd events, which began in October 1963 and lasted several weeks. On two occasions, the Martins were forced to move out of their damp quarters to live with relatives in Lawrence. However, the waterspout poltergeist followed them to their temporary residence both times.

(The town of Methuen is in the northeastern part of the state, at the junction of I-93 and I-495. The house is a private residence in Methuen.) **139**

MONOMOY ISLAND

NATIONAL WILDLIFE REFUGE The ghost of a large black horse is seen swimming in the icy Atlantic waters off this island. The horse, always surrounded by a ring of white sea foam, attempts to warn ships of dangerous rocks. It is allegedly the steed used by a pirate who lured ships close to shore here. The land pirate hung lanterns from the horse and walked it slowly back and forth in the loose sand. From a ship offshore, it appeared to be another ship, sailing in safe water. By the time the ship's captain realized what was happening, it was usually too late. The pirate made a living by salvaging the wreckage. Apparently, the horse's ghost is trying to make amends for its life of treachery.

(The park is located just south of Chatham, Massachusetts by way of Highway 28. It is necessary to take a boat from the mainland for one mile to Monomoy Island, which is at the mouth of Nantucket Sound. The park headquarters are off Tisquatum Road on Morris Island. Wildlife Refuge, Wikis Way, Chatham, MA 02633. Phone: 508-945-0594.) **36**

NANTUCKET

COFFIN HOUSE This house is named for Jared Coffin, a bank director accused of embezzling money from the local bank in 1797. He was proved innocent when a robber confessed twenty-one years later, but his life was already ruined by suspicion and gossip. His bitter ghost haunts his former home. Author Peter Benchley encountered the ghost when he lived here in the 1960s. He described it as an elderly man with long hair, dressed in eighteenth-century clothes. The ghost was sitting in a rocking chair in front of the fireplace.

(Nantucket is a large island in extreme southeastern Massachusetts. It is located about twenty-two miles off the south shore of Cape Cod. The city of Nantucket is on the north shore of the island. The house is now the Coffin House Restaurant, 29 Broad St., Nantucket, MA 02554. Phone: 508-228-2400. www.jaredcoffinhouse.com) **6, 198 (6–90)**

SIASCONSET A group of rentals on a bluff overlooking the ocean, Wade Green's Cottages have been the scene of strange phenomena. In 1985, an unmarried couple reported that an unseen presence tried to keep them from making love. The puritanical force made loud pounding sounds from a wall behind the bed, a wall that backed a huge fireplace in the kitchen.

(The cottages are located on Shell Rd. in Siasconset, Nantucket, MA 02564.) **72**

SNELLING HOUSE This 1900s house was owned by the minister of St. Paul's Episcopal Church for many years. Pastor Snelling used the third floor as a study, and had a small organ there. When he died, the organ was sold and his widow gave the property to the church. Later residents of the house have reported the ghostly sounds of organ music coming from the third floor. Christmas music is said to emanate from the area at midnight every Christmas Eve.

(Snelling House is now a private residence, at 25 Orange St., Nantucket, MA 02554.) **6**

UNITARIAN CHURCH A ghost named Seth haunts this 1809 church. He seems to be an elder churchman from a congregation long ago. Seth displays a distinct aversion to noisy children, and his phantom has chased youngsters from the church and grounds. Strange pounding sounds from the vestry and organ loft are also blamed on his cantankerous spirit.

(The church was originally the Second Congregational Meeting House Society Church. The steeple can be seen from five miles out at sea. Unitarian Church, 6 Orange St., Nantucket, MA 02554. Phone: 508-228-0100.) **6**

U.S. COAST GUARD STATION This old lighthouse is now a U.S. Coast Guard station. The nearby dormitory is haunted by a poltergeist spirit that has been known to throw pots and pans around and move other objects. The men say when they yell for the ghost to stop, it usually follows orders.

(The Coast Guard station is on the east coast of Nantucket at the old Sankaty Lighthouse. Phone: 508-228-0388.) **72, 198 (6–90)**

PITTSFIELD

BRIDGE LUNCH DINER In February and March 1958, workers and customers at this diner witnessed a phantom train pass by on railroad tracks in front of the establishment. The ghostly steam locomotive had a coal tender and pulled five coaches and a baggage car. Railroad officials confirmed that no trains of any kind were on the tracks at the times of the sightings.

(Pittsfield is in western Massachusetts, near the New York border, at the junction of U.S. Highways 20 and 7. The diner is now out of business.) **148**

SALEM

BARRACO RESIDENCE The apparition of an elderly man in dungarees has been reported by residents of this house. Sometimes, the ghost's sighing and moaning can be heard in the upstairs rooms. He is thought to be a Cuban immigrant who died in the house in 1872. He was provided refuge in the house, which was owned by the First Church of Salem.

(From Boston, take Highway 128 north sixteen miles to the town of Salem, which is the Halloween capital of the world. The city puts on a ten-day Haunted Happenings festival with over fifty city-wide events. Information is available at the Visitor Center in the Old Town Hall, 32 Derby Square, Salem, MA 01970. Phone: 508-744-0004. The Barraco house is a private residence, at 5 Carpenter St., Salem, MA 01970.) **66 (6/89, 10/90)**

OLD SALEM The apparition of alleged warlock Giles Corey appears near the Old Jail whenever something terrible is about to happen in the community. Ghosts of accused witches also foreshadow calamity on Gallows Hill. The home of Jonathan Corwin, one of the judges in the bizarre witch trials, is considered to be haunted by the spirits of those condemned there. Now known as the Witch House, it was the scene of many preliminary examinations of accused witches.

Another haunted house is the Ropes Mansion, where the ghosts of Judge Nathaniel Ropes and his wife Abigail roam the halls. He was a Tory stoned to death by angry colonists. Later, Abigail burned to death in a fire in the upstairs bedroom. She passed too close to the fireplace, and her nightgown caught fire.

Nathaniel Hawthorne, descendent of one of the witchcraft judges, was born in Salem in 1804 and always felt that the home of his cousin Susan Ingersoll was haunted. He put his impressions on paper in the famous horror novel whose name the house now bears. The House of the Seven Gables is considered to be one of the eeriest in a town full of haunted houses. While still a young author, Hawthorne encountered the ghost of an elderly reverend every day for a week at the Salem Athaeneum Library.

The Salem witch trials of 1692 to 1697 were discredited as a form of mass hysteria, when the girls pointed the finger at the wife of the governor. Nonetheless, poltergeist activity may have contributed to the paranoia that resulted in the accusations being taken seriously. At the trial of Bridget Bishop on March 24, 1692, many witnesses testified that as she was taken under guard past the town meetinghouse, a poltergeist attack took place: "A Demon invisibly entering the Meeting House, tore down a part of it; so that tho' there was no person to be seen, yet the People, at the noise, running in, found a Board which was strongly fastened with several Nails, transported into another quarter of the House." Testimony was entered at the trial of Susanna Martin that accused her of using witchcraft to invisibly attack residents at night. The Reverend George Burroughs was accused of biting and hitting people from behind. His real crime? He had written an essay entitled: "That There Neither Are Nor Ever Were Witches, who Having Made a Compact with the Devil, Can Send a Devil to Torment Other People at a Distance."

(For Old Salem tour information, call 800-441-5305. The Salem Witch Museum is at 19½ Washington Square North. Phone: 978-744-1692. The Witches Dungeon Museum, a recreation of the Salem jail, is at 15 Lynde St. Phone: 978-741-3570. The original Gallows Hill is on the northern side of Almeda St., opposite Salem Hospital.

The Witch House is at 310½ Essex St. Phone: 978-744-0180. Ropes Mansion is at 318 Essex St. Phone: 978-744-0718. The House of the Seven Gables is at 54 Turner St. Phone: 978-744-0991. www.salemweb.com/attracts.htm) **21, 24, 30, 61a, 66 (2/89), 102 (8/91), 192**

SALEM HOSPITAL Nurses, doctors, and patients have reported seeing the apparition of a confused woman in the delivery room of this modern hospital. The ghost resembles a patient who died in childbirth several years ago.

(Salem Hospital, 81 Highland Ave., Salem MA 01970. Phone: 978-741-1215.) **72**

SANDWICH

DILLINGHAM HOUSE This three-story, wood-frame house gained a reputation for being haunted and was left vacant for many years. Police have been called several times to investigate reports of strange activity there, and former residents talk of the ghosts of young children running through the house. The apparition of an unidentified, middle-aged man has been seen on the third floor. Rappings and strange footsteps are heard throughout the house. The house, built in 1790 in Sagamore and moved to its present location in 1810, was the scene of a family tragedy. Owner Branch Dillingham committed suicide here in 1813, and his wife died a few weeks later. Their nine children remained in the house and were forced to care for themselves.

(The town of Sandwich is on Highway 6A, on the North Shore of Cape Cod. Dillingham House is a private residence, at 71 Old Main St., Sandwich, MA 02563. Phone: 508-833-0065.) **134**

SOMERSET

ROBINSON APARTMENTS The back walls of the rear bedrooms on the upper and lower floors here are haunted by an "animal-like presence with claws." Witnesses report a very "uncomfortable feeling" associated with the rear wall of the building. The owner and tenants of the two-family dwelling have felt the malevolent force, which seems to draw beds in the two rear rooms toward the back wall.

(Somerset is in Bristol County, north of Fall River on Highway 138. The two-story, wood-frame house is a private residence, at 35 Hall Ave., Somerset, MA 02725.) **135**

SPRINGFIELD

ALEXANDER-PHELPS HOUSE For several months in the 1880s, Leila Alexander, a sensitive young girl whose family lived in this house, carried on a courtship with the handsome ghost of a former tenant. The man's library was full of books on the occult, and it was there that the girl first met his ghost. Leila suddenly took to sleepwalking and carrying on conversations with the ghost while in a hypnagogic state. As she stood transfixed in the backyard during a thunderstorm one night, she was struck and killed by lightning. In a letter she had written to family members, she told of the ghost's love for her from "a far-off country" to which he would retire to wait for her to be at his side. Years later, construction workers found the skeleton of a young man in a cellar beneath the library wing. Leila's family buried it next to their daughter's grave.

(Springfield is in the southwestern state, at the junction of I-90 and I-91. The house is now a private residence located on State St., between Elliot St. and Spring St. The address is 289 State St., Springfield, MA 01105.) **168**

ASHLEY HOUSE RESTAURANT The ghost of a former owner of this popular restaurant keeps a close eye on how it is run. Vincent Lanzarotto owned the eatery from 1951 until he died in 1978. He ran the place with a strong hand and supervised his employees closely. His apparition has been seen in the dining room, but the most frequent manifestation is a foul, highly localized odor that materializes if he is upset with some aspect of the current management. The unexplainable sounds of a nonexistent dinner party have been heard in the downstairs area and the apparitions of an elderly couple have been seen in the basement. The building was originally a farmhouse built by Charles Ashley in 1829. In the 1920s it was used as a tavern and inn. The old house became Vincent's Steakhouse in 1951.

(The restaurant and motel is on Riverdale Rd. which is Highway 5. Ashley House, Riverdale Rd., West Springfield, MA 01089.) **133**

TEMPLETON

GOODRICH HOUSE This two-story bread box of a house was built during the Revolutionary War by Ebenezer Goodrich. Ebenezer is a likely candidate for one of the presences that haunts this house. Loud footsteps and rapping noises have been heard late at night, and visitors once saw the ghost of a man standing at the foot of their bed. The ghost of a woman, caught lying on the bed in the guest bedroom, gazed into the face of a terrified witness and then completely vanished. Former occupants hung religious paintings throughout the house and stocked pitchers of holy water in every room.

(Templeton is fifty miles west of Boston. The house is a private residence two miles outside of town on Athol Rd., Templeton, MA 01468.) **134**

WAYLAND

VOKES THEATRE This tiny playhouse is haunted by the ghost of Beatrice Herford, a British actress who founded it in 1904. Named after comedienne Rosina Vokes, the private theater was part of Herford's estate. After she died in 1952, it became the property of a local theater group. Her friendly spirit is most often detected near her reserved box in the balcony, although some employees and patrons have heard her whispering voice or encountered her presence in the lobby and backstage.

(Wayland is fifteen miles west of Boston on Highway 20. A portrait of Beatrice hangs in the lobby of the theater. Vokes Theatre, 97 State Rd. East, Wayland, MA 01778. Phone: 508-358-2011.) **133**

MICHIGAN

BEAVERTON

RADIO STATION WGEO When this radio station bought a repossessed mobile home in 1981, it was hoping to find an inexpensive way to expand its business offices. It also acquired a ghost. An unmistakable presence started to show itself in the back bedroom, which the station used for storage. An ice-cold cone of dead air hovered in the hall near the room, and poltergeist-like pranks happened regularly. Weird electrical problems kept interrupting work, and some employees felt strangely ill at ease. Finally the phantom of a child in a yellow jacket was seen and the manager started to hear voices telling her to hurt herself. The company that sold WGEO the mobile home would not release any information on its history, and the local church refused to perform an exorcism.

(Beaverton is in central Michigan, fifty miles from Midland. Take U.S. Highway 18 northwest to Highway 18 north. The radio station is on Highway 18 north of town.) **53 (10/84)**

COLDWATER

HALSTEAD HOUSE This Painted Lady Victorian home is haunted by the ghosts of two children, who sit at the top of the maid's stairway. The Italianate house with a central cupola tower was built in the 1870s by Lorenzo Halstead, a New Yorker who set up a sewing business in the area.

(Coldwater is in Branch County, eight miles from the Indiana border on I-69. The house is owned by antique

Two ghost children sit at the top of the maid's staircase in Halstead House. See Halstead House, Coldwater, Michigan (JAMES E. RAINBOLT)

dealers. It is located at 208 West Chicago St., Coldwater, MI 49036.) **72**

DEER PARK

WESTERN RESERVE The ghost ship *Western Reserve* has been spotted in the waters off Deer Park. The three-hundred-foot-long schooner went down on April 30, 1892. It was the proud property of financier Peter Minch, who was aboard the ship with his family. Only the wheelman survived the disaster. Captain Truedell, of the Great Lakes Life Saving Service in Deer Park, dreamed the exact details of the disaster on the night it happened. He even recognized the body of Peter Minch when he found him washed up on shore near Deer Park.

(Deer Park is in the Upper Peninsula on Lake Superior, fifty miles west of Sault St. Marie. The ship went down fifteen miles west of Deer Park, after rounding Whitefish Point and Iroquois Point.) **176**

DETROIT

COLE HOUSE The back bedroom of this modern home was haunted by a nightmarish ghoul in the early 1960s. Anyone who slept in one particular room had frightening dreams or encountered the terrifying figure of a bludgeoned woman wearing a blue dress and fur jacket. Her face was that of a decomposing corpse. Bill Cole, his wife Lillian, and several friends and members of his family all witnessed the ghastly apparition. Finally, the trapdoor to the cellar started rising up by itself and belched the overpowering odor of rotting flesh. Police made a search of the entire house but turned up nothing unusual. After another horrifying encounter in 1963, the Cole family moved away.

(The gray wood-frame house is a private residence on Martin St., Detroit, MI 48210.) **41, 176**

GENERAL MOTORS PLANT In 1964, the life of a young worker in this car assembly plant was saved by the ghost of a black man, who pushed him out of the way of a giant metal-forming machine that had malfunctioned. The apparition resembled a man who was crushed to death in a similar accident in 1944.

(The incident took place at the GM Stamping Plant. For tour information, contact GM Tours, 3600 Helen St., Detroit, MI 48207. Phone: 313-923-3632.) **115**

KENNETTE BOARDING HOUSE One of Detroit's oldest ghost stories revolves around a rude and bitter woman named Marie Louise Kennette. To make a little extra money, the miserly spinster decided to take on a boarder. She could not have chosen anyone more opposite her own ways. Clarissa Jordan was a pious, churchgoing woman who firmly believed in the existence of ghosts. Clarissa spent many years trying to reform Marie, but it was not until she died that her efforts paid off. A glowing ball of light appeared to Marie one night and changed before her eyes into the form of Clarissa Jordan. By the time Marie died in 1868, she was a transformed woman. She became a firm believer in the afterlife, and a lot nicer to her amazed neighbors.

(The boarding house stood on Springwells River Rd. in Detroit.) **115**

MONGAUGON BATTLE GROUND During the War of 1812, American troops engaged British troops in a bloody skirmish here. The ghost of British officer Lt. William Muir can be seen marching through the woods with a saber raised high in his hand. His ghost first appeared to his fiancée Marie McIntosh on the day he died. He asked her to retrieve his body from a thicket in the woods and bury him. She went to the British commander, and together they discovered his body exactly where the ghost had told her. There was a gaping bullet hole in his head.

(The battle ground is near the Canadian town of Windsor, just across the border from Detroit via the Huron Bridge or the Highway 1 Tunnel.) **39, 176**

NAIN ROUGE Detroit's infamous Nain Rouge, or Red Dwarf, has been reported in the city for over two centuries. The phantom dwarf was first seen in the mid-1700s by Cadillac, the founder of Detroit. Nain Rouge was next reported in 1763 on the banks of the Detroit River. Many residents reported the Red Dwarf running through the streets in 1805 and just outside the city in 1813. The grinning ghoul was seen by several residents in 1967. In March 1976, two Detroit Edison linemen chased the dwarf but were unable to catch him. It is said that each time Nain Rouge makes an appearance in the city, some calamity befalls the residents. So far, that has proved true. Detroit has been attacked by Indians, endured catastrophic fires, and suffered other disasters after the appearance of Nain Rouge.

(Nain Rouge has been reported along the river in south Detroit, near Grand Circus Park, at Cadillac Square, and at several other areas around the city.) **111**

GRAND RAPIDS

MICHIGAN BELL TELEPHONE COMPANY This modern technical center is haunted by the ghosts of Warren and Virginia Randall, whose house once stood on the property. The young couple moved into the house in 1907. They seemed happy until Warren lost a leg in an accident at work on the Grand Rapids and Indiana Railroad. Fitted with an artificial leg, he became depressed and insanely jealous of Virginia. During one of their many arguments, Warren took off his leg and beat his wife to death. Then he opened the gas jets and slashed his throat. It was two weeks before police found their horribly decomposed bodies. The house quickly gained a reputation for being haunted, and nobody would live in it because of the couple's ghosts. It was finally torn down in the 1920s, when the telephone company built a brick office on the site. The Randalls' ghosts have been blamed for strange phone calls made late at night to Michigan Bell customers, as well as numerous unexplainable events in the building.

(Grand Rapids is in west-central Michigan, at the junction I-94 and I-96. Take I-96 to Highway 131 south and exit east on Pearl St. The Michigan Telephone Company is on the corner of Division and Fountain streets, Grand Rapids, MI 49501. Phone: 616-530-3500.) **14, 101**

PHILLIPS MANSION Ghosts of the James Phillips family haunt this mansion. The great house was built in 1864 and the Phillips lived there for 32 years. James died there of a heart attack on March 12, 1912, at the age of sixty-seven. Residents have reported luminous images floating in the bedrooms, and moving lights so bright they can be blinding. The apparition of a very thin, elderly woman and a young blond man have also made appearances.

(The two-story mansion, which has four Doric columns in front, is a private residence in the Heritage Hill section of Grand Rapids.) **53 (6/80)**

JACKSON

REYNOLDS CEMETERY Sometime between dusk on November 21 and dawn on November 22, the ghosts of a father and his daughter are said to reunite in this cemetery. The ghost of Eunice White rises from her grave and greets the ghost of her father, Jacob Crouch. They died together in a bloody mass murder that occurred near Grand Rapids on November 21, 1883. Eunice's husband and a family friend were also murdered that night. Six weeks later, Eunice's sister, her husband, and a farm hand were also found murdered. The case has never been solved.

(Jackson is in south-central Michigan, at the junction of I-94 and U.S. Highway 127. Jacob Crouch is buried at Reynolds Cemetery, on the corner of Reynolds Road and Horton Road. Eunice is buried in St. John's Cemetery in Jackson. The reunions always take place at Reynolds Cemetery.) **111**

LAKE ODESSA

OLD SHOPWELL HOUSE In 1903, Daniel and Cora Shopwell built a house on the foundation of another home that had burned down years before. They soon realized the site was haunted. Loud noises from the back of the house would wake them in the middle of the night, and the sound of a large, invisible object rolling across the porch could also be heard. The oven door would unlatch and then slam shut, and a living-room chair levitated—once with Daniel sitting in it! The Shopwells sold their home within a year of moving in. The next owners, Gottlieb and Anna Kussmaul, had more patience with the ghosts. Even their young daughter Hattie learned to accept the strange footsteps and odd noises. Once, Gottlieb had a seizure while sleeping. Anna was awakened by the ghost of a gray man hovering next to her bed. She tried to awaken her husband and quickly realized something was wrong. Had she not summoned a doctor, her husband would have died. The Kussmauls lived in the house until 1946 and often gave interviews about their haunted house. Investigators discovered that at the turn of the century, a real-estate agent with a large amount of cash was murdered in the original house, which was burned to the ground to hide the body.

(The town of Lake Odessa is midway between Lansing and Grand Rapids on Highway 16. The house stood at the corner of Sixth Avenue and Tupper Lake St. in Lake Odessa and has been replaced by a newer building.) **176**

MACKINAC ISLAND

LOVER'S LEAP The ghost of an Indian maiden haunts this 145-foot-high limestone pillar. Indian princess Michi leaped to her death from here when she found out that her lover, Geniwegnon, had been murdered by her father and a jealous suitor. Her final words were a curse on the tribe and a vow to never let them forget what had happened.

(Mackinac Island is off Michigan's Upper Peninsula, where Lake Michigan meets Lake Huron. Ferries to the island leave from Mackinac City or St. Ignace. The State Park Visitor Center is on the corner of Fort and Huron Streets. To reach Lover's Leap, follow Lake Shore Boulevard north along the western shore for one mile. The stone pillar can be seen to the east.) 36

STRAITS OF MACKINAC The ghost ship *W. H. Gilcher* has been sighted in the Straits of Mackinac, where it went down in 1892. The old coal steamer appears just within the fog off Mackinac Island. Another, older ghost vessel is said to make an appearance in the straits every seven years. It is the phantom boat of the French explorer Sebastian, who is keeping a promise to his fiancée to return to her—dead or alive. A mysterious booming sound is sometimes detected in the Great Lakes. It is called the Ottawa Drum and is said to tally the number of lives lost in the treacherous waters. The so-called Great Lakes Triangle has claimed dozens of ships and aircraft.

(The Straits of Mackinac are often icebound in the winter months. Planes that fly over the Straits, on the way to Mackinac Island, leave from St. Ignace and Pellston.) 5, 53 (8/80, 9/80), 176

MARSHALL

THE NATIONAL HOUSE INN This brick inn was built as a stagecoach stop in 1835 by Andrew Mann. A secret chamber in the basement indicates it was used as a stop on the Underground Railroad before the Civil War. After 1878, the building became a windmill and later was used as a wagon factory. In the 1920s, the hidden room in the basement was used for the sale and consumption of liquor during Prohibition. After that, the building was converted into apartments. In 1976, the building was completely restored and furnished with antiques. That was when the ghost of a lady in red began roaming the halls.

(The town of Marshall is twenty miles east of Battle Creek near I-94. The sixteen-room inn is on Fountain Circle Park and overlooks the downtown area. The National House Inn, 102 South Parkview, Marshall, MI 49068. Phone: 616-781-7374.) 72

MOUNT PLEASANT

CENTRAL MICHIGAN UNIVERSITY The five-story tower in this imposing brick building is haunted by the ghost of a nineteen-year-old cafeteria worker who died in a freak accident in the building. On June 1, 1937, Theresa Schumacher put her head through a small window in the third-floor elevator door, just as the lift descended, breaking her neck. The accident was forgotten, but for many years afterward there were reports of disembodied footsteps on the central stairway, lights going on and off for no reason, and pounding sounds in Rooms 503 and 504. Then, in 1969, Theresa's specter was seen on the fifth floor of the tower by students working for the college radio station.

(Mount Pleasant is in Isabella County in central Michigan, at the junction of U.S. Highways 10 and 27. Central Michigan University, Warriner 105, Mount Pleasant, MI 48859. Phone: 517-774-4000. www.cmich. edu) 53 (10/88)

OSCODA

AU SABLE The ruins of this community, destroyed by fire in 1911, are haunted by a mysterious, unidentified presence that locals associate with feelings of dread and evil. The feeling is so pronounced that modern witches use the site to perform secret ceremonies. However, the only apparition sighted here was of a smiling woman dressed in a winter coat and mittens. She has been reported by hunters in the area, who call her Leona. They say she was accidentally shot by a deer hunter in 1929.

(The town of Oscoda is in Iosco County, north of Saginaw Bay on Lake Huron. The ruins are inland from the town.) 111

PARADISE

SHELDRAKE The specters of former residents of this abandoned logging town walk through its ruins. The old settlement once numbered 1,500 residents, but a series of disastrous fires killed the town. The last fire was in 1926, and today only a dozen homes remain. The apparition of an old sea captain has been seen standing on the Sheldrake Dock on Whitefish Bay. Strange lights are seen in the old Palmer House, and residents of Hopkins House reported a luminous outline that moved through their bedrooms at night. The bearded ghost of a former logger, wearing bib overalls, haunts the Smith House, and the revenant of a lady in a blue veil has been sighted walking through the hallways and bedrooms of the Biehl House.

(The town of Paradise is in the Upper Peninsula, sixty miles northwest of Sault Sainte Marie on Highway 123. The ruins of the town of Sheldrake are four miles north of Paradise on the Whitefish Point Rd.) **133**

PORT SANILAC

FORESTER CAMPGROUNDS This campground is haunted by the ghost of Minnie Quay, a teenage girl who took her own life by walking off the Forester pier. She drowned herself on May 29, 1876, after her sailor lover went down with his ship in a storm. Minnie is said to beckon young girls into the water, and at least one drowning has been blamed on the ghost.

(Port Sanilac is at the junction of Highways 25 and 46 on the east coast of Michigan. The settlement of Forester is four miles north of Port Sanilac on Highway 25. The campsite is just north of Forester. The old Quay house still stands across from the Forester Inn Tavern in Port Sanilac.) **111**

SAGINAW

SAGINAW BAY The ghost schooner *Erie Board of Trade* has been spotted in Saginaw Bay. The cursed ship disappeared in Lake Huron in 1883, allegedly scuttled at the hands of a ghost. The cruel captain of the merchant ship ordered a crewman to go up the main mast in a boatswain's chair everyone knew was unsafe. The man fell to his death. Soon, the man's ghost began appearing on deck and up the topmast. On its very next voyage, the ship vanished and was never seen again.

(Saginaw is in northeastern Michigan, approximately thirty-five miles north of Flint on I-75. Saginaw Bay is bounded by Au Sable Point and Point Aux Barques on Lake Huron.) **176**

ST. CLAIR SHORES

ST. PHANOURIOS GREEK ORTHODOX CHURCH In March 1991, an inexplicable, permanent halo appeared over the head of a saintly figure in an icon here. As word spread, people began to flock to the small Greek church. Before long, over 1,500 people a week were visiting the church to witness the miracle. Many of the modern pilgrims claimed the glow from the halo cured them of terminal diseases such as cancer. The ancient icon pictures Saint Phanourios, a martyr who performed miracles to free priests who were sold into slavery in the thirteenth century.

(St. Clair Shores is a eastern suburb of Detroit on St. Clair Lake. St. Phanourios Greek Orthodox Church, P.O Box 66007, Roseville, MI. Phone: 810-294-4060.) **72**

TRAVERSE CITY

BOWER'S HARBOR INN Ever since this old mansion was remodeled into a restaurant in 1959, a ghost has walked its halls. Glasses break, lights go on and off, and objects fly through the air—all for no apparent reason. Several guests have reported seeing the reflection of a ghostly woman in an antique mirror on the premises.

(Traverse City is in northwest Michigan, at the junction of Highways 37 and 72. The restaurant is on the Old Mission Peninsula in Grand Traverse Bay. Bower's Harbor Inn, 13512 Peninsula Dr., Traverse City, MI 49684. Phone: 616-223-4222.) **111**

WYANDOTTE

SISTER ISLES The wailing sounds of three Indian maidens are still heard on this group of deserted islands. A Wyandot Indian chief banished the quarreling, disrespectful young women to these islands, where they eventually starved to death.

(The town is in southeastern Michigan, south of Detroit on the Detroit River. The islands are in western Lake Erie, northeast of Toledo, Ohio.) **111**

MINNESOTA

ALBERT LEA

OLD BORLAND RESIDENCE When James Jensen was building this house 1893, he could feel the presence of a restless spirit in the upstairs south bedroom. Something peered over his shoulder when he worked there. In the fifty-three years that the Jensens lived in the house, no one ever used the haunted room. When the Jensens left in 1946, a quick succession of fourteen owners tried to make a home of the place, but they were always driven away by some "unspeakable problem." The house sat vacant for long periods. In 1964, Dick and Anita Borland bought the place and moved in with their nine children. Just as they were getting settled in their new home, the figure of a tall, thin woman in a flowered-print dress started appearing near the upstairs south bedroom. She was seen on the small balcony outside the room, in the second-floor hallway, and most often, near a closet inside the room. Before long, none of the Borlands would sleep in the bedroom with the presence who has haunted this house for over a century.

(Albert Lea is at the junction of I-35 and I-90 on the Iowa border. The two-story farmhouse is a private residence on a hilltop just outside the town of Albert Lea.) **176**

COLLEGEVILLE

ST. JOHN'S UNIVERSITY An angry mother haunts the campus of this Catholic school for men. During con-struction of Abbey Church in the 1880s, a young monk fell from a scaffold and was killed. The mother of the dead man was never satisfied with the abbott's explanation about the circumstances of her son's death. After a heated argument at the dedication of the church, the woman was killed when her buggy overturned into a nearby lake. Afterward, strange, wet footprints were regularly found down the center aisle of the church, and people complained of feeling an agitated presence in the church. Years later, when a new church was built on the same spot, a huge crack formed down the center aisle on the day of dedication. Wet footprints are also left behind by another ghost. Brother Anselm Bartolome, who drowned at nearby Sagatagon Lake, haunts the shores of the lake, as well as the halls of the university where he taught. The small lake is also haunted by the phantom of a bear named Murro, who was a mascot at the school. The bear maimed a student who hit it with an oar at the lake, and authorities killed the animal. Since then, Murro's angry ghost roams the shoreline. Frank House is thought to be haunted by a former student, who committed suicide there. Although no ghost has been sighted, a pesky poltergeist annoys students.

(The school was founded in 1857 and moved to Collegeville in 1867. Saint John's University, P.O. Box 5000, Collegeville, MN 56321. Phone: 320-363-2011. www.csbsju.edu) **75**

CROW WING COUNTY

MILFORD MANGANESE MINE This two-hundred-foot-deep shaft is haunted by a skip-tender who never left his post. On February 5, 1924, miners dug through a wall that abutted Foley's Pond, and a rush of water flooded the mine. In fifteen minutes, the mine was under water and forty-three men had died. The seven survivors spoke of the heroism of one man, Clinton Harris, who could have escaped but remained to sound warning bells to miners on upper levels. His warning bell rang for nearly five hours after the mine was inundated. It took three months to drain the mine of water. The first miners who volunteered to go down into the shaft found an unexpected scene at the bottom of the shaft. There was the ghostly form of Clinton Harris, still clutching the escape ladder, his gaze directed upward. The men scurried from the mine and never returned.

(The mine is in Crow Wing County in the Cuyuna Range in central Minnesota. www.prairieghosts.com/ mine.html) **176**

DULUTH

GLENSHEEN On June 27, 1977, Elisabeth Congdon, the elderly owner of this thirty-nine-room mansion, was found dead in her bed. She had been smothered with her pillow. On the stairway lay the bludgeoned body of her nurse. Roger Caldwell, Elisabeth's son-in-law, was convicted of the murders in 1978. He had murdered her to speed collection of his wife's share of the inheritance. Caldwell later made a plea bargain and was released from jail in 1983, but five years later he committed suicide. Under the terms of Congdon's will, the mansion was turned over to the University of Minnesota in July 1977. Ever since, the ghosts of Elisabeth and her faithful night nurse Velma Pietila are said to walk the halls of Glensheen.

(Tours are available, but the management will not even admit to the murders, let alone the ghosts. Congdon Mansion, 3300 London Road, Duluth, MN 55802. For information, call 888-454-GLENN www.ci.duluth.mn. us/city/police/website/history/congdon) **72, 106**

GOODHUE

HOLY TRINITY CHURCH CEMETERY A ghost roamed this graveyard in the 1920s. First seen in 1922, the tall figure, shrouded in mist, followed people walking near the cemetery. The town marshal even set traps to capture the ghost, but he never succeeded.

(Goodhue is nine miles north of U.S. Highway 52 on Highway 58 in the southeast corner of Minnesota. The cemetery is a few blocks from the church. Holy Trinity Church, RR2 Box 90. Phone: 651-923-4472. Goodhue, MN 55027.) **176**

GRAND PORTAGE

WITCH TREE An ancient pine tree here has been considered to be possessed by spirits for over a hundred years. The twisted, knotted tree is considered sacred by the Chippewa Indians, who call it "Spirit Little Cedar." For generations, they have laid offerings of tobacco at the base of the tree.

(The tree is located in Cook County, at Hat Point on Lake Superior. Many local residents know of its exact location.) **75**

LAKEFIELD

LOON LAKE CEMETERY The ghosts of three alleged witches buried in this abandoned cemetery are said to roam the grounds. The most famous is Witch Mary Jane, whose head was cut off by the good citizens of Petersburg in October 1881. Of the sixty-seven original tombstones, only eighteen are still readable.

(The abandoned cemetery is south of Lakefield on Highway 86, between Sioux Valley and Petersburg. www. prairieghosts.com/loon.html) **75**

LAKE SHETEK

SLAUGHTER SLOUGH Strange dancing lights and invisible footsteps pushing down the grass are thought to be caused by the spirits of Indians massacred by white settlers here in the mid-1800s. The Indians were buried under an earthen mound in an area that is now farmland.

(The wetland covers four thousand acres in Murray County. For information, call the Minnesota Travel Line at 800-657-3700.) **75**

LAKE SUPERIOR

BANNOCKBURN Known as the "Flying Dutchman of the Lake Superior," the ghost ship *Bannockburn* is still sighted in the cold, drifting fog that covers this lake.

The freighter disappeared in November 1902, and no wreckage or other evidence of disaster has ever been found. In fact, the only evidence was to the contrary. Oddly, relatives of the twenty crew members lost with the ship received telegrams telling them not to worry, that the ship was safe despite rumors of its being lost. Today, captains on other ships on Lake Superior sometimes report the swift-moving, 245-foot-long *Bannockburn* steam past them and disappear from view in only two or three minutes.

(Lake Superior runs along the northeastern border of Minnesota. The ship often docked at Duluth.) **72**

LAMBERTON

SANBORN CORNERS GRAVEYARD The ghost of a twelve-year-old girl, accidentally buried alive in the graveyard here, roams the hillside at night. Her apparition has also been heard moaning or crying at the four-way stop at the bottom of the hill.

(Lamberton is at the junction of U.S. Highway 14 and County Road 5 in southwestern Minnesota. The graveyard is at the top of a hill near the intersection of U.S. Highways 14 and 71, a four-way stop known as Sanborn Corners.) **75**

LUVERNE

PALACE THEATER The ghost of Herman Jochims, who built this theater in 1915, has been seen by ushers and patrons. His apparition is most often encountered in the center balcony. But he is not alone. The ghost of his wife Maude is sometimes seen sitting at the pipe organ next to the stage.

(Luverne is in Rock County, on I-90 in the extreme southwest corner of Minnesota. The theater is on the corner of Main Street and Freeman Avenue, 104 E. Main St., Luverne, MN 56156. Phone: 507-283-8526. www.prairieghosts.com/palace.html) **75**

MANKATO

MANKATO STATE UNIVERSITY This coed university has spawned several ghosts. There is the ghost of a student locked in his room in Crawford Dorm, who rings a buzzer to get out, and the phantom of the main storeroom, who runs off with rolls of toilet paper. The Crawford-McElroy Complex is haunted by a 1960s ghost, who still likes to go on panty raids. No

pranksters have ever been caught faking the weird phenomena.

(Mankato is at the junction of U.S. Highways 14 and 169 in south-central Minnesota. Mankato State University, Makato, MN 56001. Phone: 507-389-2463. www.mankato.msus.edu) **75**

MINNEAPOLIS

CITY HALL The fifth floor of this Gothic municipal building is haunted by the presence of a man hanged in the Chapel Courtroom on that floor in March 1898. Though he pleaded "inherited insanity," twenty-five-year-old John Moshik was convicted of the murder of another man in a robbery that netted him fourteen dollars. As the noose was put around his head, Moshik directed the preparations for his execution, telling the guards to tighten the noose and bind his feet and legs more securely. It took only three minutes for him to die. He was the last man to be hanged in Minnesota. Today, his ghost is reported by custodians, lawyers, judges, and others who work on the fifth floor. The Chapel Courtroom soon gained a reputation for being jinxed and haunted, and it was "remodeled out of existence" in the 1950s. Ice-cold winds, odd movements, and lurking shadows still plague the fifth-floor corridors.

(City Hall covers the square block bounded by South 4th and 5th streets and South 3rd and 4th avenues in downtown Minneapolis. Moshik murdered John Lemke on the corner of Humboldt Ave. North and 47th St. Minneapolis City Hall, 350 South 5th St., Minneapolis, MN 55401. Phone: 612-673-3000. www.prairieghosts.com/guthrie.html) **72**

GUTHRIE THEATER This old opera house is haunted by the ghost of one of its former ushers. Richard Miller was an awkward English boy with few friends, when he worked here in the late 1960s. He attended the University of Minnesota, but never seemed to be accepted by the other students there. Just like in high school, he gained a reputation for being something of a nerd. The taunting and loneliness slowly took its toll. On Saturday, February 5, 1967, he strolled into a Sears store, purchased a surplus Mauser rifle and shells, and went back to his car in the parking lot. There, the eighteen-year-old boy put the gun to his head and pulled the trigger. His body was not discovered until the following Monday. He was still wearing his Guthrie Theater usher's uniform. Within weeks of his suicide, patrons in Row 18, part of the area assigned to Miller, began complaining of an usher constantly walking back and forth. They described Miller down to the large mole on his cheek. Since then, dozens of patrons, employees, ushers, actors, singers, and custodians at the theater have seen young Richard Miller walking slowly up and down the aisle in Row 18, in the catwalks, or in an exclusive section of seats called the Queen's Box. The ghost would follow witnesses with his eyes or head but never spoke or made a sound. An exorcism performed in 1994 supposedly placated his restless spirit, although an investigation in 1996 detected unexplainable electromagnetic phenomena in Row 18.

(Richard Miller attended Edina Morningside School in Minneapolis and lived in Territorial Hall at the university. His body was found in the parking lot of the Sears on Lake Street. He is buried at Fort Snelling National Cemetery. The theater is opposite the Sculpture Garden in the Loring Park area of southwest Minneapolis. Guthrie Theater, 725 Vineland Place, Minneapolis, MN 55403. Phone: 612-377-2224.) **49, 72, 80, 91**

MONTICELLO

OLD MEALEY PLACE This old farmhouse has long been considered haunted by a ghost nicknamed T. G. The initials stand for Tobias Gilmore Mealey, who built the house in 1855. Marion and Jeannette Sebey lived in the house in the 1940s and reported many strange phenomena, including lights going on and off by themselves, loud thumping sounds, and furniture that moved around in the upstairs bedroom. No one would live in the house for many years, but Bob and Marion Jameson figured they could put up with the ghost if they could get the hilltop house for a good price. They remodeled the house in 1965 and moved in. For the next ten years, they lived with loud footsteps in the middle of the night, knocking sounds on doors and windows, and a large bluish light that hovered near the front door. They avoided the upstairs bedroom at night; anyone who slept there was awakened by something tugging at the bedsheets, and the Jameson's two dogs refused even to enter the room.

(Monticello is a small town on the West Mississippi River, at the junction of I-94 and Highway 25. The white frame house, which is now a private residence, is up a dirt road off East Broadway in the town.) **176**

MOORHEAD

CONCORDIA COLLEGE The fifth floor of Hoyum, a girls' dormitory here, is haunted by an unidentified presence that calls out the girls' names while they are sleeping and appears standing at the bottom of their beds. The ghost is also blamed for a variety of mischievous deeds, including flooding the bathroom with hot water, messing up students' papers, and turning on radio and TV sets in empty rooms.

(Moorhead is on the North Dakota border, opposite Fargo on I-94. Concordia College, 901 South Eighth St. Moorhead, MN 56560. Phone: 218-299-4000. www.cord. edu) **75**

MOOREHEAD STATE UNIVERSITY During remodeling of Weld Hall in the 1970s, a construction worker fell off a ladder and broke his neck. He was alone in the building on a Friday, and his body was not discovered until the following Monday. Some time after the remodeling was completed, his ghost began to be seen in the building. The first sighting was by two night watchmen who were investigating strange noises coming from the auditorium. When they went in, they observed the white apparition of a man standing in the middle of the stage. As they approached him, the figure suddenly vanished from sight.

(Moorehead State University, 1104 7th Ave. South, Moorehead, MN 56560. 218-236-2011. www.moorhead. msus.edu) **72**

NEW LONDON

OLD DEPOT HOUSE A two-story house was once used as a train depot on the Burlington Northern route and is said to be haunted by the ghost of the agent who worked there. He died in the building around 1900. The friendly spirit of Eby Witzke has appeared only a few times in the last ninety years.

(New London is in Kandiyohi County is south central Minnesota, fifty-five miles southwest of St. Cloud on Highway 23. The house is a private residence in downtown New London.) **75**

NORTHFIELD

VANG LUTHERAN CHURCH Strange voices have been heard in this 170-year-old church. In the late 1930s

Members of a ghostly congregation haunt this 170-year-old church. See Vang Lutheran Church, Dennison, Minnesota (HEALTH TORSTVEIT)

a blurry apparition was seen crossing the church to the basement steps. No one has identified members of the ghostly congregation.

(Northfield is in southeastern Minnesota, thirty-five miles south of Minneapolis. Take County Road 9 from Dennison to Highway 56. Go south until you come to County Road 49. The church is two miles down the road. Phone: 507-789-5186.) **75**

ROSEAU

WINDEGO An ancient ghost has haunted this area for hundreds of years. The Chippewa and Mandan Indians called it the Windego. The appearance of the awesome apparition, fifteen feet tall with a shining star on its forehead, is a portent of death. The strange spirit terrorized this community from the late 1800s into the 1920s, and each appearance resulted in unexpected deaths.

(The town of Roseau is in extreme northern Minnesota at the junction of Highway 11 and Highway 89. The Windego has been reported throughout Roseau County. www.prairieghosts.com/wendigo.html) **176**

ST. CLOUD

ST. CLOUD STATE UNIVERSITY A ghostly woman in high heels haunts this coeducational teachers college. She is reported walking the corridors of Riverview Hall. Her phantom footsteps have been reported by students, custodians, and professors.

(St. Cloud is fifty miles northwest of Minneapolis, off I-94. St. Cloud State University, 720 4th Ave. South, St. Cloud, MN 56301. Phone: 320-255-0121. www.stcloud.msus.edu) **75**

A ghostly nun appears to troubled students who pass by the convent cemetery on the campus of the College of St. Benedict. See College of St. Benedict. St. Joseph, Minnesota. (HEATH TORSTVEIT)

ST. JOSEPH

COLLEGE OF ST. BENEDICT This school for women is haunted by a nun buried in the convent cemetery. She appears only to troubled students who pass by the cemetery. One of the dormitory rooms here was haunted for several years by the ghost of a sickly girl who died in the room. Disembodied sounds of crying and moaning forced administrators to seal off the room.

(St. Joseph is five miles northwest of St. Cloud. The school was established in 1912. College of St. Benedict, College Ave., St. Joseph, MN 56374. Phone: 320-363-5011. www.csbsju.edu) **75**

ST. PAUL

GRIGGS MANSION This twenty-four-room mansion, built by grocer Chauncey Griggs in 1883, is St. Paul's most haunted house. The ghostly apparition of a maid who hanged herself from the third-floor landing has been reported here since 1915. The ghost of a gardener, Charles Wade, returns to the library to consult books on gardening, and the shadowy presence of a teenage girl named Amy has been detected in the parlor. Another ghost, that of a thin man in a black suit, pops in and out of rooms during both daylight and nighttime hours. The house changes hands like a hot potato. The longest owner was the St. Paul Gallery and School of Art, which occupied the building from 1939 to 1964. Many students and teachers reported feeling the presence of spirits during that time. One student had a terrifying encounter with a ghastly, floating head in a small apartment at the rear of the house. In 1964, Griggs Mansion was purchased by Carl Weschke, founder of Llewellyn Publishing. He did extensive renovations, which seemed to increase the activity. Weschke, his maids and butler, and an investigative team from the *St. Paul Pioneer Press* all encountered ghostly manifestations in the house.

(The house is a private residence, at 476 Summit Ave., St. Paul, MN 55102. www.prairieghosts.com/ griggs.html) **101, 176**

MORIARITY HOUSE The ghost of a former owner haunted this house from 1965 to 1968. When Dick Gibbons and his wife Valjean moved into the two-story brick house, they expected to be able to enjoy a little peace and quiet. Within a few weeks, they realized they had an uninvited houseguest. A rocking chair in the library started moving by itself at regular intervals, their dog chased an invisible presence up the stairs, and objects disappeared. Neighbors confided that the house had been haunted since the death of the previous owner, Mrs. Moriarity.

(The house is now a private residence on Goodrich Ave., St. Paul, MN 55105.) **176**

WABASHA STREET CAVES St. Paul's limestone caves are haunted. The caves have been used since the 1840s for storing food, growing mushrooms, and mining silica. In 1933, the world's first underground nightclub, the Castle Royal, was opened inside one of the caves. The exquisite night spot featured a 1,600-square-foot dance floor and attracted a number of the country's most notorious gangsters. In 1934, witnesses saw three men gunned down in front of the fireplace in the Castle Royal, but by the time police arrived the bodies were gone and the blood cleaned up. The only evidence was bullet holes in the fireplace, which can be seen to this day. The ghosts of Castle Royal include those murdered hoodlums, as well as the apparition of a man in a panama hat and a ghostly couple, a man and a woman, who materialize around 3:00 A.M. in the barroom.

(St. Paul is east of Minneapolis on I-94. The entrance to the massive caves is located at 215 South Wabasha St. in downtown St. Paul. The barroom is in the central, finished cave. Phone: 612-224-1191 www. wabashastreetcaves.com) **53 (10/94)**

WINONA

ST. MARY'S UNIVERSITY The angry spirit of a Catholic priest is considered to be responsible for a number of deaths on this campus. On August 27, 1915, Father Laurence Michael Lesches sneaked up behind Bishop Patrick Heffron, who was kneeling before the altar in the chapel, and shot the bishop to death. Heffron had refused to give the fifty-five-year-old Lesches a parish of his own and accused him of being emotionally unstable. Father Lesches was committed to the State Hospital for the Dangerously Insane in St. Peter. On May 15, 1931, the charred remains of Father Edward Lynch, another enemy of Lesches, were found in his room at the college. The cause of his death was a mystery, and Father Lesches was still confined to the insane asylum, but many believe the deranged man was somehow responsible. Lesches died at the hospital in 1943. He was eighty-four years old and had spent twenty-nine years incarcerated. A new dormitory was named Heffron Hall in honor of Bishop Heffron, but it soon gained a reputation for being haunted by his murderer. The frightening ghost of Father Lesches was seen several times on the third floor of the building.

(Winona is on the Mississippi River in the southeastern corner of Minnesota, at the junction of Highways 43 and 54. Father Lesches is buried in St. Mary's Cemetery, 2.5 miles from the campus. St. Mary's University, 100 Terrace Hgts, Winona, MN 55987. Phone: 507-452-4430.) **101, 176**

WORTHINGTON

OLD BERNARDY HOUSE In the 1980s, this house was haunted by the ghost of a man who committed suicide in the attic. The house was owned by attorney Cy Bernardy, who lived there with his two college-age sons. He rented some of the rooms out to other college students. A strange presence was detected in the house, which seemed to follow people around, and loud banging sounds were heard in the attic. Then the wizened face of a man with green eyes and white hair appeared to students staying in the rooms. Soon afterward, an old diary was found under a windowsill. It apparently belonged to the man who committed suicide. Out of respect, his private thoughts were never revealed, which seemed to placate his restless spirit.

(Worthington is in Nobles County in the extreme southwest corner of Minnesota, at I-90 and U.S. Highway 59. The three-story house is now a private residence on Warren St., Worthington, MN 56187.) **75**

MISSISSIPPI

BEAUREGARD

FLAG STOP For many years along the Illinois Central railroad tracks here, a phantom man tried to stop trains by swinging a spectral light back and forth. The first encounter was in 1926, when a train heading for McComb was flagged down by a man with a lantern. When the engineer and brakeman searched the area for the flagman, no one could be found. Before long, dozens of trains were being halted by the ethereal flagman and railroad authorities initiated an investigation. They discovered that a local haunted house existed on the spot where the trains were being halted. The dilapidated old house belonged to a Dr. Rowan, who died in 1912. Dr. Rowan was in his seventies when he was run down by a train on the tracks behind his house. The engineer reported that the confused doctor had turned around and yelled "Stop!" But there was nothing the engineer could do. The area came to be known as Flag Stop by trainmen, and the sightings continued for many more years.

(Beauregard is forty miles south of Jackson on U.S. Highway 51. It is two miles north of the Wesson exit on I-55. Dr. Rowan's house, which was torn down in the 1940s, was on the south edge of town.) **227**

COLUMBUS

ERROLTON Miss Nellie Weaver, the daughter of the man who built this house in 1848, returned from the grave to put her mark on it. After she was married in 1878, she used her diamond ring to inscribe her name on a parlor window. Nellie said that she loved the house so much that she never wanted to be forgotten by it. She lived in the house until she was eighty, when she died from burns suffered when her dress caught fire from sparks from a fireplace in the rear parlor. The house fell into disrepair but was renovated in the 1950s. Unfortunately, workmen smashed the window that Nellie had inscribed. Several years later, the new owner, Mrs. Erroldine Hay Bateman, was astonished when she lifted the parlor shades and found N-E-L-L-I-E etched into the window pane. The ghost of Nellie had returned to inscribe her name exactly as it had appeared so many years before.

(Columbus is in east central Mississippi, at the junction of U.S. Highways 45 and 82. Errolton Mansion is a private residence just north of Columbus.) **101, 175, 227**

TEMPLE HEIGHTS This antebellum mansion is haunted by a ghost called Miss Elizabeth. She is Elizabeth Kennebrew, one of the daughters of Methodist minister J.H. Kennebrew, who bought the house in 1887. Elizabeth never married and lived in the house until she died. She became somewhat eccentric and was known to use Mercurochrome for lipstick and rouge, with chalk dust for facial powder. Her white apparition is seen outside an upstairs guest room and on the stairway to the fourth floor. In July 1991, during an open house for tourists, Miss Elizabeth was observed standing in the middle of the master bedroom. The house was built in 1837 by General Richard Brownrigg.

(Temple Heights Mansion is a private residence in Columbus. The house is open during the regular Pilgrimage Tours. For information, call the Columbus Chamber of Commerce at 614-221-2747.) **93**

WAVERLY Built in 1852, this magnificent mansion was abandoned from 1913 to 1962, and there are many stories about it being haunted. The ghost of Major John Pytchlyn rides his phantom horse near the estate. Pytchlyn, who died in 1835, was raised by Indians and loved to ride bareback on the nearby prairies. Further, the mirrors inside the house sometimes contain the image of Colonel George Hampton, who built Waverly. Dozens of other ghosts were seen in the unoccupied house, but the most pathetic ghost was not seen until someone moved into the old mansion. Robert and Donna Snow started seeing the ghost of a little lost girl in 1964. The indentation of the child's body was sometimes found on a freshly made bed in the upstairs bedroom, and her voice could be heard whimpering "Mama, Mama!"

(Waverly is a private residence on Mullen's Bluff on the Tombigee River between West Point and Columbus, about six miles south of Columbus.) **93, 227**

DURANT

CASTILIAN SPRINGS The ghost of a tall Confederate general materialized here on several occasions. The apparition was first reported in 1961 by a YMCA camp director. The ghost appeared in his second-floor bedroom apartment, between the recreation room and the dining room. Many other independent sightings occurred on the second floor in the next decade. The building had been used as a Confederate hospital during the Civil War, and at least forty-three bodies are buried along a dirt road about a mile from the building.

(Durant is thirty-five miles south of Winona on U.S. Highway 51 in central Mississippi. Castilian Springs used to be a YMCA summer camp. It is three miles west of Durant.) **227**

ELLISVILLE

OLD DEASON HOME Newt Knight was a Confederate deserter who led a band of 125 rebels in the Piney Woods area. As Knight's reputation grew, the Confederate Army dispatched Captain Amos McLemore to capture him. In 1862, McLemore and two other officers took up residence in the Amos Deason home in Ellisville and made it their center of operations. In September, Newt Knight sneaked into the Deason home, entered the parlor, and shot McLemore several times. The officer bled to death in a few seconds, and his bloodstains sank deep into the wood flooring. When Knight died, his guilt-ridden spirit returned to haunt this house. Later owners of the Deason house say the parlor door sometimes bursts open, but there is nobody there. They think it is Newt Knight, returning to the parlor where he committed the dastardly deed.

(Ellisville is in Jones County, seven miles southwest of Laurel off I-59. The Amos Deason home is a private residence in Jones County on the southern outskirts of Ellisville. www.prairieghosts.com/deason.html) **93, 227**

GAUTIER

TWELVE OAKS It took a hurricane to shake the ghosts loose in this house. At least four different apparitions started appearing after Hurricane Elma struck the area in 1966. The ghosts include a man seen climbing the steps; an elderly woman with curly white hair, who sits by the den window; a little girl with long blond hair; and a teenage girl, who haunts the bedrooms. The great house was built in 1869 by Henry Gautier.

(Gautier is on the Gulf of Mexico, between Biloxi and Pascgoula on U.S. Highway 90. Twelve Oaks is a private residence in town.) **93**

HATTIESBURG

HOWELL RESIDENCE When the Howell family built their ranch-style home in 1977, they were not expecting a ghost to move into their attic. The sounds of some invisible presence living in the attic became routine. Sometimes, late at night, the uninvited houseguest would come downstairs and rummage through the house. Once, their son Scott heard an invisible person come down from the attic, go outside, and start a lawn tractor. The driverless tractor smashed into the side of the Howell's Cadillac. Unfortunately the insurance company refused to pay for any damage caused by a ghost. The Howells believe their unseen visitor is Harry Blosser, an Air Force pilot who died when his B-58 jet crashed on the property in October 1959. They think his lonely spirit wandered the woods until they built their house. Then he moved in with them.

(Hattiesburg is in southeastern Mississippi at the junction of I-59 and U.S. Highway 49. The house is a private residence in the Lake Serene section of Hattiesburg.) **93**

HOLLY SPRINGS

FEATHERSTON PLACE Three ghosts haunt this quaint old house, built in 1834. The apparition of a beautiful young lady is sometimes seen in the secondfloor hallway, and the heavy footsteps of a man can be heard going halfway up the staircase and then stopping. But the most frequently sighted visitor is the elderly spirit of Mrs. McEwen, who lived with the original owners of the house, Mr. and Mrs. Winfield Scott Featherston. Mrs. McEwen's ghost is easily identified by a large white-on-black cameo she wears.

(Holly Springs is in the northwest corner of Mississippi, forty-five mile southeast of Memphis on U.S. Highway 78. Featherston Place is a private residence in Holly Springs.) **227**

JACKSON

COLSTON COMMERCIAL PHOTOGRAPHY STUDIO The many unusual phenomena reported in this two-story brick building are thought to date back to several violent deaths that occurred here. In the 1920s it served as a railroad worker's hotel. Late one night, the owner was shot in the head while sleeping in his room on the ground floor. In the 1930s, a jealous husband literally kicked a worker to death in his room. In the 1940s, the premises were used for prostitution and gambling, and several unsolved murders took place. In the 1950s, a man was killed during a shoot-out in the upstairs corridor. Unidentified skeletons are still turning up on the traumatized property.

(Jackson is in central Mississippi at the junction of I-55 and I-20. Steve Colston Commercial Photography, 1032 Spengler St., Jackson, MS 39202. Phone: 601-355-1364.) **93**

MADISON

ANNANDALE A hunchbacked servant at this family mansion vowed never to desert her beloved residence, even after she died. When the structure later caught fire, her ghost appeared at a window and refused to leave. The ghost of Annie Devlin haunted the mansion for many years after she died. She appeared to strangers coming to the door, walked the halls, and haunted her former room. People who slept in that room were awakened in the middle of the night by an unseen hand pulling the covers off the bed. When the great house caught fire twenty years after she died, firefighters and a custodian saw her at a second-floor window, peering out at the strangers in the yard, still wearing her favorite three-cornered shawl.

(Madison is off U.S. Highway 51, fifteen miles north of Jackson. The Annandale ruins are behind the Chapel of the Cross in Madison County.) **93, 223**

EPISCOPAL CHAPEL OF THE CROSS The cemetery of this picturesque brick church is where the ghost of Helen Johnstone visits the grave of her fiancé Henry Vick. The chapel was part of the Johnstone family's large estate and was to be the site of Helen's marriage. In May 1859, the month before she was to be married, her young man was killed in a pistol duel in New Orleans. The grieving bride went to his grave every day. Even after she was buried in another cemetery in 1916, her mournful form was seen sitting on an iron bench alongside Vick's grave here.

(Episcopal Chapel of the Cross, 674 Mannsdale Rd., Madison, MS 39110. Phone: 601-856-2593.) **223**

MERIDIAN

GRAND OPERA HOUSE A ghostly presence, dubbed The Lady, can sometimes be heard singing on the stage here. The theater opened in 1890, and the ghost could be Sarah Bernhardt, Norma Shearer, Helen Hayes, or any of a number of other illustrious female performers who appeared at Meridian's Grand Opera House.

(Meridian is in Lauderdale County, at the junction of I-20 and I-59. The theater building is downtown at 2206 Fifth St., Meridian, MS 39301. Phone: 601-693-5239.) **93**

MERREHOPE MANSION People walking by this mansion report seeing the apparition of a woman looking out an upstairs window. She is Eugenia Gary, daughter of John Gary, who bought the house in 1868. Although she never lived here while alive, Eugenia has taken up residence in the restored mansion. She is seen in the center hall and near the windows on the first and second floors. She usually wears a green plaid hoopskirt with a solid green blouse. She shares the house with another ghost, a former schoolteacher who haunts his room on the second floor. In the 1940s, the depressed man set up a line of whiskey bottles on the fireplace mantel and started shooting them. When the last bottle was smashed, he put the gun to his head and pulled the trigger.

(The house is owned by the Merrehope Restorations Foundation, Meridian, MS 39301.) **93**

NATCHEZ

DEVIL'S PUNCH BOWL A sinister presence here is mysteriously linked with the Mississippi River. Devil's Punch Bowl is a giant depression in the bluffs overlooking the river, a geological abnormality for which there is no scientific explanation. Considerable treasure hunting has taken place at the center of the basin, where pirate and outlaw gold is reputedly buried. At one time it was the hideout of the treacherous John Murrell gang. See Natchez-Under-the-Hill, below; Farmington, Tennessee; and Surgoinsville, Tennessee.

(Natchez is in the southwest corner of Mississippi, at the junction of U.S. Highways 61 and 84/98. The Devil's Punch Bowl is the larger of two gigantic sinks in the cliffs above Natchez, about one mile north of the city. Information on sites around Natchez is available from the Natchez Convention and Visitor's Bureau, 640 S. Canal St., Natchez, MS 39120. Phone: 601-446-6345.) **15**

DUNLEITH The ghost of a young woman who lost her heart to a visiting Frenchman stills plays her harp in his loving memory. The man was part of the delegation of Prince Louis Philippe, who visited Natchez in the early 1800s. The woman, Miss Percy, fell in love with the man and accompanied him back to France. Before long he grew tired of her, and Miss Percy returned to Natchez to live out her years in solitude. It is said she died of a broken heart and that her forlorn harp music can still be heard at Dunleith.

(Natchez can be reached from the east or west directions by Highway 84, and from the north or south directions by Highway 61. Dunleith is a two-story mansion with seven Doric columns on each side that is now a B&B. Dunleith, 84 Homochitto St., Natchez, MS 39120. Phone: 601-446-8500. www.natchez-dunleith.com) **227**

GLENBURNIE This old plantation manor house serves as the Natchez mayor's residence. The nearby woods are haunted by the ghost of Jennie Merrill, whose barefoot figure, clad in a blue cotton dress, is seen running through the trees or standing alone on the paths. Her solitary figure waits, moaning and wailing hysterically. It is believed she was shot and killed by her neighbor, Dick Dana (see Glenwood, below).

(Glenburnie is just outside Natchez. Information on plantations in the area is available from the Natchez Convention and Visitor's Bureau, 311 Liberty Rd., Natchez, MS 39120. Phone: 601-446-6345.) **5**

GLENWOOD The ruins of this old plantation harbor the ghost of a murderer. He is Dick Dana, who sits at a piano playing thunderous music, trying to drown out the cries of the woman he murdered. Jennie Merrill (see Glenburnie, above) and Dick Dana used to be neighbors, living in huge plantations just across the road from one another. But when Jennie tried to buy Dana's property out from under him, he shot her to death as she strolled in the woods between their houses. He was arrested for the deed, but a lack of evidence forced authorities to drop the case. Dick Dana's mind rapidly deteriorated, and along with it his beloved plantation. In the early 1900s, tourists paid him fifty cents apiece to tour the once proud estate, which became strewn with garbage and overrun by farm animals. It came to be known as Goat Castle.

(The ruins are located across the road from the old Glenburnie plantation near Natchez.) **5**

KING'S TAVERN Hundreds of employees and guests have encountered the presence of a ghost named Madeline here. The wooden building was constructed in the 1760s and became a tavern in 1789, when Richard King purchased the property. Madeline was his young mistress and serving girl. Her mischievous ghost intends that people never forget her. In the 1930s, three mummified skeletons were dug up in the cellar of the tavern. Two were men, and the third was a sixteen-year-old girl, thought to be Madeline. A jeweled dagger was found next to her body.

(The restaurant is in lower Natchez at 619 Jefferson St. Phone: 601-446-8845. www.prairieghosts.com/natchez.html) **93**

LINDEN This great house has been in the Conner family since 1790, and family ghosts haunt it. The sounds of a horse-drawn buggy pulling into the front driveway and the tapping of an invisible cane in the west gallery are heard to this day. The ghost of a man in a top hat has appeared in the children's bedroom many times, and the apparition of a woman has been reported on the roof of the east wing. She leaps off the edge, but disappears before hitting the ground.

(The mansion is a private residence at Linden Place, Natchez, MS 39120. 601-445-5472. www.natchezms. com/linden) **93**

LONGWOOD Dr. Haller Nutt and his wife Julia haunt their unfinished mansion. Construction was nearly complete when the Civil War broke out, forcing the Nutts to live in the basement of their magnificent house. Dr. Nutt died in 1864, and the interior of the great house was never finished. Locals dubbed the thirty-two-room, octagonal mansion "Nutt's Folly," although today it is a popular Natchez attraction and a national historic landmark. The Nutts relish the new attention lavished on their former home and have been known to appear to tour guides. Mrs. Nutt is seen on the staircase, while Dr. Nutt prefers the garden area. One groundskeeper quit recently after seeing the good doctor standing under a tree.

(The mansion is now a museum, just outside the city. Longwood Museum, 140 Lower Woodville Rd., Natchez, MS 39120. Phone: 601-442-5193.) **93, 101**

MAGNOLIA HALL The ghost of Thomas Henderson, who built this magnificent town house in 1858, haunts his downstairs bedroom. He spent his last days there, debilitated by a stroke. The imprint of his head appears on a pillow, and his hooded apparition has been spotted on the stairway.

(Magnolia Hall, now owned by the Natchez Garden Club, is at 215 South Pearl St., Natchez, MS 39120. Phone: 601-442-6672. www.natchezms.com/magnolia) **14, 93, 101**

MONMOUTH PLANTATION After restoration of this old manor house was begun in 1977, construction workers, housekeepers, and visitors sensed a ghostly presence. Heavy, invisible footsteps traipsed through the building at all hours of the day. Once, the alarm system went off for no reason, and responding policemen also reported hearing the mysterious footsteps. Most believe the ghost is General John Anthony Quitman, a previous owner who died in the house of a lingering and undiagnosed two-year illness. Now his former home is a twenty-five-room inn.

(Monmouth Plantation Inn, 36 Millrose Ave., at the J. A. Quitman Parkway, Natchez, MS 39120. Phone: 601-442-5852. For reservations, call 800-828-4531. www.monmouthplantation.com) **73**

NATCHEZ TRACE The Natchez Trace is a mysterious barren pathway that runs diagonally across much of the mideastern United States. A National Park Service signpost south of Tupelo proclaims: "Witches Dance—The old folks say the witches once gathered here to dance, and that wherever their feet touched the ground, the grass withered and died, never to grow again." Chickasaw and Choctaw legends going back nearly a thousand years warned young Indians not to set foot on the paths. More recent legends tell of a witch along the trace who ground up the skull of one of the notorious outlaws, the Harpe Brothers, and made a potion out of it. Another outlaw, Joseph Thompson Hare, told of seeing strange things along the trace, including a phantom white horse, before he was hanged in 1818. It has been estimated that Hare was responsible for murdering over a hundred people along the Trace. See Natchez-Under-the-Hill, below.

(The Trace runs from Natchez up through the northeast corner of Mississippi, on through Nashville, Tennessee, and into Pennsylvania. A plaque describing the Trace has been erected in Bluff Park, off Broadway Boulevard, in Natchez. Take Highway 61 north out of Natchez for thirteen miles to the Natchez Trace Parkway, which follows the original Trace and has numerous exhibits telling its history. For information, contact the Superintendent, National Park Service, 2680 Natchez Trace Parkway, Tupelo, MS 38804. Phone: 662-680-4025. www.nps.gov/natr) **15, 48, 72, 227**

NATCHEZ-UNDER-THE-HILL This old riverbank area is home to a shocking number of ghosts from the eighteenth and nineteenth centuries. One is the apparition of a man in a military uniform seen on the bluffs near here. He is thought to be an American spy who imparted secrets to the Spaniards when they ruled the territory. The ghosts of groups of Spanish soldiers are seen in the same area. After the Americans took over the territory, it became known as the Devil's Backbone, home to many outlaws who attacked travelers on the Natchez Trace. Joseph Thompson Hare (see Natchez Trace, above) was one of the area's most active bandits and robbed settlers, traders, and merchants of tens of thousands of dollars. The outlaw, who kept a careful journal of his experiences, once had a vision of a beautiful white horse that he felt was sent by God to make him repent his ways. However, Hare did not heed the vision and ended up on the gallows years later. Hare's own laughing ghost is most often encountered around Halloween, along with the apparition of his unfaithful mistress, whom he buried alive wearing the jewels he had given her. The woman's ghost offers gold to anyone who will save her from the clutches of Hare's gang.

Another outlaw reportedly haunting Natchez-Under-the-Hill is John Murrel (see Devil's Punch Bowl, above; and Farmington, Tennessee). His crime was stealing and reselling slaves. Sometimes he would sell the same slave many times, until the black man was recognized. Then Murrel would mercilessly kill him. In 1835, rumors spread that Murrel was planning a slave rebellion in New Orleans, which would eventually encompass the whole state. The ensuing panic resulted in the lynching of scores of suspected conspirators. The other ghosts of Natchez-Under-the-Hill are three men whose heads were cut off and displayed along the Trace as a deterrent to other criminals. Outlaw Samuel Mason was known as the Wolfman, because of a front tooth that grew horizontally and stuck out from under his lips. His head was hacked off by two fellow outlaws, who claimed a reward with the head as evidence. Micajar and Wiley Harpe were ruthless criminals who turned to crime after losing all their money in a horse race. Known as Big Harpe and Little Harpe, they were remorseless butchers, and their innocent victims often included women and children. Big Harpe once admitted to smashing a newborn baby against the wall of a cave, where one of his female companions had gone into labor. Years later, as he lay paralyzed from bullet lodged in his spine, Big Harpe told a man who had already started to saw off his head to "Cut on and be damned." But it is really the ruthless outlaws of Natchez-Under-the-Hill who are damned—damned for all eternity to wander these streets.

(Natchez-Under-the-Hill is a section of the city below the bluffs, near the river. It is bounded by Ferry, Silver, and Water streets.) **15**

POST HOUSE RESTAURANT This large house, built in 1789, is haunted by the presence of a former owner. Today, the building houses a popular restaurant. Manager Cathy Hibbs says employees and guests alike sense the unseen presence, which seems to watch over the place.

(The restaurant is in central Natchez. Post House Restaurant, Natchez, MS 39120.) **72, 101**

SPRINGFIELD Sounds of eighteenth-century music drift from the second-floor west here, and a great crashing noise shakes the house on a Sunday once a year. The second-floor west used to be a ballroom, but no one knows what causes the great crash. The house was built in 1790 by Thomas Marston Green. Andrew Jackson married Rachel Robards in the parlor in the spring of 1791. The event caused a great scandal, because the impulsive Rachel was not yet divorced from her previous husband. The house was abandoned for many years but was restored in the late 1970s by the La Salle family.

(Springfield is a private residence in rural Jefferson County, not far from Natchez.) **93**

STANTON HALL Frederick Stanton died on January 4, 1859, only a few months after moving into his splendid new home. His apparition has been seen in the garden, on the staircase, and in the hallways.

(Stanton Hall is a national historic landmark in Natchez. It is now the headquarters of the Pilgrimage Garden Club at 401 High St. Phone: 601-442-6282.) **93**

OXFORD

ROWAN OAK Author William Faulkner sought refuge within these walls in 1930, but he found his peace disturbed by the ghost of a young woman. The house was built in 1844 by Colonel Robert Sheegog. Faulkner told friends that Sheegog's daughter Judith died trying to elope with a Yankee soldier. As she climbed out her window onto a rope ladder, she lost her balance and fell to her death on the brick sidewalk below. But Sheegog never had a daughter named Judith. Faulkner made up the story to explain the strange footsteps, the sounds of objects crashing to the floor, and ghostly piano music in the parlor. Those phenomena still go on in the old house, and to date no one has found a better explanation.

(The town of Oxford is in Lafayette County in northern Mississippi, at the junction of Highway 6 and Highway 7. The house is a historical landmark on Old Taylor Rd. Phone: 662-234-3284.) **93**

Charles Hickson points out where he was taken aboard a UFO in 1973. See Alien Abduction, Pascagoula, Mississippi. (IUFOR)

PASCAGOULA

ALIEN ABDUCTION On October 11, 1973, two men fishing from a wooden pier on the Pascagoula River saw a blue light land in the open field behind them. Three five-foot-tall creatures with pincer claws and gray, wrinkled skin emerged and abducted both of them. Calvin Parker fainted immediately, but Charles Hickson watched as the figures floated them into the craft. There, the two humans were examined in minute detail by an eyelike mechanical appendage. They were then returned to the river bank and eventually reported their abduction to the local sheriff. The time was one of intense UFO activity throughout the south, and several witnesses reported seeing similar creatures. An extensive police investigation, which included lie detector tests, could find no evidence of a hoax. Parker suffered a nervous breakdown. Hickson, his wife, and their five children underwent much ridicule, and he had to quit his job at the Walker Shipyard. In 1987, the men were offered a huge sum of money to make a movie of their experience, but they turned it down. Both have undergone profound personality changes but refuse to submit to hypnotic regression and relive the experience. The day before the incident, police investigated reports of an oval object hovering over Avery Estates, about sixty miles away. A week later, a man driving on the interstate fifteen miles east of Pascagoula told police he was also abducted by a UFO. See Mobile, Alabama.

(Pascagoula is twenty-five miles east of Biloxi on U.S. Highway 90. Take the Highway 63 exit south off of I-10.

The two men were fishing off the wooden pier at the Schaupeter Shipyard. Avery Estates is sixty miles north of Pascagoula.) **55, 72, 139, 150**

SINGING RIVER The section of the Pascagoula River that passes near Pascagoula is known as the Singing River because of a mysterious buzzing sound emanating from its depths. It is said that the melodious siren call of an ancient water goddess issues from deep in the river and is joined by the low, humming sound of hundreds of other voices. The phenomenon has been witnessed by hundreds of people and is most pronounced during August, September, and October. Biloxi is the name of an Indian tribe that lived here for hundreds of years. They worshipped a mermaid deity and built a temple for their ceremonies. In 1569, Catholic missionaries forced the Indians to destroy the temple and recant their pagan beliefs. According to legend, the mermaid goddess rose from the river and called her people to join her rather than accept Christian doctrines. In a single day, every man, woman, and child in the tribe stepped into the river and drowned. Archeological evidence confirms the mass extinction, although most scholars believe it was at the hands of an enemy tribe. That does not explain the sighting by a scuba diver swimming in the waters off Pascagoula in 1988. He swears he encountered a creature half-fish, half-woman, with flowing hair and unmistakable human breasts.

(The Pascagoula River empties into the gulf between New Orleans and Biloxi. The Singing-River section is located at a bend in the river as it passes through Pascagoula.) **55, 57, 172, 196**

PASS CHRISTIAN

HAWES RUINS A phantom rowboat with four ghostly figures at the oars and the slender wraith of a woman playing a harp has been spotted just off the coast here. Sometimes, the sound of mysterious harp music mixes with the sea breeze. Some insist the place is cursed, which is why no resort or restaurant ever survives in the area. But in the 1850s, a mansion stood near the shoreline. It was built by Captain Hawes, a rich old seaman, after his ship caught fire in the gulf waters off Pass Christian. The captain and his first mate were suspected of setting fire to the ship deliberately, so they could abscond with a horde of gold brought on board by a couple from Uruguay. Julia Vinesto and her rich husband were heading for a new life in New Orleans. Julia, a beautiful, cultured woman, loved to play the harp and held daily concerts on the ship. In fact, she was playing on the deck of the ship as it burned and sank. Only the captain and four crewmen survived, but the Lady with the Harp haunted him and this ragged coastline for many years. Occasionally, the glow of a burning ship can be seen off the coast here, accompanied by the faint sound of harp music.

(Pass Christian is seven miles west of Gulfport on U.S. Highway 90. The Hawes Ruins were located on Pitcher's Point, a pitcher-shaped outcropping of coastline between the cities of Pass Christian and Long Beach.) **5, 223**

PINCKNEYVILLE

COLD SPRING PLANTATION The wine cellar of this elegant 1790s mansion is haunted by the ghost of its builder, Dr. John Carmichael. The doctor was a wine connoisseur and had assembled an enviable collection of fine vintages in his wine cellar. He left instructions that when he died his coffin was to be taken to the cellar, where the funeral guests would drink from a large keg of wine until it was fully consumed. Then, he would be buried on the property. His instructions were obeyed to the letter. Today, in the late afternoon, his presence is detected in the cellar, rocking softly in his old rocking chair, sipping on a glass of fine wine.

(The town of Pinckneyville is in the extreme southwestern corner of Mississippi, on Highway 24 on the Louisiana border. The mansion is northeast of Pinckneyville. The iron fencing and Masonic emblem over the back door were installed by Dr. Carmichael to protect the premises from "all manner of threats." The body of Dr. Carmichael was later exhumed from Cold Spring and buried in Woodville. www.prairieghosts.com/coldspring.html) **227**

PONTOTOC

LOCHINVAR The ghost of a beloved black man called Uncle Ed carries on his faithful watch over this old plantation. The estate was built in the late 1830s by Robert Gordon for his wife Mary and only child, James. When James Gordon rode off to war, he asked Uncle Ed to watch over the plantation. Every day, the old man made his rounds, and late at night, if he heard something sus-

picious, he jumped out of bed to investigate. The light from his oil lamp is still seen on the property at night.

(Pontotoc is twenty miles west of Tupelo on Highway 6. Lochinvar is a private residence north of the town of Pontotoc. The white wooden mansion has four massive Doric columns in front with a large second-floor balcony. www.prairieghosts.com/lochinvar.html) **227**

POPE

OLD MATHIS PLANTATION A monstrous black cat brought the downfall of this once proud plantation. George Mathis had a mean streak in him and treated everyone who lived with him like dirt. But one old Louisiana black man named Bo-Man got even. After Mathis kicked Bo-Man and his family off his land, the former slave put a spell on the plantation. He made a "conjure ball," a likeness of George with a tight string around its neck, and sent a black cat to haunt the man. George choked to death one night, and at his funeral a huge black cat kept circling his coffin. The mourners said the cat disappeared into thin air when they tried to swipe at it with a broom. Sid Mathis, George's son, took over running the plantation. Before long, he started hearing strange voices and was harassed by a sassy black cat. He turned the place over to a cousin, Ben Hentz, who was driven off the property by persistent scratching sounds. Many times, the thundering sound of dozens of rolling barrels woke everyone in the house, but no barrels or other cause for the dreadful noise were found. Anyone who stayed at the Old Mathis Plantation moved away. Before long it was overgrown with weeds. All that exists today is a few dilapidated wood walls and a tall brick chimney—and a big black phantom cat roaming the grounds.

(Pope is in northwestern Mississippi, seven miles south of Batesville on U.S. Highway 51. The site of the old plantation is in Panola County, south of Pope.) **227**

TUPELO

MALCO CINEMA 10 THEATER A strange presence that laughs, mumbles, coughs, and makes weird noises chases employees of this modern movie theater. Most of the activity occurs in the first two auditoriums, built in the 1960s. Witnesses say the unidentified ghost haunts the projection booths and third-row seats, and the stage area in the theaters.

(Tupelo is in northeastern Mississippi, at the junction of U.S. Highways 45 and 78. The movie house is on Cliff Gookin Boulevard, Tupelo, MS 38802. Phone: 662-842-3684.) **134**

VICKSBURG

ANCHUCA This stately mansion was built in 1837 by Richard Archer. He was an eccentric and stubborn man, who kept a stern eye on his five daughters. One daughter resembled her father so much that they called her "Archie." When she fell in love with the son of a plantation overseer who worked for him, Mr. Archer forbade the marriage and sent the boy away. His enraged daughter barely talked to him afterward and started taking all her meals in the parlor, where she ate from the fireplace mantel, standing up. The ghost of the headstrong girl is still seen there. The haunting started in 1966, when the Jack Lavender family moved into the house. Mr. and Mrs. Lavender, their daughter Mel, and their butler have seen the ghost of a young woman dressed in a long brown dress, standing close to the fireplace.

(Vicksburg is on the Louisiana border, west of Jackson I-20. Anchuca originally stood near Port Gibson in Claiborne County but the great house was moved to Vicksburg several years after Richard Archer died in 1867. Now the mansion is located at 1010 First East St., Vicksburg, MS 39180. Phone: 601-661-0111.) **227**

CEDAR GROVE A whole family of ghosts haunts this 1840s mansion. The ghost of John Klein smokes his favorite meerschaum pipe in the parlor, and his wife Elizabeth walks down the front stairs. The sounds of their ten children fill the halls. Their sixteen-year-old son died from an accidental gunshot wound on the back stairs. Two infants died in the nursery, and an older child passed away in an upstairs bedroom. A later resident, a young woman, shot herself in the ballroom.

(The inn is located on a bluff overlooking the Mississippi River at 2200 Oak St., Vicksburg, MS 39180. Phone: 601-636-1000. www.cedargroveinn.com) **93**

JUDGE LAKE HOME Judge William Lake was killed in a duel with a political adversary in October 1861. The duel took place at De Soto Point, and the judge died without letting his gentle wife know about the duel. After her husband's death, Mrs. Lake sought solace in her beautiful garden, where she spent all of her time. Her ghost lingers there to this day.

(Desoto Point is across the river in Louisiana. The single-story house has six short Doric columns on the front porch. It is located on the corner of Main and Adams streets, Vicksburg, MS 39180.) **227**

MCRAVEN HOUSE This house was headquarters for the Union occupation of Vicksburg, after the Battle of Vicksburg in July 1863. Colonel Wilson, in command of the Union soldiers, and Captain McPherson, a former resident of the city, were quartered here. McPherson served as a liaison between the occupying troops and townspeople. One night he failed to return from his rounds and was declared missing. Then, his mutilated apparition, dripping with water, appeared before Colonel Wilson and told his commander that he was murdered by Confederate sympathizers and thrown into the river. McPherson's bloodied phantom has appeared to several other occupants of the house since the Civil War. He is not the only ghost seen here. The specter of a woman with long brown hair and a plain dress appeared to very reputable witnesses in the middle bedroom, and the ghosts of Civil War soldiers have been reported in the gallery. The building was exorcised by an Episcopal priest in 1991, but the uninvited houseguests keep returning.

(The Vicksburg National Military Park is on U.S. Route 61 at Vicksburg. McRaven House is at 1445 Harrison St., Vicksburg, MS 39180. Phone: 601-636-1663.) **163**

VIDALIA

OLD VIDALIA JAIL The ghost of a woman dressed in a red gown with a flaring bustle is seen in a particular jail cell here when it is otherwise unoccupied. She is thought to be the ghost of Rose Mataz, an immoral and flamboyant young woman known as the Hungarian Razzmatazz. She spent time in the jail in 1879 for attempted robbery. Some say the devil sentenced her to eternity in her old jail cell; others say she is just seeking a little peace and quiet. Jailers and visitors have reported her apparition standing in a corner of the cell, defiantly humming a tune and cleaning her long fingernails.

(Vidalia is off U.S. Highway 49 in the southernmost heel of Mississippi. The old jail is next to the courthouse in central Vidalia.) **158**

MISSOURI

BRANSON

INSPIRATION POINT This mountain overlook, used as a Confederate lookout post during the Civil War, is haunted by the ghost of a Confederate soldier. The apparition was first seen in 1964, during an outdoor play about the Baldknobbers, a group of pro-Union vigilantes. The ghostly figure seemed to be fleeing the actors in one of the scenes. Ever since, whenever the nighttime pageant is repeated, the phantom rider reappears.

(Branson is south of Springfield in southwest Missouri. Take U.S. Highway 65 south to U.S. Highway 160 east. The site is the highest point on the road following the mountain ridge just west of Branson. The Shepherd of the Hills theme park is located at Inspiration Point.) **231**

BRIDGETON

PAYNE-GENTRY HOUSE So far, twenty-three different spirits have been encountered in this old mansion, which would make it one of the most haunted houses in America. The ghosts have been tallied by the Ghost Research Society.

(Bridgeton is a northwestern suburb of St. Louis off I-270. Payne-Gentry House, 4211 Fee Road, Bridgeton, MO 63044. Phone: 314-739-5599.) **101**

COLUMBIA

ROCK BRIDGE STATE PARK Visitors to Devil's Icebox Cave in this park report strange feelings of uneasiness, and some have encountered evil-looking apparitions that glow in the darkness. Several people have died from accidents in the cave.

(Rock Bridge Memorial State Park is located seven miles south of Columbia at 5901 South Columbia, MO 65203. Highway 163. Phone: 573-449-7402. www. mostateparks.com/rockbridge.htm) **72**

STEPHENS COLLEGE The ghost of Sarah June Wheeler returns to Senior Hall on this campus. Sarah was a student at the old Baptist Female College and was living in Senior Hall when she found an escaped rebel prisoner, Isaac Johnson, hiding in her closet. For weeks, she fed and nursed the injured man—and eventually fell in love with him. However, someone at the school turned him in to authorities. Three days later he was killed by a firing squad in front of Senior Hall. Moments afterward, Sarah climbed the bell tower and leaped to her death, the bell cord looped around her neck. Recent renovations at Senior Hall have increased the ghostly activities, and it is said that Sarah's apparition can be seen in the bell tower every Halloween at midnight.

(Stephens College, 1200 E Broadway, Columbia, MO 65215. Phone: 573-442-2211. www.stephens.edu.) **176**

SUTTON HOUSE This two-story wood-frame house was built before the Civil War and was home to the Sutton family for many generations. Later residents reported seeing the ghost of a short young woman with long brown hair wearing a gray dress. Her eerie singing sometimes filled the whole house. Sutton House gained a reputation for being haunted, and no one would live in it. Finally, in 1983, the Columbia Fire Department deliberately burned the house to the ground.

(The house was destroyed, but the stone foundation stood for several years at 4933 Lake Valley Lane, Columbia, MO 65203.) **134**

FAYETTEVILLE

LILAC HALL This old mansion became haunted in 1977. The sounds of a phantom vacuum cleaner in the living room and chains dragging through an upstairs hall are just a few of the ghost's manifestations. The image of an elderly widow wearing black has sat on beds and appeared to children in the house. She is thought to be Miss Minnie, the last owner of the house, who died in 1949.

(Fayetteville is in Lafayette County, west of Kansas City. Take the Highway 13 south exit from I-70. Lilac Hall is now a state historic site.) **53 (8/91), 68**

FLORISSANT

McCLUER NORTH SENIOR HIGH SCHOOL The Taille De Noyer building on this high school campus is said to be haunted by its former residents. The house was constructed in 1798 and witnesses report seeing ghosts dressed in clothing from the early 1800s.

(The town of Florissant is a northwestern suburb of St. Louis off I-270. McCluer Senior High School, 705 Waterford Dr., Florissant, MO 63031. Phone: 314-831-6600.) **101**

HARTVILLE

WARD FARM A well-documented poltergeist case took place on the farm of Mr. and Mrs. Clinton Ward in 1958. Most of the events centered around their nine-year-old daughter, Betty Ruth Ward. The strange events started at Betty Ruth's grandmother's house one afternoon, while they were shelling walnuts in the living room. Suddenly walnuts starting floating all around the room, crawling up the curtains, and bouncing down

from the ceiling. The two ran out of the house and went directly to the Ward residence to tell them what was happening, but as soon as they opened the front door, bowls, knickknacks, and other objects began floating in midair. Mrs. Ward's bed later rose off the floor three times—while she was lying in it. The astonishing activity persisted for nearly two weeks and was witnessed by researchers from Duke University. William Cox and Jim Bethel, both from Duke's Parapsychology Laboratory, saw the levitation of a can of shoe polish, a bar of soap, and even a pot of hot stew. They were pelted with pieces of bark, a rock, and a walnut that seemed to come from nowhere. Five witnesses saw a heavy tub of wet laundry fly off the front porch and spill clothes into the yard. Once, when the Wards went shopping in nearby Lebanon, a pair of shoes flew off a store rack and landed right at the feet of Betty Ruth. Her mother, two brothers, and a store clerk all witnessed the unexplainable event.

(Hartville is in the southwest corner of Missouri. It is located east of Springfield in Wright County, at the junction of Highways 5 and 38. The farm is private property west of town.) **105**

HOLLISTER

LAKE HOUSE The ghost of a gray-haired Peeping Tom haunts this lakeside house. His ashen face has been seen peeping in the bathroom window when young women are using the toilet. The window is eighteen feet off the ground. The lecherous phantom's vaporous form has also been seen in the hall leading to the bedrooms. He is believed to be the ghost of a man who murdered his wife and buried her in the basement of the house in the 1930s. He was known for his voyeuristic tendencies.

(Hollister is in southwestern Missouri. The town is located about thirty-five miles south of Springfield on U.S. Highway 65. Lake House is a private residence just outside Hollister, on Chalet Road, at the edge of a cliff overlooking Lake Taneycomo.) **231**

INDEPENDENCE

OLD JACKSON COUNTY JAIL Visitors to this old jail sometimes report feelings of nausea and extreme cold. Guards have reported unexplainable footsteps, growling noises, and the sounds of someone gasping for breath. The ghost of a man in a blue uniform has been detected in the center south cell. He is thought to be Deputy Marshall Henry Buggler, who was killed in a jailbreak in June 1866.

(Independence is in the southwest corner of Missouri, at the junction of U.S. Highways 75 and 169. The jailhouse is still in operation in downtown Independence at 200 S. Main St. Phone: 816-881-4400.) **66 (6/90)**

TRUMAN HOME The ghost of Harry S. Truman returns to his former home. Park employees have reported his ghost relaxing in the living room, where the odor of his favorite bourbon is sometimes detected. Harry and his wife Bess lived in the house from 1919 until their deaths. The house was built by Bess's grandfather in 1867. See White House, District of Columbia.

(Harry S. Truman National Historic Site, 223 North Main St., Independence, MO 64050. Phone: 818-254-7199. www.nps.gov/hstr) **72**

JEFFERSON CITY

PHANTOM STEAMBOAT Fishermen along the river here have reported seeing the phantom of a unique steamboat, with a duck-paddle system of propulsion, steaming up the Missouri River. The apparitions of about a dozen passengers can be seen on the deck of the ghost ship, which seems to hover a few feet over the water.

(The vessel has been seen twenty miles south of Jefferson City, in Boone County, at the confluence of the Missouri River and the Oasage River. The area is southwest of Columbia in central Missouri.) **134**

JOPLIN

DEVIL'S PROMENADE Almost every night since 1866, a strange orange ball of light bounces along this road in an easterly direction. As the light moves through the air it leaves behind luminous traces of dancing sparks. The light has been known to enter cars and buses, but paradoxically, dodges people chasing it. Loud noises also make it disappear. It has been called the Hornet Ghost Light, the Neosho Spook Light, and the Devil's Jack-O'-Lantern, and scientists who have studied the phenomenon cannot agree on a cause. In 1946, a study by the Army Corps of Engineers concluded the phenomenon was "a mysterious light of unknown origin." A 1983 report by the Ghost Research Society described the light as diamond-shaped, with a

hollow center. Some locals believe the light is the ghost of a pair of Quapaw Indian lovers who committed suicide together. Others hold that it is the lantern of a ghostly miner searching for his wife and children, who were abducted by Indians. For other nearby spook lights, see Columbus, Kansas; and Miami, Oklahoma.

(Devil's Promenade is in the village of Hornet, eleven miles of southwest of Joplin. The area is near the borders of Missouri, Oklahoma, and Kansas. This tristate region is known as the Spooksville Triangle. Follow I-44 west from Joplin. Just before the last exit at the Oklahoma border, turn south onto State Line Rd. Devil's Promenade Rd. crosses State Line Rd. after about four miles. There is an abandoned spook light museum at the site. From Neosho, follow Highway 86 until it dead-ends before Highway 43. Turn right and go two miles to the second road on the left. Turn left and go a quarter mile to Devil's Promenade. The light is visible from any point along a two-mile stretch of the road here. www.ghosts.org/ghostlights/hornet.html) **5, 15, 20, 56, 66 (7/83), 176, 196, 231**

UFO SIGHTING Two gigantic saucer-shaped UFOs were observed hovering over Joplin in January 1967. Police from Joplin, Baxter Springs, and Pittsburg, Kansas, followed the objects, which appeared to land in the Spooksville area (see Devil's Promenade, above) and then take off again. The objects moved noiselessly against the wind. Scores of credible witnesses observed the phenomenon, including the mayor of Carthage, who took one of several photographs of the floating objects. Authorities searching for evidence of a landing discovered an unusual, rippled-metal disc that measured over three feet in diameter.

(The UFOs moved at a low altitude from north of Joplin to the tristate border area known as the Spookville Triangle.) **15**

KANSAS CITY

SAVOY HOTEL The oldest continuously operating hotel west of the Mississippi is haunted by at least two ghosts. One is an elderly woman named Betsy Ward, who haunts Apartment 505. She died in the bathtub there, and now comes back to take showers. Residents have reported that the shower curtain draws closed by itself, and the faucet turns on to an empty stall. The other ghost is Fred Lightner, who haunts his former apartment in the hotel. In 1987, two witnesses reported his gray ghost standing in the hall outside his old apartment. Other residents of the hotel, which was built in 1888, have reported strange footsteps and voices throughout the building.

(Kansas City is on I-70 in western Missouri at the Kansas border. The hotel is at 219 West Ninth St., Kansas City, MO 64105. Phone: 816-842-3575.) **133**

UNIVERSITY OF MISSOURI This university's Playhouse is haunted by the spirit of a female manager who died in the arms of the stage manager in the lobby in 1957. Her footsteps and presence were detected on the stage for many years.

(University of Missouri, 5100 Rockhill Rd. Kansas City, MO 64110. Phone: 816-276-1800. www.umkc.edu) **68**

KNOB NOSTER

HERMIT LIGHT The ghost of a hermit who lived on the top of a hill here returns during stormy weather. The man died mysteriously, some say of fright, during a violent thunderstorm. He was on his way down the hill to seek shelter in town. His body was found lying next to his lantern, which was still burning. Now his ghost, still carrying the lantern, is seen coming down the path into town whenever thunderstorms rage, through the area.

(The town of Knob Noster is in Johnson County, at the junction of U.S. Highway 50 and Highway 23. Knob Noster State Park is southwest of town.) **176**

MARYVILLE

NORTHWEST MISSOURI STATE UNIVERSITY Students living in Roberta Hall dormitory make a burn mark on their doors with a hot iron to discourage nocturnal visits from the dorm's resident ghost. Roberta Steel was critically injured on April 28, 1951, after a gas tank east of the building exploded. Flames were seen seventy miles away, and the force of the explosion hurled the tank into the dormitory. After a heroic struggle to live, Roberta finally succumbed from her injuries in November 1952. But her passion to live kept her spirit alive, too, and the dorm has been considered haunted since her death. Doors and windows unlock and open by themselves, lights go off after being left on too late at night, and the volume on loud radios is turned down. People can hear Roberta playing a piano in a deserted basement room. At least once, her ghost

materialized in a room and tried to get in bed with startled coeds. When one of them pushed her away, Roberta's phantom started dancing in circles in the middle of the room.

(Maryville is thirty-four miles north of St. Joseph on U.S. Highway 71. Northwest Missouri State University, 800 University Dr., Maryville, MO 64468. Phone: 660-562-1275. www.northwestonline.org) **66 (6/94)**

OZARK MOUNTAINS

OZARK MADONNA The ghost of a barefoot woman holding a baby is seen on the ridge tops here. She is thought to be the spirit of Laurie May Maumsey, who lived in a cabin in the hills in the 1930s. Her drunken husband had threatened to beat their baby unless she gave him money. In the struggle that followed, the child fell from her arms to the stone floor and died from a concussion. The woman committed suicide shortly afterward.

(The area is the Mark Twain National Forest, which runs through Ozark and Taney counties along the Arkansas border.) **158**

PARIS

PARIS SPECTER The ghost of a woman in black, the Paris Specter, walked the streets of this village for nearly seventy years. She always appeared in October and stayed until spring. Brandishing a cane, the woman floated over sidewalks as terrified bystanders jumped out of her way. Children were not allowed out after dark, and men walked in groups of three for protection. She was first encountered by Darcy Ambrose, who saw her walk by the Ambrose House in October 1866. The last reported sighting was in 1934. Investigators have suggested she was either a formidable spinster who lived in the town, or the ghost of another woman who swore on her deathbed to haunt her faithless lover and the whole "small-minded" town.

(Paris is in Monroe County in northeast Missouri, at the junction of U.S. Highway 24 and Highway 15.) **176**

ST. GENEVIEVE

GUIBOURD HOUSE Missouri's oldest town has one of the nation's oldest haunted buildings. The phantoms of three old men dressed in eighteenth-century clothing have been reported here. The men materialize only from the waist up. Their restless spirits are blamed for moving objects and making unexplained crashing sounds in a second floor bedroom. Perhaps unrelated are strange footsteps heard in the kitchen area, which used to be slave quarters. The French settled this town in 1735 and the exquisite Guibourd House was built in the mid-1700s.

(St. Genevieve is sixty miles south of Saint Louis on the Mississippi River. Follow I-55 to Highway 32 West. Guibourd House Museum, 1 North 4th St., St. Genevieve, MO 63670. Phone: 573-883-7544. www.prairieghosts. com/g_valle.html) **175, 188**

ST. LOUIS

CURREN HOUSE This house was the scene of one of the most celebrated cases in the history of spiritualism. On July 8, 1913, Mrs. Pearl Curren sat down with her Ouija board and started moving the planchette furiously from letter to letter. The message spelled out: "Many months ago I lived; again I come. Patience Worth my name." Soon Patience began talking directly through the uneducated Pearl Curren, while Mr. Curren took dictation. Mrs. Curren reported that Patience was born in England in the 1600s, migrated to America, and was killed by Indians in Missouri. Over the next decade, Patience, as channeled through Mrs. Curren, turned out a prolific array of poems, stories, novels, and essays—four million words in twenty-nine volumes. All of the works had literary merit. According to philologists, her novel of medieval England, *Telka*, was a miracle. The book contained not a single word that entered the language after 1700. Patience was enormously popular nationwide, and even had her own magazine and fan clubs. Her voice was stilled when Pearl Curren died in 1937.

(The Curren House is now a private residence in south St. Louis.) **37, 50, 53 (11/76), 68, 149, 176, 189**

EDGEWOOD CHILDREN'S CENTER The ghost of a ten-year-old girl hovers above the ground near the old cottonwood tree here. Another presence manifests inside Rock House, the oldest building at the center. Adults living in quarters on the second floor in the east end of the building have reported an oppressive uneasiness, moving objects, and footsteps in the attic late at night. A tunnel several blocks long was recently discovered under Rock House. It is thought to date back to Civil War days, when the building was used to hide runaway slaves. The stone house, built in 1850 by abolitionist Reverend Artemus Bullard, was first used as a seminary called Webster College. In 1855, it became an orphanage known as the St. Louis Protestant Orphan Asylum. The center now provides treatment for severely disturbed, abandoned, and abused children.

(The twenty-three-acre campus of the Edgewood Children's Center is in the Webster Groves area, at 330 North Gore St., St. Louis, MO 63119. Phone: 314-968-2060.) **14, 101**

GEHM HOUSE This two-story wood house with a brick facade was built in the 1890s by a German immigrant named Henry Gehm. Gehm was a reclusive gentleman who died alone in the house in the early 1950s. In 1956, the house was purchased by the S. L. Furry family. Mr. and Mrs. Furry had been married twenty years and had two young daughters. Soon after they moved in, they started hearing unexplainable footsteps and odd noises like big birds hitting the windows. Every night at exactly 2:00 A.M., something would shake Mrs. Furry's bed and wake her up. Within a few weeks, the entire family started seeing the ghost of a lady dressed in black, enveloped in a mysterious white cloud. One of the children said the ghost periodically beat her with a broom, although it never hurt. The Furry family lived with the harmless ghost for nine years, finally moving into a newer home. In November 1965, the Walsh family moved into the house and soon encountered the same apparition, plus two others. Clare Walsh, her husband, and their two daughters started sensing the ghost of a little blond-haired girl in the attic. Then, on March 1, 1966, the ghost of Henry Gehm himself appeared and directed Mrs. Walsh to a hidden doorway in the attic. Behind the door, she found a secret chamber. It was empty. Soon after that incident, the Walshes moved out, into a brand new home, one they could be sure no one had lived in before.

(The house is located in the Webster Groves area of the city, in the 300 block of Plant Ave., St. Louis, MO 63119. www.prairieghosts.com/gehm.html) **85, 86**

LEMP MANSION In 1904, brewery tycoon William Lemp, despondent over the death of his favorite son, went into the marble office of this mansion, put a gun to his heart, and pulled the trigger. In 1920, one of his daughters, Elsa, also committed suicide with a gun. In 1922, one of his sons, William Junior, followed his father into the marble office and put a pistol to his own heart. In 1949, another son, Charles, took the family dog into the basement and shot it dead. Then, he put the revolver to his own head. He was seventy-seven when he committed suicide. The mansion was used as a boarding house for many years. In 1977, after extensive renovation, it opened as a fashionable restaurant. Workmen at the site were harassed by many strange phenomena, including slamming doors, ghostly sounds, and the "burning sensation" of staring eyes. The atmosphere was so oppressive that several workers refused to enter the old mansion. Customers and employees have witnessed water in a pitcher swirl by itself, as if stirred by an unseen hand, and have heard music issue from a piano when no one was near it. The sounds of ghostly barking have also been heard.

(Follow Broadway to Cherokee St. in downtown St. Louis. Go west, then turn north at De Menil Place. The Lemp Mansion Restaurant is at 3322 De Menil Place, St. Louis, MO 63118. Phone: 314-664-8024. www. prairieghosts.com/lemp.html) **14, 72, 101, 231**

OLD PACIFIC HOUSE HOTEL A salesman from Boston was working the St. Louis area in 1876 when the ghost of his departed sister appeared to him in his hotel room here. The eighteen-year-old girl had died of cholera in St. Louis in 1867. Her distinct form materialized in front of the man for several seconds, and he was able to detect a long scratch or mark across her face. When he returned to Boston and mentioned the encounter to his parents, his mother confessed that she had unintentionally marred the girl's face while preparing the body for the funeral. She covered the scar with makeup and was the only person who knew about it.

(The old brick building is now abandoned in downtown St. Louis.) **148**

V.I.P. GRAPHICS When Matt and Denise Piskulic bought this former police station for their graphics business, they knew the place was haunted. Built in 1904, the old station house was the scene of many traumatic events. Probably the best known was the Bobby Greenlease kidnapping case in the early 1940s. During a ransom exchange that took place at the station, the fourteen-year-old boy was murdered and three hundred thousand dollars of the ransom money mysteriously disappeared. Then, in 1945, Edward Melendes, being held for petty theft, was beaten to death in his cell

by three officers. The station was converted into a private house, and in 1960, residents started complaining of ghostly sounds such as heavy footsteps and dragging chains. In the 1970s, the Fosmire family was chased out of the house by an invisible presence in the middle of the night. They never returned. By the early 1990s, when the Piskulics moved in, phenomena also included the sounds of a baby crying in the loft, a man's sudden shriek, and a woman's voice saying "Hello" from the bathroom. Renovations only increased the paranormal activity.

(The old station house is located in the Central West End of St. Louis. V.I.P. Graphics, 14 North Newstead Ave., St. Louis, MO 63108. Phone: 314-535-1117. www. prairieghosts.com/14north.html) **53 (10/95)**

SAND SPRINGS

PHANTOM RIDER After the Civil War, people started seeing a ghostly rider and his horse in the Sand Springs area. Search parties were organized in the 1930s to try to follow the Phantom Rider, but they never succeeded. According to legend, the rider is Charles Potter, who rode his horse into a small church here one Sunday in 1865. Dressed in a Confederate uniform and mounted on a powerful steed, Potter wanted to run the preacher out of town. The preacher, Elder Maupins, led a group of violent marauders known as Maupins Raiders. Before he could confront the preacher, someone shot Potter through a window in the building. He died in the aisle of the church, and his horse ran off into the mountains.

(Sand Springs is in Pulaski County, between the cities of Lebanon and Rolla, two miles west of Roubidoux Creek.) **176**

SPRINGFIELD

FANTASTIC CAVERNS Traveling through this beautiful sacred site is said to gently recharge one's mental and physical being. The colorful, womblike cave has hundreds of stalagmites, stalactites, stone curtains, and crystal columns.

(Take I-44 to Highway 13 north and turn west at Caverns Road. For information, contact Fantastic Caverns, 4872 N. Farm Rd., 125, Springfield, MO 65803. Phone: 417-833-2010. www.fantastic-caverns.com) **99**

TOWOSAGHY

TOWOSAGHY STATE HISTORIC SITE This bleak, unimproved sacred site was a thriving religious community in A.D. 1000. Towosaghy is an Osage Indian term for "Old Town," a fifty-two-acre walled site inhabited by unknown ancient people. There are two ceremonial temple sites, one a pyramid mound and the other a ridged mound.

(Towosaghy is in the southeastern tip of Missouri. Take I-55 to Highway 80 east. Go past the town of East Prairie to Road FF, then turn south onto Road AA. Turn east on first unmarked road. For permission to visit, contact the Superintendent, Missouri Department of Natural Resources, Big Oak Tree State Park, 13640 S. Highway 102, East Prairie, MO 63845. Phone: 573-649-3149.) **99**

MONTANA

BANNACK

BANNACK GHOST TOWN The sounds of babies crying emanate from the empty Amede Bessette's House in this old town. The babies were among the fourteen infants who died here during a smallpox epidemic in the late 1880s. The apparition of a girl who drowned in Grasshopper Creek has been seen on the second-floor of the old Meade Hotel. Dogs and other pets refuse to enter the portals of the spooky redbrick building.

(The ghost town is located in the Bitterroot Range in the southwestern tip of Montana. Follow U.S. Highway 93 to Salmon and go southeast twenty-two miles on Highway 28. Turn east on Highway 324. The old town is twenty miles north of Grant. Bassette House is a wood-frame house with an attic. It is located at 4200 Bannack Rd., Dillon, MT 59725. 406-834-3413. www.ghosttowns. com/states/mt/bannack.html) **30, 54, 127**

BILLINGS

BEVERLY'S HOUSE The ghost of a teenage girl named Beverly haunts her former home. In the early 1900s, the girl was rushing to get to a Christmas Eve party on the main floor, when she tripped at the second-floor landing and fell down the stairs. Hemorrhaging internally, she died in her second-floor bedroom that same night. For many years, residents called her ghost the Witch in the Attic and blamed her for moving objects, making odd noises, and scattering presents around the den at Christmas.

(The two-story house faces east on First Ave. North, Billings, MT 59101.) **46**

LA LLORONA The ghost of a tall, dark-haired woman wearing a flowing white gown has been seen along the banks of the Yellowstone River near Billings. She has been dubbed the Weeping Woman, another variation of La Llorona, the Spanish mother who drowned her own children and is destined to roam the banks of rivers near Hispanic settlements throughout the country looking for them. See Gary, Indiana; El Paso, Texas; and Guadalupita, New Mexico.

(The river area is five miles east of Billings.) **131**

BOZEMAN

CHICO HOT SPRINGS LODGE AND RANCH In May 1986, two night watchmen at this resort hotel came upon the nebulous form of a young woman hovering near a piano in the third-floor lounge. Only the upper body of the white ghost appeared. The face of the peaceful apparition stared right at them for several minutes, enough time for one of the guards to grab a camera from a nearby table and snap a photograph. A tiny white spot appeared on the film where the ghost had stood. The same apparition had been seen by guests several times in the past, but this was the first time the Lady in White was photographed. In 1990, two other security guards followed the Lady in White from the lobby to the hallway leading to Room 349, where the presence has been reported by many employees and guests.

(Bozeman is 140 miles west of Billings on I-90. The resort is located fifty-eight miles southeast of Bozeman in the Paradise Valley, just outside of the town of Pray. Take I-90 east to U.S. Highway 89 south. Chico Hot Springs Lodge and Ranch, Pray, MT 59065. 800-HOT-WADA.) **128, 131**

MONTANA STATE UNIVERSITY The tragic death of a theater director is responsible for the haunting of the MSU Theater. In the early 1970s, the director slipped and fell down the metal spiral staircase behind the stage. He hit his head and suffered from brain damage, which left him subject to drastic mood swings. One evening, in his office next to the sound booth, he loaded real bullets in a prop pistol and shot himself. After the suicide, people reported having strange feelings in his old office, but it was not until the mid-1980s that a "blackened silhouette" started to be seen near the room. The adjoining Strand Student Union is home to another suicide ghost. The apparition of a woman wearing a 1930s dress has been spotted there and near the light room of the MSU Theater. She is believed to be the spirit of a young woman who hanged herself in the ballroom.

(The theater building is part of the student union complex. Montana State University, 1711 W. College St., Bozeman, MT 59717. Phone: 406-994-0211. www. montana.edu.) **128**

BUTTE

BUTTE-SILVER BOW COUNTY COURTHOUSE This four-story limestone building has been considered to be haunted for nearly a century. Most incidents occur under the county jail at the rear of the structure. Many of the descriptions of apparitions fit a man named Miles Fuller, who was hanged in the yard behind the jail. He was executed on May 18, 1906, for murdering a fellow prospector. When pallbearers placed the accused murderer's coffin on a funeral wagon, an uncanny crashing sound, like a bolt of thunder, was heard. The startled witnesses took the event as a sign that Fuller was innocent. Ever since, Fuller's ghost has been reported wandering the area at the rear of the Courthouse.

(Butte is in Silver Bow County in southwestern Montana at the junction of I-90 and I-15. The courthouse is in north central Butte. Phone: 406-723-8262.) **127**

COPPER KING MANSION Construction of this thirty-two-room mansion began in 1884 and took four years. It was originally the home of Senator W. A. Clark and was later used a residence for Catholic nuns. A cold presence seems to haunt the game room; a warmer spirit is felt in the old chapel. "A light-colored thing that floats and moves around" has been observed in the basement and in the first-floor hallway.

(The redbrick Victorian inn is west of Main Street and north of Park St., at 219 West Granite St., Butte, MT 59701. Phone: 406-782-7580.) **127**

HENNESSY MANSION This mansion was built at the turn of the century by department store owner D. J. Hennessy. It has been used as a dormitory for nursing students and as a fraternity house, and Hennessy's ghost has been encountered by several people over the years. His presence is strongest in the kitchen, on the basement staircase, and in a basement gymnasium.

(Hennessy Mansion, Park St. and Excelsior St., Butte, MT 59701.) **127**

MOUNT MARIAH CEMETERY The ghost of a man in a wheelchair has been seen in this cemetery. In January 1973, two police officers saw the apparition wheel itself through the locked gates at the front entrance to the graveyard.

(The cemetery is at 2415 S. Montana St., Butte, MT 59701. Phone: 406-782-1778.) **127**

CROW INDIAN RESERVATION

FORT ABRAHAM LINCOLN In May 1876, General George Custer's six-hundred troops marched from this fort to join other troops in an assault on Sioux Indians. As residents waved good-bye and watched the Seventh Cavalry Regiment ride off to the southeast, they were astonished to see almost half the troops ride off into the sky and vanish from sight, while the remaining troops were in plain view. Many interpreted the strange vision as an omen of impending doom. On June 25, at the Battle of the Little Bighorn, Custer and 264 of his troops, about half those who marched out of Fort Lincoln, were killed by the united tribes of the Sioux Indian Nation. See Little Bighorn, below.

(The Crow Indian Reservation is southeast of Billings in southeastern Montana. The reservation extends to the Wyoming border.) **72, 139**

A ghostly occurrence at Fort Abraham Lincoln was seen as a sign of impending doom for General George Custer's troops as they left the fort and traveled to the Battle of Little Bighorn. See Fort Abraham Lincoln, Crow Indian Reservation, Montana (B. A. SCHAFENBERGER)

LITTLE BIGHORN BATTLEFIELD NATIONAL MONUMENT Here in June 1876, General George A. Custer and his cavalrymen went down in defeat to Sioux Indians led by Crazy Horse and Sitting Bull. The bloody engagement is widely referred to as the Battle of the Little Bighorn, a nearby river. Visitors have been overcome by a sense of sorrow and loss on Last Stand Hill and near Battlefield Cemetery, but perhaps the strangest events take place near a section of the battleground known as Reno Crossing. This is the section of the Little Bighorn River where cavalrymen under the direction of Major Marcus Reno retreated from Indian forces, carrying as many dead and wounded comrades as they could. The ghost of Second Lieutenant Benjamin Hodgson, who died a horrible death near the crossing, has been seen by park personnel. His leg shattered by a bullet that also killed his horse, the frantic soldier tried to crawl up a steep hill, before being killed by an Indian. His body rolled down to the riverbank, where a marker now stands. Other apparitions have been encountered at Stone House, an employees' residence near the cemetery, where strange lights have also been reported. Employees' Apartments A and D are known for shimmering forms that appear at the foot of sleeping workers' beds. The apparition of a soldier, wearing a brown shirt with a black cartridge belt across

his chest, has been seen in the visitor center. The ghost of Custer himself is said to roam through the museum, making one last check of the premises before retiring late at night (see Fort Abraham Lincoln, above). In 1986, the National Park Service arranged for relics of the battle to be psychometrized by selected psychics. All the psychics described, in exacting and historically precise detail, previously unknown facts about the people who died here.

(The battlefield is in Crow Agency, fifteen miles outside of Hardin on I-90. Indians called this Little Bighorn valley "Greasy Grass." The two-story, stone building that formerly housed park personnel faces the cemetery. Reno Crossing is about five miles from the main battleground. Phone: 406-638-2621. www.nps.gov/libi) **112, 127, 131, 136, 175, 203**

FLATHEAD INDIAN RESERVATION

CHIEF CLIFF This site is sacred to Kutenai Indians. Legend says that the spirit of an aged chief looks out over his people from the cliff top. Long ago, the chief rode his horse to the top of the ridge and addressed his people, who had assembled below. He warned them of forsaking the old ways and of not respecting their elders, then punctuated his remarks by riding at full gallop over the edge of the cliff. According to Indian legend, his spirit still permeates the site.

(The huge reservation is in the Rocky Mountains of northwestern Montana. Chief Cliff is 5 miles west of Flathead Lake. It is north of the town of Elmo, at the end of a ten-mile-long mountain ridge. At its easternmost point, the ridge ends with a sheer cliff that drops 150 feet to the ground. Just below the cliff is semicircular pattern of broken rock.) **33**

FLATHEAD LAKE This region takes its name from a mysterious race of short, flatheaded, red-skinned people, who were gradually absorbed into the Salish and Nez Perce tribes. Legends say the mystery people came either from ships in the ocean or from a "burning star" that plunged into the lake hundreds of years ago. The painted rocks on the west shore of the lake have strange signs and characters in vivid color painted by the lost tribe. A skeleton found in 1934 near Forest Grove, Montana, came from an unidentified racial type that was shorter but more muscular and powerful than local tribes. Along with the bones were found beads of copper unlike any in the area, as well as other unusual jewelry.

(Flathead Lake is south of Kalispell in the northwest corner of Montana. Most of the lake is on the Flathead Indian Reservation. It is the largest body of freshwater west of the Mississippi.) **33**

FORT PECK

FORT PECK SUMMER THEATRE The ghost of a workman who fell to his death during construction of this Swiss chalet building still haunts the place. The ghostly presence has been known to support people to keep them falling down stairs or off ladders. The apparition of a man in khaki work clothes has been seen in the back balcony, and for some unfathomable reason, the same figure has been reported sleeping in the restrooms. The theater was erected in 1934, but after World War II it was used as a movie house. In 1968 it once again began staging live performances.

(Fort Peck is in northeast Montana, forty-six miles west of Wolf Point. Take U.S. Highway 2 to Highway 117 south at Nashua. Fort Peck Summer Theatre, Fort Peck, MT 59223. For information, call the Fine Arts Council at 406-228-9219. www.klt2.com/theatre. html) **128**

GREAT FALLS

BLACK HORSE LAKE Many people traveling the road along this lake report running over the phantom of a hitchhiker. The tall ghost wears bib overalls and stands with his legs apart in the middle of the road. Some have described him as an Indian with long black hair, wearing a denim jacket. After the man is struck he disappears, and there is no damage to the vehicle.

(Great Falls is in west-central Montana at the junction of I-15 and U.S. Highway 87. The lake is just outside of town.) **127**

HELENA

BRANTLY HOUSE The stern spirit of State Supreme Court Judge Theodore Brantly haunts his former home. Brantly died in 1922, and his large house was converted into apartments. Since then, caretakers and tenants in the building have reported hearing his lonely footsteps ascending the stairs to the third floor, and children have said that he watches over them. But the judge does have one vice. His ghost is blamed for stealing M&M candies if they are placed out in a dish.

(Helena is in west-central Montana, sixty-four miles north of Butte on I-15. The house is a private residence on Holt St., Helena, MT 5960. www.hauntedhouses.com/ states/mt/house.htm) **128**

CARROLL COLLEGE A locked-up bathroom on the fourth floor of St. Charles Hall is just one source of ghostly phenomena here. The room was the scene of an accident in which a young male student fell and hit his head against the sink. He died of a cerebral hemorrhage. Indelible red stains in the sink and rumors of a haunting prompted college officials to seal the room. Another student committed suicide by jumping from a window at the top of the north stairwell in St. Charles Hall. The student's ghost is said to reenact his death, over and over again. St. Albert's Hall is haunted by the spirit of a nun who died of an illness there. Glimpses of her fleeting specter are reported in the corridors on the top floor of the building, which is now the student union. The ghosts on this campus are most active when the students are suffering from emotional trauma or the stress of exams. The spirits seem attracted to their raw emotional energy.

(Carroll College, 1601 N. Benton Ave., Helena, MT 59625. Phone: 406-447-1300. www.carroll.edu) **127**

GRANDSTREET THEATER A charming phantom haunts this stone playhouse. When Clara Bicknell Hodgin died in 1905, at the age of thirty-four, residents took up a collection and donated a Tiffany window in her memory to the Unitarian Church. After the church was converted to a library, the window was removed and stored in the civic center. In December 1976, the window was rediscovered and again installed in the building, which had just reopened as a theater. It was then that Clara's spirit began to manifest. Delicate, discarnate footsteps are heard throughout the building, appliances and lights come on and go off, and her engaging presence is felt by visiting children, patrons, actors, and employees of the theater.

(The theater is off U.S. Highway 12 in downtown Helena at 325 N. Park Ave. Phone: 406-442-4270. www. grandstreet.net) **127, 128**

KLEINSCHMIDT HOUSE This house is haunted by Mary Kleinschmidt and her youngest son, Erwin. Theodore Kleinschmidt and his wife Mary built their Victorian home in 1892. Mary died in the house in 1904, and by the 1950s it was common knowledge that she was haunting her former residence. Realtors even went to far as to warn prospective buyers of ghostly activity at the house. Recent tenants have heard Mary's footsteps throughout the house. The apparition of blond-haired Erwin, clad in knickers, is usually seen in the bedrooms.

(The Kleinschmidt House is a private residence, at 1823 Highland Ave, Helena, MT 59601.) **128**

T. C. POWER MANSION

T. C. POWER MANSION This stone castle was home to Thomas C. Power, millionaire businessman and former U.S. senator. The mansion was built in 1889, and Thomas and his wife Mary lived there for many years. After their deaths, their son willed it to the Catholic Church. Later the diocese sold the building, and it became a day-care center. Caretakers, church officials, and employees at the old Power Mansion have reported seeing the apparition of a former maid in the ballroom and at other locations in the house. The ghost of Thomas Power has been sensed in the bedroom where he died.

(T. C. Power Mansion, 600 Harrison St., Helena, MT 59601.) **128**

MISSOULA

BEARMOUTH The ghost of a man dressed in an old-fashioned black coat has been seen running from behind the general store here. The phantom runs directly into the hillside and disappears. He is thought to be the ghost of the owner of a hotel that once stood on the property.

(Missoula is in western Montana at the junction of I-90 and U.S. Highway 93. Bearmouth is an old mining town thirty-two miles southeast of Missoula on I-90.) **46, 54**

GARNET This old ghost town was established during the 1860s gold rush, and by 1880 there were four thousand men living here. Ghostly honky-tonk music has been heard coming from the boarded-up windows of the old Kelly Saloon, and strange presences have been felt in the adjacent bank building. More ghostly partying has been heard coming from the boarded-up J. K Wells Hotel.

(Garnet lies at 5,800 feet elevation in the Rocky Mountains northeast of Missoula. Take I-90 southeast thirty-two miles to Bearmouth and follow the steep mountain road off Highway 200, ten miles north to Garnet. Cabins are available for rent. Contact Ghost Town Cottages, P.O. Box 8531, Missoula, MT 59807 Phone: 406-329-3914. www.ghosttowns.com/states/mt/garnet.html) **30, 46, 54, 128, 131,**

MISSOULA CHILDREN'S THEATRE A friendly spirit named George haunts this nationally acclaimed children's playhouse. Although he is sometimes blamed for making loud banging noises in the deserted shop or throwing storyboards he does not like, George is also credited with helping out during productions. Once, he whispered the correct page number to a pianist who lost her place during a recital.

(Missoula Children's Theatre, 200 N. Adams St., Missoula, MT 59802. Phone: 406-728-1911. www.mctinc. org) **128**

UNIVERSITY OF MONTANA The theater in the Fine Arts Building on this campus is haunted by a spiteful spook who likes to trick people. Brantly Hall is haunted by a female student who committed suicide after her father lost all his money in the 1929 stock market collapse. The ghost of her German shepherd has also been seen in the corridors. A phantom class of twenty students haunts Rankin Hall. Their voices and restless shuffling are heard coming from empty classrooms on the second floor. In Main Hall, also known as University Hall, a ghost disturbs custodians cleaning the restrooms by slamming stall doors, walking noisily across the floor, and making loud breathing sounds.

(University of Montana, Missoula, MT 59812. Phone: 406-243-6266. www.umt.edu) **127, 128**

ZAKOS HOUSE This has been called the spookiest house in all of Montana. James and Eleanor Zakos moved into the old Victorian house with their six children and Eleanor's mother in 1938. Immediately they began hearing a woman's bloodcurdling screams coming from the walls. The screams always came in two shrieks that started out low in pitch and rose higher "until the volume threatened to split the walls." The shrieking sounds went on day and night and came from throughout the house. The Zakoses called in the police and fire departments and hired an electrician to inspect the entire building. No one could find an explanation for the horrendous sounds. By 1941 the family had given up trying to find the source of the screams and resigned themselves to living in a haunted house. Then, in 1956, Eleanor's sister arranged to have an exorcism performed by the Reverend Andrew Landin. That seemed to have quieted the house until 1980, when Mary Zakos, who was just a baby when her family moved into the house, told reporters that she was seeing handwriting on the wall of her bedroom. Mary was herself a writer of horror and modern romance books, and her psychiatrist insisted she was somehow projecting the writing onto the wall.

(The house is a private residence at 319 South Fifth St. West, Missoula, MT 59801.) **53 (8/75), 128**

PRYOR MOUNTAINS

CROW MEDICINE ROCK The Crow Indians believe that these mountains are sacred, because they are the home of a race of Little People, who protect the tribe. The Little People are said to be great meat-lovers with sharp canine teeth. Rumors of ferocious dwarfs tearing the hearts out of horses kept enemies off Crow lands, and the tribe still makes offerings to the Little People at Medicine Rock. In 1932, a mummified dwarf sitting cross-legged in a cave was found here by two prospectors. See Pedro Mountains, Wyoming.

(The Pryor Mountains are in south-central Montana, west of Billings. The Chief Plenty Coups State Park is in the middle of the area. It is located near Pryor, thirty miles south of Billings on County Road 416 on the Crow Indian Reservation.) **131**

SHELBY

WRITING STONE Mysterious drawings on this rock wall are said to tell the future. Indian warriors about to go off to battle traveled to the site to look for their picture on the stone. If they saw their own image, it meant they would soon die. Blackfoot Chief "Old Man" Mandan became known for his ability to prophesy the future using the pictographs of the Writing Stone. Pictures on the rock also foretold the appearance of the scores of oil derricks in the area. Indians believe the enigmatic drawings were created by angels or giant multicolored birds.

(Shelby is in Toole County in northeast Montana at the junction of I-15 and U.S. Highway 2. The ancient Writing Stone is a light-colored cliff outside of town.) **33**

VIRGINIA CITY

BONANZA INN The ghost of a nun has appeared in rooms in this inn and in the building next door, known as the Bonanza House. The two buildings are said to be the most haunted in the city. The Bonanza Inn was the first county courthouse in Virginia City, but when a new courthouse was built in 1876 it became a Catholic hospital. The Bonanza House was used as a nunnery. But the ghosts seen in these buildings are far from benign. One of the rooms at the inn had to be sealed because of all the frightening poltergeist manifestations, and the apparition of a lecherous man has appeared in one of the upstairs rooms at the Bonanza House. Disembodied footsteps, eerie feelings of discomfort, and bone-chilling cold spots plague both buildings to this day.

(Virginia City is in Madison County in southwestern Montana. From Butte, take I-90 east to U.S. Highway 287 South and exit at State Highway 287 west. Bonanza Inn, Virginia City, MT 59755.) **128**

COSTUME SHOP The apparition of a little blond-haired girl has been seen dozens of times sitting on the front steps of this commercial building. Some customers of the shop have seen a ghostly little girl's dress that sometimes hangs on the racks, but when they turn around it disappears.

(Virginia City Costume Shop, Wallace St., Virginia City, MT 59755. For information on Virginia City sites, call the town hall at 406-843-5321.) **128**

LIGHTNING SPLITTER This house is called the Lightning Splitter because the rear gable is one of the highest points in town and is frequently struck by lightning. Originally a house of prostitution, the Lightning Splitter is now haunted by a demonlike creature. Locals believe the demon was summoned by a former tenant who was killed in a motorcycle accident. The man had a reputation as a drug dealer and bar brawler, and was known to dabble in satanism. The creature resembles a giant black dog and attacks residents in the upstairs bedrooms. In the same house, a "long, white, orblike thing" has been observed in the kitchen.

(The unique house, which is a private residence, has a three-gabled roof.) **128**

OPERA HOUSE This old theater building is haunted by the revenants of bygone days and at least one modern ghost. Phantom footsteps are heard as some invisible entity enters the back door and walks into the building, and employees have also hears the untraceable sounds of a deep voice laughing at around 3:00 A.M. And for some reason, the ghost of a piano player at the nearby Bale of Hay Saloon who died in 1988 has appeared on the stage at the Opera House.

(Virginia City Opera House, Virginia City, MT 59755. www.virginiacity.com) **128**

NEBRASKA

ALMA

ALMA NIGHTWALKER The ghost of a woman in a black robe haunted the streets of this town for many years at the turn of the century. She came to be known as the Alma Nightwalker. Her ghostly form was seen by dozens of people, including such notables as Congressman Ashton Schallenberger and newspaper editor H. S. Wetherald, who both encountered her apparition in March 1902.

(Alma is in Harlan County, at the junction of U.S. Highways 136 and 183 near the Kansas border.) **176**

BENKELMAN

UFO CRASH On June 6, 1884, John Ellis and a half-dozen of his ranch hands heard a strange whirring sound and saw a large flying object crash behind a ridge in back of them. They found "bits of machinery lying on the ground" which emitted a white light "so dazzling that the eye could not rest upon it." The object left a long scar on the prairie about twenty feet wide and eighty feet long, and the sand in the area was fused into green glass. One of the cowboys ventured within two hundred feet of the glowing debris and immediately fell to the ground with symptoms of radiation poisoning. His face and arms were badly blistered, and he had to be taken to the ranch where it is believed he died within a few weeks. The site continued to glow for another day, and ranchers from all over the county came to see it. On

June 7, brand inspector E. W. Rawlins visited the site. After the wreckage cooled, he examined it and found pieces of a brasslike metal that were inexplicably light and strong. One three-inch-thick piece, sixteen inches wide and forty-two inches long, weighed less than five pounds. Rawlins estimated the cylindrical craft to be sixty feet long and twelve feet in diameter. Rancher Ellis canceled his roundup to collect the debris, but no record exists as to what became of it. It is speculated that the wreckage was turned over to agent Rawlins, who sent it on to the Smithsonian in Washington.

(Benkelman is in Dundy County in the extreme southwest corner of Nebraska at the junction of U.S. Highway 34 and Highway 61. The crash site is thirty-five miles northwest of town near the Colorado state line.) **72**

HAT CREEK

HAT CREEK BATTLEGROUND The sounds of whispering Indians hidden in the tall prairie grass and a strange green mist that swirls around the Hat Creek Monument testify to the presence of spirits. Scores of Cheyenne Indians were massacred on this spot by the Fifth U.S. Cavalry. It was here that William F. Cody, also known as Buffalo Bill, killed the warrior Yellow Hand. Buffalo Bill displayed the brave's warbonnet and weapons at sideshows for many years.

(Hat Creek is also known as Warbonnet Creek. The battleground is a state historic site in northwestern Nebraska.) **131**

LINCOLN

HOBBITTSVILLE HOUSE The ghost of a little girl who drowned in a pool here is said to haunt the backyard. There is now a concrete fence around the yard to keep other children away from the pool, and some say it also keeps the ghost from leaving.

(Lincoln is in eastern Nebraska at the intersection of I-80 and U.S. Highway 77. The private house is near the corner of Sheridan Rd. and Park Ave. in Lincoln.) **72**

LAKE STREET PARK Many witnesses have reported the ghost of an elderly man walking along the shore of the lake in this park. The figure seems to fade in and out of a mist. In 1987, three independent sightings of a "blue shimmering shape" were reported near the creek that runs into the lake.

(The park and lake are at the corner of 15th St. and Lake St. in Lincoln. The creek runs through Irvingdale Park at 17th St. and Harrison Ave.) **17**

NEBRASKA WESLEYAN UNIVERSITY The ghost of Miss Urania Clara Mills haunted the C. C. White Memorial Building on this campus. The huge brick building, erected between 1903 and 1907, housed the Music Department, where Miss Mills taught from 1912 to 1936. On October 3, 1963, Mrs. Coleen Buterbaugh, a secretary to Dean Sam Dahl, was in the music building on an errand. When she entered the rooms of Dr. Tom McCourt, she was overcome by a strong, musty odor. Then she saw the apparition of a tall, thin woman reaching for some papers on the top shelf of an old music cabinet in a corner. Looking out the window, Coleen realized it was summertime, with the sun shining and flowers blooming. Suddenly the ghostly scene disappeared and the outdoor scenery returned to a gray October day. When she told Dean Dahl about her experience, he launched an investigation and discovered that those rooms belonged to Clara Urania Mills. She had died on October 3, 1936, in the room across from where her ghost was seen. The case has become a classic in the literature of the paranormal.

(The C. C. White Building was torn down in 1973. It sat across from Willard House, a girls' dormitory. When she died, Miss Mills was living at 4717 Baldwin Ave., Lincoln, NE 68504. Nebraska Wesleyan University, 5000 St. Paul Ave., Lincoln, NE 68504. Phone: 402-465-2218. www.nebrwesleyan.edu) **17, 41, 56, 134, 176**

OLD CAPTAIN'S STUDIO The ghost of a retired sea captain who rented a studio in this building has returned to his last home on land. Tenants in the building have reported seeing his form on several occasions since his death. The captain's former studio is now occupied by a lawyers' office.

(The building is at North 48th St. and St. Paul Blvd. in Lincoln.) **72**

ROBBER'S CAVE The Pawnee Indians called this cave Nahurac. It was one of five spirit caves where they could contact Tirawa, the one god of all things. They held sacred ceremonies and initiations in the caves, until white soldiers moved the Indians to reservations and burned their villages in 1858. In the 1860s, settlers and runaway slaves lived in the five-hundred-foot-long cave. In 1869 a brewery used the cool area to store kegs. In the 1870s outlaws such as Jesse James hid out there. A robber's cache of stolen goods and money was found in the cave in 1906, and Robber's Cave was a tourist attraction for many years. In one secluded chamber, visitors have reported hearing distant chanting sounds and unintelligible voices.

(Robber's Cave is a half-block south of the intersection of High St. and 10th St. at 3245 South 10th St. Lincoln, NE. 68501. For information, contact the Lincoln Historical Society at 402-471-3270.) **15, 17**

STATE CAPITOL BUILDING Visitors to the dome observation deck here report hearing the sounds of a man sobbing, usually on the southeast side of the building. There are several likely candidates for the Capitol Ghost. One is a prison inmate who had a heart attack in 1968 while stringing Christmas lights on the outside of the dome. Another possibility is a 1950s man who fell ten floors when he leaned too far over the railing of the spiral staircase. Or perhaps the spirit is that of an Indian ghost sensed in the lower basement of the building. The Indians believed the hill on which the capitol now stands was sacred.

(The state capitol is at the corner of 10th St. and Capitol Parkway, Lincoln, NE 68501 www.nebraskahistory. org) **17**

UNIVERSITY OF NEBRASKA Several buildings on this Lincoln campus are said to be haunted. The ghost of a student who fell from the overhead rigging and died on the stage at the Temple Building returns to haunt his fellow thespians. The student died in the

1940s, while preparing for a performance of *Macbeth*. Now, whenever that Shakespearean play is presented, his ghost is seen near the stage. In the 1970s, a ghostly figure was reported in the east basement studios of KUON-TV in the building. More recently, a ghost in the light booth in the auditorium faded from view in front of several witnesses. In the 1980s, unexplainable thumping sounds started coming from the attic. Pound Hall is haunted by Lucy, a 1960s hippie who leaped to her death from the fifth floor of her dorm. Her thin, wispy ghost is seen in her former room, where books open by themselves or fall to the floor for no apparent reason. Finally, a cold, unidentified presence is said to lurk in the corridors of Raymond Hall.

(University of Nebraska, Lincoln, NE 68588. Phone: 402-472-3620. www.unl.edu) **17, 95, 101**

OMAHA

O'HANLON HOUSE Loud, stamping footsteps, shaking walls, and harsh pounding at the front door have haunted this house for over a hundred years. In 1883, when the house was owned by John and Bridget O'Hanlon, workmen doing repairs discovered a human skeleton in the basement. He was thought to be a peddler who was robbed and murdered when he visited the former owners of the house. He is also thought to be responsible for all the scary phenomena that occur here.

(Omaha is on I-80 on the Iowa border. The house is now a private residence in the Omaha Heights section of Omaha.) **176**

OMAHA INDIAN RESERVATION

BLACKBIRD HILL The ghostly screams of a woman are heard here every October 17. The woman was stabbed to death by her jealous husband in a cabin that stood at the top of this hill in 1849. The woman wanted her husband to release her from her vows so she could marry an old sweetheart. In a fit of rage, the man slit her throat, and her bloodcurdling scream is said to linger on. Her lover carried her body up the hill and jumped with her into the river below. On the path where her blood spilled, grass will not grow to this day. Her screams are said to be heard every year on the anniversary of her death. Although the sizable crowd of people who gathered here on October 17, 1933, went away disappointed, her scream has been reported most other years. This is the same spot where Blackbird, the great Omaha Indian chief, is supposed to be buried, sitting upright on his favorite horse. The site was visited by the Lewis and Clark expedition in 1804.

(The reservation is in northeastern Nebraska, west of U.S. Highway 75. Blackbird Hill is eight miles north of Decatur along the Missouri River.) **49, 176**

NEVADA

CARSON CITY

BEE HIVE WHOREHOUSE The ghost of a tall, bloated woman with straggly red hair and dressed in a dirty white nightgown has been seen on the streets near the whorehouse where she once lived. Her name is Timber Kate, and she was part of a notorious saloon act with her female lover, Bella Rawhide. The two performed live sex acts in honky-tonks in Carson City, Spokane, Butte, and Cheyenne. Then young Bella fell in love with a half-breed ruffian by the name of Tug Daniels. After Bella and Tug ran away together, Timber Kate resorted to dressing as a man in white tights and lifting weights on stage, though she usually ended doing a bizarre striptease. In 1880, Bella and Tug met up with Kate in Carson City. In the ensuing showdown, Tug pulled a knife and cut open Kate's belly "from her crotch to her navel." The eviscerated woman died in excruciating pain on the whorehouse floor. Tug escaped and was never seen again. In 1882, Bella committed suicide by drinking cleaning fluid.

(Carson City, the capitol of Nevada, is at the junction of U.S. Highway 50 and U.S. Highway 395 in the west-central corner of the state. The site of the old Bee Hive Whorehouse is on north Quincy St., but Timber Kate's ghost has been seen on many of the streets nearby.) **158**

BLISS MANSION This 8,500-square-foot mansion was built on top of an 1860s graveyard. Lumber millionaire D.L. Bliss completed the three-story house in 1879, after the last bodies on the property were exhumed. Some psychics believe those disturbed pioneers still haunt the grounds.

(The mansion is now a bed-and-breakfast inn on the corner of West Robinson and North Mountain streets, across from the governor's mansion. Bliss Mansion, 710 West Robinson Street, Carson City, NV 89703. For information, call manager Ed Dilley at 775-887-8988.) **72**

BREWERY ARTS CENTER Built in 1874 by the Carson Brewing Company, this structure is now the center of cultural life in Carson City. It houses the Nevada Artists Gallery and the Donald Reynolds Theater. The building has a ghostly caretaker as well. A pleasant, discarnate voice makes suggestions and reminds workers to turn off the lights and lock doors.

(The Brewery Arts Center is at 449 West King St., Carson City, NV 89703. Phone: 775-883-1976. www.breweryarts.org) **72**

CURRY HOUSE Abe Curry left his wife behind in New York when he came west in 1850 to search for gold. It took several years for him to make enough money to bring her west, and in 1871 he built her a beautiful limestone home. But when Abe died his total wealth consisted of a single silver dollar he had in his pocket. That may be why he returns here, searching for his wife Mary, whom he left alone and destitute. See Nevada State Museum, below.

(The privately owned house is on the corner of North Nevada and West Telegraph streets, at 406 North Nevada Street, Carson City, NV 89703. The house is featured on the Kit Carson Trail Ghost Tour. For information, call 775-687-7410.) **72**

EDWARDS HOUSE The ghost of a maid keeps this place neat and clean, just as she did when she was alive. Built in 1883, the house is maintained by the spirit of a Paiute Indian woman, who dusts and folds clothes but refuses to do windows.

(The Edwards House is a private residence, at 204 North Minnesota St., Carson City, NV 89703.) **72**

GOVERNOR'S MANSION This stone mansion was completed in 1909 and has been haunted since the 1950s. That is when someone presented the governor with an antique mantel clock apparently accompanied by ghosts. Doors in the parlor started opening by themselves, and a cold, moving presence was detected. Ultimately, a housekeeper saw the ghosts of a woman and her eight-year-old daughter wandering through the room and into the halls.

(The governor's residence is at 606 North Mountain St., Carson City, NV 89703. Phone: 775-882-2333.) **72**

GUSTASSEN HOUSE Remodeling here shook some lost soul loose from the past. Now the ghost places fresh flowers on the doorstep. The ghostly figure passes through the front door, but the real-life tulips cannot follow. They are put in a vase of water and left on the front stoop.

(The house is a private residence located on the corner of Curry and West Robinson streets, at 602 North Curry St., Carson City, NV 89703.) **72**

NEVADA STATE MUSEUM Abe Curry was the head of the Carson Mint in the late 1800s. He built this rugged, fortresslike structure to house the U.S. Mint in 1869, and used the same type of stone to build his house two years later (see Curry House, above). Eventually the building became the headquarters for the Nevada State Museum and Historical Society. Curry's friendly spirit is felt by many here.

(The museum is at 600 North Carson St., Carson City, NV 89703. Phone: 775-687-4810. Tours of Carson City's haunted sites are organized from this site in October. For information, call 775-687-7410.) **72**

FALLON

GRIMES POINT ARCHEOLOGICAL AREA Shoshone shamans held sacred rituals at this earthquake fault area. The rocks are covered with ancient, indecipherable symbols. Some modern visitors have reported intense visions after sitting calmly on the rocks for an hour or so.

(Fallon is sixty miles east of Reno in Churchill County. The site is east of Fallon on Highway 50. For information on Nevada sites in general, call the State Tourism office at 800-638-2328.) **200**

FISH SPRING

KELSEY HOUSE This simple wood-frame house was the sight of several recent hauntings. The first series of encounters lasted from 1977 to 1981 and involved all members of the Kelsey family. A tall, mustached male ghost called Samual appeared in the kitchen and bedrooms. The manifestations centered around thirteen-year-old Jennifer, whose bed levitated on several occasions. The Steve and Mona Robinson family, who rented the house from the Kelseys in October 1989, also experienced ghosts. The visitations began with footsteps and the disembodied voice of an angry man. Garrett, their eleven-year-old son, was chased from the house one day after hearing the voices of two male and one female ghost coming from the upstairs bedrooms. His six-year-old brother Miles once levitated in his bed. In October 1990 the Robinson family could no longer tolerate the angry spirits and moved out of the house. The Kelseys sold the house in 1992.

(Fish Spring is south of Reno, near Virginia City off Highway 341. The house is a private residence in Fish Spring, NV 89410.) **72**

GOLDFIELD

OLD GOLDFIELD HOTEL Built on top of an abandoned gold mine, this 154-room hotel was first opened in 1908. Since then, it has undergone extensive renovations and added a few nonpaying guests. The hotel is considered to be home to several ghosts. In the downstairs employees' area at the west end of the hotel, Room 109 is a small room with a single bed. The room is haunted by the presence of a pregnant woman, believed to be a prostitute named Elizabeth who was chained in the room by George Winfield, the original owner of the hotel. After giving birth, the woman was left to die in the room and her baby was thrown down the old mine shaft at the northern end of the basement. Elizabeth's ghost turned up on a photograph taken in the room by a reporter from Las Vegas. On the first floor, the George Winfield Room is said to be haunted by his ghost. Untraceable cigar smoke and fresh ashes have been found there. George's presence has also been detected near the lobby staircase, where the ghosts of a midget and two small children have also been seen. The Gold Room is haunted by a ghost that "stabs" people. High psychic energy has been detected in the Theodore Roosevelt Room and a southwest room on the third floor. Some psychics say that the Goldfield Hotel is one of only seven portals to the "Other Side" that exist in the modern world. Unfortunately, the hotel is now abandoned.

(Goldfield is twenty-six miles south of Tonopah on U.S. Highway 95. Goldfield Hotel, 310 Sunday Ave. Goldfield, NV 89013. www.ghosttowns.com/states/nv/goldfield.html) **14, 101**

GOLD HILL

GOLD HILL HOTEL The victims of a mining accident here took up residence in the local hotel after they died. Employees and guests of the old Gold Hill Hotel have reported the apparitions since the turn of the century. One is William, thought to be the original owner, who died in a fire at the hotel in the late 1800s. He is a dark-haired man who smells of cigar smoke. The ghost of Rosie, a red-haired former housekeeper, smells like rose-water perfume. The original stone structure was built in 1859, thus making it Nevada's oldest hotel. A new addition was built in 1987.

(The fifteen-room Gold Hill Hotel is one mile south of Virginia City on Highway 342. Follow Highway 341 from Carson City or via Highway 342 from Reno. Gold Hill Hotel, P.O. Box 710, Virginia City, NV 89440. Phone: 775-847-0111. www.virginiacity-nv.org/gold_hill.html) **72**

LAS VEGAS

FLAMINGO HILTON The ghost of gangster Benjamin "Bugsy" Siegel haunts the Presidential Suite at this Las Vegas Strip hotel. It was Siegel's home for many years, and ever since his violent death in 1947, dozens of guests staying in the Presidential Suite have seen his specter in the bathroom or near the pool table. The green-colored bidet, toilets, and linoleum in the two bathrooms are the same ones that Siegel personally selected for the suite. He considered pistachio green to be a very "classy" color. See Virginia Hill House, Beverly Hills, California.

(Las Vegas is at the junction of U.S. Highway 95 and I-15. For information about the Las Vegas area, write the Las Vegas Visitors Bureau, 2301 East Sahara Ave., Las Vegas NV 89105. The Flamingo Hilton is on Las Vegas Blvd. between Flamingo Rd. and Sands Ave. at 3555 Las Vegas Blvd., Las Vegas, NV 89109. Phone: 702-733-3111.) **193**

LAS VEGAS HILTON The ghost of Elvis Presley is said to roam the area around the backstage elevators of this glamorous casino.

(The Las Vegas Hilton is at Paradise Road and Karen Avenue, north of the Convention Center, at 3000 Paradise Rd., Las Vegas, NV. 89109. Phone: 702-732-5111.) **81**

LUXOR PYRAMID Some Las Vegans believe this casino has brought bad luck to their gambling mecca. During construction of the four-hundred-foot golden pyramid, one worker was killed and several injured in separate accidents. Several construction workers refused to work at the site. Just as the pyramid was completed, Vegas World Sky Tower casino caught fire and suffered serious damage. Those who believe in the esoteric properties of the pyramid shape say the city will remain cursed until an artificial eye is placed at the capstone of the pyramid.

(The Luxor is between Tropicana Avenue and Sunset Road, at 3900 Las Vegas Blvd. South, Las Vegas, NV 89119. Phone: 702-262-4000.) **72**

NELLIS AIR FORCE BASE Air Force personnel and civilian mechanics at Jet Engine Intermediate Maintenance Facility Building 858 have reported encountering a ghostly gray figure and hearing disembodied footsteps at night. The "gray mass of dim light" hovers about five feet off the ground. At other times, it is observed as a brilliant ball of light about twenty feet off the ground. The unidentified specter has been sighted along the south wall, in the hanger bay, and in the hall leading to the break room. The building was constructed in the 1960s but has been expanded twice since then.

(The base is northeast of Las Vegas off Highway 604. Phone: 702-652-1110.) **72**

RACHEL

HIGHWAY 375 This isolated state road has become known as the Alien Highway, because of the many UFO sightings reported along its route. The area became famous in 1989, when government physicist Bob Lazar came forward with information that the government was operating a secret flying saucer base in the restricted area between Highway 375 and U.S. Highway 95 to the west. He claimed the government had nine UFOs at the site and was trying to reproduce alien technology. A place known as the Black Mailbox is the closest unauthorized persons can get to Area 51, the top-secret site at Papoose Lake, where the spacecraft and other top-secret projects are supposedly stored. The lake is twelve miles south of Groom Lake in an extremely classified area, officially known as Dreamland, on the huge Nevada Test Site and Nellis Air Force Base. In 1995, the government confiscated White Sides mountain and Freedom Ridge, which had provided views of the "nonexistent" base. The only remaining legal viewpoint is from Tikapoo Peak. However, the 7,900-foot-elevation site is difficult to reach and provides only a distant view of Groom Lake.

(The Black Mailbox is at Mile Marker 29.5. A better observation area is at the gravel turnoff at Marker 32.3. A road at Mile Marker 34.6 leads to White Sides, which is now off-limits to civilians. Freedom Ridge, two miles south of White Sides, is also off-limits. Tickapoo Peak is thirteen miles east of Freedom Ridge, 5.5 miles due southeast of the Highway 375/Groom Lake Road intersection. It is extremely dangerous and unlawful to trespass the secured area anywhere along Highway 375. For information on hiking tours to Tikapoo Peak, contact the Psycho Spy Network, HCR Box 38, Rachel, NV 89001.) **21, 34, 72, 126 (6/93,8/93)**

LITTLE A-LE-INN This restaurant and inn is the headquarters for UFO enthusiasts seeking to spot alien craft (see Highway 375, above). The roadhouse is covered with flying saucer memorabilia and sells UFO tapes, books, T-shirts, and other souvenirs.

(Follow I-15 northeast out of Las Vegas to Exit 64, Highway 93. From the east, take Exit 91, Highway 168, to Highway 93. Follow Highway 93 north one hundred miles to the intersection of Highway 375 at Crystal Springs. Take Highway 375 west to Mile Marker 9.7. Little A-Lee-Inn, HCR Box 45, Rachel, NV 89001. Phone: 775-729-2515.) **21, 126 (6/93)**

MORMON HILL At this point on March 21, 1938, angels appeared to Mormon leader Dr. M. L. Glendenning and conferred upon him the "keys of Aaron." The sacred monument is a good point for observing the Tikapoo Valley, site of many UFO reports. See Highway 375, above.

(The monument is near Hancock Summit at Mile Marker 37.6 on Highway 375.) **21**

TONOPAH

MIZPAH HOTEL The fifth floor of this 1908 hotel is haunted by a lady in red. Dozens of witnesses have seen the flamboyant phantom, thought to be a lady of the evening stabbed to death by a jealous lover.

(Mizpah Hotel, 100 North Main Street, Tonopah, NV 89049. Phone: 702-482-6202.) **72**

A glowing headstone is seen among the fifteen cemeteries clustered on the north end of town in Virginia City. See Cemeteries, Virginia City, Nevada   (B. A SCHAFFENBERGER)

VIRGINIA CITY

CEMETERIES Virginia City has fifteen cemeteries clustered on the north end of town. Sections are divided according to race, religion, social status, occupation, and fraternal organizations. People have reported sensing many discarnate souls here. A glowing headstone is sometimes seen by observers in town, but when they arrive at the graveyard to investigate, the stone is dark again.

(Virginia City is located at the intersection of Highway 341 and Six Mile Canyon Road in the mountains between Carson City and Reno. From Carson City, follow Highway 50 to Highway 341 north. From Reno, follow U.S. Highway 395 to Highway 341 and take the Geiger Grade to Virginia City. The graveyard is on the north outskirts of town, across a gully from the Ophir Mine, at Carson St. and Cemetery Rd. An RV park is near the entrance to the cemetery. The address is Virginia City RV Park, 355 North F St., Virginia City, NV 89440. Phone: 775-847-0999.) **72, 232**

DELTA SALOON The Suicide Table here is haunted by the ghost of Black Jake. The notorious gambler owned the Delta Saloon in the 1860s. One evening he lost a huge amount of money at this faro table, where he committed suicide by shooting himself. Afterward, players at the table reported seeing the ghost of Black Jake putting a gun to his head. Soon, no one would sit at the table, and it was retired from use.

(The Suicide Table is on display in the casino. Delta Saloon and Casino, 18 South C St., Virginia City, NV 89440. Phone: 775-847-0789.) **72, 232**

FOURTH WARD SCHOOL This four-story school has sixteen classrooms, two study halls, and accommodated over one thousand grammar and high school students. Built in 1875, it graduated its last class in 1936. A tardy ghost named "Miss Suzette" still walks across the school yard to the front steps, where she vanishes. A local couple even gave the phantom a ride one evening. They saw a woman in an old-fashioned clothes walking down the street and offered her a ride. She said that her name was Suzette and had to get to the school. When they dropped her off, she disappeared before their eyes. She is thought to be a teacher who worked at the school in 1908.

(The old school is on the corner of B St. and C St. in south Virginia City. For information, contact the Virginia City Chamber of Commerce, 131 South C St., Virginia City, NV 89440. Phone: 775-847-0311.) **72, 232**

LONGBRANCH BUILDING The muffled sounds of a child crying have been reported many times in this old building. Some believe the child ghost to be a little girl trampled by a stagecoach in front of the Longbranch in the 1870s. She was carried into the building, where she died. Sometimes happier sounds are heard coming from the old building. The eerie sounds of banjos playing and people laughing have been heard coming from the deserted building between 2:00 and 3:00 A.M.

(Today, the Longbranch Building is a series of shops near the assay office on the north edge of town.) **72**

MACKAY MANSION The apparition of a woman dressed in Victorian clothing has been seen sitting in a high-backed chair in the living room here. An upstairs room is haunted by the presence of child who likes to lie down on the freshly made bed. The mansion was built in 1860 and housed both the living quarters of entrepreneur John MacKay and the offices of the Gould and Curry Mine.

(The mansion is located between South D and Washington streets in south-central Virginia City. The address is MacKay Museum, 129 South D Street, Virginia City, NV 89440. Phone: 888-234-0680. www.mackaymansion.com) **232**

OPHIR MINE The ghost of Henry Comstock haunts the site where he discovered the "Comstock Lode" in January 1859. He lost millions of dollars when developers took over his claim. In the winter of 1874, an eerie light shot out from the mouth of mine and rose sixty feet into the air. Townspeople arrived to put out what they thought was a fire, but no smoke or flame could be detected. All they could see was the weird light coming from halfway down the shaft. The next morning, strange things were reported at the long-deserted seven-hundred-foot level. The cage would be summoned when no one was there, and odd sounds could be heard coming from that level. Investigators discovered the glowing ghost of Henry Comstock, who identified himself and said he was reclaiming his gold. Chunks of skin were hanging from his decomposing skeleton and "his eyes were an orange-yellow color with pupils that danced as if filled with blue flames." The ghoulish phantom continued to harass the miners, blowing out their candles one at a time in a row, calling the cage when no one was around, and filling the tunnels with his howling, insane laughter.

(The mine is south of D St., between Six Mile Canyon Rd. and Carson St., in north Virginia City. It is just south of the Virginia City cemeteries. The mountain of tailings from the Ophir Mine is easily visible.) **162**

ST. MARY'S ART CENTER The ghost of a white nun stays in the upstairs rooms here, and her face is frequently seen at an upper window. The two-story brick building used to be a Catholic hospital. One night in 1878, a patient in the psychiatric ward started a fire in which he and the nun on duty burned to death. The nun's spirit is tied to the place where she so selflessly served.

(The former hospital is in east Virginia City, at 55 North R St., Virginia City, NV 89440. Phone: 775-847-9973.) **232**

ST. MARY'S IN-THE-MOUNTAINS The distinctive footsteps of Father Meinecke are still heard coming from an upstairs alcove in the church. The priest, who has been dead for many years, walked with a cane. Both parishioners and visitors have reported hearing the inexplicable sounds.

(The Catholic church is on the corner of South E and Taylor streets at 111 South E St., Virginia City, NV 89440. Phone: 775-847-9099.) **232**

ST. PAUL'S EPISCOPAL CHURCH Many people have reported seeing the ghost of a woman with a shawl over her shoulders standing in an upstairs window here. Her agitated apparition turns from side to side, as if suffering some great distress. The church was built in 1876 on the site of a previous church that burned in the Great Fire of 1875, when two thousand buildings were destroyed in Virginia City.

(The church is on the corner of South F St. and Taylor St., across from St. Mary's.) **232**

SIX MILE CANYON The terrifying ghost of outlaw Jack Davis still haunts the secluded canyon where he buried his loot. Davis led a double life. He arrived in the area in 1859 and set up a livery stable in Gold Hill. In his spare time, he robbed stagecoaches, trains, and bullion wagons on the Geiger Grade. He built a small bullion mill in Six Mile Canyon and melted down his stolen gold. Then he sold it as legitimate gold bars and buried his proceeds so people would not catch on as to how rich he was. Finally, in 1870 he was caught trying to rob the Verdi train. In 1875 he was paroled, but two years later was shot in the back during an attempt to rob a stagecoach south of Eureka. It is thought that the outlaw's cache of buried gold coins is still in the canyon, but treasure seekers have been frightened away by the white, screaming specter of Jack Davis. Sometimes, his ghost sprouts wings and rises into the air.

(Six Mile Canyon is just east of Virginia City off Highway 341.) **175**

WASHOE CLUB The nebulous form of a blond-haired woman has appeared on the spiral staircase in this saloon so many times that patrons gave her a name—Lena. The unique staircase was built for the Millionaire's Club, an exclusive men's group which met in the building in the 1870s. Lena's ghost has also appeared in front of the wall across from the bar. The apparition of an old prospector has materialized on one of the stools at the end of the bar, and the ghost of a thirteen-year-old girl, thought to have been murdered in the basement, has appeared in an upstairs bedroom. Owners Doug and Sharon Truhill have reported a number of other unusual manifestations, including moving chandeliers and the presence of an "angry spirit" that breaks glasses.

(Old Washoe Club, 112 South C St., Virginia City, NV 89440. Phone: 775-847-7210.) **72**

WILD WEST MUSEUM This is one of the eeriest places in Virginia City. Hundreds of authentic artifacts are on display, as well as recreations of murder scenes and a spook room upstairs. The collection of skulls includes several from outlaws, such as the Apache Kid and a Zuni ceremonial skull adorned with turquoise.

(The museum is at 66 North C St., Virginia City, NV 89440. Phone: 775-847-0400.) **72**

NEW HAMPSHIRE

BENTON

RAVINE LODGE A lot of stories are told at this mountain lodge about the man who built it. Dr. Tom Benton called this his Tip-Top House when he finished it in the early 1800s. He anchored the building to the mountainside with heavy chains and iron rods, and built a laboratory to study medicine. The curious doctor is said to have searched for the elixir of youth in his mountain hideaway, and not a few Bentonites thought he experimented on kidnapped babies. There seems to be no end to the adventures of Dr. Benton, including tales of his ghost (or perhaps the immortal doctor himself) dragging heavy chains behind him, late on moonlit nights.

(Benton is in the White Mountain National Forest in Grafton County in northern New Hampshire. The town is located eight miles from the Vermont border on Highway 116. Ravine Lodge is near the top of Mount Moosilauke, nine miles south of Benton.) **49**

CONCORD

TIO JUAN'S RESTAURANT This restaurant is haunted by unidentifiable voices in the dining room and kitchen. Sometimes it sounds like a convention of invisible ghosts and goblins.

(The town of Concord is at the junction of I-93 and I-89, north of Manchester. Tio Juan's, 1 Bicentennial Square, Concord NH 03301. Phone: 603-224-2821.) **101**

EAST KINGSTON

OLD PHILBRICK HOUSE When Keri Marshall Tucker and her husband Rich began restoring their Colonial Cape home in 1988, they did not realize they were disturbing spirits in the old structure. Unexplainable loud noises, ghostly lights in vacant rooms, and the mysterious workings of antique clocks became commonplace events. Police were called on a number of occasions but never found prowlers or anything out of place. The identity of the presumed ghost has not been determined, but the Tuckers suspect members of the Philbrick family, who built the farmhouse in the 1830s.

(East Kingston in the southeast corner of New Hampshire, off Highway 108. The house is east of town off Highway 107, at 47 Depot Road, East Kingston, NH 03827.) **134**

EATON CENTER

TOLL HILL An old farmhouse on top of this hill is haunted by the ghost of a white horse. During a blizzard the horse sought shelter in the abandoned building but was trapped inside by drifting snow. The animal's body was found in the spring of 1925. For years afterward, people reported seeing the animal's ghost still trying to break out of the house.

(Eaton Center is in east-central New Hampshire, south of Conway Lake in Carroll County. Follow Highway 153 south from town 3.5 miles to East Madison. Turn

east onto Horse Leg Hill Rd. and follow it 1.5 miles to the last house on the left. This is the old farmhouse, which is now a private residence. It is known locally as the old David Thurston place, or Baird farm.) **36**

EXETER

UFO SIGHTINGS While Norman Muscarello was hitchhiking to his home in Exeter late on the night of September 3, 1965, he saw a large, round, glowing object "float down from the sky" and hover directly over two houses. Muscarello hid in a ditch until the UFO moved away. As soon as he reached Exeter, Muscarello went into the police station to report what he had seen. The duty officer radioed patrolman Eugene Bertrand to investigate. Bertrand radioed back that he was already talking with a woman in a parked car who had just seen a large UFO. Officer Bertrand returned to the station to pick up Muscarello, so the man could show him where he had encountered the object. When the two men arrived at the spot, they observed a gigantic, glowing spherical object hovering about a hundred feet above the ground. A few minutes later, patrolman David Hunt arrived at the scene and witnessed the same UFO. They described the craft as ninety feet in diameter, emitting no sounds, with brilliant red lights which flashed in sequence. The strange object moved even closer to the ground then drifted away, pausing at intervals. Finally, it disappeared to the east. This area was the site of a flurry of UFO activity that began in March 1965 and is documented in John Fuller's *Incident at Exeter.*

(The town of Exeter is just southwest of the junction of Highways 85 and 101, south of Portsmouth.) **61, 139, 190**

HENNIKER

OCEAN-**B**ORN **M**ARY **H**OUSE The ghost of a remarkable woman born on an Irish immigrant ship in 1720 still haunts the countryside where she lived out her final years. Captain Don Pedro, a notorious pirate, had captured the sailing ship *Wolf* in the waters off Massachusetts. When he saw a red-haired baby born that very day to the ship's captain, he promised to spare the ship and passengers if the child were named after his beloved mother. Thus did Mary Wallace, better known as Ocean-Born Mary, get her name. She grew into a strikingly beautiful woman, married, and had four

sons. Unfortunately Mary was widowed at an early age and had to struggle to make ends meet. Years later, Captain Pedro retired to a large house on a hill overlooking Henniker. The captain set out to search for Mary, and when he found her, asked her to marry him and live in his mansion with her children. Mary accepted and lived happily for many years. Then one day she found the bludgeoned body of her husband in their garden. Someone had murdered him, perhaps in a dispute over buried treasure. She interred her husband's body under a huge hearthstone in the kitchen. Mary died in 1814, at the age of ninety-four. She had outlived all her family, and the deserted mansion fell into ruins. The apparition of a six-foot-tall woman, with red hair and flashing green eyes started to appear in the upstairs windows or on the central staircase. Some even saw Mary's ghost riding through the hills in a phantom coach drawn by four horses. Her apparition was often seen in the yard, throwing something down the well. Later, the house was renovated and new owners moved in. Many of them reported feeling the presence of Ocean-Born Mary. Her ghost was once seen helping family members repair a garage during a fierce storm, and several subsequent owners believe her presence protects the house from harm. Recently two New Hampshire state troopers reported seeing the specter of a tall, red-haired woman wearing colonial clothing crossing the road just below the old mansion.

(Henniker is in southwest New Hampshire on Highway 114. Mary's wood-frame, two-story house is now a private residence. Mary Wallace, Ocean-Born Mary, is buried in the Centre Cemetery behind the town hall in Henniker. www.hauntedhouses.com/states/nh/house2.htm) **5, 15, 68, 69 72, 80, 82, 89, 175, 188**

LANCASTER

ALIEN **A**BDUCTION The famous Hill abduction case took place near here on September 19, 1961. Betty and Barney Hill were returning from a vacation in Canada to their home in Portsmouth, when they spotted a peculiar light in the sky. The light seemed to follow them for a while, then started getting larger as it approached. Finally, it hovered directly in front of them, about seventy feet off the ground, a hundred feet away. Barney used a pair of binoculars and saw five or more humanoid figures behind a double row of windows in the craft. The events of the next two hours were retrieved by hypnosis. They both remembered being taken aboard the vessel by eight or more aliens and physically examined. When Betty asked one of the extraterrestrials where they were from, he showed her a star map. That map, which Betty reproduced under hypnosis, strongly resembles a cluster of stars near the Zeta Reticuli constellation. The configuration was unknown to astronomers at the time.

(Lancaster is in northern New Hampshire at the junction of U.S. Highways 2 and 3. The incident started south of town on U.S. Highway 3, when the Hills spotted the light in the sky. The UFO followed them to the White Mountains and landed near Indian Head. The next thing they remembered was driving the car near Ashland two hours later. Ashland is thirty-five miles south of Indian Head on Highway 3.) **126 (7/74, 11/91), 139, 149, 190**

NASHUA

COUNTRY TAVERN The ghost of Elizabeth Ford haunts this building, which dates from 1741. She was murdered by her sea captain husband, who returned after ten months at sea to find his wife had just given birth. The enraged man is said to have buried the bodies of Elizabeth and her illegitimate child not far from the house. Elizabeth's playful ghost has been known to entertain children, help with housecleaning, and move small objects such as glasses, plates, and knickknacks. She also likes to lift the hair of women in the ladies room and hide their personal possessions. Dozens of employees and customers have sensed her presence. Elizabeth's apparition has been seen in the upstairs dining room and staring out a window in a part of the building that used to be a barn. She is described as about five feet, seven inches tall, with long white hair and wearing a flowing white gown.

(Nashua is northwest of Boston on U.S. Highway 3. The tavern is located at 452 Amherst St., Nashua, NH 03063. Phone: 603-889-5871. www.countrytavern. org) **134**

NORTH SALEM

MYSTERY HILL This thirty-acre sacred site is probably the oldest surviving settlement on the North America continent. It has been called America's Stonehenge. A 4.5-ton sacrificial altar here is grooved for the collection of blood. Underneath the altar, a speaking tube runs to a huge underground chamber, 22 feet wide and 6.5 feet high. This oracle chamber contains a drawing of an ibex and other mysterious carvings. One high-walled corridor leads to a central temple room, and the outlying stones are arranged to detect the change of seasons and the directions of the compass. The Tomb of Lost Souls is the only chamber with an east-west axis. Early colonists discovered the unusual grouping of stone walls and named it Mystery Hill. They avoided the area and had no idea of its extensive underground features. Early archaeologists assumed that Mystery Hill was built by Indians, but recent evidence suggests it was built by a Mediterranean civilization around 2025 B.C. Pieces of charcoal wedged between stones at the site have been carbon-dated at 4,000 years old, and several scholars believe the workmanship and carvings at Mystery Hill are Minoan or Phoenician. The popular G-stone at the site is actually two letters from the Phoenician alphabet, and rock carvings show outlines of Phoenician sailing vessels. The gods worshiped at this site were certainly not the gods of the American Indians. In fact, some researchers believe the site was dedicated to the ancient god Baal. After visiting the site in 1937, H. P. Lovecraft was inspired to write his famous short story, "The Dunwich Horror."

(North Salem is twelve miles east of Nashua on Highway 111. Take Exit 3 east from I-93 and follow Highway 111 for five miles to the junction of Island Pond Rd. and Haverhill Rd. Go south on Haverhill Road to the park entrance. America's Stonehenge, P.O. Box 84, North Salem, NH 03073. Phone: 603-893-8300. www. stonehengeusa.com) **15, 32, 50, 53 (11/77, 6/92), 56, 72, 99, 144, 196**

OSSIPEE

OSSIPEE TRIANGLE The frequency of mysterious events that occur in this area has led some researchers to compare it to the Bermuda Triangle. According to Indian legend, the area around Ossipee Lake was sacred. The lake is surrounded by the remains of one-hundred-million-year-old volcanoes, and there are a number of kettle lakes carved by ancient glaciers. One of these is Mystery Pond, now called Snake Pond, which some believe is so deep it is nearly bottomless. In 1800 a burial ground was discovered that contained as many as ten thousand bodies arranged in concentric circles. Some archaeologists believe the site was created by an ancient Celtic tribe. UFOs are also seen in the area. Some of them have been observed plunging into the deep ponds, which might be connected by underground caverns.

(The Ossipee Triangle includes most of Carrol County in eastern New Hampshire. At the center is Ossipee Lake.) **72**

RACCOON MOUNTAIN ROAD For over a century a phantom horse has been reported on the road that ascends this mountain near the town of Center Ossipee. Legend says it is the horse of Adam Brown, a local grist-mill owner who was murdered on the road in the 1830s. During the ambush, Brown's horse slipped off an embankment and fell into a ravine, where it died a slow and painful death. The ghostly animal is seen galloping up behind observers but never catching up.

(Center Ossipee is on Ossipee Lake in eastern New Hampshire, at the junction of Highways 16 and 25. Follow the Moultonville Rd. west out of Center Ossipee for a half-mile to the Moultonville Mill Pond Bridge. Just before the bridge, go north on the Raccoon Mountain Road.) **36**

PETERBOROUGH

MACDOWALL COLONY This artists and writer colony is haunted by the spirits of several former residents, including writers Elinor Wylie and Edward Arlington Robinson. Wylie's ghost is said to still reside in the Watson Studio building.

(Peterborough is at the junction of U.S. Highway 202 and Highway 101 in southwestern New Hampshire. The colony is one mile west of town.) **49**

PORTSMOUTH

GENERAL JONATHAN MOULTON HOME The wife of a legendary British general returned to haunt her home. Abigail Moulton was the first wife of General Jonathan Moulton, who gained a reputation as a ruthless man during the French and Indian wars of the eigh-

teenth century. Abigail died under mysterious circumstances in 1774. On the day of her funeral, her husband stripped all the jewels and rings from her corpse and immediately gave them to his second wife, Sarah Emery. That is when Abigail's ghost started showing up. One night, a white phantom grabbed Sarah's hand in the middle of the night and stripped the rings from her fingers. The angry specter disappeared before the eyes of the startled general and his new wife, and the jewelry was never seen again. General Moulton died in 1787, but that did not stop Abigail's ghost from returning. The case became so famous that John Greenleaf Whittier wrote a poem about it, entitled "The New Wife and the Old." Finally, in the 1850s the house was moved and an exorcism performed. That seemed to rid the place of its ghostly visitor.

(The house is in Hampton, which is fifteen miles south of Portsmouth in the southeastern corner of New Hampshire, at the junction of U.S. Highway 1 and Highway 51. The General Moulton Home is now a private residence in Hampton, NH 03842.) **38, 188**

SISE INN A suite in this Queen-Anne-styled inn is haunted by a peculiar spirit who likes to steal keys and throw ice cubes. Guests and employees have reported many strange phenomena associated with the suite. Keys to Suite 214 seem to disappear, and sometimes the door will not open no matter what key is used. At other times, the door is found open for no apparent reason. Trails of ice cubes lead from the ice machine into the empty room, where the ice is scattered on the floor. Once, a potted plant flew off the coffee table, which caused a terrified guest to demand an "unhaunted" room. The house was built in 1881 and was used a private residence until the 1930s. It was renovated and opened as an inn in 1986.

(Portsmouth is sixty miles north of Boston on Highway 95. The inn is in Old Town, at 40 Court St., Portsmouth, NH 03801, Phone: 877-SISE-INN. www.someplacesdifferent.com/sise.htm.) **133**

NEW JERSEY

BERNARDSVILLE

BERNARDSVILLE PUBLIC LIBRARY The ghost here is so active, the staff issued it a library card. Phyllis Parker's specter was first encountered in January 1877, in a private residence that now houses part of the library. The building had been converted from a tavern that was constructed during the Revolutionary War. Vealtown Tavern was the scene of a tragic love affair between the innkeeper's daughter and a tenant, Dr. Byram. Just after the two were married, Dr. Byram was hanged by General Anthony Wayne for being a British spy, and his lifeless body was delivered to the tavern. Not knowing what was in the large pine box, Phyllis opened it. On seeing the bugeyed corpse of her beloved, she became hysterical and suffered a nervous breakdown. Her insane weeping is still heard in the old section of the library, which consists of the meeting room and the public reading room (where the casket was opened). After renovations in 1974, employees started seeing the apparition of Phyllis moving through the old wing. A videotape recording of a séance, held in 1987 in an effort to contact her spirit, can be played back by patrons in the local history room. In November 1989, a child saw the ghost of a woman in a long white dress in the reading room.

(Bernardsville is eight miles south of Morristown on U.S. Highway 202, west of Newark. The library is downtown at 1 Anderson Hill Rd., Bernardsville, NJ 07924 Phone: 908-766-0118. www.bernardsville.org) **14, 72, 101**

BLOOMFIELD

BLOOMFIELD POLICE BARRACKS The spirit of a gambler haunts this area. He was robbed and murdered by a riverboat captain on the Morris Canal. Seen many times over the last century, the ghost is said to be still searching for his lost money.

(Bloomfield is off the Garden State Parkway north of Newark. The area is between Exit 153 and Highway 3 on the Parkway.) **72**

BURLINGTON

BURLINGTON COUNTY PRISON A cell on the third floor of this old prison is haunted by the presence of Joseph Clough, convicted of murder for beating his mistress to death with a table leg. Clough was chained to the floor of Cell 5 for many months, before he was finally hanged in the 1850s. The sounds of those heavy chains and Clough's incessant moaning are still heard in Cell 5. Sometimes, inmates see cigarettes float in midair, and several guards have reported sensing a presence in the cell when no one is physically there.

(Burlington is on the Delaware River, off U.S. Highway 130 between Philadelphia and Trenton. The prison is located on High St. Burlington City, NJ 08016.) **72**

HALL-DOANE ACADEMY This Catholic school for boys and girls is haunted by the ghost of Bishop George Washington Doane, who founded the academy 156 years ago. His presence is felt by students, teachers, and custodians. Students have nicknamed the Gothic redbrick building "Doane's Dungeon."

(The Hall-Doane Academy is owned and operated by St. Mary's Episcopal Church. Hall-Doane Academy, 145 W. Broad St., Burlington, NJ 08015. Phone 609-386-0902.) **72**

CAMDEN

MARTIN HOUSE A sixty-year-old, three-story tenement building in this middle-class neighborhood was haunted by two ghosts for nearly thirty years, until the structure was torn down. The apparitions of a woman and her small son appeared before several generations of the Martin family, who lived in the house for over three decades. The child ghost played with the Martin children and even crawled into their beds at night.

(Camden is across the Delaware River from Philadelphia. The tenement house, which has been torn down, was located at 522 North Fifth Ave., Camden, NJ 08102.) **85, 89**

CAPE MAY

CAPE MAY COUNTY HISTORICAL MUSEUM Employees and visitors at this county museum have reported encountering the apparition of a man, or hearing his deep voice. This museum is housed in a 1700s wood-frame house, built by John Holmes, the presumed ghost.

(Cape May is at the extreme southern tip of New Jersey, at the end of the Garden State Parkway. The house is the headquarters of the Cape May Historical Society, 504 Route 9 North, Cape May, NJ 08204. Phone: 609-465-3535.) **178**

HIGBEE BEACH The sand dunes on this beach are the stomping grounds of two ghosts. The most frequently seen ghost is an elderly black man, who was the slave of plantation owner Old Man Higbee. The black man's ghost is said to keep vigil over his master's grave near the beach. Sometimes, in the early morning hours, the pale gray, glowing ghost of Old Man Higbee himself is seen gliding over the dunes toward the water.

(Higbee Beach is on the bay side of Cape May, near the lighthouse.) **178**

KELTIE'S NEWS AND BOOKS The ghostly sounds of women giggling, books that fly through the air, and the apparition of a man in a white coat are a few of the unexplainable things that go on in this bookstore. The building is more than 140 years old and was moved from a beachfront lot to its present location in a downtown mall. The apparition is thought to be Dr. Loomis, a dentist who once had an office in the building in its former location.

(Keltie's News and Books, Washington Street Mall, Cape May, NJ 08204.) **178**

QUEENS HOTEL This quaint inn is haunted by an unknown presence. Objects and furniture in the Plum Room and the Palm Room have a way of moving by themselves. Sometimes an unseen presence bumps against the beds in those rooms. Both are on the third floor of this inn, which used to be a fancy gambling hall and whorehouse. In those days, the ladies' quarters were found on the third floor.

(The bed-and-breakfast inn is in the Historic District, at 601 Columbia Ave., Cape May, NJ 08204. Phone: 609-884-1666.) **178**

WASHINGTON INN This house was already a century old when it was opened as an inn in the 1940s. The building was renovated many times and was once moved to another position on the property, only to be returned to its original location. The foyer to the inn is the most haunted spot. The gentle voice of a long-dead woman is heard, and sometimes she even calls employees by name. They have christened the ghost Elizabeth.

(The inn and restaurant is at the corner of Washington St. and Jefferson St. at 801 Washington St. Cape May, NJ 08204. Phone: 609-884-5697. www.washingtoninn.com) **178**

WINTERWOOD GIFT SHOP The spirits of two spinster sisters will not leave their family home. Their soft voices and dainty footsteps continue to be heard throughout the house, which was built in 1722 by Joshua Hildreth. A white-robed figure has been observed drifting from the front lawn to a burial plot on the property, and another misty form has been seen floating in a doorway inside the house. They are thought to be the Hildreth sisters. Hester Hildreth died in 1948, and her sister Lucille joined her in 1954. The two were as inseparable in life as they are in death.

(The house is on U.S. Highway 9, about six miles north of Cape May, at the southernmost tip of the state. Hildreth House is now Winterwood, a Christmas gift shop in Rio Grande. A wooden plaque on the side of the building details its history. Winterwood Gift Shop, 518 Washington St., Cape May, NJ 08204. Phone: 609-884-8949.) **178**

WINWARD HOUSE INN The Wicker Room on the third floor of this charming inn is haunted by the ghost of a temperamental Irish maid. The usually friendly spirit has been encountered by a number of guests, one of whom reported finding the ghost sitting defiantly on her bed. The house was built in 1905 by Philadelphia lawyer George Baum. It became a boarding house in 1940 and was remodeled into an inn in 1977.

(Winward House Inn, 24 Jackson St., Cape May, NJ 08204. Phone: 609-884-3368. www.windwardhouseinn. com) **178**

DENNISVILLE

HENRY LUDLAM INN Henry Ludlam built this house in the late 1700s. The building is haunted by his descendants, Jonathan and Rachel Ludlum. The unexplained events include the sound of shattering glass. Jonathan was known to be a cavalier gentleman, who some say made his living as a pirate on the Delaware Bay.

(Dennisville is on Highway 47 in Gloucester County, south New Jersey. The Henry Ludlam Inn is just south of Dennisville at 1336 Highway 47. Phone: 609-861-5847.) **178**

ELIZABETH

UNION COUNTY COURTHOUSE The pathetic and confused apparition of Hannah Caldwell has been seen in this old courthouse. Hannah was killed by a stray musket ball during the Revolutionary War.

(The town of Elizabeth is just south of Newark on I-95. The courthouse is off U.S. Highway 1/9 Union County Courthouse, 2 Broad St., Elizabeth, NJ 07201 908-659-4100.) **72**

HACKENSACK

RIVERSEDGE MANOR The ghost of General F. W. A. Von Steuben, a German supporter of the Colonies during the Revolutionary War, appeared to a tourist in his former home in 1951. He was seated in a chair in a second-floor parlor, then got up and talked to the woman. In a faraway voice, the revenant asked several questions about George Washington and the affairs of the nation. Von Steuben seemed very surprised when told the date, and then suddenly vanished from view.

The ghost of General Von Steuben, a Colonial supporter, appeared in his former home, dubbed Riversedge Manor. See Riversedge Manor, Hackensack, New Jersey (STEVE HEALEY)

(Hackensack is east of Paterson in northeast New Jersey. Take the Highway 17 exit off I-80. The house is a historical museum one mile north of Hackensack. Riversedge Manor, Riversedge, NJ 07646.) **86**

HOWELL TOWNSHIP

PINE BARRENS These are the haunts of the Jersey Devil. The Devil is a furry creature with two-foot-wide bat wings, the head of a horse or ram, and a long tri-pointed tail. It is the size of a large crane with a thick neck and has long hind legs with three toes. Legend says the mutated beast was found in 1735 by Abigaile and Arthur Leeds, who raised it as their own child. After they died, the Jersey Devil survived in the wild pine barrens, perhaps breeding with other animals. In 1951 a group of people gathered at the Duport Clubhouse in Gibbstown witnessed the creature staring in a window. In 1960, the Jersey Devil was encountered near Mays Landing. Sightings in the Pine Barrens reached a peak in 1975 to 1976. According to writer Henry Charlton Beck: "Where stunted pines of burned-over forest are revealed in darksome pools, the Jersey Devil lurks."

(Howell Township is on the east central coast of New Jersey. Follow Highway 33, south of Asbury Park at Ocean Grove, west to Howell Township. The Jersey Devil was raised at Leeds Point, which is in Whitesbog, near Smithville. The Devil has been reported in the cemeteries, coastal pinelands, and marshes throughout Howell Township.) **15, 34, 139, 149, 175**

MIDLAND PARK

CRAYHAY MANSION Built in 1864, this is one of New Jersey's most famous haunted houses. Most of the ghosts originate with the Crayhay family, who lived here from 1906 to 1934. The spirit of Max Crayhay, who committed suicide in the barn, haunts the downstairs hall. The presence of a neighbor girl named Rose haunts the upstairs hallway. She fell to her death while trying to climb out an upstairs window to elope with a servant who had gotten her pregnant. The ghost of an elderly woman, thought to be a former owner shot and killed in a robbery, was seen in an upstairs bedroom. Also, the wraith of a small boy who died in an accident here is seen throughout the house. The phantom of a yellow and white cat frequents a small room on the third floor and can be felt as a warm spot wherever it goes. Artist Ethelyn Woodlock lived here for twenty-seven years and used to open the house for tours. Hundreds of people witnessed ghostly manifestations. The attempts of Catholic, Episcopal, and Buddhist priests and psychics, such as Ingo Swann and Karlis Osis, to free the building of its spirits have proved unsuccessful.

(The three-story, mansard-roofed house, also known as the Pink House, is a private residence, on Franklin St. Midland Park, NJ 07432.) **53 (5/88), 72, 135**

MORRISTOWN

JIMMY'S RESTAURANT Built in 1749 by John Sayre, this family estate passed into the hands of Samuel Sayre in the early 1800s. In 1833, he hired Antoine LeBanc, an unemployed sailor from the West Indies, as a farmhand. Thinking the family had a large sum of money,

LeBanc killed Samuel, his wife, and his young daughter Phoebe. LeBanc was caught and hanged. The house gained a reputation for being haunted, which continued when it was turned into a restaurant in 1949. Unexplainable phenomena still occur at the eatery, although there is some debate as to the identity of the ghost. The owners prefer to think of it as innocent little Phoebe Sayre, but others insist it is the vengeful spirit of Antoine LeBanc.

(The restaurant, formerly the Society Hill Restaurant, is at 217 South St., Morristown, NJ 07960. Phone: 973-455-7000. www.jimmysmorristown.com) **101, 135**

PYRAMID MOUNTAIN HISTORICAL AREA Psychics believe this park is the source of the most powerful earth energy in New Jersey. A glacial feature known as Tripod Rock is said to focus the invisible energy. The 160-ton boulder is supported 2.5 feet off the ground by three smaller rocks. Some evidence suggests that the site was used by ancient people to determine the summer solstice.

(Pyramid Mountain is five miles north of the intersection of I-80 and I-287. For maps and information, write the Morris County Park Commission, P.O. Box 1295, Morristown, NJ 07960. Phone: 973-326-7600. www.parks.morris.nj.us) **99**

WATER'S EDGE CAFE Several ghosts lodge at this turn-of-the-century inn, but they did not make themselves known until the 1960s, when an Englishman bought the building. The most frequent visitor is the dark figure of a heavyset man that appears in the lounge or on the staircase. The presence once spoke to the proprietor and told him that his name was Armon Hirsuit, although no one has been able to find a record of such a person's existence.

(The café is on Lake Swannanoa in Jefferson Township, Morris County.) **72**

NEWARK

CENTRAL STATION Regularly at midnight on the tenth day of nearly every month during the 1870s, a ghost train pulled into this Victorian railroad depot. No one ever saw anything, but hundreds of witnesses reported hearing the engine's whistle and the screeching of iron wheels against the rails as the invisible train passed through the station. On one occasion, nearly six hundred people witnessed the phenomenon, but fortunately, the so-called Express Train to Hell never stopped to pick up passengers.

(The station is off Clinton Ave. in Newark.) **142**

NEWARK HOUSING DEVELOPMENT One of the most documented cases of poltergeist activity lasted two weeks in the apartment of Mrs. Mabelle Clark. It all began on May 6, 1961, when her thirteen-year-old grandson, Ernest Rivers, was doing his homework on the kitchen table. To his amazement, a pepper shaker floated from the stove and landed beside him. For the next two weeks, plates, cups, bowls, glasses, ashtrays, and other fragile objects sailed across the tiny apartment and smashed to the floor. Mrs. Clark tried to keep the unexplainable events secret, because she did not want to be evicted from the apartment where she had lived for twenty years. But before long, representatives from the Newark Housing Authority were knocking at her door. When the officials beheld the unseen force wrecking havoc on the apartment, they brought in a team of investigators. Word of the case spread, and hordes of reporters and curiosity seekers descended on the building. There were so many people around that over fifty paranormal events were observed by multiple witnesses. Professor Charles Wrege of New York University witnessed many of the events and declared that he thought it was impossible that anyone could be faking them. On May 12, a heavy steam iron floated from the linen closet into Mrs. Clark's bedroom, in full view of two persons. On May 13, Dr. Wrege saw a table lamp fly across the living room and a glass rise in midair, break to pieces, then fall to the floor in slow motion. That same evening, Ernest's uncle, William Hargwood, was attacked by a sudden barrage of small objects. The phenomena stopped when young Ernest was removed from the apartment. Parapsychologists surmised that the adolescent was the source of the poltergeist activity. He was a deeply troubled youth, whose mother had murdered his prizefighter father five years earlier. Just before the poltergeist activity began, Ernest's mother escaped from a woman's reformatory and was not apprehended until a month later.

(The four-room apartment is on the first floor of the large housing development complex on Rose St., Newark, NJ 07108. www.haunted-places.com/newjersey.htm.) **108**

PHILLIPSBURG

HUNT HOMESTEAD The ghost of a woman wearing a dark cloak and hood passes by the kitchen window here. She proceeds toward the back door and then vanishes into thin air. The woman's apparition has followed the same routine hundreds of times. The phenomenon began shortly after the building was renovated in 1976. Parts of the house were built in 1772 by Edward Hunt, but the main structure was completed in 1825 by his grandson. The man died in the house in 1864, and his wife Mary Insley Hunt lived there until her death in 1882.

(Phillipsburg is on Highway 57, across the Delaware River from Allentown, Pennsylvania. The Homestead's mailing address is Box 135, RD No. 1, Phillipsburg, NJ 08865.) **14, 101**

Sunnybank was home to Albert Payson Terhune. The ghost of his beloved mongrel has been spotted on the property. See Sunnybanks, Pompton Lakes, New Jersey (STEVE HEALEY)

POMPTON LAKES

SUNNYBANK Sunnybank was the home of Albert Payson Terhune for more than thirty years. The noted author wrote many popular stories about dogs and raised collies on his country estate. One day in March, 1916, two of his prized collies, Lad and Rex, got into a horrible battle. The fighting started in the woods and moved to the front lawn, where both dogs tore savagely at each other. Rex had Lad pinned and was gnawing at his throat, when Terhune took a hunting knife and stabbed Rex. Rex died immediately, and it took Lad months to recover. About a year afterward, a friend visiting Terhune described a peculiar-looking, mongrel collie dog he had seen on the property. The description fit Rex perfectly, even to a large scar he had. Later another friend saw the ghost of Rex at the feet of Terhune, who was sleeping in a chair. The phantom dog was looking up at his master with "a kind of pleading adoration."

(Sunnybank is now part of the Terhune Memorial Park in Passaic County in Wayne, New Jersey. In Wayne Township, follow the Hamburg Turnpike one mile past U.S. Highway 202 intersection to Terhune Drive. Go up the hill half a mile to the park entrance.) **36, 37, 50, 53 (6/77)**

PORT MONMOUTH

SPY HOUSE A ghostly lady in white descends the stairs from the attic here and walks into the Blue and White Room on the second floor. Once inside, the apparition leans over a nonexistent bed or crib and tucks in the covers. Then, she turns slowly away and vanishes. In July 1975, in the same room, a group of visitors saw the lid on a sewing machine pop open and the machine start to operate with no one pumping the foot pedal. An unidentified presence also haunts the entrance room on the first floor, as if it is waiting for someone to arrive. The ghost of a full-bearded man with a top hat has been seen in the first floor hall. Although parts of the two-story wooden house date back to 1648, the main structure was built in the late 1690s by Daniel Seabrook. The house remained in his family for 250 years, and today it is considered to be one of the nation's most haunted places. There have been over seventy sightings of ghosts here. The place is called Spy House, because the British believed someone in the house was spying on their naval operations in 1778. They even attempted to burn the house down to stop the spying activity. However, the real spy was a man named John Stillwell, who lived nearby on Garrett's Hill.

(Follow the Garden State Parkway to Highway 36. Go east for ten miles to Port Monmouth, which is on Sandy Hook Bay. The address of the Spy House Museum is 119 Port Monmouth Rd., Port Monmouth, NJ 07758. Phone: 732-787-1807.) **86, 133**

RINGWOOD

RINGWOOD MANOR This majestic mansion was built in 1807 and is home to at least two ghosts. The first is thought to be General Robert Erskine, who built the first house on this property in 1762. The second might be Jackson White, a strange and restless spirit.

Two ghosts haunt this 1807 mansion. See Ringwood Manor, Saddle River, New Jersey (STEVE HEALEY)

He was a mixture of black, Indian, and white, the descendant of runaway slaves who settled in this valley during the Civil War. The ghosts' distinctive footsteps are heard throughout the house, and the downstairs corridors and the upstairs hallway outside the main bedroom are the most frequently haunted areas. See Ringwood Manor Cemetery below.

(Ringwood is on the Saddle River near Saddle Brook, which is just east of Paterson in northeast New Jersey. Go east on I-80 from Paterson and take the Highway 17 North exit. Follow Highway 511 to Sloatsburg Rd. in Bergen County. Take Sloatsburg Rd. to Ringwood Rd. West, which leads to Ringwood Manor Park. Ringwood Manor, Saddle Brook, NJ 07662. www.hauntedhouses. com/states/nj/house.htm) **89, 101**

RINGWOOD MANOR CEMETERY On dark, moonless nights, the ghost of Robert Erskine can be seen sitting on top of his tombstone here. Sometimes he swings a lantern in one hand, and at other times he manifests as a blob of blue light. The strange light has been known to follow cars on Ringwood Road or escort visitors from his grave back to the bridge that leads out of the cemetery. General Erskine built Ringwood Manor in 1762 and is buried in the small family cemetery there. One night not long after he was buried, a brick mysteriously popped out of the side of his vault. It is said his spirit escaped the grave that night and has never returned. See Ringwood Manor, above.

(The cemetery is in Ringwood Manor Park. Just before the manor house, turn left onto Farm Rd. and park. Follow the dirt road on foot to the graveyard.) **15, 72**

TOMS RIVER

GARDEN STATE PARKWAY This highway is haunted by the Parkway Phantom, the ghost of a man waving his arms as he tries to cross the road. He is very tall and wears a long topcoat belted at the waist. The strangest thing is the way the phantom bends its arms from the elbows, moving both at the same time. According to researcher Mark Sceurman, it looks like a "macabre football cheer." The sightings date back to 1955, when the Garden State Parkway was first completed. The state police will not comment on the reports but do admit to a larger than usual number of accidents in the area. Most of the sightings take place at Exit 82 at Highway 37 and along an eight-mile stretch of the Garden State Parkway in the vicinity of the Toms River Barracks of the New Jersey State Police.

(The town of Toms River is in east central New Jersey at the junction of the Garden State Parkway and Highway 37.) **72**

TOTOWA

LAUREL GROVE CEMETERY Numerous passing motorists have seen the ghost of a young woman in a white wedding gown walking down the road near this cemetery.

(Totowa is in Passaic County, across the Passaic River from Browertown Rd. in West Paterson. The cemetery is east of Exit 55 on I-80.) **72**

UNION

GALLOPING HILLS GOLF COURSE The specter of a headless horseman has been reported by several credible witnesses here. It is unlikely that he is looking for golf balls.

(Union is a southwest suburb of Newark, in the Kenilworth area. The town is at the junction of the Garden State Parkway and U.S. Highway 22. Galloping Hills

Golf Course, Galloping Hill Rd., Union, NJ 07083. Phone: 908-686-1556.) **72**

WOODSTOWN

SEVEN STARS TAVERN This old tavern, built in 1762, was once called the most haunted house in New Jersey. A bevy of noisy ghosts can be heard climbing the stairs to the attic rooms. The restless spirits sound as if they are arguing with one another, and the sounds of pushing and shoving fill the hallway. Farm workers who stayed at the home in the 1930s reported seeing the ghost of a man with a rope around his neck. Hideous gurgling sounds came from the ghost and bloody foam oozed from his mouth. He pointed plaintively to the noose around his throat, as if he wanted them to remove it. The ghost is said to be that of a Tory spy hanged from an attic beam just before the Revolutionary War.

(Woodstown is in Salem County in southwestern New Jersey, at the junction of U.S. Highway 40 and Highway 45. The two-story brick building is now a private residence on the corner of Kings Highway and Woodstown-Auburn Rd. near Woodstown.) **101, 168**

YELLOW FRAME

YELLOW FRAME CHURCH Local legend says the ghost of a former minister returns to haunt his church at night. The preacher died after giving his first sermon here and was buried in the churchyard. Sometime in the early 1800s, his body was exhumed and moved two miles away to the Johnsburg Cemetery. No one knows why the body was moved, but many believe his spirit is returning to its original resting place. The ghost is especially active around Halloween, when eerie organ music and lights flashing on and off are reported by people walking by the church at night.

(Yellow Frame is in northwestern New Jersey, on Highway 94 in southwest Sussex County. The church is located on Yellow Frame Rd., Yellow Frame, NJ 07860.) **87**

NEW MEXICO

ALAMOGORDO

ALAMOGORDO FIREBALLS Strange green fireballs that darted about in the sky were observed here from the 1950s through the 1970s. A "flap" of spectacular sightings occurred in 1957. Several sightings were reported over the Mescalero Apache Reservation in October of that year. At 1:00 P.M. on November 4, a glowing oval object flew over Highway 54 near Orogrande and caused cars to stall. The automobiles' lights, radios, and engines all failed at the same time. An electronics engineer in one of the cars reported that he felt waves of heat as the object passed overhead. The exposed portions of his skin later became reddened and itchy. At the same location, at 9:20 A.M. on November 7, a couple spotted an identical object and reported that their speedometer appeared to malfunction. All of the UFO reports led famous meteor researcher Dr. Lincoln La Paz to set up a research project to study them. Although the sightings have never been explained, Air Force security personnel treated them very seriously. See Lubbock, Texas.

(Alamogordo is at the junction of U.S. Highways 54 and 70 in Otero County, in south-central New Mexico. Many sightings occurred near Vaughn and at various locations in the Sacramento Mountains east of town. The reservation is about thirty miles north of Alamogordo in the Three Rivers area. Orogrande is another thirty miles north of Three Rivers on U.S. Highway 54. The UFOs flew out of mountains to the north of road. This UFO-haunted region is just east of where the first atomic explosion took place in 1945.) **126 (11/90), 150, 190**

HOLLOMAN AFB In 1971, an alien spacecraft is reported to have landed on this Air Force base, which is in an area known for numerous UFO sightings. The alleged landing took place in the middle of a UFO "flap," a period of intense sighting activity.

(The base is next to the White Sands National Monument southwest of Alamogordo on U.S. Highway 70. www.holloman.af.mil) **150**

ALBUQUERQUE

ALBUQUERQUE PRESS CLUB This log mansion was built in 1903 by architect Charles Whittlesey. In 1920, it became home to Arthur Hall and his new wife, Cliffy Hall. She later divorced him and married Herbert McCallum in 1935. Cliffy lived in the house until 1960, when she sold it to the Lambda Chi Alpha Fraternity. In 1973, it was purchased by the Albuquerque Press Club. Since then, numerous employees and guests have encountered the ghost of Cliffy McCallum, whom they affectionately call "Mrs. M." Her revenant usually appears at the bar, where bartenders leave a shot of gin just for her.

(Albuquerque is in central New Mexico, at the intersection of I-25 and I-90. The Albuquerque Press Club is located on the western edge of the high land east of the city

at 201 Highland Park Circle Southeast. Phone: 505-243-8476.) **64**

KiMo Theater This unique pueblo deco building was constructed in 1927 by Oreste Bachechi and soon became Albuquerque's premier movie house. In 1951, the boiler in the basement exploded, demolishing a section of the lobby and killing a young boy. Ten years later, a fire destroyed part of the stage area. The movie house closed in 1968, although the stage is still used by local performing arts groups. Today, it is customary to bring in doughnuts on opening nights and leave one for the boy's spirit. When the ritual is not adhered to actors report an invisible presence on stage that trips them or moves props. Today, a long string of hard, dusty doughnuts hangs on a water pipe backstage. The boy's apparition, wearing a striped shirt and blue jeans, has been seen on the lobby staircase, and the unidentified ghost of a woman wearing a bonnet has also been reported walking the halls.

(KiMo Theater, 423 Central N.W., Albuquerque, NM 87102. Phone: 505-848-1370.) **64**

Luna-Otero Mansion This great house was built in 1881 on land granted to the Luna and Otero families from the King of Spain in 1692. In the 1970s, the mansion was remodeled into a restaurant, and it was then that the ghost of one of the original family members, Josefita "Pepe" Otero, began to appear. Several employees have seen her very real-looking apparition, dressed in 1920s clothing, in two former bedrooms on the second floor, an attic storeroom, as well as at the top of the stairs leading to the second-floor bar.

(The restaurant is twenty miles south of Albuquerque off I-25 in Las Lunas. Luna Mansion Restaurant, P.O. Box 789, Los Lunas, NM 87031. Phone: 505-865-7333.) **64**

Maria Teresa Restaurant Numerous ghosts haunt this old building. A busboy quit after encountering a whole roomful of spirits sitting in the Board Room, but braver employees have learned to live with the apparition of a man wearing a dark suit in the Chacon Room, a nonexistent woman reflected in the mirrors of the Zamora Room, and a ghostly piano player in the Armijo Room. The structure was built in the 1840s by Salvador Armijo and was remodeled into a restaurant in 1977. Recently, plumbers discovered a cache of

old human and horse bones buried under the floorboards in the bar.

(Maria Teresa Restaurant & Bar, 618 Rio Grand Blvd., Albuquerque, NM 87102. Phone: 505-242-3900.) **64**

Petroglyph State Park This sacred site is covered with ancient rock drawings that hold special meaning to modern Indians.

(The site is on Atrisco Road in northwest Albuquerque. Phone: 505-839-4429. www.nps.gov/petr) **72**

Quarai Mission Visitors to this seventeenth-century Spanish mission are surprised to find the ghost of a conquistador still guarding the ruins. He enters through one of the gaps in the adobe walls and is surrounded by a blue-white light. He wears a tabard bearing the symbol of the Calatrava, a Spanish military religious group. He was first sighted in 1913, when he pointed his finger at a startled tourist and said (in Spanish): "Frequent this place, traveler on a mystic journey."

(The ruins of Quarai are southeast of Albuquerque, in the Manzanos Mountains at Punta de Agua.) **231**

Wool Warehouse Theater Restaurant This old wool warehouse was converted to a dinner theater in 1984. The unidentified ghost of a man in a double-breasted, cream-colored suit has appeared near the stage during performances.

(The theater restaurant is at 502 First St. NW, Albuquerque, NM 87102.) **101, 135**

BANDELIER

Bandelier National Monument The Anasazi first settled in this beautiful canyon ten thousand years ago. The Tyuonui Ruins look like a miniature Machu Pichu, surrounded by green forests and mountains. The Great Kiva was a site of public religious ceremonies; Ceremonial Cave was where private initiation rituals took place. An ancient ceremonial circle, the Shrine of the Stone Lions, is sacred to nearly every tribe in the southwest. The Cochin, Hopi, Ildefonso, Santa Domingo, and Zuni Indians all believe the spirits of their ancestors can be contacted here.

(The park is north of Santa Fe. Take Highway 502 south from U.S. Highway 285, then follow Highway 4

into the park. For information, contact Bandelier National Monument, HCR-1 Box 1 Suite 15, Los Alamos, NM 87544. Phone: 505-672-0343. www.nps. gov/band) **72, 99**

CHACO CANYON

CHACO CANYON NATIONAL PARK A strange, naked ghost haunts this national park. Visitors and employees have seen the apparition of a very tall, naked man emerging from the Sipapu, sacred holes in the ground inside ceremonial kivas. The holes are said to be connecting points to the Other Side. At other times, the phantom is bathed in a blue light and dripping with moisture. Once, a park ranger tried to arrest the naked man, only to see the giant disappear into thin air. Hopi Indians believe the giant ghost is a genius loci, a spirit of place that feeds off the energies of Mother Earth. Other spirits, the ghosts of the Anasazi people, are also sensed here. Some evidence links the short-statured, long-headed Anasazi with ancient Egyptian and Phoenician cultures that possibly inaugurated the Mayan culture. Fajada Butte was considered sacred by the Anasazi. They created an astronomical observatory there now known as the Sun Dagger and left behind mysterious etching on stones at the site. Pueblo Bonito is a five-story, eight-hundred-room cliff dwelling built around A.D. 900. It contains thirty-seven kivas and is situated to take advantage of solar energy. The partially excavated Una Vida has one hundred rooms and eight kivas. Chetro Ketl has five hundred rooms and sixteen kivas. Casa Riconada was built to be used only for worship and magical initiation. The perfectly round structure is sixty-six feet in diameter and fourteen feet deep. Psychics consider Chaco Canyon to be one of the centers of Harmonic Convergence on the planet.

(There are seventy-five ancient structures in Chaco Culture National Historic Park, which is in northwest New Mexico, fifty-four miles south of Bloomsfield. Follow Highway 44 and Highway 57 through the 35,000-acre park. Information is available from the Chaco Culture National Historic Park, State Route 4, Box 6500, Bloomsfield, NM 87413. Phone: 505-786-7014. www. nps.gov/chcu) **15, 53 (7/93), 99, 200, 203**

CHIMAYO

EL SANTUARIO DE CHIMAYO This small chapel is sometimes called the American Lourdes. It is built on top of a piece of land known for its healing and magical powers. Indians went to the site to avail themselves of the healing energies, and Spanish priests felt its spiritual power. The chapel was built in 1816 by Bernardo Abeyta, who was visited by an angel. The heavenly messenger told the farmer that two priests had been murdered on the property. Abeyta searched and found part of a robe and a large crucifix that belonged to the martyrs. The townspeople carried the six-foot-high green cross to Santa Cruz to be displayed, but the cross magically reappeared back in Chimayo at the same spot where the farmer had discovered it. This happened three times before Abeyta decided to build a chapel around the site. The miraculous cross still rests behind the altar in the Santuario.

Abeyta was a disciple of a Central American religious leader named Equipulas, who taught that Christ was dark-skinned like his own people. One of the ceremonies of the sect included healing with sacred mud from a mineral springs in Guatamala. Abeyta carved a Black Christ for his chapel and claimed the dirt on his property was holy. Since then, thousands of people have visited the site to take some of the sacred soil from an earthen well in the El Posito annex. The mysterious well is always full to the brim, no matter how much dirt is taken. The place is littered with crutches and wheelchairs left behind by those miraculously cured of their afflictions.

(The town of Chimayo is north of Santa Fe, ten miles east of Espanola on Highway 76. For further information, contact El Santuario de Nuestro Senor De Equipuias, P.O. Box 235, Chimayo, NM 87522. Phone: 505-351-4889.) **9, 144, 200**

CIMARRON

COLFAX GHOST TOWN The Weeping Lady of Colfax is the apparition of a woman who appears in the back row of the combination church and schoolhouse here. Her spirit still grieves for her ten-year-old son, who died of an unknown illness in the late 1800s. Inconsolable grief killed the mother within a month of her son's death.

(From I-25, exit onto Highway 58 for Cimarron, which is forty miles southwest of Raton in the north corner of New Mexico. The ghost town is at the intersection of the Old Dawson Rd. and Highway 64, about ten miles northeast of Cimarron. www.ghosttowns.com/states/nm/colfax.html) **231**

DAWSON CEMETERY The cemetery of an old silver boomtown is haunted by the ghosts of miners killed in cave-ins. Two separate mining disasters killed most of the men in Dawson, which was abandoned at the turn of the century. It is said that the light from their bright carbide lights can be seen hovering above their graves at night.

(Follow Highway 64 northeast from Cimarron for ten miles to the Old Dawson Road. Go north for five miles on the dirt road www. vivanewmexico.com/ghosts/dawson. html) **231**

The Bat Masterson Room is one of several haunted rooms in the St. James Hotel. See St. James Hotel, Cimarron, New Mexico (ST. JAMES HOTEL)

ST. JAMES HOTEL Opened in 1880, this gambling hall and saloon saw plenty of action, as the bullet holes in the tin ceiling attest. At least twenty-six people were killed here. Notable early visitors included outlaws Clay Allison, Black Jack Ketchum, and Jesse James, as well as Wyatt Earp, Buffalo Bill, and Annie Oakley. The building was remodeled into a hotel in 1985, although not all the rooms are for rent. The management keeps a nasty ghost locked up in Room 18. Whoever he is, the ghost does not like to be disturbed and sometimes manifests as a swirling energy field to keep people out. A gentler presence haunts Room 17. She is Mary Lambert, wife of the original owner who died in the room while still young. Sometimes a drifting wave of fragrant perfume manifests in the room. No one has been able to identify the odor or its source. A friendly spirit, whom the owners have dubbed the Little Imp, likes to torment new employees in the kitchen and dining room. Described as

a small man with a pockmarked face, the Little Imp has been known to burst glasses, relight candles, and move objects in front of nervous new hires.

(The hotel is near the intersection of U.S. Highway 64 and Highway 21 at 17th and Collinson streets in Cimarron. The mailing address of the St. James Hotel is Route 1 Box 2, Cimarron, NM 87714. Phone: 505-376-2664.) **14, 53 (3/88), 72, 101, 211**

CLOUDCROFT

THE LODGE The restaurant in this eighty-five-year-old inn is named after a ghost named Rebecca, and her portraits, including a stained-glass window, are scattered throughout the establishment. Dozens of employees and guests at this mountain resort have recognized the apparition of a woman wearing a long dress roaming the halls. Rebecca was a beautiful young maid with striking blue eyes and red hair, murdered by a jealous lumberjack at the inn in the 1930s. Rebecca is a flirtatious, mischievous spirit who likes to use the telephone in Room 101, the Governor's Suite. Guests in that room sometimes receive phone calls from nowhere, and operators at the resort say that the line to Room 101 is often lit up, even when no one is in the suite. Rebecca's presence is also felt in the Red Dog Saloon, where ashtrays move by themselves and flames appear in the fireplace with no logs or other source of fuel.

(Cloudcroft is fifteen miles east of Alamogordo on U.S. Highway 82. The Lodge is a three-story mountain inn overlooking Cloudcroft at an elevation of nine thousand feet. The Lodge, 1 Corona Place, Cloudcroft, NM 88317. Phone: 505-682-2566. For reservations, call 800-395-6343. www.thelodge-nm.com) **41, 53 (4/85), 135, 175**

CORRALES

RANCHO DE CORRALES RESTAURANT Employees and many customers here are aware of a strange presence that haunts the old section of the building. A bloody shoot-out between members of the Emberto family took place there in April 1898. It started when the son killed his father's mistress. The father then shot and killed his wife, blaming her for prompting the murder. In the ensuing gun battle, the father was also killed. The Embertos were buried on the property, and their inflamed family passions are felt to this day.

(Corrales is outside Albuquerque. The old hacienda now houses a restaurant in Corrales. It was formerly known as the Territorial House. Rancho de Corrales, Corrales, NM 87048. Phone: 505-897-3131. www. premiersystems.com/ranchos) **231**

CUBA

REED CANYON Trail Creek in this peaceful canyon is a deserted area haunted by the ghosts of settlers moving west after the Civil War. The sounds of whips and wagon wheels rolling over the steep hills sometimes last for hours. Barking dogs, crying babies, laughing children, and busy people shouting commands at one another are heard along the trail. Sheepherders, tree cutters, and campers have all heard the preternatural sounds. The canyon is named after a man who built a stone cabin in the mountains and charged outlaws a high price to hide out there. Reed died in 1900, but the ruins of his house remain.

(The town of Cuba is eighty miles northwest of Albuquerque. Take Highway 126 east from Cuba thirty miles to Trail Creek, which runs through Reed Canyon, which parallels Calavaries Canyon. Ojitos Mesa is an area of frequent reports.) **135**

DULCE

CATTLE MUTILATIONS Dulce was the cattle mutilation capital of the world in the late 1970s. Dozens of unexplainable cases occurred here. On June 14, 1976, a rancher found a three-year old cow with its sex organs, tongue, and an ear removed. Within five hundred feet of the carcass, investigators found "a mysterious trail of suction-cup-like impressions" that were four inches in diameter and twenty-eight inches apart. A mutilated eleven-year-old bull was found on the same property on April 24, 1978. Identical ground markings were discovered, backed up by several independent UFO sightings. Podlike tracks were also found near a mutilated bull on the ranch of Manuel Gomez in 1976. At that site, unidentified round objects appeared in the sky on two photographs developed by magazine photographer Howard Burgess. On April 8, 1979, two Apache tribal officers on patrol near Dulce saw an unidentified craft hover about fifty feet off the ground and shine a powerful white light on the cattle below.

(Dulce is near the Colorado border in Rio Arriba County, on U.S. Highway 64.) **139**

JICARILLA INDIAN RESERVATION This Chiricahua Apache reservation is said to be protected by the spirit of a white wolf that can take the form of a man. The wolf appeared in the summer of 1984, when the tribe was threatened by a power-hungry local sheriff, and again later, when a minister visited the reservation to drive out the evil he thought was in the minds of the Indians. Both times the white wolf appeared and drove the intruders away.

(The reservation is just south of Dulce. Highway 537 runs through the center of the area.) **131**

UNDERGROUND ALIEN BASE Buried deep in the desert here are caverns allegedly populated by alien beings. Numerous abductees have reported being taken to the alien base here to be examined, and most of them have seen members of our own military present. According to some reports, the aliens are carrying on genetic experimentation in a secret agreement with the government. In 1969, according to ex-Naval Intelligence Officer Milton Cooper, a confrontation took place between the aliens and our own scientists in which sixty-six humans died.

(Dulce is in northern New Mexico on the Colorado border, about 130 miles northwest of Santa Fe on U.S. Highway 64. The alien base is supposedly located near the Continental Divide, south of Dulce on the Jicarillo Indian Reservation. The site is said to be connected to Los Alamos by an underground shuttle.) **1**

FARMINGTON

UFO SIGHTINGS The entire population of this town (five thousand people) observed a formation of hundreds of UFOs perform astonishing aerial maneuvers. The UFOs appeared before noon on March 18, 1950, and returned that same afternoon. Observers described the objects as "spaceships" and estimated their speeds in excess of one thousand miles per hour. Witnesses included the mayor, newspaper reporters, and highway patrolmen.

(Farmington is in the northwestern corner of New Mexico on U.S. Highway 64.) **139**

GUADALUPITA

LA LLORONA La Llorona, the frightful wailing woman who searches through all eternity for the children she drowned in a river, has been reported several times in this area. In the 1930s, a whole family saw a tall ghost with flowing black hair rise from a ravine, cross the road, and walk on top of the water of a nearby creek. See Billings, Montana; El Paso, Texas; and Gary, Indiana.

(Guadalupita is on Highway 434 in Moro County, fifty miles north of Las Vegas, New Mexico. The phantom was seen between Mora and Guadalupita, crossing Lucero Rd. She has also been spotted in the Apache Ridge area, and along the old Santa Fe trail near Garcia St.) **131**

LAS CRUCES

DOUBLE EAGLE RESTAURANT The ghost of a petite young lady, wearing a black skirt and white blouse, has been spotted in the Carlotta Room. She is thought to be a maid named Inez, who was killed by a stray bullet from a skirmish that took place on the plaza in 1849. A grislier version of events is that she was killed by a member of the Maese family. One day the mother caught her young son in bed with Inez. In a fit of rage, the woman grabbed a pair of scissors and started stabbing at the bed. Before she realized what she was doing, she had killed both her son and the maid. The spirit of Inez remained quiet until the room was remodeled in the 1980s, after which the ghost of Inez began gliding across the floor. The frightening apparition was also seen reflected in mirrors, and a photograph of her ghostly form hangs in the Carlotta Room. Inez sometimes manifests as a cold spot in the tiny room, which only seats eight people. Unexplainable noises, such as the sounds of pottery breaking and disembodied voices, are also heard in the area. At least a dozen guests and employees have observed supernatural phenomena. On October 24, 1989, amazed witnesses saw eighty glasses fly off a back shelf onto the floor, but only three of them broke. The house was built in 1825 and converted into a restaurant in the 1970s.

(Mesilla is in south central New Mexico, about forty miles from the Mexican border. It is just south of Las Cruces. The single-story, brown adobe restaurant is at 2335 Calle De Guadalupe St. Phone: 505-523-6700.) **101, 112, 134**

PEPPERS RESTAURANT Patrons and employees at this popular Mexican restaurant have reported seeing misty apparitions floating through the main dining room. No explanation has been found.

(Las Cruces is at the junction of I-10 and I-25 in southwestern New Mexico. It is about sixty miles northwest of El Paso on I-25. Peppers Restaurant, 308 Calle De Guadalupe, Mesilla, NM 88002. Phone: 505-523-4999.) **72**

ROSWELL

INTERNATIONAL UFO MUSEUM AND RESEARCH CENTER The Roswell City Council officially endorses this museum, which features a recreation of the famous saucer crash near Roswell, a display of UFO phenomena from the 1940s to the present, and a research library. It also has an auditorium for lectures, reading rooms, and a gift shop. Over 1,500 tourists a month visit the center. See UFO Crash, below.

(Roswell is in Chaves County in southeast New Mexico at the junction of U.S. Highways 285 and 70/380. International UFO Museum, 114 North Main St., P.O. Box 2221, Roswell, NM 88202. Phone: 505-625-9495. www.iufomrc.com) **72**

UFO CRASH In 1947, Roswell gained notoriety as the site of a UFO crash. On the night of July 2, 1947, during a fierce thunderstorm, rancher William Brazel heard a tremendous explosion. When he investigated the next morning, he found pieces of metal strewn about his property. The pieces were as light as balsa wood but could not be dented, even with a sledgehammer. Brazel called the Roswell Army Air Field who sent out intelligence officer Jesse Marcel to collect the debris and bring it back to Hanger 84 at the base. Four bodies were also found and taken to the infirmary for examination. An official press release said that evidence of "flying discs" had been found, but soon the Army said that the debris was not from a UFO, but rather were pieces of a downed weather balloon. Supposedly, the metal was taken to Wright Patterson AFB (Dayton, Ohio), for further analysis. Rumors spread that the Air Force had recovered an entire craft with alien bodies and stored them in Hanger 18 at Wright Patterson. To his dying day, Jesse Marcel insisted that the pieces were of extraterrestrial origin. In January 1994, the General Accounting Office launched an investigation into allegations that the government is withholding information about the UFO crash. They admitted that all the files on the incident had been shredded by unknown persons. Yet another UFO is said to have crashed near Aztec in May 1948. That, too, was allegedly covered up by the government. See International UFO Museum, above; Alamogordo Fireballs, Alamogordo, New Mexico; and Lubbock, Texas.

(The alleged crash site is in Lincoln County about eighty miles northwest of Roswell, near Corona. Roswell Army Air Field has been abandoned, but Hanger 84 and the infirmary building are still standing. Aztec is in the northwest corner of the state, at the junction of Highway 544 and U.S. Highway 550. To arrange a tour of the Roswell crash site, call 505-623-4043.) **53 (1/91, 9/91), 72, 126 (9/90, 1/91, 7/91, 2/92, 4/92, 3/95, 5/95, 6/95, 9/95), 150, 190, 203**

SANTA FE

ALTO STREET The phantom of a headless caballero haunts this street. The hapless cowboy brandishes a sword as he rides his horse down the road to the Santa Fe river. It is said he lost his head to two Spanish witches, after complaining about a love potion they gave him.

(Santa Fe is in north central New Mexico, sixty-five miles northeast of Albuquerque on I-25. The phantom has been sighted on Alto St. and along the riverbank.) **231**

CAMACHO HOUSE This house is haunted by a mischievous presence that likes to grab ankles and trip people. Tenant Patricia Camacho has seen the impression of an invisible person in the comforter on her bed and has heard the voices of a group of people coming from an empty basement. The unearthly voices have also been heard by visitors to the house, which was used as a brothel and gambling hall in the 1920s.

(The small adobe house is a private residence, at 507 Apodaca Hill St., Santa Fe, NM 87501.) **65**

CASA REAL HEALTH CARE CENTER This senior health-care facility was built in 1985 on top of an old penitentiary graveyard next to another haunted building (see St. Vincent Hospital, below). Employees, patients, and visitors to the 112-bed convalescent center have complained of an oppressive, uncomfortable feeling that emanates from the place. Strange cold spots move through the rooms, and unexplained moaning sounds have been heard in the north and south wings.

(Casa Real Health Care Center, 1650 Galisteo St., Santa Fe, NM 87501. Phone: 505-984-8313.) **65**

CHURCH OF SAN MIGUEL The old bell at this church was the source of a miracle in the mid-1800s. A blind man attended the church at noontime every day. His fervent prayers are said to have caused the bell to ring with no one pulling the rope. During the ringing, the man regained his sight. He was later able to accurately describe statues and icons inside the church, but he was blind again as soon as the ringing stopped. Catholic officials described the miracle as a visitation of the Holy Ghost. The bell was cast in Spain in 1356 and fell from the old spire in 1872. It was left where it landed and is currently on display on the church grounds.

(Church of San Miguel, 401 Old Santa Fe Trail, Santa Fe, NM 87501. Phone: 505-983-3974.) **231**

DELONEY NEWKIRK FINE ART This one-story building has been haunted by strange voices and unexplainable sounds for many years. The gentle voices are heard only during the winter months. According to director Kate Norton, there is an uneasy feeling about the place after hours, and employees refuse to spend the night in the building.

(Deloney Newkirk Fine Art, 634 Canyon Rd., Santa Fe, NM 87501. Phone: 505-982-1468. www.collectors guide.com/sf/g291.html) **65**

DEVIL HOUSE A young man who engaged in devil worship in this house got more than he was bargaining for. Michael joined a gang of satanists from Cerrillos and was soon overcome by evil. He performed rituals in his bedroom and once sacrificed a dog there. Then one evening, two figures, like "huge, winged birds or bats" appeared in his room and beat him unconscious. When he was released from the hospital, Michael tried to quit the group, but never succeeded. In September 1988, the twenty-three-year-old committed suicide by slitting his throat. Prospective tenants inspecting the house reported feeling uneasy there, and a few felt they were being slapped by an invisible hand. A priest blessed the house, and current residents have reported no problems.

(The house is a private residence, at 934 Lopez St. Santa Fe, NM 87501.) **65**

GRANT CORNER INN This three-story house was built in 1905 and was home to judge Arthur Robinson and his wife for many years. It was used as an office building in the 1950s and became an inn in 1982. Custodians, guests, and visitors have reported a number of ghostly encounters over the years. Unexplainable sounds of heavy objects falling to the floor, doors banging shut, and loud footsteps are heard throughout the building. Police have been called on several occasions. The gray form of a woman has been spotted in the second floor hall, and strange happenings have been reported in Rooms 4 and 8 of the inn.

(The Grant Corner Inn is on the corner of Grant Ave. and Johnson St., at 122 Grant Ave., Santa Fe, NM 87501. Phone: 505-983-6678. www.santafe.org/grantcorner) **65**

LA FONDA HOTEL A dining room in this hotel is haunted by the ghost of a salesman, who lost his company's money in a card game a hundred years ago. The distraught man leaped to his death down a deep well. The well was located just outside an old gambling hall known as the Exchange House. Today, the La Plazuela dining room of the La Fonda Hotel is situated directly over the old well. Guests and employees have reported the strange sight of a ghostly figure that walks to the center of the room and seems to jump into the floor and disappear.

(The hotel is located on the main plaza in Santa Fe. La Fonda Hotel, 100 E. San Francisco, Santa Fe, NM 87501. Phone: 505-982-5511. www.lafondasantafe.com) **231**

LAGUNA PUEBLO MISSION The coffin of a murdered priest keeps popping up through the church floor here. Father Juan Padilla was murdered by Indians in 1733 and was buried beneath the floor at the Islata Pueblo Church. Before long, his coffin, hollowed out of a cottonwood tree, rose out of the earth in front of the altar. It rose again twenty years later, and again in 1889. Then, on Christmas Eve 1914, it poked through the floor again. Two investigations were conducted by the Bishop of Santa Fe, but no conclusion was reached as to the nature of the phenomenon.

(Laguna Puelbo Mission, Santa Fe, NM 87501.) **231**

LA POSADA DE SANTA FE HOTEL The land on which this modern hotel stands was farmed by Spanish settlers as far back as 1610. The land became the property of the Baca family in the early 1800s. German merchant Abraham Staab acquired the site in 1876 and built a house for his family. His wife Julie died in 1896 at the age of fifty-two. Abraham died in 1913, but the spirit of his wife never joined him. Her ghost is still seen on the second floor of her former home.

(La Posada Hotel, 330 East Palace Ave., Santa Fe, NM 87501. Phone: 505-986-0000. www.laposadadesantafe. com) **65**

LA RESIDENCIA This nursing home originally housed the community hospital (see St. Vincent Hospital, below). The muffled crying of a little boy who died in Room 311 is still heard by nurses. The child and his father both died of injuries suffered in an automobile accident on Interstate 25. The eerie sounds from Room 311 are so frequent that administrators try to keep the room unoccupied. When the state museum began storing Indian artifacts in the basement here, some nurses refused to enter the area. Strange sounds emanate from the basement rooms, and two nurses once saw a wall there ooze fresh blood.

(The building is on the corner of Palace Ave. and Paseo de Peralta at 820 Paseo de Peralta, Santa Fe, NM 87501. Phone: 505-983-2273.) **65**

LEGAL TENDER SALOON This old saloon and vaudeville hall is haunted by several ghosts. A lady in white, dressed in an elegant white gown, is seen floating up the steps to the balcony in the Parlor Room. A little girl ghost in a long dress sits alone on the stairs. A man in black, killed by a stray bullet in the rowdy gambling hall, has been seen helping himself to a drink at the bar. The building was constructed in 1881 and was called the Annex Saloon. In the 1950s, it was known as the Pink Garter. It became the Legal Tender Saloon in 1969.

(The Legal Tender Restaurant and Saloon is located in Lamy, eighteen miles southeast of Santa Fe. Phone: 505-982-8425.) **65**

PERA BUILDING Many locals consider the Public Employees Retirement Association (PERA) building to be haunted. Some will not go near it, because it is built on an old Spanish-Indian graveyard. In fact, two levels of the five-floor building were constructed belowground in the middle of the graveyard. Unseen hands are said to reach out and trip people on stairways, and unexplained cries and moans echo through the halls. Once the ghost of a tall, thin woman appeared in a third floor corridor. At least one janitor has quit because of the ghostly activity.

(The building is off Agua Fria St., near the banks of the Santa Fe River at 1120 Paseo de Peralta. For information, call 505-827-4700.) **65, 131, 231**

ST. VINCENT HOSPITAL The ghost of a very short Hispanic man, dressed in old-fashioned clothing, appeared several times to a nurse on the top floor of this three-story modern hospital. The ghost of a woman wearing a black mantilla was observed with the man. The ghostly couple seemed confused and in need of some kind of help. The hospital was built in 1977 on top of an old penitentiary graveyard (see Casa Real Health Care Center, above). A more recent hospital operated on this same tract of land also reported paranormal activity (see La Residencia, above).

(St. Vincent Hospital, 455 Saint Michaels Dr., Santa Fe, NM 87501, 505-983-3361. www.stvin.org) **65**

STAAB HOUSE The ghost of a wealthy socialite still lingers near her expensive crystal and gold knick-knacks. Although Mrs. Staab died in the 1880s, it is believed that she could not leave her possessions behind, so she stayed with them. She roams the house as a moving cold spot, an icy wind so cold it can extinguish candles. Her quiet sobbing is sometimes heard as well.

(The house is a private residence in the La Posada section, at 330 East Palace Ave., Santa Fe, NM 87501.) **231**

TEN THOUSAND WAVES HEALTH SPA Shortly after owner Duke Klauch moved into his home on this property, he started hearing loud metal banging sounds like heavy chains being dragged across the floors. The frightening sounds always occurred around 3:00 A.M. Once, a visitor noticed a dark presence in a bedroom and felt a heavy weight pin her to her bed. In 1981, an employee encountered the white ghost of a woman standing in one of the spa rooms. Klauch bought the property from Elizabeth Zinn, whose grandmother was buried on the land. Moreover, Elizabeth's daughter had committed suicide in the corral a few years earlier. At 3:00 in the morning, the young woman walked into the corral and shot herself in the head with a pistol. Within a year, her despondent father hanged himself from a beam in the living room. At Klauch's request, three priests from St. Francis Cathedral performed a thorough exorcism rite that included every building on the premises. The crucifix they used still hangs next to a Japanese bell on the wall behind a counter at the main entrance to the establishment.

(The Japanese-style spa is located 3.5 miles downtown from Santa Fe at 3451 Hyde Park Rd. Phone: 505-982-9304.) **65**

THREE SISTERS BOUTIQUE The ghost of a Catholic nun known as Sister George haunts this modern Western-wear shop. Sister George, a member of the Sisters of Loretto order, was known for her unselfish assistance to those of need in the community. After she died in the early 1970s, her spirit started manifesting in the old Opportunity School building, where she had spent many years. The old school was purchased by Best Western Corporation and turned into shops, but several tenants complained of hearing footsteps when no one was around, and of noticing strange electrical problems such as lights going on and off for no reason. Oddly, some shop owners reported that an extra ten-dollar bill regularly appeared in their cash registers. Today, most of the ghostly activity seems to be centered around the Three Sisters Boutique. The clothing shop was named for Sister George and two other nuns who ran the original school.

(Three Sisters Boutique, 211 Old Santa Fe Trail, Santa Fe, NM 87501. Phone: 505-988-5045.) **65**

SHIPROCK

HIGHWAY 666 This is the highway to hell according to witnesses who have seen a phantom car appear out of nowhere during the full moon. Paranormal investigator Avery Teicher says the ghost car has run scores of vehicles off the road and is responsible for at least five deaths. There is also a mad trucker who drives the highway and intentionally runs people down. If that were not enough, packs of demon dogs whose teeth are so sharp they shred tires have been known to attack anyone who pulls off the road along Highway 666. The apparition of a frail girl in a nightgown has also been seen on the highway. When people stop to help her she vanishes from sight. Funeral directors and police records indicate an unusual number of dumped bodies are found along this stretch of road, which also has one of the state's highest accident rates.

(Shiprock is in the extreme northwest corner of New Mexico, at the junction of U.S. Highway 64 and U.S. Highway 666. The Highway to Hell runs from Shiprock south to Gallop. U.S. Highway 666 is a two-hundred-mile-long road that runs from Utah to New Mexico through

southwestern Colorado. It used to run into Arizona, but officials there decided to rename it Highway 191 after complaints by motorists.) **72**

SHIPROCK MOUNTAIN This beautiful mountain peak sometimes appears to float in midair, which is why white settlers named it Shiprock. The Navajo call it "Rock with Wings" and consider it sacred. According to legend, it was here that the Slayer of Enemy Gods killed two ferocious dragons that lived on a hidden ledge on the mountain. The male and female dragons were transformed into an eagle and an owl—a profound allegory of the psychological changes necessary for individuals to become whole.

(The mountain rises to 7,178 feet fifteen miles southwest of Shiprock off Highway 504. It can also be seen from U.S. Highway 666.) **144, 200**

SOCORRO

CLOSE ENCOUNTER A highway patrol officer allegedly encountered a UFO with extraterrestrial entities near this desert community. Patrolman Lonnie Zamora was chasing a speeding car at 5:45 P.M. on April 24, 1964, when he saw a blue flame on the horizon. He thought it came from a shed used to store dynamite, so he abandoned his pursuit and drove back along a bumpy dirt road to check out the shed. Sergeant Chavez had been monitoring his radio and also headed for the location of the explosives shed. When Zamora rounded a bend in the road, he discovered a car-sized metallic egg sitting in an arroyo 450 feet away. Two very short humanoid figures wearing white suits stood next to the craft. They immediately ran back into the UFO, which started emitting a deafening, high-pitched screech. Suddenly the object zoomed off in a southwest direction. Sergeant Chavez arrived to find a badly shaken Zamora sitting alongside the road. The Air Force investigated the site and discovered burned bushes and four imprints from the craft's landing pods, but their extensive survey failed to explain the incident. Metal scrapings sent to the Goddard Space Flight Center in Maryland were identified as a zinc-iron alloy not naturally occurring or currently manufactured on earth. An independent investigation discovered a dozen additional witnesses who saw the object descend.

(Socorro is in south-central New Mexico at the junction of I-25 and U.S. Highway 60. Zamora was half a mile south of Socorro on Park St. when he observed the object land. The object was seen descending over Highway 85 at the same time by independent witnesses. Zamora encountered the aliens 1,650 feet southwest on the dirt road that connects Old Rodeo St. and U.S. Highway 60.) **139, 150, 190, 191**

TAOS

BENT HOUSE MUSEUM When an angry mob protesting the Mexican War appeared in front of Governor Bent's home on January 18, 1847, he went outside to reason with them. He was shot with bullets and arrows, and scalped by Indians. His family escaped by digging through an adobe wall and fleeing from a neighbor's house. The men who killed the governor were caught and hanged, but their ghosts still haunt his residence. Their dim outlines and angry voices have been reported late at night here.

(Taos is on U.S. Highway 64, sixty miles northeast of Santa Fe. The museum is on the main plaza in Taos. For information, call the Taos Chamber of Commerce at 800-732-TAOS. www.taoschamber.com) **231**

KIT CARSON HOUSE MUSEUM The friendly ghost of Kit Carson has been detected in his former home. The three-room house was expanded to accommodate his children, and Carson's domesticated ghost is said to be very kind to women and children. The frontiersman moved to Taos in 1825. He died in 1868 at the age of fifty-nine.

(Carson House is only two hundred yards from the Bent House Museum at 222 Ledoux St. Phone: 505-758-5440.) **231**

LAS PALOMAS DE TAOS ADOBE When actor Dennis Hopper and his wife lived in this 125-year-old house in the late 1960s, they both encountered the ghosts of the couple who originally built the place. The ghosts of Mabel Dodge Luhan and her husband Tony were seen moving through a wall in the hall outside the bathroom, and earlier, their laughing apparitions had been observed floating in another room. Other residents blamed Mabel's presence for moving statues and furniture in the house. The privileged matriarch lived in the house for forty-four years, until her death in 1963. The Rainbow Room in the old adobe home was used by Indians for various rituals, and the ghost of an Indian girl has been seen there. She is said to have died of natural causes in the room many years ago.

(The adobe is a private residence in the north section of Taos.) **231**

WHITE OAKS

HOYLE'S CASTLE This abandoned house is a poignant reminder of a lost love. In the 1880s, Andy Hoyle built the brick mansion for his mail-order bride, a woman he had fallen in love with after she answered his ad in an eastern newspaper. But after she arrived something went wrong. Within a few weeks, she boarded a stagecoach and headed back to her home on the east coast. Andy was crushed by her departure. One day, he simply disappeared, leaving his magnificent mansion abandoned. However, some say his ghost haunts the lonely old building waiting for his promised love to return.

(White Oaks is eighty miles east of Socorro on U.S. Highway 380. The ghost town is in the mountains north of the highway. Hoyle's Castle still stands in the middle of the abandoned town.) **30, 112**

WHITE SANDS

ALKALI FLATS Tracks of giant humanoid creatures were found here in 1931. The thirteen prints measured sixteen to twenty-two inches long and eight to twelve inches wide. The stride was about five feet with a separation width of two feet. The prints were about 2.5 inches deep in 1931, but by 1974, they stood 1.5 inches *above* ground. The surrounding soil had eroded away around the compacted prints, leaving behind eerie pedestals of alien footprints. By 1981, the prints stood over two inches high. Archaeologists consider the unexplainable footprints to be at least ten thousand years old. The area is protected for further scientific study.

(Alkali Flats is in the eastern foothills of the San Andres Mountains in the Great White Sands area.) **139**

NEW YORK

ALBANY

CHERRY HILL For many years, residents of this mansion have reported a ghostly figure wandering the lower floor. The specter has also been seen walking the terrace on the property. Investigators suspect the house was the scene of a murder many years ago, but the identity of the ghost has never been uncovered.

(Albany is about 160 miles north of New York City on I-87. Cherry Hill, South Pearl St., Albany, NY 12207.) **102**

LINDENWALD Many people have tried to identify the ghost of Lindenwald. Some say it is a butler who hanged himself in the orchard, or a woman who was murdered at the gatehouse. Others believe the spirit here is none other than Aaron Burr, who hid out in the house after killing the immensely more popular Alexander Hamilton in a duel (see Quantum Leap Café, Francis House, and Morris-Jumel Mansion, New York City). A white apparition has been observed by many residents of the historic house, which was built in 1797 by Judge William Van Ness. Strange odors in the kitchen and the sounds of violin playing in an empty second-floor bedroom have also been reported. Recently, a hidden room was discovered in the attic. Inside was a rocking chair, a pig whittled out of wood and a faded calling card bearing the name of Aaron Burr.

(Lindenwald is a private estate near the town of Kinderhook, about twenty miles south of Albany on the Kinderhook River. 1013 Old Post Rd., Kinderhook, NY 12106. 518-758-9689. www.nps.gov/mava) **188**

LOUDON COTTAGE Abraham Lincoln's ghost has appeared in this clapboard cottage several times. Locals say that his spirit was brought to Loudonville by his blood and brains, his very life force, which spattered on the dress of Clara Harris. Clara sat next to the President on the night he was assassinated (see Ford Theatre, District of Columbia). When the traumatized young woman returned to her parent's home in Loudonville, she hung the dress in a closet and had it walled shut. Clara went on to lead a tragic life. Her husband murdered her in front of her terrified children, because he was jealous of the attention she gave them. The man spent the rest of his life in an insane asylum. The hysterical specter of Clara Harris has also been seen in Loudon Cottage. See Rathbone House, District of Columbia.

(The cottage is in Loudonville, a northern suburb of Albany, at U.S. Highway 9 and Osborne Road. Loudon Cottage is a historical landmark in Loudonville.) **72**

NEW YORK CENTRAL RAILROAD TRACKS The ghostly outline of Abraham Lincoln's funeral train travels the New York countryside here. After the president was killed on Good Friday, April 14, 1865, the train carrying his body and three hundred mourners started a tour which reportedly has never ended. It was a bumpy ride for the presidential corpse. The body was moved seventeen times, and thousands of hysterical people crowded by to view it. At one point, his body was even kidnaped and held for ransom. The ghost train is said to follow the historic route on April 27 of every year. Although Lincoln's ghost has never been spotted on the phantom train, hundreds of other ghosts make the journey. A band of skeleton musicians plays distorted dirges on a flat car following the funeral wagon. The steam engine has a wide smokestack with a polished brass boiler and is manned by a crew of skeletons. The other cars carry hundreds of blue-coated soldiers, some with coffins on their backs. It is said that the tracks seem to be covered with a black carpet, and that when the ghost train passes through a railroad station, all the clocks stop. See Lincoln's Tomb, Springfield, Illinois.

(Lincoln's funeral train traveled 1,700 miles, from Washington, north through New York, and on to Springfield, Illinois. The ghost train, however, never makes it to Springfield, which lends credence to the belief that Lincoln is not really buried there.) **5, 31, 42, 115, 163, 176, 183**

STATE CAPITOL BUILDING

STATE CAPITOL BUILDING The Assembly Chamber of this august building is haunted by a strange presence nicknamed George. His roaming shadow is also seen on the fifth floor of the building. The ghost moans, jingles keys, opens doors, and rattles doorknobs. Several elevator operators and custodians have requested transfers after encountering the ghost. In 1981, television station WNYT held a séance in the Assembly Chamber late at night. Unusual sounds were recorded, and a cold draft of air moved through the area. The psychic reportedly contacted the spirit of a night watchman, Samuel Abbott, who died in a fire in the building in 1911.

(The capitol building was constructed in 1868. State Capitol Building, Albany, NY 12223. Phone: 518-455-4100.) **53 (2/85), 101, 135**

AMITYVILLE

DeFeo House The famous and controversial "Amityville Horror" case took place in this house. One night in November 1974, twenty-four-year-old Ronald DeFeo shot and killed his parents, two brothers, and two sisters. DeFeo told police he heard voices that ordered him to kill his family. He was sentenced to six consecutive life terms in prison. In December 1975 the house was purchased by George and Kathy Lutz.

Within a month, the Lutzes abandoned the house and moved in with friends. Rumors started to spread, and the news media promoted the idea that the house was possessed by evil spirits. In 1977, the Lutzes commissioned Jay Anson to write *The Amityville Horror*, which was made into a hit movie and four sequels. However, investigators were unable to confirm any of the spectacular claims made by the Lutzes. In all likelihood, the Lutzes moved out because they realized they could not afford the mortgage payments and then capitalized on the sensational publicity. The ASPR investigated the site and found no evidence of paranormal activity. The present owners of the house have reported nothing unusual.

(Amityville is at the junction of Routes 27A and 110 in southwest Long Island. The house is a private residence at 112 Ocean Ave., Amityville, NY 11701.) **31, 37, 50, 53 (5/78), 68, 69, 96, 149, 148**

BINGHAMTON

HIGHWAY 17 A dangerous curve on this state highway, known as "Devil's Elbow," had a deadly reputation in the 1930s. It was the scene of numerous accidents and several fatalities. One evening in late October, a book salesman approached the area in a heavy rainstorm. He was driving slowly because he knew how treacherous the curve could be, when he saw a woman on the side of the road. She had a scarf over her head and wore a white coat. Although she was not hitchhiking, he pulled over to ask if she needed a ride. She thanked him, opened the door, and got into the front seat. She asked to be let out at a house just past Devil's Elbow. She was shivering so badly that the driver wrapped his jacket around her shoulders. When he pulled over to the house, he noticed that both the girl and his jacket had disappeared. Only a puddle of water remained on the passenger's side. In disbelief he walked up to the house and knocked on the door. He was determined to retrieve his jacket. When an elderly woman came to the door, he told her about picking up the girl in the white coat and bringing her to that address. The woman told him there was nothing she could do. Whenever it storms in late October, her daughter tries to come home again. She was killed in a crash at Devil's Elbow ten years earlier. Other tales of the Lady in White on Highway 17 continued to be told for the next fifteen years. This case is typical of "Vanishing Hitchhiker" stories told throughout the United States.

(Binghamton is on the Pennsylvania border at the junction of I-81 and I-88. Devil's Elbow is fourteen miles east of Binghamton on Highway 17.) **183**

BUFFALO

BUFFALO NAVAL PARK The USS *Sullivan* in this naval dry dock is haunted. The World War II battle ship is named for the five Sullivan brothers, who died together when their light cruiser was torpedoed in 1942. When the ship named for them was mothballed, the five brothers started to haunt it. Workers and guards have encountered their restless spirits on numerous occasions, especially on Friday the thirteenth. Sometimes they hear the sounds of a ghostly craps games or a disembodied voice whispering "Hey you!" Five luminous forms have been seen floating down passageways and weird electrical phenomena still occur on the floating iron hulk. In 1993, a guard reported encountering the ghastly ghost of George Sullivan, the oldest Sullivan brother. His face and clothes were burned, and he was walking on air, not touching the deck.

(The ship, Number 537, is mothballed at the Buffalo Naval Park on the Niagara River at one Naval Park Cove, Buffalo, NY 14202. Phone: 716-847-1773. www. buffalonavalpark.org) **72**

HOLIDAY INN The ghost of a little girl who was burned to death in a house that once stood here now haunts the modern motel built over the ashes of her home. Guests, maids, managers, and bellboys have all witnessed Tanya's playful spirit. People usually report her jumping on beds in empty rooms or running through the halls at night. Manager Scott Swagler says: "Our housekeepers have stories about Tanya that could fill a book."

(Buffalo is on the Niagara River in extreme western New York. The hotel is on Grand Island. Take the Grand Island exit off I-190 just west of Buffalo. Holiday Inn, 100 Whitehaven Rd., Grand Island, NY 14072. Phone: 716-773-1111.) **72**

OLD FORT NIAGARA The Battle of Fort Niagara took place in 1759. British troops had French and Indian soldiers pinned down for two weeks. But that did not stop two Frenchmen from dueling over the attention of a beautiful young girl. Their sword fight was so fierce that the winner severed the head of his opponent. The head bounced on the cobblestones and rolled into a deep well. The ghost of headless Henri LeClerc has been seen on numerous occasions ever since, walking the battlements of Fort Niagara, searching for his lost head. It is said that when the full moon is at its highest point, the phantom of Henri climbs out of the well, and walks awkwardly into an old brick building, called the French Castle.

(Youngstown is twenty miles north of Buffalo on Highway 93. Old Fort Niagara is a state historic site located in the Fort Niagara State Park, P.O. Box 169 Youngstown, NY 14174. Ghost tours are held in October. Phone: 716-745-7611. www.oldfortniagara.org) **101, 168, 183**

CHENANGO RIVER VALLEY

CHENANGO QUARRY The shore around this deep, dark pool of water is haunted by the ghost of a big, red-faced man dressed in turn-of-the-century clothing. He is Jabez Mighty, a powerful millionaire who lived in a mansion called China Hall, and once ran for governor of New York. He was known as a ruthless, ambitious, and amoral man, and ended up cheating his five brothers out of all their inheritance and acquiring expensive real estate in a number of shady deals. He ruined so many lives that he was one of the most hated men in New York state. As Jabez grew older, he started cashing in all his holdings and buying gold. Late at night, his figure could be seen carrying iron boxes along paths leading to the bottomless waters of Chenango Quarry. One night he told his manservant, "I can't take it with me. But I'll know where it is, always." Jabez Mighty died on November 1, 1890 at the age of seventy-five. His ghost still returns to guard the deserted quarry near his home.

(The Chenango River Valley runs between Oneida Lake and Binghamton. The quarry is just outside the tiny town of Cincinnatus, which is at the junction of Highway 23 and Highway 26, just across the Chenango County line in Cayuga County.) **157**

CHENANGO RIVER The ghost of Manonah, an Oneida Indian chief, appears regularly along the banks of the Chenango River on the Earlville-Poolville Road. The ghostly Indian's first appearance was May 2, 1830, when he warned settlers not to fish the waters of the

Chenango River. Then on May 2, 1880, he rose out of the mists to tell a fisherman that he was violating the Oneida fishing grounds. By May 2, 1930, the word was out and the local fishermen were too afraid to fish the river after dusk. The same thing happened on May 2, 1980. Maybe someone will have the guts to challenge the spirit of Manonah on May 2, 2030.

(Earlville is forty-five miles southeast of Syracuse. Take Highway 92 southeast to U.S. Highway 20. Go south on Highway 46/12B to Earlville.) **72**

GEORGETOWN An ornate house with icicle lattice-work hanging from its eaves was begun here in 1855 by spiritualist Timothy Brown. Brown was a firm believer in spirits and the human ability to communicate with them, and he wanted to build a home suitable for departed souls. Brown insisted he was guided by spirits in building the house, which took fourteen years for him to complete. According to witnesses, when Brown would attempt to hammer a nail in the wrong place, "the spirits would not let him do it." On the upper floor of the house was a large séance room known as Free Hall, where traveling mediums would come to contact spirits. Thousands of spiritualists from all over the world traveled to Georgetown to behold the Spirit House. Timothy Brown joined the spirit world himself in 1885, dying at the age of seventy.

(Georgetown is in south Madison County at the junction of Highway 26 and Highway 80. Spirit House is now a private residence next to the Georgetown Baptist Church on South Main St., Georgetown, NY 13072.) **72**

COBLESKILL

BULL'S HEAD INN The ghost of a woman in a white nightgown has been seen in the first floor dining room here. That area used to be the bedroom of Mrs. John Stacy, when she lived in the house from 1920 to 1966 with her husband. Mrs. Stacy was an active member of the Women's Christian Temperance Union and is blamed for the peculiar phenomena that have plagued the inn ever since it acquired a liquor license. Her ghost has appeared to bartenders and tossed napkins and silverware at the bar. The Bull's Head Inn was opened in 1802 but became a private residence in 1839. It was reopened as an inn in 1966.

(Cobleskill is thirty-five miles west of Albany at the intersection of Highway 145 and I-88. The inn is at 2 Park Place, Cobleskill, NY 12043. Phone: 518-234-3591.) **133**

CUTCHOGUE

WICKHAM FARMHOUSE In 1988, on the night John and Anne Wickham awoke to find the ghost of man standing over their bed, they sealed the door and moved into another bedroom. The house has been considered haunted since 1854, when James and Frances Wickham were hacked to pieces by an insane farmhand. The footsteps of the ax murderer, creeping through the second floor hall on that fateful night, are still heard. The farm has stayed in the family since the murders, but no one uses the master bedroom anymore.

(Cutchogue is in extreme eastern Long Island, on Route 25 on the Great Peconic Bay. The farmhouse is a private residence in Suffolk County.) **72**

EMMONS

UNDERGROUND RAILROAD The Underground Railroad here helped slaves escape into Canada in the 1850s. One of the stops on the Underground Railroad was a house in Emmons that was connected to the river by a long tunnel. The tunnel was badly weakened by spring rains and collapsed one night while six slaves were making their way up to the house. No one was able to rescue any of the men, who had come tragically close to tasting their freedom. Today, some people hear the cries of terror and agony coming from the slaves buried beneath the streets of central Emmons. The eerie phenomenon seems most frequent during heavy rains in the springtime.

(The town of Emmons is in Delaware County, in south-central New York.) **183**

GLEN COVE

MORGAN HALL Banker J. P. Morgan's lavish estate on Long Island eventually became the home of a ghost. The mansion was built by Morgan in 1910 and used by the Russian Embassy after his death. When the Russians gave up the mansion, the Catholic Church converted it into a convent and school. Soon thereafter, women postulants in rooms on the third floor of the mansion began complaining of loud footsteps coming from the hallway and attic at all hours of the night. Rumors spread that the mansion was haunted. In October 1965, windows on the third floor opened and closed by themselves, and the women reported an invisible, icy-cold figure moving through their rooms. Finally, the ghost of girl wearing a long black dress appeared to one of the novice nuns. It was J. P.'s daughter Alice, who died of typhoid fever in the house while a young girl.

(Glen Cove is in northern Nassau County on Long Island. Morgan Hall is a private mansion in town.) **85**

WINFIELD HALL F. W. Woolworth built this sixty-two-room, palatial mansion in 1917 and died two years later. An eccentric man who believed he was the reincarnation of Napoleon, Woolworth died of infected teeth because he was too afraid to go to the dentist. He was not afraid of dabbling in the occult, however. He reportedly kept a black mirror, used in satanic rituals, in the master bedroom. The family's marble coat of arms above the fireplace cracked through the painted face of his daughter Edna Winfield, on the same night she committed suicide. Two fuzzy white mists thought to be Woolworth and his daughter have appeared at séances held in the house, and ghostly organ music is sometimes heard drifting through the hallways.

(Winfield Hall was purchased by the Reynolds family [of the Reynolds Aluminum Company] in 1929. From 1964 to 1976, it housed the Downs School, a modeling and stewardess training facility. The Italian Renaissance building is now the headquarters of the Pall Corporation.) **136**

GREENBURGH

BRANDYWINE BATTLEGROUND The ghost of a decapitated soldier clad in a blue Revolutionary War uniform has been spotted here frantically searching for his lost head. The soldier rides a ghostly horse along the Hudson River, at the site of a bloody battle during the War for Independence.

(Most sightings are in the southern Hudson Valley or near the New York–Pennsylvania border, along the Delaware River.) **78, 113**

HEMPSTEAD

ST. PAUL'S GREEK ORTHODOX CHURCH An icon of the Virgin Mary in the bedroom of twenty-two-year-old Pagona Catsounis began to shed tears on the evening of March 6, 1960. The devout woman had recited her evening prayers, when she noticed tears pouring down the cheeks of the Virgin Mary. The teardrops were witnessed by her husband and the family's pastor, who proclaimed it a miracle. In the next

week, over four thousand people visited the Catsounis home to witness the crying Virgin Mary. The icon shed copious tears for the entire week and then suddenly stopped. On March 23, the icon was moved to St. Paul's, where an average of 3,500 people a day came to view it.

(Hempstead is in central Nassau County on Long Island. The Catsounis family lived in an apartment in Island Park. The six-by eight-inch icon was enshrined on the altar of St. Paul's Greek Orthodox Church in Hempstead at 110 Cathedral Ave. Phone: 516-483-5700.) **56, 139**

HUDSON

DIETZ HOUSE This house, built in the 1830s, is haunted by Mabel Parker, a woman who moved into the house in 1904 and lived there for more than fifty years. During the time the Jay Dietz family lived in the house, Mabel's ghost was often heard walking up the stairs into the hall and entering a second-floor bedroom, where she was apt to pull the covers off anyone sleeping in her old room.

(Hudson is in Columbia County, thirty miles south of Albany on I-87, at Exit 21. The house is now a private residence in Old Town, on South 6th St., Hudson, NY 12534.) **80**

HUDSON VALLEY

HUDSON CORRIDOR The lower Hudson River Valley is one of the nation's UFO hotspots. Ossining west to Stony Point and then north along the river to Newburgh and Poughkeepsie has been an area of intense UFO activity since the mid-1970s. Researcher Philip Imbrogno has catalogued over six thousand sightings in his book *Night Siege: The Hudson Valley UFO Sightings*. One repeatedly sighted object during the 1980s was a triangular-shaped UFO the size of a football field that stopped traffic on major highways as it slowly passed overhead. Hundreds of reports of alien abductions accompanied the sightings. See Kent Cliffs, below.

(The Hudson Corridor begins just northeast of New York City and runs into western Connecticut. U.S. Highway 9 and U.S. Highway 9W run through the center of the New York area, while I-84 cuts through the area in western Connecticut.) **53 (6/94, 9/95)**

KENT CLIFFS Colonists arriving here believed the nearby stone structures were built by Druids, and stayed away. The rock caves were probably constructed during the period between 2000 B.C. and A.D. 500, and there is some evidence that Druids did actually build them. The caves are made of huge carved limestone and granite boulders. The largest chamber is located in Fahnestock State Park, just outside Kent Cliffs. This small town is at the center of paranormal activity and the point of origin for many UFO sightings in the Hudson Corridor. The area shows many magnetic anomalies and strange ghostly figures have been reported near the sites. Cloaked phantoms have been seen surrounding the Balanced Stone, and short gray alien creatures have been reported along Magnetic Road. A red-glowing phantom was encountered at the Double Capstone Chamber. Other strange beings, including Viking-like ghosts and dwarfs in hooded robes have been seen at other sites.

(Kent Cliffs is in Putnam County, northeast of West Point at the junction on Highway 301. Balanced Rock is located just off Highway 116 in North Salem, which is on the Connecticut border southeast of Kent Cliffs. Magnetic Road is in Croton Falls, which is halfway between Kent Cliffs and North Salem. The Double Capstone Chamber is just off Highway 301 outside Kent Cliffs.) **53 (6/94)**

HYDESVILLE

FOX SISTERS The worldwide spiritualist movement began here in March, 1848, in a case that became known as the Hydesville Haunting. The Fox family lived in a ramshackle house on the outskirts of Hydesville. John Fox was a blacksmith and farmer. He and his wife shared their small home with two daughters, fifteen-year-old Margaretta (Maggie) and eleven-year-old Catherine (Katie). Unexplainable knocking sounds started in the girls' room one night and soon became a regular event. When the two girls realized the strange sounds could do them no harm, they started asking the mysterious noisemaker questions using a preset code. To everyone's surprise, the spirit replied correctly to such questions as how old were the Fox sisters. It also told of being murdered by John Bell, one of the former tenants of the house. The spirit said Bell had murdered him for five hundred dollars and that his body was buried in the cellar. Mr. Fox reportedly found human teeth and pieces of skull buried there. A former servant of Bell, Lucretia Pulver, told police that a young peddler had stayed at the house in 1844 and then mysteriously disappeared. After that, Lucretia refused to

work alone in the house, because she thought it was haunted. When the Bells moved out, a Mrs. Lafe took up tenancy. She moved out after only a few months, insisting the house was haunted by the ghost of a young man. Nonetheless, authorities would not prosecute Bell, who lived only a few miles away, based on ghost sightings and the rappings of a disembodied spirit. As word spread of the phenomenon, hundreds of people came to Hydesville to witness the tapping entity, and many were allowed to question the spirit themselves. The girls nicknamed him "Mr. Splitfoot," although he indicated his initials were "C. R." and that he was from Orleans County in northwest New York.

An older sister, Leah, organized nationwide tours in which the three Fox sisters gave demonstrations and lectures, but the strenuous schedule was too much for the two younger sisters, who suffered from alcoholism and mental deterioration. Katie died in 1891 at the age of fifty-six, and Maggie followed her a year later, at the age of fifty-nine. Whether or not the Fox sisters somehow faked their contact with the Other Side, they fired enthusiasm for spiritualism for the next fifty years, as thousands of people engaged in seances and table-tapping experiments in an effort to establish a "spiritual telegraph" with the dead. Finally, in November 1904, children playing in the cellar of the deserted Fox house caused the east wall to collapse, burying one of them under dirt and rubble. Rescuers discovered that a false wall had been built a few feet from the original wall. Behind the partition, they found an old peddler's tin box and the headless corpse of a man. The original house burned to the ground in 1955 but was rebuilt and moved to Lily Dale as a tourist attraction in 1968. (See Lily Dale, below.)

(The tiny settlement of Hydesville is in upstate New York, about thirty miles east of Rochester in Wayne County.) **6, 37, 40, 44, 56, 72, 68, 69, 179, 189, 196, 204, 212**

LAKE PLEASANT

ELM LAKE Philip Rhinelander, Jr., built a sawmill and hundred-acre estate on Lake Pleasant in the early 1800s. He was an extremely jealous man. He kept his wife a virtual prisoner on the property, and there were rumors that he had killed a peddler and a servant who got too close to her. Mary Golden Rhinelander died on September 7, 1818. Philip kept his wife's body in a crypt near the house, and took her body to New York City with him when he moved there in 1823. For the next fifty years, the ghost of Mary Rhinelander often haunted the Elm Lake house, even appearing in broad daylight to men working in the fields. After the house burned down in 1874, the appearances lessened, although sometimes she is still seen roaming the remote ruins of her Elm Lake estate.

(Lake Pleasant is in the Albany area, in eastern New York. The sawmill site is near a bridge on the main highway over the Sacandaga River at Lake Pleasant. The house nearby overlooked tiny Elm Lake. The densely forested land is now owned by the International Paper Corporation.) **49**

LEEDS

SALISBURY MANOR This blue-stone mansion was built by William Salisbury in 1730. He was a stalwart Christian and stern man, who went too far in punishing one of his servant girls. He repeatedly warned Anna Swartz that he would not stand for her late-night merrymaking. One night, he went to a dance held at a neighboring farmhouse and demanded that Anna accompany him home. To humiliate her further, the heartless man tied his servant to a rope attached to a second horse he had brought with him. His servant walked behind the animal for several miles, until something spooked the horses. Salisbury was thrown from his horse, but Anna's horse galloped away, dragging her behind. The poor girl died a horrible death, and Salisbury was sentenced to hang for her murder. However, because of his high standing in the community, his sentence was delayed until he reached the age of ninety-nine. In the meantime, he was ordered to wear a noose around his neck to remind him of the sentence. Salisbury wrapped the noose in fine red silk and facetiously carried out the decree. He died in 1801 at the age of eighty-seven. For many years, the ghost of a gray horse, dragging something behind it, was seen galloping on the road to Salisbury Manor. After Salisbury died, his ghost joined the gray stallion, to ride forever along the haunted road.

(Leeds is at the junction of Highway 23B and Five Mile Woods Road in Greene County. Take Exit 21 of the New York State Thruway. The town is 2.5 miles west of the exit. Salisbury Manor is a private residence. For Salisbury Manor tour information, contact the Greene County Promotion Department, P.O. Box 467, Catskill, NY 12414 518-943-3223. www.greene-ny.com) **36**

LILY DALE

LILY DALE ASSEMBLY Lily Dale is a 167-acre spiritualist settlement founded 116 years ago. Members say there is something special about Lily Dale, especially a spot known as Inspiration Stump, that fosters communication with departed souls. During an 1884 séance at the old tree trunk, a guitar was taken into the air and carried about by a spirit. Lily Dale is also the headquarters of the Spiritualist Church, and from June through Labor Day, thousands of mediums gather here to attend classes, hold séances, meditate, and conduct healings. Free public séances, called Message Services, are provided, as well as individual readings that cost about thirty-five dollars an hour with any of the thirty mediums who have passed the assembly's certification process.

(Lily Dale is about forty-five miles southeast of Buffalo on Cassandra Lake. Take the Fredonia exit off I-90 south to Lily Dale. The Maplewood Hotel is in the compound. Phone: 716-595-2505.) **72**

MOHAWK VALLEY

BEARDSLEE CASTLE Guy Roosevelt Beardslee built this mansion, a replica of an Irish castle, in 1860. The last Beardslee family member left the manor in the 1940s, and the structure was converted into a restaurant. Since then, dozens of customers and employees have reported all sorts of ghostly manifestations. Balls of light and ghostly figures, some blue and white, others dark green and red, have been observed floating through the rooms. The ghost of former owner Anton Christensen has been seen in the upstairs corner where he committed suicide by hanging himself. The source of a terrifying scream, "a cross between a scream and a howl" that sometimes fills the hallways, has never been found. The shadow of a large man is seen walking on the top floor and off the main lobby. Sometimes his apparition appears as an "X-ray ghost," in which only his skeleton shows up. Flying tableware and napkins have also been observed, as well as chairs that move by themselves. The origin of some of the disturbances might date back as far as the 1700s, when a French fort stood here. It is said that Indians tunneled under the outpost with barrels of gunpowder to destroy it but were killed when the explosives ignited prematurely.

(The Beardslee Castle Restaurant is in the Mohawk Valley. It is located seventy-five miles west of Albany, on

Highway 5 between St. Johnsville and Little Falls. Phone: 315-823-3000.) **134**

HENDERSON HOUSE This replica of an ancient Scottish castle is haunted by the stalwart lady who had it built on land she inherited from her parents. Harriet Douglas Cruger was a hot-tempered woman who once had the bed she shared with her husband sawed in half to make a point. No one wanted to cross the red-haired lady, a fact which makes it seem odd that her relatives failed to follow her last wishes. When she died in 1870 at the age of eighty, she left instructions that she was to be interred in a sarcophagus in the basement of her castle home. Instead she was buried in a cemetery, and her sarcophagus was taken outside and used as a horse trough. One day not long after her death, the stone trough was destroyed by a bolt of lightning. Doors started slamming with an angry bang, the way they used to when she was alive. Things began to go wrong unless they were done the way "Aunt Harriet" preferred. To this day, they say Harriet Douglas Cruger's home is still her castle.

(Henderson House is a private residence off I-90 in the Mohawk Valley.) **187**

MOHAWK RIVER The ghost of an Indian in a phantom canoe is seen paddling in the middle of the Mohawk River. The white-haired Indian is thought to be the last of the Mohawks, a tribe of Algonquian Indians that settled in this valley. The Indian died in 1789.

(The section of the Mohawk River where the phantom is seen runs southeast from Utica to Schenectady.) **115**

NEWFANE

VAN HORN MANSION The ghost of Malinda Van Horn haunts the opulent brick mansion where she died in 1837. Her apparition has been seen in the upstairs bedroom and standing by a hall window. Malinda has even been spotted standing in the middle of the street in front of the house. During renovations, workers encountered her smoky figure under an archway on the second floor. The men refused to return to work, and a new crew had to be hired.

(The town of Newfane is in extreme western New York, twenty-eight miles north of Buffalo on Highway 78. Van Horn Mansion, 2165 Lockport-Olcott Rd., Newfane, NY 14108. Phone: 716-778-7197.) **72**

NEW LEBANON

SHAKER BUILDINGS The ghosts of a strict sect of Quakers who built a community of twenty buildings here in the 1800s still roam the grounds. The last Shaker members left the area in the 1940s, and their old settlement became a summer camp. A Sufi spiritual sect acquired the land in 1975 and set up the Abode of Message Center in the eastern half of the compound. The westernmost buildings are used by a private high school called the Darrow School. Both of the new tenants have been visited by the peaceful spirits of those who once lived on these grounds. The ghost of a woman wearing an apron is seen in the ruins of the carriage house, near the school, and the Sufis have sensed the presence of many spirits from the days when the celibate, nonmaterialistic Shakers lived in their buildings.

(The Shaker buildings are located on a dirt road that leads off U.S. Highway 20 about thirty-miles east of Albany and six miles west of Pittsfield, Massachusetts.) **135**

NEW YORK CITY

ABIGAIL ADAMS SMITH MUSEUM Unexplainable footsteps and other strange sounds here have led some to speculate that Abigail Adams Smith still walks the halls of her former home.

(Abigail Adams Smith Museum, 421 East 64th St, New York, NY 10021. 212-838-6878. For general information on New York City, call the Visitor's Bureau at 212-397-8200.) **72, 101**

BARKER HOUSE This brownstone apartment house was built in 1859. Its first owner, Alanda Hanna Barker, lived there with her two sisters for over fifty years. In the 1970s, the building was used as a whorehouse, and it was voted one of the ten most interesting bordellos in New York by one magazine. In 1978, the house was purchased by Carole Boyd and Sandi Summer, who renovated the building for use as a town house. Before long, objects began moving under their own volition, and the sounds of classical music could be heard drifting through the house. Often the suffocating smell of lavender would arise from nowhere. Many other inexplicable events occurred before Sandi came across the ghost of a twelve-year-old girl with long blond hair, wearing a nightgown, standing in her bedroom. The women called the ASPR, who investigated the house. Their twenty-nine-page report concluded the house was indeed haunted, with the back room on the third floor the center of the activity. Other ghosts started to appear in the house. They included a tall, thin man wearing 1700s clothing, a man who built boats in the garden, a grieving woman in black, a wild-acting woman, and a furry dog. One other intriguing fact about this case: Neighbors have reported seeing ghostly prostitutes walking the street in front of the building.

(The three-story brownstone is a private residence in Manhattan on East 26th St.) **134**

BAY RIDGE APARTMENTS Something about the Makuta family seems to attract departed spirits. The family has lived with a gaggle of ghosts for many years. Their first otherworldly visitor was Linda's grandfather, policeman William Mahoney, who died in 1980. The ASPR investigated the Makutas in 1985, and three psychics who examined the apartment all agreed on the presence of several other departed spirits in the household. A ghost named Otto followed the family when they moved here. So did the spirit of a woman named Eileen, who keeps asking for the police to be called. The restless spirit suspects someone has murdered her. The ghost of a woman named Clarisse waits at the top of the stairs for a letter to come, and the wraith of a six-year-old girl is sometimes seen next to her. Another ghost, that of an elderly woman in a blue dress, followed the family home after they attended a performance of *Godspell* at a local church. Kevin and Linda Makuta and their children Justin and Lauren have lived with the ghosts so long, they have gotten used to them, although they have a hard time finding babysitters.

(The Makuta apartment is a private residence at 544 Bay Ridge Parkway, Brooklyn, NY 11209.) **135**

BELASCO THEATER The old Belasco Theater was considered to be one of America's most haunted places for nearly fifty years. The ghost of owner David Belasco was seen for many years after his death in 1931. The sounds of an empty backstage elevator could be heard going up to his ten-room suite, where he took showgirls for private "auditions," and the sounds of wild parties were heard coming from the empty chambers. Though his theater once hosted some of America's best vaudeville acts, it eventually became a sleazy striptease joint known as the Follies. Then in 1965, patrons and workers started reporting the ghost of a redheaded lady

wearing a white negligee. She sometimes appeared descending a circular staircase and once threw a vase across the manager's office. She was thought to resemble a former stripper, who had hanged herself in the basement of the club. She continued to haunt the area, even after the decrepit theater was torn down.

(The Belasco, later known as the Follies, was located at 111 West 44th St., New York, NY 10036. Phone: 212-239-6200.) **72, 102, 116, 188**

BOWNE HOUSE This national landmark is haunted by an unidentified presence. The 330-year-old-house is said to be home to a colonial ghost, which the site's education director has characterized as "friendly or positive."

(The Bowne House Historical Society operates the house, which is located in the Flushing section of Queens.) **72**

CENTRAL PARK During the winter months, the ghosts of two sisters haunt the Wollman Ice Rink here. Rosetta and Janet Van der Voort lived in a brownstone mansion in Manhattan in the 1800s. The two were inseparable, and during the winter they spent endless hours together skating figure eights on the ice in Central Park. When they grew older, they lived alone together in their large house. They had no friends or close relatives and died within months of one another in 1880. Their ghosts were first spotted during World War I skating side by side on the frozen lake in Central Park. They were both dressed in huge bustles: one in a red dress, the other in a purple dress. The skating ghosts have been seen many times since, their silver skates gliding just above the ice in a never-ending series of figure eights.

(The Wollman Ice Rink is a frozen pond in south Central Park at 59th St. The Van der Voort mansion is on 14th St., just off Fifth Avenue. For general information, contact the New York Convention and Visitor's Center, 2 Columbus Circle, New York, NY 10019. Phone: 212-397-8222.) **158**

CLINTON COURT An old potter's graveyard here is haunted by several ghosts. Old Moor, a mutinous sailor executed by the British, was the first ghost to appear. In the 1820s, when the building was a carriage house for Governor George Clinton, Old Moor's appearance frightened a coachman's wife so badly that she fell down a winding stairway and died—only to become another ghost haunting the courtyard. Old Moor also frightened one of Governor Clinton's children, who fell from the second floor porch to her death. Recently, the presences of the child's ghost and the spirit of a colonial officer named Walker have been detected in the courtyard. See Havoc House, below.

(Clinton Court can be accessed by entering the narrow passage at 420 West 46th St. into a large courtyard. The quaint building at 422[h] West 46th St., is the former carriage house. The winding stairway to the second floor still exists. The neighborhood is in the Hell's Kitchen district of Manhattan.) **89, 91**

CLINTON STREET BROWNSTONE A one-hundred-year-old building here is said to be haunted by the ghost of a young girl who died while her father was attempting to perform an abortion on her. Cesa Rist was the daughter of a doctor who once owned the house. When she became pregnant by her boyfriend, her father tried to abort the baby at home. Cesa died during the operation. She was buried in the family plot in Denver, Colorado, but her spirit was drawn back to New York.

(The house is a private residence in the 300 block of Clinton St., Brooklyn, NY 11200.) **80, 91**

THE DAKOTA This Gothic apartment building was built in 1884. It is where Roman Polanski filmed *Rosemary's Baby* (1966), although the castlelike structure has long had a reputation for being a supernatural site. In 1965, workers renovating Apartment 77 encountered the ghost of a ten-year-old boy walking in a hallway between two bedrooms. The child's ghost was accompanied by a "strange outdoorsy, fresh-yet-musty odor" and was seen on several occasions by multiple witnesses. In the 1960s, Boris Karloff and Judy Holliday lived at the Dakota. The apartments also became the home of John Lennon, who was shot to death by a crazed gunman in the doorway of the building on December 8, 1980. Numerous reliable witnesses have reported seeing his ghost on the sidewalk in front of the Dakota.

(The Dakota is on the corner of 72nd St. and Central Park West in Manhattan. Phone: 212-362-1448.) **101, 136, 149, 186**

DAVINCI'S PIZZA RESTAURANT The phantom of a Madison Avenue advertising executive whose life was ruined by alcohol leaves empty martini glasses on the bar here and scribbles ad slogans on the walls. The man committed suicide after becoming an alcoholic, and his ghost still wants a drink every now and then.

(The posh restaurant and bar is at 44 Waters St. in Manhattan. Phone: 212-635-2424.) **82**

DEGELDERN HOUSE The ghost of a young girl haunted this old brownstone in the 1960s. The ghost was described as sixteen years old, with braided blond hair and wearing an old-fashioned blue dress. The apparition was most often seen on the heavy wooden staircase near the first floor. The Worm family and the DeGeldern family both reported sensing the dead girl's presence. The house was built in 1894, and no one was able to identify the spirit.

(The five-story brownstone is a private residence on West 87th St. in Manhattan.) **82**

EMPIRE STATE BUILDING This skyscraper was the scene of many suicides until the protective barriers at the top of the building were raised higher, but the ghosts of those who leaped to their deaths are said to haunt the observation deck. Recently the apparition of a woman in her twenties, wearing bright red lipstick and dressed in 1940s clothing, was seen in the elevator and on the deck. She is thought to be a woman who committed suicide here after learning that her lover was killed in Germany during World War II.

(The Empire State Building is located at 350 Fifth Avenue at 34th St. The 1,250-foot-high observation deck is on the 102nd floor. Phone: 212-736-3100.) **38**

FIRE STATION NO. 2 This eighty-eight-year-old firehouse is home to the ghost of a middle-aged fireman who wears an old-fashioned helmet and a double-breasted red shirt. The apparition has a mustache and salt-and-pepper hair. He has been spotted in a fourth floor storage room, on the stairs, and in a basement coal bin. In 1991, a fireman was awakened at 2:30 A.M. by the specter of the dead man staring down at him over his bed. In 1992, William Tobin, a twenty-five-year veteran with the New York Fire Department, told reporters that he saw the ghost in a long, narrow storage room on the fourth floor.

(The four-story firehouse is across the street from the Poe House in Greenwich Village. Fire Station No. 2, 84 West 3rd St., New York, NY 10012.) **72, 198 (11-93)**

A middle-aged fireman haunts his old firehouse. See Fire Station No. 2, New York City, New York
(B. A. SCHAFFENBERGER)

FRANCIS HOUSE Both Aaron Burr's attempt to become president of the United States in 1800 and his run for governor of New York four years later were foiled by his powerful archenemy, Alexander Hamilton. The two men's hatred for one another came to a head on July 4, 1804, when they faced each other in a pistol duel. Hamilton was mortally wounded and taken to the home of his physician, John Francis. His doctor's house became the site of the famous patriot's funeral. Although the original quarters no longer stand, some residents at the apartment building on the site say it is haunted. See Quantum Leap Café and Morris-Jumel Mansion, New York City; and Lindenwald, Albany.

(The apartment building is located at 27 Jane St. in the Greenwich Village section of New York City. Hamilton actually died at 80[h] Jane St., now a hardware store. He is buried in the graveyard at Trinity Church.) **37, 42, 86**

GARROWAY HOUSE Television personality Dave Garroway's six-story house was haunted by the ghost of an evil old man in the late 1960s. Every night the agi-tated ghost would open every door in the house, even if they were locked. Concerned that the entity would harm their children, the Garroways called in medium Ethyl Meyers. Although she held a séance, the medium believed she was unsuccessful at dispelling the angry spirit.

(Dave Garroway and his family lived in a house on East 63rd St. in New York City for many years.) **89**

GAUNT RESIDENCE Barrie Gaunt, a tenant in a basement apartment here in the 1960s, lived with a ghost for several years. A moving fog seemed to follow him, and some invisible presence poked at guests sleeping in the bedrooms. During an investigation in 1964, Hans Holzer and Sybil Leek contacted a spirit named Miss Boyd. According to records, a woman named Boyd lived there with her father. She died in the house in 1886 while looking for a deed to the property. Apparently, she was still looking for it eighty years later.

(The building is now a private residence in Greenwich Village on Charles St., New York, NY 10014.) **82**

GAY STREET PHANTOM Residents of this apart-ment building have sensed a shadowy entity moving up and down the stairways, and once, several witnesses encountered the apparition of a man in a black suit standing on the steps in front of the building. The ghost smiled politely and then disappeared. The apparition of a man in a top hat and tails has been reported inside the house as well. Author Walter Gibson believes the spirits are psychic impressions he left behind when he wrote *The Shadow* mystery series here in the late 1940s. The Shadow was Gibson's crimefighting hero. His alter ego, Lamont Cranston, often wore a dark cape and top hat.

(The apartment building is in Greenwich Village at 12 Gay St., New York, NY 10014.) **72, 89**

HAVOC HOUSE The basement apartment of this townhouse was the home of actress June Havoc from 1962 to 1969. She noticed many strange things at the rear of the house, including unexplained tapping and banging noises from the kitchen. It sounded as if some-one were looking through the cabinets for something to eat. Former tenants had nicknamed the ghost Hun-gry Lucy.

(The Victorian apartment building is a private resi-dence on the corner of 44th St. and 9th Ave. at 428 West 44th St., New York, NY 10036.) **81, 86, 89,101**

HOTEL DES ARTISTES This old Manhattan hotel is haunted by a noisy ghost who likes to touch people. The outgoing spirit's cloudlike apparition has been reported by several tenants here.

(Hotel Des Artistes, 1 West 67th St., New York, NY 10023.) **101**

HOUDINI HOUSE The ghost of magician and psychic investigator Harry Houdini is seen in his former New York apartment. Before he died on October 31, 1926, he left secret code words with several people, whom he promised to contact from beyond the grave (see Houdini Mansion and Hollywood Hotels, Hollywood, California).

(The brownstone house is a private residence at 278 West 113th St., New York, NY 10026.) **72**

JAN JUS PLAYHOUSE An unfriendly spirit is said to haunt this theater building. Author Marvin Kaye encountered the Jan Jus Phantom in 1973 and has since written several books about ghosts. The theater is home of the comedy company Chicago City Limits.

(Jan Jus Playhouse, 351 East 74th St., New York, NY 10021. Phone: 212-288-6743.) **102**

MARTHA WASHINGTON HOTEL A twelfth-floor room at the Martha Washington is reportedly occupied by the stubborn spirit of an elderly lady who once lived there. Later tenants at this women's hotel said they could hear the ghostly lady turning newspaper pages late at night. Eileen Courtis, who stayed in the room for six months, said the unfriendly ghost once held a pillow over her face while she was sleeping. Courtis believed the spirit hated anyone staying in "her" room. She might be right. At least two previous tenants were found dead in the room.

(The women's residence is at 30 East 30th St., in Manhattan. Phone: 212-689-1900.) **80, 87**

MCGOWAN'S GHOST An attic darkroom in this studio apartment is haunted by the ghost of a man who was hanged from the rafters there. Tenants of the apartment reported the greenish phantom on numerous occasions. The ghost is believed to be that of General Samuel Edward McGowan, a Union officer in the Civil War. McGowan was strangled to death in this apartment by the boyfriend of his mistress, Mignon Guychone. The man hanged McGowan's body from the attic rafters to make it look as if the Southerner committed suicide. General McGowan's body was taken back to South Carolina and buried there. But his ghost haunts the site of his insidious murder.

(General McGowan is buried in Long Cane Graveyard in Abbeville, South Carolina. The studio is on the top floor of the Victorian apartment building at 226 Fifth Ave., New York, NY 10001.) **86, 89**

MEDICAL ARTS BUILDING A malevolent presence in the penthouse apartment here has been blamed for driving tenants mad. The oppressive atmosphere is thought to be the legacy of socialite Edna Champion and her French lover, Charles Brazelle, who lived together in the building and had a secret passageway connecting their apartments. Their bitter arguments eventually cost them their lives. Both died from injuries suffered at each other's hands.

(The building is at 57 West 57th St., New York, NY 10019.) **212**

MERCHANT-HOUSE MUSEUM This ornate, three-story brownstone was the home of the Tredwell family for a century. Seabury Tredwell, who made a small fortune in the hardware business, built the imposing brownstone in 1830. He and his wife Eliza had six daughters and two sons, and Mr. Tredwell was known as a strict disciplinarian. He ruled his house with an iron hand, which might be why one of his daughters killed herself when she became pregnant out of wedlock. Seabury died in 1865, and for many years the only resident of the house was his eccentric spinster daughter Gertrude, who died in 1933 at the age of ninety-three. The unique house, with two cellars and a secret tunnel to the river, is one of the few surviving brownstone mansions furnished just as it was in the nineteenth century. It was not long after the Historical Landmarks Society turned the Tredwell home into a museum that caretakers and docents began reporting the ghostly figure of Gertrude Tredwell materializing in the canopy bed in the front bedroom and near the fireplace in the parlor. Other active areas include the kitchen and ground floor at the rear of the house. Over the last thirty years, Gertrude's ghost has been reported by a variety of other witnesses, including journalists, photographers, and psychic researchers.

(The museum is operated by the Historical Landmarks Society. It is located between Lafayette St. and the Bowery at 29 East 4th St., New York, NY 10003. Phone: 212-777-1089.)

www.merchantshouse.com/house.htm) **85, 87, 89, 101**

MORRIS-JUMEL MANSION The ghost of an angry old lady haunts this stately home. Some believe that beautiful Eliza Jumel murdered her aging husband Stephen in 1832. A year later, the rich widow married politician Aaron Burr. That marriage lasted another year. Eliza accused the seventy-seven-year-old Burr of adultery and was granted a quick divorce. Burr died a year later. Eliza had accumulated a vast fortune but was shunned by New York society. Living alone in her stately mansion, she went insane and died in 1865 at the age of ninety-three. Many times over the years, people have reported the ghosts of both Eliza and Stephen Jumel roaming through their mansion. The ghost of the crazy old lady has been seen at the third-floor windows shouting at noisy children on the street below. On January 19, 1964, a whole group of school children witnessed her phantom on the balcony. Two other ghosts seen on the third floor are of a servant girl who leaped to her death from the balcony, and the spirit of an unknown presence, possibly a soldier or Aaron Burr himself (see Quantum Leap Café and Francis House, New York City; and Lindenwald, Albany). Another ghost may preexist the Jumels'. In 1993, the ghost of a Revolutionary War soldier was witnessed on two separate occasions on the top floor by school teachers taking their classes on tours through the building. The mansion was built in 1765 by a British colonel named Roger Morris. The Jumels bought it in 1810.

(Morris-Jumel Mansion is in the Washington Heights section of Harlem on Manhattan's West Side. It is a historic site preserved by the City of New York. Follow 162nd St. to Jumel Terrace. The mansion is on the corner of Edgecombe Ave. and 160th St., at 1765 Jumel Terrace, New York, NY 10032. Phone: 212-923-8008.) **14, 42, 72, 82, 86, 89, 101, 188**

MUSEUM OF THE AMERICAN INDIAN This museum has a number of haunted items in its collection of over one million Indian artifacts. One is a sacred buffalo horn. In 1938, a member of the Water Buster sect of the Gros Ventres Indians of Montana donated his tribe's most cherished relic to this museum. The horn is said to allow one to experience the consciousness and power of a buffalo. By holding the horn and calling forth its power, the initiate will have visions and dreams of being in the body of buffalo.

(The National Museum of the American Indian is operated by the Smithsonian Institute. It is located in the Old Custom House in Lower Manhattan at 1 Bowling Green. For directions and information, call 212-668-6624. www.nmai.si.edu/hreye/index.html) **72**

NATHAN HALE PLAQUE Sensitive people have been overcome by feelings of mayhem and violence here. The impressions do not stem from any modern-day encounter on the busy street corner but from an act of violence that occurred on this spot nearly 225 years ago. This is where convicted spy Nathan Hale was executed by a British firing squad.

(The commemorative plaque is on the side of the Hotel Biltmore at the corner of 43rd St. and Vanderbilt Ave. in Manhattan. For information, contact the Office for Metropolitan History, 246 West 80th St., New York, New York 10024. Phone: 212-799-0520.) **86**

PALACE THEATRE The ghost of a tightrope walker has been seen swinging on the dress-circle rim at this theater. Louis Borsalino, part of the "Four Casting Pearls" act, fell to his death while performing on the tightrope here in the 1950s. The ghost's screams and images of a man falling to his death have been reported by people peering through peepholes in the curtain.

(The theater is at Broadway and 47th Street. Palace Theatre, 1564 Broadway, New York, NY 10036. Phone: 212-730-8200.) **94**

POE HOUSE Edgar Allan Poe lived in this house from 1844 to 1845, but the famous horror author is not the presence that haunts it. It has been suggested that the spirit is that of an insane woman kept hidden in the house after Poe moved out. Unexplainable pounding and thumping sounds, and a woman's incoherent ramblings have been reported in the attic. See Fire Station No. 2, above; and Poe House, Baltimore, Maryland.

(The four-story, plaster-facade house is a private residence in Greenwich Village, at 85 West 3rd St., New York, NY 10012.) **72, 198 (11–93)**

QUANTUM LEAP NATURAL FOOD RESTAURANT The ground floor of this three-story building is reputed to be haunted. The ground floor is divided into a duplex loft. At the rear of the lower room, several employees and customers have observed the ghost of a young man with penetrating black eyes, wearing a ruffled white shirt. He is thought to be the spirit of American statesman Aaron Burr. Up to the 1830s, the building was part of Burr's stables. See Fire Station No. 2, Francis House, and Morris-Jumel Mansion, New York City; and Lindenwald, Albany.

(The café is near Sullivan St., next door to Fire Station No. 2, in Greenwich Village. The natural food restaurant was previously known as Café Bizarre. Quantum Leap Natural Food, 88 West 3rd Street, New York, NY 10012. Phone: 212-677-8050.) **72, 82, 89, 101, 188**

ST. BARTHOLOMEW'S CHURCH The figure of Christ suddenly appeared on a wall here in February 1932. The clearly discernible image, about 1.5 feet tall, showed a white-robed Christ coming out of a rockhewn tomb, with a wooden cross in the background. The image was discovered by Reverend Dr. Robert Norwood, just after he concluded a Lenten sermon on the mystical significance of Christ's resurrected body. Hundreds of visitors filed into the church to witness the image, which the reverend conjectured was created by the force of thought of his parishioners.

(The figure of Christ can be seen in the light marble of the sanctuary wall at St. Bartholomew's Church in Manhattan. St. Bartholomew's, 109 East 50th St., New York, NY 10022. Phone: 212-378-0200. www.stbarts.org) **56**

ST. MARK'S IN-THE-BOWERY The first church on this site was built in 1660 by New York's first governor, Peter Stuyvesant. He was buried in a vault here in 1672. The old church was torn down and another church built on the same spot in 1799. The new church is now home to four ghosts. The apparition of a woman parishioner appears in the center aisle in the middle of the nave. Another woman ghost in a wide skirt stands near the rear entrance. A ghostly form has also been seen in the balcony next to the organ. The apparition of a man with a wooden leg, who walks with a cane, is none other than Peter Stuyvesant. The Bowery was originally the road to his farm. After he died at the age of eighty, his ghost was reported walking on his former property. Today, people who live in the area, tourists, and homeless people report encountering his apparition strolling down the sidewalks of the Bowery.

(The ghost of Peter Stuyvesant is most often seen walking down Stuyvesant Ave. toward Cooper Square. St. Mark's in-the-Bowery is a Catholic church open to the public. It is located in lower Manhattan on the corner of Second Ave. and Tenth St. on St. Mark's Square. St.

Mark's in-the-Bowery, 131 East 10th St., New York, NY 10003. Phone: 212-533-4650.) **15, 89, 91**

ST. PAUL'S CHAPEL The sidewalk in front of this Catholic church is haunted by the apparition of one of America's most revered photographers, Mathew Brady. He loved to walk the streets of New York, and his ghost has been reported approaching people on the sidewalk, as if he were going to ask them something. This was where Brady set up his first photography "studio," where he spent many hours soliciting business from people dressed up for dinner, pushing baby carriages, or just strolling down Broadway. He used all his money to finance twenty photographers, who recorded the horror and anguish of the Civil War. His priceless negatives were confiscated by the government when Brady fell behind on the rent of his storage space. It was only after his death in 1876 that people recognized his great contribution.

(Take Broadway south to Fulton St. The Episcopal chapel is on the corner of Fulton St. and Broadway. The church graveyard is at Vesey St. and Broadway. Brady is buried at Arlington National Cemetery. St. Paul's Chapel, Fulton and Broadway, 211 Broadway New York, 10038. Phone: 212-602-0874.) **15**

TIMES SQUARE The ghosts of two Royal Air Force officers have been sighted walking on the sidewalks here. The two are always looking at their watches and seem like flesh and blood people, until the stroke of midnight, when they disappear into thin air. One witness said the apparitions told him they were killed over Berlin in World War II and had always wanted to see Times Square.

(Times Square is on Broadway at 45th St. in Manhattan.) **39**

TWAIN HOUSE Mark Twain once stayed at this old apartment house, but it is the ghosts of murdered children that haunt the place. Just before World War II, two immigrants killed their young child by starvation and bizarre torture, such as making the child walk around in circles for hours while tied to a rope looped over the top of a chair. The house seemed to take on the child's twisted life force, and several tenants felt strangely uncomfortable in the house. Former tenant Joan Bryant Bartell wrote a book about the building's ghosts, entitled *Spindrift*. She committed suicide shortly after moving out, and her book was published posthumously in 1974. In 1987, another little girl, seven-year-old Lisa Steinberg, was beaten to death in a third-floor apartment here.

(The apartment building is in Greenwich Village at 14 West 10th St., New York, NY 10011.) **72**

NIAGARA

DEVIL'S HOLE This twenty-foot-deep cave got its name because of the dark, evil presence many have detected here. Seneca legend attributes the feeling to the Evil One, the master of dark spirits. It has been a scene of massacre and disaster for over three centuries. French explorer LaSalle ignored warnings against visiting the cave and was murdered in 1687. British troops were massacred by Indians near the cave in 1763, and many Indians died in battles that followed. Since the 1850s countless people have lost their lives in freak accidents near the cave. Nearly every year, someone is killed by falling or drowning near the haunted cave.

(Devil's Hole is north of Niagara off U.S. Highway 62, between the Whirlpool Rapids and Lewiston on the Niagara River Gorge. The site is opposite Niagara Glen near the Canadian border.) **53 (6/92)**

NIAGARA CORRIDOR This area is one of the most UFO-haunted sites in North America. Electrical disturbances have been associated with UFO activity here since 1956. In fact, the massive East Coast power blackout of November 9, 1965, is said to have originated with the sighting of a red oval object hovering over power lines at Clay, New York. In any case, something sucked two hundred thousand kilowatts from the lines, causing relays to trip throughout the network and putting twenty-six million people in the dark.

(The area covers northwestern New York and southeastern Ontario in Canada. Clay is near Syracuse in upstate New York. The corridor circles Lake Ontario with its hub at Niagara Falls. Power disturbances and UFO encounters have taken place at Cherry Creek, east of Toronto, St. Catherines, Niagara, and many other cities in the area.) **150**

NIAGARA FALLS The spirits of these magnificent falls are sensed near the Three Sisters, three tiny islands at the west edge of Goat Island. Iroquois shamans made sacrifices of food and goods at the Three Sisters and communed with the Great Spirit of Thunder Waters. Modern psychics say anyone can hear the voices of the spirits here if they listen carefully.

(Follow I-190 to I-190 over Grand Island to the Robert Moses Parkway and follow the signs to the Falls. For information, write the Niagara Falls Chamber of Commerce, 345 Third St., Niagara Falls, NY 14303. Or call Niagara County Tourism at 800-338-7890.) **44, 99**

NORTH SALEM

BALANCED ROCK This sacred site consists of a ninety-ton, 2,400-cubic-foot boulder of pink granite balanced on several limestone supports. Archaeologists have discovered three circular earthen rings surrounding the dolman rock and a series of underground chambers that radiate spokelike from its center. They believe the area had great religious significance to an unidentified ancient people.

(North Salem is located on Highway 116 in Washington County near the New York City border at Croton Reservoir. Follow Keeler Lane from town to the site. Further information can be obtained from the Middletown Archaeological Research Committee, P.O. Box 98, Middletown, NY 10940.) **72, 144**

NYACK

ACKLEY HOUSE This eighteen-room mansion is said to be full of ghosts, and the Appellate Division of the New York Supreme Court agreed. The court officially ruled the house, which had a nine-year history of ghostly visitations and poltergeist events, to be haunted. In 1989, Jeffrey Stambovsky put down $32,000 to buy the mansion for his wife and young son. After signing the contract, he found out that the house was supposedly haunted by dozens of ghosts, including Revolutionary War soldiers and a cheerful apple-cheeked Santa Claus type who occasionally left little presents for families living there. Stambovsky asked to be released from the $650,000 deal, but owner Helen Ackley refused. According to the courts, the house was considered to be haunted and the prospective buyer should have been informed of that fact. The house is currently rented by the Greenwald family, who have yet to report any ghostly encounters.

(Nyack is on the Hudson, 10 miles north of Yonkers. The Victorian mansion is on the Hudson River at 1

Laveta Place, Nyack, NY 10960.) **53 (10/94), 72, 198 (9–92)**

OYSTER BAY

RAYNHAM HALL John Andre, a British major during the Revolutionary War, is one of Long Island's best-known ghosts. He has haunted this house for over two hundred years. During the British occupation of Oyster Bay in 1778, Andre spent many hours at Raynham Hall visiting with the Townsend family, who owned the house and shared it with Lt. Colonel John Simcoe, commander of British forces. One day, while Andre was conferring with Simcoe, one of Townsend's daughters overheard them talking about a payment in gold to Benedict Arnold, the American commander at West Point. Benedict Arnold had agreed to surrender his troops to John Andre for a payment in gold. The Townsends relayed the information to George Washington, who captured Andre at the rendezvous point. Benedict Arnold escaped aboard a British ship, but Andre was later hanged. Colonel Andre has haunted Raynham Hall ever since.

(Oyster Bay is on Long Island. Follow the Long Island Expressway to Exit 41 north, Route 106, which becomes South St. in Oyster Bay. Raynham Hall, 20 West Main St., Oyster Bay, NY 11771. Phone: 516-922-6808. www.sinpak.com/raynham) **14, 101**

PORT WASHINGTON

CARLTON STREET A seventy-five-year-old wooden house in this residential neighborhood was home to a ghost in the 1960s. The specter always appeared on the second floor, usually in the hallway or in one of the bedrooms. He was described as a tall young man, wearing dark clothing. Once, he pushed a woman down the stairs, and she was laid up for several months. The youthful apparition also interrupted a couple engaged in intimate relations in one of the upstairs bedrooms, and a thirteen-year-old girl who lived in the house frequently saw a "big boy walking back and forth in the hallway all night." Her sister said the specter opened the door while she was taking a bath. Other owners reported strange creaking sounds in the hallway and a second-floor bedroom door that opened by itself no matter how securely it was shut.

(Port Washington is on Route 101 south of Sands Point in northern Nassau County on Long Island. The house is located on Carlton Street near the waterfront, just off Main St. It is situated midblock and is now a private residence.) **85**

POUGHKEEPSIE

CHRIST EPISCOPAL CHURCH The rectory of this church was considered to be haunted by Bishop James Pike. The library was the most active spot. Overhead objects seemed to move, candles were blown out, doors shut by themselves, and strange noises abounded. Once a bat materialized in the library and later disappeared. See Grace Cathedral, San Francisco, California.

(Poughkeepsie is seventy miles north of New York on U.S. Highway 9. Christ Episcopal Church, 20 Carroll St., Poughkeepsie, NY 12603. Phone: 914-452-8220.) **89**

ROCHESTER

GANONDAGAN This site is said to "tingle with energy, touching all who visit with its powerful vibration." The area is sacred to the Iroquois people and was once the home of Jikonsasaeh the Peace Queen, who was responsible for uniting six warring tribes into the Seneca nation. The Peace Queen was a disciple of the prophet Deganawidah, whose teachings were studied by Benjamin Franklin and formed the basis of our present federal system. The site consists of three large terraces of oak, hickory, and pine trees. Markers along the five miles of trails explain the history of the region.

(Rochester is on Lake Ontario in extreme northern New York. Ganondagon is twelve miles southwest of Rochester, in the Finger Lakes area. From I-90, take Exit 44 to Highway 332 South. Turn west on County Road 41 and follow it into the park. For information, contact the Ganondaga State Historic Site, 1488 Victor-Holcomb Rd., Victor, NY 14564. Phone: 716-924-5848. www.ganondagan.org.) **144**

WERNER HOUSE The ghost of a former owner has been encountered in this old house. For over thirty years at the beginning of the century, tenants witnessed a ghostly ritual in the house. Almost every night, the sounds of a man's heavy footsteps would come down the attic stairs and walk out the back door. Fifteen minutes later, the invisible presence would return and retrace his path to the attic room. The house was originally a barn. In the 1890s, a farmer, despondent over the death of his wife, climbed to the loft and hanged himself. His spirit continued to reenact the fateful night, even after the barn was remodeled into a house.

(The house is a private residence, located at 45 Ringle St., Rochester, NY 14619.) **53 (12/81)**

RYE

THE CEDARS This Victorian house was built in 1860 by Jared Peck. The many unusual phenomena reported here since the turn of the century have included the movement of heavy objects, noises like chains rattling, and doors slamming shut. Once a sharp knife flew across the kitchen floor and a heavy ashtray levitated softly to the floor of an upstairs bedroom. One of the ghosts is thought to be of a former family member, who was kept locked in a small bedroom on the third floor. The other is the spirit of a woman who died in the house. This later ghost mysteriously appeared on a frame of film made at the house for a television news program. Her form also materialized during a modeling session staged there for an artist.

(Rye is east of Yonkers in Westchester County. The town is located off the New England Thruway, I-95, at the Connecticut border. The house is a private residence located on Barberry Lane, Rye, NY 10580.) **80, 89**

SEAFORD

HERRMANN HOUSE Police officers, reporters, and parapsychologists witnessed intense poltergeist activity in this six-room, ranch-style home for five weeks in 1958. The activity began on February 3 around 3:00 P.M. when bottles started popping open and pouring their contents out onto the floor. Jimmy Herrmann and his wife Lucille at first thought some odd chemical reaction was causing the phenomenon, until they witnessed the bottles moving across counters and flying across the room. When the poltergeist seemed to be harassing their two children, twelve-year-old James Junior and thirteen-year-old Lucille, the couple called the police. Patrolman James Hughes and Detective Joseph Tozzi both witnessed the strange events. They requested the Long Island Lighting Company to conduct an electromagnetic survey of the house, and had samples of liquids in the house analyzed at the police lab in Mineola. The building department surveyed the house and capped the chimney to rule out downdrafts. The fire department checked an old well in the front of the house and reported that the level had not changed in five years. RCA sent a test truck to search for radio frequencies. No one discovered anything unusual. The poltergeist activity increased in power as bottles, figurines, knickknacks, lamps, and other objects were observed levitating or crashing to the floor. Then the poltergeist seemed to concentrate on the boy's room. A picture frame on his wall kept leaping to the center of the floor, his dresser moved against the door, and a heavy bookcase turned upside down and wedged between the bed and a radiator. The news media named the poltergeist Popper, because of the dozens of bottle-popping incidents, and curiosity seekers from all over the nation converged on the premises. Researchers William Roll and J. G. Pratt from Duke University documented sixty-seven separate events. The last event occurred on the evening of March 10 at 8:14 P.M. The top of a bleach bottle unscrewed and flew several inches away. That was the last time the Herrmann family heard from Popper.

(The town of Seaford is located on Long Island in Nassau County, at the south end of Route 135 on South Oyster Bay. The house is a private residence in Seaford.) **40, 68, 100, 105, 108, 109, 175**

STATEN ISLAND

CONFERENCE HOUSE Strange phenomena have been reported at the historic Conference House for the last 150 years. On September 11, 1776, Benjamin Franklin, John Adams, and Edward Rutledge met at the home of British commander Lord Howe to work out a peace treaty in the Revolutionary War. The peace plan failed, and the colonies went on to win their independence. Conference House, called Bentley Manor at the time, was built in 1687 by Captain Christopher Billopp. Since the 1850s, people have reported strange murmuring and moaning sounds, as well as the screams of a young girl. Legend says Christopher Billopp, Captain Billopp's grandson, in a fit of anger murdered a servant girl on the attic staircase. Sensitives have described Billopp's ghost as a fat man in a fur coat with black trousers and high boots.

(Take the Staten Island ferry from New York to Staten Island, then the SIRT train to Tottenville. The Conference House, which overlooks Raritan Bay, is now a public museum. Conference House Museum, 7455 Hylan Boulevard, Tottenville, NY 10307. Phone: 718-984-2086.) **86**

CRAWLEY MANSION The owner of this Victorian mansion was killed by a vengeful ghost in 1870. Mrs. Dartway Crawley lived alone after her husband took off to California in search of gold. Her maiden name, Magda Hamilton, would have been easily recognized by New Yorkers of the time. She was a police informant who broke a notorious "smugglers doll" diamond gang. One of the criminals indicted was Franchon Moncare, a young French girl who posed as the child of Ada Danworth. The innocent-looking Franchon carried her fragile china doll, filled with $250,000 in jewels, right through customs. The two women lived together in a beautiful mansion on Staten Island and worked with Boss Tweed's gang in a number of robbery and smuggling operations. Magda Hamilton joined Franchon in a caper to rob a Chicago millionaire, and afterward became an accepted member of the gang. After Magda turned in her old gang members, she and her new husband bought the old mansion. One night, shortly after Franchon had died in prison, the tiny Frenchwoman's ghost appeared in Magda's bedroom and shoved a china doll down her throat, suffocating her. Franchon's ghost was still being seen on the property nearly a century later. New York Harbor authorities have received dozens of reports from witnesses in passing boats of a ghostly figure on the widow's walk high on top of the old Crawley mansion.

(Staten Island is off south Manhattan. Take the Bayonne Bridge or the ferry. The house sits on Sandy Hook on the island. The headquarters of the smuggling ring was in Chinatown in Manhattan, at 20 Mott St.) **158**

STONY BROOK

COUNTRY HOUSE RESTAURANT This old farmhouse was built in 1710 and was used as a stagecoach station in the 1800s. The building, known as haunted for many years, became a restaurant in 1960. The latest owner asked the Psychical Research Foundation to investigate. Medium Rita Allen contacted the spirit of a young woman hanged by the British as a spy during the Revolutionary War. The ghost has been tentatively identified as Annette Williamson, allegedly buried in a small graveyard on the property. Her presence has been felt on the staircase and in the kitchen, where a towel once floated in front of several witnesses. One skeptical newsman had a glass of wine thrown in his face by the unseen spirit.

(Stony Brook is in Suffolk County on Long Island. Follow I-495 to Exit 62 North and take Route 25A into Stony Brook. The Country House Restaurant is on Route 25A and Main Street, Stony Brook, NY 11790. Phone: 631-751-3332. www.stonybrookvillage.com/Listing/Contyhse.htm) **14, 101**

STONY POINT

HUDSON RIVER The ghost of the Revolutionary War general "Mad" Anthony Wayne has been observed riding through the tunnels and woods of the countryside here on his beloved horse Nag. Blue and orange sparks fly out from the stallion's horseshoes when they strike hard pavement. Sighting his ghost presages a stormy night, much like the night Wayne rode his horse through Storm King Pass to warn American soldiers of an impending attack. See Walker House; Ticonderoga, New York; Valley Forge, Pennsylvania; Lake Memphremagog, Vermont; and Loudoun County, Virginia.

(The general has been seen riding along the banks of the Hudson River between Storm King Mountain and Stony Point.) **158**

WALKER HOUSE Danton Walker discounted all the old stories about the old house he bought. He was more concerned with fixing it up as a vacation retreat from his hectic job as a Broadway columnist. At one time the house was barracks for revolutionary war soldiers, and the former headquarters of General "Mad" Anthony Wayne stood nearby. In 1944, two years after he took possession, Walker started hearing the sound of heavy boots, and pictures fell off the walls for no reason. He sensed something unearthly about the house and refused to sleep there anymore. By 1952, the place was known nationwide as haunted. Eileen Garrett, a famous Irish medium, contacted Walker and asked if she could investigate. Almost immediately after entering Walker's house in November 1952, Mrs. Garrett fell into a trance and contacted a Polish mercenary soldier who had served in the Revolutionary War. The soldier, Andreas, had been captured by British soldiers, beaten horribly, and left to die in the house. See Hudson River; Ticonderoga, New York; Valley Forge, Pennsylvania; Lake Memphremagog, Vermont; and Loudoun County, Virginia.

(Stony Point is thirty miles north of New York on the Palisades Interstate. The house is located in Rockland

County, a few miles outside Stony Point on the Hudson River.) **37, 39, 40, 78, 158, 212**

SYRACUSE

FIREHOUSE ENGINE COMPANY NO. 18 Strange footsteps on the stairs and a ghostly presence at the rear of the second-floor dormitory have haunted this brick fire station for many years. Firefighters have named the ghost Tyler Green, after a dead fireman. The building was constructed in 1927 on a historic Revolutionary War and Indian trail. An Indian burial ground is located nearby.

(The haunted fire station is at 176 West Seneca Turnpike, Syracuse, NY 13205.) **134**

Several ghosts, including a lady in white, haunt this historic theater. See Landmark Theatre, Syracuse, New York (THE LANDMARK THEATER)

SYRACUSE AREA LANDMARK THEATRE Shortly after renovations were completed here in 1978, employees began reporting the apparition of a pale young lady, dressed entirely in white, in the upper balcony. Sometimes she seemed so real that ushers asked her to leave the area, only to see her disappear from sight. Psychics say she is the spirit of a woman who worked at the theater and spent all her life wanting to be an actress. The ghost of Oscar Rau, who worked as an electrician at the theater, has been observed near the lightboard. A ghostly blue light has been seen by many witnesses near the banister that runs along the back of the auditorium, in the catwalk access hallway, and on the stairs leading to the downstairs dressing room. Psychics say the Turkish Room, also known as the Red Room, is

haunted by the passions of a violent love triangle. Scary events have occurred in the basement catacombs, but the most negative area in the theater is the Walnut Room. Employees report feeling extremely uncomfortable in the room, where fires have erupted and unusual cold spots appear. The original Loew's State Theater opened in 1928 and seated 2,896 people. The restored theater is on the National Register of Historic Places.

(Take I-81 north to the Salina Street exit downtown. Syracuse Landmark Theatre, 362 South Salina St., Syracuse, NY 13202. Phone: 315-475-7979. http:// landmarktheatre.org/Landmark) **14, 53 (7/80), 101**

TARRYTOWN

SUNNYSIDE The ghost of Washington Irving appeared at his former home. Several years after his death in 1859, three witnesses saw his apparition walk through the parlor and disappear into the library. His ghost also roamed the stacks of books at the Astor Library in New York City, where Irving wrote *The Legend of Sleepy Hollow.*

(Tarrytown is in Westchester County, ten miles north of New York City, on U.S. Highway 9. Sunnyside is located on the Hudson River in Tarrytown at West Sunnyside Lane No. 9. 914-591-8763. The Astor Library was at Lafayette Place in Manhattan. www.hudsonvalley.org/ web/sunn-main.html) **56, 199**

TICONDEROGA

FORT TICONDEROGA One of the most famous ghosts in history appeared on a battlefield here. The story began in Scotland, when a young man pounded on the door of Major Duncan Campbell's castle and asked for refuge from his pursuers. The honorable Scotsman promised to hide the man and kept his promised, even when he discovered the man had murdered Duncan's own cousin, Donald Campbell. From that night forward, the ghost of Donald appeared to Duncan and implored him to surrender the murderer to the authorities. But the honorable Duncan kept his promise. Finally the fugitive left the area. That night, Duncan awoke to a brilliant flash of light. In its midst he saw the specter of his cousin, who told him: "Farewell, Duncan Campbell. Farewell till we meet at Ticonderoga." Duncan could not fathom the cryptic meaning of the message until many months later. His battalion,

The legend of Duncan Campbell, immortalized in Robert Louis Stevenson's *The Master of Ballantrae*, hinged on a ghostly appearance on the battlefield at Fort Ticonderoga. See Fort Ticonderoga, Ticonderoga, New York
(FORT TICONDEROGA MUSEUM)

Scotland's Black Watch (the 42nd Regiment of Foot), had been called up to help the British drive the French from North America. They were to travel up the Hudson River to attack Fort Ticonderoga. There on the bloody battlefield, the ghost of his cousin appeared to Major Campbell one last time. "Farewell, Duncan Campbell," the apparition said. Two weeks later, on July 17, 1758, Duncan died of wounds he suffered at Ticonderoga. Though the British outnumbered the French five to one, they went down in a humiliating defeat. The legend of Duncan Campbell became the basis of Robert Louis Stevenson's *The Master of Ballantrae*. Some say Donald's and Duncan's ghosts still appear here. Another ghost still seen at this old fort is that of its commander in the 1770s, General "Mad" Anthony Wayne. His form is reported in the commandant's dining room and sitting in an old wing chair near the fireplace. Sometimes he is seen pacing the rampart facing Mount Defiance. (See Stony Point, New York; Valley Forge, Pennsylvania; Lake Memphremagog, Vermont; and Loudoun County, Virginia.) The ghost of Wayne's lover, Nancy Coates, is said to wander these grounds, too. She committed suicide by walking into the lake after Wayne turned his attentions to a young British girl.

(Ticonderoga is in northeastern New York, in Essex County on the Vermont border. Duncan Campbell is buried at the Union Cemetery at Fort Edward, New York. Follow I-87 to Highway 74 and go east twenty-five miles to

the old Fort Ticonderoga, which is north of Mount Defiance, at the head of Lake Champlain. Fort Ticonderoga, Fort Rd. Box 390, Ticonderoga, NY 12883. Phone: 518-385-2821. www.fort-ticonderoga.org) **5, 7, 53 (1/86), 68, 158, 162**

WATERTOWN

THOMPSON PARK This city park is said to be a portal to another dimension. Nothing unusual was reported here until the 1930s, when WPA workers built a series of stone walls leading up a grassy hill. People soon began experiencing eerie feelings on the hill, which is situated between a golf course and a swimming pool. Locals named the area Lightlines, after the odd sensations felt by people walking in the grassy space between two rows of trees here. Strange sounds and ghostly forms started to manifest in the area. Mist-covered shapes, sometimes on horseback, were reported. In the 1970s, people began suffering physical effects at Lightlines. One eighteen-year-old vanished from the top of a hill in plain sight of several eyewitnesses. Twenty minutes later, he reappeared, totally disoriented, at the bottom of the hill.

(The park is in Watertown, which is east of Lake Ontario in northern New York state. Take Exits 45 through 45 from I-81 into town. The park is at 600 William T. Field Dr. Phone: 315-785-7775.) **99**

WEST POINT

U.S. MILITARY ACADEMY The Superintendent's House is said to be haunted by Molly, the ghost of a former maid, who goes from bedroom to bedroom rumpling up newly made-up beds. The 47th Division Barracks of the 4th Regiment area is haunted by the figure of a handlebar-mustached soldier in an 1830s uniform. The ghost, who sometimes carries a musket rifle, was first seen on October 21, 1972, walking through the door to Room 4714. The next night he was seen again by two cadets sleeping in the room. Cadet Captain Keith Bakken investigated and found the room to be unexplainably cold. He assigned an upperclassman to share the room with the two freshmen cadets. Again the ghost appeared, partially coming through one of the walls into the room. Other cadets who spent the night in the room also witnessed the uncanny figure. The haunting lasted until mid-November 1972, when the commanding officer ordered all of the furniture removed from Room 4714 and declared it off-limits.

(The academy is located in Orange County in south-eastern New York, fifty miles north of New York City on U.S. Highway 9W, on the west bank of the Hudson River.) **42, 72**

WHITEHALL

SKENE MANOR The apparition of a woman in a full-skirted dress, wearing a distinctive ring on her right hand, appears for a few seconds and then turns into a glowing ball of light. Finally, the image of a skeleton forms, while on her bony finger the ring can still be seen. She has appeared in the dining area, and some-times just her hand, wearing the huge ring, material-izes, in the fountain behind the bar. She is Colonel Skene's wife. When she died, the colonel placed her body in a lead-lined coffin, which he kept in the house. After the old mansion became a restaurant, the owner placed the coffin behind the bar and built a fountain around it.

(Whitehall is northeast of Glens Falls, on U.S. Highway 4 at the head of Lake Champlain in northern Washington County. Skene Manor is now a restaurant. A four-story clock tower marks the gray-stone Gothic manor just outside Whitehall. Skene Manor Restaurant, 8 Potter Terrace, Whitehall, NY 12887. Phone: 518-499-1906.) **162**

NORTH CAROLINA

ASHE COUNTY

DEVIL'S STAIRS This landmark is the site of many unusual phenomena, which began happening in 1910, after two deaths took place here: a black miner was accidentally killed in a dynamite explosion, and an unwanted baby was murdered by its mother. Several apparitions have been sighted, including a phantom rider who jumps on the back of living horses as they trot by.

(Ashe County is in the extreme northwest corner of North Carolina, bordering Tennessee and Virginia. Devil's Stairs is a rocky steppe near the White Top and Konnarock Mountains. The site is near the tiny town of Oak Grove.) **121**

ASHEVILLE

REED HOUSE Reed House was built in 1892 by Samuel Harrison Reed, the lawyer for George Vanderbilt, whose opulent Biltmore estate lies nearby. Reed's simple but elegant Victorian mansion is haunted by a ghost who passes its time playing pool on a table in the game room, which lies between the parlor and the library. The crack of balls hitting each other can be heard at all hours of the day or night, and it is impossible to keep a set of racked balls from splitting apart. Other haunted rooms include the Circus Room, the Lavender Room, and the back stairs hallway.

(Asheville is in the western tip of North Carolina, at the junction of I-26 and I-40. Reed House is now a bed-and-breakfast inn in the Biltmore District, two miles south of town on U.S. Highway 25. Take Exit 50B North on U.S. Highway 25 and turn east on Irwin St., then north on Dodge St. Reed House Bed & Breakfast Inn, 119 Dodge St., Asheville, NC 28803. Phone: 828-274-1604.) **101, 168**

STARNES AVENUE APARTMENTS Furniture belonging to the owner of this building seemed to be possessed by her spirit after she died. The woman, an avowed atheist, refused last rites as she lay dying in her room. Residents of the apartment insisted that her wheelchair moved about her room by itself and occasionally smashed against the door, as if wanting to get out. Other furniture was also affected, including an antique rocker that constantly moved back and forth. The events continued for several months in the late 1950s.

(The apartments are located on Starnes Ave., Asheville, NC 28801.) **8**

BATH

CUTLAR FARM Hoofprints from a horse whose rider was killed in a race here still mark the place where he died. On October 13, 1813, Jesse Elliot was thrown from his horse after he supposedly made a pact with the devil to win the race or die trying. Jesse's head struck a tree and he died on the spot. The field has been in the Cutlar family for over 150 years, and the hoofprints are still there. Nothing grows in the impressions, and hogs will not eat corn thrown over the marks. Even the side of the pine tree where Jesse hit his head is said to have died, while the opposite side continues to grow.

(Bath is in northeastern North Carolina, off I-95. Ed Cutlar's farm is on private property, located one mile west of Bath. The hoofprints are 250 feet from his farmhouse.) **169**

BEAUFORT

HAMMOCK HOUSE This huge log hall became the center of social life for many sea captains and naval officers in the early 1700s. But the sturdy building has been deserted for many years, since a tragic mistake spawned ghostly phenomena. Blobs of glowing light move from room to room and the sounds of men fighting with swords can sometimes be heard. Bloodstains on the upper stairway turn a deep red when it is foggy or humid, and no amount of scrubbing or detergents have ever been able to wash them away. The blood is that of Carruthers Ashby, who was slain by Captain Madison Brothers after he caught the man in the arms of his fiancée. What the quick-tempered Captain Brothers did not realize was that Carruthers was the woman's brother, and they had not seen each other for years.

(Beaufort is on U.S. Highway 70 on the middle Atlantic coast of North Carolina, at Cape Lookout. Hammock House faces Beaufort Inlet. www.historicbeaufort. com/history.htm) **220**

BENTONVILLE

HARPER HOUSE In 1905, two hunters in the Bentonville Woods near the old Harper House saw a ghostly reenactment of a bloody Civil War battle. Witnesses Jim Weaver and Joe Lewis described an engagement that took place on the Bentonville Battleground during the early days of the Civil War. Details of the ferocious battle were later verified by surviving veterans. The confrontation between sixty thousand of Sherman's troops and meager Confederate forces lasted from March 19 to March 21, 1865. Many of the casualties were treated at the nearby Harper home, which served as a hospital for both sides. The two hunters saw the woods around them fill with the scenes and sounds of battle. As they ran past Harper House, they saw strange lights and fiery ghosts in the windows.

(Bentonville Battleground is just off U.S. Highway 701. The park is located thirteen miles south of the town of Smithfield. Harper House is at the center of the park. The site is east of U.S. Highway 701 in Johnston County.) **169**

BROWN MOUNTAIN

BROWN MOUNTAIN LIGHTS Some say the strange lights on this even-crested mountain are caused by the restless spirit of a man whose corpse was found near the bottom slope; others believe the lights are UFOs. Scientists say they are some sort of unknown electromagnetic discharge. The red and white shooting lights are only seen during the autumn months on moonless nights. The phenomenon was first observed by Cherokee Indians around 1200. The site was studied by German scientist Gerard de Brahm in 1771. In 1913, interest in the phenomenon resulted in a study by the U.S. Geologic Survey. Another study was conducted in the 1970s by the Oak Ridge Isochronous Observation Network. Both groups reached similar conclusions: Some of the sightings were caused by train and truck lights refracting from areas beyond Brown Mountain. The studies did not attempt to explain the hundreds of sightings that occurred before trains and trucks ran through the area, and concluded that a large percentage of the modern reports remained unexplainable. The lights usually appear around 7:00 P.M. and last for about thirty seconds before disappearing. Local resident and former congressional candidate Ralph Lael claims to have encountered alien beings on the mountain in 1962, and some people believe there is an underground alien base here.

(The area is located in Burke County, in the western part of the state, between Morganton and Lenoir, on Highway 181. It is marked by a Forest Service sign, which explains the history of the lights. Ralph Lael owns the Outer Space Rock Shop Museum on Highway 181 outside Morganton. www.ghosts.org/ghostlights/brownmtn. html) **1, 20, 34, 55, 66 (7/84), 68, 70, 72, 165, 171, 196**

CAPE HATTERAS

CARROLL DEERING On January 30, 1921, the cargo schooner *Carroll Deering* went aground on the North

Carolina coast at Diamond Shoals. The ship floundered in good weather with her sails still set. Rescuers found no one on board the vessel, except for two cats. A dinner meal had been served in the crew's mess hall, but it had not been touched. No members of the crew were ever seen again, but for many years afterward, residents along the coast at Diamond Shoals reported seeing the mysterious ghost ship running aground.

(Diamond Shoals is on the middle Atlantic coast, off Pamlico Bay. The area is visible from the ferries to Cape Hatteras.) **51, 70**

HATTERAS BEACH The ghost of Theodosia Burr Alston has been seen walking the beaches here. She was lost in a shipwreck off the east coast in 1812. Theodosia was traveling to New York to meet her father, Aaron Burr, the famous American patriot. Theodosia, married to the governor of South Carolina, left Georgetown for New York aboard *The Patriot*. The ship apparently wandered off course and was lost. Some have even suggested it disappeared in the Bermuda Triangle. While the remains of the ship were never found, the ghost of Theodosia returned to the beaches of Cape Hatteras, leading to speculation that she drowned in the waters offshore. See Quantum Leap Café, Francis House, and Morris-Jumel Mansion in New York City.

(Cape Hatteras National Seashore is on the Outer Banks, which is the ocean coastline that makes up the eastern border of North Carolina. For information on camping at National Park Service sites, call 919-441-6644. The cape is just off Pamlico Sound. Theodosia's ghost has been reported as far south as Brookgreen Gardens in South Carolina.) **42, 70, 159, 162**

CHAPEL HILL

UNIVERSITY OF NORTH CAROLINA A blood-stained rock is all that remains of a tragic love story played out in 1833. Undergraduate Peter Dromgoole was hopelessly in love with a beautiful girl from Chapel Hill. They often met at a wooded hill on the western edge of town. A friend of Dromgoole also became infatuated with the girl, and the two students decided to settle the matter with a pistol duel. They faced each other on that same wooded hill. Dromgoole was hit in the chest and bled to death, collapsing on a large, flat rock. His friend and their seconds buried the boy's body next to the rock—a deed they would confess sixty years

later. After her lover's disappearance, the forlorn girl spent hours weeping on the rock at their old meeting place, unaware that his body lay directly beneath. Today, the rock sits in front of an old stone building that students consider haunted. They have named it Dromgoole's Castle.

(Chapel Hill is southwest of Durham on U.S. Highway 15/501. University of North Carolina, Chapel Hill, NC 27514. Phone: 919-962-1630. www.unc.edu) **70, 169**

CHARLOTTE

FOUNDERS COLLEGE The ghost of a young girl, dubbed Louise, haunted Chambers Hall here. The green-eyed, slender girl was seen by several students and professors in the 1930s. She lived in the town of Salisbury and died young, which made her all the more tempting to grave robbers, who sold her corpse to the medical school at Founders College.

(Charlotte is in southwestern North Carolina at the junction of I-77 and I-85. Founders College was on a small campus at the center of town.) **125**

MACINTOSH MINE A ghost shut down one of North Carolina's richest gold mines. The MacIntosh Mine, at 450 feet deep, was one of the most dangerous in the area, and the owner had to pay premium wages to get anyone to work it. Johnathon MacIntosh told the miners that he had used the finest timbers to support the walls of the deep hole, when in fact many of the timbers had rotted away. After miner Joe McGee was killed in a cave-in at the mine's second level, his ghost appeared to the other miners and warned them of the dangers. The ghost was seen so many times within the mine and at the miners homes that no one would work the mine, and it was abandoned. The owner went insane, knowing that a fortune in gold was within his grasp but his own greed and a persistent ghost had kept it from him.

(The MacIntosh Mine was located on a hill near historic Reed Mine in Mecklenburg County.) **172**

REED MINE America's first gold rush began here in 1799, when twelve-year-old Conrad Reed discovered a seventeen-pound nugget in Meadow Creek on his father's farm. The Reed Mine became one of the world's leading producers of gold. But in the early 1800s the mine gained a permanent resident. The ghost of Eleanor Mills has haunted the place ever since her husband dumped her body down the main shaft. William Mills loved his wife despite her constant nagging. When she tripped on her dress and struck her head on an oak bench, her husband lay down on the floor next to her dead body and wept himself to sleep. He awoke to her shrill voice coming from the corpse's motionless, ice blue lips. Terrified, the burly man threw her lifeless body down a deep, vertical tunnel known as Engine Shaft. Yet her nagging voice never stopped. Years later, people could still hear her: "It's so cold, it's so dark down here. Help me out!"

(The old Reed Mine is a National Historic Site northeast of Charlotte. Take Highway 24/27 east out of Charlotte for twenty miles to Highway 200 north. Follow the road eight miles to the mine.) **167**

WHITE OAKS This double-winged, wood-frame house was built by tobacco king James Duke. The ghost of Jon Avery, a later owner of the house, is said to have kept a rendezvous in the garden here. The married man and his paramour had been coming to the spot at midnight on the anniversaries of their first meeting. He promised her that they would meet whether "dead or alive." It was not until after their third meeting that the woman learned John had already been dead a week when he showed up for their last rendezvous.

(White Oaks, or Duke Mansion, was converted to private condominiums. It is located in the Eastover district at 400 Hermitage Rd., Charlotte, NC 28207.) **101, 168**

CONCORD

GOLD HILL The old Randolph Mine at Gold Hill is haunted by two ghosts. One is the ghost of Aaron Klein, murdered in the mine in 1842. Klein was often tormented with anti-Semitic pranks, but one night a fellow miner, jealous of his affections for a young woman in the town, lured him to the mine and pushed him down the 850-foot shaft. Klein's body was never discovered, but a shimmering yellow light started appearing at the mouth of the mine. Klein's murderer, Stan Cukla, seemed to be very bothered by the unexplained light and could be seen late at night picking through the rubble at the bottom of the pit. Then, one morning Cukla's lifeless body, smashed almost beyond recognition, was found at the bottom of the shaft.

Gold Hill's second ghost appeared over a century later. In January 1954, two witnesses saw a grisly sight near the mine. Pieces of a body seemed to float in midair just ahead of them. A head, arms, legs, feet, and other body parts, bathed in a strange luminescence, were suspended several feet above the ground, as the ghastly assemblage moved toward them. The head, eyes rolling, mouth moving, drifted within a few feet of the terrified couple. Suddenly, with sound of a cracking whip, the horrific vision vanished. Local residents were not surprised when the couple identified the strange apparition as Joe Newman, brother of wealthy mine owner Walter George Newman. Joe died in a mysterious explosion that blew him and his house to pieces. It was widely believed that Walter killed him to gain sole control of the mine. After Walter died in 1918, his ghost joined his brother's odd specter, to emerge from the old Newman Mine at dusk and walk the darkened streets of this tiny town.

(The town of Concord is about twenty-five miles northeast of Charlotte on U.S. Highway 29. Gold Hill is a small community not far from Concord.) **167, 169**

CULLOWHEE

JUDACULLA ROCK This sacred site is a complete mystery to modern archaeologists. No one knows who made the hieroglyphic symbols on the fourteen-foot-wide soapstone boulder. The strange symbols include seven-fingered hands, human figures, and geometric shapes. According to Cherokee legend, the rock was created by a one-eyed giant called Judaculla. The symbols codified laws of hunting and respect for the balance of nature.

(The town of Cullowhee is south of Asheville in Jackson County. Follow Highway 107 south out of Cullowhee for 3.5 miles to Caney Fork Rd., then go east for three miles to the site. For further information, contact the Jackson County Chamber of Commerce, 116 North Central St., Sylva, NC 28779. Phone: 828-586-2155. www.nc-mountains.com) **144**

FAYETTEVILLE

SLOCUMB HOUSE The apparition of a beautiful young woman wearing a black dress has been seen floating up and down the staircase of this elegant house. Built in 1800 by A. S. Slocumb, the house was used as a bank in the 1820s. The ghost is allegedly the fiancée of a murdered man whose body was hidden in a vault in the basement. During the Civil War, the vault became the entrance to a tunnel that led all the way to the Cape Fear River.

(Fayetteville is in Cumberland County, in southeastern North Carolina. It is located at the junction of I-95 and U.S. Highways 301 and 401. The house is a private residence in Fayetteville.) **169**

FLATWOODS

HIGHWAY 19W This winding mountain road is haunted by the phantom of an open wagon, pulled by four horses. The ghostly rig has been blamed for a number of accidents. Just before impact, the wagon, the team of horses, and the man and woman driving them completely vanish from sight. Legend says the two hapless ghosts are a settler couple who were ambushed by Indians one night near Hacker's Creek, which runs along Highway 19W.

(Flatwoods is a wooded area in Yancey County, north of Asheville. Highway 19W runs from Bald Creek north into the Bald Mountains.) **72, 166**

FLETCHER

CALVARY EPISCOPAL CHURCH The ghost of a frightened young woman on a palomino horse appears momentarily on the roads near this church and then vanishes at a fast gallop, as if pursued by someone. Where the highway is paved, she rides on the gravel shoulder of the road. The girl has long blond hair and wears a flimsy gossamer gown, over which she wears a heavy Confederate cape. The ghost is thought to be a woman who died soon after learning that her lover had been killed in the Civil War. In the spring of 1865, the Phantom Rider was blamed for the deaths of twenty-three troops under the command of General Stoneman. The troops followed the ghostly rider right into the midst of a rebel ambush. The Union general organized a search party to capture or kill the girl, but the soldiers were never able to catch up to her. When they got within firing range, their bullets passed right through her. Over the years, the ghost of the Phantom Rider has been seen many times. Sometimes, witnesses can see dozens of bullet holes in her heavy, flapping cape.

(The town of Fletcher is ten miles south of Asheville on U.S. Highway 176. The phantom rider has been seen between the towns of Arden in Buncombe County and Fletcher in Henderson County, and also on the church

driveway beyond the wrought-iron gate. Calvary Episcopal Church, Hwy 25 at Old Airport Rd., Fletcher, NC 28732. Phone: 828-684-6266.) **172**

GREENSBORO

U.S. HIGHWAY 70 UNDERPASS The ghost of a beautiful young lady has appeared here since 1923. Wearing a white evening gown, she stands next to the underpass and waves frantically for someone to stop. Those who do find a lovely girl named Lydia, who asks for a ride to an address in High Point. She has been at a dance in Raleigh and is eager to get home. Just as they approach the house, the girl vanishes from sight. Drivers who inquire at the house are always told the same thing: Lydia died in a car wreck many years ago at the U.S. Highway 70 underpass.

(Greensboro is in north-central North Carolina, at the junction of I-40 and I-85. The underpass is on U.S. Highway 70 near Jamestown, between Greensboro and High Point.) **169**

HENDERSONVILLE

CULPEPPER RUINS Hunters in this area have reported seeing the dancing ghosts of a couple celebrating their wedding night in the ruins of an old homesteader house. In the 1890s, an elaborate wedding took place here, but the bride died of scarlet fever just a couple weeks later.

(Hendersonville is twenty miles south of Asheville on U.S. Highway 176. The basement foundation of the old Culpepper homestead is in the woods off Highway 25, south of Hendersonville.) **166**

HICKORY NUT GORGE

CHIMNEY ROCK Cherokee legends spoke of mysterious flying Little People, who inhabit this gorge, The first recorded sighting by white men was in 1806. Another sighting occurred in 1811, and sporadic encounters have occurred ever since. The Little People are described as short, white-robed figures who float across the mountainside near Chimney Rock. Witnesses report feeling slightly exhausted, although strangely at peace, after sighting the creatures.

(Hickory Nut Gorge is in the Pisgah National Forest in western North Carolina. Chimney Rock is a chimney-

shaped outcropping about halfway up the gorge. Phone: 828-877-3265. www.chimney-rock.com) **72, 172**

HOT SPRINGS

SHUT-IN CREEK This area is haunted by disembodied voices and an enigmatic light that rolls down hills like a barrel. Strange things have happened here ever since a man was killed by poison fumes in a primitive manganese mine over ninety years ago.

(Hot Springs is on the Tennessee border in Madison County, northwest North Carolina. Shut-In Creek is four miles outside town, near Black Mountain. The manganese mine was at Dry Branch.) **166**

KADESH

KADESH METHODIST CHURCH. Music comes from the organ here, even when no one is in the church. The ghostly organist plays beautiful but unrecognizable melodies from the old pipe organ. The phenomenon started one November morning after World War II and has reoccurred several times since.

(The town of Kadesh is a tiny community in the hills of northern Cleveland County, north of Shelby, near the South Mountains State Park.) **169**

KINSTON

BATCHELDER'S CREEK In May 1863, the 25th Massachusetts Regiment slowly made its way to join up with other Yankee regiments in an assault on a small Confederate outpost in the Gum Swamp. As the Northern troops approached Batchelder's Creek at the entrance to the swampland, a mysterious electric wind came up from nowhere and split the regiment right down the middle. When the devil wind was gone, two hodgepodge piles of terrified soldiers were hiding in the ditches on either side of the dirt road. The officers quickly reassembled their men, but as soon as the regiment took its first step forward, the electrifying wind rose again, wreaking the same havoc. An official report described the encounter to superiors, who attributed the phenomenon to flocks of owls.

(The town of Kinston is in eastern North Carolina, at the junction of U.S. Highway 70 and Highway 11. The creek is in a pine forest near Kinston. Gum Swamp is eight miles south of the city.) **163**

MACO

ATLANTIC COAST RAILROAD CROSSING Hundreds of witnesses have seen the fabled Maco Light, and their stories are always the same. A distant light starts moving back and forth in the darkness. The flickering light resembles an old railroad lantern. Occasionally the sound of a train is heard, followed by a deafening crash. The phenomena occur near a spot where in 1867 a real train stalled on the tracks and was hit from behind by a speeding locomotive. Some believe the light is from the lantern of conductor Joe Baldwin, who tried to warn the approaching engine of the blockage. Baldwin, who was decapitated in the accident, was the only casualty. Sometimes, the light does not appear for almost a month, but it always returns.

(Maco is in Brunswick County, in the extreme southern corner of North Carolina, twelve miles northwest of Wilmington on U.S. Highway 74/76. Baldwin is buried in the Catholic cemetery near the tracks. The railroad crossing is just outside the town of Maco, over the old Wilmington-Florence-Augusta tracks. The line is now part of the Atlantic Coast Line Railroad. More information on the site can be obtained from the Southeastern North Carolina Beach Association, Wilmington, NC 28401.) **78, 82, 86, 89, 90, 164, 169**

MARSHALL

CHUNN'S TAVERN The ghost of a former tavern owner walks through the mists along the river here. In the mid-1800s, the tavern and inn was known as an evil place where travelers often disappeared. The man who ran the establishment robbed and murdered his well-off guests and buried their bodies in the surrounding woods. After the place was abandoned, locals reported seeing ghosts roaming the ruins. They warned of one particular phantom, that of the former owner, who would attack unlucky travelers in the area.

(Marshall is in Madison County, twenty miles north of Asheville. The old tavern no longer exists, but Chunn's ghost appears near the river on the French Broad, from Marshall to Painted Rock, near Hot Springs.) **172**

MOORE COUNTY

ALSTON HOUSE Built in 1770, this large plantation house has gained a statewide reputation for being haunted. A strange light has been observed leaving the ground and flying high into the air. Unexplainable footsteps, whispering in the fireplace, and high-pitched vibrating sounds have been heard many times over the years. In 1781, a small battle was fought between British troops and the owner of the house, Colonel Philip Alston. He was arrested but later paroled. Alston left the area a few years after that, when he was implicated in a murder. Many believe the ghost of the maverick colonel is responsible for the odd happenings.

(Alston House, also known as the House in the Horseshoe, is located on a sharply curving bend of the Deep River in northern Moore County, which is in central North Carolina Alston House, 324 Alston House Rd., Sanford, NC 27330. Phone: 910-947-2051.) **187**

MOORHEAD CITY

CRAB POINT In the swirling mists here are seen the figures of a woman and a Confederate soldier. They are Emeline Pigott and Stokes McRae, lovers who met here in 1862, just before Union forces overran Fort Macon. Emeline served the south by conveying secret messages to Confederate sympathizers. She was later imprisoned, and before she was released, McRae died at Gettysburg. His body was brought to the prison for her to identify but she refused, so he was buried as an unknown soldier. After the Civil War, Emeline was released and lived many years as a lonely spinster. Just before she died, she left instructions that she wanted to be buried next to the grave of the unknown soldier, and that is where she rests to this day.

(Moorhead City is on Bogue Sound on the south-central coast. Crab Point is on the Outer Banks of the North Carolina coast east of Moorhead City.) **163**

OCRACOKE

OCRACOKE INLET Legend says that every September on the first night of the new moon, a flaming ghost ship sails past this ocean inlet three times. The spectral light is from an old sailing vessel that brought refugees from the Rhine Valley to the New World in the early 1700s. While anchored off the coast here, the crew mutinied and robbed all the immigrants of their valuables. Then they set the ship afire, pulled up anchor, and abandoned her. The vessel drifted out to sea, but the screams of its passengers could be heard for miles

away. The ship was last sighted in September 1999. It always moves in a northeasterly direction.

(The ship is sighted off the northern shore of Ocracoke Inlet on Pamlico Bay. It is always traveling northeast. For ferry information, call 919-928-3841.) **220**

PISGAH MOUNTAINS

BLUE RIDGE PARKWAY The ghosts of two young lovers haunt these hills. In an effort to break up the courtship of Jim Stratton and Mary Robinson, Mary's father reported Jim to the authorities for operating a still. Mary and Jim fled together into the wilderness, where it is thought they froze to death in the deep snow. In the winter months, the ghosts of Jim and Mary are seen on the mountainside. Sometimes his phantom is kneeling at her feet, pledging his undying love.

(The Pisgah Mountains are northeast of Asheville in western North Carolina. The Blue Ridge Parkway runs along the western rim of the range.) **96**

RALEIGH

ANDREW JOHNSON HOME Andrew Johnson was born in this house in 1808. Johnson became the seventeenth president when Lincoln was assassinated in 1865. The light of a ghostly candle is sometimes seen in the single downstairs window of his old family home.

(Raleigh is in central North Carolina, at the junction of I-40 and U.S. Highway 1. The small, gambrel-roof house is located on Mordecai Square in Raleigh. A stone marker identifies the landmark. The mailing address is 1 Mimosa St., Raleigh, NC 27604. Phone: 919-834-4844.) **168**

EXECUTIVE MANSION In 1970, Governor Bob Scott decided to replace the massive old wooden bed in his second-floor bedroom at the Executive Mansion with a modern, king-size bed. He moved the old bed, which had been built in 1891 to the precise specifications of Governor Daniel Fowle, to a little-used room on the third floor. Fowle had died in the bed while he was still governor, and some have suggested that his spirit remained there. Soon, strange rapping sounds were heard coming from the wall where the headboard of Fowle's bed had rested. The persistent knocking started around 10:00 P.M., increased in frequency, and did not cease until late at night. The timely rapping continued through the rest of Bob Scott's administration, and he admitted that his family had nicknamed the poltergeist Governor Fowle's Ghost. The phenomenon promptly ceased when a new administration took over, and Fowle's bed was moved back to the second floor.

(The Executive Mansion is in downtown Raleigh, a few blocks northeast of the State Capitol, on North Blount Street, between Lane Street and Jones Street. The address is 200 North Blount Street, Raleigh, NC 27601. Tour information can be obtained by contacting the Capitol Area Visitor Center, 301 North Blount St., Raleigh, NC 27601. Phone: 919-733-3456. www.prairieghosts.com/raleigh.html) **14, 101, 168**

Mordecai Manor Built in 1785 by Joel Lane, this house is named for Moses Mordecai, who married Lane's daughter Ellen. The old manor house is said to be haunted by a woman in a long, black, pleated skirt, wearing a white blouse and black tie.

(The two-story mansion, with a balcony on the second level, is located on Mordecai Square. The mailing address is Capitol Area Preservation Society, 1 Mimosa St., Raleigh, NC 27604. Phone: 919-834-4844.) **101, 168**

Poole's Woods The phantom of a white horse and rider is seen galloping through these woods. William Poole rode his magnificent horse through the woods of his 1,600-acre estate every evening at 5:00 P.M., until Union soldiers confiscated the animal during the Civil War. The devastated Poole left instructions in his will that the seventy-five acres of woodland where he rode his beloved horse be preserved without a single tree being removed. After his death, a ghostly white horse was seen along the road from Raleigh to his estate and in the woods surrounding his mansion. In the 1920s the woods were sold to commercial developers, but the trees proved worthless owing to internal rot. The ghost of a horse, sometimes with a rider on its back, is still seen in the area.

(The woods are located three miles southeast of Raleigh. The Poole mansion is no longer standing, but Poole Road begins just east of the capitol building and runs to the southeast from New Bern Ave.) **101**

ROAN MOUNTAIN

Ghostly Choir The heavenly sound of a choir singing has been heard on the top of this mountain since the 1770s. The music is clearest just after a thunderstorm and is said to grow in intensity before it reaches a wild crescendo. Historically, local herdsmen have attributed the singing sounds to angels.

(Roan Mountain is in the Bald Mountain Range located in Mitchell County along the Tennessee border.) **169**

ROANOKE ISLAND

Fort Raleigh National Historic Site In the dark forests near old Fort Raleigh, a mysterious silver-white doe has been sighted for hundreds of years. The strange animal is said to be the ghost of Virginia Dare, the first English child born in the New World. She was part of the ill-fated Sir Walter Raleigh colony that arrived in Virginia in 1587. Their ship, under the command of John White, returned to England for badly needed provisions, but immediately on its arrival the vessel was ordered into service in the Spanish War. It was three years before it was able to return to the colony. When White finally landed on Roanoke Island, there was no trace of the 110 settlers he left behind. The only hint was the seven letters "C-R-O-A-T-O-A" carved on a post. Some researchers believe that the cryptic message signifies that the starving colonists joined with, or were massacred by, the Croatan Indians. An old Indian legend holds that a blue-eyed white child named Virginia was adopted by the tribe. As the girl grew into a beautiful maiden, she aroused jealousy among the young braves of the tribe. A medicine man named Chico used a magic necklace to turn Virginia into a young doe, to prevent her from marrying any of the tribe members. One heartsick brave, Okisko, stalked the white doe for many years, hoping she would return to her human shape. The ghost of Virginia Dare supports the assimilation theory. Other evidence, such as the rare birth of blue-eyed, blond-haired Indians, suggests the same. (See Melungeons, Hancock County, Tennessee.) The colony's desperation produced yet another ghost. From the 1600s to modern times, many people have reported seeing the phantom of a three-masted sailing ship off the shores of Roanoke Island.

(Roanoke Island is off the northeast coast in Croatan Sound. Follow U.S. Highway 64 to the island. The lost settlement was in the Maneteo area at North West Point on Roanoke Island, four miles north on U.S. Highway 158. The ghost of Virginia Dare is most often encountered

north of Fort Niagara, along the Thomas Hariot Trail.) **5, 36, 55, 70, 172, 220**

SALISBURY

KING'S MOUNTAIN ROAD The apparitions of two British soldiers dressed in Revolutionary War uniforms have been seen galloping on phantom horses along this road. They are said to be James and Douglas Duncan, two couriers sent by Major Ferguson on King's Mountain to request reinforcements from Lord Cornwallis in Charlottesburg. The British couriers never delivered the urgent plea for backup, and the Americans won a decisive victory at King's Mountain. The two men were murdered by American sympathizers at a tavern where they paused for refreshment, but their spirits continued their journey. Stagecoach drivers, hunters, motorists, and later Kings Mountain residents told strange tales of encountering two spectral horseback riders, who stop short and seem to be asking for directions. Their cadaverous phantoms are always dressed in soiled British uniforms. Sometimes, green-skinned corpses are seen kneeling over a crude map at the forks of roads.

(The town of Salisbury is on I-85 in Rowan County, between Greensboro and Concord. The ghosts have been seen on the road between King's Mountain and Charlotte, near the town of Salisbury. They were murdered at an old inn that stood at the South Fork of the Catawba River, and are most often seen in October, at the forks of roads in the area.) **162, 172**

SILER CITY

DEVIL'S TRAMPING GROUND A perfect circle here, forty feet in diameter, is said to be formed by the eternal pacing of the devil himself, as he ponders new evils for mankind. No tree or plant will grow there, and twigs or branches placed on the path are said to be gone by next daylight. Surrounding brush grows just up to the edge of the circle. Early settlers attributed the barren earth to Indians holding ceremonies there, but the circle remained long after the Indians disappeared. A recent study by the North Carolina Department of Agriculture showed the dirt within the circle to be completely sterile, leading to speculation that the Devil's Tramping Ground is really the world's oldest surviving UFO crop circle. See Delphos, Kansas.

(Siler City is in central North Carolina, at the junction of U.S. Highways 64 and 421. The Devil's Tramping

Ground is along Buies Creek in Chatham County in central North Carolina, just west of Siler City. Take Highway 421 south nine miles to County Road 902. Go west six miles to Harper's Crossroads, and turn north on Glendon Road. Turn left on next paved road, which is County 1100.) **49, 70, 99, 169**

SMITHFIELD

HANNAH'S CREEK SWAMP Exactly fifty ghosts haunt a small island in the middle of this swamp. Their ghastly forms are seen hanging from trees. The men were members of David Fanning's Marauders, a group of northern plunderers who ravaged the area after Sherman's troops burned a path through the South. They were caught camping on the island by Confederate troops led by Colonel John Saunders, whose parents they had recently murdered. The colonel had the men hanged from the limbs of trees on the island.

(Smithfield is twenty-four miles southeast of Raleigh on U.S. Highway 70. The swampland is just outside Smithfield in Johnson County.) **169**

MILL CREEK BRIDGE Spectral lights danced on this bridge in the 1950s. Old timers in the area say the luminescent flashes are the ghost of an old black man being lashed by his cruel master. In May 1820, Master Lynch and one of his slaves, Old Squire, were clearing land near the wooden bridge here. Lynch lashed at the slave with his whip one too many times, and the large black man struck back at his master with a hoe. Old Squire buried Lynch under the bridge, and before long, people started noticing strange things at the wooden crossing. Lanterns would go out as the bridge was traversed, and weird sounds emanated from under it. Once, a man's cane was snatched from his hand as he stepped onto the bridge, only to be returned to him when he reached the other side. Old Squire confessed to the murder on his death bed.

(Mill Creek is just outside Smithfield in Johnson County.) **169**

SMOKY MOUNTAINS

TSALI The ghost of an Indian has been sighted in these hills for nearly 150 years. Tsali was a Cherokee Indian who organized his people to resist attempts by the U.S. Government to resettle their tribe on a reservation in Oklahoma. In 1838, cavalrymen under General Winfield Scott started rounding up the Indians and forcing them to march to Oklahoma. Many died on the march or were killed by soldiers for resisting, but Tsali and a band of followers escaped into the mountains. General Scott sent word that if Tsali surrendered the rest of his band could remain free. When Tsali did surrender, Scott had him shot by a firing squad.

(The Great Smoky Mountains National Park is in the western tip of North Carolina, along the Tennessee border. Tsali's ghost appears in October and early November in the evening mists of the valleys and hilltops of the Great Smoky range in northwestern North Carolina. Historical marker Q3 tells his story. Phone: 865-436-1200. www. nps.gov/grsm) **165, 183, 223**

A train wreck near Bostian's Bridge is replayed in ghostly detail to witnesses each year on the anniversary of the disaster. See Bostian's Bridge, Statesville, North Carolina (STEVE HEALEY)

STATESVILLE

BOSTIAN'S BRIDGE A passenger train wreck that occurred near here on August 27, 1891, is said to be repeated at 3:00 A.M. on the anniversary of the disaster. Witnesses report hearing the sounds of twisted metal, steam pipes rupturing, and the screams of helpless passengers, but find no evidence of an accident. Sometimes the ghost of baggage master H. K. Linster appears and asks for the correct time, so he can set his gold watch. Passenger train number nine was heading from Salisbury to Asheville, when it derailed off the old Bostian's Bridge and fell into the ravine ninety feet below. Scores were injured and thirty people killed, including baggage master Linster.

(Statesville is at the junction of I-40 and I-77 in western North Carolina. The bridge is east of town.) **172**

THOMASVILLE

SAN-MOR COMPANY The apparition of a fifty-year-old man is frequently observed in this furniture factory building. The six-foot-tall ghost, wearing a checkered long-sleeved shirt and khaki pants, has been seen by workers and visitors here over a hundred times. Workers nicknamed the spirit Lucas, short for Lucifer. The twenty-thousand-square-foot, cinder-block building was constructed in the 1940s on the site of a barn on the Peace family farm. Their fifty-year-old retarded son hanged himself in the barn and swung from the creaking beam for over a day before anyone discovered his body.

(Thomasville is a southwestern suburb of High Point on U.S. Highway 29/70. The former San-Mor Company site is at 20 Peace St., Thomasville, NC 27361.) **101, 135**

TOWN CREEK HISTORIC SITE

TOWN CREEK INDIAN MOUND This sacred site was home to Creek Indian priests and contained temples, burial grounds, and council buildings. Purification rites practiced at the site included extended fasting and meditation. The reconstructed thatched-roof main temple sits atop an earthen pyramid, where the community soul was believed to reside.

(The state historic site is located near Mount Gilead off Highway 73 on Highway 3. For more information, contact the Town Creek Historic Site, 509 Town Creek Mound Road., Mount Gilead, NC 27306. Phone: 919-439-6802. www.sandhillsonline.com/history/mound. htm) **144**

WARSAW

ATLANTIC COAST LINE RAILROAD TRACKS A phantom train runs along these tracks. Complete with whistle and headlight, the locomotive approaches crossings and then completely disappears from sight. The train is thought to be one that overturned after derailing here in November 1906. A protruding timber from a sidelined flatbed had accidentally thrown a switch that caused the wreck. Engineer Gilbert Horne and his fireman were scalded to death when the boiler ruptured, and a man in the baggage car died of a broken back. The ghost train, nicknamed Shoo Fly by locals, was spotted many times rushing down the tracks near where it derailed. After a while, engineers habitually slowed their trains when approaching the area, not knowing what to expect.

(Warsaw is in Duplin County in southeastern North Carolina. It is thirteen miles east of Clinton on Highway 24. The tracks are just outside of town.) **169**

WILMINGTON

CHAMBER OF COMMERCE Wilmington's official welcome center is home to a ghost, who was once photographed descending a staircase in the building. Known officially as the Price-Gause House, the place has been considered haunted ever since it was built in 1843. Immediately after moving in, the Gause family heard strange footsteps on the stairs and traced an eerie tapping sound that moved along the walls. They finally decided to live with the unidentified presence. Later residents came to the same conclusion. An investigation in October 1967 documented several mysterious sounds and yielded the startling photo of a misty human form walking down the stairs.

(Wilmington is on the extreme southern tip of North Carolina, at the south end of I-40. Wilmington Chamber of Commerce, One Estel Lee Place, Wilmington, NC 28401. For information, call 910-762-2611. www. wilmingtonchamber.org) **159**

FORT FISHER The ghost of Confederate General William Whiting is said to roam the ruins of the fort he once commanded. Whiting was mortally wounded in a massive Federal attack on the stronghold in 1864. The embattlement protected the last river route used by blockade runners to supply Southern troops, and its fall to the North spelled the end of the Confederacy. Whiting's gray-clad figure is seen at dusk on the old parapet, gazing back to the road.

(Fort Fisher is now a state historic site in New Hanover County. It is south of Wilmington on a peninsula between the Cape Fear River and the ocean. The fort is located where the highway ends at the tip of the peninsula at Kure Beach. Phone: 910-458-5538.) **169**

NEW HANOVER COUNTY PUBLIC LIBRARY The second-floor wing of this library is haunted by the ghost of a short woman whom some believe to be a former patron who frequented the local history room. Her form has been sighted by three employees in the last few years. Ghostly footsteps, moving books and pamphlets, and the unexplained sound of pages turning are attributed to the spirit of a man who lived in a home that stood on the property in the nineteenth century. He was killed in a duel, and his nervous ghost was heard pacing about in the house for many years. The library moved into the present building, a former department store, in 1982.

(New Hanover County Public Library, 201 Chestnut Street, Wilmington, NC 28401. Phone: 910-341-4390.) **72, 101, 135**

ST. JAMES EPISCOPAL CHURCH Samuel Jocelyn's grave appears peaceful enough from the surface. But what unimaginable horror did the youth experience when he awoke inside his coffin in March 1810? Apparently a fall from his horse put Jocelyn into a comatose sleep just long enough for him to be buried alive. Several times in the days immediately following his funeral, Samuel's trembling ghost appeared to his closest friend, Alexander Hostler, and begged him to open his grave. Finally, the driven Hostler enlisted the assistance of another friend and dug up the coffin. When they opened it, they found the lifeless body turned over on its stomach. Samuel Jocelyn had indeed been buried alive.

(The graveyard is just south of the church. St. James Episcopal Church, 25 S. 3rd Street, Wilmington, NC 28401. Phone: 910-763-1628.) **159, 165**

THALIAN HALL The ghosts of two men and a woman, all dressed in frilly Edwardian costumes, haunt the center seats in the first balcony of the Thalian Hall theater. Their presence has also been felt backstage, in the corridors, and in the lobby. The Thalian Theater Group was formed in 1788, and the present building was constructed in 1858. The group is the oldest theater company in the United States. Thalian Hall is also one of America's architectural treasures. The design of its graciously curved auditorium and floating balcony was later copied by the architect of Washington's Ford Theater.

(The theater is in west central Wilmington at 310 Chestnut St. Phone: 910-343-3660. www.thalianhall. com) **162**

WINSTON-SALEM

BROTHERS HOUSE A cellar in Brothers House, which used to be part of a home for Catholic monks, is haunted by the ghost of a young brother who died helping dig it out. On March 25, 1786, Brother Andreas Kremser was killed when a wall of earth collapsed on him. Kremser was sixteen years old when he left Pennsylvania to join the brothers and practice his shoe-cobbler trade. After he died, the brothers often heard the tapping of his shoemaker's hammer. Later, his red-jacketed figure was seen drifting through the cellar, and his ghost was dubbed Little Red Man.

(Winston-Salem is north central North Carolina, at the junction of I-40 and U.S. Highway 52. Brothers House is in Old Salem, near the junction of U.S. Highway 52 and 311 in Winston-Salem. General information on the Winston-Salem area is available by calling 800-331-7018.) **169**

OLD SALEM The ghost of a Texan who died in a room of the Salem Tavern has been seen walking in the first-floor hallway. Before the Civil War, guests, maids, and the innkeeper all reported seeing the apparition, who asked that his brother be notified of his death. With that done, the haunting in the 212-year-old building ceased. But ghosts are still reported walking near the much more modern blacksmith area, which is not far from the tavern.

(The tavern and blacksmith shop are part of the Old Salem restoration. Old Salem Inc., Box F Salem Station, 600 South Main St., Winston-Salem, NC 27108. Phone: 336-721-7300. www.oldsalem.org) **72, 165**

NORTH DAKOTA

ABERCROMBIE

FORT ABERCROMBIE Ghosts of both soldiers and Indians have been reported walking through the restored buildings of this old fort. It was established in 1857 to protect wagon trains moving westward. The stockade was repeatedly attacked by Sioux Indians in 1862.

(Abercrombie is twenty-five miles south of Fargo in extreme southeastern North Dakota. The Fort Abercrombie Museum is just northeast of town. Fort Abercrombie Historic Site, 816 Broadway, Abercrombie, ND 58001. Phone: 701-553-8513.) **102**

A glowing cross appears inside this deserted church. See Absaraka Methodist Church, Absaraka, North Dakota (HEATH TORSTVEIT)

ABSARAKA

ABSARAKA METHODIST CHURCH A mysterious luminous cross forms inside this deserted church. Witnesses describe it as "a big light in the sign of the cross." The phenomenon was first noticed after new windows were installed in 1953. The glowing cross appeared several nights in a row in November 1987 and was seen by dozens of people, who came from miles around to observe it. The church was built in 1888 and has been closed since 1983, though it opened for a centennial celebration in 1988. Although the effect seems to be caused by the refraction of light through the frosted windows, many people admit to being deeply moved by the sight.

(Absaraka is in Cass County in the northeast corner of North Dakota, twenty-two miles west of Fargo, north of I-94. The abandoned Methodist church is at the edge of town.) **16, 72**

AMIDON

BLACK BUTTE This rock formation is a hundred feet high and eight miles in circumference. It used to be called H. T. Butte, because it was located on the largest horse ranch in the state, the H. T. Ranch. One of the cowboys who worked at the ranch was Bob Pierce, who was known as "Crazy Loon" for the breakneck speed at which he rode horses. He probably died on horseback, because his ghost is seen on moonless nights, riding a phantom horse right up the sides of Black Butte. Sometimes the chilling sounds of wolves are heard as well.

(Amidon is in southwestern North Dakota. Take U.S. Highway 85 south from I-94 for twenty-six miles. Black Butte is south of town on the west side of U.S. Highway 85. The Butte View State Campground is about twenty miles south of town on U.S. Highway 85. For information, contact the North Dakota Department of Tourism at 800-435-5663. www.ndtourism.com) **175**

ASHLEY

UFO SIGHTINGS Many of North Dakota's most recent UFO incidents have occurred near this small farming town. Several UFO crop circles have been found in the area, and numerous well-witnessed UFO sightings have occurred. A half-dozen mysterious crop circles, one nearly a hundred feet in diameter, were discovered in the area during 1990 and 1991. In June 1993, Donald Krumb was driving east of town when he spotted some strange lights coming from a ditch along the road. His pickup truck stalled and everything in it shut down for about ten seconds. The next day, he returned to the site and found all the grass flattened in a circular pattern. During the same week, several witnesses reported seeing bright white lights flying in a U-shaped pattern south of town.

(Ashley is in McIntosh County near the South Dakota border, at the junction of Highway 11 and Highway 3. The UFO-haunted area includes McIntosh, Logan, and Dickey counties.) **72**

BISMARCK

HOLY HILLS This site has been considered sacred for hundreds of years. Sioux Indians considered the area to be full of nature spirits that worked at night deep below the ground. Mysterious clicking sounds emanating from the ground and hills here have never been explained. The sounds stop when modern vehicles approach the site.

(Bismarck is in central North Dakota, on the Missouri River, at the junction of U.S. Highway 83 and I-94. Holy Hills is three miles southwest of Cannon Ball, which is on the Missouri River south of Bismarck.) **175**

LIBERTY MEMORIAL BUILDING This 1920s building is haunted by a ghostly presence known as the Stack Monster. The building used to house the state historical society and was used to store and exhibit thousands of Indian and pioneer artifacts, skeletons, and old books. It is thought the ghost was brought to the building with one of those items. Feelings of dread, unexplainable footsteps and voices, and strange shadows have plagued workers here for the past twenty-five years. The building is now home to the North Dakota Department of Tourism.

(The Liberty Memorial Building is located on the grounds of the state capitol in central Bismarck, at 604 East Blvd., Bismarck ND 58505. Phone: 701-224-2525.) **175**

FARGO

ENGINE NO. 571 For many years at the turn of the century, Northern Pacific Railroad engineers were terrified of locomotive number 571. Throughout the state, railroad workers knew it simply as the "Hoodoo." Several trainmen had died in the engine, which was involved in three wrecks. When the steam locomotive plunged into the Green River in 1892, it was believed to have absorbed some kind of evil energy. That same year, engineers started seeing a hideous goblin that perched itself near the pilot and prevented water from being sprayed to cool down the coals.

(Engine no. 571 was based in central Fargo. General information on the state is available from the Greater North Dakota Association, 1430 35th St. SW, Fargo, ND 58103. Phone: 800-382-1405.) **53 (5/92)**

NORTH DAKOTA STATE UNIVERSITY Ghostly disturbances on the third floor of Ceres Hall are blamed on a man who committed suicide there. Sometime during World War II, the man hanged himself from a heating pipe.

(The university was founded in 1890 and covers 21,000 acres in this small city. North Dakota State University, 1301 N. University, Fargo, ND 58105. Phone: 701-237-7752. www.ndsu.nodak.edu) **72**

UFO SIGHTING A remarkable UFO dogfight took place in the skies above Fargo on October 1, 1948. Lieutenant George Gorman engaged an unidentified "globular" object that appeared to be under intelligent control. The Air National Guard pilot chased it in his P-51 fighter for over thirty minutes. The object easily outmaneuvered his jet. The UFO made 90-degree and 180-degree turns at speeds in excess of six hundred mph.

Several observers on the ground followed the object, which they described as a sharply outlined ball of light zigzagging through the sky at a high rate of speed. Gorman followed it to an altitude of fourteen thousand feet but had to give up the chase when his plane started to stall. Nine months earlier, another Air National Guard pilot, Captain Thomas Mantell, died in the crash of his P-51 after he followed an identical UFO to over fifteen thousand feet in the skies above Kentucky.

(Forgo is in Cass County, on the Minnesota border at the junction of I-29 and I-94. Witnesses included pilots and ground personnel at Sky Ranch Flying Field and Hector Airport.) **72, 126 (5/86, 10/88, 4/90), 190**

GRAFTON

NOCTURNAL UFO Police tracked a giant red UFO through this city on September 25, 1961. The round object appeared from the east and traveled through town in the early morning hours. It hovered as close as five hundred feet above the ground, then disappeared over the Grafton Airport. Air Force personnel at Grand Forks could not offer an explanation for the sightings. The incident was part of a flap, or wave of sightings, that occurred from North Dakota to Kansas in 1961.

(Grafton is in Walsh County in the northeastern corner of the state, twenty-five miles north of Grand Forks on U.S. Highway 81.) **50, 53 (1/62)**

GRAND FORKS

ALTRUE HOSPITAL This old hospital building is haunted by several apparitions. The staff elevator sometimes runs under the direction of a woman who died in the hospital and seems to be trying to get out. With no one in the elevator, it runs by itself, opening at random floors. Sometimes the female apparition is seen inside the elevator, just as it begins to open. In the former psychiatric ward, strange "shadows" set off the door alarms. When seen on video cameras, the apparitions appear to slide under the door and reappear on the other side.

(Altrue Hospital, South Columbia Rd., Grand Forks, ND 58201. Phone: 701-780-5187.) **72**

ST. ANNE'S GUEST HOME This old building was originally a convent. Left vacant for many years, it was eventually turned into a nursing home. For many years, people have reported the ghostly figure of a woman in the bell tower windows, although the tower is completely sealed off. Many believe the apparition is Sister Mary Murphy, who threw herself from the tower in 1978.

(St. Anne's Guest Home, 524 North 17th St., Grand Forks, ND 58203. Phone: 701-746-9401.) **72**

UNIVERSITY OF NORTH DAKOTA There have been several sightings of the ghost of a girl, usually without legs, floating up one of the tunnels that connect Wilkerson Dining Hall to five dormitories on this campus. In 1988, three students saw her apparition in the West Hall tunnel. They described her as about five feet five inches tall, with short dark hair, wearing a nightshirt. In December 1962, before the tunnels were constructed, a young coed froze to death about sixty feet from West Hall. It is thought she slipped on the ice while trying to make her way to the dining hall around 2:00 A.M.

(Grand Forks is far-eastern North Dakota, on the Minnesota border at the junction of I-29 and U.S. Highway 2. University of North Dakota, Box 8095 University Station, Grand Forks, ND 58202. Phone: 701-777-2011. www.und.nodak.edu) **72**

KINDRED

WHITE CLADS Dozens of sightings of mysterious white-robed figures, called White Clads by locals, were reported in rural areas near this town in August 1976. White Clads are usually seen carrying candles and assembled in forests, alongside roads, or near bridges. It was never determined whether the White Clads were phantoms or some type of cultists, although a ritually mutilated bull discovered near Enderlin lends credence to the latter theory. A least five other cases of animal mutilation have been reported in conjunction with sightings of White Clads. See Valley City, below.

(Kindred is southwest of Fargo in Cass County, six miles west of I-29 on Highway 46. The White Clads were seen by motorists on Highway 46 between Kindred and Enderlin. They were also reported at nearby Millsite Park, along the Sheyenne River and crossing a bridge over railroad tracks. The sightings included other communities in the Red River Valley, all the way to Lake Park, Minnesota.) **50, 53 (2/77), 72**

LAKE SAKAKAWEA

LAKE SAKAKAWEA STATE PARK There have been multiple monster sightings in this park. A large, serpentine creature has been reported in the lake, which Indians call Devil's Lake. A nine-foot-tall gorilla like animal has been sighted in the woods. The Bigoot has been tracked as far south as the Cannonball River and has also been reported in the Killdeer Mountains.

(Lake Sakakawea is a widening of the Missouria River near the Fort Berthold Indian Reservation in western North Dakota. The Cannonball River is a tributary of the Missouri beginning about twenty-five miles south of Bismarck. The state park is north of Pick City, which is thirteen miles west of U.S. Highway 83 on Highway 1806. Phone: 701-487-3315. www.state.nd.us/ndparks/Parks/LSSP.htm) **16**

MINOT

HOME SWEET HOME This antique shop is located in a four-story building that is haunted by two apparitions. The first is a man who hanged himself in the attic. Now sealed off by a locked door, witnesses have reported icy winds and other unexplained activity there. Candy in old jars in the attic moves from dusty jar to dusty jar, yet there are never any fingerprints left by someone opening the jars. The other ghost is a man who drowned in the river behind the building. The accident happened at 4:39 A.M. and that is when, some say, the horrible event replays itself in an otherworldly scene.

(Home Sweet Home, 103 Fourth Ave. NW, Minot, ND 587033. Phone: 701-852-5604.) **72**

MINOT AIR FORCE BASE Airmen at three different missile silos in northern North Dakota observed and tracked two UFOs on August 24, 1966. One object was white and the other displayed multiple colors. The UFOs seemed to be inspecting the military sites and sometimes hovered near the ground for extended periods. The mysterious objects were observed for over four hours, and ground personnel trying to investigate the sightings reported extensive radio interference. A similar multicolored UFO was observed near Parshall on October 27, 1967. In November 1961, four men, two with very high security ratings, observed a UFO landing in a field. When they investigated they found several humanoid figures on the outside of the craft. One of the men fired his gun at an occupant of the craft who seemed to be waving them off. The humanoid fell to the ground and was carried back into the UFO, which then departed the area. A government investigator debriefed the men and took samples of their clothing, but no report on the incident was ever made public.

(Minot is in Ward County in northwest North Dakota. It is at the intersection of U.S. Highways 2, 52, and 83. The air force base is twelve miles north of town on U.S. Highway 83. www.minot.af.mil) **72, 126 (10/91)**

RICHARDTON

WILD PLUM SCHOOL A teacher and eight students witnessed a spontaneous outbreak of poltergeist activity in this rural schoolhouse. It began when pieces of coal in a bucket started flying about the room. When the teacher picked up the coal, she found that each piece "trembled" in her hand. Then the coal scuttle tipped over, and a large dictionary on the teacher's desk began to move. Finally, the window shades began to smolder and the bookcase suddenly erupted into flames. Teacher Pauline Rebel called for help from other school officials, who also witnessed the phenomena. The incident took place in April 1944 and became one of the best-documented cases of its kind on record. A thorough investigation by the state fire marshal could find no reason for the events. Samples of the coal were sent to the FBI forensics lab in Washington, D.C. No signs of fraud were revealed, and all the witnesses passed lie detector tests. *Time* magazine suggested that the Wild Plum phenomenon might be explained by applying "the principle of increasing entropy [disorder]," a tenet of atomic physics popularized at the time.

(Richardton is in southwest North Dakota, fourteen miles east of Dickinson on I-94. The schoolhouse is north of town in Stark County.) **72**

VALLEY CITY

WHITE CLADS Sightings of hooded, white-robed figures carrying candles were reported by rural residents here during the summer of 1976. They were part of the White Clads phenomenon that plagued North Dakota in the late 1970s (see Enderlin, above). Mutilated sheep and cows were discovered on some farms near Valley City.

(Valley City is in Barnes County in eastern North Dakota. The city is forty-five miles east of Fargo on I-94.) **50, 53 (2/77)**

OHIO

ADAMS COUNTY

SERPENT MOUND STATE MEMORIAL This sacred site, considered to be one of the most powerful in the world, was built on the edge of a crater formed when a meteor struck the earth over three thousand years ago. The Great Serpent Mound was used for worship by both the Adena and Hopewell Indians as far back as 1200 B.C. The man-made raised earthen snake is 1,348 feet long, 20 feet wide, and 5 feet tall. The jaws of the uncoiling snake open seventeen feet wide to devour a huge oval egg. This is not a burial ground but a sacred site intended only for worship. In cultures around the world, the coiled serpent represents creativity, enlightenment, and immortality. Several people have reported encountering both evil and pleasant spirits here. In 1983, a noted archaeologist working at the site experienced a psychic epiphany that opened his mind to the spiritual world. An almost identically shaped serpent intaglio is located in Rice County in the middle of Kansas, and some researchers believe the earthen serpents are somehow associated with ancient legends of Cibola, the Seven Cities of Gold described by the Aztecs. See Lost Dutchman Mine, Superstition Mountains, Arizona.

(The site is in south central Ohio, near Columbus in Adams County. The mound is just off Highway 73 in Locust Grove. Serpent Mound State Memorial 3850 State Route 73, Peebles, OH 45660. Phone: 937-587-2796. www.ohiohistory.org/places/serpent) **53 (7/94), 66 (10/89), 99, 122, 144**

WICKERHAM INN Hundreds of witnesses have seen the Headless Ghost of Wickerham Inn. Built in 1797 by Peter Wickerham, the inn was the scene of a bloody murder in the early 1800s. A stage driver was robbed and murdered in his room one night, but his body was never found. Within a few weeks, people reported seeing a decapitated phantom roaming the halls on the second floor. Finally, during renovations in 1922, the headless skeleton of a man was found beneath the cellar floor.

(The brick inn is on the old Zanes Trace, near West Union in Adams County.) **230**

AKRON

SUMMIT COUNTY JUVENILE DETENTION HOME The ghost of a former matron still makes her rounds in this home for juvenile delinquents. Eula Bonham was killed by nine girls during an escape that took place on November 27, 1955. Her conscientious ghost still patrols the halls and has been known to levitate contraband cigarettes or food from the hands of offenders.

(Akron is fifteen miles south of Cleveland on Highway 8. Summit County Juvenile Detention Home, Akron, OH 44300.) **230**

BELLBROOK

LITTLE SUGAR CREEK This haunted creek is home to two ghosts. The headless phantom of James Buckley has been seen walking down this stream. His phantom silently implores witnesses to help him find his severed head. The Englishman had a cabin in the woods here and was beheaded by robbers in the 1880s. His severed head was discovered lying in the middle of the road, but his ghost has yet to claim it. The other spirit dates from the same period. She was a young servant girl who became pregnant by the mayor. When the man denied the baby was his, she took the infant to Little Sugar Creek, held it tightly, and jumped into the water. Now, during the month of June, the apparition of the woman walks the bank and can sometimes be heard humming a lullaby.

(Bellbrook is in Greene County, five miles southeast of Dayton on Highway 725. The female ghost is seen near Magee Park, which is north of Highway 725 on Little Sugar Creek Rd.) **229, 230**

BOWLING GREEN

BOWLING GREEN STATE UNIVERSITY The Joe E. Brown and Eva Marie Saint Theaters on this campus are haunted by a ghost named Alice. She is said to have been a coed killed in an accident during her performance in *Othello*. Stage managers make a point of verbally inviting her to all performances and leaving a stage light burning for her. If the ritual is neglected in any way, the theater is plagued with loud noises, crumbling sets, and electrical problems. Several members of the theater company have encountered Alice's pallid specter, her long hair flowing gracefully over her shoulders. In 1986, her apparition was observed on the stage stairwell during a performance of *Othello*. Another ghost haunts the Chi Omega Sorority. Her name is Amanda, and she is said to be a freshman who died in a train accident on the night she was to be pledged. Her brown-haired ghost is seen in the kitchen and in a room dedicated to her memory.

(Bowling Green is in Wood County, fifteen miles south of Toledo on Highway 25. BGSU, Bowling Green, OH 45403. Phone: 419-373-2222. www.bgsu.edu) **229**

BUCYRUS

OLD HANLEY FARM The beautiful ghost of Ethyl Hanley, the nineteen-year-old daughter of a family that farmed here in the early 1900s, has been seen roaming the hills overlooking her home. Dressed in white, her silent form appears momentarily, leaving behind the scent of lilacs. Ethyl had planned to marry civil engineer Frank Burbank. The two postponed their marriage for several years so he could complete his education, but a few days before the ceremonies the young girl was killed in a tragic accident. She was thrown from a carriage and cracked her head on a stone bridge abutment. Locals say that it was Frank's deep mourning that brought her spirit back.

(Bucyrus is in Crawford County in north-central Ohio, at the junction of U.S. Highway 30 and Highway 4. Hanley's ghost has been seen on the grassy bluffs overlooking the Sandusky River southeast of town.) **158, 176**

CAMBRIDGE

U.S. HIGHWAY 40 Two headless ghosts haunt this modern highway. One is a laborer who worked on the construction of the roadway. The man was robbed and murdered by a fellow employee, and his decapitated corpse was buried under the road. His ghastly phantom is still seen by motorists traveling the highway. The other is a woman who lived in a cabin near the old trail in the late 1890s. She was beheaded by her husband in a violent argument, and soon afterward, the headless apparition of Lady Bend was seen riding sidesaddle on a magnificent white horse.

(Cambridge is in Guernsey County in eastern Ohio, at the junction of I-70 and I-77. The phantom laborer stalks a stretch of Highway 40 called Deep Cut, which lies between Cambridge and Old Washington. The headless lady is seen on U.S. Highway 40 at Lady Bend Hill, on the third bend from the top.) **229**

CINCINNATI

CORNELL PLACE APARTMENTS This Victorian mansion was the site of out-of-control passions at the turn of the century. A man committed suicide here, and a doctor's daughter was found slain on the stairway. Unexplainable footsteps and disembodied voices attest to the spirits walking the halls. The mansion was built in the 1850s and gained a reputation for being haunted in the 1880s. For many years, no one would live in it. The building was sold to the Ealy School for Girls in 1900 and became an apartment building after World War II.

(Cincinnati is in the southwest corner of Ohio. The apartments are located at 3517 Cornell Place, Cincinnati, OH 45220.) **80, 87**

CLEVELAND

DRURY MANSION This fifty-two-room mansion, built in 1912, now serves as a halfway house for convicts. Police and inmates alike believe the place is haunted. Ethereal presences seem to roam freely throughout the building, although the ghost of woman wearing a long brown dress seems to be confined to the main stairway.

(Cleveland is on Lake Erie in northern Ohio. The mansion is in east Cleveland, across from the Drury Theater at 8625 Euclid Ave., Cleveland, OH 45215. www. prairieghosts.com/oh-cleve.html) **230**

MASON COURT APARTMENTS The ghost of a woman who was murdered in an argument with her husband haunted her old apartment for many years. The Thomas Todd family moved into the apartment in November 1957 and were bothered by screaming sounds and moaning from the cellar. They opened a trapdoor in the kitchen floor and inspected the area but found nothing wrong. The eerie sounds continued. Then, one evening in March 1958, the kitchen trapdoor opened by itself, with one of the Todd children standing on top of it. That was enough for the Todds. They nailed the door shut and moved out that same night. On March 31, Thomas brought fifteen people into the house to witness the uncanny phenomena. In front of them, the trapdoor burst open, ripping the hinges loose and pulling up the nails. Two gray fingers protruded through holes in the floor. Police investigated the scene and discovered nothing amiss, but no one would live in the house after that.

(The abandoned house stood for many years at 4207 Mason Court Southeast in Cleveland before being torn down.) **176, 229**

ST. CLAIR STREET The ghost of a popular grocer haunted this street for many years in the late nineteenth century. Reuben Weisberger's apparition was seen several times after his death, roaming St. Clair Street. He was usually following his wife Rosa. The well-documented haunting started on July 13, 1870, when Rosa went to medium Silvie Heitmen. The medium allegedly contacted her dead husband's spirit, which never again left Rosa's side.

(St. Clair St. runs through central Cleveland.) **41, 176**

SQUIRE'S CASTLE This three-story stone house was intended as a caretaker's cottage on the 525-acre summer estate of Fergus Squire, one of the founders of Standard Oil. In the early 1900s he vacationed here with his family, although his wife detested their country home. She missed the social life of the city and was terrified of untamed nature. She always had trouble sleeping on the property, and late one night she wandered into the trophy room. Apparently, one of the stuffed animals frightened her, and in her attempt to flee, she tripped and broke her neck. Her husband was devastated and never completed his plans to build a great castle on the land. He sold the property in 1922. Locals, with a sarcastic twist, named the cottage "Squire's Castle" and claim that Squire's wife is doomed for all eternity to wander the house she so hated. Her anguished screams are heard late at night, and the eerie red light from her lantern is seen moving slowly from room to room.

(Take I-90 to Highway 91 South and exit at Highway 6, then go east to Chagrin River Rd. to the Squire's Castle Picnic Area. The address of Squire's Castle is North Chagrin Reservation, Cleveland Metroparks System, Cleveland, OH 44144. For information, call the Sanctuary Marsh Nature Center at 216-351-6300. www. prairieghosts.com/oh-squir.html) **14, 101**

TIEDEMANN CASTLE This Gothic, turreted mansion has a long history of psychic disturbances. Doors explode off their hinges, chandeliers spin around, mirrors fog up for no reason, and lights turn themselves on and off. The unexplainable crying of babies is heard, a ghostly cloud moves through the upstairs hall, and the apparition of a woman in black has been seen several times staring out a tiny window in the front tower room. The manifestations are thought to be connected with Hannes and Luise Tiedemann, who built the great house in 1864. The family lived there for thirty-three years, and several family members died in the house. After Hannes died in 1908, the building came into the hands of the German Socialist Party, which used it for meetings and club functions for the next fifty-five years. In 1968, the house was bought by the Romano family. The Romano children immediately made contact with the ghosts in the house, although Mrs. Romano declared the third and fourth floors off-limits after frightening tramping sounds were heard and a friend witnessed a gray mist moving in the halls. The family consulted a Catholic priest, who said that the house contained evil spirits. He refused to perform an exorcism but did advise them to move. The Romanos finally found a buyer in 1974, and the building became the headquarters for the Universal Christian Church. Dozens of people, including members of news media, observed unexplainable phenomena in the house. Many refused ever to set foot in the building again. It was sold to Cleveland Police Chief Richard Hongisto in 1978, but his family moved out in less than a year. Since 1979, George Mirceta has owned the haunted house. He quickly accepted the fact that the place was haunted. He gives tours on weekends and keeps a logbook of strange things experienced by visitors.

(The Tiedemanns are buried in Riverside Cemetery. Their mansion, also known as Franklin Mansion, is located at 4308 Franklin Blvd. NW, Cleveland, OH 44113.) **176**

COLUMBUS

CAMP CHASE CONFEDERATE CEMETERY A mournful lady in gray, dressed in an antebellum traveling suit, visits the grave of Benjamin E. Allen. Allen was with the 50th Tennessee Regiment, and fresh flowers have mysteriously appeared on his grave for many years. The Lady in Gray has been seen drifting through trees and other solid objects near his grave and the Tomb of the Unknown Soldier. During a Civil War ceremony in 1988, the untraceable sounds of a woman's weeping were heard by dozens of witnesses.

(Columbus is in Franklin County at the center of Ohio. The cemetery is on Sullivant Ave. For information, contact the Hilltop Historical Society, 2456 West Broad St., Columbus, OH 43204. Phone: 614-276-0060.) **229**

KELTON HOUSE This house was built in 1852 by Fernando Cortez Kelton. It stayed in his family until 1975, when his granddaughter died. Her spirit never vacated the premises. The apparition of Grace Bird Kelton has been reported in the old house and her soft footsteps are sometimes heard in the attic. She rearranges the furniture and keeps the house spotless.

(The house is owned by the Junior League; tours are available. The address is 586 East Town St., Columbus, OH 43215. Phone: 614-464-2022. The Columbus Landmarks Foundation conducts ghost tours in October. For information, call 614-221-0227. www.fofs-oura.org/ Example/kelton.htm) **229**

OLD GOVERNOR'S MANSION The apparition of a black woman wearing an old-fashioned dress has been seen in the restaurant and on the stairs here. She is thought to be a former maid in the house, which served as the governor's mansion from 1920 to 1957.

(The mansion is on East Broad St. in downtown Columbus. For information, contact the Ohio Historical Society, 1982 Velma Ave., Columbus, OH 43211. Phone: 614-297-2300. www.ohiohistory.org.) **230**

PALACE THEATRE A séance was held here to try to contact the spirit of Thurston the Magician who, it was believed, haunted this old theater. However, the medium contacted the ghost of an elderly man who had died of a stroke in the theater. A powerful presence was also detected in the middle of the second-floor balcony by ghost-hunter Chris Woodyard. After recent renovations, the ghostly activity reached a new high.

(The Palace Theatre is in downtown Columbus at 34 West Broad St. Phone: 614-469-1331. www.capa.com/ venues/palace.html.) **230**

RESCH HOUSE This house was the site of unexplainable poltergeist activity for several months in 1984. It all started in March, when the TV and microwave kept running even when unplugged. Then the shower started turning on by itself, chairs overturned, and eggs flew across the kitchen and spattered against the walls. John and Joan Resch and their six children were terrified. Efforts by Mormon elders to dispel the presence with prayer were not successful. After an electrician could find nothing wrong with the house wiring, the family called the police. Before long, forty reporters had descended on the house and witnessed many of the unbelievable events. An investigation by the highly respected Psychical Research Foundation concluded that Tina, the Resch's fourteen-year-old adopted daughter, was the source of the phenomena. They took her back to North Carolina, where she produced a wide variety of psychokinetic manifestations. The case became one of the best-documented instances of spontaneous psychokinesis ever investigated.

(The Resch House is a private residence in Columbus.) **53 (9/84), 176**

ST. MARY'S OF THE SPRINGS For many years, the third-floor dormitory of Old Motherhouse was haunted by an unseen presence, which moved down the aisle from the doorway to a small closet in back of the room. The area had originally served as the chapel for the convent, and the closet used to be a confessional.

(The nunnery is in west Columbus. Phone: 614-253-3347.) **229**

THURBER HOUSE When humorist James Thurber was still in college, he lived here with his family. At 2:00 A.M. on November 17, 1915, the family heard loud footsteps in the downstairs rooms. The sound seemed to circle the kitchen table and was heading for the stairway. Two of the younger boys investigated and saw a ghost coming up the stairs. Convinced it was actually a burglar, Mrs. Thurber threw a shoe through a neighbor's window and asked them to call the police. Eight policemen broke down the front door but found no intruder. Grandfather Thurber, who was sleeping in the attic, ended up shooting one of the police officers in the shoulder. During this anxious period, it was reported that electricity "leaked" from overhead light fixtures. Thurber later wrote about the incident in a short story entitled "The Night the Ghost Got In."

(Thurber House Literary Center is one block west of the East Broad Street exit of I-71. The address is 77 Jefferson Ave., Columbus, OH 43215. Phone: 614-464-1032. www.thurberhouse.org) **14, 229**

CROWN CITY

METHODIST CHURCH On a wide lawn next to this church, several witnesses saw a house materialize in the summer of 1953. Sometimes, the single-story phantom building had a ten-foot bush in front of it. As witnesses approached it, the ghostly structure disappeared. Research revealed that a house had never stood on the spot.

(Crown City is a small town in south Ohio, south of Jackson. The church is located in Crown City.) **148**

DAYTON

MEMORIAL HALL The spirit of a custodian who died after falling into the orchestra pit has haunted this auditorium for the last thirty years. The ghost of Old Drake is blamed for strange noises, lights going on by themselves, and invisible footsteps coming from the catwalks.

(Dayton is in Montgomery County in western Ohio. Ghost bus tours of the Dayton area are held in October.

Call 513-426-5110 for information. Memorial Hall, 125 East First St., Dayton, OH 45402. Phone: 937-225-5898.) **229**

PATTERSON HOMESTEAD Loud footsteps in the basement, doors that open by themselves, and mysterious odors led workers in this restored 1816 farmhouse to suspect the place was haunted. Then, in 1989, a tourist saw the ghost of a man wearing black riding boots on the third floor. Workers identified him as the ghost of Colonel Robert Patterson, and have made him welcome in his former home.

(The museum is operated by the Montgomery County Historical Society. Patterson Homestead, 1815 Brown St., Dayton, OH 45409. Phone: 937-222-9724.) **229**

SINCLAIR COMMUNITY COLLEGE Strange presences are detected in the cafeteria, which is built on top of the old city gallows. Ghosts tug at people's clothing in Blair Hall, where the sound of disembodied laughter is sometimes heard. Custodians have reported voices coming from the deserted third floor of Building Seven. Even the security office is haunted. The apparition of a former chief of security was seen by his fellow officers there. Why ghosts are attracted to the modern buildings of this community college is anyone's guess.

(Sinclair Community College, 444 West Third St., Dayton, OH 45402. Phone: 937-512-2924. www.sinclair.edu) **229, 230**

STIVERS MIDDLE SCHOOL The Ghost of Stivers is a former teacher whose fully clothed body was found in the swimming pool in the 1920s. It is widely believed that she was killed by a senior boy, who disappeared that same day. Today the swimming pool is boarded over, but in the classroom built on top of it and in the third-floor corridor, the teacher's ghost still walks. Sometimes only her high-heeled footsteps are heard; at other times, the glowing figure of a woman in white is seen.

(The school is at 1313 East 5th St. in Dayton. 937-223-3175. Phone: 513-223-3175.) **230**

UNITED STATES AIR FORCE MUSEUM At night in this military museum, objects move by themselves, and guards report hearing unexplainable voices and other eerie sounds. Parts retrieved from *Lady Be Good,* a B-24 that crashed in the Libyan desert during World

Strange movements, lights, and sounds plague the United States Air Force Museum. The pilot of the *Black Maria* helicopter is sometimes seen in the cockpit. See United States Air Force Museum, Dayton, Ohio. (JAMES E. RAINBOLT)

War II, are said to move by themselves and could be the source of other paranormal activity at the museum. Seven crewmembers died in the crash. Strange lights are observed in another B-24, the *Strawberry Bitch*. The helicopter *Hop-Along* is haunted by its former copilot, whose ghost is seen flipping switches, trying to get the craft to take off. Bloodstains can still be seen on the seat where he died. Another helicopter, the *Black Maria*, is haunted by a similarly traumatized presence. He is thought to be a pilot hit by gunfire while flying a dangerous mission in Vietnam. Military police have reported seeing the ghost of a little Japanese boy standing next to *Bockscar*, the bomber that dropped the A-bomb on Nagasaki. Some investigators believe the old Air Force relics on display at the museum attract the spirits of departed crew members.

(From Dayton, take Highway 75 or Highway 675 south to the base. U.S. Air Force Museum, 1100 Spaatz St., Wright Patterson Air Force Base, Dayton, OH 45410. Phone: 937-255-3284. www.wpafb.af.mil/ museum) **229**

UNIVERSITY OF DAYTON The apparitions of children and a priest have been seen near the Chapel of the Immaculate Conception on this urban campus. In the 1850s, the site was occupied by St. Mary's School for Boys.

(University of Dayton, 300 College Park Ave., Dayton, OH 45409. Phone: 937-229-1000. www.udayton. edu) **229**

VICTORIA THEATRE The ghost here, called Vicky, is believed to be the spirit of an actress who disappeared mysteriously from her dressing room in the early 1900s. She was never seen again, but her presence is still felt in the Victoria Theatre. People smell her rose perfume, or hear her footsteps and the rustle of her petticoats as she crosses the stage. Her apparition has been seen in the ladies restroom and the reception room, both on the third floor.

(Victoria Theatre, 138 North Main St., Dayton, OH 45402. Phone: 937-228-3630. www.victoriatheatre. com) **229**

WOODLAND CEMETERY A glowing tombstone here is home to the ghost of a young girl. During the daytime, her distinctive apparition has been seen hovering over the grass and skipping down the pathways on the cemetery grounds. She is blond, has a blue sweater tied around her waist, and wears Nike tennis shoes.

(Woodland Cemetery, 118 Woodland Ave., Dayton, OH 45409. Phone: 937-222-1431.) **229**

DELAWARE

ROBINSON ESTATE In 1825, an ex-pirate captain by the name of John Robinson started building an opulent mansion on a piece of bottom land near the Scioto River. Rumors spread of iron chests full of gold being carried into the structure, along with expensive furniture and oil paintings. The villagers of Delaware kept their distance, and that was the way Robinson liked it. The only other person ever seen at the estate was a young Spanish girl, whom Robinson treated brutally. Then one spring, locals noticed that there was no activity at the mansion, and the place was becoming overgrown with weeds and vines. They entered the house and found the library spattered with bloodstains and all the paintings slashed except for a lone portrait of the Spanish girl. No bodies were ever found, and the estate was eventually destroyed by treasure seekers. But the ghost of the Spanish girl haunts the old estate. She is most often seen around 5:00 P.M., wearing a lace dress and brocades, sobbing hysterically near the ruins of the mansion or among the willows along the riverbank.

(Delaware is located in central Ohio, fifteen miles north of Columbus on U.S. Highway 23. The Robinson Estate was located on the banks of the Scioto River, just north of the Franklin-Delaware County line.) **5, 176**

DEXTER CITY

JOHNNY APPLESEED Ohio's most famous ghost is sometimes seen in September visiting his family's cemetery. He is also seen near a monument erected to his memory in September 1942. Johnny Appleseed was a real person, who followed the teachings of Sweden-borg and believed in the spiritual essence of all things. He spent his life trading bags of apple seeds for parcels of land and died a rich man, but his gray-bearded ghost is always barefooted, wearing an old pair of pants held up by a single suspender.

(Dexter is in southeastern Ohio, twenty-nine miles south of Cambridge on I-77. The Appleseed family cemetery is south of Dexter. The Appleseed Monument is on Highway 21, on the Noble–Washington county line.) **229**

DOYLESTOWN

ROGUES' HOLLOW The phantom of a headless horse has been seen on Clinton-Doylestown Road just east of here. The animal was killed when it ran into a low-hanging branch of an oak tree during a thunder-storm. The oak tree itself is haunted. The face of the devil himself was reported glaring down from its branches. When the tree was felled, a ghost oak tree started to appear in the same spot. Doylestown is also the home to the headless ghost of a man who was crushed to death by the waterwheel of the Chidester Wool Mill. Other ghosts, apparently of overworked coal miners, have been reported from time to time over the years. In the mid-1800s, over fifty coal mines were dug into the gentle hills here. When the mines were abandoned, they were taken over by rats, outlaws, moonshiners—and ghosts.

(Doylestown is ten miles southwest of Akron, off Highway 585. From Doylestown, Clinton St., South leads directly into Rogues' Hollow. Hometown Rd. is the main pathway through the old mining settlement, where several of the town's seven original saloons have been converted into private residences.) **15**

EAST LIVERPOOL

BEAVER CREEK STATE PARK Part of an 1830s canal system, known as Gretchen's Lock, is named for the ghost of a young Dutch girl. She died of malaria on August 12, 1838, and on the anniversary of her death, her ghost is said to walk the towpath of this lock. Jake's Lock is haunted by the charred phantom of a lock keeper who was struck by lightning while patrolling the canal. A ghastly ghost walks the ruins of Spruceville, a deserted settlement within the park. Esther Hale was to be married in August, 1837, but her lover never showed up. Her badly decomposed body was found in her cabin four months later, still dressed in her wedding gown. Ever since, her white skeleton, wearing a dirty wedding gown, is seen darting in front of cars or jumping out to touch the living.

(East Liverpool is on the Ohio River in Columbiana County, thirty-five miles south of Youngstown on U.S. Highway 30. The park is eleven miles north of East Liverpool at 12021 Echo Dell Rd., East Liverpool, OH 43920. Ghostly trail rides are conducted by Harmony Hills Riding Stables, 12243 Sprucevale Rd., East Liverpool, OH 43920. Phone: 330-385-6191.) **229, 230**

ELMORE

ELMORE BRIDGE The headlight from a motorcyclist who was decapitated in an accident near this bridge in 1918 can still be seen. The man had just returned from the war, when he discovered that his girlfriend had married another man. He sped off on his motorcycle, lost control on a curve near the bridge, and plummeted down a ravine. Both his headlight and his head were severed in the crash. The phantom headlight races down the road and suddenly disappears halfway across the bridge.

(Elmore is in Sandusky County, fifteen miles southeast of Toledo on Highway 51. The bridge is across the middle branch of the Portage River east of town.) **68, 176**

GALION

BROWNELLA COTTAGE The apparition of a woman in a white dress has been seen on the stairs and in the second-floor turret bedroom of this homey cottage. She is Ella Brown, wife of Episcopalian Bishop William Brown. The agnostic bishop was expelled from the church in 1924 for exposing his disbelief in anything supernatural, including God. Oddly enough, the bishop's ghost has been reported as well.

(Galion is west of Mansfield in Crawford County. Take U.S. Highway 30 west to Highway 598 South. The cottage is a private residence in Galion. For information, contact

the Galion Historical Society, P.O. Box 125, Galion, OH 44833.) **229**

GALLIPOLIS

OUR HOUSE This elegant old tavern, now a museum, was built in 1819. Volunteers and visitors have reported hearing unaccounted-for footsteps in the front hall. Sometimes the sound of a woman's singing comes from the empty ballroom on the second floor.

(Gallipolis is on the Ohio River in Gallia County, at the southeast end of U.S. Highway 35. Our House is on the banks of the river, south of town. Our House Museum, 432 First St., Gallipolis, OH 45631. Phone: 614-446-0586.) **230**

GAMBIER

KENYON COLLEGE This respected liberal arts college has enough ghosts to fill a classroom. An insomniac student who committed suicide haunts Norton Hall, while a freshman who hanged himself in Lewis Hall is blamed for poltergeist activity there. A student who died before she could start classes at the college is said to move the furniture at Manning Hall, and the ghost of a male student who fell down the elevator shaft at Caples Hall has been seen in the rooms of several coeds. Werthheimer Hall is haunted by a ghost who likes to work out and jog; Shaffer Hall has a ghost who likes to swim. Even after the building was changed into a dance studio in 1984, the sounds of the swimming ghost could still be heard. Security guards at Hill Theater have investigated a number of strange occurrences there. The building is thought to be haunted by the spirits of two people killed in a drunk-driving accident at the site. The legless apparitions of nine students killed in a 1949 fire float through the first-floor corridors of Old Kenyon Dorm, and the fourth floor is haunted by a Delta Kappa Epsilon fraternity pledge who died during his initiation. Freshman Stuart Pierson was killed by a train on the Kokosing River railroad trestle on October 28, 1905. His specter is seen peering out a round window on the fourth floor, on the anniversary of his death. So many ghosts walk this campus that some students call the twin columns flanking Middle Path the "Gates of Hell," and believe the basement of Mather Hall contains a doorway to the Other Side.

(Gambier is in central Ohio in Knox County, five

miles east of Mount Vernon on Highway 229. Kenyon College, Gambier, OH 43022. Phone: 740-427-5000. www. kenyon.edu) **229**

GEAUGA COUNTY

PUNDERSON STATE PARK The ghost of a teenage girl who drowned in Punderson Lake in 1977 has been observed walking along the shore. Her seaweed-covered phantom is seen emerging from the water, walking a short distance, then returning to the lake. Ghosts also walk in Punderson Manor House Lodge. Their footsteps are reported by custodians and rangers, and the ghost of a bearded man in work clothes has appeared at the foot of an employee's bed in the middle of the night. Other ghostly presences have been detected in the Blue Room, the King Arthur Room, and the Great Hall. The apparitions of children, accompanied by a woman in a blue cape, have been reported in the Manor House Restaurant.

(The park is thirty-eight miles east of Cleveland in Newbury. Take Highway 422 to Auburn Corners and head north on Highway 44. Punderson Manor House Lodge, 11755 Kinsman Rd., Newbury, OH 44065. Phone: 440-564-9144.) **230**

GRANVILLE

BUXTON INN This quaint inn is haunted by several active spirits. It was built in 1812 by the founder of Granville, Orrin Granger. His ghost was once discovered inside the kitchen pantry trying to steal a piece of apple pie. Granger's gray-haired apparition, wearing knee britches, has also been spotted at other locations in the inn. During renovations in 1972, workmen were startled by the presence of a ghostly woman in a blue dress who appeared regularly, around 6:00 P.M. She is thought to be Bonnie Bounell, the innkeeper from 1934 to 1960. The elegant woman sang in the opera at one time. Her presence has been detected on the upper balcony, in the ballroom, on the stairway, and in Room 9, where she died. Sometimes she is seen in other guest rooms, peering over the edge of the bed at night. Another deceased innkeeper, Major Buxton, has made a few appearances on the second floor of the inn. He owned the place from 1865 to 1905 and apparently still thinks he holds the deed.

(Granville is in Licking County in central Ohio. It is

six miles west of Newark on Highway 16. Buxton Inn, 313 East Broadway, Granville, OH 43023. Phone: 614-587-0001. www.prairieghosts.com/oh-buxt.html) **66 (10/89), 101, 176, 230**

HINCKLEY

HINCKLEY LIBRARY This 1845 mansion belonged to Vernon Stouffer, founder of the Stouffer food corporation. It became a public library in 1973, and during renovations several staff members reported ghostly manifestations. The apparitions of a young woman in an old-fashioned blue dress and a man in a hat were seen on the stairway. A workman encountered a ghostly figure on the basement stairs. Others have felt strange presences on the upper floors and witnessed poltergeist effects, such as paper clips flying across the room. It has been suggested that the ghosts are Dr. Nelson Wilcox and his sister Rebecca, who lived in a cabin on the site during the Civil War.

(The town of Hinckley is near Akron in northeast Ohio. Hinckley Library, Ridge Rd. and Center Rd., Hinckley, OH 44233. Phone: 216-278-4271.) **72**

HIRAM

GARFIELD HOUSE When this house was moved to its present location, the ghosts of President James Garfield and his wife Lucretia started to appear. The house was built in 1836 and served as a faculty boarding house for the Western Reserve Eclectic Institute until 1867. Garfield lived there when he became a teacher and principal at the institute in 1856. That same year he married Lucretia, and they both lived in the house until 1861. The house had several owners after the school closed and in 1958 was willed to Hiram College. Bruno and Dorothy Mallone bought it in 1961, and had it moved from the campus to their property outside of town. Almost immediately, strange things started happening in the house. The dining-room light flickered whenever Garfield's name was mentioned. Then, the unaccountable odor of cigar smoke and strange footsteps were detected in the parlor. The eerie effects increased in frequency, and the Mallones called in psychics to investigate. Several seances were conducted in which Garfield's spirit was contacted. The general impression was that James Garfield is not happy in the afterlife. He thinks he was betrayed by close friends who arranged his assassination.

(Hiram is in Portage County in northeastern Ohio, twenty-five miles southeast of Cleveland. Take I-480 to Twinsburg, then take Highway 82 east to Hiram. The Greek Revival mansion is a private residence overlooking Garfield Road just outside town.) **175**

JOHNSON'S ISLAND

UNION PRISON The ghosts of Confederate officers imprisoned here under frigid and inhumane conditions still walk the island. Scores of the ghostly gray figures gather in the oak trees and sing soulful renditions of "Dixie." Mexican workers who spoke no English mysteriously started singing the Southern anthem one summer morning. Apparitions have also been observed near the Confederate Soldier Monument and hovering over the cemetery. The old compound was designed to hold one thousand prisoners, but actually confined up to fifteen thousand men at one time.

(The three-hundred-acre island is in Lake Erie, three miles north of Sandusky and half a mile south of the Marblehead Peninsula. For further information, contact the Ohio Historical Society, 1982 Velma Ave., Columbus, OH 43211. Phone: 614-466-1500.) **163**

LAKE ERIE

BESSIE Bessie is the name given to a monstrous serpent said to swim in the waters off northern Ohio. The beast has been sighted over twenty-five times since 1985 and is described as thirty-five to one hundred feet long, with a tubular body and a long neck. Its weight has been estimated at two hundred tons. The dark green creature is said to smell like putrefied garbage. In August 1992, Bessie was blamed for attacking a sailboat and killing three people. Survivors Matty Jentol and Allison Sullivan said the monster's head was as big as a car. A $102,000 reward has been offered for the humane capture of the beast.

(Many of the sightings have taken place near Maumee Bay, at the lakeside community of Huron, and off Cedar Point near Sandusky. www.monstertracker. com/news.cfm) **72**

LEBANON

FORT ANCIENT This giant earthen "fortress" was never inhabited or defended. It was used by an unknown people as a ceremonial center with a capacity of up to twelve thousand participants. Tall poles at the heads of two limestone serpents indicate the winter and summer solstices. The site is said to be psychically charged and visitors walking along the Path of Transformation have reported feeling an electric energy rising up from out of the ground.

(Lebanon is in Warren County, seven miles northeast of Cincinnati on U.S. Highway 42. Fort Ancient State Memorial is on the Little Miami River, six miles southeast of Lebanon on Highway 350. For information, contact the Fort Ancient Museum, 6123 S.R. 350, Oregonia, OH 45240. Phone: 800-283-8904. www.ohiohistory.org/ places/ftancien) **99**

GLENDOWER STATE MEMORIAL This restored 1850s mansion is visited by a ghostly group of energetic young adults. Their voices and footsteps are heard approaching the front door, but no one is there when the door is opened. In 1991, a volunteer heard the sounds of a roaring fire coming from an empty fireplace.

(The memorial is on U.S. Highway 42, just southwest of Lebanon. Glendower State Memorial, 105 S. Broadway St, Lebanon, OH 45036. Phone: 513-932-5366.) **230**

MCCONNELSVILLE

MCCONNELSVILLE OPERA HOUSE This old opera house dates back to the Civil War and was used as a stop on the Underground Railroad. Restoration in the early 1960s stirred up some dust, as well as a few ghosts. Construction workers reported the sounds of a lady singing and playing a piano that sat covered and undisturbed in a corner of the building. As work continued, the apparition of a man in a white suit started to appear in the back of the auditorium. On one occasion, nearly forty witnesses saw his white apparition floating high in the rafters. Further renovations brought forth the misty form of a graceful lady, floating high in the scenery drops.

(McConnelsville is in Morgan County, thirty miles southeast of Zanesville on Highway 60. The 1890 Opera House is at 15 West Main St., McConnelsville, OH 43756. Phone: 740-962-3030.) **229**

MIDDLETOWN

SORG OPERA HOUSE Entrepreneur Paul Sorg built this theater in 1891 and reserved a seat for himself through all eternity in the first row of the first balcony. That is where his apparition, dressed in evening attire, is most often seen. Sometimes during rehearsals, he is sensed backstage or high in the catwalks.

(Middletown is in Montgomery County, on I-75 between Dayton and Cincinnati. Sorg Opera House, 57 South Main St., Middletown, OH 45042. Phone: 513-425-0180. www.sorgopera.com) **229**

MILAN

EDISON BIRTHPLACE MUSEUM Visitors to this museum have reported hearing the voices of angels or encountering a strange bioelectricity. Thomas Alva Edison spent the last years of his life working on an apparatus to communicate with the dead, and many believe the inventor came back from the dead to direct its construction. For many years, volunteers worked on the device using instructions received from mediums, but the effort to assemble Edison's telephone to the Other Side was finally abandoned in 1959.

(Milan is southeast of Sandusky. Take U.S. Highway 250 South, to Exit 7 at I-80/90. Go south two miles to Highway 113 and follow it east to the town. Thomas Edison Birthplace Museum, 9 Edison Dr., Milan, OH 44846. Phone: 419-499-2135. www.tomedison.org) **229**

MOUND CITY

MOUND CITY NECROPOLIS This City of the Dead, dating back to 200 B.C., is one of the best-preserved Hopewell sacred sites. The dead are here because the mound builders believed that the afterlife and our present existence converged at this place. The twenty-three earthworks have been called a "simulacrum of the Otherworld," and the site is said to be spiritually charged. The thirteen-acre park has self-guided tours and an observation deck. Excavations have yielded many mysterious artifacts, including a prehistoric shaman's ceremonial death mask.

(The park is three miles north of Chillicothe on Highway 104. The site is forty-five miles south of Columbus on U.S. Highway 23. For information, contact the Mound City Group National Monument, 16062 Ohio Route 104, Chillicothe, OH 45601. Phone: 740-774-1125. www.nps.gov/hocu) **53 (6/94), 72, 144**

NEWARK

OCTAGON EARTHWORKS This unique sacred site consists of a 1,200-foot wide octagon and a 1,200-foot diameter circle connected to a large square and another circle. Although archaeologists have no explanation for the geometric figures, they bear a striking resemblance to symbols used by European alchemists to describe the stages in the squaring of the circle, a mystical formula for psychological perfection. The 3,200-year-old, four-square-mile site also contains burial mounds and animal effigies. It is believed that thousands of people took part in mystical ceremonies here. Astronomically, the sighting stones at the site appear to be laid out according to the twenty-eight-day lunar calendar.

(Newark is in central Ohio, east of Columbus in Licking County. Follow Highway 79 from southwestern Newark to the mound site and museum. For information, contact the Mound Builders State Memorial, 99 Cooper Avenue, Newark, OH 43055. Phone: 740-344-1920. www.ohiohistory.org/places/newarkearthworks/octagon. cfm) **144**

OAKVILLE

WALINGHAM FARM The problems at this wooden Victorian farmhouse began in 1891, when the owner found pieces of a skeleton in the basement. He threw the old bones into a lime kiln. Soon, the family started hearing terrified screams in the early morning hours and bells chiming from nowhere. Then, furniture moved across rooms, and a dismembered hand was seen on the staircase. Finally, the ghost of a bloody, beaten man started to materialize. The family's dog attacked the ghost and was thrown to the ground with a broken neck. During a dinner party not long afterward, groans were heard coming from an upstairs room and blood started to drip from the ceiling above the dinner table. The family moved out the next day, and their deserted home became known as possessed by demons. When investigator Horace Gunn spent a night there, he awoke to see the bloodied head of a man floating above his bed. He ran into the hallway, but was grabbed by cold, invisible hands and choked into unconsciousness. When he was discovered the next day, he was severely traumatized and incoherent. He never fully recovered from the experience.

(Oakville was a town near Mansfield in the nineteenth century. The Walingham Farm is on private property just outside of town in Mansfield County.) **51, 72, 115**

OXFORD

MIAMI UNIVERSITY The area around old Fisher Hall is said to be haunted by the presence of Judge Elam Fisher, for whom the building was named. The ghost is blamed for the disappearance of a number of items, as well as a former student. Sophomore Richard Tammen vanished without a trace from his room in Fisher Hall on April 19, 1953, and has never been seen again. But Fisher's ghostly presence is still reported on the grounds where the building once stood.

(The town of Oxford is in Butler County, about twenty miles northwest of Cincinnati on U.S. Highway 27. Miami University, East High St., Oxford, OH 45056. Phone: 513-529-2531. www.muohio.edu) **229**

PIKE COUNTY

BIG ROCK This granite, flat-topped hill is haunted by the spirit of a magnificent gray wolf known as Old Raridan. The hill was originally called Great Buzzards Rock, because it was the dying place of wolves in the area. For some strange reason, hundreds of the animals came here to die. Settlers pushing into the area gradually killed off many of the wolves, until just Old Raridan and his mate remained. In 1801, hunters with dogs cornered the pair and shot them. Mortally wounded, Old Raridan grabbed his mate by the nape of the neck and dragged her lifeless body up to Big Rock, where they both died.

(Pike County is in south-central Ohio. The site is in the Lake White State Park, 2767 State Route 551, Waverly, OH 45690. For further information, call the Ohio Tourism Office at 800-282-5393.) **176**

RICHLAND COUNTY

MALABAR FARM STATE PARK The ghost of Ceely Rose stares out the windows of the old white farmhouse in this park. In 1896, her parents, brother, and sister all died of arsenic poisoning, and Ceely was found guilty. She spent the rest of her life at an asylum for the criminally insane but returned after death to walk the halls where the tragedy took place.

(Richland County is in north-central Ohio. The park

is near Pleasant Hill Lake near the junction of Highway 95 and Highway 603, at 4050 Bromfield Rd., Lucas, OH 44843. Phone: 419-892-2784.) **229**

MOHICAN STATE PARK The ghoulish phantom of a Mohican Indian warrior still looks for victims—with a tomahawk ready at his side. Around his neck he wears a ghastly necklace made up of ninety-nine human tongues. The crazed Indian was on his way to collect his one-hundreth trophy when he was attacked and killed on the old stage road near Killbuck Swamp.

(The park headquarters is at 249 Main St., Loudonville, OH 44842. Phone: 419-994-5125. The park is on the Clear Fork River at 3116 State Route 3.) **229**

SOMERSET

ST. JOSEPH'S CHURCH The ghost of a dead priest appeared to many of his brothers here. He was seen standing at the foots of their beds or in the sacristy while the priests were preparing for Mass. When it became impossible to keep the altar candles lit, the fathers recited special Masses for the dead priest, assuming he was guilty of some great sin. But the dead priest may have only wanted to fulfill his earthly commitments. When the priests completed the backlog of the priest's personal schedule of Masses, the disturbing manifestations stopped.

(Somerset is in Perry County, eighteen miles northeast of Lancaster on U.S. Highway 22. The church is also known as Old Priory and is the oldest Catholic church in Ohio. St. Joseph's Church, 5757 State Route 383, Somerset, OH 43783. Phone: 740-743-1317.) **229**

WARREN

WARREN CITY HALL This city building was once the mansion of Bish Perkins and his Aunt Lizzie. After the mysterious death of a servant girl, Bish committed suicide. Today his Aunt Lizzie is seen roaming the grounds with a lantern.

(Warren is in Trumbull County, northwest of Youngstown on U.S. Highway 422. A Ghost Tour of the city is held in October. Warren City Hall, Warren, OH 44481. For information, call 330-399-1212.) **229**

WAYNESVILLE

QUAKER MEETINGHOUSE Unexplainable kitchen noises, musical sounds, and the ghost of a small woman in old-fashioned clothes haunt this historic building. The ghost is said to have the ability to look out windows on all sides of the building at once.

(Waynesville is twenty-nine miles northeast of Cincinnati on U.S. Highway 42. The meetinghouse and Quaker Cemetery are below Maple St. in Waynesville. Ghost Tours of the city are conducted by Historically Speaking, P.O. Box 419, Waynesville, OH 45068. For information, call 513-897-8855.) **230**

STETSON HOUSE ANTIQUE SHOP This six-room frame cottage, built in the early 1880s, is haunted by a small, dark-haired woman and a large-nosed man. The woman has been seen outside the front door, where she dissolves into a wall. The man has been observed peeking out an upstairs window. The ghosts have broken mirrors and moved old antiques around the shop. Lousia Stetson Larrick, who lived here in the 1860s, and John Stetson, son of the famous Philadelphia hat maker, are believed to be the two ghosts of Stetson House.

(Stetson House is at 234 South Main St., Waynesville, OH 45068. Phone: 513-683-1023.) **66 (10/89), 135, 230**

WAYNESVILLE FIREHOUSE The ghost of an elderly gentleman who donated the land on which this fire station was built is said to make nightly rounds through the building, just as he did when alive. The man's shuffling footsteps are heard coming in the side door, walking around the fire engines, climbing the stairs to the top floor, then returning to the ground floor and out the door.

(The fire station is Firehouse #1 in central Waynesville.) **230**

XENIA

EDEN HALL This thirty-two-room, three-story mansion is haunted by spirits who like to have a good time. Recent residents have reported the ghostly sounds of partygoers laughing and talking, traipsing up and down the stairway, and dancing on the third floor. The house is currently owned by the Paul Cozatt family, who have become accustomed to living with the raucous spirits. Eden Hall was built in 1840 by Abram Hivling and was the center of social activity in Greene County for over a century.

(Xenia is in Greene County, ten miles east of Dayton on U.S. Highway 35. The mansion is near the corner of East Second and South Monroe streets. Eden Hall, 235 East Second St., Xenia, OH 45485. Tours are by appointment only. Phone: 937-376-1274.) **230**

ZANESVILLE

CONVENT OF ST. THOMAS The apparition of an unidentified nun has been reported by several sisters living at this convent. The ghostly nun kneels at the altar rail in front of the tabernacle.

(Convent of St. Thomas, 130 N. 5th St., Zanesville, OH 43702. Phone: 740-453-3301.) **229**

OKLAHOMA

ARAPAHO

ARAPAHO CEMETERY George Smith always lamented that his daughter had died before she could be saved by accepting the Lord. Robina Smith died in a freak car accident in 1936, when the car in which she was riding hit a creamery truck on U.S. Highway 183. When police finally arrived, they discovered a horrific scene. Several of the victims had frozen to death on the icy pavement, and Robina's head was impaled on the floor-mounted gearshift lever in the car. After her father died in 1972, his spirit returned to haunt his daughter's grave. Dozens of reputable witnesses have reported hearing George's voice coming from her grave: "Oh no! Oh my God! Robina has not been saved!" The phenomenon continues to this day.

(Arapaho is in Custer County in western Oklahoma, five miles north of Clinton. Take the U.S. Highway 183 north exit from I-40 at Clinton. The cemetery is east of town.) **53 (2/82)**

CENTRAHOMA

MCWETHEY HOUSE This small house was the site of remarkable poltergeist activity in the summer of 1990. On June 15, Bill and Maxine McWethey and their two daughters were sitting in the front yard when they were pelted by a shower of rocks that seemed to come from nowhere. The spectral rock-throwing went on even after the family moved indoors, and continued off and on for weeks. The rocks varied in size from pea-sized to golf ball-sized, although pennies, nickels, dimes, quarters, nails, screws, eggs, bottles, and other items were also hurled through the air by the invisible force. The poltergeist strengthened and started pulling off sheets and bedcovers. It was heard to make a high-pitched mewling sound or whisper *"Psst"* if it wanted to draw someone's attention. The paranormal events were witnessed by dozens of reporters, police, neighbors, and psychic investigators. Many of the effects centered around eighteen-year-old Twyla McWethey.

(Centrahoma is in Coal County in south-central Oklahoma, twenty-three miles southeast of Ada on Highway 3. The single-story, white wood-frame house is a private residence in town.) **72**

GUTHRIE

TERRITORIAL GOVERNOR'S MANSION This old mansion is haunted by a speaking ghost, who hollers back with a faint "Hello" from the downstairs hallway when strangers walk around on the second floor. Witnesses have also observed various objects floating up the central staircase. The ghost is thought to be a member of the family of one of Oklahoma's early territorial governors.

(Guthrie is twenty miles north of Oklahoma City at the junction of I-35 and Highway 33. Old Territorial Governor's Mansion, Guthrie, OK 73044.) **72**

HEAVENER

HEAVENER RUNESTONE STATE PARK Strange symbols carved into a stone dating as far back as A.D. 600 seem to imply the Quachita National Forest is haunted. The eight glyphs are from an Old Norse alphabet known as runes. Cryptographers have come up with a variety of translations, such as: "Earth Spirit's Dale," "Valley of the Gnomes," and "Magic to Gloi." Other runestones dating from around A.D. 1015 have been found in Poteau and Shawnee, Oklahoma. More evidence of pre-Columbian European visitors to the area has been discovered just across the Oklahoma border in Picture Canyon, Colorado.

(Heavener is in Sequoyah County near the Arkansas border. It is eleven miles south of Poteau, at the junction of U.S. Highways 59 and 270. Follow Morris Creek Rd into the park. For information, contact the Heavener Runestone State Park, Route 1 Box 1510, Heavener, OK 74937. Phone: 918-653-2241. Picture Canyon is near Springfield, Colorado off U.S. Highway 287. For information, contact U.S. Forest Service, P.O. Box 127, Springfield, CO 81073. Phone: 719-623-6691.) **32, 53 (6/94), 99, 203**

LAWTON

APACHE CEMETERY Geronimo was captured and imprisoned at Fort Sill until his death. He is buried at the Apache Cemetery. Although his apparition has never been seen in the cemetery, his noble spirit is still felt by many psychically attuned visitors at the site.

(Lawton is in Comanche County in south-central Oklahoma. The cemetery is just north of old Fort Sill, which is now part of the U.S. Army Artillery and Missile Center. Phone: 405-442-8111.) **98**

ELK MOUNTAIN Spirits of the dead are said to guard an underground cave with a thick iron door, hidden somewhere on this mountain. The Cave with the Iron Door is said to contain Spanish gold, as well as two hundred thousand dollars hidden there by Jesse James, and another five hundred thousand dollars hidden by Belle Starr. A Mexican expedition searched for the Spanish treasure in the 1850s, and in the early 1900s two cowboys stumbled on the iron door, but could not find it when they returned with tools to open it. In 1908, an old woman with a huge iron key came to the area looking for the treasure cave. She claimed a dying outlaw gave

her the key and told her where the iron door was located. Sporadic sightings of the iron door in the side of Elk Mountain have continued for the last eighty years.

(Elk Mountain is in Comanche County, about thirty miles west of Lawton off of U.S. Highway 62. The lost treasure site covers the Treasure Lake area and Elk Mountain between the towns of Indiahoma and Hobart. The area is in the Witchita Mountains Wildlife Refuge. For more information about Oklahoma sites, contact the Oklahoma Tourism Department, at 15 N Robinson Ave., #801, Oklahoma City, OK 73105. Phone 405-521-2406. www.otrd.state.ok.us) **49**

NANCY'S ANTIQUES AND MONEKA ANTIQUES A gray wood-frame house is haunted by the presence of a robber killed in the dining room. The large house was constructed in 1892 and served as a Rock Island Railroad boarding house for many years. During that period, a robber broke into the house during suppertime and demanded everyone's money. The burly railroad men got the upper hand, and the would-be thief died in ensuing struggle. Not wanting to get into trouble with the authorities, the men loaded the body onto a northbound train, where it was later found by strangers and buried in an unmarked grave. Today, the robber's specter and other ghosts from the building's colorful past haunt the rooms along the east and north sides, upstairs and down. The sightings became more frequent when Nancy War remodeled it into an antique shop with a small tea room restaurant.

(The site is located in the town of Waurika, which is fifty-three miles southeast of Lawton. Take Highway 7 to Pumpkin Center, then go south on Highway 65 to Highway 70 east. Nancy's Antiques and Moneka Antiques, Highway 70 East, Waurika, OK 73573. Phone: 580-228-2575.) **72**

MIAMI

SPOOKSVILLE TRIANGLE This twenty-mile-sided triangle of strange multicolored light phenomena runs from Joplin, Missouri to Columbus, Kansas to Miami, Oklahoma. The area is traversed by Highway 66 and the Spring River. The lights have been observed regularly for over a hundred years. Most often they are seen hovering over certain deserted roads and fields. Legend says the Miami Light is the lantern of a farm girl who disappeared into the fog one night and was never seen again. See Joplin, Missouri; and Columbus, Kansas.

(Miami is in Ottawa County, in the extreme northeast corner of Oklahoma, fifteen miles from the Missouri border on I-44. The lights have been observed as far west as Quapaw, Oklahoma. www.prairieghosts.com/spooksville. html) **20, 176, 231**

NOWATA COUNTY

NOWATA MONSTER The creatures that live between the Sandstone Hills and the Ozark Plateau in northeastern Oklahoma have terrorized residents for decades. The hairy, upright-walking beasts were first spotted in 1974 in the community of Watoya, just outside the town of Nowata. Since then, whole families of the Bigfoot creatures have been sighted. They range in size from six feet to nine feet tall and give off a horrible odor. In 1975, the creature clan was sighted near Noxie. One angered Bigfoot attacked a hunter, and another damaged a pickup truck. The foul-smelling animals have been seen by dozens of witnesses, including hunters, sheriff deputies, and National Guard troops.

(Nowata County is in the northeast corner of Oklahoma. The desolate region is in the Coo-Wee-Scoo-Wee district of the old Cherokee Nation. The town of Nowata is forty-five miles northeast of Tulsa on U.S. Highway 169. Watova is six miles south of Nowata on U.S. Highway 169. Many sightings have taken place near Oologah Lake at Double Creek Cove, two miles south of Nowata.) **50, 53 (12/76, 6/84)**

OKLAHOMA CITY

BROADWAY BOULEVARD Evidence of a sophisticated ancient civilization was found here in June 1967. Road workers discovered a buried mosaic floor, about three feet below ground, that covered several thousand square feet. The perfectly laid stones formed a diamond shape that points directly to the east (see Heavener Runestone State Park, Oklahoma). Post or foundation holes, exactly two rods apart, were also found.

(Oklahoma City is at the center of Oklahoma, at the junction of I-35, I-40, and I-44. The site is at Broadway and 122nd St., along the Broadway Boulevard extension between Edmund and Oklahoma City.) **194**

PAWHUSKA

CONSTANTINE THEATER Phantoms of the Old West are blamed for supernatural activity at this old vaudeville theater, built in 1894. The raucous cowboy spirits are said to toss objects and make loud banging sounds, as if a fistfight were going on.

(Pawhuska is in Osage County in northwest Oklahoma, forty-two miles east of Ponca City on U.S. Highway 60. Constantine Theater, Pawhuska, OK 74056.) **72, 101**

SPIRO MOUNDS

SPIRO MOUNDS ARCHEOLOGICAL SITE This sacred site might date back to A.D. 1 but archeologists know it was occupied by an Indian culture from A.D. 850 to 1450. Religious ceremonies centered around a cluster of twelve earthen mounds built in a circular array. The rituals involved the burial of and caring for departed souls. Ceremonies used giant crystals and symbols such as the falcon and the sun. Over five hundred burial chambers have been discovered at the site. Today, many psychics say the area is charged with etheric energy. Shimmering sheets of blue light have been seen by dozens of witnesses over the Craig Mound. Once, a phantom team of giant cats was seen pulling an empty wagon over the mound.

(Spiro is in Sequoyah County in far-eastern Oklahoma. Take the Sallisaw exit, U.S. Highway 59, south from I-40. Follow it sixteen miles to Highway 9, then go east to the town of Spiro. The 138-acre site is three miles east and four miles north of town in LaFlore County. Take SH-9 east of Spiro to the Mayo Lock and Dam Rd. Spiro Mounds Interpretive Center, Route 2 Box 339AA, Spiro, OK 74959. Phone: 918-962-2062.) **32, 99**

OREGON

ALBANY

CONSER LAKE A seven-foot-tall, white-haired creature with webbed feet was first reported here in 1958. Reports of the creature, which came to be called the White Bigfoot, were so common in the 1960s, that posses of up to two hundred people were formed to hunt it down. It has been described as a polar bear or white gorilla, and people have clocked the monster moving at speeds over thirty-five miles per hour. It has been dubbed the "Hairy Ghost" because of its elusiveness.

(Albany is five miles north of Corvalis on Highway 99W in northwest Oregon. The small, private lake is 6.5 miles from Albany. It is between Dever-Conner and Millersburg, about four miles northwest of the old pulp mill visible from I-5. For more information on Bigfoot, contact the Bigfoot Research Project, P.O. Box 126, Mt. Hood, OR 97041. Phone: 503-352-7000,) **77**

ASHLAND

LITHIA PARK The diffuse blue light that wanders through this park at night is thought to be the spirit of a young girl raped and murdered here in 1875. The spooky light has been reported for more than a century. In 1975, a car passed through the misty form, which was standing in the middle of a winding road near the park. All the passengers reported feeling a damp coldness penetrate them as the car "struck" the ghost.

(Ashland is in southwestern Oregon in Jackson County, ten miles south of Medford on I-5.) **77**

OREGON SHAKESPEAREAN FESTIVAL A tall male apparition appears on the third floor of the Elizabethan Playhouse. The friendly ghost is said to sing madrigals almost every night. Further, the ghost of Charles Laughton appeared at an 1964 performance of *King Lear* staged at the theater. He had always wanted to play Lear at the Ashland festival but died before it was staged. During the next performance of the play, an eerie vibrating sound moves from the audience onto the main stage.

(Oregon Shakespearean Festival, 15 South Pioneer St., P.O. Box 158, Ashland, OR 97520. Phone: 541-482-2111. For ticket sales, call 541-482-4331 www.orshakes. org) **77**

PIONEER STREET The ghost of the Dog-Faced Boy has been seen near parked cars along this street several times in the last thirty years. The boy was a deformed child who supported himself by selling pencils and stealing from cars. He is thought to have been murdered near here in 1926, after being caught stealing from someone's vehicle.

(The Dog-Faced Boy has been reported on Pioneer St., and in the parking lot of Lithia Park, site of the old Chautauqua Theater, which was replaced by the Oregon Shakespearean Festival Theater in 1935.) **77**

BLUE MOUNTAINS

TOLLGATE Researchers tracked a group of four Sasquatch monsters in this area from 1982 to 1987. Their footprints ranged in size from sixteen to eighteen inches. The first footprints were found near Elk Wallow in 1982. In 1986, three different sets of tracks started appearing. These included a set of twelve-inch footprints thought to belong to a young Bigfoot. A supposed sleeping lair was discovered, as well as significant damage to shrubs and trees. Different footprints were discovered near Tollgate in 1986, and a sighting occurred on a road about twenty miles to the north of the resort town.

(The Blue Mountains are about 170 miles east of Mount Hood. Highway I-84 goes through the mountains between Pendleton and LaGrande. Tollgate is located in the northeast corner of Oregon in the Umatilla Wilderness Area. Take Highway 11 northeast from Pendleton, sixteen miles to Athena. Go east twenty miles on Highway 204 to Tollgate.) **110**

CANNON BEACH

BANDAGE MAN The phantom of a man completely wrapped in bandages haunts this small community. The bloody figure, smelling of rotting flesh, jumps into vehicles passing on a road outside of town. Bandage Man has appeared in pickup trucks, sedans, station wagons, and even sports cars. Sometimes the mummy breaks windows or leaves behind bits of foul-smelling bandages. Some believe he is the ghost of a dead logger, cut to pieces in a sawmill accident.

(Cannon Beach is in Clatsop County in the extreme northwestern corner of the state. It is seventy-three miles northwest of Portland on U.S. Highway 26. The mummy appears on the short approach road connecting U.S. Highway 101 to Cannon Beach. The phantom always vanishes just before reaching town.) **77**

CRATER LAKE

WIZARD ISLAND Shamans were the only members of the Klamath Indian tribe who dared approach this sacred lake. They assembled on Wizard Island to perform secret ceremonies. According to legend, the spirits of the World Below live in this lake, while the spirits of the World Above live at Mount Shasta (see Mount Shasta, California). The deep, sky blue Crater Lake was created by the collapse of a giant volcano nearly seven thousand years ago.

(Crater Lake National Park is in the Cascade Mountains in southwestern Oregon. From Medford, follow Highway 62 north into the park. Boats leave for Wizard Island in the summer months from the base of Cleetwood Trail. Camping is available at the Mazama Campground, P.O. Box 7, Crater Lake, OR 97604. Phone: 541-594-2511. www.nps.gov/crla.) **99**

EUGENE

SOUTH EUGENE HIGH SCHOOL A seat near the center of the auditorium of this high school is haunted. In 1957, student Robert Granke fell from a catwalk to his death onto the seats below. Now, students who sit there report a "chilling presence," as if they were sharing the spot with an invisible person. The huge empty space between the auditorium ceiling and roof is also haunted. Stage managers have reported strange sounds and a mysterious blue light moving around in the area. Once, a brick mysteriously fell from the overhead crawl space into the haunted seat, narrowly missing a student about to sit down.

(Eugene is in Lane County in western Oregon, at the intersection of I-5 and Highway 126. South Eugene High School, 400 E. 19th Ave., Eugene, OR 97404. Phone: 541-687-3201.) **77**

FLORENCE

HECETA HEAD LIGHTHOUSE The ghost of a frail old lady floats across rooms and through closed doors in the caretaker's house here. Sometimes the spirit screams in the middle of the night or rattles dishes in the cupboard. At other times, the Lady in Gray eavesdrops from the stairs or spies through closed windows. Once, a repairman fixing a broken window in the attic saw her float up in front of him. He jumped off his ladder and never returned. The owners then heard the swishing of a broom and found all the broken pieces of glass swept into a neat pile on the attic floor. Spanish explorer Bruno Heceta discovered this coastal point in 1775, and the lighthouse was built in 1894.

(Florence is on the Oregon coast, fifty miles west of Eugene on Highway 126. The private site is six miles north of the town of Florence on U.S. Highway 101. www. hecetalighthouse.com) **77**

FOREST GROVE

PACIFIC UNIVERSITY The ghost of Vera, a former music student who died in Knight Hall, is said to still haunt the building. The ghost's singing and piano playing can be heard echoing through the halls here. In the 1960s, watchmen investigating the sounds encountered the form of a woman enveloped by a shimmering blue light. In the 1980s, the spirit grew stronger, and even voiced its displeasure at some students' performances at the keyboard. Vera's presence has been witnessed by students, reporters, and professors at the college. Assistant director of admissions Jeff Grundon has experienced firsthand some of the phenomena and now believes there is indeed a ghost in Knight Hall. According to the school's public relations director, Steve Sechrist, several parapsychologists are currently studying the phenomenon.

(Forest Grove is ten miles west of Portland on Highway 8. Knight Hall is a three-story Victorian house with a rear stairway from the second-floor patio to the third-floor attic. The university is at 2043 College Way, Forest Grove, OR 97116. Phone: 503-359-2218. www.pacificu. edu) **72, 135, 148**

PHANTOM BUGLER The phantom of a burly man has been blamed for several deaths in the woods outside of Forest Grove. The muscular outdoorsman lived in the woods and carried a brass bugle around his neck on a leather strap. In 1910, his mauled body was found on a path where he had apparently been attacked by a mountain lion. His mangled bugle, which he used to club the animal, was found lying beside him. Today, the man's angry ghost roams the woods, beating anyone he encounters with his heavy brass bugle.

(The phantom bugler stalks the woods around Forest Grove in Washington County.) **49, 77**

FORT STEVENS

FORT STEVENS STATE PARK The ghost of a man carrying a bright flashlight haunts the stone walkway known as Battery Russel at Fort Stevens. The phantom makes a noise like heavy, clanging chains while he makes his rounds late at night. Some witnesses have discerned the form of a man behind the bright beam of light he carries, only to see the phantom disappear as he approaches.

(Fort Stevens State Park is on the Pacific Ocean at Hammond Peninsula, west of Astoria on the extreme northwest tip of Oregon. From Portland, follow U.S. Highway 30 about eighty-five miles north to Astoria and cross the bridge west of town into the park which is on Ridge Mountain Rd. Phone: 503-861-1671.) **77**

GOLD HILL

OREGON VORTEX People have felt there was something not quite right about this hill for hundreds of years. Indians called it the "Forbidden Ground," and white settlers in 1864 talked of "something wrong" here. The unease felt by people on the hill may have made them receptive to paranormal experiences. John Litster, a Scottish physicist, for instance, came to the site in 1914, and spent the rest of his life studying what he considered to be "aberrations in the light field and gravity." The site became a tourist attraction in 1930, and thousands of people have experienced both entertaining illusions and the authentic effects of the Oregon Vortex. The House of Mystery on the site was used as an assay office for a gold mining company until it collapsed sideways in a thunderstorm. The strongest vortex concentration is said to be directly behind the building. The whirling energy is believed to distort photographs taken there. In a 1994 investigation, William Moffitt concluded that the site exhibits some genuine phenomena, but compared with other sacred areas it is "a lesser vortex infused with commercialism."

(Gold Hill is just off I-5 between Medford and Grants Pass. The site is on Sardine Creek Rd., four miles east of Highway 234. The site is just north of town. For information, contact Oregon Vortex, 4303 Sardine Road, Gold Hill, OR 97525. Phone: 541-855-1543. www. oregonvortex.com) **13**

JACKSONVILLE

HERMAN HELMS HOUSE Two ghosts haunt this old wood-frame house, which dates back to 1862. One is an elderly lady who walks through the halls weeping; and the other is a little girl who sits at the bottom of the stairs, also crying. The lady is Herman Helms' wife Augusta Englebrecht Helms, who is mourning the family's numerous tragedies. Epidemics, murder, and suicide claimed a dozen members of the Helms clan in the late 1800s. Mrs. Helms herself died in the house in

1911, at the age of seventy-two. The little girl ghost is her youngest daughter, Herminne. She died of small-pox in 1868. Because of the epidemic, the child was buried in the front lawn. When an addition to the house covered her grave site in 1878, her tombstone was moved into the basement of the new section. See Ella Rooming House, Portland, Oregon.

(Jacksonville is five miles west of Medford in Jackson County. The Jacksonville National Historic Landmark is one mile southwest of town on Highway 238. Helms House, Oregon St., Jacksonville, OR 97530.) **77**

JOHN MILLER HOUSE When this house was remodeled after a fire destroyed the second floor, the ghost of a former owner started to appear. The house was built in 1860 by gunsmith John Miller, but a later occupant haunts it. A man who owned the house in the late 1800s was caught cheating at cards. That was a serious offense in this mining town, and the man was found hanging from a noose on his front porch the next morning. His white apparition is sometimes seen sitting on a bed, and his lonely footsteps can be heard late at night in the hallway.

(The house is a private residence on East Main St., Jacksonville, OR 97530.) **77**

LA GRANDE

HOT LAKE HOTEL The ghosts of former tenants walk the corridors of this deserted resort at night. Footsteps on the upper floors, the sounds of a piano, and an occasional scream echo through the empty building. Sometimes it sounds as if the departed spirits are throwing a party on the third floor. The hotel was built next to the 205-degree sulfurous Hot Lake in 1851. The first structure was gradually expanded into an elegant gabled building in 1907, when Dr. W. T. Phy established a health spa at the site. A fire in 1934 destroyed the ballroom and library, and all that is left today is a neglected and unfriendly brick building next to a few smaller houses.

(La Grande is fifty miles southeast of Pendleton, through the Blue Mountains, on I-84. The hotel spa is on private property at the bottom of a large hill in the Grand Ronde Valley. It is seven miles southeast of LaGrande, between LaGrande and Union, off Highway 203 at 65182 Hot Lake Lane. Phone: 541-963-5253.) **53 (7/95), 77**

LINCOLN COUNTY

NEAHKAHNIE MOUNTAIN The spirits of massacred Spanish pirates guard a lost treasure on the coast here. In the early 1700s, Indians watched as two sailing vessels fired "thunder" at each other. One of the ships was badly damaged and ran aground near this mountain. They watched as men from the ship buried a heavy black chest in the sand. Later, they befriended scores of these "white and black men." But the arrogant Spanish pirates wasted no time in wearing out the Indians' hospitality. One night a band of 1,500 united Tillamook, Clatsop, and Nehalem Indians descended on the sailors' camp and killed them all. They buried the bodies on the beach next to the black chest. Mysterious markings on rocks on Neahkahnie Mountain may hold clues to the whereabouts of the lost treasure chest. A giant *W* with a mile-long base formed with mounds of rocks has been found here, as well as several smaller rock carvings of the letter. The Indians believe the spirits of the lost sailors guard their treasure, and, indeed, since 1900, five people have died in separate accidents while searching for the lost chest.

(Lincoln County is along the middle-western coast of Oregon, from Cape Perpetua to Neotsu. Neahkahnie Mountain is located near the ocean in north Lincoln County. Skeletons of several men were found in the remains of an old sailing vessel buried at Three Rocks Beach.) **49, 77**

MCMINNVILLE

TRENT FARM On May 11, 1950, Paul Trent's wife spotted an unusual flat-shaped object in the sky above their farm. The object was noiseless, left no vapor trail, and appeared to be about thirty feet in diameter. Paul ran into the house, got his camera, and was able to take two pictures before the UFO shot out of sight. The photographs were studied by a variety of scientific and university groups and have never been proved fake. According to Dr. William Hartmann, they show "an extraordinary flying object, silvery, metallic, disc-shaped, tens of meters in diameter and evidently artificial."

(The town of McMinnville is west of the Willamette River, about thirty miles southwest of Portland on Highway 99W. The Trent farm is on private property in Yamhill County.) **72, 139, 149, 150, 190**

This picture was taken by Paul Trent who, with his wife, in 1950 spotted "an extraordinary flying object, silvery, metallic, disc-shaped, tens of meters in diameter and evidently artificial." See Trent Farm, McMinnville, Oregon (IUFOR)

MONMOUTH

WESTERN OREGON STATE COLLEGE The Theater Building of this liberal arts college is haunted by the ghost of George Harding, the school's first professor of theater. The site was originally a gymnasium, and Mr. Harding's ghost did not move in until the Theater Building was erected. His slow, methodical footsteps can be heard pacing across the stage, and he is known to sabotage productions not up to his exacting standards.

(Monmouth is in Polk County in west Oregon, twenty-five miles south of McMinnville on Highway 99W, sixty miles from Portland, twenty miles from Salem. Western Oregon State College, Monmouth, OR 97361. Phone: 503-838-1220.) **77**

MULTNOMAH FALLS

UPPER MULTNOMAH FALLS The spirit of an Indian maiden who leaped to her death from the 542-foot-high Upper Falls is felt here. She sacrificed herself after being told by an old medicine man that it was the only way to stop the spread of a deadly epidemic among tribe members. The sickness left the Indians, but the girl's spirit never left the falls.

(The Falls are at Columbia Gorge, twenty miles east of Portland on I-84. For information, contact the Greater Portland Visitors Association, 26 Southwest Salmon, Portland, OR 97204. Phone: 877-678-5263. www.pova.com) **99**

NEWPORT

YAQUINA BAY LIGHTHOUSE This deserted three-story lighthouse is haunted by the ghost of a murdered sea captain. The crew of the whaling ship *Moncton* took over the ship in January 1874 and cast Captain Evan MacClure adrift in a rowboat off the coast here. The captain was never seen again, but his ghost started making appearances at homes and taverns all along the coastline. The legend of Oregon's wandering ghost grew until dozens of people had reported seeing the red-haired man with "the face of a skeleton." The ghost told one housewife that he was just looking for "a place to stay and someone to join him in death." The Newport Lighthouse, abandoned in 1874, was just the kind of place Captain MacClure had in mind. Not long after his ghost moved in, a young woman named Zina was picnicking here with friends. After she ran back into the lighthouse to get her gloves, she was never seen again. Captain MacClure's apparition, and that of a young woman in a white dress, would be encountered by scores of witnesses over the next 120 years.

(Newport is on the central Oregon coast, fifty-four miles west of Corvallis on U.S. Highway 20. A movie shown summers at the lighthouse mentions the ghosts. Phone: 541-574-3100.) **72, 77**

OREGON CITY

BARCLAY HOUSE Several ghosts haunt the former home of Dr. Forbes Barclay. The apparition of a small red-haired boy appears to be so real that residents have called police, and his phantom dog even leaves paw prints on the carpets. Another ghost in the house, called "Uncle Sandy," is thought to be the brother of Dr. Barclay. Uncle Sandy stays near his old bed, where encounters with his spirit are most likely to take place. See McLoughlin House, below.

(Barclay House Museum is on a hill overlooking Oregon City, which is a small town in the Willamette Valley south of Portland. From I-205, take the Oregon City exit and turn left at McLoughlin St. Follow 10th St. to the top of the hill and take 7th St. left to Center St. The address is 719 Center St., Oregon City, OR 97045. Phone: 503-656-5146.) **14, 68, 101**

MCLOUGHLIN HOUSE The hulking ghost of Dr. John McLoughlin walks through the upstairs hall and bedroom of this old mansion. He founded Oregon City in 1829 and built this house in 1845. Standing six feet five inches tall, with shoulder-length hair, McLoughlin was an imposing figure. He was also a remarkably generous man, serving as the community's doctor, mayor, and investor. Not long after he moved into his new house, though, the U.S. Congress divested him of all his holdings because he was a Canadian citizen. He died on September 3, 1857, a bitter and broken man. After his death, his home was used as a camp for Chinese laborers and later became a whorehouse. In 1909, the house was moved to a hilltop location and restored as a museum. In the 1970s, the graves of McLoughlin and his wife were also moved to the new estate. That was when the ghostly manifestations started. In addition to sightings of McLoughlin's tall, dark shadow, objects in the house seem to move by themselves, and disembodied footsteps are heard on the stairway and upstairs. On the anniversary of the date and time of his death, September 3 at about 9:35 A.M., his portrait above the downstairs fireplace radiates a brilliant golden aura as the sun strikes it. The ghost of a woman has been reported standing by an upstairs window, and a phantom dog scampers through the first-floor halls. See Barclay House, above.

(The McLoughlin House Museum is next to Barclay House. From I-205, take the Oregon City exit and turn left at McLoughlin St. Follow 10th St. to the top of the hill and turn left at 7th St. Turn left again at Center St. The address is 713 Center St., Oregon City, OR 97045. Phone: 503-656-5146.   www.mcloughlinhouse.org) **14, 66 (10/90), 68, 133**

PENDLETON

PENDLETON PUBLIC LIBRARY The ghost of Ruth, a former librarian here, haunts this building. In the late 1940s or 1950s, Ruth was working one Sunday when the library was closed and became suddenly ill. She passed out and was not discovered until the next day, when she was transported to a hospital and died. Rumors that she was despondent over a failed love affair and ate a can of lye in the basement have been proven false. In any case, her dainty footsteps are still heard at the library, and her ghost knocks books from shelves, turns on lights, and opens windows.

(Pendleton is twenty-seven miles southeast of Hermiston on I-84 in northwestern Oregon in Umatilla County. The library is the former Umatilla County Library. Pendleton Public Library, 214 North Main St., Pendleton, OR 97801. Phone: 541-276-1881.) **72, 77**

PORTLAND

BUTTERTOES RESTAURANT The ghost of a woman in a high-collared dress, with her hair bobbed up, has been encountered so many times that employees here named her Lydia. Sometimes only the top half of the ghost appears; other times, only her old-fashioned, black shoes can be seen. A waitress quit after seeing the apparition, a cook was touched by the ghost, and four people renting rooms have encountered the female phantom. Lydia is known to dislike jokes about her and seems to go out of her way to show herself to unbelievers.

(Portland is on I-5, in the northwest corner of Oregon. The former restaurant is now a private residence, at 1244 Southeast Belmont St., Portland, OR 97214.) **134**

BELLA ROOMING HOUSE Another tragedy struck the Helms family here on January 6, 1907 (see Herman Helms House, Jacksonville, Oregon). Emma and Anna, daughters of Herman Helms, operated a rooming house here. On the fateful morning, Emma's estranged husband, Fred Martin, burst into the sitting room and killed Emma with a gun. As Anna tried to escape, he mortally wounded her. Then, he ran into the cellar, put the gun into his mouth, and pulled the trigger. His suicide note requested that he be buried next to his sister-in-law Anna, with Emma's body "as far from us as possible." The tangled web of emotions from that day still hangs over this old haunted house.

(The boarding house is at 655 Southwest Washington St., Portland, OR 97205.) **77**

OLD HOOD RESIDENCE At around 2:00 A.M. on December 22, 1973, Marles Hood let her estranged husband Billy in the front door of her apartment. Shortly afterward, he beat her savagely and then shot her to death. As his five children lay whimpering in their beds, he turned the gun on himself and committed suicide. No one knows exactly what made Billy crack that night, but a lot of people do believe that he never left the scene of the crime. The house has been considered to be haunted ever since the gruesome incident. In 1985, a couple purchased the vacant house at a bargain price, without knowing of the murder-suicide. In 1987, their three-year-old daughter started seeing a ghostly lady tucking in her bed at night. Next to the nice lady, the child saw the dark figure of a man who never smiled or moved around much. That was the start of a series of unexplainable events, including freezing-cold spots, electronic equipment strangely malfunctioning, the booming sound of an angry man's voice, and eerie footsteps late at night. By 1992, the family had grown accustomed to living with the ghosts, whom, they believed, meant them no harm.

(The house is a private residence, at 2107 North Watts St. Portland, OR 97217.) **72, 175**

PORTLAND STATE UNIVERSITY One of the older buildings on this ninety-two-acre campus is believed to be haunted. Students passing through the halls of Wald-schmidt Hall have reported hearing footsteps behind them when no one is there, and seeing the fleeting apparition of a dark figure lurking in corners.

Portland State University, 5000 North Willamette Blvd., Portland, OR 97203. Phone: 503-725-3511. www.pdx.edu) **72**

ST. JOHN'S THEATER An unidentified presence has been encountered by actors and employees at this theater house. The ghost has been reported backstage and in the main auditorium.

(St. John's Theater, 8704 North Lombard St., Portland, OR 97203. Phone: 503-286-1768.) **72**

WHITE EAGLE CAFÉ & SALOON This old tavern and whorehouse, built in 1899, is haunted by a wide variety of ghostly presences. The basement and second floor are sites of much strange activity, including objects tossed out of nowhere, groping invisible hands, old coins materializing on the floors, and teardrop-shaped apparitons. An invisible presence walks down the corridor from the bar, enters the men's room, and flushes the toilet. The phantom flushing continued even after a new toilet was installed. The unexplainable crying of a woman is heard on the second floor. There are many candidates for the ghosts here. The basement used to house black prostitutes, while the second floor housed white prostitutes. A tough Chinese bouncer, who kept the peace among the surly customers, disappeared while working one night and was never seen again. An abandoned ten-year-old boy named Sam was taken in by one of the owners. Sam worked as a roust-about housekeeper and died in the 1930s at the age of thirty in his second-floor bedroom. The room was sealed for many years with all his belongings locked inside. Chuck Hughes bought the building in 1978 and quickly became a believer in ghosts.

(The two-story brick building is in Old Town. It was known as the Risko Brothers Soft Drink Emporium during Prohibition. White Eagle Café & Saloon, 836 North Russell St., Portland, OR 97227. Phone: 503-282-6810.) **72, 101, 135, 198 (6-90)**

YELLOW BRICK ROAD ANTIQUES This antique shop is housed in a fourteen-room former funeral home in which some unseen presence pushes people, lifts hats off their heads, plays pranks, and makes odd swooshing noises in the walls. The ghost is believed to be a caretaker who died in the building years ago.

(The store is between Foster and Woodstock streets in Portland. Yellow Brick Road Antiques and Collectible Store, 5916 Southeast 91st Ave., Portland, OR 97266.) **72**

SALEM

GOVERNOR'S MANSION When Governor Neil Goldschmidt moved into this mansion in 1987, he was duly warned about the ghost there. Former owners spoke of the apparition of Thomas Lively, a millionaire commodities broker who built the Tudor-style mansion in 1925. Every three or four days at around 7:30 A.M., his ghost, wearing a blue-gray robe, made an appearance in the master bedroom. Although Goldschmidt later admitted to needing "all the help he could get" in running the strange household, no governor has yet admitted to seeing the ghost.

(Salem is in Marion County in northwest Oregon, forty miles south of Portland on I-15. The mansion is located in the Fairmont Hill section of the city, at 533 Lincoln St., Salem, OR 97301.) **53 (1/89)**

TILLAMOOK

T̲ILLAMOOK̲ L̲IGHTHOUSE̲ This lighthouse was built in 1880 on top of a jagged rock that the local Indians considered to be possessed by evil spirits. A few weeks before the cornerstone for the lighthouse was laid, twenty-five people lost their lives when several fishing boats sank at the mouth of the Columbia River during a storm. Witnesses reported seeing a ghostly boat sail through the floating wreckage, as if collecting the souls of those who died. Lighthouse keepers at Tillamook started reporting "low, chilling groans from the stair cylinder leading to the lantern," and the place soon gained a reputation for being haunted. In the 1950s, a coast guard crew reported sighting a ghost ship in the fog immediately below the lighthouse. The lighthouse was abandoned in 1957. Since 1980, it has been used as a depository of cremated human remains.

(The Tillamook Lighthouse is on Tillamook Rock, one mile seaward of Tillamook Head. The area is located on the Pacific Ocean, about twenty miles south of the mouth of the Columbia River in the northeast corner of Oregon. Phone: 503-220-0202.) **77, 187**

T̲ILLAMOOK̲ S̲PIT̲ Residents of the seaside community of Bayocean observed a phosphorescent frigate sail into their bay in 1912. Several witnesses saw the phantom ship approach to within a hundred feet of shore, then disappear. The sighting presaged bad luck for the community, which gradually washed away into the sea.

(Bayocean was a large town on the Tillamook Spit, a four-mile-long peninsula that separates Tillamook Bay from the Pacific Ocean. The town was founded in 1910 but was gradually washed away by beach erosion. By 1954, there was nothing left of the once-proud settlement. The sighting of the phantom ship occurred near the present rockfill dike on the south end of the Tillamook Spit.) **77**

WALLOWA LAKE

W̲ALLOWA̲ M̲ONSTERS̲ A black serpentine creature with the head of a hog has been seen swimming in this lake since the early 1800s. In the 1950s, reports were received of two creatures feeding on bluebacks at the head of the lake. One was sixteen feet long and the other was eight feet long. Their weight was estimated at several hundred pounds each. Legend says the horned lake serpents lie in wait for anyone to cross the deepest part at the lake's center. Not a single drowning victim has ever been recovered from the lake. Because of the stories, Nez Perce Indians will not go out on the water, although they fish the streams that run into it.

(The park is in Wallowa County in northeastern Oregon. From LaGrande, follow Highway 82 north about eighty miles to the park, which is at the northeastern edge of the Eagle Gap Wilderness Area, Wallowa Lake State Park, 72214 Marina Lane, Joseph, OR 97894. Phone: 541-432-4185.)

WASCO

J̲OHN̲ D̲AY̲ R̲IVER̲ The ghost of Mary Leonard haunts the riverbank here. She and her husband owned a hotel on this site in the 1880s. It is said they robbed several wealthy guests at their hotel and buried the bodies nearby. Mary was sent to jail for murdering her own husband, and when she was released spent the rest of her life searching the riverbank for buried loot. Strange floating lights are seen in the area, as well as the ghost of an old lady with long white hair.

(Wasco is a tiny town in northern Oregon, off U.S. Highway 197 south of the Dalles, in Wasco County. The site is where the Oregon Trail crossed the John Day River, just east of Wasco.) **77**

WELCHES

W̲ELCHES̲ R̲OADHOUSE̲ Tenants and visitors to this mountain cabin have witnessed the presence of a female ghost. She is described as wearing a full-length dress, with her hair done up in a bun. The ghost has been spotted looking out over the river from a second-floor window and in the upstairs bedrooms. One cocaine-using tenant claimed the ghost appeared to him on numerous occasions and warned him that she did not want "anything negative" happening in the house. The house was built in 1890 by Samuel Welch, who founded the town. Some believe the presence in the house is a former caretaker who became pregnant by an escaped prisoner she hid there. When the man wanted to leave, she became hysterical and flung herself out the north door, where she ran into a tree and broke her neck.

(Welches is forty-five miles northwest of Portland on U.S. Highway 26. Welches Roadhouse is on Roberts Ave., Welches, OR 97067.) **134**

This controversial photograph is held by ufologists to be a picture of a UFO about twenty-two feet in diameter. See Diamond Peak, Willamette Pass, Oregon (IUFOR)

WILLAMETTE PASS

DIAMOND PEAK On November 22, 1966, a biochemist traveling across the Willamette Pass pulled off the highway to take some pictures of the scenery. When he saw a fuzzy object start to move upward from the valley, he took a single picture before it zoomed out of sight. His photo showed a metallic object about twenty-two feet in diameter. Surprisingly, three separate images of the object appeared on the film in the split second that the shutter was open. One explanation is that the object moved by fading in and out of our space-time, much like the motion of atomic particles in quantum physics. The photo remains controversial with ufologists. Dr. J. Allen Hynek and photoanalyst Adrian Vance pronounced it genuine; a 1990 study by Dr. Irwin Wieder concluded that it was a picture of a road sign taken from a moving vehicle.

(Willamette Pass is in the Columbia Gorge region, southeast of McMinnville on Highway 221. The photo was taken at the five-thousand-foot elevation of Diamond Peak.) **72, 126 (4/87, 1/94)**

YONCALLA

APPLEGATE HOUSE This enormous house was built between 1852 and 1856 by lumber mill operator Charles Applegate. Today, the ghosts of Charles, his wife Melinda, and their fifteen children haunt their former home. Disembodied voices and footsteps are heard throughout the house, and the swishing sounds of long skirts come from empty hallways. The crying of babies can be heard in the dusty attic. Fiddle and banjo music is heard in the deserted parlor. The apparitions of a man in baggy pants and women wearing white have also been encountered in the parlor.

(Yoncalla is in Douglas County in western Oregon. It is on Highway 99, just off I-15, forty miles south of Eugene. The house is just northeast of Yoncalla, at the end of Applegate Rd.) **77**

PENNSYLVANIA

ADAMSTOWN

MAIN STREET A weird variety of ghosts walk the streets of this old Pennsylvania Dutch town. The phantoms of headless pigs have been reported in the streets near the old Echtenach distillery. Hundreds of swine were fattened off grain residues from the distillery, and then unceremoniously slaughtered. A more appealing black puppy ghost also roams the streets nearby. The little doggy follows people for a block or so, then vanishes. Two women ghosts, called Weiss Fraa (White Lady) and Schwatz Fraa (Black Lady), are also seen in the central district. When followed, the pair of apparitions starts walking toward the cemetery.

(The town is on the border of Berks and Lancaster Counties, twelve miles southwest of Reading on U.S. Highway 322.) **2**

ALBURTIS

INN AT MAPLE GROVE Lighting a fire in the fireplace here seems to perturb the spirit of an Indian buried beneath the hearthstone. The hapless Indian was lynched for showing affection to a white girl. He was strung up in what is now the main dining room of the old Maple Grove Hotel. The ghost and its stories are featured on the inn's logo and menus.

(Alburtis is in Lehigh County in southeastern Pennsylvania, fifteen miles southwest of Allentown off Highway 100, between Allentown and Reading. Inn at Maple Grove, 2165 State St., Alburtis, PA 18011. Phone: 610-682-4346.) **3**

OLD HENSINGERSVILLE HOTEL A ghost nicknamed Bucky haunts this two-hundred-year-old building. The unidentified presence seems to be centered in the kitchen of the house, although footsteps and other manifestations occur near the bar and in upstairs bedrooms.

(The former hotel is now a private residence on the corner of Mountain Rd. and Hensingersville Rd., just outside Alburtis.) **3**

ALLEGHENY MOUNTAINS

CHESTNUT RIDGE Some investigators believe that this mountain ridge is a doorway to another dimension. Certainly the area has attracted an unusual number of sightings of UFOs and other strange creatures. A UFO seen by thousands of witnesses crashed near Kecksburg on December 9, 1965. The entire area was cordoned off and military personnel commandeered a farmhouse near the site. That same night, the 662nd Radar Squadron from the Oakdale Army Facility hauled away a huge object hidden under a tarp on a flatbed truck. They later denied that they had found anything. A flap of over five hundred sightings from 1988 to 1990 brought hundreds of UFO watchers to the area. The first Bigfoot sighting in the area was in 1931 at Indianhead in Fayette County. Since 1972 there have been sightings every year. There were twenty-eight reports in 1988 alone. Three-toed footprints, thirteen to twenty-one inches long, have been found in connection with the sightings. The creatures are described as red-eyed, hairy humanoids who make high-pitched chirping or crying sounds.

(Chestnut Ridge is a two-mile-wide, one-hundred-mile-long section of the Allegheny Mountains that originates in Preston County, Virginia, and runs through southwestern Pennsylvania. The ridge cuts through Fayette, Westmoreland, and Indiana Counties. Most of the UFO sightings have been near the towns of Ligonier, Latrobe, and Derry. Highway 711 parallels Chestnut Ridge, and I-80. The Pennsylvania Turnpike crosses the middle of the area near Pittsburgh. To report sightings, call the Pennsylvania UFO Hotline at 724-838-7768.) **15**

ALLENTOWN

CEDAR CREST COLLEGE A ghost named Wanda haunts Butz Hall. She is said to have committed suicide in the building in 1956. Afterward, her ghost was seen wandering the halls by students and custodians.

(Allentown is in Lehigh County in southeastern Pennsylvania. It is located at I-78 and the Northeast Extension of the Pennsylvania Turnpike. Cedar Crest College, 100 College Drive, Allentown, PA 18104. Phone: 610-437-4471. www.cedarcrest.edu) **3**

KING GEORGE INN AND RESTAURANT The ghosts of a woman and small child, dressed in 1700s-style clothing, have been seen walking from the entrance hallway into the dining room here. The unexplainable sounds of a baby crying have been heard in the kitchen and near an old well in the basement.

(The inn and restaurant is just outside Allentown on Highway 222, between Easton and Reading. King George Inn, 3141 Hamilton Blvd., Dorneyville, PA 18104. Phone: 610-435-1723.) **3**

MAGNOLIA'S VINEYARD RESTAURANT This 1850s building is named for the ghost of a young woman who walks its halls. Magnolia Evans was the daughter of a Union major-general, who came across a wounded Confederate soldier in the vineyard behind her home. She nursed the man back to health and eventually fell in love with him. The two sweethearts agreed to meet after the war, but he never returned. Magnolia's ghost

is seen along the banks of Jordan Creek, at the spot she was to meet her lover.

(The restaurant is along Jordan Creek in the town of Guthsville, in South Whitehall Township, just north of Allentown in Lehigh County. Magnolia's Vineyard Restaurant, 2204 Village Rd., Orefield, PA 18069. Phone: 610-395-1233.) **3**

MUHLENBERG COLLEGE The ghost of Bernheim House is Oscar Bernheim, a former registrar who willed his house to the college. His apparition is seen in the attic, basement, rear garden, and third-floor bedroom, where he died.

(Muhlenberg College, 2400 Chew St., Allentown, PA 18104. Phone 610-821-3100. www.muhlenberg.edu) **3**

ALTOONA

BAKER MANSION Elias Baker was a nineteenth-century iron mill owner who ruled his family with an iron hand. When he denied his daughter Anna permission to marry a common millwright, she refused to marry anyone and died a spinster in 1914. Years later, museum docents put an old wedding dress on display in Anna's winter bedroom, and it seemed to summon her back from the grave. The dress moved within its airtight glass case, and satin slippers outside the case shuffled around by themselves. Employees found the bedcovers rumpled in the mornings, as if someone had slept there overnight.

(Altoona is in Blair County in Pennsylvania, at the junction of U.S. Highways 22 and 220. The mansion is now a private residence in central Altoona.) **72, 102**

BARTONSVILLE

INTERNATIONAL EATERY An unidentified presence dubbed "Veronica" by the owners haunts this small restaurant. Her appearance coincided with the purchase of an old wooden writing desk, which now sits in the lobby. Her wispy white apparition has been seen several times floating from the kitchen toward the walk-in refrigerator.

(Bartonsville is in eastern Pennsylvania, in Pike County off I-84. The restaurant is on Highway 611, Bartonsville, PA 18321.) **180**

Fantastic phantoms, such as the brilliantly shining ghost of a ten-foot-tall man, haunt this peak. See Hawk Mountain Sanctuary (South Lookout), Berks County, Pennsylvania (TRACEY JOHNSON)

BERKS COUNTY

HAWK MOUNTAIN SANCTUARY Many fantastic phantoms roam this historic peak. The brilliantly shining ghost of a ten-foot-tall man has been reported by several drivers along the two-lane road to the mountaintop, and the phantoms of settlers butchered by Indians in the mid-1700s are said to stalk the grounds at night. Ghosts have also been seen peering out of windows in the old headquarters building in the nature sanctuary, which at one time was the home of Mathias Schambacher. In the middle nineteenth century, Schambacher and his wife operated an inn in their house, although their guests had a way of checking in and not checking out. Schambacher confessed to robbing and killing several peddlers, soldiers, and other travelers, and then burying their bodies in the woods around his house. However, the most active ghost in the house is that of a young girl who fell down the stairs and died in the center of the living room. She is seen floating eighteen inches above the present floor. Some years after the accident, the house was remodeled and the living room floor lowered eighteen inches. But of course, the ghost had no way of knowing that.

(Berks County is in southeast Pennsylvania, in the Reading area. The mountain is between Ecksville and Bailey's Crossing in Berks County. Schambacher is buried in the New Bethel Church graveyard. Hawk Mountain Sanctuary, 1700 Hawk Mountain Rd., Kempton, PA 19529. Phone: 610-756-6000. www.hawkmountain.org) **2, 3, 180**

A veiled ghost entices drivers here onto the approach to the Old Birdsboro Bridge, which was torn down long ago. See Old Birdsboro Bridge, Berks County, Pennsylvania (TRACEY JOHNSON)

OLD BIRDSBORO BRIDGE For over a century, the ghost of a woman wearing a veil has appeared to drivers here. Before the wooden bridge was torn down, she appeared to buggy riders crossing into Birdsboro. Some witnesses reported that she spoke to them about the reality of life after death. Today, the same ghost entices people to join her on the Other Side. She motions drivers to continue onto the old approach to the now nonexistent bridge.

(The area is near Baumstown, on the South Baumstown Rd. at the sharp turn that leads to Highway 82.) **2**

WITCHES' HILL What we know today as crop circles were called *Hexen Danz* by the Pennsylvania Dutch. The flattened circles of wheat were blamed on dancing witches. This mountain was where the witches gathered, especially on May 1, or *Walpurgis Nacht*. Their phantoms, along with strange balls of light, are still seen on this hilltop, which locals call *Hexenkopf*, or Witches' Head.

(The eight-hundred-foot-high mountain crest runs between Virginville and Windsor Castle in Williams Township. Follow Hexenkopf Rd., along the bluff, which overlooks Stout Valley. The area is west of Allentown and north of Reading.) **2**

A woman ghost is seen near the tombstone of George D. Fahrenbach, a Civil War soldier buried in the Haag Cemetery. See Haag Cemetery, Bernville, Pennsylvania (TRACEY JOHNSON)

BERNVILLE

HAAG CEMETERY Several witnesses have reported seeing the apparition of a woman near the tombstone of George D. Fahrenbach. The Civil War soldier lived from 1846 to 1919, and the identity of his ghostly admirer has never been determined.

(Bernville is in Berks County on Highway 183, north of Blue Marsh Lake. Haag Cemetery, Bernville, PA 19506.) **2**

BETHLEHEM

LEHIGH UNIVERSITY A cantankerous ghost pesters students and employees at the Linderman Library. He is thought to be an elderly gentleman who frequented the library and made a general nuisance of himself.

(Bethlehem is just east of Allentown in eastern Pennsylvania. Lehigh University, 27 Memorial Dr., Bethlehem, PA 18015. Phone: 610-758-3100. www.lehigh.edu) **3**

LEITHSVILLE INN The ghost of a man lynched for an unknown crime in the eighteenth century haunts the barn where he was hanged. Guests and owners of this old inn have encountered his presence in the lobby and in the barn, which is now a garage.

(The inn is southwest of Bethlehem in Northhampton County, at the junction of Highway 412 and Flint Hill Road, 2006 Leithsville Rd., Hellertown, PA 18055. Phone: 610-838-8155.) **3**

MORAVIAN COLLEGE The old tunnels under the south campus of this Christian college are said to harbor a number of noisy spirits who sometimes disrupt classes with loud banging sounds. An old couch in Main Hall, a women's dorm, is haunted by the spirits of an elderly couple, who are occasionally seen seated on the sofa. Single Brethren's House is haunted by a Revolutionary War nurse, and Comenius Hall, on the main campus, is home to the ghost of a young man who died during World War I. The apparition of a girl named Alicia is seen in the attic rooms of Phi Mu Epsilon sorority. She died after being pushed down the steps in an argument with her boyfriend.

(The sorority is on Main St. in north Bethlehem. Moravian College, 1200 Main St., Main St. and Elizabeth Ave., Bethlehem, PA 18018. Phone: 610-861-1320. www.moravian.edu) **3**

WALDHEIM An unknown black shape stalks the halls of this singing club, founded in 1891. The presence is most often detected in the old barn, members' lounge, and kitchen. Members have named the shy apparition Beethoven.

(The clubhouse is south of Bethlehem, on Highway 412 in south Northhampton County.) **3**

BLAIRSVILLE

PACKSADDLE GAP This valley is haunted by the ghost of a man who accidentally shot his girlfriend. The man mistook her for a deer and has been reliving the moment since the turn of the century.

(Blairsville is thirty-three miles east of Pittsburgh on U.S. Highway 22/119. Take the Old William Penn Highway east from Blairsville for two miles, then turn south through Strangford. Follow Highway 2002 for 1.5 miles south to an overlook of Packsaddle Gap.) **184**

BOYERTOWN

RHOADS OPERA HOUSE On January 13, 1908, a terrible fire swept through this theater during a Sunday-school benefit production. Over 170 men, women, and children died. The tragedy attracted attention throughout the country as newspapers told of "the horrible smell of roasted flesh" in the fire that claimed whole families. Nearly 150 gravediggers stood by the next morning. The charred remains of many unrecognizable individuals were deliberately mixed with ashes from the building itself to make sure all bodies were claimed. Those ashes, with pieces of bone and body parts, were buried in a common grave. Reports of ghostly cries issuing from the burned site kept police busy for weeks. One woman's house was allegedly besieged by restless spirits from the fire. Three officers were required to escort an elderly man away from smoldering debris. He said his wife's ghost told him to come to a certain spot in the ruins to talk to her.

(Boyertown is located in Berks County, east of Reading at the junction of Highways 73 and 562. The common grave is in Fairview Cemetery. The building was rebuilt on the same spot in midtown. Rhoads Opera House 113 Grist Mill Rd., Boyertown, PA 19512. Phone: 610-367-7824.) **2, 49**

The 170 men, women, and children killed in the tragic fire that destroyed the Rhoads Opera House were buried in a common grave here at the Fairview Cemetery. See Rhoads Opera House, Boyertown, Pennsylvania (TRACEY JOHNSON)

BRISTOL

BORDENTOWN ROAD Midnight Mary is the name given to the ghost of Bordentown Road. Her white form is seen gliding across the road or walking on the water of Manor Lake. Sometimes she is seen hitchhiking in a dripping wet prom gown. She is allegedly the ghost of a young girl who died on the way back from a prom dance when the car in which she was riding went off the road into the lake. Her boyfriend's body was dredged from the water, but her body was never found.

(Bristol is in extreme southern Bucks County, just northeast of Philadelphia on U.S. Highway 13. The road runs near Manor Lake in Tullytown, three miles northeast of Bristol on U.S. Highway 13.) **72**

MARGARET GRUNDY MEMORIAL LIBRARY The river path behind this modern library is haunted by a lantern-carrying ghost by the name of Bonaparte. In the 1800s the Keene mansion stood here, and the beautiful Sarah Keene was the subject of many young men's thoughts. Not the least of these was Joseph Bonaparte, brother of Napoleon. He traveled by rowboat down the Delaware River to court the young lady, who never returned his attentions. His broken spirit is said to still haunt the riverbank.

(Margaret Grundy Memorial Library, 680 Radcliffe St., Bristol, PA 19007. Phone: 215-788-7891.) **97**

ST. JAMES EPISCOPAL CEMETERY An old iron chair next to the tombstone of Merritt P. Wright is called the Witch's Chair. Legend says that if you sit in the chair at midnight during the month of October, the arms of a witch will encircle you. Not far from the dreaded chair is the grave of Gertrude Spring, thought to be the source of the Midnight Mary legend (see Bordentown Road, above). The young girl died in May 1935 in a car accident on the Bristol Pike.

(The cemetery is on Cedar St. Bristol, PA 19007.) **72**

SUNBURY The specter of a lady in a white dress with a blue sash has been seen by residents of this historic house. Just down the road, the ghosts of two horse thieves haunt the spot where they were hanged during the Revolutionary War.

(The house is a private residence south of Bristol, overlooking the Neshaminy River on Newportville Rd. The horse-thief ghosts haunt the intersection of Newportville Rd. and Ford Rd.) **97**

CANADENSIS

AMERICAN LEGION HALL The spirit of former American Legion member Sam Everett is blamed for poltergeist effects here, such as moving ashtrays, unexplainable footsteps, and playing cards that mysteriously change color.

(Canadensis is in Monroe County in eastern Pennsylvania. It is located eighteen miles north of East Stroudsburg on Highway 447. The Legion Hall is on Spruce Cabin Rd. Phone: 570-595-2030.) **180**

PINES HOTEL A tall, well-dressed gentleman ghost has confronted maids cleaning the cottages here. The hotel was built in 1908 and surrounds an old graveyard.

(Pines Hotel, Evergreen Rd., P.O. Box 217 Canadensis, PA 18325. Phone: 570-595-7172.) **180**

COLEBROOK

CONEWAGO CREEK The iron furnace here was built in 1791, and in the early 1800s was managed by a cruel ironmaster. One night, in a drunken rage, he asked that his seventeen hound dogs be readied for a fox hunt. When the exhausted dogs would not perform, he threw them all into the roaring flames of the furnace. For years, people heard the ghostly animals howling in the night, and some saw the "Hounds from Hell" come back to hunt for their evil master. The original iron furnace was dismantled in 1858, but a similar furnace still stands in Cornwall.

(Conewago Creek is in Colebrook, just off Highway 117 in Lebanon County, which is southeastern Pennsylvania. The Ironmaster's Mansion is now a private residence. The Cornwall Furnace and Museum is a few miles east of Colebrook on Highway 322.) **36**

DOUGLASSVILLE

FAIR'S WINGS OF WIND RESTAURANT This restaurant was formerly known as the Brinton Lodge, and the moving apparition reported on the second and third floors here is thought to be Caleb Brinton, who operated the exclusive restaurant in the twenty-eight-room building from 1927 to 1975. Brinton handpicked his guests from society's elite, and his ghost is said to be upset that the new owners allow commoners to enjoy the remodeled restaurant.

(The town of Douglassville is about ten miles southeast of Reading on U.S. Highway 422. Fair's Wings of Wind Restaurant, Douglassville, PA 19518. Phone: 610-326-9828.) **2, 72**

DOYLESTOWN

BUCKS COUNTY COMMUNITY COLLEGE The ghost of a woman has been reported at Tyler Hall on this campus. She is believed to be former administrator Stella Tyler, for whom the building was named.

(The college is twelve miles southeast of Doylestown on Highway 413. Bucks County Community College, Swamp Rd. Newtown, PA 18940. Phone: 215-968-8000. www.bucks.edu) **102**

EASTON

CHURCHMAN'S BUSINESS SCHOOL The ghost of a woman was seen so many times near this building that she became known simply as Easton's Ghost. Although never identified, the apparition was seen on the steps of the old First Presbyterian Church and inside the parsonage. Most sightings occurred in the 1940s and 1950s. The church buildings later became part of a business college.

(Easton is on the New Jersey border, fifteen miles northeast of Bethlehem on U.S. Highway 22. The business college is near Center Square in the town. Churchman's Business School, 355 Spring Garden St., Easton, PA 18042. Phone: 610-258-5345.) **3**

EASTON PUBLIC LIBRARY During construction of this building in 1903, workers uncovered the graves of 514 people. Most of the bodies were moved to other cemeteries, but at least thirty were left unclaimed. Two prominent former citizens, Elizabeth Bell "Mammy" Morgan and William Parsons, were reburied in graves with markers on the library grounds. Mammy Morgan is buried on the west lawn and Parsons is buried on the front lawn. The other corpses, and any unidentified pieces of bodies, were unceremoniously dumped into an underground concrete vault on the property. Today, the library is haunted by the misplaced souls. Doors slam shut and open suddenly, filing cabinet drawers swing open for no reason, and unseen hands run through the hair or touch the shoulders of patrons and staff. And over the years, many people have reported the ghost of Mammy Morgan roaming the library grounds.

(The burial vault is under a telltale depression in the northeast part of the driveway that exits the library. The library is on the corner of Church St. and 6th St.

515 Church St., Easton, PA 18042. Phone: 610-258-2917.) **3, 14, 101**

NORTHHAMPTON COUNTY COUNTRY CLUB

Dressed in a long black dress and black bonnet, the ghost of Margaret Getter walks in the vicinity of this country club. The club was built over an old quarry, where Margaret's bludgeoned body was found in February 1833. Her husband was convicted of her murder and hanged from a gallows built on a small island across from the town of Easton. His ghost is also seen walking alone on the small island.

(The country club is on the William Penn Highway, just outside Easton, Getter's Island is in the Delaware River near Bushkill Creek at 5049 William Penn Highway. Phone: 610-252-9618) **3**

STATE THEATRE

This old theater building has had a diverse history. It was built as a bank building in 1873, then was remodeled into a vaudeville house in 1910. It became a movie house in 1914. In 1926, it was extensively remodeled and opened as the State Theatre, which featured a variety of live performances. In the 1930s, it again operated as a movie house. In the 1960s, it was a porno parlor. In the 1970s, it became a rock music hall. Finally, in 1989, it was remodeled once more into a prestigious theater with live stage performances. Along the way, the theater gained a ghost. Today, the spirit of Fred Osterstock, who managed the building from 1926 to 1956, is encountered by patrons, actors, janitors, and even board members. The theatrical company officially dedicated the building to "Fred and his ghost," when the theater reopened in 1989.

(The State Center for the Arts, 453 Northhampton St., Easton, PA 18042. Phone: 610-252-3132. www.statetheatre.org) **3**

EAST STROUDSBURG

ANALOMINK ROOMING HOUSE

Coed students from East Stroudsburg University have shared their rooms at this boarding house with the ghost of a young woman. The sightings began in the 1980s, and eventually the specter came to be known as Beattie. Her tall white form resembles a young woman dressed in a blouse and slacks. Beattie has been seen in the downstairs kitchen, the stairway, and the upstairs bathroom.

Once she materialized from a radiator in the downstairs living room and floated into the kitchen, in front of several astounded witnesses.

(East Stroudsburg is off I-80, near the New Jersey border on U.S. Highway 209. The house is at 151 Analomink St., East Stroudsburg, PA 18301.) **180**

EAST STROUDSBURG UNIVERSITY

A mysterious icy-cold presence is blamed for the strange phenomena that happen in the Fine Arts and Performing Center at this university. Campus police keep a log of the displaced objects, defaced name plaques, and disembodied voices that plague the auditorium. Hawthorne Residence Hall is said to be haunted by another unidentified presence.

(East Stroudsburg University of Pennsylvania, 200 Prospect St. East, East Stroudsburg, PA 18301. Phone: 570-422-3542. www.esu.edu) **180**

PHI SIGMA KAPPA FRATERNITY HOUSE

Fraternity members call her Mrs. Booth. She is the ghost of an unidentified owner whose ashes are entombed in one of the fireplaces in this old Victorian house. Her apparition is seen near the fireplace and on the second and third floors.

(Phi Sigma Kappa House, 91 Analomink St., East Stroudsburg, PA 18301.) **180**

SIGMA PI FRATERNITY HOUSE

A ghost named Margie has harassed fraternity brothers staying in a third-floor room ever since it was remodeled in the 1960s. A cremation urn was found hidden between the plaster walls and accidentally spilled on the floorboards. The spirit of the dead person treated so disrespectfully is believed to be responsible for a number of poltergeist effects.

(The fraternity house is on the corner of Smith St. and Analomink St., East Stroudsburg, PA 18301.) **180**

GETTYSBURG

CASHTOWN INN

The ghost of an unidentified Civil War soldier has been seen walking in the halls of this inn. His footsteps are heard in the attic, and he likes to knock at the door of Room 4 in the middle of the night. The spirit was most active during restoration of the inn, but he still makes himself known in the early summer months.

The ghost of a Civil War soldier haunts the halls of the Cashtown Inn and knocks on the door of Room 4 in the middle of the night. See Cashtown Inn, Gettysburg, Pennsylvania (TRACEY JOHNSON)

(Gettysburg is in Adams County, near the Maryland border, thirty-eight miles south of Harrisburg on U.S. Highway 15. The inn is eight miles west of Gettysburg at 1325 Old Route 30, Cashtown, PA 17310. Phone: 717-334-9722. www.cashtowninn.com) **141**

EISENHOWER HOME Dwight and Mamie Eisenhower bought this old farmhouse in 1950 and lived here after leaving the White House. After Ike died in 1969, Mamie continued living in the house until her death in 1979. By 1982, enigmatic events and Mamie's apparition at the Eisenhower home had prompted two National Park Service employees to threaten to quit their jobs. Mamie's ghost had appeared in a corner in the living room and near a window in her bedroom. The Park Service asked a Washington psychic, Anne Gehman, to investigate. She confirmed the presence of other spirits in the house that included the former president, a maid named Rose Wood, Mamie's mother, and Quentin Armstrong, the settler who built the farmhouse. She also claimed that Mamie's ghost was worried that part of the yard was going to be torn up for a parking lot. The Park Service later canceled plans for the parking lot.

(The house is adjacent to the Gettysburg battlefield and is administered by the National Park Service. Eisenhower Home, 97 Taneytown Rd., Gettysburg, PA 17325. Phone: 717-338-9114. www.gettysburgguide.com/ike/ike.html) **136**

GETTYSBURG COLLEGE The ghosts of Civil War sentries have been seen by students and faculty in

Pennsylvania Hall. The apparitions have been seen in the cupola and hovering over the roof. Two administrators who were working late one night took the elevator to the first floor. But the elevator bypassed the first floor and went directly to the basement. When the doors opened, they saw a makeshift hospital full of wounded Civil War soldiers. In one corner was a grotesque pile of severed arms and legs. As a bloody surgeon approached them as if to ask for help, they frantically started pushing elevator buttons. The doors closed just in time. Apparitions of children are seen on the third floor of Stevens Hall. A thin young girl ghost looks at herself in mirrors, and a phantom Blue Boy has been seen by many witnesses over the years. The building was used as a college-prep school for children from 1911 to 1935. Brua Hall, the college's theater building, is haunted by a ghost called "The General." The elderly Civil War officer is seen lounging in a phantom chair at centerstage, or peeking out an eastern window in the building.

(Gettysburg College, 300 N. Washington St., Gettysburg, PA 17325. Phone: 717-337-6100. www.gettysburg.edu) **72, 141**

Devil's Den in Gettysburg National Military Park is haunted by the phantoms of scruffy Texas soldiers who died defending the area against Union troops. See Gettysburg National Military Park, Gettysburg, Pennsylvania (TRACEY JOHNSON)

GETTYSBURG NATIONAL MILITARY PARK In just two days of hand-to-hand fighting that ended here on July 3, 1863, over fifty thousand Americans killed each other. The bloodiest battle of the Civil War was fought by Confederate troops under General Robert E. Lee and Union troops under General George Meade.

During the height of the battle, reinforcements from the 20th Maine Division neared Gettysburg but were unsure in which direction to travel. A glowing horseman in a tricornered hat appeared at a fork in the road to lead them. At first the men thought it was a Union general, but then they realized it was the ghost of George Washington. Before long, the northern troops were in a strategic position on a hilly slope called Little Roundtop. They turned away an advancing Confederate flank in what turned out to be one of the decisive engagements of the battle. Hundreds of men had witnessed the apparition, and the Union Army even launched a formal investigation at the request of Edwin Stanton, Secretary of War. General Oliver Hunt and several other officers swore that the apparition bore the face of George Washington. Colonel Joshua Chamberlain, who was directly in charge of the troops, said: "we know not what mystic power may be possessed by those who are now bivouacking with the dead. I only know the effect, but I dare not explain or deny the cause. Who shall say that Washington was not among the number of those who aided the country that he founded?"

Other, less prestigious, ghosts also haunt the battlefield. A headless officer on horseback is still seen at Little Round Top, and the wraith of a woman in white is seen near Spangler's Spring. She is said to have committed suicide at the spot in 1880, after she realized an adulterous love affair would never work out. Nearby, the Culp Farm is haunted by the footsteps of some invisible presence that runs back and forth on the second floor. A policeman once saw a phantom horseman ride through the Angle and disappear. Visitors to the maze of boulders known as Devil's Den have reported encountering the phantoms of scruffy soldiers from Texas, who died defending the area against Union troops. Some have even provided photographs of shaggy-haired cavalrymen sitting on the large rock in Devil's Den. The terrified spirits of frightened soldiers are still felt hiding in the attic and cellar of Weikert House, an old stone house in the center of the park. To the north, a window in the kitchen of Hummelbaugh House makes strange vibrating sounds. The house served as a crude operating room, where the limbs of hundreds of soldiers were quickly amputated and tossed through the window into a grotesque pile on the ground. For many years the National Cemetery was haunted by a cavalryman who was upset that his marker made no mention of his Medal of Honor. As soon as the tombstone of Captain William Miller was properly inscribed, the haunting stopped. The far-off sounds of babies crying and eerie footsteps on the stairs are heard at Cemetery Lodge. For decades, the building housed the unclaimed personal items of men killed at Gettysburg.

(Gettysburg National Park is on business route U.S. 15 at Gettysburg. Phone: 717-334-1124. Little Round Top is at the southernmost section of the park. Spangler's Spring is just east of Baltimore Pike. Culp Farm is at the intersection of Fairfield Road and York Road. Devil's Den is situated west of little Round Top. Weikert House is located just south of the Pennsylvania Monument. Hummelbaugh House is north of the Monument. Cemetery Lodge is at the entrance to the Gettysburg National Cemetery, near the intersection of Emmitsburg Road and the Baltimore Pike. For information on Ghost Tours at the park, call 717-337-0445. www.ghostsofgettysburg.com) **53 (6/83), 72, 141, 162, 163**

The Five Locks Section of the Schuylkill Canal is haunted by a locktender's daughter who drowned here. See Schuylkill Canal, Hamburg, Pennsylvania (TRACEY JOHNSON)

HAMBURG

SCHUYLKILL CANAL The Five Locks section of the Schuylkill Canal is haunted by a locktender's daughter. The young woman fell, or jumped, off the edge of the locks and drowned. Her apparition is seen hovering over the water or walking along the towpath. Some witnesses report that she moves her head slowly from north to south, as if she is looking for someone.

(Hamburg is in southeastern Pennsylvania, twenty-

five miles west of Allentown at the junction of U.S. High-way 22 and Highway 61. The locks are south of Hamburg on the Schuylkill River.) **2**

HARRISBURG

CHARMING FORGE The hallway between the kitchen and the servants' quarters in this ironmaster's mansion is haunted by the spirit of a young servant girl who burned to death when her skirt caught fire from the kitchen fireplace. Unexplainable footsteps are heard on the central staircase and on the back stairway leading to the third floor. The second floor bedrooms are haunted by the ghost of a man in an old fashioned tricornered hat. The mansion was built in 1777 by George Ege at the site of his uncle's iron foundry.

(Harrisburg is at the junction of I-76 and I-81 in southeast Pennsylvania. The mansion is a private residence on Tulpehocken Creek, near Wormleysburg, which is just outside Harrisburg.) **2**

INDIAN ECHO CAVERNS

INDIAN ECHO CAVERNS PARK The ghastly ghost of a glaring Indian holding the severed head of a bearded white man appears in the Rainbow Room of this five-million-year-old cave. The apparition has been seen by over a dozen witnesses since 1987. Other shadowy forms have been reported in the same chamber. Susque-hannock Indians believed the Rainbow Room was home to evil spirits and rarely entered the area. However, they used the 110-foot-wide Indian Ballroom for initiation ceremonies, and felt good spirits reside at Crystal Lake, a serene body of water 125 feet underground.

(The caverns are in southeastern Pennsylvania. Take the Middletown-Hummelstown exit from either I-80, I-283, or U.S. Highway 322. The site is one mile south of Hummelstown. For information, contact Indian Echo Caverns, 368 Middletown Rd., Hummelstown, PA 17036. Phone: 717-566-8131. www.indianechocaverns. com) **99**

KUTZTOWN

KUTZTOWN STATE COLLEGE This college's central administration building, Old Main, is haunted by the spirit of Mary Snyder. She died of heart failure in a fifth-floor room, just days before her graduation in June 1895. In the 1970s, coeds living in a Whiteoak Street

residence reported encountering the ghost of a woman who used to live in their apartment.

(Kutztown is fourteen miles southwest of Allentown on U.S. Highway 222. Kutztown State College is on College Hill, Kutztown, PA 19530. Phone: 610-683-4060. www. kutztown.edu) **2, 3**

LANCASTER

ROCK FORD This eighteenth-century Georgian mansion harbors a disturbing presence. The house was built by General Edward Hand in 1793. He died in the house in 1802, and his son committed suicide there a few years later. The house quickly became known as haunted and no one wanted to live in it. Even penniless immigrants offered free lodging refused to stay overnight. The house was subsequently turned into a museum.

(Lancaster is forty miles west of Philadelphia on U.S. Highway 30. Rock Ford is four miles south of Lancaster on the Conestoga River at 881 Rock Ford Rd., Lancaster, PA 17608. The mansion is open to the public. Phone: 717-392-7223.) **86**

LATROBE

ST. VINCENT'S ABBEY The ghost of a Benedictine monk began haunting this church on September 18, 1859. He appeared nightly in the chamber of one novice for over a month. The same ghost materialized during a Mass and told the assembled faithful that the idea of purgatory was in error: no such probationary state existed after death. It appeared once more to two men on the abbey road during summer of 1936.

(Latrobe is thirty-eight miles southeast of Pittsburgh on U.S. Highway 30. St. Vincent's Abbey, 300 Fraser Purchase Rd., Latrobe, PA 15650. Phone: 724-539-8629. www.stvincent.edu) **201**

LEHIGHTON

RUSTY NAIL BAR Patrons see the face of a former owner in an old leather-covered cabinet door here. The face of the man started to appear after he committed suicide in the building. The cabinet is at the heart of the tavern, at the center of the barroom under the cash register.

(Leighton is in eastern Pennsylvania, eighteen miles north of Allentown on Highway 9. The bar is in Palmerton, which is three miles east of Lehighton on Highway

248. The tavern is at 939 Hazard Rd., Palmerton, PA 18071. Phone: 610-826-6061.) **3**

MERCER

CANDLEWOOD This former tavern inn is haunted by the ghost of a peddler who was robbed and murdered in the 1850s. The room with his bloodstains was haunted by his presence for many years. The structure was built as a farmhouse in 1833 by John Crill. In 1845, it was remodeled into a tavern by Adam Boston.

(Mercer is near the Ohio border in northeastern Pennsylvania, at the junction of U.S. Highways 19 and 62, east of Sheron. The house is a private residence 2.75 miles south of Mercer on South Pitt St., Mercer-Slippery Rock Pike, Mercer, PA 16137.) **184**

NEW HOPE

INN AT PHILLIPS MILL The phantom of a woman in a long, narrow-waisted, high-collared dress brushes against people on the stairway here. She has also been seen sitting in an old rocker in the upstairs hall. The inn is a converted barn, built in 1756 by Aaron Phillips.

(The town of New Hope is in Bucks County, near the New Jersey border, about thirty minutes from I-95 on U.S. 202. In October, the city holds a Ghost Tour of haunted sites. The inn is located north of New Hope. Inn at Phillips Mill, 2590 River Rd., Phillips Mill, PA, 18938. Phone: 215-862-9919.) **97**

LOGAN INN One of the oldest tavern inns in America is haunted by at least four ghosts. Room 6 of this sixteen-room inn is home to a glowing apparition, which exudes an overpowering scent of lavender. The basement, dining room, and bar are the haunts of a tall Revolutionary War soldier. The shadowy form of a little girl roams the parking lot. Once, the vaporous figure of a man in knee britches was encountered on the stairway to the basement men's room. The ghost bowed, then vanished. Built in 1722 by John Wells, the inn has been a source of ghost stories for over 150 years.

(The inn and restaurant is downtown near the river, across the street from the Bucks County Playhouse. Logan Inn, 10 West Ferry St., New Hope, PA 18938. Phone: 215-862-2300. www.loganinn.com) **97, 134**

PICKETT HOUSE The ghost of Joseph Pickett, a famous American artist, has haunted the house where

he lived since his death in 1918. His apparition is seen in an upstairs bedroom, which used to be his studio. Pickett's ghost has also been reported walking along a tow-path that runs next to the canal and in front of another brick house a few doors down from where he used to live. That house belonged to his cousin.

(The building was home to the Living Earth crafts shop in late 1970s. The private residence is located near the canal on Mechanic St., New Hope, PA 18938.) **78, 97**

NEWTOWN

GEORGE SCHOOL This prestigious private school harbors a dark presence that no light can penetrate. It is said that at a certain spot in the middle of the basement floor in Tate House, all candles or flashlights extinguish themselves, plunging the visitor into darkness. Beneath the floor lies the grave of a Hessian soldier. Tate House was built in 1756 by Anthony Tate. His son, Dr. James Tate, inherited the house in 1781. When the ambitious doctor heard that a German soldier had died of disease while in prison, he decided to exhume the body and dissect it. When he was finished, he buried the corpse in the cellar of his house. Ever since, people going into the old cellar are suddenly plunged into darkness; they hear heavy footsteps rush up the stairs and cross the hallway to the front door, as if something were trying to escape.

(Newtown is northeast of Philadelphia at the junction of Highways 413 and 332. George School, 1690 Langhorne Newton Rd., Newtown, PA 18940. Phone: 215-579-6547. www.georgeschool.org) **97**

OLEY

LONG LANE The phantom of a young girl in a white gown lingers here, waiting for her lover to return from the Revolutionary War. The young people were to be married, but the man was killed in battle. Her ghost is reported only in the months from May through July.

(Oley is five miles northeast of Reading on the Stoney Creek Mills Road, at Highway 662. Long Lane connects the town to the Oley Turnpike.) **2**

OLEY FORGE When this old ironmaster's mansion was restored in the late 1960s, four ghosts started appearing. One was former owner Colonel John Lesher, who brought along a male servant and his large dog. Also seen is a little girl, who can sometimes be heard singing "Twinkle, Twinkle, Little Star."

(The mansion is a private residence in the Oley Valley, near Spangsville.) **2**

SACRED OAK A powerful presence in this great oak tree was revered by Indians and white settlers alike. Even today, people come to the base of the two-hundred-year-old tree to perform rituals, meditate, and share in its energy.

(The huge chestnut oak is at the rear of a private farmyard on Friedensburg Road in the Oley Valley.) **2**

PHILADELPHIA

ALLEN'S LANE The ghost of a Revolutionary War soldier galloping down the street with his severed head gripped tight next to his saddle has been seen late at night on this narrow street. The first sighting was by two British soldiers in 1775, and in 1986 two policemen reported seeing the ghost.

(The street is located in central Philadelphia.) **85**

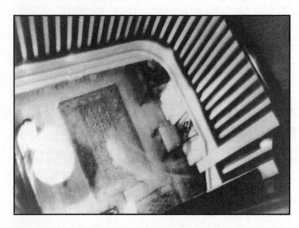

This photograph is ostensibly one of the many ghosts, malevolent and benign, who haunt Baleroy, a magnificently furnished mansion. See Baleroy, Philadelphia, Pennsylvania (BALEROY)

BALEROY The powerful spirit of the Blue Room is not to be trifled with. A two-hundred-year-old blue-upholstered wing chair in the room belongs only to Amelia, as the ghost is called. Anyone else who sits in it soon dies. At least four deaths have been blamed on the deadly curse. A cold ectoplasm sometimes hangs in a doorway from the Reception Room into the Blue Room. Another nasty ghost, that of an elderly lady with a cane, has been reported hovering in a corner in the second-floor hallway. But there are friendlier spirits here. The ghost of Thomas Jefferson has appeared beside a tall clock in the dining room, and the figure of a friendly monk dressed in a brown habit has materialized in the second-floor master bedroom. Ghostly presences have materialized at several séances held at Baleroy. The house is owned by descendants of Civil War General George Meade and is filled with his possessions, as well as many items that belonged to Napoleon Bonaparte.

(Evening and afternoon tours of the magnificently furnished mansion can be arranged. Baleroy is in the Chestnut Hill section, at 111 West Mermaid Lane, Philadelphia, PA 19118.) **14, 72, 101**

BELMONT HOUSE This four-story house was once part of the clubhouse of the Belmont Race Track, which was built in the late 1800s. When the racetrack shut down, the clubhouse was moved here in two pieces, which became large homes next to each other. Later, this house functioned as a whorehouse. Former residents have reported the apparition of a young woman wearing dark clothing, who ascends the staircase to a third-floor bedroom.

(Merion Station is a suburb of Philadelphia. Belmont House is a private residence, at 511 Winding Way, Merion Station, PA 19066.) **135**

BOLTON MANSION Many visitors to this mansion have seen the ghost of a woman stalking the grounds, apparently looking for a lost child. Meanwhile, the apparition of a young girl has been reported inside the house, running from window to window, as if looking for someone. While the ghostly activities are assumed to be related, the identity of these restless spirits remains a mystery.

(The mansion is in Levittown, a suburb of Philadelphia. Follow Levittown Parkway west to New Falls Rd., south. Turn east on Holly Drive. Bolton Mansion is located at 84 Holly Dr., Levittown, PA 19055.) **14, 72, 101**

CHURCH OF ST. LUKE A statue of Jesus Christ sitting twelve feet above the altar here bled human blood from its hands for nearly a year in 1975 to 1976. The twenty-eight-inch statue was X-rayed and its arms broken off and inspected, but no tubes or other signs of fakery were uncovered. The fluid was analyzed and found to contain human blood. The dark red blood wept from the plaster wounds in the hands of the statue, and priests and doctors testified to the authenticity of the phenomenon. About a year later, the owner of the statue, Mrs. Ann Poore of Lynwood, developed bleeding stigmata in her own palms.

(Eddystone is eight miles southwest of Philadelphia on Highway 291. Church of St. Luke, Eddystone, PA 19013. Phone: 215-874-2251.) **7**

CRIER IN THE COUNTRY RESTAURANT A mischievous presence here disrupts preparation for festive events, and the sounds of ghostly dinner parties fill the halls when empty. Once a shadowy form tried to encompass a boy sleeping in the third-floor bedroom. Many unexplained events occur in the Lydia Room and in the ladies' restroom. The building has a long history. It was built as a house in 1740 and was expanded in 1861. It became a retirement home in the late 1940s and has been used as a restaurant since 1968. Lydia Pennell, one of the early owners, buried her three grandchildren on the grounds. The bodies were later moved to a graveyard a few blocks away. During the Revolutionary War, two colonists were hanged nearby, and during the Battle of Brandywine, British troops camped on the grounds.

(The restaurant is in Glen Mills, which is seventeen miles southwest of Philadelphia on U.S. Highway 1. The Battle of Brandywine took place north of Chadds Ford. Crier in the Country Restaurant, Crier in the Country Lane, Glen Mills, PA 19342. Phone: 610-358-2411. www.crierinthecountry.com) **134**

DAVY ESTATE This beautiful Victorian mansion, built in the 1880s, is haunted by the ghost of a former servant girl. The spirit appeared to several members of a respected banking family in the 1960s. William Davy, his wife Mary, and his father William Senior all encountered the strange presence, usually in a third-floor bedroom. They described the ghost as a dull white light in the shape of a young servant girl, often accompanied by a strong odor of bayberry. Attempts to uncover further details about the ghost have not been successful, although there is evidence that the third-floor bedroom door was broken down at some time in the past.

(The mansion is in north Philadelphia, not far from Temple University, in an area originally part of the Wright's Farm acreage.) **5**

GENERAL WAYNE INN A gaggle of ghosts haunt this 1704 inn. Countless customers, reporters, psychics, and employees have seen them or felt their presence. In the basement alone there are ghosts of eight Hessian soldiers, two women, a small boy, a black man, and an Indian. Even the apparition of Edgar Allen Poe has been seen writing by a window here. One of the ghosts reached out to a man in another city. Michael Benio, of Olyphant, told researchers that a ghost from the inn appeared repeatedly in his bedroom, begging for a Catholic burial. The ghost was a Hessian soldier named Ludwig, who was buried in a wall in the basement. Benio got permission from the owners to dig for Ludwig's remains, but a building inspector halted the excavation after only two days.

(The inn is eight miles from downtown Philadelphia in Merion. The inn and restaurant is at 625 Montgomery Ave., Merion, PA 19066. Phone: 610-664-5125. www.hauntedhouses.com/states/pa/house2.htm) **101, 135**

HEILBRON MANSION The ghosts of a distraught mother and a murderous farmhand are said to haunt the site of this mansion, built in 1837 by Joseph Edwards. The farmhand, Elisha Culbert, allegedly raped and strangled fourteen-year-old Margaret Edwards in 1864. The body was found in a creek by her mother, who later hanged herself from an upstairs window of the house. The farmhand was hanged from a tree on the property by a local mob. The incident was the subject of the book *Night Stalks the Mansion*, by Constance Westbie and Harold Cameron.

(The mansion burned down some years ago, but there are plans to restore it. It was located west of Ridley Creek in Middleton Township, Delaware County, southwest of Philadelphia. The address of the restored residence is 559 West Rose Tree Rd., Middleton, PA 15757.) **72**

LOUDOUN Built by Thomas Armat in 1801, this mansion stands on top of the graves of Revolutionary War soldiers buried after the Battle of Germantown. Their spirits might be responsible for the tall columns and balls of white light that move through the house and grounds. The more defined apparition of a woman has been seen walking through the house and on the front porch, sipping tea. She is thought to be Maria Dickinson Logan, the last of the Armat family, who gave the mansion to the city when she died in 1939. Maria's younger brother, Willie, who died at the age of eleven, is also thought to be in residence. His playful spirit is believed to move small objects, rearrange books in the library, and hide visitors' possessions.

(Loudoun sits on Neglee's Hill in Germantown. The mansion is on the northwest corner of Germantown Ave. and Apsley St. The address is 4650 Germantown Rd., Germantown, PA 19144. Phone: 215-843-3388.) **14, 78, 101, 168**

NORTHHAMPTON NURSERY Ghostly children haunt this building. Their footsteps, voices, and sometimes crying are heard throughout the house. Their origin is unknown.

(Richboro is five miles north of Philadelphia on Highway 232. The nursery is at 100 Almshouse Rd., Richboro, PA 18954. Phone: 215-364-7040. www. northamptonnursery.com) **97**

PITTSBURGH

KDKA-TV STATION This modern television studio is haunted by the ghost of its former facilities director, Julian Drob. He died in May 1963 of a sudden heart attack at the age of fifty. He apparently left behind a lot of unfinished projects, because his presence lingered on to help out those who took over his work. Late at night the lights would go on in his old office, and two porters witnessed papers turning over one by one on the top of his desk. Others felt his perfectionist spirit guiding them in the daily operation of the station.

(The studio is at 1 Gateway Center, Pittsburgh, PA 15222. Phone: 412-575-2200.) **72, 82**

KIRK HOUSE The ghost of a man has been reported looking out the front window here. In the corner of the window is his signature, written with a diamond. James Kirk was general auditor of the Baltimore and Ohio Railroad, when he built this wood-frame house in 1885. The house is an exact replica of his wife's childhood home in Baltimore. Today, his ghost stares blankly at the old railroad tracks.

(Kirk House is in Glenshaw, a suburb of Pittsburgh in Allegheny County. The house is a private residence, at 1001 Glenshaw Ave., Glenshaw, PA 15116.) **184**

MILLVALE CROATIAN CATHOLIC CHURCH In 1934, witnesses saw a ghostly figure pass in front of the altar at this picturesque stone church. Later, respected Yugoslav artist Maxim Hvatka saw the ghost while painting a fresco near the altar. Unexplained cold spots also moved around at the front of the church. Some researchers have suggested that the spirit was that of a Father Ranzinger, who built the first Catholic church in Millvale on this same spot. Father Ranzinger's wooden church burned to the ground in a mysterious fire.

(The church is in Millvale, a suburb north of Pittsburgh on Highway 28 and the Allegheny River.) **89, 102, 187, 201**

SHIELDS HOUSE The spirit of Captain William Shields is said to return to his family mansion, which was completed in 1854. He was killed leading a Union charge at the Battle of Chancellorsville in May 1863, but his body was never recovered for a proper burial. William is most often seen in the front ground-floor room to the right of the entrance. Once, his ghost and the apparitions of his wife and three other female family members were seen huddled around the sofa in the living room. The phantoms stopped their conversation and looked at the frightened witness as if she were eavesdropping. The woman ran screaming from the room.

(The two-story brick house with two chimneys and a front veranda is a private residence located in Sewickley. The town is on the Ohio River, three miles northwest of Pittsburgh on Highway 65.) **211**

POCONOS

HENRYVILLE INN When the living abandoned this once-bustling inn, the ghosts took over. The specter of a screaming woman awakens caretakers in the middle of the night, and at least two other ghosts are said to haunt the place. One is a maid who hanged herself from the basement steps. Another is a man burned to death when he jumped into a flaming bale of hay he had doused with gasoline.

(The former inn is on private property at the intersection of Highway 191 and Highway 715 in the Pocono Mountains of eastern Pennsylvania. Henryville Inn, Henryville, PA 18332.) **180**

INN AT BUCK HILL FALLS The second and third floors of this inn, built in 1898, are haunted by an unidentified presence that chases maids and security personnel.

(The large inn is in Monroe County in the Pocono Mountains. The Inn at Buck Hill Falls, 35 Falls Dr., Buck Hill Falls, PA 18323. Phone: 570-595-5000.) **180**

MERWINSBURG This town is named for the Merwin family, some of whom still haunt their historic inn. Built in 1756, the three-story house is generally known to be haunted. White apparitions have been seen in an upstairs bedroom and in the hall, where music "coming from far away and long ago" can sometimes be heard.

(The town is just off Highway 115 in western Monroe County. The former inn is now a private residence, still known as Merwin's Place.) **180**

SHAWNEE INN ON THE DELAWARE This modern resort was built on top of an old fort that dates back to the early 1700s. The central structure of the fort, now called the Fort Deputy Building, was erected in 1726 and is home to the restless ghost of a woman who has pestered security guards for years. Another building, which stood on Hollow Road where the Shawnee Mountain Ski Area sign is located, was haunted for fifty years by the ghost of a man who hanged himself on the back porch.

(The luxury inn and resort is in the village of the same name, along the Delaware River in the Poconos. The Fort Deputy Building at 1 River Rd., Shawnee-on-Delaware, PA 18356. Phone: 570-424-4000. www.shawneeinn. com) **180**

SKYTOP LODGE Indian Ladder Falls near this lodge are said to be haunted by the spirits of Indians who escaped their white pursuers by climbing the falls in the 1700s.

(The inn is near Buck Hill Falls, off Highway 390. The Trout Stream Trail leads 1.75 miles to Indian Ladder Falls. Skytop Lodge, Skytop, PA 18323. Phone: 570-595-7401. www.skytop.com.) **180**

STARTING GATE SKI SHOP This old homestead building was once part of the Underground Railroad network, which assisted runaway slaves in finding freedom. It later became a house of prostitution and then a speakeasy. Today, besides being haunted, it serves as a combination ski shop and Indian museum. An unobtrusive ghost is sometimes seen in the Indian museum section, and owners have named the benign presence Eli. The museum also contains a life-size recreation of Mesingwah, a Bigfoot creature said to roam in the Pocono forests.

(The ski shop/museum is on Highway 209, just north of Marshall's Creek in Pike County. Starting Gate Ski Shop, Bushkill, PA 18324. Phone: 570-223-6215.) **180**

TANNERSVILLE INN After renovations here in the 1970s, waitresses began reporting a mysterious presence in the dining room. Before long, employees were calling the playful spirit Mabel. Then guests on the second floor started seeing a "smoky energy" swirling around in some of the rooms. Before long, the tornadic energy started to form the image of a young man, who appeared at the foot of beds. A medium identified the ghost as a black man who died in a carriage accident on Learn Road over 140 years ago.

(The Tannersville Inn is in Monroe County, between Learn Rd. and Highway 611, Tannersville, PA 18372. Phone: 570-629-3131.) **180**

POTTER COUNTY

TWIN SISTERS In 1618, Indians here captured and beheaded a Frenchman, part of a mining party led by explorer Etienne Brulé. The Indians' attempt to drive the white men from their lands worked, except the spirit of the dead man did not move on. According to Indian legends, the Frenchman's ghost returns to Twin Sisters every October, on the night of the full moon. Indian legend soon became white man's fact, and many sightings of the Headless Frenchman have occurred near an abandoned smelter here. The ghost was last reported in October 1948.

(Twin Sisters was named for two huge white-pine trees that grew at the head of Hammersley Fork Valley in the East Fork District of Potter County. Ruins of the stone chimney and pit of the old smelter are located about one mile into Hammersley Valley, between Sartwell Creek and Fishing Creek.) **49**

READING

CENTRAL CATHOLIC HIGH SCHOOL An unidentifiable shadowy presence has been reported by students and custodians at this high school. The ghost has been seen lurking in the corridors, classrooms, and the outside garden area.

(Reading is in southeastern Pennsylvania, forty-five miles northwest of Philadelphia on U.S. Highway 422. Central Catholic High School, 1400 Hill Rd., Reading, PA 19602. Phone: 610-373-4178.) **2**

CLOVER ALLEY Ghostly screams and moaning sounds are heard coming from an old house here, where a woman was murdered in the early 1900s.

(The private residence is in Clover Alley, between Tenth St., and Moss St.) **2**

HAMPDEN FIRE STATION A former fire chief haunts his old firehouse. Edward Dell served the Hampden Volunteer Fire Department for nearly forty years, until his death on December 2, 1953. But Dell's footsteps are still heard in the building, and sometimes the sounds of a billiard game come from the empty den. Dell's picture has a way of falling off the wall on the anniversary of his death, and sometimes firemen are awakened by his ghost shaking their beds, just seconds before an alarm comes in.

(The fire station is on the corner of Eleventh St. and Greenwich St., Reading, PA 19604.) **2**

HAMPDEN RESERVOIR The apparition of a young woman wearing a long dress has been seen walking on the rim of this reservoir. Police investigators say that her silhouette is sharp, but she fades away when approached.

(The reservoir is in northeast Reading.) **2**

LOCK NO. 49 The ghosts of a woman and her three children are seen along the towpath of this canal lock. She is Mrs. Phillip Bissinger and her children are Phillip, Lillie, and Mollie. On the afternoon of August 17, 1875, Mrs. Bissinger tied large rocks to herself and her three children, embraced them tightly, and jumped into the murky waters of Lock No. 49. All of them drowned, but their disconsolate spirits have returned to seize anyone who walks this area at night. Recently, a reporter for the *Reading Eagle-Times* was temporarily enveloped by a powerful, unseen presence at Lock No. 49.

(Lock No. 49 is in the Union Canal in Reading. The incident occurred near Gring's Mill.) **2**

SAYRE

BURIAL MOUND The skeletons of several humanoid creatures seven feet tall, with horns on their heads, were discovered here in the 1880s. Estimates place their burial at around A.D. 1200. The bones were found by a Pennsylvania state historian, a Presbyterian dignitary, and two professors who were investigating the burial mound. Some of the skeletons were sent to the American Investigating Museum, a forensic institution in Philadelphia.

(Sayre is in Bradford County, on the New York border, at the north end of U.S. Highway 220 in northeastern Pennsylvania.) **139**

SOMERSET

OLD MANNER HOUSE The Manner family could not understand why they got this huge Victorian mansion so cheaply. Although the house had been vacant for two years, it was lavishly furnished and in excellent condition. But as soon as they moved into the house in 1966, Mrs. Manner felt uneasy. She awoke every night at precisely 2:00 A.M. with a feeling of dread. She started seeing the ghosts of an immaculately dressed man and an elderly woman, who both passed through doors and walls with ease. The apparitions fit descriptions of the previous owners, who had died in the house. The couple's fourteen-year-old son and six-year-old daughter were afraid to be left alone. Strange noises were heard at all hours of the day, and the overpowering scent of flowers would suddenly permeate the whole house. The Manners asked for help from police and their minister, but things only got worse. Finally, a third ghost appeared: the image of a burly man with tortured eyes, covered with blood, trying to pull himself up the central stairway. The Manners moved out the very next day. The family that next lived in the house also reported uncanny phenomena.

(Somerset is fifty-five miles southeast of Pittsburgh on I-70/76. The Old Manner House is a private residence off Highway 281.) **72, 85**

STROUDSBURG

BONSOR ROAD Locals call this road Suicide Ridge, because of all the people who have taken their lives here. In the 1930s, a father and son named Werkheiser hanged themselves from a tree along the road. Another man hanged himself in the Saylorsburg playground, and a fourth suffocated himself with carbon monoxide from his car in a garage on Bonsor Road. Recently, a resident suffering from cancer took his own life. The ghosts of suicide victims have been reported all along the road, and several ghostly encounters have occurred in the Old Finkbeiner House.

(Saylorsburg is in Ross Township, Monroe County, in eastern Pennsylvania. It is seven miles south of Stroudsburg on Highway 33. Bonsor Rd. is northwest of town. It

has also been known as Sullivan Rd. and the Wilkes-Barre to Easton Turnpike. The Old Finkbeiner House is a private residence, across from Sobers Meat Market on Highway 115.) **180**

OLD MEISSE HOUSE This 125-year-old house is haunted by the sounds of a baby crying and footsteps that keep pace with people walking in an upstairs hall. The Ralph Meisse, Sr., family have credited their resident ghost with watching out for their young son and daughters, tucking the children in at night, and preventing accidents.

(Scotia is five miles southwest of Stroudsburg on Highway 33. The two-story frame house is a private residence on Fenner Ave., Scotia, PA 18354.) **180**

STROUDSMOOR GENERAL STORE When the old Highland Inn was remodeled into a general store and private residence, ghostly activities started to occur on the third floor. The owner blames the manifestations on the Snowy Mountain Ghost, which, according to local legend, protects people living in the area.

(The store is located in the Stroudsmoor Country Inn complex, which is south of Stroudsburg on Highway 191. Phone: 570-421-6431. www.stroudsmoor.com) **180**

UNIVERSITY PARK

PENNSYLVANIA STATE UNIVERSITY The ghost of a mule haunts the Watts Hall dormitory on this campus. Old Coaly, as the mule is called, was one of the original pack mules that worked to build the university in the 1850s. Coaly lived to a ripe old age, and when he died his remains were preserved and displayed in the Old Main Building. After the building was destroyed by fire in the early 1900s, Coaly's remains were stored in the basement of Watts Hall. Then, in the 1960s, Coaly's skeleton was once again put on display, this time at the Agricultural Building. Ever since, Old Coaly's ghost has been reported standing in the hallway outside the storage room back in Watts Hall. Sometimes, his noisy braying is heard coming from behind the locked door. Another haunted spot on this campus is in Runkle Hall. A third-floor room there was the scene of poltergeist activity in the fall of 1994. A resident assistant reported loud banging sounds, lights blinking on and off, and a disembodied voice that spoke incoherently. She also said that her mattress and pillow were "breathing"—

rising and falling in a regular pattern. The university investigated but could find no explanation.

(The 540-acre campus is ninety miles from Harrisburg. Penn State University, 201 Shields Building, University Park, PA 16802. Phone: 814-865-5471. www.psu. edu) **72**

VALLEY FORGE

PENNSYLVANIA HOUSE Some residents of this apartment hotel say it is haunted. They report hearing the sounds of ballroom dancing and seeing unexplainable moving shadows.

(The Valley Forge area is in Chester County in the southeast corner of Pennsylvania, just northwest of Philadelphia. The hotel is four miles northwest of the town of Valley Forge on Highway 23. Pennsylvania House, 226 E. High St., Phoenixville, PA 19460. Phone: 610-933-5700.) **3**

The ghost of General Anthony Wayne has been spotted near the statue erected in his honor at Brandywine Battlefield in Valley Forge National Military Park. See Valley Forge National Military Park, Valley Forge, Pennsylvania (TRACEY JOHNSON).

VALLEY FORGE NATIONAL MILITARY PARK The phantom of General Anthony Wayne, on his trusty horse Nab, has been reported roaming the battlefield area here. His ghost has also been encountered near the statue erected in his honor at Brandywine Battlefield. (See Stony Point and Ticonderoga, New York; Lake Memphremagog, Vermont; and Loudoun County, Virginia.) Phantom sentries have been seen on the hillside at Valley Forge, as well as the ghosts of spies who have been executed here.

(The park is at the junction of I-76 and U.S. Highway 422, just northwest of Philadelphia. Valley Forge National Military Park, P.O. Box. 953, Valley Forge, PA 19481. Brandywine Battlefield is north of Chadds Ford, near the Delaware border on U.S. Highway 1. Phone: 610-459-3342. www.nps.gov/vafo) **78, 162**

WALNUTPORT

LOCK NO. 23 A lady in white has been seen floating over the water in the canal at this lock since the 1940s. The apparition is sometimes seen walking along the towpath, where she once chased a frightened witness into the water. She is also encountered near the restored lock tender's house at the boulder marking Lock No. 23.

(Walnutport is six miles southeast of Lehightown on Highway 145. The site is at Lock No. 23 in the Lehigh Canal, which runs through Walnutport.) **3**

WILKES-BARRE

HAZLETON MINE In August 1963, two men trapped for fourteen days in a mine cave-in reported encountering angelic apparitions, who came to their aid. David Fellin and Henry Throne survived the ordeal thanks to two phantasms that appeared on the fourth day. The entities, dressed as "utility linemen," materialized through a doorway made of bright blue light. After the miraculous appearance, the men were no longer afraid and waited patiently for rescuers. In the face of considerable skepticism, the men maintain to this day that they did not imagine the ghosts.

(Wilkes-Barre is in Luzerne County in eastern Pennsylvania. Hazleton is twenty-three miles south of Wilkes-Barre on Highway 309. The men were trapped at the three-hundred-foot level of the Hazleton Mine, which is in the Nescopeck Mountains in Luzerne County.) **82**

SMURL HOUSE This duplex house was built in 1896. The Smurl family bought the house in 1973 and settled in for twenty-five years of terror. Jack and Janet Smurl lived in one half, and Jack's parents, John and Mary Smurl, lived in the other half. In January 1974, strange events began to take place in Jack and Janet's section of the house. Unexplainable claw marks were found in the bathroom, an unusual stain appeared on the carpet, and the television set burst into flames. In 1975, their oldest daughter, Dawn, started seeing ghosts hovering in her bedroom. The weird phenomena continued until February 1985, when a hideous, faceless ghoul appeared. The dark creature, which they called the "Old Hag," was about five feet tall and could walk through walls. It regularly attacked members of the family and even beat the Smurl's dog. Scaly creatures sexually attacked both Jack and Janet, and pig noises started coming from inside the walls. The Smurls called in paranormal investigators, and when the news leaked out, crowds of reporters and curiosity seekers showed up and nearly destroyed their home. Within a few days, fifty-three people had witnessed unexplainable events at the Smurl residence. More than fifty exorcisms were performed on the house, but it was not until 1989, a year after the Smurls moved out, that the paranormal activity ceased.

(The house is in West Pittston, which is in Luzerne County in northeastern Pennsylvania, six miles east of Wilkes-Barres on U.S. Highway 11. The house is a private residence, at 328-330 Chase St., West Pittston, PA 18643.) **47, 66 (6/88), 68, 72**

RHODE ISLAND

BLOCK ISLAND

BURNING EYES Fiery apparitions haunt the residents of Block Island. The phantom known as Burning Eyes has burning embers for eyes and is usually discovered on the back porches of houses late at night. During the hard winters here, the bodies of deceased people used to be stored at the back of houses, so they could be buried when the ground thawed. Burning Eyes is believed to be one of those spirits, who lingered longer than the spring thaw.

(All of the sightings of Burning Eyes have been in the town of Block Island on the eastern coast.) **72**

PALATINE LIGHT As the Dutch ship *Palatine* approached the coast of North America in 1752, it ran into a series of fierce storms. The frightened crew decided to mutiny and abandon the ship. They killed the captain and stole the valuables of the passengers, and left the ship to run aground off Block Island. A band of pirates who made a living plundering ships run aground seized the opportunity to raid the ship. But one hysterical woman refused to leave the floundering *Palatine*. When the pirates set fire to the vessel and the tide lifted the blazing ship off the reef and back out to sea, the woman was left screaming on the deck. Mysterious lights and burning ghost ships were sighted near the island for many years afterward. In 1969, dozens of witnesses described a great fireball in the ocean, and, to this day, the light from the burning *Palatine* is reported

by residents of Block Island. John Greenleaf Whittier penned a long poem about the Palatine Light, which concludes: "Now low and dim, now clear and higher/Leaps up the terrible Ghost of Fire/Then, slowly sinking, the flames expire/And wise Sound skippers, though skies be fine/Reef their sails when they see the sign/Of the blazing wreck of the Palatine!"

(Block Island is off the south coast of Rhode Island. It lies eleven miles from Long Island, in the Rhode Island Sound, between Montauk and Gay Head. The island can be reached by ferry from Galilee, Rhode Island, which is near Point Judith. A schedule is available from Interstate Navigation Co., 14 Eugene O'Neil Dr., New London, CT 06320. Phone: 203-442-7891. Once on the island, follow Corn Neck Rd. North to the State Beach or Settler's Rock Grove. A brochure on the island can be obtained from the Chamber of Commerce, Drawer D, Block Island, RI 02807. Phone: 401-466-2982. www.block-island.com) **20, 37, 42, 57, 69, 139, 158**

CRANSTON

SPRAGUE MANSION Ghosts have been seen in this mansion since 1925, when an apparition was reported descending the staircase. Later residents told of a ghost in the wine cellar and complained of an unseen force that flung off their blankets in the middle of the night. One room in particular, called the Doll Room because of the collection of porcelain dolls there, is the source of many unnerving phenomena, including eerie footsteps, lights that go on by themselves, and a ghostly presence. The house was built in 1790 by William Sprague, who operated a cotton mill and bleachery on the property. One evening William got a fish bone caught in his throat and died during surgery to remove it. His sons Amasa and William Junior made a highly successful business from their inheritance. William Junior became a U.S. senator, while his brother tended the business. Then, in 1864, Amasa was found brutally beaten to death. A man whom Amasa had prevented from obtaining a liquor license was executed for the murder, but one of the accused's brothers later confessed to the crime. As a result of the miscarriage of justice, Rhode Island passed a law forbidding capital punishment. One of Amasa's sons went on to become governor, and the other became a brigadier general and U.S. senator. After the Civil War, the Sprague fortune dwindled and the house was sold. The family's checkered history is believed to have spawned the ghostly activity at Sprague mansion.

(Cranston is five miles southwest of Providence on Highway 2. Take Exit 16 from I-95 and go west on Highway 12 to Highway 2. The private mansion is at 1351 Cranston St., Cranston, RI 02920. Phone: 401-944-9226.) **14, 101**

EXETER

CHESTNUT HILL CEMETERY The phantom of a nineteen-year-old girl whose grave was violated stalks this old family graveyard. Mercy Brown died on January 18, 1892, but two months later her father, George Brown, dug up her grave believing that she might be a vampire, responsible for the deaths of his wife and oldest daughter and the strange weakness suffered by him and his son. Actually, they all suffered from tuberculosis, but George Brown believed a vampire had sucked the life force from them. Brown and a group of friends, including the district medical examiner, found evidence that Mercy had moved in her coffin. When the doctor removed her organs and squeezed blood from her liver and heart, it was enough to convince Brown that his daughter was indeed a vampire. To keep her from rising from the dead, he burned her heart and liver on a rock near the open grave. Then he used the ashes as a medicine to cure himself and his son. The desperate remedy failed. Over the years many witnesses have reported seeing a strange blue light moving slowly through the cemetery. It is believed to be Mercy's spirit, displaced from her violated grave.

(Exeter is in central Rhode Island, off Exit 5 from I-95, near the Kent-Washington County line. Take Highway 102 toward Exeter and follow signs to the Chestnut Hill Baptist Church, behind which lies Rhode Island Historical Cemetery No. 22. Brown's grave is at the center of the small cemetery. Chestnut Hill Baptist Church, Exeter, RI 02822.) **15, 53 (8/85)**

NARRAGANSETT

OLD WEDDERBURN HOUSE This four-story, white clapboard house was built by a rich sea captain, Japhet Wedderburn, in 1830. He lived there with his housekeeper Huldy Craddock for a long time, until he brought home a bride from one of his trips to Spain. Dona Mercedes was a tiny, dainty woman very unlike the robust housekeeper who had ruled the house for so many years. When Captain Wedderburn returned from a two-year journey, Huldy told him his wife had sailed back to Spain because she was so lonely. On his next sea trip, Wedderburn died of a heart attack and the house was sold. For over fifty years, residents of the house complained of seeing the ghost of a childlike woman dressed in a black veil. She appeared around dusk, looked out the front windows for a few seconds, then turned and disappeared. In 1925, when the house was being renovated, it was decided to replace the hearthstones in the library fireplace. Underneath the fireplace floor, workers found a hole with a wooden box in it. Inside, they found a small female skeleton with an old tortoiseshell Spanish comb and the wispy remains of a black lace mantilla.

(Narragansett is in Washington County in south Rhode Island, on Highway 1A on the southeastern coast. The house is located on Front St. in Narragansett, RI 02882.) **158**

NEWPORT

THE BREAKERS The ghost of Mrs. Cornelius Vanderbilt haunts her former home. The mansion was built in 1895 and was once owned by the Vanderbilts. Today tourists and employees at the museum believe Mrs. Vanderbilt's spirit never left.

(Newport is on the south coast of Newport Island on Rhode Island Sound. Take Highway 114 south from Prov-

idence to the island. *The Breakers Museum, Newport, RI 02840. Phone: 401-847-1000. www.newportmansions. org/gildedage/thebreakers.html)* **102**

PORTER MANSION This great house was built by Mrs. Mary Porter in 1848, but it is haunted by the ghost of lawyer Richard Washburn Child, who died in the building on January 31, 1935. He served as President Harding's Ambassador to Italy and even collaborated with Mussolini on his autobiography. Child's ghost has been seen on the third floor, the stairway, and in the first floor hallway.

(The old mansion was converted to apartments. It is located at 25 Greenough Place, Newport, RI 02840.) **101, 187**

THE SPRAY On July 3, 1898, Joshua Slocum landed his thirty-six-foot sloop, the *Spray*, at this seaside port after being at sea for three years and covering 46,000 miles. Not only was he the first lone sailor to travel around the world, but he was probably the first sailor ever to turn his ship over to a ghost to pilot it. During a fierce, three-day storm in the Atlantic, Slocum finally succumbed to exhaustion and could no longer control his craft. He gave up the wheel and collapsed on his bunk belowdecks, certain he would die in his sleep. But Slocum awoke to feel the *Spray* being piloted smoothly by an expert hand through the raging seas. When he went back on deck, he saw the phantom of a tall, heavy man, wearing fifteenth-century clothing, at the helm of his ship. The man identified himself as the helmsman of the *Pinta*, one of the three ships under the command of Christopher Columbus. Then, the phantom vanished into thin air. Moments later, the fury of the storm subsided and Slocum was able to continue his record-breaking cruise.

(The sloop was registered in Boston and docked at Newport. Slocum departed from Yarmouth, Nova Scotia, on July 2, 1895.) **96**

SOUTH CAROLINA

BARNWELL

BOYLSTON SPRINGS This is the only place in America legally owned by God. The site was deeded to God by farmer Lute Boylston in July, 1944, and duly recorded in the Barnwell County Courthouse. Indians were the first to treat the springs as sacred, and early settlers and Revolutionary War soldiers came to partake of the spring's healing powers. Thousands of people still make the pilgrimage each year.

(Barnwell is in southwestern South Carolina at the junction of U.S. Highway 278 and Highway 70. The springs are in Barnwell County.) **57**

BISHOPVILLE

SCAPE ORE SWAMP In June 1988, the first encounter with South Carolina's Lizard Man occurred here. While changing a flat tire on a road that runs through this dismal bog, Christopher Davis was approached by a red-eyed, greenish-black, reptilian creature that stood over seven feet tall. A farmer's sighting in Brownsville became the most publicized encounter, though dozens of people eventually reported seeing the beast. A thorough investigation by police and news media from around the country failed to explain the sightings, although one plaster cast of a webbed footprint was declared a hoax by biologists. Most sightings have taken place within Scape Ore Swamp, which incidentally was named "Escaped Whore Swamp" during the

Revolutionary War, after a group of British soldiers eluded their American pursuers by taking a route through the wetland.

(Bishopville is not far from Columbia. From I-20 east, take the Highway 15 exit north one mile to Bishopville. All of the sightings have been in Lee County, most in the swamp area and along Highway 15.) **15, 57**

CAMDEN

GRAY LADY The beautiful, though frightening, apparition of the Gray Lady walks the streets of this peaceful town. The young lady is an ancient ghost. She appeared to members of the De Saurin family in France for hundreds of years before showing up among descendants who settled near Camden. Her name is Eloise De Saurin, and she died at a convent, where her father had sent her less than a year earlier to prevent her marrying a young man who was not Catholic. Shortly after her death, her ghost appeared to her father, who committed suicide by plunging a dagger into his chest. Then, she appeared to her brothers to help them escape from the St. Bartholomew's Day Massacre in Paris. She has appeared to numerous family members over the years, most often in times of danger or death. When the family lost its estate, the ghost started frightening the new residents and now is said to walk the streets of Camden as well.

(Camden is twenty-four miles east of Columbia, off

I-20. The Gray Lady is most often reported at the Court Inn and on the roads nearby. The old inn has been torn down, but at one time it was known as Lausanne, the De Saurin family estate.) **172**

CHARLESTON

CHARLESTON NAVAL BASE The ghost of a slave girl has been seen standing near a clump of old trees along the river here. She is waiting for a slave boy in a rowboat to take her away to freedom. She promised to give the boy a cache of jewelry belonging to Mrs. Thomas Shubrick, whom she served as a personal slave. But the boy snatched the jewels and pushed off into the river alone. The desperate girl returned to the manorhouse and set it on fire to cover her crime. In March 1796, the Belvidere mansion and all its furnishings burned to the ground.

(The base is three miles outside of Charleston. The site is along River Rd. in a group of Live Oak trees on the Cooper River landing.) **117, 159**

CITY HALL Charleston's most prestigious ghost roams the corridors of City Hall. General Pierre Gustave de Beauregard, the famous Confederate general, was widely known for his high ethical standards. Beauregard once discovered that a respected citizen had embezzled money from the state. He found the money hidden in the man's mansion and forced him to return it. It is said that the general's ghost returns to search for similar shenanigans at City Hall.

(Charleston City Hall is on the northeast corner of Meeting St. and Broad St. 80 Broad St., Charleston, SC 29401. Phone: 843-577-6970.) **159**

FENWICK HALL Ann Fenwick spent her last years in this house going from room to room, pleading for the ghost of her dead husband to appear. Her father Lord Edward Fenwick disapproved of her secret marriage to a stable worker, and ordered the man hanged. That happened over 250 years ago, but recently, after the great house was restored, Ann's gentle spirit returned to the East Parlor and staircase.

(Fenwick Hall is in central Charleston.) **117**

HEYWARD HOUSE James Heyward's ghost walks in the library of his Charleston home. The young man died in 1805 in a hunting accident. His rifle went off by mistake, and the bullet severed his jugular vein. His apparition, clad in a green hunting coat, has been seen several times by later owners of the house.

(The house is now a private residence, at 31 Legare St., Charleston, SC 29401.) **117**

LADD HOUSE Built in 1732, this white-stucco house is home to two ghosts. One is Dr. Joseph Brown Ladd, who lived here in the 1780s. A rush of cold air announces his entrance, then the sound of his footsteps are heard. Sometimes the doctor's ghost whistles his favorite tune, an old English ballad, which is heard in the darkened hallways. The sensitive young physician left behind dozens of love poems, which were later published. But perhaps the good doctor took life too seriously. He died in 1786, in a senseless pistol duel brought on by a disagreement over the talents of a young Shakespearean actress. The other ghost is of a little girl, a member of the Savage family who lived here in the 1830s. She is sensed in the second-floor drawing room and on the piazza sidewalk below.

(Charleston is on the south-central coast of South Carolina, at the south end of I-26. For more information about Charleston sites, call 800-853-8000. Built in 1732, Brown House is surrounded by a brick wall, but the large screened-in porch on the second floor can be seen from the street. It is now a private residence, at 59 Church St., Charleston, SC 29401.) **117, 165, 168**

MEDWAY South Carolina's oldest building is still home to the Dutchman who built it. Jan Van Arrsens built the stone house for his wife in 1686. Today his ghost smokes an invisible pipe near the fireplace in the upstairs south bedroom. A later resident of Medway haunts the downstairs north rooms. She is the bride of a young man killed in a hunting accident, and she still waits by the window for his safe return.

(The Medway Estate is in Charleston.) **117**

ST. PHILIPS GRAVEYARD The ghost of a gray man is seen leaning against headstones in this distinguished cemetery. He is thought to be a slave named Boney, who was granted his freedom in recognition of his heroism. In 1796, he climbed the side of the church to put out a fire on the steeple shingles. An instant hero, Boney spent the rest of his life lounging around the church grounds. He was buried on his former master's Waccamaw River plantation.

(St. Philips is at 142 Church St., Charleston, SC 29401. Phone: 843-722-7734.) **159**

SIMMON'S ALLEY The lonely ghost of an angry, frustrated woman haunts the alley where her house once stood. Ruth Lowndes Simmons moved into the house on the night of her marriage, a union that would never be consummated. Francis Simmons loved another but had already proposed marriage to Ruth. In the early 1800s, a man's word was his bond, and Francis went through with the ceremonies. The couple rarely spoke, and before long he moved to another house. Ruth's lonely nights and bitter emotions made their mark here, and people still report hearing her carriage pull up to the empty house.

(The house stood at 131 Tradd St., in Charleston. An alley occupies the site today.) **117**

SWORD GATE This imposing gate is haunted by the stern lady who had it built. Madame Talvande ordered the gate built in 1838 to keep the girls in her boarding school from meeting boys at night or eloping with their secret lovers. She is said to be still on the lookout for trespassers.

(The crossed-sword-and-spear wrought iron gate is at 39 Legare St. in Charleston.) **117**

YEOMAN'S HALL This modern development of large homes was built on the ruins of Goose Creek Plantation. The ghost of Mary Hyrne, an old Irishwoman who spent her last years at Goose Creek, appeared to later residents of the plantation whenever something occurred that met with her disapproval. The pious ghost showed up if anyone blasphemed, worked on the Sabbath, or missed church. Over the years, her phantom was forgotten until she started showing up in the central clubhouse of the housing development. Witnesses described the disapproving figure as an elderly lady wearing a tiny white hat and an old-fashioned black dress.

(Yeoman's Hall is just south of Charleston.) **117**

COLUMBIA

AIRPORT HIGH SCHOOL The tall, thin ghost of a man with his hands on his hips is seen in the halls here. He is George Pair, the school's first principal. The high school was built in 1958 and Pair died in 1962. He worked hard to get the school built and is said to protect the premises from harm. Most sightings have occured in the "300s" corridor. Custodians, students, and visitors have reported encountering the stern ghost.

(The high school serves the Cayce-West Columbia area. Airport High School, 1315 Boston Ave., West Columbia, SC 29170. Phone: 803-822-5600.) **121**

HIGHWAY 76 The ghost of a girl carrying a canvas travel bag haunts this lonely stretch of highway. Concerned motorists see her walking down the dark road and stop to ask if she needs a ride. She graciously accepts and gets into the car. Then she tells the driver she is going to visit her ailing mother in Columbia and mentions an address there. But just on the outskirts of the city, the girl vanishes from sight. A couple who checked out the address described the girl to the man who answered the door. He said the girl was his sister. She had died in an accident on the way to visit her sick mother. The incident happened to several independent witnesses over a three-year period in the 1950s.

(The city of Columbia is at the center of South Carolina, at the junction of I-20 and I-26. The ghost was first seen southeast of the city, on Highway 76 between Columbia and Sumter streets over the wateree River Bridge. The address given by the girl was on Pickens St. in Columbia.) **165, 183**

DAUFUSKIE ISLAND

DAUFUSKIE ISLAND An apelike creature has been sighted by residents on this undeveloped island. The Bigfoot has been observed and tracked near the Moss Creek Plantation and the Daufuskie Lighthouse.

(The South Carolina island is sixteen miles from Savannah, at the mouth of the Savannah River. Moss Creek Plantation is along Highway 278 on the island. Boat tours leave from Savannah or Hilton Head. For information, call 800-398-7687.) **159**

HAMPTON PLANTATION The ghost of Hampton House makes itself known "by a remarkably regular series of sounds" coming from the bedroom over the dining room area: first, a quiet rocking sound, then three distinct raps, and finally the creepy sound of a body being dragged from a northwest to a southeast corner of the room. Sounds of a man's sobbing and a chair that rocks itself are reported in the library downstairs. The house was built in 1735 by a family of strict Huguenot immigrants, the Rutledges. In the 1830s, John Henry Rutledge, disconsolate because he was not allowed to marry the woman he loved, sat down in a rocker in the library, put a gun to his head, and pulled

A disconsolate ghost sobs in the library of Hampton House where a man committed suicide 150 years ago. See Hampton Plantation, Georgetown, South Carolina
(GEORGE COUNTY CHAMBER OF COMMERCE)

the trigger. In 1937, one of his descendants, Archibald Rutledge, explored the old passageways in the house and found barrels of valuable antiques, including hundreds of gold coins dating from 1795. No one has ever been able to explain the strange sounds that emanate from the bedroom.

(Hampton is nineteen miles south of Georgetown on U.S. Route 17. Signs mark the turnoff for Hampton at Rutledge Rd., near the South Santee Bridge. Hampton Plantation, 1950 Rutledge Rd., McClellanville, SC 29458. Phone: 803-546-9361.) **14, 101, 159, 187**

HENRY MILLER HOUSE This Revolutionary War era house is haunted by the stubborn presence of a young British soldier who died in the house. Several tenants have reported ghostly manifestations on the second floor.

(The Henry Miller House is on U.S. Route 17. For tour information, contact the Georgetown Chamber of Commerce, P.O. Box 1776, Georgetown, SC 29442. Phone: 803-546-8436.) **14**

HERIOT TARBOT HOUSE This house is haunted by a ghost named Sad Lady. She is an unidentified woman found buried on the property in an unmarked grave.

(Heriot Tarbot House is a private residence on U.S. Route 17, near Hampton Plantation. Meetings are held at the County Library Courtyard to discuss the history of haunted houses in the area.) **14**

WEDGEFIELD PLANTATION MANOR This Revolutionary War manorhouse is haunted by a ghost of a headless British sentry. He died in 1781 from the swift and razor-sharp sword of the legendary American rebel Francis Marion, also known as the Swamp Fox. Marion broke into the house to rescue an American prisoner and killed the guard to gain entry. According to witnesses, the headless torso of the guard reeled and tottered about, then fell and struggled like a chicken that had just had its neck wrung. The ill-fated soldier was buried in the garden near the main house. Seven weeks later, the guard's grisly ghost started to appear, stumbling through the garden with a pistol in his hand, searching for his head. He was also seen on the porch of the old house and in the front yard. Strange noises such as the thundering hooves of many horses sometimes presage his appearance. His appearances are not frequent since the main house was replaced by a mansion in the 1930s, although occasionally someone reports the headless apparition of an eighteenth-century British Dragoon tottering about the yard.

(The residential resort community is on the Black River, five miles north of Georgetown off U.S. Highway 701. Wedgefield Plantation, 129 Clubhouse Lane, Georgetown, SC 29440. Phone: 448-2124. www.wedgefield.com) **14, 159, 843**

HILTON HEAD ISLAND

BAYNARD PLANTATION When William Baynard died of yellow fever in 1849, he was entombed in the templelike Baynard Mausoleum, located in Zion Cemetery. There he rested peacefully until the Civil War, when Yankee marauders searching for family valuables broke into his crypt and removed his body. After that, Baynard's spirit never rested again. He is still seen leading a ghostly funeral procession from Braddock Point Plantation down the old road, past the ruins of Baynard Plantation, to his empty mausoleum. His black-draped carriage stops at each plantation along the way. Baynard steps out, both hands covering his face, and walks slowly to the gate. There he pauses, and after a short while returns to his carriage. Bringing up the rear of the procession is a line of loyal servants dressed in red velvet and silver trim. The ghost of William Baynard's mistress haunts the Eliza Tree, from which she was hanged for poisoning Baynard's wife. Eliza's lifeless body was placed in a metal cage and suspended from the tree for all to see.

(Hilton Head Island is at the extreme southwestern tip of South Carolina. Take the Highway 462 exit from I-95 to Highway 278, which leads across to Hilton Head Island. The funeral procession follows Highway 278. The Baynard Mausoleum is in Zion Cemetery at the intersection of Highway 278 and Matthews Drive. The Eliza Tree is the large oak at the intersection of Matthews Drive and Marshlands Rd. The Baynard Plantation ruins are on Baynard Park Rd., eight miles past the entrance to Sea Pines Plantation on Highway 278.) **159**

MYRTLE BEACH

ALL SAINTS WACCAMAW CEMETERY The ghost of Alice Flagg has been encountered many times near the Flagg family plot here (see the Hermitage, below). Her marker is inscribed with only one word: Alice. For over a hundred years, romantic teenagers from throughout the south have visited her grave to place flowers there. Some walk backward around her grave thirteen times, hoping to awaken her sleeping spirit. It has even been suggested that some of the bouquets are placed there by the ghost of her dead brother.

(Myrtle Beach is thirty-four miles northeast of Georgetown on U.S. Highway 17. The church cemetery is on Highway 255, about three miles west of Pawleys Island.) **14, 55, 159, 168, 175**

HERMITAGE South Carolina's most famous ghost can be found here. The house was built in 1848 by Dr. Allard Belin Flagg. He lived there with his mother and sixteen-year-old sister Alice. Dr. Flagg was very dominant and protective of his younger sister. When Alice was engaged to a traveling salesman shortly after her debutante ball, she had to wear the ring on a ribbon around her neck to hide it from her brother. But the girl took sick with malaria, and her brother discovered the ring. In a fit of rage, he tore the ribbon from her neck and hid the ring. As Alice lay on her deathbed, all she asked for was her engagement ring, but it was never returned to her. Today, her spirit returns from the dead to look for it. Her face has been seen looking out the round window from her second-floor bedroom and reflected in

mirrors in the house. See All Saints Waccamaw Cemetery, above; and Wachesaw Plantation, below.

(The Hermitage is located on U.S. Highway 17, south of Myrtle Beach at Murrell's Inlet. The mailing address is: The Hermitage, Route 1 Box 29A, Murrell's Inlet, SC 29567. Phone: 803-357-1205.) **14, 55, 101, 159, 162, 165, 172, 175**

HUNTINGTON BEACH STATE PARK The spirit of a ten-year-old boy can still be heard crying for help along a marshy section of beach here. He died in the 1930s when a huge stone crab grabbed his arm and would not let go. The boy drowned when the tide came in, because no one was able to hear his cries above the surf. Locals have named his ghost Crab Boy.

(Follow Highway 17 south for the park. The park is at 16148 Ocean Highway, Murrells Inlet, SC 29576. Phone: 843-237-4440.) **15, 159**

WACHESAW PLANTATION In the 1920s, workers here discovered the bodies of several adult and child Indians buried in a kneeling position. In all, nine corpses were uncovered. They all had grotesque grinning expressions, with beads stuffed into their eye sockets. Archeologists identified them as Waccamaw Indians buried around 1600. Soon after their graves were disturbed, the ghosts of the Indians started appearing to residents of Wachesaw. Strange shadows, enveloped by white mists, moved about the area, and laborers reported the apparitions of Indians fighting over the unearthed relics. The ghostly visions continued for several years. The plantation was a gift to Dr. Allard Belin Flagg when he married Penelope Bentley Ward in 1850. Flagg's mother continued to live in his former residence. See Hermitage, above.

(The plantation is now a private resort community. Follow U.S. Highway 17 in Murrell's Inlet to Wachesaw Road. The plantation is two miles back, next to the Wacca Wache Marina at 1623 Pond Rd., Murrells Inlet, SC 29576. Phone: 888-922-0027. www.wachesaw.com) **159**

NEWBERRY

BUNCOMBE ROAD The infamous Hound of Goshen has chased people and animals along this road for over a century. The ferocious white phantom leaps out of bushes or passes right through wrought-iron gates to pursue trespassers. The animal ghost has been seen most often on Goshen Hill, near the abandoned home of Dr. George Douglas, who is said to have moved away just to be rid of the Hound from Hell.

(The town of Newberry is about thirty miles northwest of Columbia on I-26. The Hound of Goshen has been spotted along a five-mile stretch of the old Buncombe Rd., which runs between the church cemetery and Goshen Hill just outside Newbury.) **164, 165**

PAWLEYS ISLAND

HAGLEY ESTATES The ghosts of a bride, a groom, and a Civil War soldier have been seen walking the roads of this residential community. The soldier, thought long dead, returned to Hagley Plantation on the night of his sweetheart's wedding to another man. The soldier still loved the woman deeply, and he believed that drowning himself in the ocean was the only honorable thing to do. But when the bride found out he committed suicide she, too, jumped off the dock to her death. Out of despair, the groom followed her. The horror of the triple suicide still haunts this old plantation.

(Pawley's Island is on the Grand Strand, eleven miles northeast of Georgetown on U.S. Highway 17. Hagley Estates is off Highway 17, at the south entrance to Pawley's Island. The ghosts are seen along Hagley Boulevard and in the woods around the Hagley Landing. For more information, contact the Georgetown County Chamber of Commerce, 1001 Front St., Georgetown, SC 29440 Phone: 800-777-7705.) **159, 165**

LITCHFIELD PLANTATION MANOR This old manor house is haunted by the ghost of a man who lived and died here before the Civil War. The apparition of Dr. John Hyme Tucker has been seen walking the halls of Litchfield many times by later owners and their employees.

(Litchfield Manor is just outside Georgetown, near All Saints Church. Litchfield Manor, P.O. Box 290, Kings River Rd., Pawley's Island, SC 29585. Phone: 843-237-9121. www.litchfieldplantation.com) **14, 165**

PELICAN INN Sometimes on the second-floor piazza of the Pelican Inn or along the deserted dunes nearby, the thin figure of a man in a gray fishing cap and working clothes is encountered by startled tourists. But locals know and welcome him. He is the Gray Man, a faceless apparition, whose presence always warns of approaching, dangerous storms. His first appearance was followed by a fierce gale in 1804. Thereafter island residents headed for the safety of the mainland whenever they saw him. Gray Man appeared just before the devastating hurricanes of 1806, 1822, 1893, 1916, 1954, 1955, and 1989, and he is credited with saving thousands of lives. He has also appeared at residents' homes and on the beach. Some say he is the ghost of Percival Pawley, the founder of the island; others say he is the ghost of a young man who died here in 1800. The romantic man was riding to see his fiancée on the North Island, when his horse tripped and threw him into a pit of quicksand, where he drowned.

(Evan's Pelican Inn, 506 Myrtle Ave., Pawley's Island, SC 29585. Phone: 843-237-2298.) **5, 68, 72, 86, 90, 164, 165, 175**

SOUTH DAKOTA

BADLANDS

BADLANDS NATIONAL PARK The Badlands are an eternal reminder of the power of the spirit world over human affairs. This is where thousands of Indians came to perform the Ghost Dance, a sacred ceremony that lasted for days and was intended to imbue the tribe members with indomitable spiritual energy. In fact, the power of the Ghost Dance religion prompted the United States Cavalry to try to crush the ceremonies, a plan that led to the Wounded Knee massacre in 1890 (see Pine Ridge Reservation, South Dakota). But the Badlands are still sacred to the Sioux, who originally called the area Mako Sica, or "Land Bad to Travel Through." The constant wind forms surrealistic sculptures out of the soft rock, and the remains of prehistoric animals have been exposed in some areas. Legend says that the barren area was formed in a single day, when the earth heaved forth fire to stop senseless fighting between two tribes that once lived here.

(The Badlands National Monument is in southwestern South Dakota. From I-90, take Exit 110 or 131 to Highway 240, which leads to the Cedar Pass Visitor Center. For information, contact Badlands National Park, P.O. Box 6, Interior, SD 57750. Phone: 605-433-5361. www.nps.gov/badl) **33**

BEAR BUTTE

BEAR BUTTE STATE PARK This uniquely shaped mountain has been worshiped by Indians for thousands of years. In fact, some of the artifacts found here are ten thousand years old. The 400-foot-high, 4,422-foot-long butte resembles a gigantic sleeping bear. The site was a source of spiritual energy for Cheyenne and Sioux medicine men. In fact, the Cheyenne base their entire religion on Bear Butte. They believe the odd-shaped mountain holds the secret to understanding the power of natural creation, which they incorporate in their artwork by making use of the sacred number four. Shamans and their young initiates still hold vision quests, sweat lodges, and sacred ceremonies near the mountain. In 1994, more than two hundred Sioux Indians staged a protest at Bear Butte State Park. They demanded that access to sacred areas on Bear Butte be limited to Native Americans, but park officials declared that it would be impossible to differentiate among the fifty thousand visitors to the site each year.

(Bear Butte State Park is in Meade County in western South Dakota. Take I-90 to Highway 34 East, twenty miles northwest of Rapid City. Follow Highway 34 for four miles to Highway 79. Then take Highway 79 north for three miles into the park. For further information, contact the Bear Butte State Park, Box 688, Sturgis, SD 57785. Phone: 605-347-5240.) **144**

BELLE FOURCHE

BELLE FOURCHE HIGH SCHOOL During nighttime hours, witnesses see a dark apparition moving about in the halls and rooms of this high school. The ghost is said to be an elderly janitor who fell to his death while fixing a light in the gym. Sometimes the light he was working on sways eerily or flickers on and off by itself.

(Belle Fourche High School, 1301 12th Ave., Belle Fourche, SD 57717. Phone: 605-723-3350.) **72**

This memorial to Native Americans is a sacred site in the making. See Crazy Horse Monument, Black Hills, South Dakota (B. A. SCHAFFENBERGER)

BLACK HILLS

CRAZY HORSE MONUMENT This is a sacred site in the making. The memorial to American Indians is being sculpted from a solid granite mountain and will eventually be 563 feet high and 641 feet wide. The project began in 1939, when the shrine to the American presidents was completed at Mount Rushmore. The Sioux considered Mount Rushmore a sacrilege to their sacred Black Hills, and asked sculptor Korzcak Ziolkowski to create a more fitting memorial. The project was dedicated in 1948 and work continues, made possible by donations from around the world. The site includes a large model of the completed project and the Indian Museum of North America, which represents eighty tribes.

(The monument is sixteen miles from Mount Rush-

more on U.S. Highway 16/385. Take U.S. Highway 16 south from Rapid City to U.S. Highway 16/385 South. For information, contact Crazy Horse Monument, Avenue of the Chiefs, Crazy Horse, SD 57730. Phone: 605-673-4681. www.crazyhorse.org) **144**

SPIRIT HILLS Sioux Indians considered the Black Hills to be home to a variety of spirits, and the Lakota Indians believe they are the heart of the planet. At night, the black rocks are said to turn into ghosts that sing unrecognizable songs. Rock paintings made before the Indians arrived teach medicine men how to use the hidden powers to heal and where to find crystal caves full of sacred objects. There are seventy-two crystal caves in the area, of which Jewel Cave is the largest. Only sixty-nine miles of the cave have been explored, and geologists estimate there are hundreds of miles of deep tunnels yet to be discovered. The Sioux consider Harney Peak, which they call the "Hill of Thunder," to be possessed by evil spirits and will not climb it. They say the dreaded Thunderbird often stops there. Another legend tells of a giant white man with a stride of twenty feet, who lives inside the mountain.

(The Black Hills run from western South Dakota to northeastern Wyoming. For information about the area, contact the South Dakota Department of Tourism, Capitol Lake Plaza, 711 E. Wells Ave., Pierre, SD 57501. Phone: 605-773-3301. www.travelsd.com) **33, 144**

DEADWOOD

BULLOCK HOTEL The ghost of Deadwood's first sheriff, Seth Bullock, walks the halls of the hotel he founded. Bullock was sheriff in the 1870s and died here in 1919. Since then over thirty people have seen his ghost. Guests, employees, and managers of this hotel have encountered the tough old sheriff "whose gaze could stop fights."

(Bullock Hotel; 633 Main St. Deadwood, SD 57732. Phone: 605-578-1745. For reservations, call 800-336-1876. www.bullockhotel.com) **72**

GREEN DOOR BROTHEL This Wild West museum is said to be haunted by the voices and footsteps of long-dead hookers and their clients. Townspeople are grateful that the spirits have the decency to stay inside the building.

(Deadwood is in Lawrence County near the Wyoming

border, twelve miles west of Sturgis on U.S. Highway 85. Sturgis is twenty miles northwest of Rapid City on I-90.) **101**

HILL CITY

HILL CITY HIGH SCHOOL This high school building is haunted by the ghost of a student who committed suicide by leaping off the roof. The distraught spirit is seen by students and custodians, and sometimes his disembodied voice is heard. The apparition is sighted most frequently on the anniversary of the the teenager's death.

(Hill City High School, 464 Main St., Hill City, SD 57746. Phone: 605-574-3000.) **72**

MITCHELL

DAKOTA WESLEYAN UNIVERSITY An old dormitory on this university campus is haunted by a former student. The male student jumped to his death during a fire at Graham Hall decades ago, but his frantic spirit still lingers on the grounds.

(Dakota Westleyan University, 1200 W. University, Mitchell, SD 57301. Phone: 605-995-2600.) **72**

PIERRE

SIOUX RIDER Passengers on trains traveling through the prairies surrounding Pierre reported seeing the ghost of a Sioux Indian brave with yellow and red war paint on his face riding a black horse alongside the tracks. The horse seemed to run above the ground, and over the years learned to keep up with the speeding trains. The sightings started in the mid-1800s and continued through the 1940s. Famous artist Frederick Remington reported seeing the Indian rider, and one salesman saw the phantom five times in 1943.

(Pierre is at the center of South Dakota, near the junction of U.S. Highways 14 and 83. The phantom rider has been reported in Hughes, Stanley, Lyman, and Jones counties.) **158**

PINE RIDGE RESERVATION

PINE RIDGE INDIAN RESERVATION In 1889, a Paiute prophet named Wovoka had a vision that was to change history. He prophesied the coming of an Indian messiah who would resurrect dead Indians, bring back the buffalo herds, and restore peace to the land. Each spring, the messiah would renew the youth of all good men so that no one would age past forty. Wovoka's followers performed a dance with the spirits, called the Ghost Dance, in which they fell into a trance and danced until they dropped. (See Badlands National Park, Badlands, South Dakota). The new religion spread rapidly across the Plains and united all the Indian tribes. That is what frightened the white men, who decided it was time to disarm the Indians. One of the earliest operations in this new effort was the rounding up of three hundred Hunkpapa Sioux at Wounded Knee Creek on December 29, 1890. While disarming the assembled Indians, a disturbance broke out and men of the Seventh Cavalry opened fire. Four Hotchkiss guns, each of which fired fifty two-pound explosive shells a minute, were trained on the crowd of men, women, and children. In fighting for their lives, the Indians managed to kill twenty-nine soldiers with their bare hands. Fleeing women were tracked down and slaughtered, and all the bodies were thrown into a single pit. The incident broke the spirit of the Indians and spelled the end of the new religion. Wovoka died in 1932, although some of his ideas survive in Southwest peyote rituals. The land here is considered sacred to the Indian nation that almost grew out of his teachings.

(The Pine Ridge Indian Reservation is south of the Badlands National Park in Shannon County. It is located in southwestern South Dakota off U.S. Highway 18. Wounded Knee Camp is near Wounded Knee Creek on the Pine Ridge Indian Reservation, Manderson, SD 57756.) **62**

RAPID CITY

ALEX JOHNSON HOTEL Built in the 1920s, this stately hotel is haunted by several ghosts. The eighth floor is haunted by the apparition of a woman who is blamed for moving objects and making frightening crying sounds. Sometimes a piano on the floor starts playing by itself. The ghost is thought to be that of a woman who, full of despair, jumped out of her window on her wedding night. The hotel is also haunted by another female suicide victim, a former hotel manager who leapt to her death from the roof in the 1930s. There is also an unidentified ghost who likes to stand at the foot of a particular room's bed at night. The top floor of the hotel, which is used only for storage, is plagued by a poltergeist. Furniture stored there moves around, lights turn on and off, and one employee reported having a chair thrown down the stairwell at him from the top floor doorway. Not surprisingly, several employees have quit because of the ghostly phenomena.

(Alex Johnson Hotel, 523 6th St., Rapid City, SD 57701. Phone: 605-342-1210.) **72**

SIOUX FALLS

SIOUX FALLS COMMUNITY PLAYHOUSE This theater is haunted by a janitor who hanged himself in the rafters. His name was Larry and many people have experienced his presence in the old building. His ghostly footsteps are heard late at night, he turns faucets on and flushes toilets to get attention, and seems to frequent the small balcony area. Next door, the Actors Studio also has a ghost. That building is haunted by a customer killed when it was the Rainbow Bar and Grill. He was dancing with a woman whose husband was in the military during World War II. The soldier came back to surprise his wife and caught them together in the bar. In a fit of rage, the solider killed the man. But the man's former haunt became his present haunt and his ghost lingers on. The happy-go-lucky spirit can sometimes be heard whistling "Twinkle, Twinkle Little Star."

(Community Playhouse, 305 N. Phillips Ave., Sioux Falls, SD 57104. Phone: 605-336-8306. Actors Studio, 315 N. Phillips Ave., Sioux Falls, SD 57104. Phone: 605-336-7418.) **72**

ELLSWORTH AIR FORCE BASE A small antenna building on this modern Air Force base is haunted by an unknown presence. Objects move about on their own, lights go on and off, coffeepots unplug themselves, and strange shadows are seen. Several airmen have reported seeing dark brown eyes staring at them. No face has ever been discerned, but the presence does have a predilection for females. Visiting WAF officers have been patted on the rear by the unseen phantom. Unlike the other antenna buildings that are staffed by one person, this building is always staffed by at least four people, and it is common knowledge that women should steer clear.

(Rapid City is in western South Dakota at the junction of I-90 and U.S. Highway 16. The base is eight miles northeast of town. Ellsworth Air Force Base, Rapid City, SD 57701. Phone: 605-385-1000. www.ellsworth.af. mil) **98**

STEVENS HIGH SCHOOL A ghost nicknamed Sparky haunts the storage room and stage in the auditorium here. The haunted area sits on the spot where a whole family died in a house fire. Sparky is blamed for lighting up chairs with a strange aura and dropping nails from the cement ceiling.

(Stevens High School, 1200 44th St., Rapid City, SD 57702. Phone: 605-394-4025.) **72**

TENNESSEE

ADAMS

JOHN BELL FARM What is widely regarded as America's greatest ghost story began in an isolated farmhouse in 1817. A malicious and powerful force plagued the Bell family for four horrible years and ended in the only murder by a poltergeist ever recorded in the United States. The problems started when John Bell sighted a strange, doglike animal in his cornfield. When he aimed his rifle at it, the creature dissolved into thin air. A few weeks later, the family began hearing scratching on the doors and windows as if something were trying to get in, then gnawing and thumping sounds started coming from inside the house. Within a year, the mysterious presence had grown so strong that the whole farmhouse shook with clashing and clanging sounds, loud garbled utterances, and tortured gasps. Most of the activity seemed to center around thirteen-year-old Elizabeth "Betsy" Bell. While her brothers Richard, Joel, William, and Drewry were harassed by the poltergeist, Betsy suffered brutal yanking on her long hair and invisible blows to her face that left ugly bruises. Another brother, John Junior, and the mother, Lucy Bell, were never bothered by the spirit, which the family called Kate. As Kate grew in strength, John Bell appealed for help to the family minister, James Johnson, who performed an exorcism. When that did not work, the minister organized a committee of parishioners who kept watch over the Bells and documented the supernatural assaults. They dubbed the presence the Bell Witch, and before long the whole countryside descended on the farm, hoping to witness the inexplicable phenomenon. One witness described the voice of the spirit in these words: "It commenced whistling when spoken to, in a low, broken sound, as if trying to speak in a whistling voice, and in this way progressed. The voice gradually gained strength in articulating and soon utterances became distinct in a low whisper so as to be understood in the absence of any other sound." Even future President Andrew Jackson came to the Bell farm to dispel the spirit, although he left in defeat after having dishes and furniture hurled at him. "I wish no more dealings with that torment," he said. The added attention caused the Bell Witch to grow even stronger. Betsy started having seizures and lost consciousness, during which time a disembodied voice thundered through the house: "I am a spirit from everywhere. I am in the air, in houses, any place at any time. I've been created millions of years. I was once very happy, but I have been disturbed and made unhappy." Then the voice would quote from scripture and attack local residents for their immoral behavior.

The voice directed the brunt of its attack on John Bell and declared that he must die. Some say the Bell Witch was the spirit of Kate Batts, a cantankerous woman to whom John Bell had proposed marriage when he lived in Halifax, North Carolina. The woman's body was found near a well on her property in the late 1770s, and soon afterward, John married Lucy Williams and moved to Tennessee. Whatever the true identity of the Bell Witch, John Bell was mercilessly beaten by the unseen foe and his tongue became so swollen that he could barely eat. Before long, he was bedridden and sinking fast. The doctor prescribed a tonic, but the Bell Witch bragged that it switched the tonic with a dark-colored poison. "I've got him this time," it bellowed, "He will never get up from the bed again." John Bell fell into a coma and died on December 21, 1820.

The murderous spirit left the house, promising to return in seven years. It kept its promise and returned in 1827 for two weeks. Then it promised to return to bring havoc to the lives of John Bell's descendants in 107 years. Joel Bell encountered further manifestations in 1852, and his son felt he was visited by the Bell Witch in 1861. But in 1935, the year the witch promised to return, nothing happened, although many of the Bell descendants alive in that year have met violent or unusual deaths. In the 1980s, the apparition of a dark-haired woman was seen gliding over part of the former Bell property, and descendent Carney Bell has reported many strange events at his home in Springfield, Tennessee. A cave on the former Bell land, dubbed the Bell Witch Cave, is still haunted by the sounds of chains rattling and inhuman screams. The apparition of a girl, floating across Highway 41, has been "struck" by several bewildered motorists, and eerie balls of lights have been reported hovering over the old Bell farm.

(The town of Adams is thirty-six miles north of Nashville on U.S. Highway 41. John Bell's farmhouse was demolished by fearful local residents, but the Bell property still exists. It is located in Robertson County along the Red River, near the Kentucky state line. A Tennessee Historical Commission road marker on U.S. Highway 41 commemorates the site of the Bell farm, and a stone monument has been erected in memory of the Bell family. A smooth gravel driveway leads up to where the house once stood. Tours of the Bell Witch Cave, located in a cliff overlooking the Red River, has been conducted by the present owner, W. M. Eden of Adams, Tennessee. John Bell is buried in the cemetery at Adams. Betsy Bell died in 1890 in Panola County, Mississippi, at the age of eighty-six. www.bellwitch.org) **5, 12, 15, 31, 37, 53 (1/92), 55, 57, 58, 68, 69, 72, 78, 162, 166, 183, 186, 188, 189, 204, 223, 228**

ATHENS

TENNESSEE WESLEYAN COLLEGE Students have reported hearing strange voices and seeing dark fig-

ures moving near the spot where two trees grew side by side for 165 years. In 1780, a British officer wounded at the Battle of King's Mountain was found by Cherokee Indians and taken back to their village. He was nursed back to health by the chief's daughter Nocatula and later joined the tribe and married her. He was named Connestoga, meaning "the Oak." When Connestoga was killed by a jealous tribe member, Nocatula took her own life to be at his side through all eternity. The chief buried the lovers together, and in a symbol of undying love placed an acorn in Connestoga's hand and a hackberry in Nocatula's. From these seeds grew two large trees. In 1945, the diseased hackberry tree had to be cut down, and by 1950, the oak had withered and died.

(The town of Athens is in southeastern Tennessee, forty-five miles northeast of Chatanooga off U.S. Highway 11. A metal marker commemorates the spot where the two trees grew. Wesleyan College, Box 40, Athens, TN 37303. Phone: 423-745-5872.) **228**

BIG SPRINGS

NEW HOPE MISSIONARY CHURCH An isolated poltergeist event took place in this church in the late 1800s. During an unusually boring sermon one Sunday, a smoking barrel suddenly materialized inside this church and rolled down the aisle toward the pulpit. Then the barrel totally disappeared, leaving behind only thick smoke. The incident terrified the congregation and frightened away all the horses tied to hitching posts outside the church. No evidence was ever found of the barrel, despite a thorough search. Before long, hundreds of curiosity seekers descended on the small community.

(Big Springs is in Rutherford County in central Tennessee, near Murfreesboro. The original building was torn down in 1901 and a new church erected nearby. New Hope Missionary Church, Big Springs, TN 37037.) **228**

BLOUNTVILLE

SULLIVAN COUNTY NEWS A ghost nicknamed George has haunted this one-story brick building since the late 1940s. During working hours, the front door opens and closes by itself, and the apparition of a man in a neat gray suit has been spotted coming in the back door. One editor fired a gun twice at the ghostly intruder. The ghost has not been identified.

(Blountville is in Sullivan County in the northeastern tip of Tennessee. Take the Highway 126 south exit, five miles south of Bristol on I-81. Sullivan County News, Main St. Blountville, TN 37617. Phone: 423-323-5700.) **55, 134**

BOLIVAR

PARRAN HOUSE The ghost of a former owner is still seen rocking quietly in his favorite rocking chair on the porch of this quaint old house, nicknamed the "Wedding Cake" by locals. Before Dave Parran died in 1936 (at the age of eighty-six), he spent all his time porch-rocking and greeting neighbors as they passed in front of his house in which he had lived for seventy-five years. His ghost has also been heard rummaging through the house in the late hours of the night.

(Bolivar is in southwestern Tennessee, sixty miles east of Memphis on U.S. Highway 64. The single-story Wedding Cake House is on Bills St. Dave Parran's old rocker still sits on the porch. Bolivar is in Hardeman County in southwestern Tennessee.) **228**

CHAPEL HILL

L & N RAILROAD CROSSING Hundreds of witnesses have reported seeing a mysterious ball of light that travels in a straight line along the tracks here. Once, it passed right through the body of a young man who was watching from alongside the tracks with some friends. The light hit him with a thud and paralyzed him for a few seconds. In the 1970s, four witnesses saw the light pass through a car stalled on the tracks. The light always grows dimmer when it moves through an object. The only documented tragedies in the area are the Ketchum murder of 1940, in which a mother of two disappeared from her home. The suspect in the case committed suicide and the woman's body was found a year later. Tales of a flagman decapitated near the crossing have never been documented.

(Chapel Hill is located in central Tennessee, fifteen miles south of Murfreesboro on U.S. Alternate Highway 31. The light is seen near a dirt road that takes a sharp dip as it crosses the L & N tracks west of town. Witnesses usually face north as the light approaches.) **228**

CHARLESTON

LOST MONK The hooded ghost of a Catholic monk haunted this town for many years after he was killed in a train wreck. The accident happened during the Flood of 1867, when the rising waters of the Hiwassee River washed out the tracks outside of town. A passenger train derailed and fell into the ravine. There was no hospital in Charleston, so the injured were taken to homes and a morgue was set up in the train depot. Dozens died despite the efforts of a local doctor who worked until he dropped. The body of a young Catholic monk from Baltimore was never recovered, and only the doctor knew the reason for his disappearance. He had stripped the flesh from the man's dead body, boiled and bleached the bones, and made a skeleton to hang in his office. It was not long before the monk's ghost came looking for his bones. Most of the sightings of the hooded ghost were in the building where the doctor's office was located. Dr. J. Lake McClary, who became the town's doctor many years later, encountered the dismal ghost on several occasions. When the building was demolished in 1932, crews found a brown habit and rosary hanging from a stud between walls.

(Charleston is south of the Hiwassee River in southeast Tennessee, thirty-one miles northeast of Chatanooga on U.S. Highway 11. The train derailed near the present Coon Hunters Association Building.) **228**

CHATANOOGA

CHICKAMAUGA-CHATANOOGA MILITARY PARK Old Green Eyes is the name of a demon who hides in the bushes in this park. The humanoid creature has glowing green-orange eyes with fanglike teeth. It wears a cape, which is partially hidden by its waist-length hair. The ghoul was first seen prowling among the corpses after Civil War battles. Since then, the phantom has been reported by both rangers and park visitors, and in the 1970s it caused two separate automobile accidents when it was spotted alongside a road. Old Green Eyes is most often encountered on Snod-grass Hill, site of a bloody Civil War battle. In September 1863, over 35,000 men died there in three days of fighting. The ghost of a lady in white is also seen roaming the grounds. She is said to be searching for her sweetheart, who died in the carnage.

(Chatanooga is on the Georgia border in southeast Tennessee. The park is ten miles south of Chatanooga on U.S. Highway 27. Phone: 706-866-9241. www.nps.gov/chch) **15, 66 (4/83)**

CLEVELAND

CRAIGMILES MAUSOLEUM, The white stone of this impressive mausoleum is stained with blotches of dark red, which locals say bled from the stone itself in response to the tragedies suffered by the Craigmiles family. The first stains were noticed after the interment of Nina, the seven-year-old daughter of John Henderson Craigmiles and Adelia Thompson Craigmiles. She died on October 18, 1871, when the carriage in which she was riding plowed into the side of a passing train. Another catacomb in the mausoleum contains the body of the Craigmiles' infant son, who died shortly after he was born. The father died of blood poisoning in 1899, and his wife joined him when she was struck by an automobile in 1928.

(The city is located in the extreme southeast corner of Tennessee, twenty-three miles northeast of Chatanooga on I-75. The mausoleum is located in the churchyard. St. Luke's Episcopal Church, 320 Broad St., Cleveland, TN 37311. Phone: 423-476-5541.) **228**

DUCKTOWN

COPPERHILL MINE ROAD On the road leading from the Copperhill Mine to Chatanooga, a phantom wagon train has appeared. The drivers are said to be the ghosts of men who hauled copper ore down this old trail. Several of the drivers were ambushed and killed by robbers.

(Ducktown is in the extreme southeast tip of Tennessee. The town is located thirty-nine miles from Cleveland on U.S. Highway 64/74. The old mine road is south of town off Highway 68.) **166**

ISABELLA COPPER MINES The cries of desperate miners wailing in unison can sometimes be heard coming from the bottom of this abandoned mine. The men died here in the 1890s, when a fresh-air pump failed.

(The mines are near Copperhill on the Georgia border south of Ducktown.) **166**

ELIZABETHTON

WATAUGA RIVER BRIDGE The ghoulish phantom of a hooded figure in a monk's robe, with a skull for a face, haunts the area under this old bridge. Reports date back to the 1930s, when two young lovers seeking solitude under the bridge were stabbed to death by an unidentified madman. For the last sixty years, people have encountered an evil presence lurking in the shadows under the bridge and near Stony Creek.

(Elizabethton is in the eastern tip of Tennessee, four miles east of Johnson City on Highway 91. The steel-girder bridge spans the Watauga River on the road between Elizabethton and Watauga Lake.) **147**

FARMINGTON

MURRELL'S HIDEOUT A simple house here served as the meeting place for the infamous John Murrell outlaw gang. In an argument over money one night, a member of the gang was shot and killed. Nobody could ever wash out the bloodstains off the wall, although a later resident, Mrs. W. C. Ransom, hid them with wallpaper. During a thunderstorm in 1968, the house caught fire and burned down, but the outlaw's ghost is said to haunt the premises. See Natchez, Mississippi.

(Farmington is a small town in Williamson county in central Tennessee. The ruins of the house, including a stone fireplace, still exist in the forest south of Farmington.) **228**

FRANKLIN

CARNTON MANSION This unique house, with seven square columns in the front and the back, is one of the most haunted places in Tennessee. Rebel yells and the dark shadows of Civil War soldiers are just a few of the phenomena reported here. Perhaps the source is the hastily dug graveyard not far from the house. Legend says that there were so many dead bodies stacked up that they stood erect next to each other in a ghastly column. The grounds contain the remains of as many as 1,700 Confederate soldiers killed at the Battle of Franklin on November 30, 1864. One of them still walks across the back porch into the yard, and sometimes the apparition of a woman in white is seen at the same location. The floating head of a former cook has appeared in the hall near the kitchen, and another soldier has been seen in one of the bedrooms. Yet another ghost of Carnton Mansion is said to be a young girl murdered here in the 1840s.

(Franklin is fifteen miles south of Nashville on Hills-boro Road, U.S. Highway 431. The Carnton Mansion is at 1345 Carnton Lane in Franklin, TN 37064. Phone: 615-794-0903. www.carnton.org) **14, 101, 168**

CARTER HOUSE The ghost of Annie Vick Carter, one of the daughters of the man who built this mansion in 1830, has been seen running through the upstairs hall and down the stairway. The ghost of a son has been seen several times in the bedroom where he died. Tod Carter was mortally wounded on the lawn of Carter House while fighting for the Confederacy at the bloody Battle of Franklin. Over 8,500 men died in a single day on the lands surrounding Carter House.

(Carter House is a national historic landmark on U.S. Highway 31 south of Franklin. Carter House, 1140 Columbia Ave., Box 555, Franklin, TN 37064. Phone: 615-791-1861. www.carter-house.org) **14, 101**

GORDONSBURG

MERIWETHER LEWIS PARK The spirit of the governor of the Louisiana Territory, Meriwether Lewis, is still felt by psychics visiting here, and his mysterious death on October 11, 1809, is still controversial. His body was found outside Grinder's Stand, a family's log cabin which offered shelter to travelers. Meriwether was taking his memoirs to Washington where they were to be published. A mule had run off with Meriwether's papers, and out of frustration he is said to have shot himself in the side and again in the head. He lingered on the edge of life all night. A terrified woman inside the cabin heard him mutter, "It's so hard to die." But years later, evidence surfaced that he might have been murdered during a robbery. His gold watch turned up in Louisiana. A suddenly rich Grinder family bought land and slaves in western Tennessee. Finally, in 1839, Meriwether's relatives received a trunk containing his lost papers. His mysterious death took place on a section of the fabled Natchez Trace. See Natchez, Mississippi.

(Gordonsburg is in south-central Tennessee, fifteen miles west of Columbia on U.S. Highway 412. A round granite pillar marks Lewis's grave. Ruins of the Grinder's house are 230 yards south of the monument. The park is located off the Natchez Parkway outside Gordonsburg.

Meriwether Lewis Park, Hwy 20 Natchez Trace Parkway Hohenwald, TN 38462. Phone: 601-680-4025. TN 38465.) **228**

HANCOCK COUNTY

MELUNGEONS The lost race of Melungeons, who have copper-red skin, narrow faces, and fine, straight hair, lives in the mountains here. Scholars have linked them with the Lost Tribes of Israel, the Phoenicians, and the Mayans, but clan members trace their ancestry to Sir Walter Raleigh's colony on Roanoke Island. See Fort Raleigh National Historic Site, Roanoke Island, North Carolina.

(The Melungeons live in the southern Appalachian Mountains of Hancock County, along the Virginia border in northeastern Tennessee.) **57**

JOHNSON CITY

EAST TENNESSEE STATE UNIVERSITY The specter of Sidney Gilbreath has been seen by custodians and students in Gilbreath Hall. He was the founding president of the university, which opened in 1911. His red-glowing ghost has been seen looking out of the attic window and moving through the building, turning off lights and closing windows. Invisible footsteps follow maintenance workers in Mathes Hall, and the ghost of a former English teacher haunts Burleson Hall. She taught Shakespeare there for decades, before she put a gun to her head and killed herself in the early 1970s. Ever since, Christine Burleson has haunted the building where she spent so many years. Her spirit is said to have taken over a portrait of her father, which hangs on the second floor. The painting's distinctly feminine eyes follow all who walk by. For an entire month in 1988, her moans inexplicably filled an office in the building. Another campus building, Cooper Annex, was haunted for forty-five years by an unusual entity. It was described as a female version of James Walters Carter, the only son of George and Mayetta Carter. The Carters had always wanted a girl, and they seem to have gotten one in the ghost of their son. Jimmy's ghostly presence was so strong in the building that the university had it demolished in 1984.

(Johnson City is in the extreme eastern corner of Tennessee. The town is located at the junction of I-81 and U.S. Highway 11E/321. East Tennessee State University, Johnson City, TN 37614. Phone: 423-929-4213.) **147**

JOHN SEVIER CENTER On December 24, 1989, a fire in this apartment hotel killed sixteen elderly people. Their ghosts continued to haunt the building for several years. The apparition of a white-haired old lady has been seen waving, in slow motion, from a window on the fourth floor. Another spirit, named the Watch-Ghost, appears to people who try to steal things from empty rooms in the building. The luxury hotel was built in 1924 by financier John Sevier. It became a retirement home in 1978.

(The building is at 141 E. Market St., Johnson City, TN 37601. Phone:423-926-3161) **147**

MOUNTAIN HOME VETERANS HOSPITAL An old soldier dressed in a uniform of the Spanish-American War walks the roads on the grounds of this veteran's hospital. Mountain Home was built in 1903 to provide care for Civil War veterans. Memorial Hall Theater is haunted by several modern ghosts, including a former projectionist and actors who move about on the empty stage.

(Veteran's Affairs Medical Center at Mountain Home, P.O. Box 4000, Mountain Home, TN 37610. Phone: 423-926-1171.) **147**

TIPTON-HAYNES FARM RECREATION AREA A cave in this park is a hotbed of ghostly manifestations. On summer nights, the glow of ethereal campfire is seen, and around it ghostly figures gather. They are the revenants of pioneers long dead, and of Indians who sought shelter within the widemouthed cave. Neolithic people probably used the cave as far back as 12,000 B.C. The apparitions of Cherokee Indians are reported here, as well as members of the James Needham expedition of 1673. Even the ghost of Daniel Boone has been seen stoking a fire in front of the cave entrance.

(Tipton-Haynes Farm is a historic park operated by the Johnson City Recreation Department. It is located off the old Erwin Highway at 2620 S. Roan St., Johnson City, TN 37605. The cave is one hundred feet east of the restored farmhouse. Phone: 423-926-3631. www.tipton-haynes.org) **147**

JOHNSON COUNTY

FIDDLERS ROCK This rock outcropping, also known as Screaming Rock, makes an eerie, high-pitched screeching sound on cold winter days. Legend says that the sounds are the ghost of Old Martin playing tunes on his fiddle. He was such a good fiddle player that he could stop babies from crying, make mules sing, cure ailing people, and charm snakes. He used to sit on this ledge and play for the snakes. Huge rattlesnakes would crawl out from under rocks, mesmerized by his music. But one night Old Martin never returned from the ledge. A search party found his swollen body on a trail near the ledge, his skin covered with dozens of fang marks.

(Johnson County is in the extreme eastern tip of Tennessee. Fiddlers Rock is located over a precipice near the top of Stone Mountain in Johnson County between Mountain City and Laurel Bloomery, off Highway 91. www. prarieghosts.com/fiddler.html) **121, 171, 228**

SONGO HOLLOW This area has been considered haunted by the ghosts of a man and his wife since the 1860s. Samuel Songo lived with his wife in a small cabin here. He was shot and killed by someone hiding in the underbrush, for reasons never determined. On realizing her husband was dead, Samuel's wife took a hunting knife and plunged it into her abdomen. She bled to death in the doorway.

(Songo Hollow is a large gap near Roan's Creek in Doe Mountain, which is located in eastern Johnson County. A ruin of stones on a little knoll is all that is left of Samuel Songo's cabin.) **121**

KINGSPORT

LONG ISLAND An Indian curse made this sacred island unfit for white man and forever home to the ghosts of Cherokee braves. Their ancient campfires illuminate young warriors dancing in circles, as reported by modern visitors to the island. But white men should beware: The curse says that no white man will ever find peace on the island. Since 1796, when the Indians gave up the island, it has been home to violence, larceny, and murder. Even today, police are mystified by the extremely high crime rate here.

(Kingsport is on the Virginia border in the eastern corner of Tennessee, nineteen miles northwest of Johnson City on I-181. Long Island is in the Holston River at Kingsport, in upper east Tennessee. Half the island is a national historic park, but the other half is occupied by the Tennessee Eastman Waste Disposal Plant.) **147**

NETHERLAND INN ROAD The phantom of an antique Ford haunts this road. The car is seen lying turned over in the middle of the road. Sometimes the apparition of Hugh Hamblen is also spotted, waving other drivers to slow down and be careful. But Hamblen was not driving that evening. He was struck and killed by the car one foggy night in 1922 as he walked back along the road where his son had been injured in a previous accident.

(The road runs along the waterfront in Kingsport, near the Tennessee Eastman Plant.) **147**

ROTHERWOOD MANSION In the last 125 years, the apparition of Rowena Ross has been seen by literally hundreds of people. Rowena never recovered from the death of her true love, a man who drowned in the Holston River on the day they were to be married. She went on to marry two years later, but that husband died of yellow fever. Ten years later she married again. When her only daughter was just six years old, Rowena committed suicide. Her ghost, known as the Lady in White, is most often spotted near the front flower bed or on the riverbank searching for her drowned fiancé. The mansion was built by Rowena's father Frederick in 1818. By 1847, he had lost all his money and was forced to sell the mansion to Joshua Phipps, a cruel slave owner. It is said that Joshua was suffocated when a swarm of flies came in his bedroom window and landed on his face, but his funeral was even more horrific. The horses drawing his casket to the cemetery were somehow unable to move forward, as if they were pulling a great weight. The sky suddenly darkened and a great black dog jumped out from under the caisson canopy, terrifying scores of people attending the funeral. Ever since, the hound from hell is heard howling near Rotherwood Mansion on stormy nights.

(The historic private mansion overlooks the Holston River in Kingsport. www.prairieghosts.com/kings. html) **147**

MEMPHIS

BELLEBOIS MANSION The apparition of Raike Gaston, known as the "Longest Boy in Tennessee," has been seen along roads, canebrakes, woods, and savannas throughout the state. His tall figure appears just long enough to carve his trademark, a rake head, into tree bark. Raike was born in 1815, the illegitimate son of gambler Forbes Gaston and his mistress Nan Raike. The boy ran away at the age of twelve, but he was already the size of man in height and other proportions,

and he had a man's appetites. By the time the boy was eighteen, he stood six feet ten inches tall and had sired a whole crop of illegitimate children. At the age of twenty-five, Raike was a living symbol of freedom and the Dionysian lifestyle, although he spent much of his time hiding out from irate husbands. When he was twenty-nine, he was informed that he had inherited his father's plantation estate in Memphis, called Bellebois, but the itinerant lad turned it over to a distant uncle. Raike froze to death in a ditch near Osceola, when he was in his thirties. His free spirit continues to roam the countryside near Memphis and along the Mississippi River, where many still catch a glimpse of the barefoot boy, with no shirt, wearing tight butternut britches.

(Memphis is in the extreme southwestern tip of Tennessee. The old mansion is a private residence in Shelby County, outside of Memphis.) **15**

BRINKLEY FEMALE COLLEGE This woman's college was haunted by the ghastly phantom of a little girl with sunken eyes and unkempt hair. Wearing a moldy, wet, pink dress, the apparition first appeared on February 21, 1871, to student Clara Robinson, who was practicing piano in the music room. The ghost followed her when Clara went screaming into the halls. One week later the ghost appeared to the same woman, as well as teacher Jackie Boone and another student. The child ghost told them of a large glass jar buried under a stump at the front of the building, but the apparition warned them not to open the jar for sixty days and to keep it at the home of Clara's father, a lawyer. They dug up the jar and waited. Meanwhile, news spread of the ghost. People were afraid to go out at night, and sightings of the Girl in Pink were coming in from as far away as Missouri. The jar was to be opened in public at the Greenlaw Opera House. However, a few days before the big event, a thief accosted Mr. Robinson in his backyard and threatened to kill him unless he told him where the jar was hidden. The jar was hid in the privy in the backyard, and the thief made off with it. The only verification of the strange events is in county records. The college was formerly a mansion built by Colonel Davis, who sold the property after the death of his young daughter, Lizzie.

(The building that housed the college was on DeSoto St., now South Fifth St., in central Memphis. The mansion was demolished in 1972. Brinkley's pink ghost has been reported throughout the city.) **175, 228**

The ghost of Elvis has been seen all over the world, or so it seems, and he has not neglected Graceland, his former home. See Graceland, Memphis, Tennessee (STEVE HEALEY)

GRACELAND The ghost of Elvis Presley has been seen wandering the grounds here. In fact, his active spirit has been reported in distant places all over the world, and hundreds of people claim to be in almost constant contact with him. Sociologists have commented half seriously that the phenomenon could be the beginning of a new religion. Over seven hundred thousand visitors a year tour his former home. Elvis died in his bathtub at Graceland on August 16, 1977. He is buried in the Meditation Garden along with his mother, father, and grandmother.

(The Presley residence is at 3734 Elvis Presley Blvd., Memphis, TN 38116. Phone: 901-332-3322. www.elvis-presley.com) **72, 81**

ORPHEUM THEATER The ghost of a twelve-year-old girl killed in a car accident near this theater in 1921 seems to be attracted to the site. She is most often seen sitting in Seat C-5 and wearing a white dress. Actor Yul Brynner saw her when he performed here in *The King and I*. In 1977, the cast of *Fiddler on the Roof* saw her so many times that they held a séance in the balcony to contact her spirit. Audience members saw her apparition during an organ concert in April 1979. Employees have gotten used to working around the ghost of the little girl named Mary and take all the strange events and harmless pranks in stride. When a parapsychology class from Memphis University investigated the site in 1979, they found evidence of at least six other ghosts haunting the old playhouse.

(The little girl was run down on Beale St. Orpheum Theater, 203 South Main St., Memphis, TN 38173. Further information is available from the Memphis Development Foundation, P.O. Box 3370, Memphis, TN 38173. Phone: 901-525-3000. www.orpheum-memphis. com) **101, 133, 175**

MURFREESBORO

STONES RIVER NATIONAL BATTLEFIELD The ghosts of Civil War soldiers killed in a bloody battle here in January 1863 roam the grounds. Strange feelings and shadowy figures are most often encountered by park rangers and visitors at tour stops four and six. One ghost stands behind a clump of bushes, then moves out into plain view, only to fall to the ground and disappear. He is assumed to be a soldier shot while trying to surrender.

(Murfreesboro is twenty-seven miles southeast of Nashville. The 350-acre park and museum is located at 3501 Old Nashville Highway, Murfreesboro, TN 37129. Phone: 615-893-9501. www.nps.gov/stri) **15**

NASHVILLE

HAWKINS HOUSE The John Hawkins family witnessed a variety of poltergeist phenomena, including loud banging sounds and moving objects, when they lived in this house in the 1960s.

(The house is a private residence, at 1627 Ninth Ave. North, Nashville, TN 97208.) **72, 101**

OLD STONE FORT PARK

OLD STONE FORT ARCHEOLOGICAL PARK This sacred site was settled by an unknown people in 1500 B.C. The site was not a fortress but a religious center of great significance to the prehistoric people. Stone walls four feet tall surround forty acres of hallowed ground. A ditch connecting Big and Little Duck Rivers encircled the entire site with water. The entrance lines exactly with the sunrise of the winter solstice. Scientists suspect the land was considered sacred even before the fort was built.

(The site is five miles southwest of Manchester in south-central Tennessee. Take Highway 55 west from I-24 and follow the signs. Old Stone Fort Archeological Park, 732 Stone Fort Dr., Manchester, TN 37355. Phone: 931-723-5073.) **99**

PIGEON FORGE

PIGEON RIVER According to Cherokee legend, a race of Little People live in the forests along the banks of the Pigeon River and the streams that flow into it. The mysterious race of people are said to stay young forever and never grow larger than a child. See Hickory Nut Gorge, North Carolina.

(Pigeon Forge is in eastern Tennessee in Sevier County, twenty-five miles southeast of Knoxville on U.S. Highway 321/441.) **164**

PINSON MOUNDS

PINSON MOUNDS STATE ARCHEOLOGICAL AREA This sacred site was constructed by unknown people around A.D. 1. The most remarkable feature is Saul's Mound. At seventy-two feet, it is the one of the tallest mounds in North America and probably took over three years to build. Gigantic oak trees now grow on the oval-shaped mound. The oval shape is found throughout the park, which leads some to speculate that the site was a mystical place used for rejuvenation ceremonies. Further evidence for this view comes from the positioning of Ozier's Pyramid, which is perfectly aligned with the sunrise of the spring equinox.

(The site is in western Tennessee, northeast of Memphis. Take Exit 45 south from I-40 into the park. Pinson Mounds State Archeological Area, 460 Ozier Rd., Route 1 Box 316, Pinson, TN 38366. Phone: 901-988-5614. www.state.tn.us/environment/parks/pinson) **99**

REELFOOT LAKE

KALOPIN Kalopin was a clubfooted Chickasaw Indian chief. In 1811, he asked Copish, chief of the Choctaws, for the hand of his daughter in marriage. When the Choctaw chief refused, Kalopin returned to the camp at night and kidnaped his daughter. As Kalopin approached his own village, he heard the beating drums of welcoming ceremonies. Then, he heard a deafening roar as the earth shook beneath his feet. Within minutes a mountainous wave of water swept the valley and inundated the settlement. The devastating earthquake created a lake that stands to this day, and along its banks people still hear the tom-toms welcoming Kalopin and his new bride. The haunting sounds come from deep in the lake named after the unlucky warrior. In Chickasaw, Kalopin means "clubfoot" or "reelfoot."

(Reelfoot Lake is in the northwest corner of Tennessee, west of Union City on Highway 22.) **228**

RUGBY

HISTORIC RUGBY This utopian community was founded in 1880 by the English social reformer Thomas Hughes. The ghostly presence of its former residents has been detected many times by employees and tourists here. Room 13 of the old Chaucer's Tabard Inn was haunted by the ghosts of the married couple that managed it. The husband slit the throat of his wife as she lay sleeping in their bed, then took his own life with a gun. Years later, when the inn caught fire and burned down, his suffering spirit cried out from the room, which was the last to be consumed by the flames. Some of the furniture from Room 13 was saved and moved into the new inn, called Newbury House. Guests there have reported being awakened by the figure of a man leaning over their beds. In the 1960s, another ghost started to make itself felt at Roslyn, one of the private residences in the compound. The apparition of a hawk-nosed woman in an old-fashioned dress walks the halls and sobs. The glowing ghost of a tall man wearing a shroud has been reported in an upstairs bedroom. A phantom carriage with four black horses and a ghostly driver is sometimes seen rolling along overgrown High Street, which runs in front of Roslyn. A snoring ghost who pulls the covers off freshly made beds has been detected in the Kingstone Lisle House. The ghost of Eduard Bertz, a perfectionist German librarian, is sensed during the twilight hours in the Thomas Hughes Free Public Library. The original seven thousand volumes of the Victorian Collection, which he organized from 1881 to 1883, are still housed at the library.

(Historic Rugby is in northeastern Tennessee. Take U.S. Highway 27 north from I-40 at Harriman. Follow U.S. Highway 27 to Elgin and go west seven miles on Highway 52 to Rugby. The town is near the Big South Fork National River Recreation Area. The library is on Central Ave. in Rugby. The mailing address is Historic Rugby Incorporated., P.O. Box 8, Rugby, TN 37733. Phone: 423-628-2441. www.historicrugby.org) **15, 72**

SAVANNAH

CHERRY MANSION In June 1976, several witnesses saw the apparition of an elderly gentleman dressed in a white suit walk up to a metal historical marker in front of this old mansion. The man carefully studied the marker, then disappeared into thin air. The house itself has been the site of weird noises such as heavy footsteps moving across the front porch, and the ghost of a Union officer has been seen peering out an upstairs window.

(Savannah is located in the southwestern part of the state. It is located 130 miles east of Memphis on U.S. Highway 64. The town is about ten miles across the river from the Shiloh National Park Battleground. Cherry Mansion is a private residence in Savannah.) **228**

SEWANEE

UNIVERSITY OF THE SOUTH The ghost of a headless student, called the "Phantom Gownsman," roams the buildings on this campus. Students who have been inducted into the Order of the Gownsmen wear dark gowns as part of their academic attire, and the ghost is thought to be a member of the group decapitated in a car accident many years ago. He was living in the old Wyndcliff Hall at the time, but his ghost has been spotted outside Forensic Hall, in St. Lukes Hall, and at other places on campus. His floating head is said to appear during exam periods. One student described the head bouncing down stairs and counting each step as it went.

(The town of Sewanee is northwest of Chattanooga in southeastern Tennessee. Take I-24 to Exit 134 and follow U.S. Highway 41A/64 west six miles. University of the South, 735 University Ave., Sewanee, TN 37375. Phone: 931-598-5931. www.sewanee.edu) **121**

SHELBYVILLE

EAKIN HOUSE The ghost of Lucretia Pearson Eakin haunted this house for nearly forty years. She lived in the house with her husband for half a century and died at home in the 1890s. Lawyer Ernest Coldwell bought the house after her death and lived there for many years with his wife and daughter. Lucretia's ghost became so familiar to the family, they called her Aunt Crecy. She helped them care for the house by straightening pictures or shutting windows just before it rained. In 1931 a fire destroyed her old sitting room on the second floor, and her ghost has not been seen since.

(Shelbyville is in south-central Tennessee, fifty-five miles southeast of Nashville on U.S. Alternate Highway 41. The former two-story Eakin residence is a now one-story brick house at 610 North Jefferson St., Shelbyville, TN 37160.) **228**

SURGOINSVILLE

LONG DOG The eerie phantom of a long white hound has been seen near here. Legend says it belonged to a family of settlers passing through eastern Tennessee in the early 1830s. While they were camped one night, notorious outlaw John Murrell (see Farmington, Tennessee; and Natchez, Mississippi) and his gang sneaked up and killed everyone in the party. Murrell even strangled a large hound that tried to protect the family. A few years later, travelers along a stage route that ran from Bristol to Nashville began reporting the glowing ghost of a dog that ran out from under a white oak tree near Surgoinsville and followed alongside the wagons. A few times it even jumped up into the back of moving wagons, but the dog always vanished from sight at a particular spot in the road. The luminous animal was sighted so many times that people started to look for it. Once, a man swung at the dog with a fence rail, which passed right through it.

(Surgoinsville is on the Holston River in the northeastern corner of Tennessee, eighteen miles southwest of Kingsport on U.S. Highway 11W. The white oak tree still stands on a small hill next to the road near Surgoinsville.) **228**

SWEETWATER

LOST SEA CAVE This ancient cave was considered sacred to the Cherokee Indians, who used a cavernous chamber deep inside the mountain for secret ceremonies. The massive cave contains the largest underground lake in the world. No one knows for sure how deep it is, but the main body of water is 800 feet long by 220 feet wide. So far, over thirteen acres of the Lost Sea have been explored. The cave was home to giant Pleistocene jaguars eight feet long and weighing over five hundred pounds. The bones and tracks of one of the twenty-thousand-year-old cats were discovered here in 1939.

(Sweetwater is in Loudon County in eastern Tennessee, thirty miles southwest of Knoxville on U.S. Highway 11. Lost Sea Cave is open to the public. It is located at 140 Lost Sea Rd., Sweetwater, TN 37874. Phone: 423-337-6616. www.thelostsea.com.) **57**

WARTRACE

HOTEL OVERALL This old hotel is home to a white apparition that has appeared on the stairway. Manager George Wright reports that the ghost has been seen by employees and at least one guest.

(The town of Wartrace is located in Bedford County in south-central Tennessee, midway between Shelbyville and Manchester on Highway 64. The hotel is on Main St. Hotel Overall, P.O. Box 266, Wartrace, TN 37183. Phone: 423-389-6407.) **72, 101**

TEXAS

ALICE

U.S. HIGHWAY 281 The ghost of a lady in black haunts a section of this modern highway. She is Leonora Rodriquez, wife of Don Raul Ramos, who lived in a hacienda at Falfurrias in the 1700s. At the time the area was a flat chaparral cut by a single dirt road. Leonora was hanged from a large oak along that road, by her husband's vaqueros. Don Paul had accused the woman of becoming pregnant by another man. Now her spirit haunts the place where she died. The ghost is seen along the road wearing the same black dress she wore the night she was murdered. Numerous motorists have pulled off the road to help the forlorn phantom, only to see her vanish.

(Alice is in Jim Wells County in southern corner of Texas, thirty-one miles west of Corpus Christi on Highway 44. The Lady in Black is most often reported on U.S. Highway 281 at the Farm Rd. 141 underpass, south of Alice.) **202**

ALPINE

DELORES MOUNTAIN This mountain is named for a tall, dark-haired woman whose ghost is seen here. She was working as a servant girl in a large house outside Laredo in the 1880s when she fell in love with a sheepherder, who spent many weeks away from her tending sheep in the mountains. While they were apart, the two lovers lit brush fires to communicate their love over the great distance. Unfortunately the Apaches also saw the fires. They attacked and killed the sheepherder. After her lover's murder, Delores still climbed the mountain to light her fire, hoping against hope to see a reply in the far-off peaks. She did so until she was old and gray, and her ghost continues to kindle a flickering flame to this day.

(Alpine is in Brewster County in the southwestern corner of Texas, at the junction of U.S. Highway 67/90 and Highway 118. Delores Mountain is near Fort Davis, twenty-three miles north of Alpine on Highway 118.) **202**

FORT DAVIS NATIONAL HISTORIC SITE The ghost of lovely Alice Walpole has been seen here since Civil War days. In 1861, when this fort was being used by Confederate troops, the young Alabama beauty disappeared. She was searching for white roses along Limpia Creek when she was abducted by Apache Indians. No body was ever found, but her ghost started showing up a few days later. She was most often seen outside the quarters where the women did their needlework. The mysterious odor of roses presages her appearance. Sometimes, even now, out-of-season white roses are found within the compound.

(The old fort is in north Fort Davis on Highway 17 and can be reached by I-10 on the north or U.S. Route 67/90 on the south. Fort Davis, P.O. Box 1456, Fort Davis, TX 79734. Phone: 915-426-3224. www. fortdavis.com) **163**

MARFA LIGHTS These famous floating balls of light have been seen in the mountains near here for over 150 years. The greenish-yellow lights appear just above the horizon at dusk and sometimes split into two or more separate lights. Apache legends say the lights are the spirit of Chief Alsate, who was condemned to wander the area after he offended a tribal god. (See Los Chisos Mountains, Big Bend, Texas) White settlers attributed the lights to the ghostly lanterns of a family that got lost in the wilderness in the 1850s. Marfa was established in 1881 as a watering stop on the Texas and New Orleans Railroad, and the first modern sighting was reported by a cowboy, Robert Ellison, in 1883. Recently, a driver on U.S. Highway 90 reported that one of the glowing balls entered his speeding car through an open window and stayed in the automobile for two miles. In July 1989, *Unsolved Mysteries* set up sophisticated monitoring equipment at the site and monitored the lights, but all their guest scientists could agree upon was that the phenomenon was not manmade. Mutual UFO Network (MUFON) researcher Dennis Stacy has cataloged reports in which the lights seem to display intelligent behavior, such as following people or vehicles.

(The town of Marfa is in Presidio County, twenty-six miles west of Alpine on U.S. Highway 67/90. The lights have appeared in an area southwest of Chinati Mountain, on Mitchell Flat, near Twin Peaks, and over the flat prairie north of the Cuesto Del Burro Mountains. A roadside plaque on U.S. Highway 90, eight miles east of Marfa, commemorates the mysterious phenomenon. An abandoned Air Force base is near the site. The best viewing locations are near the U.S. Highway 90 plaque, on the large plateau just east of Marfa and west of Alpine, and on Mitchell Flat southwest of Marfa. www.ghosts. org/ghostlights/marfa.html) **15, 68, 126 (11/87), 150, 175, 194, 202, 231**

ANGLETON

BAILEY'S PRAIRIE This section of Texas prairie was named for the ghost that haunts it. Brit Bailey spent his life trying to homestead the land here, and before he died he asked to be buried upright, so he could continue walking the land in the afterlife. Since his death in 1833, his ghost has been spotted many times doing just that. Settlers in the area claimed he sometimes peered into their windows in the early evening hours. After 1850, his spirit took the form of a glowing ball of light floating over the prairie. Brit Bailey's Light is still seen today.

(Angleton is thirty-three miles south of Houston on County Road 521. Bailey's Prairie is five miles west of the town of Angleton in Brazoria County.) **194**

AURORA

MASONIC CEMETERY According to some reports, there is an extraterrestrial being buried in this cemetery. In 1897, *The Dallas Morning News* published an article saying that a UFO sailed across the downtown section of Aurora and crashed into a windmill on the property of Judge Proctor. There was a terrific explosion that destroyed the windmill, a water tower, and the judge's garden. The craft was constructed of a "strange metal" and records were found written in some "unknown hieroglyphics." The pilot was killed, but his remains were definitely not human. According to the paper, he was buried in Aurora on April 18. The story was not rediscovered until 1966 and was generally thought to be a hoax. However, in 1973, an unusual boulder was found in the Masonic Cemetery. It had the vague outline of an arrow with three small circles. Many believed it was the tombstone marking the alien's grave, but cemetery officials insisted the grave contained the remains of a man named Carr who died of spotted fever in 1897, and secured an injunction to prevent any unauthorized digging at the site. About that time, fragments of metal unearthed at the crash site were examined by a professor from North Texas University who declared the pieces to have very unusual characteristics. But another analysis at the Canadian Aeronautical Establishment concluded there was nothing unusual about the metal.

(The tiny town of Aurora is in Wise County, northwest of Fort Worth off U.S. Highway 81/287. The cemetery is just north of town.) **72**

AUSTIN

CAPITOL CITY PLAYHOUSE An energetic ghost haunts this theater. The unidentified spirit rearranges furniture, moves stage lighting, and displaces small personal items.

(Austin is in southeastern Texas, sixty miles northeast of San Antonio on I-35. Capitol City Playhouse, 214 West 4th St., Austin, TX 78701. Phone: 512-472-2966.) **72**

DRISKILL HOTEL The flirtatious ghost of a Texas man is said to haunt the top floor of this majestic hotel where he entertained his lady friends. The old elevator still makes calls to that floor for no reason, and female guests have reported the playful spirit in several rooms on that floor. The rock group Concrete Blond encountered his presence when they stayed at the hotel on a road tour.

(Driskill Hotel, 604 Brazos St., Austin, TX 78701. Phone: 512-474-5911. www.driskillhotel.com) **72**

GOVERNOR'S MANSION The small North Bedroom here is haunted by a governor's nephew. The mansion was built in 1853 by the fourth governor of Texas, Elisha Pease, but the ghost is Governor Pendleton Murrah's nineteen-year-old nephew, who committed suicide in his bedroom in 1864. The lovesick lad put a pistol to his head when a niece of Mrs. Murrah refused his hand in marriage. Afterward, servants refused to enter the room, which they said was haunted by the boy's anguished spirit. No one could sleep in the ice-cold room because of unexplainable banging sounds, so Governor A.J. Hamilton had it sealed after the Civil War. It was reopened in 1925 and the muffled sobbing of the heartbroken boy can still be heard, especially on Sundays, the day he ended his misery. The Houston Bedroom in the mansion is said to be haunted by none other than Sam Houston, the third governor of Texas. The statesman's shadow lurks in the corner of the room. His restless spirit was encountered by both the wife and daughter of Governor Mark White in the 1980s.

(The Governor's Mansion is in downtown Austin on the corner of 10th St. and Colorado. 1010 Colorado, Austin, TX 78701. Tours: 512-463-5518. www.governor. state.tx.us/Mansion) **72, 202**

HARRY MANN ROAD In an effort to placate superstitious property buyers, the name of this rural road was changed from "Hairy Man" to "Harry Mann" in the 1980s. The road's original name referred to the dozens of sightings of the Hairy Man Ghost, perhaps a Bigfoot creature, reported here. Once, several witnesses saw Hairy Man chasing a goat down the middle of the road.

(The road runs through Round Rock, a suburb just northwest of Austin.) **72**

LITTLEFIELD HOME The ghost of Mrs. George Washington Littlefield is said to haunt her former home. Her footsteps have been heard in the upper hall-

ways, and she is said to haunt the living room where she sometimes picks out a few notes on the grand piano.

(The house is on the University of Texas campus at 24th St. and Whitis Ave, Austin, TX 78712. For information, call 512-471-1711.) **72**

METZ ELEMENTARY SCHOOL Demolition of this old brick schoolbuilding released a frenzy of ghostly activity. Work on the seventy-five-year-old school began in 1990, but progress was hampered by equipment problems and unusual accidents. Bulldozers broke down just as they approached the building, men fell off ladders pulled away by unseen hands, tools disappeared, and freak accidents happened every day. Something would shake the bottom of ladders when workers climbed them. After workers encountered the ghosts of children writing on blackboards in the classrooms or hiding in the washroom stalls, half the crew quit and the rest refused to work inside. The Torres Construction company contacted a Catholic evangelist who performed an exorcism, but shortly afterward, one of the owners was killed when a wall "exploded" on him. The work was finally completed, nearly six months behind schedule. But that may not be the last of the ghosts. Foreman Joe Torres transplanted a tree from the site to the front yard of his daughter's home. Now, people claim to hear the voices of children coming from that tree.

(Construction of the Metz Elementary School was completed in 1992. It is located at 84 Robert T. Martinez, Jr. St. Phone: 512-414-4408.) **72, 198 (15-95)**

OTTINE SWAMP A tall, gray, hairy creature has been spotted in the swamp and around the Warm Springs Foundation building here. For want of a better name, locals call it "The Thing." One night, the monster violently shook a trailer home parked on the edge of the swamp, but it never bothered anyone at the campground in nearby Palmetto State Park. The creature leaves strange tracks that look like a woman's hand without a thumb. Most of the sightings took place in the 1970s.

(The swamp is southeast of Austin along the San Marcos River, just south of Luling.) **202**

UNIVERSITY OF TEXAS The ghost of Dallis Franz, a famous pianist and professor at this university, haunts Jessen Auditorium in the Old Music Building. The professor taught here from the 1940s through the 1960s, and his presence is felt by many current students and staff at the auditorium where he produced so many well-received musicals.

(University of Texas, University Station, Austin, TX 78712. Phone: 512-471-3434. www.utexas.edu) **72**

WESTLAKE A phantom wagon driven by a ghostly cowboy roars through the hills of this modern housing project, where an old rancher's house is haunted by two ghosts from the 1860s. The teamster was bushwhacked by three men, and the wagon carried off into the prairie by the frightened horses. At Eanes-Marshall House, Howard Marshall's hearty laughter is still heard, and the figure of his wife Viola Eanes has been spotted along the banks of Eanes Creek. Both have been dead over a century.

(The exclusive housing development is called Lago Vista. It is in Austin on the old Eanes-Marshall Ranch Phone: at Lago Vista. Phone: 512-267-7952.) **202**

ZACHARY SCOTT KLEBERG THEATER Unidentified spirits haunt the stage area at this theater. The poltergeists are blamed for moving props, changing lighting, and stealing the actors' personal possessions and then returning them.

(Zachary Scott Kleberg Theater, 1510 Toomey Rd., Austin, TX 78704. Phone: 512-476-6378. www.zachscott. com) **72**

BELLEVILLE

HIGHWAY 36 A steam locomotive emerges from a fog near here and pulls a string of freight cars across the highway. But there is no crossing gate, warning lights, or even tracks. The ghost train was first witnessed by Thomas Phillips of Pasadena, Texas, on January 10, 1960.

(Belleville is thirty-five miles west of Houston. Take the Highway 36 North exit from I-10 and go eight miles to Belleville, at the junction of County Road 949. The incident occurred south of Belleville on Highway 36.) **194**

BIG BEND NATIONAL PARK

BRUJA CANYON This canyon has been thought haunted for hundreds of years. *Bruja* is Spanish for "witch," and the area can certainly be considered bewitched. Photographs taken here often cannot be developed, and unexplained flickering lights are observed. In 1978, two hikers encountered the silent apparition of a Mexican man wearing a serape and sombrero. Both witnesses sensed a "dangerous but non-malevolent power coming from the man."

(The park is in Brewster County in the southwestern tip of Texas. Follow U.S. Highway 385 South ninety-eight miles from I-10 at Fort Stockton. Bruja Canyon cuts through Mesa de Anguilla, about a day's hike west of Terlingua Abaja. Big Bend National Park, TX 79834. Phone: 915-477-2251. www.big.bend.national-park.com) **53 (1/85)**

LOS CHISOS MOUNTAINS The name Los Chisos means "the ghosts," and these mountains are said to be home to several lonely spirits. The deserted mountain passes here are home to the phantom of Apache Chief Alsate. He was executed by a Mexican firing squad in the early 1800s. (See Marfa Lights, Alpine, Texas) Sometimes one can hear the sobbing of an Indian maiden who drowned herself in a mountain pond rather than be defiled by her white kidnappers. The foothills are also haunted by a very unusual ghost—a bull named Murderer. One day in 1891, two cowboys got into an argument about who owned a maverick bull found grazing near their herds. Their heated words turned into a shoot-out, and Fine Gilliland shot Henry Powe to death. Gilliland headed for the Glass Mountains, where two Texas Rangers hunted him down and killed him. Nobody wanted to claim the disputed bull. Instead, they branded it "Murderer—1891" and let it go. But the bull, or its ghost, kept returning and soon became legend in these parts. It appeared to Powe's son and at the Wentworth Ranch bunkhouse, where Gilliland had stayed. Every time there was a fatal shooting in the area, the ghostly bull showed up in the saloon in Alpine. Several people tried to capture Murderer, but none succeeded. For the next thirty years, it seemed that anyone who came upon the bull turned into a cold-blooded killer. To this day, some claim to see the phantom black bull silhouetted against the Texas horizon in the Big Bend territory.

(The site of the branding, Leoncita, is between Alpine and Fort Stockton, thirty miles east of Fort Davis. The location is on private property north of the Santa Fe Railroad tracks that parallel Highway 67. Gilliland Canyon is in the Glass Mountains, which are located twenty-five miles northeast of Alpine, east of Highway 51. The canyon is located on private ranch land. The ghost bull was also sighted in the Chisos Mountains in the Big Bend

National Park. The headquarters are at Panther Pass. From Alpine, follow U.S. Highway 67/90 east to Marathon, then take Highway 385 South and go west on Highway 90. At Panther Pass Rd., go south three miles to the park headquarters.) **36, 59, 115**

TERLINGUA ABAJA This crumbling ghost town has been the site of several eerie encounters. Most of the buildings are adobe with the exception of the church, which is built of stone. The cemetery has twenty graves, including several infants who died in the harsh conditions here.

(The isolated adobe ghost town is on Terlingua Creek on the Mesa de Anguilla, near Santa Elena Canyon. Only experienced hikers should attempt the trip. www.ghosttowns.com/states/tx/terlingua.html) **53 (1/85)**

CENTERVILLE

U.S. HIGHWAY 75 Some unexplainable force lifted an automobile traveling on this major highway and then set it back down facing the opposite direction. Louis Johnson of Houston was driving the U.S. Highway 75 on April 19, 1963, when some tremendous force lifted his car up off the pavement, picked it up, spun it around, and placed it on the opposite side of the road in the opposite direction. Several other motorists witnessed the inexplicable phenomenon, which occurred on a sunny, windless day.

(Centerville is one hundred miles south of Dallas on I-45, at the Highway 7 junction. The area is located on U.S. Highway 75, which parallels I-45, midway between Centerville and Madisonville. Mr. Johnson was originally traveling south toward Madisonville.) **194**

CLIFTON

ST. OLAF'S CHURCH A ghostly congregation fills this deserted church. Their voices and singing are often reported in the empty building, which was constructed in 1886 and abandoned in 1917 when another church was constructed closer to town. The site was investigated in 1977. Everyone present could hear the eerie voices, though nothing turned up on tape.

(Clifton is twenty-eight miles northwest of Waco, on Highway 6 at the junction of County Road 219. The church is in Cranfills Gap, near Norse, sixteen miles west of Clifton. The site is in the Bosque Valley in east-central Texas.) **202**

CORPUS CHRISTI

FORT LIPANTITLAN STATE HISTORIC SITE This old Mexican fort was home to a living apparition known as the Lady in Green. As Marcelino Garcia lay dying from wounds suffered when Texans captured the fort, the ghost of his wife appeared near his bed for several days in a row. Dozens witnessed the strange phenomenon, yet the woman was still alive in Mexico City. A friend's letter had informed her of her husband's plight, and somehow her spirit managed to be at his side. Even after he died, the Lady in Green continued to walk through the door and over to his former bed. For twenty-five years, the uncanny image appeared at Fort Lipantitlan, and only stopped in 1860, on the day the woman died.

(Corpus Christi is on the Gulf of Mexico, 144 miles southeast of San Antonio on I-37. Fort Lipantitlan is in Jim Wells County, twenty-eight miles northwest of Corpus Christi on County Road 624. Phone: 512-547-2635.) **202**

HEADLESS HORSEMAN HILL The ghost of a headless cowboy riding a steaming horse has been seen for over a hundred years here. The cowboy is said to be a horse thief captured by a posse and crudely beheaded because the men could not find a suitable tree from which to hang him.

(The hill is above the Old City Cemetery in San Patricio, twenty-four miles northwest of Corpus Christi.) **202**

ROBSTOWN A gigantic black bird with no feet has been reported flying around this small Texas community. Reports were so numerous in the 1970s that several Fortean researchers traveled here to catch a glimpse of the creature. But Mexicans of the area already knew what it was. The bird was the legendary Lachusa, the whistling giant that appears to evil people. The greater the evil, the longer Lachusa will linger. See Washington, Texas.

(Robstown is twelve miles west of Corpus Christi on Highway 44.) **59**

CROSBY

WILLIAMS HOUSE When Jean and Ben Williams moved into their new house in 1983, they were curious about strange markings on the oak tree in their front yard. Soon, they started hearing unexplainable footsteps and voices in the house. Moving shadows roamed the house and a black substance oozed from the walls of the master bedroom. They discovered that their house was built on top of an old African-American graveyard called the Black Hope Cemetery. Neighbors confirmed the sightings of ghosts and some experienced phenomena in their own homes. Before the Williams family moved out in 1987, five members had died under mysterious circumstances. The Williamses sued the developer and wrote a book about their experiences, called *The Black Hope Horror*.

(Crosby is seventeen miles northeast of Houston on U.S. Highway 90. The Williams House is a private residence in a subdivision on Hilltop Drive in the Newport area of Lake Houston.) **66 (10/88), 72, 221**

CROSBYTON

STAMPEDE MESA A phantom herd of Texas longhorns stampedes over this mesa late at night. The area got its name in 1889, when over 1,500 cattle stampeded in the middle of the night. The spooked cattle headed right over a hundred-foot cliff at the southern end of the mesa. The carnage was increased the next day, when cattlemen rounded up a homesteader they thought had caused the stampede. Unceremoniously they tied him to a blindfolded horse and forced it over the edge of the cliff. By 1891, cowboys were reporting a herd of ghostly cattle stampeding over the mesa at night. Some also observed a ghostly rider accompanying the herd. Before long, cattle drivers were going miles out of their way to avoid the place.

(Crosbyton is in western Texas, thirty miles east of Lubbock on U.S. Highway 82. Stampede Mesa is flat prairie land located eighteen miles southeast of Crosbyton in Blanco Canyon in Crosby County. Some maps show Blanco Canyon as White Canyon. The mesa is bounded by the White River and the McNeil Branch. The entire Stampede Mesa area is on a private ranch owned by L. R. French.) **36, 59, 202, 231**

DALLAS

SNUFFERS RESTAURANT An unidentified ghost has been seen by guests and employees in this popular restaurant. The phantom emerged after remodeling and usually appears in the hallway that connects the old building with the new addition.3526

(Dallas is in northeastern Texas at the junction of I-30

and I-45. Snuffers Restaurant, Greenville Ave, Dallas, TX 75206. Phone: 214-826-6850 www.haunted-places. com/current.htm **72**

WHITE ROCK LAKE The ghost of a woman in a white evening gown dripping with water has terrorized residents here for many years. The ghost often appears to young couples parked in cars along deserted roads, although she has also appeared at residents' homes. In September 1962, Dale Berry answered the doorbell twice to find no one there. On the third ring, he opened the door to see the screaming apparition, who disappeared, leaving behind only a puddle of water. The wandering ghost's identity has never been discovered.

(The town of White Rock Lake is a northeast suburb of Dallas, near the junction of Northwest Highway and Buckner Blvd. The lake is in a city park off of Buckner Blvd. The ghost has also been seen hitchhiking in the Lakewood section of town, on Gaston Ave.) **59, 90, 194, 202, 231**

DEL RIO

DEVIL'S RIVER The Wolf Girl of Devil's River was born over 150 years ago to Mollie Pertul Dent. Mollie had accompanied her husband to the Beaver Lake area to trap. Searchers found their bodies in May 1835. He was killed in a thunderstorm and Mollie died in childbirth. Wolves had eaten parts of the bodies and apparently had carried off the baby. Then in 1845, reports of a feral child roaming with a pack of wolves began to circulate. A group of hunters captured the naked wolfchild, whose body was deformed from running on all fours, and locked her in a cabin. The wild girl went crazy and broke out. The next sighting was by a surveying party in 1852. As late as the 1930s, there were reports of human-looking wolves in the area. Then, in 1974, a bow hunter in the area claimed to have seen the Wolf Girl again, this time as a white apparition.

(Del Rio is on the Mexican border in southwestern Texas, at the junction of U.S. Highways 90 and 277/377. The Wolf Girl has been seen in the old San Felipe Springs area, along the banks of Devil's River, which is about twelve miles from Del Rio. The river flows out of the Buckhor Draw into the Rio Grande. Phone 1830-395-2133. www.tpwd.state.tx.us/park/devils/devils.htm) **49, 131, 202, 231**

DENTON

MILLS COMMUNE This community of fourteen houses is located on sacred Indian ground and is the stalking grounds of an ethereal dragon. The artists' and writers' retreat averages about fifty residents on ten acres of land owned by Susan Mills. Residents report many manifestations of the dragon in clouds, in the smoke from campfires, and at the regular meetings of members. A Chinese friend identified a photograph of the dragon as a Ming dragon. *Ming* means "light" in Chinese. The dragon phantom appears white during the day and blue at night.

(The town of Denton is thirty miles north of Fort Worth on U.S. Highway 377. The community is located off Mills Road in east Denton.) **202**

EAGLE PASS

LA CHIMENEAS RANCH This old ranch stands on the ruins of a Spanish fort, which was built in the early 1800s by the Vegas family. Screams, sounds of fighting and struggle, and wispy phantoms have haunted the site since the 1860s. The violence of years gone by have left their mark here.

(Eagle Pass is on the Mexican border in southwestern Texas, fifty-five miles south of Del Rio on U.S. Highway 277. The ruins are twenty miles northeast of the town of Eagle Pass, toward Crystal City. It is on land now owned by the Chittim Ranch.) **202**

EL PASO

FRANKLIN MOUNTAIN Spanish padres from the Paso del Norte Mission worked a rich gold mine in this mountain in the 1600s. In 1680, during a revolt of the Pueblo Indians, the padres hid all their gold and valuables in the mineshaft and sealed it with red clay. Many Spanish were killed in the rebellion, and before long no one was alive to remember the exact location of the old mine. Today, people still search for the Lost Padre Mine and encounter the ghosts of the Catholic priests who mined these hills so long ago.

(El Paso is on the Mexican border, in the extreme western tip of Texas on I-10. Franklin Mountain State Park, 1331 McKellingon Canyon Rd., El Paso, Tx 79930, Phone: 915-566-6441.) **59**

LA LLORONA The ubiquitous ghost of a weeping woman, described as a shrouded, faceless lady with long white fingernails, has been sighted in the streets of this city. La Llorona was desperately in love with a man, who ordered her to get rid of her children if she wanted to live with him. She can still be seen in her flowing black dress, wandering along the banks of the Rio Grande River where she drowned them. She is always looking for her lost children but has been known to pause long enough to seduce and then murder young men. See Billings, Montana; Gary, Indiana; Guadalupita, New Mexico.

(La Llorona is seen on both sides of the Rio Grande River here, as well as in several Hispanic settlements throughout the United States.) **37, 72, 112**

THOMAS JEFFERSON HIGH SCHOOL In 1947, the devil is said to have made an appearance at an underclass dance here. The Master of Darkness was driving a convertible when he asked a girl walking down the street if she wanted to go to the dance. The girl's mother had refused to allow her to go to the function and the girl was pouting. She accepted the invitation but only danced one tune before her partner twirled her out an alley door. When other students heard screaming, they investigated and found the girl bleeding to death from deep claw marks. Next to her a large burning bush glowed menacingly. The witnesses were overcome by feelings of a malevolent presence. This story is typical of urban legends in which the devil shows up in our everyday world.

(Thomas Jefferson High School, 4700 Alameda Ave., El Paso, TX 79905. Phone: 915-532-4963.) **121**

FORT WORTH

FORT WORTH BOOKS & VIDEO Strange lights, unexplainable footsteps, and an unseen presence are experienced by customers in this bookstore. Manager Steve Kerby has no explanation for the strange activity.

(Fort Worth is in northeastern Texas at the junction of I-20 and I-35. Fort Worth Books & Video, 400 Main St., Fort Worth, TX 76102.) **101**

FREDERICKSBURG

ENCHANTED ROCK STATE NATURAL AREA Enchanted Rock is a billion-year-old mountain of pink granite that makes strange crackling sounds at night. Evidence suggests that people have been worshipping here for ten thousand years. Indians considered it to be a gateway to the spirit world, and shamans came here on vision quests. Kiowa, Comanche, and Apache Indians call the spirit of the Enchanted Rock "Gahe" and believe the mountain is imbued with supernatural force by the Great Spirit.

(Fredericksburg is fifty-five miles northwest of San Antonio, on U.S. Highway 87. The park is in south-central Texas, sixteen miles north of Fredericksburg. Take Highway 16 to Ranch Rd. 965, fourteen miles south of Llano. Follow the road south for eight miles to the site. For further information, contact the Enchanted Rock State Natural Area, 16710 Ranch Rd. 965, Fredericksburg, TX 78624. Phone: 915-247-3903.) **99, 144, 202**

GALVESTON

ASHTON VILLA This Italianate mansion was built in 1859 by James Moreau Brown. His lovely daughter, Bettie Ashton Brown, is said to haunt her old home to this day. Bettie was a free spirit even when alive. She traveled alone throughout the world, smoked in public, and never married, though she picked her escorts from a long list of admiring suitors. Until Bettie's death in 1920, Ashton Villa was the scene of many parties and gala dinners. Today, her presence is sensed most strongly on the center stairway and in the hallway on the second-floor landing. In the Gold Room and near an alcove in the living room, furniture moves and clocks stop for no apparent reason. An employee saw Bettie's ghost on the landing in 1991. She was wearing a turquoise evening gown and carrying an ornate Victorian fan in one hand. According to Ashton Villa's manager Lucie Testa the ghostly activity intensifies on February 18, Bettie's birthday.

(Galveston is on the Gulf of Mexico, thirty-five miles southeast of Houston on I-45. Ashton Villa is in Galveston's historical district, at 2328 Broadway, Galveston, TX 77550. For further information, contact the Galveston Historical Society, 2016 Strand, Galveston, TX 77550. Phone: 409-765-7834. www.galveston.com/historichomes/ashtonvilla.shtml.) **72, 101, 168**

FLYING DUTCHMAN The most famous ghost ship in the world was sighted in Galveston Bay twice in 1892. Legend says the captain of the *Flying Dutchman,* Bernard Fokke, made a pact with the devil to reach the Indies in ninety days. His maniacal form is sometimes seen at the helm.

(The phantom ship was sighted in south Galveston Bay.) **96**

SAMUEL MAY WILLIAMS HOME Samuel May Williams was Governor Stephen Austin's secretary, and he used his influence to buy up land and ships during the Texas War for Independence. After the war, he became the state's first banker and gained a reputation for being a ruthless businessman. In fact, some historians have described Williams as the "most hated man in Texas." The man refused to give up his ill-gotten gains even after his death in 1858. Within weeks of his demise, his former slaves reported seeing him sitting in his rocking chair on the L-shaped front porch. Tourists and employees have sensed his dark spirit in his upstairs bedroom, and neighbors report seeing a light in the window late at night or a mysterious figure walking on the narrow balcony that surrounds the third floor observation room.

(Samuel May Williams Museum, 3601 Bernardo de Galvez Ave. P, Galveston, TX 77500. Phone: 409-765-7834.) **72**

WITWER-MOTT HOUSE Built in 1884 by Captain Marcus Mott, this house has been in the Witwer family for the last forty years. Neal Witwer, born in the house in 1947, blames a ghost in the attic for destroying his first marriage. It all started when a new tenant moved in. The man strongly resembled the captain's son, who was rumored to have murdered his father. For whatever reason, the boarder's arrival coincided with the emergence of a ghost. Every night at 3:00 A.M., loud voices and banging sounds came from the attic. Then, the ghost of a bearded man started to appear to Witwer's wife and call out to her in the middle of the night. For two weeks, regular séances were held to try to placate what was assumed to be Mott's spirit. Instead, another presence emerged, a female ghost who focused her attention on the new boarder, Before long, neither the boarder nor Witwer's wife could stand to live in the house. Neal Witwer's wife divorced him, and his tenant moved away. Strangely, the ghosts moved on as well.

(The Witwer Photographic Studios occupy the premises in front of the old house. Witwer-Mott House, Tremont St., Galveston, TX 77550.) **202**

GONZALES

COURTHOUSE CLOCK The tower clock at the center of this town is still haunted by the spirit of Albert Howard, hanged on the gallows behind the Old County Jail on March 18, 1921. Howard became obsessed with the courthouse clock as his execution drew nearer, and he put a curse on the clock that would toll his death. Shouting that the clock would never work properly, would never again count the time against anyone, he walked up the gallows steps. He was the last man hanged in this county, and the clock has never worked properly since the day he died. Despite large sums spent for its repair, the courthouse clock has never since read the correct time, nor have all four faces of the clock agreed on the same hour.

(Gonzales is sixty-five miles east of San Antonio, on U.S. Highway 183, south of I-10. The Gonzales Chamber of Commerce is now housed in the old County Jail building, where Howard pronounced his curse. The courthouse is on the main square in town.) **202**

HEMPSTEAD

LIENDO PLANTATION RANCH Jose Liendo received the original Spanish grant for this land, but he sold it in 1849. In the early 1870s, it was owned by Elizabet Ney, a renowned German sculptress. She, her husband, and the ashes of their only son, Arthur, are buried in a family plot on the ranch. When little Arthur died of diphtheria, his parents cremated him in the living-room fireplace and placed his ashes in an urn on the mantel. Ever since, the boy's gasping ghost has been seen in the white guesthouse next to the ranch house. It was there the child lay quarantined, struggling for a deep breath, his lonely cries filling the crisp night air.

(Hempstead is thirty-eight miles northwest of Houston on U.S. Highway 290. The ranch is private property four miles northeast of Hempstead on Whiting Chapel Road Phone: 979-826-3126. www./liendo.org/plantat. html) **202**

HENDERSON

HOWARD MANSION This three-story brick house was erected in 1851 by James Howard. Shortly after restoration in 1968, the ghost of his wife was seen floating over the stairway to the upper floors. The ghost paused and looked directly at one of the curators, as if thanking her for saving the Howard home from the wrecking ball.

(Henderson is in Rusk County, in northeastern Texas at the junction of U.S. Highways 79 and 259. The Howard Mansion Museum, South Main St., Henderson, TX 75652. For information, call 903-657-6925. www. hendersontx.com/howard.html) **90, 101**

JULIA IDESON BUILDING This 1926 building is haunted by the ghost of a caretaker who used to work at the Galveston Public Library when it was housed here. Everyone called him Mr. Cramer, and he lived in a small room in the basement with his dog, whose name was Pete. After hours, Cramer would wander throughout the building playing the "Blue Danube Waltz" on his violin. Soon after he died in the mid-1930s, people began hearing the sounds of his violin at all hours of the day and night. The sounds would start in the basement and reach a crescendo in the rotunda. Renovations in the 1970s seem to have lessened the phenomenon, although people still report hearing his footsteps and the sound of his dog's toenails on the floor. Cramer is also sensed near a large oak tree, which he planted on the north side of the old library.

(The Old Public Library, now the Julia Ideson Building, is at 500 McKinney St. in downtown Houston. Phone: 713-222-4900.) **72**

U.S. ARMY MEDICAL TRAINING CENTER Service Club Number Two at this Army training center is haunted by a playful ghost. Since 1960, employees and guests have heard the mysterious presence clearing its throat and watched as it opened and closed windows. The ghost tampers with unmanned typewriters and plays solitary Ping-Pong. Unexplained noises and musical sounds similar to a flute have been reported. The ghost is such a regular part of activities here that patrons have named it Harvey. In 1951, a young trainee committed suicide by hanging himself in a small storage room in the building, but there is nothing to connect him to the manifestations that occur in the clubhouse.

(The large cement-block building is known as Service Club No. 2 and is open to enlisted men and trainees of the U.S. Army Medical Training Center at Fort Sam Houston. Fort Sam Houston was established in 1876 and is the birthplace of the Army Air Corps. Phone: 713-963-0593.) **72, 185**

LA PORTE

TRINITY BAY Nearly two hundred years ago, at the mouth of the Neches River near La Porte, pirate Jean Laffite buried a treasure said to consist of gold and precious jewelry. Many people believe that his ghost still guards the horde. The first modern reports came in the 1920s, when several treasure seekers told of being choked and threatened by the belligerent phantom. One man died of a heart attack in his sleep a few days after the harrowing experience. Another said that he had "seen Hell and all its horrors" and never wanted to return to the site. Some La Porte residents have been awakened in the middle of the night by Laffite's ghost, dressed in a red coat, standing at the foot of their beds. The notorious pirate built his headquarters, which he called Maison Rouge, at La Porte. Laffite was pardoned by President Madison in 1816 and moved to Galveston Island. In 1820, the U.S. Army evicted him from the island because he was accused of attacking American vessels in the Gulf of Mexico. He is thought to have died in Yucatan in 1826.

(La Porte is five miles east of Houston, on Highway 225. Trinity Bay leads to the Gulf of Mexico at Galveston Island. The treasure site is near Sabine Lake, north of the Galveston Bay.) **202, 231**

LUBBOCK

LEVELLAND SIGHTINGS A series of UFO flyovers occurred on a major highway near the town of Levelland in November 1957. The gigantic oval objects caused automobiles traveling on the highway to lose all their electrical power and stop dead in the road. The incidents coincided with numerous sightings of unidentified flying objects in the Sacramento Mountains of New Mexico. All the sightings occurred within the notorious Lubbock Triangle. See Lubbock Lights, below.

(Lubbock is in northwestern Texas at the junction of I-27 and U.S. Highway 84. The town of Levelland is in Hockley County, twenty-three miles west of Lubbock on Highway 114. The Sacramento Mountains are about 180 miles southwest of Levelland. www.interoz.com/lubbock/lubmag/UFO.htm) **72, 150, 190**

LUBBOCK LIGHTS The Lubbock Triangle has been called one of the most UFO-haunted areas in North America. In August and September 1951, hundreds of

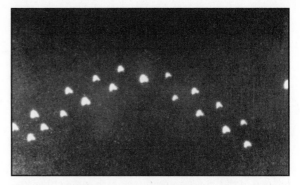

The lights of a wing-shaped craft, believed to be a nocturnal UFO, have been witnessed here by hundreds of people. See Lubbock Lights, Lubbock, Texas (IUFOR)

people observed the lights of a "wing-shaped craft." The town became famous for the Lubbock Lights when a photograph of the nocturnal UFO formation was taken by Carl Hart, Jr. On the evening of August 25, an employee of the Atomic Energy Commission and his wife saw a wing-shaped UFO with blue lights pass over Albuquerque, New Mexico. Within minutes of the Albuquerque sighting, a woman in Lubbock described the same object, a sighting confirmed by two college professors observing the sky that evening. Explanations that the lights were a natural occurrence, such as the bellies of birds glowing in the nighttime sky, seem ludicrous to those who witnessed them. See Amarogordo and Roswell in New Mexico.

(The Lubbock Triangle is bounded by the towns of Lubbock and Alpine in Texas and Albuquerque in New Mexico.) **139, 150**

ST. JOHN NEUMANN CATHOLIC CHURCH In February 1988, three parishioners here reported that the Virgin Mary had appeared to them to ask them to become messengers of prayer and love. Furthermore, Mary said she would reveal herself on August 15, 1988, at the Feast of Assumption Festival, which celebrates Mary's ascension into heaven. Nearly twenty thousand people gathered, and thousands claimed to have seen the face of Mary in a mass of sunlit clouds. Scores of the faithful reported miraculous healings, and several others claimed their rosaries changed from silver into gold.

(St. John Neumann Catholic Church, 5802 22nd St., Lubbock, TX 78504. Phone: 806-799-2649.) **57, 68**

WHITEFACE During a UFO flap in this area in 1975, rancher Darwood Marshall found oddly mutilated cattle. On March 10, the bloodless body of a heifer was discovered with its neck twisted grotesquely skyward, its internal organs neatly removed, and its navel cored out. A few days later, he found a similarly mutilated steer. Both animals were found in thirty-foot circles of scorched or flattened vegetation. Radiation surveys by the sheriff's department and personnel from Reese Air Force Base showed slightly increased levels of radiation within the circles.

(The Marshall Ranch is south of Whiteface, a small town outside Lubbock.) **72, 139**

McALLEN

OLD McALLEN HIGH SCHOOL Several former students who were killed during World War II returned as a group to haunt their old high school. The ghostly students most often appeared in the first-floor corridor. Witnesses described the four apparitions as a red-haired girl in a green print dress; a blond-haired, blue-eyed boy; a shy boy with large brown eyes; and a dark-haired thin boy. The youthful ghosts had apparently returned to the best life they had known in their short time on earth.

(McAllen is at the southern tip of Texas, at the junction of U.S. Highways 83 and 281. The L-shaped brick school was built in 1913 and replaced with a new building in the 1970s.) **84**

NECHES RIVER

GHOST RIDERS The ghost riders started haunting the Texas plains in the 1870s, when a cattleman driving his herd to market came across a new homestead blocking his normal route. It was a time of intense hatred between ranchers and farmers, and the cowboy was so angry that he stampeded his cattle right through the farm house, crushing everyone inside. Their screams are still heard whenever the phantom longhorns are sighted above the dusty plains. The legend inspired the popular song, "Ghost Riders in the Sky."

(Rio Nueces, or the Neches River, runs from Real County, northwest of San Antonio, to Lake Corpus Christi in Live Oak County. The south Texas desert area around the river is full of deserted canyons and abandoned settlements.) **115**

EL MUERTO Thousands of people have reported seeing this grotesque cowboy since the 1840s. His headless torso, clad in buckskin and rawhide chaps, rides a black, red-eyed mustang. The vaquero's gruesome decapitated head is strapped to his saddle horn, partially hidden by a dusty sombrero. Called El Muerto, the headless one, he is thought to be the ghost of a Mexican bandit named Vidal, who harassed Texas ranchers after the Battle of San Jacinto. The cowboys tracked down the outlaw and beheaded him. Then they placed his head inside his sombrero and tied it to the saddle of an unbroken stallion, which galloped off across the prairie.

(The phantom vaquero has been spotted in southwest Texas, at Bull Head and Alice, near the deserted Candelaria Mission, and along the banks of the Neches River.) **5, 58, 59**

LADY IN BLUE The mysterious ghost of a Catholic nun appeared to the Caddos and Jumanos Indians living along the Neches River in the 1620s—many years before Spanish explorers discovered the area. When the Spanish finally arrived in 1680, the Indians crossed their chests in the sign of the cross and were proficient in many aspects of catechism. They explained that a ghostly lady in blue, wearing a cross and a long blue habit, appeared to them and taught them about Christ. Amazed explorers later discovered a nun in Spain, Sister Maria Coronal de Jesus of the Agreda Convent, who insisted she traveled out of her body to converse with savages in the Americas. She accurately described many of the landmarks of New Mexico and Texas. The case remains once of the oddest on record.

(The phantom Catholic sister was reported by tribes along the Neches River and in the Rio Grande Valley from Texas to New Mexico.) **50, 53 (11/60), 162, 203, 231**

PORT ISABEL

PADRE ISLAND The spirits lingering on this island are probably all searching for lost treasure. Tourists visiting this giant sandbar have been finding Spanish jewels and gold coins for the last century, along with encountering the ghosts of long-dead treasure seekers. The artifacts, which originate from dozens of ships sunk in the Gulf, are churned up by storms and deposited on the beaches here. A whole city has even been discovered under the sand. The town of Southmost was buried by tons of sand during the hurricane of 1875 and was unveiled by the blowing winds of another hurricane in 1961. John Singer, brother of the sewing-machine tycoon, was shipwrecked here in 1847. He liked the island so much that he established a cattle ranch. During digging of the foundation for his house, he discovered a metal chest filled with eight hundred thousand dollars worth of doubloons and jewels. Just after the start of the Civil War, Singer fled the island for the Texas mainland and buried the treasure, along with his own sizable fortune, in a huge cast-iron bathtub between two oak trees. When he returned after the war, the trees were gone, and he spent the rest of his life searching for the treasure. To date, it has not been found.

(Port Isabel is on the Gulf of Mexico at the extreme southern tip of Texas, twenty-three miles northeast of Brownsville on Highway 48. The island is a three-mile wide, 132-mile long sandbar near the mouth of the Rio Grande River off Port Isabel. John Singer's ranch was twenty-three miles north of Brazos Santiago Pass.) **194**

SAN ANGELO

ANGELO STATE UNIVERSITY Strange footsteps and the sounds of a man and woman arguing are heard late at night in the deserted second-floor hallways of the Administration/Journalism Building on this 268-acre campus. Several students and university employees have reported seeing the shadowy ghost of a young woman in the halls near Room 200. In 1976, a young coed was stabbed to death after an argument with an ROTC cadet. He was a photographer with the school paper, and she also worked there. The beautiful girl spurned the man's advances, and in a fit of rage he grabbed a pair of scissors and plunged them into her chest. Then, he dragged the body into Room 200 and ran to a priest to confess his crime. Apparently he was not forgiven, for the lonely ghost of the murdered girl still stalks these hallways.

(San Angelo is in south-central Texas, southwest of Abillene, at the junction of U.S. Highways 87 and 277. Room 200 is now the Housing Office. Angelo State University, 2601 West Ave. North, San Angelo, TX 76909. Phone: 915-942-2211. www.angelo.edu) **72**

FORT CONCHO MUSEUM Construction on this remote outpost started in 1867. The fort was abandoned in 1889 and the buildings were turned into private residences. Today, the ghosts of its former

occupants are still struggling to make a go of it. The footsteps of invisible soldiers are heard in the old barracks, and a shadowy apparition has been seen walking there. Lights play games in the headquarters and courtmartial room. The presence of the camp's surgeon, Captain William Notson, is sensed in the primitive post hospital. The museum library, formerly Officer's Quarters No. 7, is haunted by the luminescent spirits of several transients who were murdered in the building in the 1890s. One library staff member claims the ghosts locked her out several times by latching the heavy nineteenth-century lock.

Fort Concho Preservation and Museum, 630 S. Oakes St., San Angelo, TX 76903. Phone: 915-657-4441. www. fortconcho.com) **14, 72, 101**

SAN ANTONIO

ALAMO When this mission was first established in 1718, it was known as San Antonio de Valero. It is thought that spirits dating back to its founding kept the old Franciscan mission from being destroyed over a century later. On March 6, 1836, after thirteen days of siege, Mexican forces led by General Antonio Lopez de Santa Anna overran the Alamo and killed every armed defender at the outpost. He ordered all 184 bodies dumped into a mass grave and left orders that the Alamo itself be torn down to the ground. But when Mexican engineers started tearing into the walls, ghostly hands protruded to stop them and workers fled in fear. Some of the phantom hands held glowing "torches," and a thundering voice called out promising a horrible death to anyone who desecrated the walls. Today the Alamo still stands, much as it was on that fateful day in 1836, and tourists staying at the nearby Menger Hotel still report seeing grotesque apparitions emerging from the old mission walls.

(San Antonio is south-central Texas at the junction of I-10 and I-35. The Alamo, 300 Alamo Plaza, San Antonio, TX 78201. Phone: 210-225-1391. www.thealamo. org) **53 (9/94), 198 (6-90)**

BROOKS HOUSE A pipe-smoking ghost haunts this Victorian house. Former residents have reported smelling pipe smoke and hearing the footsteps of the ghost just before he makes an appearance. In 1967, the tall, mustached figure tried to crawl in bed with a woman sleeping in an upstairs bedroom, but she made it clear she did not want any company and the apparition vanished. Once, the ghost was asked to leave the bathroom while a lady undressed. The amorous, though polite, specter has been sensed by both guests and residents of the house, but no one has ever identified him. The house was built in 1890 by the Hertberg family, and purchased in 1909 by the Brooks family. It was the home of Cadet Sidney Brooks, Jr., for whom Brooks Air Force Base was named. The twenty-two-year-old pilot died on November 13, 1917, when he crashed during a training exercise.

(Brooks House, a state historical landmark, is a private residence near the San Antonio River in Old San Antonio. For information, contact the San Antonio Historical Society, 135 Lanark Dr., San Antonio, TX 78218. Phone: 210-655-2898.) **186**

MILAM SQUARE The ghoulish figures of hooded skeletons with pitch black holes for eyes haunt this modern plaza. They are the ghosts of Spanish settlers and Indians who battled for this land. In 1718, Milam Square was the site of a Catholic cemetery that held the bodies of many of those who died in the violence. Today, their spirits are said to rise again in response to feelings of hatred or anger in persons who walk the sidewalks where they rest. The phantoms have also been reported along San Saba Street and Commerce Avenue.

(Milam Square is just north of El Mercado St., in downtown San Antonio.) **202**

OUR LADY OF GUADALUPE CHURCH In June 1992, a statue of the Virgin Mary in this Catholic church started to shed tears from her right eye. Hundreds of parishioners and visitors witnessed the phenomenon, and the archbishop declared it a miracle.

(Our Lady of Guadalupe Church, El Paso St., 1321 San Antonio, TX 78202. Phone: 210-226-4064.) **72**

STINSON FIELD GRAVEYARD An old cemetery near Stinson Field is haunted by the ghost of a Chinese woman. The woman was seven feet tall and was teased mercilessly because of it. In the late 1930s, she committed suicide. Now, her apparition hovers nears her grave in this abandoned graveyard. For many years, an unidentified admirer placed flowers on her grave.

(The overgrown graveyard is on Mission Rd. near Stinson Field.) **198 (6-90)**

VILLAMAIN RAILROAD TRACKS The ghosts of children haunt this rural railroad crossing. They were victims of an accident in which a freight train hit a school bus. As a memorial, streets in the area were named after those who died. It is said that the ghosts try to push cars across the tracks to safety. An investigation led by Melissa Fuentes provided startling evidence. She parked her car on a dirt road facing the tracks and sprinkled flour all over the car. To everyone's amazement, small handprints appeared on the windshield. In 1995, a national television show sprinkled baby powder on a car parked at the tracks. In front of their cameras, a child's handprint appeared.

(The tracks cross Villa Main St. on a small hill near the Stilnson Airport, which is just south of San Antonio.) **72**

WITTE MUSEUM Employees here find doors mysteriously unlocked, personal items moved, and other evidence of poltergeist activity. Some have seen a gray figure moving through the halls. The best candidate for the presence is Ellen Schulz, founder of the museum, who was always moving about straightening up things.

(Witte Museum, 3801 Broadway, San Antonio, TX 7820. Phone: 210-357-1900. www.wittemuseum.org) **198 (6–90)**

SAN MARCOS

SAN MARCOS BRIDGE This bridge is haunted by the ghost of a Confederate soldier toting a muzzle-load rifle. His ghost has been reported walking near the bridge since the 1920s. In 1939, two men fixing a flat tire on the bridge were startled by the shirtless figure of a tall man wearing a rebel cap. Because the man was carrying a rifle, one of the two businessmen went for a gun in the car, but the apparition disappeared before he could confront it. Legend says the ghost is a man who lived in a cabin near the bridge before the Civil War. When he and his brother went off to fight for the South, they promised each other that they would return home—no matter what happened.

(San Marcos is located forty-seven miles northeast of San Antonio on I-35. The bridge is over the San Marcos River on the road between San Marcos and Nixon.) **186**

SARATOGA

BRAGG ROAD LIGHT The Bragg Road Light, also known as the Big Thicket Light, has mystified observers for nearly fifty years. The light seems to sway back and forth, as if someone were carrying a gas lantern. It begins as a flickering yellow light in the distance and changes to a brilliant white as it approaches. Then it turns bright red and disappears. Bragg Road was once the gravel bed for Santa Fe railroad tracks that ran through the town of Bragg, which was settled by railroad workers and their families in 1901. The town was torn down and tracks dismantled in 1934, after the railroad discontinued the route. Legends explaining the light are plentiful. Some say the light is the ghost of Jake Murphy, a brakeman beheaded when he fell underneath a train here. Others tell of four Mexican laborers killed by a foreman who wanted their money. Or perhaps the light is a lantern carried by the phantom of a hunter lost long ago in the bogs. Whatever the explanation, the phenomenon has been observed by hundreds of witnesses.

(Saratoga is in Hardin County, thirty-nine miles west of Beaumont on Highway 105. Bragg Road is an eight-mile-long dirt pathway through a thicket that lies between the Neches and Trinity rivers. From Saratoga; follow Highway 770 west for two miles to Highway 787. Turn north on Highway 787 and travel 3.5 miles to Bragg Rd. Information can be obtained by calling the Big Thicket Museum, at 409-274-5000.) **15, 202, 231**

THORNDALE

SAN GABRIEL RIVER The banks of this river are haunted by the ghost of a man protecting a cache of gold that was never his in the first place. After a band of outlaws discovered they were being followed by Texas Rangers, they broke into a cabin along the river and murdered the old hermit they found there. Then, they dug a deep hole and buried their loot with the old man's body. Before long, a strange yellow light was seen moving between the cabin and the riverbank. Many believe it is the ghost of the murdered man guarding the outlaws' treasure.

(Thorndale is in east-central Texas, thirty miles east of Round Rock on U.S. Highway 79, off I-35 north of Austin. The old Snively-Pope cabin is just outside Thorndale on the banks of the San Gabriel River. The ruins are said to be still haunted.) **59**

TYLER

BEAIRD HOUSE This modern ranch house, built in the 1950s, was the site of mind-boggling poltergeist activ-ity from 1965 to 1968. In July 1965, hordes of giant June bugs repeatedly attacked the Beaird family while they slept in their beds. The attacks stopped as soon as the lights were turned on. Hundreds of bugs littered the floors, but most of the bugs were already dead and dried up. Small objects floated in midair, and unidentifiable, high-pitched voices were heard in the house. Then the voices of seven dead people, all known to the family, began resonating from inside the walls. An invisible force pulled covers off beds in the middle of the night, punched holes in walls, and unscrewed plugs on gas lines in the house. Police investigated the house on several occasions but could find no cause for the phenomena. The family was finally forced to move out of the house, and subsequent owners reported nothing unusual.

(Tyler is in northeastern Texas, seventy-five miles east of Dallas off I-20. The house is a private residence on Elizabeth Dr., Tyler, TX 75701.) **87, 90**

VICTORIA

SUTTON'S MOTT This picnic grove got its name from the cantankerous ghost who is seen there. William Sutton was a goatherder who lived in the area in the 1850s. He was murdered one Sunday while walk-ing up the church steps in the nearby town of Goliad. Since then, his ghost has haunted this serene patch of live oak trees. Horses and dogs refuse to enter the grove, and tales of drifting phantoms and ghostly bod-ies hanging from trees abound. Some believe Sutton returns to protect a strongbox of gold he buried here.

(Victoria is in southeast Texas, ninety-five miles north of Corpus Christi on U.S. Highway 77. From I-10, follow U.S. Highway 77 for sixty-one miles south.) **59**

WASHINGTON

MOTHMAN A strange creature has been sighted in this region many times, although it has also been reported as far away as West Virginia. The winged crea-ture is shaped like a man and is gray. Observers are gripped by a strange feeling of terror, a weird kind of fear that "the whole experience is just not right." See Robstown, Corpus Christi, Texas; and Point Pleasant, West Virginia.

(Washington is in southeastern Texas, between Hous-ton and Bryan. Take Highway 6 to Novasota and go southwest five miles on Highway 105 to the Washington turnoff.) **139**

WAXAHACHIE

CATFISH PLANTATION RESTAURANT The sign at
the entrance to this quaint restaurant reads: "If you
have a ghostly experience, please tell us!" The quaint
Victorian house was built in 1895 by a farmer named
Anderson. His daughter Elizabeth was strangled to
death on her wedding day in the 1920s. She died where
the ladies' room is now located and became one of the
ghosts of Catfish Plantation. There are two others.
One is a farmer named Will, who died in the house in
the 1930s. The other is an elderly lady named Caroline
Mooney, who died in the house in 1970. The three
ghosts are responsible for the bone-numbing cold spots
that move silently through the house, as well as flying
objects and slamming doors. Elizabeth's kindly presence is felt mostly in the dining room, where she likes
to reach out and touch people. Will's apparition is often
seen on the front porch, and Caroline's angry spirit is
detected in the kitchen. Ever since Melissa and Tom
Baker remodeled the house into a Cajun eatery in 1984,
dozens of employees, customers, and newspeople have
witnessed paranormal manifestations here.

*(Waxahachie is twenty miles south of Dallas on 1–35.
The restaurant is at 814 Water St., Waxahachie, TX
75165. Phone: 214-937-9468.)* **53 (5/94), 101, 133**

WINK

OIL FIELDS The unlikely ghost of a Russian cossack haunts the oil fields around this small town.
Nicholi was a count whose family had escaped from
the Russian Revolution. He brought his family and his
fortune to Texas to learn the oil business from the
ground up. He started out as a roustabout laborer, then
became a tool pusher. All the while, he kept his fortune
in gold hidden away in an abandoned coyote den. Or
so the rumors went, and they were enough for a band
of roughnecks, who kidnapped the cossack and his
butler. Both died rather than divulge their secret.
Before long, the ghost of Nicholi started to appear
near the oil derricks, in the barren prairie outside of
town, and even walking down Hendricks Boulevard.
Dozens of townsfolk saw the ghost over the years. One
of the more well-known witnesses was rock and roll
star Roy Orbison, who saw the ghost on a dirt road
east of town in 1950. According to legend, the cossack's treasure is still buried in the prairie, three to five
miles due east of Wink.

*(The town of Wink is in Winkler County in western
Texas. Take the Highway 115 exit at Pyote on 1–20 about
fifty miles southwest of Odessa. The town celebrates Roy
Orbison Day each year. For more information, contact
Wink City Hall, Wink, TX 79789. Phone: 915-527-
3441.)* **72**

UTAH

BRIGHAM CITY

DOVE CREEK CAMP This abandoned labor camp is haunted by the sounds and voices of Chinese workers who died laying tracks for the first transcontinental railroad. The sinkholes left from their primitive huts can be found throughout this area. Phantom headlights from old ironhorse steam engines have been reported traveling the tracks here for over a century. Engineers expecting collisions have seen the lights pass right through their trains.

(Brigham City is in Box Elder County in northern Utah, thirteen miles north of Ogden on I-84. The sinks of Dove Creek are near Kelton and can be reached by the very primitive Central Railroad Grade, near the Golden Spike National Historic Site at Promontory Point, thirty-eight miles west of Brigham City on Highway 83. Phone: 435-471-2209. www.nps.gov/gosp) **101, 131**

This park in Southeastern Utah is filled with interesting geologic formations and sacred sites. See Canyonlands National Park, Canyonlands, Utah (B. A. SCNAFFENBERGER)

CANYONLANDS

CANYONLANDS NATIONAL PARK This region in southeastern Utah is filled with sacred sites. This is the area of the Valley of the Gods and the Valley of the Goblins. From the surreal landscape of Bryce Canyon to the crimson cliffs of Kolob Canyon, this thirty-thousand-square-mile park beckons to all seeking natural spirituality. Many New-Age enthusiasts travel to Chesler Park to meditate among the bizarre columns of sandstone. The thirty-square-mile maze is a twisting series of rock canyons that are said to change one's state of consciousness—if you can survive the treacherous trip. The phantoms of wild mustangs haunt Dead Horse Point, where cowboys fenced off hundreds of the animals and left them to die of thirst.

(The Canyonlands are south of Moab in southeastern Utah. Take Highway 191/163 from Monticello to Highway 211. Go west on Highway 211 into the Canyonlands. For information, contact Utah Canyonlands, 2282 S. West

Resource Blvd., Moab, UT 84532. Phone: 435-719-2313. www.canyonlands.national-park.com) **99, 144**

HOVENWEEP

HOVENWEEP NATIONAL MONUMENT This sacred site is a group of six Anasazi dwellings shaped like castle towers. The Square Tower Group, Hovenweep Castle, and Unit-Type House were used as astronomical observatories to determine when certain religious ceremonies should take place. At Holly Group, on the morning of the summer solstice, rays of light illuminate drawings of the sun, a snake, and a human twin figure. Different patterns of light illumine the symbols at the spring and fall equinoxes. The ancient ones' deep reverence for nature and the mystical heavens is easily felt in this serene national park.

(Hovenweep National Monument is off U.S. Highway 666, now renamed U.S. Highway 262, in southeastern Utah. For information, contact Mesa Verde Area Parks, McElmo Route, Cortez, CO 81321. Phone: 970-562-4282. www.nps.gov/hove.) **99, 144**

NEWSPAPER ROCK

NEWSPAPER ROCK STATE PARK White settlers named this enormous boulder Newspaper Rock because it contains hundreds of ancient symbols and writings. Some of the pictographs show animals, while others portray six-toed feet. Most are mystical symbols. Unfortunately no one has ever been able to translate the glyphs, although they appear to have some spiritual significance.

(Follow U.S. Highway 191 south out of Moab for forty miles to Highway 211. Go west thirty-six miles into the park. For information, contact Utah State Park Southeast Office, 125 West/200 South, Moab, UT 84532. Phone: 435-259-8151. www.desertusa.com/newut/du_newut_vvc.html.) **144**

SALT LAKE CITY

OLD DESERET Visitors and guides at this former settlement have reported dozens of ghostly encounters in recent years. The buildings were part of the original colony established by Brigham Young, who led Mormons west after their leader, Joseph Smith, was murdered by an Illinois mob in 1844. Before Brigham Young's forest farmhouse was moved to the historical

park, his ghost haunted his residence for fifteen years. After it was moved, the house was taken over by his nineteenth wife, Ann Eliza Webb. Her petite apparition, dressed in black, is seen peering out of the dining-room window of the house. After Ann Eliza divorced Young, she toured the country denouncing him and the Mormon Church. At nearby Jewkes-Draper Home, the ghostly sounds of children at a party are heard, and the apparition of Mary Fielding Smith has been observed many times standing in the doorway of Smith House. Sometimes Mrs. Smith is seen wagging her finger angrily, perhaps because her house was set facing the wrong way when it was moved to the park.

(Salt Lake City is at the junction of I-15 and I-80 in north-central Utah. For information on the area, call the Visitors Bureau at 801-521-2822. Old Deseret is located in the This Is the Place State Park, 2601 Sunnyside Ave., Salt Lake City, UT 84108. Take the Foothills Exit from I-80 and go west three miles to the park. For information, call 801-584-8391. For tour reservations, call 801-582-2443.) **134**

UTAH STATE HISTORICAL SOCIETY The state's historical society is housed in a former railroad station full of ghosts. The Denver & Rio Grande Railroad Depot, built in 1910, was considered to be haunted by the 1940s. The ghost of a black-haired lady wearing an old-fashioned purple dress haunts the ladies room and the Rio Grande Café inside the depot. She was struck by a train in the station when she tried to retrieve an engagement ring her boyfriend had thrown on the tracks. In 1980, two people heard footsteps and saw the ghost of a man on the ground floor. An invisible presence who walks the balcony and lobby in the late evening hours has been detected by security officers. Once, a whole group of ghosts having a party in the basement of the building was interrupted by a security guard getting off the elevator.

(Christine Guston, a secretary at the society's library, keeps track of the ghost reports. Utah State Historical Society, 300 South Rio Grande St., Salt Lake City, UT 84101. Phone: 801-533-3500.) **14, 101**

ZION NATIONAL PARK Native Americans consider this 229-square-mile sacred site a colossal temple in which to worship, meditate, and talk to the gods. Modern psychics believe the park is a door to the ethericrealm through which are channeled the energies of the earth's Light Towers, such as the Pyramid of Giza,

Mount Sinai, Ayers Rock, and Mount Shasta (see Mount Shasta, California). They believe the crystalline peaks in Zion contain the coded matrix for the future evolution of the human spirit. The Smithsonian Butte Back Country Byway passes through some of the most sacred sites, including the peaks of the East and West Temple, and the rock formations North Guardian Angel and The Watchman.

(Follow I-15 northeast from St. George to Highway 9, which leads into the park. For information, contact Utah Parks Division, TW Recreation Services, 451 North Main St., Cedar City, UT 84720. Phone: 801-586-7697. For information on the Smithsonian Butte Back Country Byway, call the BLM Cedar City District at 801-586-2401.) **99**

VERMONT

BENNINGTON

LONG TRAIL People seem to vanish into thin air when they set out along Vermont's Long Trail. Many cases of persons who have mysteriously disappeared have been reported over the years. Middie Rivers, who knew the area extremely well, disappeared on November 12, 1945, and was never seen again. Bennington College student Paula Welden vanished on the trail in December 1946. James Telford was last seen here on December 1, 1949. Frances Christman was lost to the trail on December 3, 1950. The only missing hiker whom searchers ever found was Frieda Langer. She was murdered on the Long Trail in 1950. There are allegedly many other instances of disappearances in this area from the 1930s to the present that have not been documented.

(Bennington is in the extreme southwest corner of Vermont, at the junction of U.S. Highway 7 and Highway 9. All of the incidents have taken place on the Vermont Long Trail in the Green Mountains east of Bennington. The stretch runs from the town of Pownal to Glastonbury Mountain.) **72, 139**

BRISTOL

BRISTOL NOTCH Bone-chilling cries and howls have been heard coming from Ghost Shaft at this landmark. Bristol Notch has scores of deep shafts dug by villagers who searched in vain for Spanish silver said to be buried here. A little boy fell down one of the abandoned shafts and died. His dog, who would not leave the spot, also died soon afterward. The boy's final cries and the dog's mournful howling are still heard.

(Bristol is in central Vermont, nine miles southeast of Vergennes on Highway 17. Bristol Notch is south of town.) **102**

BURLINGTON

UNIVERSITY OF VERMONT The ghost of a medical student named Henry haunts Converse Hall, where he committed suicide in the 1920s. In 1986, a psychic was called in to release his earthbound spirit. At Bittersweet House, which houses the university's environmental program, the ghost is Margaret "Daisy" Smith. Daisy lived there from the 1930s to the 1950s. She named the house Bittersweet in memory of her husband, who died in an automobile accident shortly after they were married. Her apparition is usually dressed in an ankle-length skirt and high-collared blouse.

(Burlington is on Lake Champlain in northwest Vermont, at the junction of I-89 and Highway 7. Bittersweet House is on the corner of South Prospect and Main streets. University of Vermont, 194 South Prospect St., Burlington, VT 05401. Phone: 802-656-3370. www.uvm.edu) **72**

CHITTENDEN

EDDY HOUSE This old farmhouse, formerly the home of the Eddy family, has been called the "Spirit Capitol of the Universe," and more than five hundred ghosts are said to have materialized in a room set aside for séances. Julie Ann and Zephaniah Eddy always thought their two sons, William and Horatio, were a bit odd. An invisible hand seemed to rock their cradles, the boys spent hours playing with invisible children, and they were not allowed to attend school because of the variety of poltergeist effects that plagued their classroom whenever they were present. Then Zephaniah hit upon the idea of exhibiting his haunted children. He toured the country with the boys and their two sisters, who were less psychically gifted. He asked the children to go into a trance and then poured boiling water on them to prove the phenomenon was genuine. He scarred William for life by placing red-hot coals in his hands. He even poured hot wax over the children's mouths to show that they were not throwing their voices. Crowds never protested the brutal treatment, but they did attack the Eddys on religious grounds, saying the brothers were possessed by the devil. One mob in Danvers, Massachusetts, threw stones and fired guns at them. William was hit in the legs with a blast from a shotgun. In Cleveland, Ohio, a mob tried to tar and feather the Eddys.

In 1874, after their father died, the brothers opened their home to anyone who wished to test their powers or attend séances, which were held every night of the week except Sunday. They charged ten dollars per week for lodging and attracted scores of people from all over the world. Visitors included Henry Steel Olcott of the *New York Sun* and famed spiritualist Madame Helena Blavatsky. Guests had free run of the house and were encouraged to inspect the premises carefully. Without fail, the brothers produced a bewildering array of spirits and apparitions. Some séances were held outdoors at Honto's Cave, named for the ghost of an Indian girl who inhabited it. Besides Honto, many other phantoms appeared above the cave, floating twenty-five feet in the air. Eventually the brothers closed down their home and lived off their savings. Horatio died in 1922 and William died in 1932. To this day, no one has been able to explain how the Eddy brothers produced their colorful display of ghostly presences.

(The large white farmhouse is now a private residence just outside of the town of Chittenden. It was moved from the original site and turned to face away from the road.) **189**

CUTTINGSVILLE

BOWMAN HOUSE This large estate and family graveyard were owned by John P. Bowman, a wealthy farmer who left an endowment for the upkeep of the grounds and mansion. He also left behind a few ghosts. The ghost of an unidentified woman has been seen in the house, and there is a darkened stain at the top of the staircase that brings feelings of dread to anyone who stands there. Once, a little girl touring the house with her family stuck out her tongue at one of the paintings and it flew off the wall and hit her, in full view of several witnesses. No one is allowed to stay on the property after dark.

(Cuttingsville is in south-central Vermont, twelve miles southeast of Rutland on Highway 103. There is a Haunted Mansion bookshop on the property. Bowman House, Highway 103, Cuttingsville, VT 05738.) **102**

LAKE CHAMPLAIN

CHAMP Champ is a lake monster that has been sighted regularly since the early 1800s. In August 1878, six people in a yacht described it as having "two large folds just back of the head projecting above the water, and at some distance, say fifty feet or more behind, two or more folds at what was apparently the tail." The creature is said to be "thicker than two horses," with a long neck, very similar in appearance to an elasmosaurus, a prehistoric marine reptile. In July 1977, Sandra Mansi took a detailed color photograph of Champ. On October 6, 1980, the town of Port Henry, at the southern end of Lake Champlain, passed an ordinance forbidding the harassment of Champ or any other sea monsters in the body of water. As if feeling more secure, the lake creature made a record number of appearances in 1981. Nearly forty people witnessed Champ that year, and four more photographs resulted. Since then, an average of three reports a year are received by authorities. In 1993, four witnesses saw Champ come within twenty-five feet of their boat.

(Champ inhabits the one-hundred-mile long Lake Champlain, between Vermont and New York. www.strangemag.com/champ.html) **34, 44, 139, 148, 198 (5–90)**

LAKE MEMPHREMAGOG

GENERAL WAYNE'S GHOST Trappers and fisher-men have reported seeing General "Mad" Anthony Wayne's ghost, dressed as an Indian scout, glide across the water here. The peculiar apparition has his arms outstretched with a bald eagle perched on each hand. See Stony Point and Ticonderoga, New York; Valley Forge, Pennsylvania; and Loudoun County, Virginia.

(Lake Memphremagog straddles the Quebec-Vermont border at Newport, which is at the northern end of I-91.) **68**

ST. JOHNSBURY

FARR HOUSE An abandoned house here can be seen shaking "from cellar to roof" on moonlit winter nights. Locals say Jake Farr's old house trembles in fear, as he did in 1880 just before his wife shot him. Jake took to molesting their pretty sixteen-year-old daughter Molly and eventually got her pregnant. He told the sheriff that Molly was not really his daughter, so he was not prose-cuted. The baby died during birth, and Sally sent her daughter to a trade school in Massachusetts. Then she set out to murder her husband. Jake wasted away for fear of eating poisoned food and could not sleep for fear that his wife would stab him in the middle of the night. Before long, Jake was trembling constantly, because his wife's hatred was eating away at him. His fear was so great that somehow he passed it on to that old house. One day, while reading a newspaper on the porch, a bullet rang out from a neighbor's orchard across a gully from Jake's house. The bullet went right through the front page of his newspaper into Jake's heart. Sally moved to Burlington, and the sheriff never found Jake's murderer. Locals still talk about how good Sally Farr was with a rifle, and how her vengeful ghost is still seen in the neighbor's orchard or crossing the road late at night.

(St. Johnsbury is in Caledonia County in northeast Vermont, at the junction of I-91 and I-93. The house is on the road between St. Johnsbury and Waterford Town-ship.) **157**

INWOOD MANOR The apparition of a woman in a candy-striped dress floated up the stairs here, then turned around and smiled before she vanished. Not long after, the ghost of a small child appeared on the cellar steps. The ghosts are thought to be a mother and daughter who drowned in a nearby river. The encoun-ters happened shortly after Ron Kaczor and Peter Embarrato started renovating their thirty-two room inn. Guests and visitors still report odd goings-on at the remote resort.

(The twenty-acre resort inn is on the Connecticut River, twenty miles south of St. Johnsbury on Highway 5. Inwood Manor, Inwood, VT 05821.) **134**

WASHBURN'S BARN Many witnesses have seen the ghostly figures of four outlaws hanging from the star pole at the top an old deserted barn on the farm of Uriah Washburn. Washburn's son Dabby fed the four men poisoned root beer and strung up their bodies for the whole county to see. The four reprobates were Ter-rance Blunt, Andrew Marr, Frank Ballard, and Cal Longstreet. They terrorized the Vermont countryside in the 1830s and were wanted for a variety of robberies and other crimes, including the rape and murder of three young women. When they asked to spend the night in the Washburn barn, young Dabby recognized them from wanted posters and decided to claim the reward for himself. His trophies hung from the barn for days, and for the next hundred years, people reported seeing their blackened figures still hanging there.

(The old barn is in a private field in Waterford Town-ship.) **158**

STOWE

EMILY'S BRIDGE This covered bridge, built in 1844, was named after the ghost that haunts it. In the late 1800s, Emily Smith died here. Some say she was tram-pled by a team of horses; others say she killed herself by jumping off the bridge or perhaps by hanging herself from a roof beam. The most accepted scenario is that she died in an accident after being rejected at the altar by her fiancé. She rode after him in a buggy that over-turned on the bridge. Although the cause of her death remains unknown, locals say there is no doubt about her ghost. In 1969, plans for a housing development were canceled when it was discovered that nobody wanted to live near the haunted bridge. Sometimes Emily mani-fests as a flickering white light, other times as a mysteri-ous breeze that leaves one stunned or mesmerized.

(Stowe is in north central Vermont, sixty miles east of Burlington. Take I-84 to the Colbyville and go north twenty-six miles on Highway 100. The bridge spans Gold Brook on Gold Brook Rd. a few miles outside of town.

Gold Brick Rd. loops off Highway 100, north of town.)
134, 175

WATERBURY

OLD STAGECOACH INN The ghost of Margaret
Spencer, a wealthy socialite who died at the age of
ninety-eight, haunts Room 2 in this inn. After her death
in 1947, her apparition, wearing a white shawl, started
appearing in her former bedroom.

*(Waterbury is in north central Vermont, twelve miles
northwest of Montpelier on U.S. Highway 2. Old Stagecoach Inn, 18 N. Main St., Waterbury, VT 05676. Phone:
802-244-5056. www.oldstagecoach.com)* **72**

Unexplained footsteps haunt the White House of
Wilmington, now an inn. See White House of Wilmington,
Wilmington, Vermont (WHITE HOUSE OF WILMINGTON INN)

WILMINGTON

WHITE HOUSE OF WILMINGTON This house
was built in 1915, but strange things did not occur until
after it was remodeled into an inn. Manager Bob Gri-
nold has reported unexplained footsteps and other
sounds, as well as a shadowy presence walking the
halls.

*(Wilmington is in the south corner of Vermont, on
Highway 9 between Bennington and Brattleboro. White
House of Wilmington, 178 Route 9 East, Wilmington,
VT 05363. Phone: 802-464-2135. Reservations can be
made by calling 800-541-2135. www.whitehouseinn.
com)* **72, 101**

WOODSTOCK

CALENDAR ONE The sanctity of this site is easy to
feel. At the center of a circular earthen ring is a spring
bubbling with incredibly pure water. The ring itself is
divided into eight alignments marking the exact sunrise
and sunset times of the summer and winter solstices,
and the spring and autumn equinoxes. A mysterious
stone chamber and earthen mound are fifty yards away.
Two large stones stand to the east, and to the west is a
granite wall. Some of these stones display strange symbols, similar to markings found at European sacred
sites. Archeologists have discovered nearly two dozen
deliberate alignments with celestial bodies here, but
they have no idea who made them. Their age has been
estimated to be between one thousand and three thousand years old.

*(Woodstock is in Windsor County in east-central Ver-
mont. Take U.S. Highway 4 to Woodstock, eighteen miles
west of White River Junction on Highway 106. The site is
on private land ten miles north of the town. For information on arranging a visit, contact the American Institute
for Archeological Research, 24 Cross Rd., Mt. Vernon,
NH 03057. Phone: 603-673-3005.)* **72**

VIRGINIA

ABINGDON

MARTHA WASHINGTON INN The ghost of a riderless horse has been observed on moonless nights waiting for its owner on the south lawn of this inn. In 1864, Confederate soldiers ambushed a band of Union troops passing through Abingdon. As they made their escape, one of the Union soldiers was hit by a bullet. He was carried into this building, which served as a hospital at the time. The soldier died about midnight, but throughout the night the horse waited in vain for its owner on the lawn. By the next day the animal was nowhere to be found. The manor house was built in 1832 and served as a women's college and Civil War hospital. It became a sixty-one-room inn in 1935.

(Abingdon is in Washington County in the Southern Highlands of Virginia, at the junction of I-81 and U.S. Highway 19. Martha Washington Inn, 150 West Main St., Abingdon, VA 24210. Phone: 540-628-3161. For reservations, call 800-533-1014. www.marthawashingtoninn.com) **73**

ALEXANDRIA

BROWN HOUSE Several ghosts in Revolutionary War dress have been witnessed in this house in the last century. The house originally belonged to Dr. William Brown, America's surgeon general during the War for Independence.

(Alexandria is in the northeast corner of the state. U.S.

Highway 1 leads through the center of town. Brown House, 212 South Fairfax St., Alexandria, VA 22309.) **72**

A boy ghost, perhaps the ghost of Lee himself, is seen at Robert E. Lee's boyhood home. See Lee's Boyhood Home, Alexandria, Virginia (PHOTRI)

LEE'S BOYHOOD HOME Parts of this building date back to the 1760s, which might explain why so many ghosts have been reported here. In 1962, residents began encountering the ghost of a playful four-year-old boy who appeared only during daylight. At one time the house was occupied by Robert E. Lee, who lived there as a boy. Some say the ghost might be

Robert returning as a child or perhaps the ghost of his brother Phillip, who died at the age of four. Robert lived in the house until he was nearly eighteen, and his brother died after falling down a flight of stairs at another Lee home, fifty miles from Alexandria (see Stratford Hall, Westmoreland County, Virginia). Whoever the ghost is, he likes to play jokes. The doorbell sometimes rings by itself, and objects have a way of getting displaced for no reason. In two separate instances, snowflakes have fallen from midair onto visitors. The giggling boy's voice is heard throughout the house; his presence is most often detected in the downstairs hall, underneath the second-floor landing. Residents also reported the phantom of a black dog, sometimes seen in the backyard playing with the boy. Other witnesses have reported the ghosts of two little girls who could be the departed spirits of Lee's sisters.

(The house is administered by the Lee-Jackson Foundation, who officially deny any haunting. Boyhood Home of Robert E. Lee, 607 Oronoco St., Alexandria, VA 22314. Phone: 703-548-8454. www.leeboyhoodhome. com) **14, 43, 101, 188**

RAMSAY HOUSE The apparition of William Ramsay appears at an upstairs window in his former home. The Scottish merchant was the founder and first lord mayor of Alexandria.

(The house is now home to the Alexandria Visitors Center, 221 King St., Alexandria, VA 22314. Phone: 703-838-4200. Ghost Tours start from this site during summer evenings. www.alexandriacity.com/visitorscenter. htm) **78, 101**

SCHAEFER HOUSE The screaming ghost of Laura Schaefer is said to be heard at 2:00 A.M. at the top of the stairs here. Sometimes sobbing sounds are heard or footsteps racing down the stairs. Laura was dressing for her wedding one day, when she got too close to her bedroom fireplace and her dress caught fire. She died on the first floor at the foot of the stairs.

(The house is now a realty office, at 107 North Fairfax St., Alexandria, VA 22309.) **72**

SWOPE HOUSE During the War for Independence, this house belonged to Colonel Michael Swope of the Continental Army. He was captured by the British but eventually exchanged for Wellington Franklin, the Loyalist son of Benjamin Franklin. Upon his release, he was forced to walk the one thousand miles back to his home

in Alexandria. The endeavor cost the colonel his health, and he died soon after arriving home. Swope's ghost has never forgiven the British. According to later tenants and realtors, the colonel's ghost, usually in the form of a "hostile, bone-chilling cold spot," appears in the middle of the stairway to prevent any Englishman from occupying his house.

(Swope House is a private residence, at 212 Prince St., Alexandria, VA 22309.) **72**

AMELIA

HAW BRANCH PLANTATION This 15,000-acre plantation was one of the biggest in the South. The mansion was built in 1745, but after the Civil War the estate was reduced and the house fell into disrepair. Today it is one of the most haunted locations in America. In 1964, the property was purchased by the McConnaughey family, whose ancestors had lived in the house fifty years earlier. On November 23, 1965, they were awakened to bloodcurdling screams coming from the attic. The horrifying unexplained sounds were repeated every six months, on May 23 and November 23. In 1967, the apparition of a slim girl in a white full-length dress began to appear in the house. The Lady in White was finally identified as Harriet Mason, their great-grandmother. In 1969, a cousin gave the family an old portrait of a distant relative named Florence Wright, to hang in the restored mansion. The portrait was done in charcoal and had only hues of gray, and the McConnaugheys hung it over the fireplace in the library. Soon after the picture was placed on the wall, strange voices were heard throughout the house. Not long afterward, one of the family members saw the Lady in White materialize directly in front of the portrait, as if she were admiring it. Gradually, pastel colors began to appear on the drab charcoal sketch; it was turning into a full-color portrait!

Many other odd things have occurred here, including thumping noises from the moat, eerie footsteps late at night, and the unexplained scent of roses or oranges in various rooms. Once, the phantom of an enormous white bird with a wingspan of over six feet, appeared on the moonlit lawn. Another time, the ghost of a man carrying a lantern walked out of the barn. As the spirit approached the observers, the ghost disappeared, but they could still see a lantern levitating in midair. More recently, a visitor encountered two apparitions. One was a thin man who walked with a limp, and the other was a cavalier gentleman in riding boots, who screamed "Help me!"

(Amelia is in central Virginia, twenty-six miles west of Richmond on U.S. Highway 360. The mansion is a private residence open to visitors. It is just off U.S. Highway 360. The mailing address is Box 188, Amelia, VA 23002. Phone: 804-561-2472.) **58, 72, 78, 101, 102, 139, 207**

AMHERST

REBEC WINERY The 250-year-old house next to this winery is haunted by a male ghost who likes to climb into bed with people. The unidentified presence has been reported by owners Richard and Ella Hanson. The house was built in 1742 and has been in their family since 1877.

(Amherst is in western Virginia, twelve miles north of Lynchburg on U.S. Highway 29. Tours are available of the winery, which is five miles north of Amherst on U.S. Highway 29. Phone: 804-946-5168.) **205**

SWEET BRIAR COLLEGE The ghost of Miss Indiana Fletcher Jones walks the campus of the women's college she founded in 1901. The shadowy form of "Miss Indy" is most often reported near the dining room and beside the upstairs fireplaces in Mount San Angelo, a Victorian mansion that was her home.

(The college is located two miles south of Amherst. Sweet Briar College, Sweet Briar, VA 24595. Phone: 804-381-6142. www.sbc.edu) **205**

WINTON COUNTRY CLUB The spirit of Sarah Henry, mother of patriot Patrick Henry, is felt in her former house, now part of a country club. Her ghost has been detected in the bedroom directly above the living room and in the halls. She is buried in a grave on the property.

(The country club is in Clifford, which is about five miles northeast of Amherst on Highway 151. Winton Country Club, Clifford, VA 24533. Phone: 804-946-5134.) **205**

ARLINGTON CEMETERY

ARLINGTON MANSION The ghosts of the families of George Washington Parke Custis, adopted son of George Washington, and Robert E. Lee haunt this elegant house. The property was confiscated by the Fed-

eral government during the Civil War, but apparently the Custis and Lee families still consider it their own. The ghostly sounds of children playing are heard in the Morning Room, and the specter of a cat has been reported by employees. Other mysterious things, such as disembodied footsteps and candles that blow themselves out, are reported regularly.

(Arlington is just north of Alexandria, directly across the Potomac from Washington. The mansion is part of the general tours. For information, write George Washington Memorial Parkway, Turkey Run Park, McLean, VA 22101. Phone: 703-289-2500. www.arlingtoncemetery.com/arlhouse.htm) **72**

ROBERT F. KENNEDY GRAVE At the conclusion of the funeral services for the slain senator in June 1968, mourner Bobby Darin felt compelled to remain by the grave. The popular singer was a great fan of the Kennedys and was overcome with grief at Bobby's premature death. At 12:45 P.M., Darin was suddenly enveloped by a brilliant light that formed a ball of energy that passed right through him. Darin felt an "emotional cleansing" that profoundly altered his future behavior. He was convinced that Kennedy's spirit had reached out to him.

(Take I-95 to the Washington Beltway and exit at I-395 toward the cemetery. Arlington National Cemetery, Fort Meyer, VA 22211. Phone: 703-695-3250.) **193**

TOMB OF THE UNKNOWNS Psychics have reported sensing a powerful energy vortex on the grassy hill between the Tomb of the Unknowns and the Nurses' Memorial. The strongest spot is an open area on the southeast slope of the hill, between the evergreen trees and the tombstones. The etheric energy is said to recharge one spiritually and physically.

(The Tomb of the Unknowns is directly across the Potomac from the Lincoln Memorial.) **99**

BOWLING GREEN

OLD MANSION INN This one-and-a-half-story brick house was built in 1670 by British Colonel John Waller Hoomes using a royal land grant. The colonel's ghost is said to have appeared to each of his descendants just before they died. The ghost of his only daughter, Sophia, is frequently seen riding in a coach to her father's estate. The most active ghost at the inn is a later resident named Mrs. Woodford. The poor woman had a bad heart, and her husband actually scared her to death one night. He donned a hideous jack-o'-lantern costume and climbed into her window. Her screams are still heard coming from the downstairs bedroom. The sound of phantom hoofbeats on the grounds always seems to presage some disaster, and a lot of other paranormal activity has been reported. No remodeling has been done to this well-preserved pre-Georgian inn since 1770. The inn sits in the middle of 126 acres of three-hundred-year-old pasture and woodland.

(Bowling Green is in Caroline County in eastern Virginia, forty-two miles north of Richmond on U.S. Highway 301. Take Exit 104 from I-95 and follow Highway 201 for eleven miles northeast. Old Mansion Inn, State Highway 2, P.O. Box 835, Bowling Green, VA 22427. Phone: 804-633-6873.) **72, 206**

CHARLES CITY

BERKELEY PLANTATION Berkeley Plantation was founded in 1619 by thirty-eight settlers from Berkeley Castle in England. The manor house was built by Benjamin Harrison in 1726. Both George Washington and Abraham Lincoln were guests at the plantation. During the Civil War, General McClellan's Federal troops occupied Berkeley after retreating from Richmond. After the war, the plantation was bought by John Jamieson, a Scotsman who served as a drummer boy for McClellan. In 1927, the estate was inherited by his son Malcolm and has been in the Jamieson family ever since. Visitors to the restored mansion have reported seeing and hearing the ghost of a little drummer boy. The apparition of a tall, gaunt man has been seen walking along the riverbank, sometimes walking side by side with the little drummer boy along the old picket fence that runs up the hill to the cemetery. See Old Berkeley Cemetery, below.

(Charles City is on the James River in eastern Virginia, thirty-seven miles southeast of Richmond on Highway 5. Berkeley Plantation, 12602 Harrison Landing Rd., Charles City, VA 23030. Phone: 804-829-6018. www.berkeleyplantation.com) **101, 168, 205, 209**

BERRY HILL This old mansion is so haunted that no one wants to live here. Strange footsteps and the terrifying presence of an invisible entity have kept people from spending the night in the house. Some believe the ghost is the son of the original builder, who resents the estate's being taken out of the hands of his family.

(The Berry Hill plantation manor is now a museum. It is located near Westover, twenty-two miles west of Williamsburg, on Highway 5. For information, contact the Virginia State Travel Service, 901 E. Byrd St., Richmond, VA 23219. Phone: 804-786-4484.) **90**

EDGEWOOD The ghost of Lizzie Rowland still waits for her lost lover to return from the Civil War. Her apparition is seen behind a curtain, peering out an upstairs window. The house was built in 1849 by Lizzie's father, Spencer Rowland.

(Lizzie Rowland is buried in the Westover Churchyard. Edgewood is now a bed-and-breakfast inn. It is located a quarter-mile from Berkeley Plantation, on Highway 5. Edgewood Plantation, 4800 John Tyler Highway, Highway 5, Charles City, VA 23030. Phone: 800-296-3343. www.edgewood-plantation.com) **101, 205, 209**

GREENWOOD This seventeenth-century plantation home is haunted by the ghosts of Governor John Tyler, Sr., and his wife. They have been seen on the second floor of the house, in a bedroom now christened the Haunted Chamber.

(The T-shaped, two-story house is half a mile from the Charles City County Courthouse, along the James River, in Charles City. Greenwood, Highway 5, Charles City, VA 23030.) **101, 209**

OLD BERKELEY CEMETERY This graveyard is the final resting place of members of the original Berkeley colony and the families of plantation owners over the centuries. The ghost of a redheaded drummer boy, about twelve years old, is seen on the hilltop here. He beats his drum softly and looks out over the James River.

(The cemetery is across from Berkeley Plantation, above the James River. Further information is available from the Virginia Division of Tourism, 202 North Ninth St., Richmond, VA 23201. Phone: 804-786-4484.) **168**

SHERWOOD FOREST The Gray Lady haunts this presidential estate, which has been in the John Tyler family for over 150 years. But the Gray Lady was here long before the tenth president took up residence in 1842. She is thought to be a governess who lived in the house in the late 1700s. Her ghostly presence is detected rocking in a wooden rocker in the second-floor nursery, in the Gray Room, and on the servants' stairway.

(The plantation is owned by the Tyler family. Tours are available. The estate is northeast of the James River, opposite Brandon Marsh, just off Highway 5. Sherwood Forest, Highway 5, Charles City, VA 23030 Phone: 804-829-5377. www.sherwoodforest.org) **101, 209**

A haunted portrait hangs peacefully in a second-floor bedroom here at the Shirley Plantation, but when it is moved to another location the frame rattles violently on the wall. See Shirley Plantation, Charles City, Virginia (EVERETTE EVANS/PHOTRI)

SHIRLEY PLANTATION Martha Pratt was a daughter of Edward Hill II, who built the great house now called Shirley Plantation in 1723. When she married an Englishman and settled in England, all she left behind was an unsigned portrait of herself. By 1858, family descendants had noticed an unusual property of the painting. Whenever Aunt Pratt's portrait was removed from its spot on the second floor, the frame would start shaking violently. They moved it to a bedroom on the third floor, stored it in the attic, and hung it on the first floor, but the portrait was never "happy" unless it was back in the second-floor bedroom. In 1974, the Virginia Tourist Office put the touchy painting on display at Rocke-feller Center, along with other items related to psychic phenomena in the state. Martha Hills' portrait created quite a sensation. Spectators saw it moving constantly. It swayed back and forth so violently that other exhibits were also vibrating. The phenomenon was documented on an NBC-TV national news broadcast. The painting caused such hysteria that it was removed from the display. That did not stop Martha Hill. Dozens of office workers near the storeroom in

which the painting was locked heard incessant knocking sounds coming from the room. When officials retrieved the painting, its frame was so badly damaged that it was sent for repair to Linden Galleries in Richmond, Virginia. The same eerie vibrations were reported by workers there. Finally, the portrait of Martha Hill was returned to the Shirley Plantation, where it hangs, peacefully, above a mahogany chest in Martha's second-floor bedroom.

(Shirley Plantation is on the James River, southeast of Richmond, on Highway 5. Follow signs to the plantation grounds. The mailing address is 501 Shirley Plantation Rd., Charles City, VA 23030. Phone: 800-232-1613. www.haunted-places.com/virginia.htm) **14, 78, 101, 102, 168, 209**

WESTOVER The friendly ghost of Evelyn Byrd lingers at her old estate. She died of unknown causes in 1736 at the age of twenty-nine. Before her untimely death, she promised a friend she would try to return "in such a fashion as not to frighten anyone." That is exactly what she did. Her smiling apparition has been seen in the southeast bedroom, in a narrow passage under the three-story mahogany staircase, in the hallways, on the pantry stairs, in the gardens, and in a nearby poplar grove. She usually wears a white gown or a green velvet dress, but she always appears smiling and then slowly fades away. Evelyn Byrd's ghost has been sighted regularly for over three hundred years. Her lineage includes such American notables as Admiral Richard Byrd and Senator Harry Byrd. The ghost of another relative, William Byrd III, has been seen at the stroke of midnight, slumped over in his favorite chair in his bedroom. Distraught over financial matters, he committed suicide there in 1777. His first wife, Elizabeth, had been crushed to death a few years earlier, when a massive cabinet fell on top of her. Her plaintive wailing is still heard on occasion, echoing through the halls of Westover. The house was built in 1730 by William Byrd II and was named for the son of Thomas West, governor of Virginia.

(Westover is east of the Shirley Plantation, not far from the Berkeley estate, on Highway 5. Evelyn is buried at Westover Church, up the river a quarter-mile west of the house. Westover, 7000 Westover Rd., Charles City, VA 23030. Phone: 804-829-2882. www.jamesriverplantations.org/Westover.html) **5, 14, 78, 87, 90, 101, 187, 208, 209**

CHARLOTTESVILLE

ASH LAWN President James Monroe haunts his former home. The rocking chair of the president is often seen rocking slowly with nobody sitting in it. When the house became a museum, the embarrassing chair was locked in storage.

(Charlottesville is located in Albemarle County in central Virginia, at the junction of I-64 and U.S. Highway 29. The museum is five miles southeast of Charlottesville, on the east slope of Carter's Mountain.) **90, 205**

CARRSGROVE The ghost of a devoted mother haunts a second-floor bedroom in this mansion. She took poison in the room, sitting next to the bed of her little girl, whom she thought was dying of cholera. The girl survived, but the mother died. The sounds of the woman's disconsolate sobbing still fill the upstairs halls. The stone house was built in 1748 by David Reese. James Monroe, who became president in 1817, lived here from 1799 to 1808. Descendants of Aaron Burr acquired the property in 1955.

(Carrsgrove is on the National Register of Historic Places. It is located in central Charlottesville.) **82, 86, 205**

CASTALIA The revenant of a short woman with dark hair, wearing a striped dress, was seen on several occasions here. She has been observed in the upstairs bedrooms, the Chintz Room, and the Lavender Room.

(Castalia Mansion is a private residence a few miles from the center of Charlottesville.) **205**

CASTLE HILL The Pink Bedroom in this huge house, built by Dr. Thomas Walker in 1765, is the center of ghostly activity. Numerous residents over the years have heard unexplained noises coming from the room. Poetess Amelie Rives told of the strange odor of perfume that sometimes drifted through the room when she lived in the house. Writer Julian Green left the house in a hurry one morning after he encountered something strange there. He was never able to talk about it. Others have seen the rocking chair in the Pink Bedroom rock contentedly by itself or have witnessed other poltergeist-like phenomena, such as moving or disappearing objects. The ghost seems to be that of a young, somewhat playful, woman, but no one has ever identified her. Her apparition is described as "a charming-looking woman dressed in the fashion of long ago, and carrying a tiny fan."

(Castle Hill Mansion is a private residence outside Charlottesville, in Albemarle County.) **82, 89, 205**

THE FARM An event that took place over two hundred years ago has left a lasting impression in this colonial farmhouse. Psychics and sensitives report feeling uneasiness and high emotional energy near the fireplace. It apparently originated with a British officer, Colonel Banastre Tarleton, who spent the night of June 14, 1781, sleeping in front of the fireplace, after avoiding an ambush by Continental soldiers under the command of Captain John Marson.

(The Farm is a two-story brick house in central Charlottesville. It has been designated a city historic landmark.) **86**

MICHIE TAVERN This building has been a stopover for thirsty travelers since 1784, and two-hundred-year-old ghosts are still having a party on the third floor. The ballroom there is haunted by sounds of laughter, music, and the clinking of invisible glasses.

(Michie Tavern is about seventeen miles from Charlottesville on the Old Buck Mountain Rd. in the Earlysville area. Michie Tavern, 683 Thomas Jefferson Parkway, Charlottesville, VA 22902. Phone: 804-977-1234. www.michietavern.com) **92, 101, 205**

MONTICELLO When no one is around, the spirit of Thomas Jefferson returns to his beloved Monticello. Guards have reported hearing the sounds of cheerful humming in the empty building. It was a habit Thomas Jefferson kept beyond the grave. The third president is buried in the family cemetery here.

(The Thomas Jefferson Visitor Center at Monticello is three miles southeast of Charlottesville on Highway 20. Phone: 804-984-9800. www.monticello.org) **92, 101, 205**

SUNNY BANK This imposing Palladian mansion is home to the ghosts of two young women. They first made their presence known in the early 1900s with sounds of footsteps, the noise of sink basins filling, and the movement of furniture. By the 1920s, they were materializing before startled residents. The ghosts of Betty Dew and Constance Cazenove appear in the bedrooms in which they died. The house has been in the

Andrew Hart family for two centuries, and both apparitions are believed to be relatives.

(Sunny Bank is a private residence in Albemarle County, near South Garden. It is eighteen miles from Charlottesville.) **205**

CHESTERFIELD

PHYSIC HILL This L-shaped house was built in 1815 by Dr. John Walke and is named for a series of physicians who lived here. The ghost of Martha Branch Walke, Dr. Walke's first wife, is said to haunt the house. She died in 1841 at the age of fifty-two and is buried on the property. Her restless spirit is blamed for the sounds of pacing footsteps and heavy objects flying through the air. In 1984, a painter saw Martha's ghost standing near the window in her former bedroom.

(The town of Chesterfield is seven miles south of Richmond on Highway 10. Physic Hill is just outside Chesterfield. It is located off Winterpock Road in Chesterfield County at 14300 Physic Hill Rd.) **101, 207**

WREXHAM HALL The phantom is of a lady in red haunts this house, which is actually composed of two houses, both built in the mid-1700s. The Lady in Red is most often seen on the front porch, although her footsteps are sometimes heard on the main stairway and in the upstairs hall.

(Wrexham Hall is private residence. It is located south of the Chesterfield Courthouse on Highway 10.) **101, 207**

COLONIAL BEACH

BELL HOUSE Alexander Graham Bell inherited this house from his father, Alexander Melville Bell, in 1905. Both men were noted inventors. The Bell House was sold many times and gradually gained a reputation for being haunted. Neighbors reported seeing the face of Melville Bell in the front windows of the deserted house, and tenants admitted to encountering a "white, wispy presence" on the stairs and in the bathroom.

(The town of Colonial Beach is in Westmoreland County. It is located on the Potomac River, thirty miles east of Fredericksburg on Highway 206/205. Bell House is a private residence at 821 Irving Ave., Colonial Beach, VA 22443. Phone: 803-224-7000. www.thebellhouse.com) **206**

ELKTON

ELKTON POLICE DEPARTMENT This old police station is haunted by eerie moaning sounds and unexplainable footsteps. The phenomena occur in the basement office and the hall leading to the washrooms. In 1981, a dispatcher reported a presence in the building that turned calendar pages and made itself known in other disturbing ways. The two-story brick building served as a hospital during the Civil War. The morgue was located in the basement.

(Elkton is in Rockingham County in northern Virginia, seventeen miles east of Harrisonburg on U.S. Highway 33, at U.S. Highway 340. The police station is at 173 W. Spotwood Ave. in Elkton. Phone: 540-298-9441.) **205**

ESSEX COUNTY

BLANDFIELD This eighteenth-century mansion is haunted by the ghosts of several members of the Beverley family. For over two hundred years, their wispy apparitions and moving balls of light have been seen here. One of the women apparitions wears a long flowered dress and is seen in the upstairs hall; another, wearing a dark skirt, is seen in the downstairs hall. A male figure haunts the downstairs library. The brick mansion was built by Robert Beverley in 1774. The ghosts of Beverley family members also haunt Avenal, their summer home in Fauquier County.

(Essex County is in eastern Virginia southwest of the Rappahannock River. The mansion is a private residence off U.S. Highway 17 on the Rappahannock River.) **90, 206**

ELMWOOD This two-story brick plantation house has been home to the Garnett family since 1774. It was deserted or housed only caretakers from 1870 to the 1940s. During that time, ghostly activity reached its peak. When the house was once again inhabited, the ghosts of a man and woman dressed in lacy, old-fashioned cloths started crashing parties. No matter what music is playing, they dance the minuet together in the ballroom. They waltz down the stairs into the garden and float away, disappearing behind a clump of boxwood bushes. The ghostly couple reportedly takes no notice of the other guests, although it is the festive mood that seems to attract them.

(The plantation is situated in the rolling hills of the Rappahannock River. It is in Essex County, near the town of Tappahannock, at the junction of U.S. Highways 17 and 360.) **164, 208**

LINDEN HOUSE Renovations of this 250-year-old inn stirred up some sleeping spirits. Strange aromas drift through the brick building, and disembodied footsteps are heard on the third and fourth floors. When orange-yellow lights started moving through the hallways, the owners had a priest come out to bless the place. But the strange manifestations continue.

(The bed-and-breakfast inn is located north of Tappahannock on Highway 17. Linden House Inn, P.O. Box 23/Rt. 17, South Champlain, Va 22438. Phone: 800-622-1202.) **206**

MOUNT AIRY MANSION Colonel John Tayhoe III was the wealthiest man in Virginia in the late 1700s and early 1800s. The mansion on his tobacco plantation estate was also one of the most beautiful, and like his town house in Washington, DC (see Octagon, District of Columbia), his Virginia home is considered to be haunted. In the 1850s, descendants of Tayhoe reported seeing the apparition of a white-haired woman in one of the upstairs bedrooms. Mary Leiper, a governess hired by the family, was drawn to the room when the Tayhoes were away. She decided to spend the night there rather than in her assigned room downstairs. When the Tayhoes returned, the governess related how she was awakened in the middle of the night by deep moaning sounds, and discovered the ghost hovering at the foot of her bed.

(Mount Airy Mansion is a private residence east of Tappahannock, near Warsaw. It is located across the river on U.S. Highway 360.) **14, 206**

ST. MARGARET'S GIRL SCHOOL For generations, students here have told stories of encountering Blue Lady, who walks the halls of St. Margaret's. The apparition is thought to be the spirit of a deceased nun.

(The private school is in Essex County in Tappahannock at 444 Water Lane. Phone: 804-443-3357. www.sms.org) **206**

FAIRFIELD

MCDOWELL CEMETERY The headless phantom of a soldier in a long overcoat has been reported walking

A headless phantom walks in the graveyard at McDowell Cemetery. See McDowell Cemetery, Fairfield, Virginia (GORDON TING)

out of the old graveyard here. The cemetery is the site of the Massacre of Balcony Downs in December 1742, when Captain John McDowell and seven of his militiamen were killed and butchered by a marauding band of Onandaga and Oneida Indians.

(Fairfield is in Rockbridge County in western Virginia. It is on U.S. Highway 11, between Lexington and Stuarts Draft. The cemetery is off U.S. Highway 11 in Fairfield. It is not the main town cemetery. The overgrown McDowell Cemetery is set back about three hundred feet from the highway.) **205**

FORK UNION

CAREBY HALL This eleven-room house is haunted by the presence of Dr. William Hatcher, founder of Fork Union Military Academy. He built the house in 1897 and lived here until he died in 1912, at the age of seventy-eight. For many years after his death his daughter kept his study untouched, as if she were expecting him to return any moment. Her high expectations were rewarded. His presence has often been detected in his old den or near an upstairs window, by family members, academy personnel, and former tenants. Sometimes sounds of someone whistling a tune come from the empty house, and invisible footsteps shuffle across the floors. The most frequently reported phenomenon is a glowing fog that forms behind the upstairs front window. See Hatcher Hall, below.

(Fork Union is in central Virginia, at the junction of U.S. Highway 15 and Highway 6. Take Exit 136, U.S.

Highway 15 south, from I-64. The academy opened in 1898. Fork Union Academy, P.O. Box 278 Fork Union, VA 23055 Phone: 804-842-3212. www.fuma.org) **186**

HATCHER HALL The ghost of Dr. William Hatcher has been seen in the administration building of the military academy he founded. In 1960, a guard was investigating the sounds of a door opening and closing on the second floor of the building, when the apparition of Dr. Hatcher brushed his shoulder. The ghost had a full gray beard, wore a black overcoat, and swung a cane or umbrella as it walked down the hall and disappeared. An official report was filed. See Careby Hall, above.

(Hatcher Hall is the main building on the campus of Fork Union Military Academy. It houses the administration offices and classrooms. Phone: 804-842-3212.) **186**

Old Fort Monroe is home to many Civil War—era ghosts. See Old Fort Monroe and Casemate Museum, Fort Monroe, Virginia (FORT MONROE CASEMATE MUSEUM)

FORT MONROE

HOTEL CHAMBERLIN The ghost of a woman named Ezmerelda haunts the storage area on the eighth floor of this old hotel. She died in a fire in the hotel in 1920. Her apparition is frequently seen staring out the windows of the cluttered storage rooms. She is described as a beautiful woman with long, light brown hair, wearing a white robe.

(Fort Monroe, the nation's oldest continuously garrisoned fortress, is on the Chesapeake Bay at the southeastern tip of Virginia. It is across the Hampton Roads Bridge from Norfolk, at the end of U.S. Highway 258, adjacent to Hampton. From I-64, take Exit 268 at Hampton, and follow the signs to Fort Monroe. Phone: 804-723-6511. www-tradoc.monroe.army.mil/monroe/chamb2) **145, 146**

OLD FORT MONROE AND CASEMATE MUSEUM This heptagonal stone fortress was built in the early 1800s and is surrounded by a deep moat. Many Civil War—era ghosts haunt the grounds. The most famous are in Old Quarters No. 1, where the ghosts of Abraham Lincoln and Ulysses S. Grant roam. Matthew Lane is known as Ghost Alley. It got its name from the luminous specter of the "Light Lady," Camille Kirtz, who haunts the street where her husband caught her in the embrace of a Frenchman. Captain Wilhelm Kirtz pulled his gun to shoot the Frenchman, but shot his wife instead. The lane was the back entrance to the Tuileries, the officers' quarters, where the couple lived. After the Civil War, Jefferson Davis was shackled and

imprisoned in a cell in the Casemate. The plump ghost of his wife Varina Lee has been spotted looking out a bedroom window across from his casemate cell. The ghost of Edgar Allan Poe is said to wander through the site of his old barracks, Building No. 5. He returned to Fort Monroe for a poetry reading just a month before he died. Two other famous military men whose revenants have been seen at Fort Monroe are General Lafayette and Captain John Smith. Some of the private residences in Fort Monroe are also haunted. The ghost of a small boy haunts the upstairs of an old house inside the fort next to the moat wall; at another residence, a whole family saw a heavy marble side table float into the air and smash against the fireplace.

(Fort Monroe is an active Army command, although many of its buildings are open to the public. There is a hotel and restaurant on the premises. The main entrance is on Ingalls Road. Three sides of Fort Monroe face the Chesapeake Bay. Fort Monroe Casemate Museum, Box 341, Fort Monroe, VA 23651. Phone: 804-727-3391.) **14, 101, 145, 146, 163, 208**

FREDERICKSBURG

AQUIA CHURCH This brick church was constructed in 1754 but was struck by fire as soon as it was finished. The interior was completely rebuilt by 1757. During the Revolutionary War, when the church was not being used, highwaymen raped and murdered a young woman in the chapel. They cornered her in the belfry, where her lifeless body lay undisturbed for several years. When the church reopened, bloodstains were found on the chapel floor and her skeleton was discovered in the steeple. For nearly two hundred years, her frightened apparition has been seen running up the steeple stairway or peering out the belfry window. According to legend, the ghost caused a death in the 1890s. A young man who went into the belfry one night to confront the ghost was found dead of fright the next morning.

(Fredericksburg is in northeastern Virginia, at the junction of I-95 and U.S. Highway 17. The church is twenty miles north of Fredericksburg in Stafford County. An annual tour of haunted locations in Fredericksburg is conducted by the preservation society. For information, contact the Fredericksburg Visitor Center, 706 Caroline St., Fredericksburg, VA 22405. Phone: 800-678-4748.) **206**

CHARLOTTE STREET The frightening apparition of the Headless Blue Girl haunts a section of this street. She was seen by numerous independent witnesses in May 1974. The "concentration of bluish light" had the form of a woman without a head and floated down the odd-numbered side of the street toward Federal Hill mansion. See Federal Hill, below.

(Fredericksburg is forty-five miles south of Washington and fifty-five miles north of Richmond on I-95. From I-95, take the Highway 3 exit. The ghost was reported in front of 507, 511, and 513 Charlotte St. in Fredericksburg.) **206**

A white lady walks a path on these grounds that has become known as Ghost Walk. See Chatham Manor, Fredericksburg, Virginia
(FREDERICKSBURG DEPARTMENT OF TOURISM)

CHATHAM MANOR The apparition of a white lady walks a path on these grounds that has become known as Ghost Walk. Chatham was built in 1771 by William Fitzhugh. He named it after a close friend, William Pitt, the Earl of Chatham. Another English friend of Fitzhugh brought his daughter to live at Chatham in an effort to break up her romance with a commoner. But the man followed her to America, and the two planned to elope from Chatham Manor. He gave her a rope ladder and waited in a small boat in a nearby river. Unfortunately, none other than George Washington, another close friend of Fitzhugh, was staying there at the same time. He learned of their plans from a maid and had his men arrest the suitor. The girl returned to England with her father and later married. But she vowed to return to Chatham Manor to look for her lover. Her ghost was first sighted there on the day she died, June 21, 1790, and returns every seven years on the anniversary of her death to wander along the path to the river, looking for her lost love. The Lady in White is next due to appear on June 21, 2000.

(Follow Williams Street south to Chatham Manor, also known as Lacy House. Ghost Walk is the path at Chatham that leads to a high bluff overlooking the Rappahannock River. Chatham Manor, 120 Chatham Lane, Fredericksburg, VA 22405. Phone: 540-654-5121. www.nps.gov/frsp/chatham.htm) **14, 101, 102, 206**

FEDERAL HILL A flamboyant Scottish ghost haunts Federal Hill. He is Alexander Spotswood, the state's governor from 1710 to 1722. Spotswood was responsible for the death of pirate Edward Teach, also known as Blackbeard. Spotswood's ghost started appearing in the stately house in the 1920s and has been seen many times since. His appearances are always the same. He suddenly materializes standing next to an old sideboard cabinet. He is dressed in white-plaited hunting britches tied with a black rope, and he seems to be mixing drinks on the sideboard tabletop. See Charlotte Street, above.

(The historic house is a private residence on Charlotte Street in Fredericksburg. For further information, contact the Fredericksburg Visitor Center, 706 Caroline St., Fredericksburg, VA 22405. Phone: 800-678-4748.) **206**

FREDERICKSBURG BATTLEFIELD In December 1862, Confederate troops under General Robert E. Lee easily withstood the assault of General Ambrose Burnside's troops by taking cover on a wide, stone-walled ridge known as Marye's Heights. Over nine thousand Federalists died, compared with fifteen hundred deaths on the Confederate side. One South Carolina soldier, Sergeant Richard Kirkland, risked his own life to bring canteens of water to dying Union soldiers, whose moans filled the air during lulls in the shooting. The cries and mournful pleas of those dying soldiers are heard to this day, and the ghostly figure of brave Sergeant Kirkland, the Angel of Mayre's Heights, can be seen still coming to their aid.

(The battlefield is part of the Fredericksburg and Spotsylvania Military Park. Follow I-95 to Highway 3 east. The Visitor Center is at 1013 Lafayette Blvd., Fredericksburg, VA 22405. Phone: 540-371-0802. www.nps.gov/frsp) **163**

KENMORE The ghost of a man who died in the 1780s is haunting his former home. Colonel Fielding Lewis married Betty Washington, the only sister of our first president, and they started building this magnificent mansion in 1752. With eleven children to feed, Fielding spent many hours in his upstairs bedroom going over accounts and fretting about money. His ghost, clad in Revolutionary-era attire and studying documents, is most often seen there, but he also makes his presence felt in the downstairs hall, where doorknobs turn mysteriously and heavy footsteps pace, although there is no one to be seen.

(Follow William Street, Highway 3, to Washington Ave. Kenmore is located on the corner of Lewis St. and Washington Ave. at 1201 Washington Ave., Fredericksburg, VA 22401. Tours are available. Phone: 540-373-3381. www.kenmore.org) **14, 78, 101, 206**

LAMB'S CREEK CHURCH A woman in white is seen kneeling at the chancel rail here. The sightings date back to the Civil War when the church, built in the 1770s, was used as a stable by Union forces. The church was restored in 1908, although today the building is rarely used.

(The church is in Graves Corner, thirteen miles east of Fredericksburg on Highway 3.) **206**

LE LAFAYETTE RESTAURANT The ghost of a young child, possibly a little girl, has been seen at this Georgian-style mansion. Sometimes a child's voice is heard singing. Footsteps are heard, chairs rock by themselves, and windows and doors fly open or slam shut. Poltergeist activity, such as china flying across the room and glasses crashing to the floor, has also been reported. The distinctive house, with its two towering chimneys, was built in 1770 by Scottish merchant John Glassell. It was the childhood home of Nell Herndon, who later became President Chester Arthur's First Lady.

(The restaurant, also known as the Chimneys Tavern, is across from the Fredericksburg Visitor Center, at 623 Caroline St., Fredericksburg, VA 22401. Phone: 540-373-6895.) **14, 102, 206**

LITCHFIELD The wraith of an eight-year-old girl is seen drifting through this simple wood-frame house. Sometimes her gentle voice can be heard singing in the attic. She has long brown hair and wears an old-fashioned dress with high-button shoes. Since the 1920s, the sounds of an invisible carriage pulling up to the front of the house have been heard. Who the child is and what the relevance is of the carriage sounds have never been determined. The six-room, two-story house was built in 1802 by the Dade family.

(The house is a private residence twenty miles east of Fredericksburg, at the intersection of Highway 206 and Highway 218 in King George County.) **206**

MARMION The apparition of a woman dressed in a white dress is seen in this early-eighteenth-century mansion. She has been seen in the upstairs bedrooms, descending the stairs, and in the dining room. She is believed to be twenty-two-year-old Kate Pollock, who died in childbirth in October 1821. Kate and her baby are buried on the property.

(Marmion is two-story mansion is east of Fredericksburg, two miles west of King George on Highway 3. Historical marker J63 on Highway 3 explains the background of the house.) **206**

MONROE LAW OFFICE The ghosts of James Monroe and Thomas Jefferson were seen walking through the front door of this building in the late 1960s. The sighting is said to have coincided with the appearance of a large crack in the front door of the building, where Monroe practiced law from 1786 to 1789.

(The museum is at 908 Charles St., Fredericksburg, VA 22401. Phone: 540-654-1043. http://departments.mwc.edu/jmmu/www) **206**

RISING SUN TAVERN A playful poltergeist here tugs at dresses and knocks off hats. Many guests and employees of this eighteenth-century tavern have encountered the presence, but no one seems to know who or what it is. The poltergeist once literally pulled the rug out from under a tour guide. The house was built in 1760 by Charles Washington, youngest brother of George.

(Rising Sun Tavern, 1306 Caroline St., Fredericksburg, VA 22405. Phone: 540-371-1494. www.apva.org/apva/rising.html) **14, 102, 206**

ST. GEORGE'S EPISCOPAL CHURCH The apparition of a mysterious lady dressed in a dark dress and wearing a veil has been seen kneeling at the altar here.

(St. George's Episcopal Church was founded in 1720. It is located on Princess Anne St., between George and Caroline streets at 905 Princess Anne St. Phone: 540-373-4133.) **14, 206**

SMYTHE'S COTTAGE AND TAVERN The ghost of a tall man with long black hair, wearing a full-length black coat, has been seen on the outdoor patio here. Another ghost is sometimes seen in the front of the house directly across the street. That phantom is Tootie Ninde, who died of cancer in 1982. Her ghost has been observed crawling up the stairs or staring out a front window. Smythe's Cottage is a three-room house built in 1850 which probably served as a blacksmith's shop. According to owner Lonny Williams, faint ringing sounds like iron being formed on an anvil can sometimes be heard in the front dining room during the early evening hours.

(Smythe's Cottage is featured in the October Ghost Walk sponsored by the Historic Preservation Club of Mary Washington College. The 1830s tavern restaurant is on the corner of Faquier and Princess Anne streets at 303 Faquier St., Fredericksburg, VA 22401. Phone: 540-373-1645.) **206**

WASHINGTON HOUSE The ghost of Mary Ball Washington, the extremely possessive mother of George Washington, lingers in the house where she spent the last seventeen years of her life. Her ghost has been detected in the kitchen and on a boxwood path behind the house. A hostess reported hearing the rustling of Mary's skirts as her spirit moved from room to room closing doors. Mary died of breast cancer in 1789, at the age of eighty-one years.

(Mary Washington is buried a few blocks from her home at Meditation Rock. The historic house is on the corner of Charles St. and Lewis St., at 1200 Charles St., Fredericksburg, VA 2401. Phone: 540-373-1569. www.apva.org/apva/mwash.html) **206**

WILLIS HOUSE The ghost of a Yankee soldier nicknamed "Yip the Yank" has been seen several times in this two-story Colonial house. He was killed in the building in 1862 during bitter street fighting in Fredericksburg, and was buried in the garden of Willis House.

(The 1740s house is a private residence at 1106 Princess Anne St., Fredericksburg, VA 22401.) **206**

GLOUCESTER COUNTY

CHURCH HILL Generations of the Throckmorton family have lived in this frame manor house, and the spirit of one family member will never leave. Elizabeth Throckmorton died soon after she was buried. Everyone thought Elizabeth had died of lovesickness, pining away for an Englishman her father had forbidden her to see. But she was really only in a catatonic state and awoke as grave robbers were trying to take her rings. The frail girl managed to climb out of her premature grave, only to freeze to death on the front porch of the house. No one heard her feeble knocking on the massive front door, and a raging blizzard did her in. Now, whenever it snows, servants and family members hear the sounds of Elizabeth running up the stairway to the warmth of an upstairs fireplace. Though she died just outside the front entrance, her spirit made it safely inside.

(Gloucester County is on the east coast of Virginia on the Chesapeake Bay. It can be reached by following U.S. Highway 17 north from Hampton or southeast from Fredericksburg. Church Hill Plantation is a private residence in Gloucester County. It is located on a bluff overlooking the Ware River off County Road 3/14. The family burial plots are in the garden on the property.) **72, 208**

PAYNTON HALL Fairfax Dalton built this spacious house in the early 1700s and lived there with his wife Lettitia Brundage and their daughter Caro. He and Lettitia fought violently, and Mrs. Brundage was rumored to be responsible for the "accidental" deaths of both Fairfax and Caro. In 1745, a black maid poisoned Lettitia. For many years after the series of deaths at Paynton Hall, bloodstains would appear on the marble landing where Fairfax fell to his death, and, in the 1800s, a small-figured ghost was known to trip people and cause accidents. After Paynton Hall burned to the ground, the ghosts remained. Today, terrible screams may be heard coming from its ruins.

(The overgrown foundation of this old mansion is not far from Rosewell in Gloucester County. The area is near the York Plains Ford Battleground.) **158**

ROSEWELL This deserted mansion was once among the finest of Colonial homes. The five-story redbrick estate was built in 1725 by merchant Mann Page. It was gutted by fire in 1916, but the ruins still stand. Visitors have reported seeing the ghosts of linkboys standing near the doorway late at night and spirits moving down the Corinthian stairway. Sometimes harpsichord music is heard, and the apparition of a woman in red is seen running toward the old garden area.

(The ruins of Rosewell Mansion lie near the confluence of the York River and Cater's Creek in Gloucester County. A family graveyard lies directly behind the house. The area is the source of several recent ghost sightings.) **158, 208**

WHITE MARSH PLANTATION There were many supernatural manifestations here after the Civil War. Most were attributed to the restless souls of over 1,500 slaves buried in a graveyard in the peach orchard. But after extensive renovations in 1948, the ghost of the original woman of the house started to appear. Evelina Tabb's apparition was often seen folding children's clothes near a chest of drawers in one of the bedrooms. Once, a neighbor brushed against the phantom on the stairs, and the swishing sound of the Evelina's taffeta skirts can sometimes be heard in the hallway. The Georgian mansion was built in the 1750s by members of the Tabb family, several of whose children died here.

(The plantation house is a private residence along the Ware River in Gloucester County.) **90, 208**

HAMPTON

DENTAL OFFICE The ghost of a dead dentist haunts the office where he allegedly committed suicide in the 1970s. Although a new dentist took over the office, employees sensed the dead man's presence and even heard the sounds of the drill when no one was using it. A clairvoyant who said she had contacted the dentist's spirit said he had returned to let his mother know he

had not killed himself. He was a secret abuser of nitrous oxide, or laughing gas, and had overdosed while alone in the office one night.

(The town of Hampton is on the Chesapeake Bay. It is located in the extreme southeast corner of Virginia, at the junction of I-64 and U.S. Highway 17. The office is at 1420 King St., Hampton, VA 23669.) **145**

FERNANDEZ STUDIO This modern photographic studio is haunted by a curious ghost, who peeks over the shoulders of employees to see what they are doing. The impolite male ghost has been visiting the studio since the early 1970s, and he seems to prefer the darkroom. The studio opened in 1969 and specializes in restoring antique photos.

(Fernandez Photographic Studio, 1297 North King St., Hampton, VA 23669. Phone: 757-723-1297.) **145**

PHOEBUS FIRE STATION This old firehouse is haunted by Fire Engine Charlie. Charlie is a dead fireman, whose spirit can be heard walking through the upstairs halls or playing pool in the game room.

(The firehouse is in central Hampton at 122 S. Hope St., Hampton, VA 23663.) **145**

HANOVER COUNTY

FORK CHURCH Mary Love Alrich, wife of the rector who came to the church here in 1869, died in childbirth in 1872. Ever since, when there is an infant in the rectory, Mary's soft footsteps are heard in the second-floor nursery, and her loving presence is sensed throughout the house.

(Hanover County is north of Richmond in east-central Virginia. The brick Episcopal church, built in 1842, is in St. Martin's Parish. It is at the confluence of the North and South Anna rivers.) **206**

SCOTCHTOWN This barn-shaped mansion was built in 1719 by Charles Chiswell. His son John Chiswell killed a man in a drunken brawl in October 1766 and is thought to have committed suicide afterward. He is buried in a small graveyard on the property, but his distressed spirit is felt in the house. Dolley Payne, future wife of the fourth president, James Madison, lived in the house for a short time with her parents. (See Dolley Madison House, Lafayette Square; Octagon, Northwest Washington; and Rose Garden, White House, all in the District of Columbia.) Then in 1771, Scotchtown became the home of patriot Patrick Henry. Within months of moving in, Patrick's wife Sarah Shelton Henry went insane. She had to be kept locked up in two basement rooms, where she died in 1775. Her presence is still detected in the area, and her white apparition was once seen in a first-floor backroom.

(The estate is twenty-seven miles north of Richmond in Hanover County, five miles past Ashland on Highway 54. Scotchtown, 16120 Chiswell Lane, Beaverdam, VA 23015. Phone: 804-227-3500.) **78, 101, 206**

HARRISONBURG

LAYMAN AVENUE HOUSE A ghost named Max stays in this house to protect it from his evil sister, who altered his will so she could inherit the building. The German's guttural voice, groaning sounds, and shuffling footsteps have been reported by tenants for many years. Max explained his motivation at a séance arranged by the current owners.

(Harrisonburg is in northwest Virginia, at the junction of I-81 and U.S. Highway 33. The house is a private residence, at 537 Layman Ave., Harrisonburg, VA 22801.) **205**

STONEWALL COTTAGE The Dovel ancestral home is haunted by departed family members including the ghost of an elderly aunt who knocks her clay pipe against the fireplace. The revenant of former owner Mary Dovel Stephens returned to Stonewall shortly after her death in 1902.

(Stonewall Cottage is a private residence located north of Harrisonburg, on the Valley Turnpike.) **205**

LANCASTER COUNTY

VERVILLE An old well in the garden of this 1740s house is the source of Verville's hauntings. For nearly a century, residents told of the apparitions of a woman and a small child, who rose up out of the well, walked into the house, and climbed the stairs to the Blue Room on the second floor. Once in the room, the ghosts disappeared in a blaze of light. The strange ritual ceased in 1907, when the well was filled in, but unexplained lights, eerie noises, and the sounds of children's voices are still reported in the old house.

(Lancaster County is on the Chesapeake Bay in extreme northeastern Virginia. It lies at the mouth of the Rappahannock River. The mansion is a private residence in Lancaster County, nine miles north of the town of Kilmarnock, on Highway 300.) **72, 205**

LEXINGTON

VIRGINIA MILITARY INSTITUTE Strange moaning sounds and even tears have been reported coming from Moses Ezekiel's bronze statue, "Virginia Mourning Her Dead," at the center of the campus. Also haunted by the state's Civil War dead is a mural in Jackson Memorial Hall. But the most horrendous presence here is the Yellow Peril, a phantom with "a hideous yellow face and bleeding scar." The ghoul haunts the third floor of the VMI Barracks. The men's military college was established in 1839.

(The town of Lexington is located in Rockbridge County, in east-central Virginia, at the junction of I-64 and I-81. Virginia Military Institute, Lexington, VA 24450. Phone: 540-464-7000. www.vmi.edu) **205**

LOUDOUN COUNTY

IVON ESTATE The frightening phantom of a great black bear haunted this mansion for over 150 years. The stone manorhouse was built in the 1750s by Thomas Mason. Soon after it was completed, servants, family members, and houseguests started seeing a huge bear in the house. Sometimes the bear would materialize late at night at the foot of someone's bed. A deserted cave was found on the property, but no one ever saw a living bear. The haunting continued into the 1900s, when the Arthur Chichester family lived there. The last family to live in the house, the John Kirkpatricks, fled in the middle of the night after encountering the animal's ghost. Even after the mansion was destroyed by fire, the hulking bear continued its rounds on the property.

(Loudoun County is in extreme northern Virginia. The estate is in Loudoun County near Leesburg, which is twenty-two miles northwest of Arlington, on Highway 7. The mansion burned down in 1926. The former estate and cave are now on private farmland 3.5 miles from Leesburg on Highway 7.) **36**

NOLAND RUINS Colonial farmer Philip Noland started building his dream house in the late 1770s, but was forced to abandon the project when he ran out of money. Two escaped Hessians from the prison camp at Saratoga were tracked to the unfinished house and shot to death in the cellar there. Their ghosts are said to prowl the area at night, and frantic pounding can sometimes be heard on the cellar walls. The ubiquitous ghost of General Anthony Wayne is also said to return to these premises. Noland was a close friend of the general, who visited the building several times to check its progress. See Stony Point and Ticonderoga, New York; Valley Forge, Pennsylvania; and Lake Memphremagog, Vermont.

(The half-built brick house is near Rogue's Rd. in Loudoun County.) **68, 158**

LURAY

OLD CORRY HOUSE This whitewashed brick house was built in the early 1800s by Winston Pardue. After Winston died, his wife Della married Ham Corry and bore him a daughter, Hetty. Hetty was nineteen years old when her mother died. Shortly after that, her father died after he was accidentally hit in the head with a horseshoe while playing the game. Miss Hetty lived on alone in the big house. Her one delight was making wild-grape jam, and the only love in her life was for a wounded prisoner who stumbled into her home in 1864. She nursed the man back to health, but when he recovered, he tried to rob her. He crept up behind her one evening with a rifle, while she was boiling grapes. She tossed the boiling concoction into his face, grabbed the gun, and shot him to death. Much later, residents in her old house began reporting odd noises in the kitchen and mysterious purple stains on the floor. Hetty's ghost was seen walking up the stairs to the attic or bending over the stove in the kitchen, stirring some of her deadly grape jam.

(The town of Luray is in Page County in northern Virginia, near the Shenandoah River on U.S. Highway 211. The Curry house is located on Staunton Rd., Luray, VA 22835.) **158**

LYNCHBURG

POSTON HOUSE "A plethora of psychic manifestations" took place in this small brick house owned by the Reverend Smith family in 1839. Pots, pans, and silverware flew about the kitchen, and flour bags burst open. Bedsheets were piled onto the floor, and the house was kept in utter disorder by an unseen presence. A nanny ran screaming from the house when a cradle with a baby in it would not stop rocking by itself. Hundreds of people went to the house to see the mysterious rocking cradle.

(Lynchburg is in Campbell County in east-central Virginia, at the junction of U.S. Highways 29 and 460. The house is a private residence on the corner of Jackson and Eleventh streets, at 1104 Jackson St., Lynchburg, VA 24504.) **205**

WILLIAM BASS ELEMENTARY SCHOOL Students and teachers here see doors open and close by themselves and report the mysterious disappearance of personal belongings. In 1992, a security firm monitoring the school recorded strange voices coming from the empty building.

(William Bass Elementary School, 1730 Seabury Ave., Lynchburg, VA 24502. Phone: 804-522-3769.) **72**

MANASSAS

OLD TOWN INN A ghost nicknamed Miss Lucy haunts Room 52 in the old section of this building. Sometimes she wanders into Room 50 or 54 or strolls through the restaurant. Guests and employees have witnessed her playful antics many times. She is blamed for strange scratching sounds, messing up beds, unplugging appliances, and similar pranks. In July 1991, a couple was awakened in the middle of the night by a heavy presence on their bed. An hour later, the husband levitated out of bed and was dropped on the floor. That morning, the same couple encountered Miss Lucy in the restaurant.

(Manassas is in northeast Virginia, twenty-seven miles west of Arlington on Highway 28. Old Town Inn, 9403 Main St., Manassas, VA 22110. Phone: 888-869-6446.) **66 (10/92), 72**

MATHEWS COUNTY

OLD HOUSE WOODS These haunted woods are named for an ancient house that stood here before the Revolutionary War. Witnesses have reported strange floating lights, a ghastly skeleton, and the apparitions of soldiers, some wearing suits of armor. The three ghosts seen at White's Creek are said to be renegade indentured servants, who robbed and murdered emissaries from Charles II of England in the 1650s. As heir to the throne, Charles had contemplated moving to Virginia after the execution of his father by Cromwell. He was rumored to have sent gold on ahead. British gold is at the heart of another haunting in these woods. The ghosts of two British soldiers are seen here. The two were entrusted with a large sum of money and gold to be taken to a British ship, just before the defeat of Lord Cornwallis at Yorktown in 1781. When the soldiers were ambushed and killed by Americans, they had already buried the British treasure. Finally, a third haunting heralds bad weather. The strange apparition of Storm Lady, who is dressed in a flimsy nightgown, hovers over the tops of the tallest pine trees when a storm gale is approaching the area.

(Mathews County is on the Chesapeake Bay in extreme eastern Virginia. The village of Mathews is on Highway 14. Old House Woods is five miles from Mathews, near Diggs, a quarter-mile from the bay. Most reports have occurred near the county road, about halfway through the fifty-acre woods, and along the bay-shore road.) **162, 208**

MIDDLEBURG

FOXCROFT SCHOOL From its founding in 1914, the campus of this girls' school has been haunted by the ghost of Jane Ball Kyle, wife of a plantation owner who built Brick House in the 1700s. Legend had it that Jane went insane and was kept chained in the attic and ultimately died when she fell down the attic stairs and broke her neck. She was believed to be buried in an unmarked grave in the orchard next to her husband, who died much later. After many reports of a crazy female ghost roaming the halls of Brick House, the school's founder Charlotte Haxell Noland became convinced that the specter must be Jane Kyle. She ordered the orchard dug up and found the bodies of the Kyles. Through the middle of Jane's forehead was a bullet hole. Noland sent the skull to the Smithsonian Institution, where ballistics experts determined that the bullet was pre-Revolutionary War. Today, Jane Kyle's grave is commemorated with a brass plaque. As late as the 1970s, her ghost was encountered in Court Dormitory, at Brick House, in the old orchard near her grave, and other places on campus.

(Middleburg is in northern Virginia, thirty-two miles west of Alexandria on U.S. Highway 50. The school is within the village limits. Foxcroft School, P.O. Box 5555 Middleburg, VA 20118. Phone: 800-858-2364. www. foxcroft.org) **205**

MIDDLETOWN

BELLE GROVE PLANTATION The ghost of a woman in white has been seen standing by the fireplace, looking out the front window, gliding through the hallways, or walking down the flagstone path from the pig room to the smoke house. She is Hetty Cooley, wife of Benjamin Cooley, who lived in the house in the 1860s. Hetty married Benjamin after he had moved into Belle Grove. A black servant, Harriette Robinson, deeply resented sharing control of the house with Benjamin's new wife. In May 1861, she cornered Hetty in the smoke house and beat her to death. Harriette was sentenced to hang for the murder but was released from prison by Union soldiers. Hetty's ghost seems to be reliving the last few hours of her life over and over again.

(Middletown is in Frederick County in the northwest corner of Virginia. Take I-66 from Arlington or I-81 from Harrisonburg. Middletown is two miles north of the junction of I-66 and I-81 on U.S. Highway 11. Go south through the city of Middletown and turn west onto Highway 727 to the plantation museum. Belle Grove, Box 137336, Middletown, VA 22645. Phone: 540-869-2028. www.bellegrove.org) **15, 78, 101**

MOUNT VERNON

WOODLAWN PLANTATION This old plantation manor house is haunted by two hundred years worth of ghosts. Cloudlike forms have been seen and photographed in the great Center Hall. The Lafayette Bedroom, on the second floor in the south wing, is haunted by the ghost of fifteen-year-old Agnes Lewis, who died in 1820. Her spirit likes to rearrange furniture in her former room. In the 1930s, her ghost was accused of taking a crying baby out of its crib and placing it on top of a dresser. In 1992, an employee came across a shadowy apparition looking out a window in the same room. The back staircase to the south wing's second floor is haunted by another girl ghost. Witnesses say she seems to be about six years old. A well dug in the basement floor has been dubbed the "Well of Souls." When the well is covered, there seems to be an increase in paranormal activity in the house, as if the door somehow prevents spirits from returning to their underworld abode. Woodlawn Plantation was a gift from George Washington to his foster daughter Eleanor Parke Custis when she married in 1799. Her descendants lived in the house until 1846. In the next sixty years, the property went through a variety of owners, and once stood completely abandoned for over six years. Extensive renovations were made in 1902, 1910, and 1948.

(The Mount Vernon area is located south of Alexandria at the end of the Washington Memorial Parkway.

Woodlawn is in northern Virginia on the old Mount Vernon estate. It is at 9000 Richmond Highway in Mount Vernon. Phone: 703-780-4000.) **120**

WASHINGTON'S PLANTATION In 1780, George Washington confided to his aide Anthony Sherman that a beautiful female apparition appeared to him and revealed America's future. The strange vision inspired Washington's poetic farewell address in which he warned the against "permanent alliance with foreign powers, big public debt, a large military establishment, and the devices of small, artful, enterprising minorities to control or change government." There have been numerous reports of Washington's ghost here. Most describe him riding his favorite horse across the estate to his stables on Mount Vernon, just as he did on the wintry night he died.

(Washington's Plantation covered a great territory of land from the District of Columbia nearly to Williamsburg. His house at Mount Vernon still stands. Phone: 703-780-2000. www.mountvernon.org) **4, 67**

NEWPORT NEWS

CARTER'S GROVE PLANTATION The downstairs drawing room here is haunted by a persistent presence. Whenever white carnations are placed in the room, they are ripped to pieces at night and scattered over the floor. The room where the odd event occurs is known as the Refusal Room, because two presidents were turned down by their prospective brides in the room. Mary Cary turned down George Washington's proposal, and Rebecca Burwell denied Thomas Jefferson here. The house was built by Robert "King" Carter in the early 1750s.

(Newport News is on the Chesapeake Bay in the extreme southeastern corner of Virginia, opposite Norfolk at the mouth of the James River. The mansion is outside the city limits of Newport News, in James City County. www.williamsburg.com/plant/carter.html) **101, 209**

NORFOLK

CHESAPEAKE BEACH VOLUNTEER FIRE DEPARTMENT The spirit of Ben Bishop is blamed for setting off alarms and sirens on equipment at this community fire station. Doors on fire engines open and close by themselves and some unseen hand turns on the sirens. The manifestations began in 1971, immedi-

ately after the twenty-four-year-old firefighter was killed in a automobile accident.

(Norfolk is at the junction of U.S. Highways 17 and 58/460 in the extreme southeastern corner of Virginia. Chesapeake Beach is off U.S. Highway 60 near Norfolk. Chesapeake Beach Volunteer Fire Department, 2444 Pleasure House Rd., Chesapeake Beach, VA 23455. Phone: 757-460-7509.) **208**

ST. PAUL'S CHURCH The gravestone of Mrs. Martha Duncan and her two infant children tells a ghostly tale. They died in a house fire on May 12, 1823. Thousands of miles away, David Duncan saw his wife and two children in a vision enveloped by flames, begging for his help. At the time, he was reading a book of poetry in his quarters on a merchant ship. The lines he was reading when his three loved ones' pleading apparitions appeared to him are on their tombstone: "Insatiate archer, could not one suffice? Thy shaft flew thrice and thrice my peace was slain."

(The church is in central Norfolk. St. Paul's Church, 201 Saint Pauls Blvd., Norfolk. VA 23505. Phone: 757-627-4353) **208**

U.S. NAVAL SHIPYARD Military and civilian employees here call their ghost John Paul, because he is dressed like Revolutionary War hero John Paul Jones. The apparition has been reported in Buildings 29, 31, and 33. In 1918, a sailor broke his leg trying to flee the specter. The drydock was built in 1767, and the buildings where phenomena occur all have components taken from old sailing vessels. Drydocks 1 and 2 are haunted by three British soldiers whose graves were unearthed near the docks in 1971. Ghostly voices and the sounds of sewing machines are heard in the old sailmakers loft, where misty white forms and ethereal flames have also been reported. Quarters B' is haunted by a neat ghost, who returns keys to their proper place on a hanger near the front door. The USS *Forestal* is a haunted ship that often docks at Norfolk. The one-thousand-foot-long aircraft carrier, which carries a crew of 4,700 men, is haunted by a ghost sailors have nick-named George. His presence stalks No. 1 and No. 3 Holds and is blamed for moved objects, unseen taps on the shoulder, slamming doors, and lights switched off for no apparent reason. Once, the poltergeist grabbed the leg of a sailor climbing a ladder and would not let go. Another sailor had to pull his terrified shipmate to safety. Some suggest that the haunting is the result of an accident that occurred on July 25, 1967. A torpedo from an F-4 Phantom jet sitting on deck was mistakenly fired into the fuel tank of another plane. The resulting fire killed 134 men.

(The Norfolk Navy Base Complex is located in west Norfolk on Willoughby Bay. I-564 leads into the center of the complex. Tours are available. Phone: 757-444-7637.) **96, 208**

PETERSBURG

CENTRE HILL A whole regiment of ghosts traipse through this house every January 24th at precisely 7:30 P.M. At that moment, the door of the downstairs office opens and a rush of footsteps mixed with the clattering of sabers ascends the staircase to a room above the office. Then in about twenty minutes the strange clamor descends the stairs, goes out the front door, and slams the door behind. The ghostly brigade is thought to be Confederate troops ordered to evacuate the city in 1865. The sounds were first reported on January 24, 1866, by Union soldiers occupying the house. During the rest of the year, the house, built in 1823 by Robert Bolling, is haunted by the ghost of a beautiful lady, who looks out the upstairs window above the front door. She has also been reported in an upstairs bedroom, where she has been known to pull the covers off people sleeping there.

(The town of Petersburg is in Dinwiddie County, twenty-six miles south of Richmond on 1-85, Centre Hill is owned by the City of Petersburg and is at the center of an eight-acre park.) **163, 207**

DODSON'S TAVERN This house was built in 1753 by John Dodson and remained in the family until 1972, when Colonel John Cargill Peagram died at the age of ninety-one. The ghost of the Colonel has returned to make sure his ancestral home is taken care of. Burglar alarms go off for no reason, and books from Peagram's extensive library are found about the room, as if he is still reading them.

(The restored tavern is at 311 High St., Petersburg, VA 23803.) **101, 207**

TRAPEZIUM HOUSE The city of Petersburg bought this house in 1972 and completely restored it. In 1981, they reopened it as the "ghost storytelling house of Virginia." But people who go there to hear ghost stories should not be afraid. This house is the one place in Virginia where one should be safe from ghosts. The archi-

tectural oddity was built by Charles O'Hara, whose West-Indian servant convinced him that spirits could inhabit only right-angled buildings. So the O'Hara house has no right angles at all. None of the walls are parallel, doors and windows are all framed crooked, and the stairs and floorboards are cut at a slant.

(Trapezium House, 244 North Market St., Petersburg, VA 23803. Phone: 804-733-2404.) **102**

POQUOSON

COMMONS There is a patch of ground here where nothing grows. It is the spot where the body of Dolly Mammy was found in 1904. The woman had gone out to bring in her cows, when she got caught in deep mud and suffocated. She haunted her two lazy daughters for many years afterward. Extremely loud banging sounds marked the beginning of the haunting. Once, the girls awoke to find their hair tightly braided together. Another time, their bed levitated off the floor. Later, the spirit called out the names of the teenage girls. The Mammy house was visited by dozens of curiosity seekers, who witnessed the unexplainable sounds and moving objects. An officer from Fort Monroe investigated the phenomena and declared the disturbance to be of "supernatural origin."

(Poquoson is between Seaford and Yorktown, northwest of Hampton, on Highway 171. The Poquoson Commons are at the center of town.) **208**

PORTSMOUTH

DAUGHTERY HOUSE A violent poltergeist attacked the residence of Charles and Annie Daughtery in September 1962. The elderly couple witnessed flying bottles and vases for two days before they called police. The flying objects, along with a levitating carpet and moving furniture, were witnessed by scores of neighbors, police, and news media representatives. One day, nearly twenty thousand people showed up in front of the house to witness the phenomena. The case was investigated by Duke University parapsychologist William Roll, who traced the outbursts of psychic energy to the Daughterys' great-great-grandson.

(Portsmouth is in the southeastern corner of Virginia, just west of Norfolk in Elizabeth Bay. The Daughtery House was torn down because no one would live there. It was located at 949 Florida Ave., Portsmouth, VA 23707.) **208**

GAFFOS HOUSE Late at night the front door of this house opens and an unseen presence lumbers up three flights of stairs, then slams the attic door behind it. It is said that the young daughter of a grizzled old sea captain died of yellow fever in the attic room. He used to come home from the sea and pause in front of his house, staring at the attic dormers, wondering if his beloved daughter were dead or alive. The captain's presence has been detected on numerous occasions by residents George and Mary Alice Gaffos.

(The house is a private residence at 218 Glasgow St. Portsmouth, VA 23704.) **101, 168, 208**

GRICE-NEELY HOUSE The tombstone that serves as a step at the front entrance to this house alerts the visitor to the fact that this house has long been possessed by spirits. The most active presence is a black slave, who has appeared to several residents. The shirtless apparition seems confused and lost. The bricked-up window at the back of the house was part of an effort in the 1850s to free the house of ghosts. A medium instructed residents that when the next person died in the building, he should be taken out of the house through the back window. Then the window should be sealed with bricks. That, said the medium, would prevent any spirits from returning to the house. Apparently the desperate maneuver did not work.

(The three-story brick house is a private residence in Olde Towne, at 202 North St., Portsmouth, VA 23704.) **208**

MAUPIN HOUSE The ghosts of pit-bull dogs are seen playing in the backyard here, and the revenant of a former servant walks in the garden. Miles Portlock, a slave who died in 1939 at the age of ninety, was seen by a young servant girl in the 1940s. The house was built in 1885 and has been in the Maupin family ever since. In fact, the ghost of the first mistress of the house, Edmonia Maupin, is still seen in an upstairs bedroom.

(The three-story brick house is a private residence, at 328 Court St., Portsmouth, VA 23704.) **208**

TRINITY EPISCOPAL CHURCH An apparition appeared to Trinity's Reverend John Braidfoot several times after the Revolutionary War and told him he would die on February 6. The good reverend, in perfect health, died in his room on that exact day. The cemetery of this stately church is the starting place for the

annual Old Portsmouth Ghost Tour, held on the last Friday in October.

(Trinity Episcopal Church, 500 Court St., Portsmouth, VA 23704. Phone: 757-393-0431.) **168, 208**

RICHMOND

GAINES MILL BATTLEFIELD As late as 1991, bodies of hastily buried Confederate soldiers were found in this area. The largest and bloodiest engagement in General George McClellan's campaign to capture Richmond took place here in June 1862. Skeletons from decomposed bodies littered the ground two years later. The ghosts of the dead left so long unburied are said to still cry out.

(Richmond is in east-central Virginia at the junction of I-64 and I-95. The Gaines Mill Battlefield is part of the Richmond National Battlefield Park, 3215 E. Broad St., Richmond, VA 23223. Phone: 804-226-1981. www.nps. gov/rich.) **163**

GLASGOW HOME This stately Greek revival-styled house was built in 1841. Its most prominent resident was author Ellen Glasgow, whose family moved there in 1888. She lived in the house until she died on November 21, 1945. Her ghost joined several other restless spirits that she encountered while growing up in the old house. In her autobiography she describes an evil, disembodied red face that sometimes appeared above the second floor landing, as well as many other ghostly phenomena witnessed by family members and visitors over the years. See Hollywood Cemetery, below.

(The 2½-story, four-chimney, stucco-covered house is a private residence, at 1 West Main St., Richmond, VA 23220.) **101, 168, 207**

GOVERNOR'S MANSION The Virginia Governor's Mansion has been haunted since the early 1890s, when Governor Philip McKinney first saw the apparition of a beautiful young woman wearing a flowing taffeta dress. The ghost has been seen several times over the years and has even been chased by butlers and other people in the house. She has been spotted near an upstairs bedroom, descending the stairway, and in the basement. Several governors have detected her presence, including Linwood Holton, who was governor in the 1970s.

(The mansion is off Lakeside Ave. in central Richmond.) **101, 164, 207**

HAWES HOUSE For many years, the ghost of a small woman dressed in gray was seen floating along the hall and disappearing at the venetian blinds. Author Mary Virginia Hawes reported seeing the ghost when she lived in the house as a young girl. The apparition was encountered by family members more than fifty times. They dubbed her the "Tortoiseshell Ghost" because of a large tortoiseshell comb she wore in her hair. Later, when the house became an orphanage, the ghost was reported drifting between rows of beds in the dormitory. Then, during construction near the front entry, workers found the grave of a woman directly beneath the drawing room window. Under her skull was a carved tortoise-shall comb.

(The house was in the Hawes family from 1840 to 1875. It later became St. Paul's Orphanage. The address of the building is 506 East Leigh St., Richmond, VA 23219.) **101, 207**

HOLLYWOOD CEMETERY Strange moaning sounds have been reported near the great stone pyramid that marks the mass grave of eighteen thousand Civil War soldiers, most of whom remain unknown. Nearby, the spirit of a cast-iron dog is said to guard the grave of a little girl. The child loved to play with the statue, which stood outside of a store on Broad Street. When she died in an epidemic in 1892, the store owners donated the cast-iron statue to her memory. The sounds of barking dogs are also heard at the grave of author Ellen Glasgow, whose two pet dogs were interred with her body. See Glasgow Home, above.

(The entrance to the cemetery is on Cherry St. in Richmond. Hollywood Cemetery, Cherry St. South, Richmond, VA 23220. Phone: 804-648-8501.) **207**

LIGGON HOUSE For many years, the apparition of a black servant was seen walking down the stairs here. He was shot and killed by the six-year-old daughter of John Liggon sometime in the late 1850s. The little girl told the slave that he could not accompany the family on a shopping trip, but when the servant appeared at the top of the stairway ready to go, the child grabbed one of her father's guns and said: "I told you, you couldn't go." Then she pulled the trigger.

(A private residence, the Liggon House, 2601 East Franklin St., Richmond, VA 23223.) **101, 207**

MANCHESTER RESCUE SQUAD BUILDING In the early 1990s, this county facility was haunted by a mysterious presence employees nicknamed Clarence. The poltergeist opened and closed doors, caused crashing sounds in the kitchen and walls, and drummed out rhythmic sounds for long periods in the men's bunk room. The source of the psychic energy was never determined.

(The former rescue squad headquarters is in Henrico County, at 3213 Broad Rock Rd., Richmond, VA 23224.) **207**

PINE FLASH In a wood cottage behind the main house here, footsteps are heard descending a staircase, and a heavy mass of free standing cold air roams the downstairs rooms. The ghostly presence is thought to be Patrick Henry, the famous American statesman. Pine Flash was one of his estates, and he lived in the cottage for many months while the main house was being rebuilt after a fire.

(Pine Flash is a private residence fifteen miles from Richmond, in Hanover County.) **86**

QUEEN ANNE COTTAGE This small house was built sometime before 1732 by Charles Fleming, but ghosts did not start to appear until it was moved to another location on the same property in 1935. Residents began hearing strange footsteps and feeling an unseen presence in the rooms. It is believed to be the spirit of a man named Pierson, who was killed in a 1922 car crash on the Old River Road near the cottage.

(The cottage, also known as Rock Castle, is located on a bluff overlooking the James River in Goochland County. The site is off Highway 600, near Tuckahoe Plantation.) **101, 207**

REVEILLE HOUSE A gallery of ghosts haunts this early-1800s house. The large front room to the right of the hall is home to an unidentified ghost, who likes to walk through the house at night and turn doorknobs or switch on lights. The basement dining room is haunted by a little old lady dressed in a bonnet and cape. A ghost wearing skirts walks up the attic stairway, and a wardrobe in an upstairs bedroom seems to be possessed by another spirit, who knocks frantically on the doors. The neighbors report seeing a white figure floating in front of windows in the house.

(The house is now a church office in west Richmond. It is located behind the Reveille United Methodist Church, Cary Street Rd. Richmond, VA 23220.) **101, 207**

STATE CAPITOL BUILDING Guards and visitors here have reported hearing the muted sounds of sobbing and moaning coming from the walls. The temple-like structure has been in service continuously since October 1788. On April 27, 1870, the gallery collapsed, crushing sixty-two people to death and injuring more than 250.

(The state capitol is off the Mechanicsville Turnpike in east-central Richmond.) **207**

TALAVERA This two-story house was built in 1838 by farmer Thomas Talley. Edgar Allan Poe frequently visited Talley's daughter, Susan. Poe's reading of "The Raven" to Susan so frightened the servants that they all ran out the back door. The author died two weeks later, on October 7, 1849. Many people who have lived in the house believe it to be haunted, but no one has been able to identify the spirit of Talavera as Edgar Allan Poe.

(The house is now home to the Young Preservationists. The address is 2315 West Grace St., Richmond, VA 23220.) **101, 207**

TUCKAHOE PLANTATION Portions of this house date back to the early 1700s, and some of the ghosts do, too. A lace peddler haunts the Southeast Chamber, where he was allegedly murdered. The ghost of Little Gray Lady emerges from a cupboard in the Burnt Room, or enters through the hall door into the dining room. In 1982, a visitor saw a ghost in the laundry room, and a group of friends came across a white apparition hovering over the garden. The ghost of a lonely bride walks along a turfed path named Ghost Walk in her honor. She is thought to be young Mary Randolph, who was forced to surrender her love for an overseer and marry an elderly gentleman in the 1730s.

(Tuckahoe is a private residence in Goochland County, fifteen miles west of Richmond, on River Rd.) **101, 207**

TWIN OAKS HOUSE The ghost of a man with a distinctive chin beard haunts this house. Records indicate the property was originally the site of two small graveyards containing nineteen bodies; legend says there might be money buried there, too. In 1821, bank teller Dan Green was accused of taking over five hundred thousand dollars of bank funds but was later acquitted. Some believe the terrified teller buried the money on his property and never claimed it. Now his ghost returns for the loot. Recently the Donald Wiltshire family reported inexplicable noises and several shadowy apparitions in the house. The house is on a street named for Monument Church, under which rest the remains of seventy victims of the tragic Richmond theater fire, which occurred in 1811.

(Monument Church is on Broad St., between 12th and College streets. The old wood-frame house is a private residence, at 6321 Monument Ave., Richmond, VA 23226.) **72, 90, 101, 207**

WHICHELLO This old roadhouse tavern is haunted by the ghost of a bludgeoned innkeeper. The man's body, his head crushed by an ax, was found in his room in 1850. He was interred in a tunnel beneath the huge brick chimney, and it is said his ghost guards a cache of gold buried with him. Whichello was built in 1827.

(The house is a private residence, at 9602 River Rd., Richmond, VA 23229.) **101, 207**

SALEM

CROCKETT HOUSE This house has a built-in babysitting presence. The ghost of a short, elderly woman started appearing to the Robert and Nedra Crockett family in the 1960s, when they brought home their baby boy, Edgar. When the Crocketts failed to wake up for a 2:00 A.M. feeding, Nedra was awakened by a shaking bed and found the ghost standing next to her. Another time, when Edgar was almost three years old, the Crocketts were going Christmas shopping and did not notice that Edgar had sneaked out of the car. He went back in the house to change his shoes and was left home alone. When the Crocketts realized he was not in the car, they rushed home to find him in the library, calmly drawing pictures. The old lady had appeared to the child and told him his parents would return soon. She suggested he color pictures until they got home. The Crocketts called the ghost Mrs. Anderson, after an 1830s owner of the house. After renovating the house, another ghost turned up. Their five-year-old daughter, Luella, started seeing the ghost of an elderly gentleman sitting in her father's chair when it was empty. Long before the Crocketts moved in, the house had a reputation for being haunted.

(Salem is a western suburb of Roanoke located at the junction of U.S. 11/460 and Highway 311 in western Virginia. Take Exit 140 from I-81. The three-story brick

house is a private residence, at 229 Union St., Salem, VA 24153.) **135**

FRUIT OF THE BLOOM WINERY A brick ranch-style home, a mobile home, and an older house on this parcel of land are all haunted. Most of the property is owned by Jim and Barbara Guthrie, who operate a small winery here. A ghostly man's voice singing old tunes is heard at all hours of the night. Footsteps move through the buildings, doors slam, and chairs move by themselves. Strange circular, floating lights have appeared in parts of the brick home, which was built in 1971. The apparition of a dark-skinned boy with short hair and wearing blue jeans has appeared several times since 1976, and visiting relatives reported encountering an angry male ghost in October 1978.

(The property is located three miles west of Salem on County Road 11460. The Guthries' winery is identified by a sign. Fruit of the Bloom Winery, 4780 Vintage Lane. Salem, VA 24153. Phone: 540-380-2795.) **135**

STEVENSBURG

SALUBRIA MANSION The apparition of a woman with long black hair has been seen floating through the upstairs hall with her arms stretched out in front of her. She has also been seen in a full-length mirror in a bedroom on the same floor. She is thought to be the ghost of Lady Spotswood, widow of Sir Alexander Spotswood (see Federal Hill, Fredericksburg, Virginia). She could also be the spirit of Mrs. Hansborough, who hanged herself in Lady Spotswood's former bedroom. The house was built in the 1760s.

(Stevensburg is in Culpepper County in north Virginia, thirty miles west of Fredericksburg, on Highway 3. The mansion is a private residence in the town of Stevensburg.) **206**

SURRY

BACON'S CASTLE This plantation mansion is called Bacon's Castle because it was turned into a fortification in 1676 by the notorious rebel Nathaniel Bacon. It was here that Southern poet Sidney Lanier kindled his romance with Virginia Hankins in 1863. They spent many hours reading poetry in the Old Brick Church on the grounds. The war ended their budding romance, and they went their separate ways, but continued send-ing one another love poems for many years. Some say the intense love they kindled but never consummated still burns at Bacon's Castle. A strange ball of warm light has been sighted on the grounds many times. The orange ball forms above the house, then circles over the Old Brick Church, and finally enters the house through the single garret window on the west side. Locals had seen the light for many years after Virginia died, and in 1986 it was witnessed by a large group of tourists.

(Surry is near the junction of Highways 10 and 31 in Surry County, between Petersburg and Portsmouth in southeast Virginia. The mansion is five miles southeast of Surry, in Smithfield, at the intersection of Highway 10 and County Road 617. The address is Bacon's Castle, P.O. Box 364 Smithfield, VA. 23883. Phone: 757-357-5976. www. apva.org/apva/bacon.html) **101, 168, 208, 209**

VIRGINIA BEACH

ADAM THOROUGHGOOD HOUSE The oldest brick building in the nation is haunted by its original owners. Built in 1636 by Adam and Sara Offley Thoroughgood, the two-story, four-room house is still their home. Sara's ghost is seen carrying a candle near windows, and Adam's ghost, dressed in a brown suit, walks the halls. Once, thirty tourists witnessed four glass candle domes levitate and fall to the floor.

(Virginia Beach is at the extreme southeastern edge of the state, adjacent to Norfolk at the junction of U.S. Highways 58 and 60. The house is now a museum located at 1636 Parish Rd., Virginia Beach, VA 23455.) **101, 135, 208**

ASSOCIATION FOR RESEARCH AND ENLIGHTENMENT The Seer of Virginia Beach, Edgar Cayce, practiced his gifts of healing and prophecy here until his death on January 3, 1945. The mild-mannered psychic uttered his cures and predictions while in a hypnotic trance. Someone would ask him questions, and his replies were recorded by a secretary and stored in vaults at the site. Cayce is said to have predicted the stock market crash of 1929 and the rise of Nazi Germany, although some of his predictions, such as the spread of Christianity in China, have yet to come true. Cayce gave readings from 1910 through 1944, and most of his material has been preserved by the Association for Research and Enlightenment. Edgar Cayce saw apparitions several times when he was alive, and his own ghost is said to have appeared at the center in 1976.

(Association for Research and Enlightenment, 67 Atlantic Street, 215 E. 67th St., Virginia Beach, VA 23451. Phone: 757-428-3558. www.are-cayce.com) **53 (2/76), 72, 189**

LONGVIEW The ghost of a Civil War soldier is blamed for such odd phenomena as doors opening and closing, lights going out throughout the house, and a bell pull in the dining room that has a mind of its own. James Howard Whitehurst was wounded in the head at the Battle of New Market and spent his final years confined to a bed in an upstairs room here. The house was built in 1792.

(The old house is a private residence across from the old Princess Anne Courthouse in Virginia Beach, VA 23451.) **208**

TANDOM'S PINE TREE INN The mischievous ghost of a lady gambler shot to death at this inn in the 1930s is still seen by waitresses, cooks, and customers at the present roadhouse. She most often appears during the late evening hours. The ghost likes to hang out in the ladies room or the dining room.

(Tandom's Pine Tree Inn, 2932 Virginia Beach Blvd., Virginia Beach Beach, VA 23451. Phone: 757-340-3661.) **208**

WITCH DUCK ROAD This road is named in memory of an accused witch, who was tried by water dunking in July 1706. If Grace Sherwood floated in the water, she was supposed to be a witch. If she sank, she was innocent. Grace floated like a cork bobber and was promptly incarcerated in the county jail. The accused witch died in 1740, but many legends tell of her returning to the spot of her water trial, to try once more to prove her innocence.

(Witch Duck Road runs to the Lynnhaven River. It is Exit 2 on the Virginia Beach Expressway, Highway 44.) **208**

WARRENTON

EDGEHILL The ghost of Colonel William Chapman, second-in-command of the infamous Mosby's Raiders, returns to haunt his former home. Chapman's apparition has been seen in the library, and he is thought to

be responsible for opening locked doors and making loud noises late at night. The house was built in 1840 by James Eustace Jeffries, the father of Chapman's wife Josephine.

(The town of Warrenton is in northern Virginia, at the junction of U.S. Highways 211 and 15/29. Edgehill is a private residence, about six miles north of Warrenton, on Highway 17.) **206**

LORETTO A lady in gray walks the central stairway at night in this old house. She holds a dim candle to light her way. In one of Loretto's upstairs bedrooms, heavy furniture moves by itself to block the door. Music and laughter from a nonexistent party are heard on the main floor. The three-floored house was built in 1741 by Elias Edmonds and is also known as Edmonium. The mansion was built on top of an old Indian burial ground, and many bones and artifacts have been found in the cellar.

(Loretto is a private home located on the Old Bethel Road, four miles from Warrenton in Fauquier County.) **206**

OLD GAOL This foreboding old county jail is home to a restless presence that is heard walking around inside the empty rooms. The ghost of a short, elderly man with a white beard has been encountered in one of the cells. The jailhouse was built in 1808 and expanded in 1823. When it was remodeled into a museum in 1964, workmen encountered the ghost of a little girl. She appeared to be covered in slime.

(Gaol is the British spelling of jail, and is pronounced the same. The Old Gaol Museum is at Ashby and Waterloo Streets, Warrenton, VA 22186. Phone: 540-347-5525.) **206**

WAYNESBORO

EASTON HOUSE This house has been dubbed the Ghost Hotel, because of the many recurring ghostly manifestations that occur here. Ever since Bill and Marie Easton moved into the house in 1967, they have been plagued by discarnate footsteps, appliances operating by themselves, and unexplainable crashing sounds. When their children started talking to invisible presences named Mark and Amy, the Eastons called in a medium. The psychic contacted a bevy of confused spirits in the 245-year-old house, including two Civil War lovers named Mark and Amy.

(Waynesboro is located in west-central Virginia, twenty-one miles west of Charlottesville, on I-64. The house is a private residence near Waynesboro in Augusta County.) **205**

SWANNANOA This Renaissance mansion is an internationally known retreat and center for spiritual meditation. World leaders such as the queen of England, Pope John Paul II, and Margaret Thatcher come here. Regular visitors include Henry Kissinger, Ted Kennedy, and Elizabeth Taylor. So many powerful people show up here that some believe it to be the meeting place for the Council of Thirty, an alleged secret organization that rules the world. The fifty-two-room mansion was built in 1911 by millionaire James Dooley. It was purchased in 1948 by Dr. Walter Russell, after a mystical vision led his wife Lao to the site. Psychic manifestations have been reported near the thirty-foot statue of Christ and on the marble staircase at the front of the building.

(Swannanoa is a private retreat on top of Afton Mountain, near Rockfish Gap.) **205**

WESTMORELAND COUNTY

STRATFORD HALL Ghosts of the family of Robert E. Lee haunt these grounds. The apparition of his father Light Horse Harry Lee has been seen scrutinizing a ledger in one of the outbuildings and at a desk in the library. The ghosts of Robert's sister-in-law Ann Lee and her small daughter Margaret have been seen upstairs. The child died at the age of two, after falling down the stairs. Security guards have reported the angelic figure of a small boy near the front gate, in the old slave quarters, and in the Dependency Building. The boy is thought to be Phillip Lee, Jr., son of Phillip Ludwell Lee. The boy died in 1799 after falling down the same stairway that would claim the life of Margaret some twenty-one years later. Stratford Hall was built in the 1730s by Thomas Lee. See Alexandria, Virginia.

(The 1,600 acre Stratford Hall estate is a private estate, located on a bluff overlooking the Potomac River in Westmoreland County, which is in the Northern Neck section of Virginia, between the Potomac and Rappahannock Rivers. Phone: 804-493-8038. www.stratfordhall. org) **206**

WEST POINT

COHOKE CROSSROADS A strange ghost light appears regularly here. It first appears in the distance and then gets brighter as it approaches, but the light disappears instantly if anyone gets too close. It usually travels between the iron railings of the railroad tracks at Cohoke Crossroads. Some say it is the light of a brakeman killed in a train accident. Others believe it to be a train carrying wounded Confederate soldiers from the Battle of Richmond in 1864. The train vanished and was never accounted for.

(West Point is King William County in eastern Virginia. It is located at the head of the York River, at the junction of Highways 33 and 30. Take Exit 220 from I-64. www.ghosts.org/ghostlights/cohoke.html) **208**

WILLIAMSBURG

COLLEGE OF WILLIAM AND MARY A ghost named Lucinda roams Phi Beta Kappa Hall here. She was billed to start in a campus production of Thornton Wilder's *Our Town*, when news came that she had died in an automobile accident. Now Lucinda's apparition returns to the playhouse wearing a variety of costumes from the play. Her ghost has been spotted drifting across the stage, in a small room underneath, and on the balcony. The ghost of a Revolutionary War soldier who died of gunshot wounds in a small back room on the third floor is also seen in the building. At Brafferton Building, the disenchanted spirits of Indian boys are felt. In the eighteenth century, the young boys were taken from their tribal lands and sent to the school to learn Christian behavior. The ghost of one boy who escaped from the second floor at night to run free over the grounds is still reported on the William and Mary campus. Many of the boys died from diseases related to poor diet and unsanitary conditions. The spirit of a French soldier is heard descending the stairs from the third to the second floor in the President's House. Recently, retired president Davis Paschall confessed to seeing the apparition of the college's first president, Reverend James Blair, materialize in his bedroom late one night in 1969.

(Williamsburg is between Richmond and Hampton, on U.S. Highway 60 in James City County. Follow the Williamsburg exit off of I-64 to the college and Williamsburg Colonial Village. College of William and Mary, P.O.

Box 8795, Williamsburg, VA 23185. Phone: 757-221-4000. www.wm.edu) **72, 101, 145, 208, 209**

GAOL This old jail, built in 1704, was used as a holding area for murderers, pirates, thugs, and other felons from throughout the Virginia colony. They were brought to Williamsburg to stand trial for their crimes. Oddly, the ghosts of two women haunt the jail today. Their spirits are said to reside on the second floor of the jailer's quarters. The women's animated conversations and the thumping of their heavy shoes are heard coming from the deserted room.

(Colonial Williamsburg is a restoration of 160 buildings on 175 acres. The address is: Williamsburg Colonial Village, P.O. Box 1776, Williamsburg, VA 23187. Phone: 804-229-1000. The jail is at 310 S. England, St. Williamsburg. www.history.org/almmanackplaces/hb/hbgaol.cfm) **78, 208**

HANGMAN'S ROAD The unaccountable sounds of moaning and the creaking of heavy wooden wagon wheels fill the night air along this road. Many witnesses have reported the eerie sounds, but few know how the road got its name or where the sounds originate. It was at this site that fourteen convicted pirates were hanged in 1719. The unfortunate men were part of what was left of Blackbeard's gang, after the illustrious pirate was beheaded in 1718. The outlaw's head was impaled on a spike and displayed at Blackbeard's Point, not far from Hangman's Road.

(Hangman's Road is off Colonial Landing Road, just outside Williamsburg. Blackbeard's Point is the tiny peninsula between Sunset Creek and the Hampton River.) **145**

LUDWELL-PARADISE HOUSE The ghost of Mad Lucy Ludwell comes back to her old home to take a bath. The sounds of someone bathing in an empty second-floor bathroom have been reported by numerous residents over the last hundred years. It was a several-times-a-day ritual with the eccentric Lucy Ludwell, who took possession of her grandfather's house in 1805. By 1812, the fantasy-prone woman was taking her baths in the state mental asylum.

(The brick two-story Ludwell-Paradise mansion is in the Williamsburg Colonial Village. For information, call 800-447-8679. www.history.org/almanack/places/hb/hbludw.cfm) **101, 209**

NICHOLSON HOUSE The presence of noted violinist Cuthbert Ogle is still felt in the house where he lived in the mid-1700s. Cuthbert's ghost gently touches people on the shoulder and makes loud scratching sounds at night. The two-story frame house was built by Robert Nicholson, who took in boarders for many years. Ogle died on April 23, 1755.

(Nicholson House is on York St. in Williamsburg.) **208**

PEYTON RANDOLPH HOUSE This two-story Colonial house is haunted by the ghost of an upset woman who always appears in the red oak-paneled bedroom at the rear of the building. She is seen wringing her hands in anguish at the foot of the bed. The same scene plays over and over again to astonished visitors. No one has ever identified her, but Randolph House has a tragic past, including the death of several small children and two suicides. The sound of crashing glass has been reported on the first floor, and untraceable moaning has been heard coming from the basement. To complicate matters further, the ghost of a former lady docent, attired in her Colonial uniform, has been seen by some employees. The house dates back to around 1715.

(The Peyton Randolph House faces Market Square in Williamsburg. www.history.org/almanack/places/hb/hbran.cfm) **14, 101, 145, 175, 209**

WELL'S CORNER A phantom touring car with an old-fashioned rumble seat is seen parked alongside the road here. Standing in the street, bent over the engine compartment, is a man dressed in a dark suit. Motorists sometimes honk to alert the man to their passing, but he never looks up. As they pass, the man and the old-time car vanish. The apparition is a gentleman struck by a car here in the early 1930s while working on his engine at the side of the road.

(The area is in James City County near the intersection of County Roads 631 and 610, also known as Forge Road.) **145**

WYTHE HOUSE This house was built in 1755 as a wedding gift to George Wythe from his wife's father. The ghost of a later resident, Ann Skipwith, can be heard running up the stairs. Her ghost is observed coming out of the closet in her bedroom wearing a satin gown and red shoes. Lady Ann was walking to a governor's ball with her husband Sir Peyton Skipwith, when she broke a strap on her fancy shoe. She fell into such disconsolate despair that she returned to her bedroom and took her own life. Late at night, custodians and other employees have seen Ann's apparition on the staircase or seated at her dressing table.

(Ann Skipwith is buried at Bruton Parish Church. Wythe House is on the west side of Palace Green. For tour information, contact the Williamsburg Colonial Village, Williamsburg, VA 23185. Phone: 804-229-1000. www. history.org/almanack/places/hb/hbwythe.cfm) **14, 78, 101, 145, 175, 209**

WINCHESTER

OLD RAG MOUNTAIN The ghosts of two women are seen crossing clearings and roads in the woods near this gentle mountainside. The first sightings occurred in 1925, when a country doctor encountered the specters on several occasions. Soon, others were seeing the women as well. One of them is fashionably dressed; the other is younger and appears as a diffuse shade. Locals say they are the spirits of Marie and Lucy Carwell, who lived at the Pheasant Hill Plantation before it burned down in 1865. After the fire Marie became a recluse and lived in a dilapidated cabin on the mountain until the 1880s.

(Winchester is in Frederick County in the extreme northern corner of Virginia, at the junction of I-81 and U.S. Highway 17/50.) **157**

SHENANDOAH STAGE The phantom of a red-painted stagecoach pulled by four white horses is seen on the roads here. Sometimes the blackened remains of a driver can be seen through the billowy dust that envelops the coach. The stage was stolen on May 24, 1862, by a northern spy attempting to warn the Union army of an impending attack by General Stonewall Jackson. With Confederate soldiers in hot pursuit, the stage was struck by a sudden bolt of lightning from a dark, grumbling cloud. The driver was killed instantly, his charred remains frozen in time.

(The ghost stage passes along U.S. Highway 11, the former Valley Pike, heading toward Winchester from New Market. It was struck by lightning near the crossroads at Mount Jackson.) **166**

YORKTOWN

CRIER BUILDING This converted office building is home to a ghost named Nicholas. Nicholas is buried in the front lawn at a spot marked by his tombstone. Workers inside have reported hearing his footsteps, usually upstairs, or sensing his annoying presence when they are trying to concentrate.

(Yorktown is on the York River, fifteen miles southeast of Williamsburg at the junction of U.S. Highway 17 and the Colonial National Historic Parkway. The brick office building is downtown. Phone: 757-898-2410. www.nps. gov/colo) **145**

MOORE HOUSE Ghosts were not reported in this eighteenth-century house until the Park Service began restorations in the 1930s. Maintenance workers and tour guides began sensing an invisible presence. Deep depressions appear on freshly made beds in an upstairs bedroom or in the cushion of a red velvet chair in the parlor. Psychics investigating the site have reported the presence of Augustine Moore, Jr., whose father bought the house in 1739. Augustine was only twenty years old when he was hit by a stray bullet during the Battle of Yorktown. He lingered in excruciating pain for several days before he finally expired in the upstairs bedroom.

(The house is now a historic museum at the Yorktown Battlefield in east Yorktown.) **209**

U.S. NAVAL WEAPONS STATION Men on watch on the perimeter of this naval base report hearing strange sounds, such as struggling horses and women's screams. They are witnessing a scene that took place here a century ago. The daughter of Virginia Governor Edward Digges and her lady friends were returning from Yorktown one evening when their carriage ran off the Old Williamsburg Road into the Black Swamp. Within minutes, the carriage, horses, and screaming women sank beneath the muddy quagmire.

(The Navy base is northwest of Yorktown, between I-64 and the Colonial National History Parkway.) **145, 208**

YORK HALL The ghost of a British soldier killed in the Battle of Yorktown in 1781 makes his presence known in this 250-year-old house. Long-dead family members also return to the estate. Recently a woman's loud sobbing was heard coming from an empty third-floor room. This old mansion was home to the Nelson family and later to three generations of the Captain George Preston Blow family.

(The National Park Service now operates York Hall as a museum. It is on a hill overlooking the York River, on the corner of Main St. and Nelson St., Yorktown, VA 23690.) **101, 145, 209**

WASHINGTON

BELLINGHAM

NOOKSACK RIVER During a salmon run in September 1967, many sportsmen in this area witnessed a bigfoot creature. The nine-foot tall, hairy creature was observed sitting on a stump in a bog, wading through knee-deep water, and trying to pull a large net full of fish ashore. Tracks found in the sand measured thirteen and a half inches long with a forty-five-inch stride. Indian legends have long told of hairy ghosts that traverse the area.

(The sightings occurred in central Whatcom County, in the Mount Baker National Forest near Marietta. Follow Highway 542 east from Billingham to the Nooksack Campground, just east of Glacier.) **139**

COPALIS BEACH

DEEKAY ROAD On the night of July 26, 1969, Deputy Sheriff Verlin Herrington encountered a hairy, apelike creature standing in the middle of the road. Herrington stopped his patrol car and aimed a powerful spotlight at the bigfoot. It had brownish-black hair, pendulous breasts, a leathery face, and distinct hands and feet. He estimated the animal to be seven and a half feet tall and weigh 325 pounds. The officer returned to the scene the next day to photograph an eighteen and a half-inch footprint.

(Copalis Beach is on the central coast south of the Pacific Beach State Park, four miles north of Grays Harbor on Highway 109. The deputy was driving toward Copalis Beach from Humptulips on Deekay Rd.) **139**

EVERETT

THE EQUATOR This old schooner is haunted by figures of the sailors of yesteryear. Ghostly, floating lights appear on deck. Built in the 1880s, the eighty-one-foot schooner is now being restored as a museum. During a recent séance on board the vessel, psychics contacted two surprising ghosts. In 1888, author Robert Louis Stevenson leased the *Equator* for a six-month cruise around the Pacific islands with his family. He loved the ship and the islands so much that he vowed never to return to England. At one point, King Kalakaua of Hawaii, whom Stevenson considered to be one of his closest friends, was an honored guest on the schooner. Stevenson's ghost and that of King Kalakaua are said to be enjoying each others' company on the *Equator* to this day. See Kona, Hawaii Island, Hawaii.

(Everett is off I-5, twenty-five miles north of Seattle. Follow the Broadway exit north to Hewitt Ave. and turn west and go to Marine View Drive. The schooner is docked at the 10th St. Boat Dock, Everett, WA 98205.) **15**

GEORGETOWN

GEORGETOWN CASTLE This turreted stone mansion was built in 1889. It is haunted by a crazy old lady who materializes with one hand choking her own throat while striking out at witnesses with the other. The tall woman wears a full-length white dress, and her eyes "burn like coal." The self-strangling ghost has been observed by as many as fifty people over the years. She has been identified as Sarah, the granddaughter of the man who built the castle. The woman went insane when her Spanish lover killed their illegitimate baby and buried it under the back porch.

(Georgetown is near Seattle in the Puget Sound area. The castle is at the center of town.) **173**

MARYHILL

HORSETHIEF LAKE STATE PARK A rock painting here depicts the large-eyed goddess Tsagaglala, "She Who Watches." The site was sacred to the Wishram Indians. Legend says Tsagaglala was turned into stone by Trickster Coyote, who was jealous of the love her people felt for her.

(Maryhill in south-central Washington, near The Dalles of Oregon, at the intersection of U.S. Highway 97 and Highway 14. The park is in the Columbia River Gorge, twenty miles west of Maryhill on Highway 14 Phone: 509-767-1159. www.parks.wa.gov/horsthef. htm) **72**

WASHINGTON STONEHENGE Although not a sacred site in itself, this full-sized replica provides a unique appreciation for one of the world's most mysterious spots. It was built in 1920 by Samuel Hill, who turned his mansion on the premises into a museum of European art and Native American artifacts. Modern Druids have performed many rituals here.

(Stonehenge is two miles northeast of Maryhill, across from the Maryhill State Park, on Highway 14. For information, contact the Maryhill Museum of Art, 35 Maryhill Museum Dr., Goldendale, WA 98620. Phone: 509-773-3733. www.maryhillmuseum.org) **99, 196**

MOUNT RAINIER

UFO SIGHTING The modern UFO era began here on June 24, 1947, when Kenneth Arnold sighted nine disc-shaped, metallic objects, later dubbed "flying saucers" by the press. (The term had been used as early as 1878, by a farmer describing an object that passed over Denison, Texas.) The objects Arnold observed traveled close to the mountaintops at tremendous speed. Using two mountain peaks for reference,

Arnold calculated their velocity to be over 1,600 mph. Ten days later, a United Airlines pilot reported seeing a formation of five similar UFOs near Boise, Idaho. The area throughout the northern Cascade mountains, known as the Northwest Frontier by ufologists, is still considered to be one of the most likely places in North America to see a UFO. In August 1970, a scientific expedition discovered a naturally heated underground chamber in the mountain that some ufologists say is evidence of an underground alien base at Mount Rainier.

(The 14,410-foot-high Mount Rainier is in the Mount Rainier National Park, which is in Pierce County, southeast of Tacoma. Highway 410 leads through the park. Arnold was flying from Chehalis to Yakima. The objects came from the north of his plane, from the vicinity of the Mount Baker National Forest. They approached along the snow border on the southwest slope of Mount Rainier.) **1, 50, 53 (3/48), 126 (11/81), 139, 150, 190**

MOUNT ST. HELENS

APE CANYON In an area known for its bigfoot sightings, prospectors working a small mine were terrorized by two of the creatures in 1924. The group first noticed eighteen-inch-long footprints in the snow around their cabin. Then one evening, two ferocious apelike creatures tried to break into their cabin. The windowless cabin was fortified against heavy snow and avalanches, and the beasts were unable to break in. The four miners abandoned their claim the next morning and headed for the safety of civilization.

(The 8,365-foot-high Mount St. Helens is in Skamania County. It is part of the Mount St. Helens National Volcanic Monument, east of Longview in southwestern Washington. U.S. Highway 12 and Highway 503 lead into the desolate preserve. Ape Canyon is on the east side of Mount St. Helens Phone: 360-274-2100. www.fs. fed.us/gpnf/mshnvm) **139**

SPIRIT LAKE After cleansing itself of human habitation in the volcanic eruption of 1980, this lake is once again home to spirits, including the souls of those who died in the violent blast. The lake has always been avoided by Indians, who believed they heard voices coming from its depths. A monster named Seatco was said to live in the lake, and a ghost elk was believed to lure men close enough so Seatco could grab them.

(Spirit Lake is eight miles north of Mount St. Helens, in the Mount St. Helens National Volcanic Monument.) **173**

SAN JUAN COUNTY

ORCAS ISLAND Creaking beds and low moaning sounds suggest the presence of a very passionate ghost at the Rosario Resort on this island. The spirit of Alice Rheem, who lived in a mansion that is now part of the resort, returns to reenact good times in her room. She lived here in the late 1930s and died from alcoholism. Her husband built a mansion on the isolated island to try to control his libidinous wife, but his efforts only made her wilder. Her ghost, clad in a skimpy red nightgown, reappears in her old room. In 1987, three traveling entertainers were kept awake all night by the sounds of lovemaking from the room, which was empty at the time. They said the activity started just before midnight, after the light in the room went on and off three times.

(San Juan County is made up of the San Juan Islands in the East Sound, eighty-five miles north of Seattle. The resort is located on Orcas Island. From I-5, take Exit 230. Follow the road to Anacortes, where the ferry for Orcas Island departs. Rosario Resort, Orcas Island, 1400 Rosario Rd., WA 98245. Phone: 360-376-2222. www. rosarioresort.com) **14, 101**

Al and Lotte Wilding, pictured here, sold their farm on Shaw Island when poltergeist activity became too much for them. See Shaw Island, Washington.
(AP/WIDE WORLD PHOTOS)

SHAW ISLAND For nearly thirty years an old farmhouse on this island was haunted by the ghost of Fritz Lee, who died in an upstairs room during the 1918 flu epidemic. Fritz was buried on the property, and his mischievous ghost has been blamed for poltergeist activity reported in his former room. Al and Lotte Wilding first noticed strange things there in 1959, about a year after they moved in. Before long, they only used the room for storage. An unseen presence was heard moving about in the room, objects moved in sudden jerks, and radios tuned themselves to certain stations. In 1987 the Wildings put their farm up for sale but warned prospective buyers that their house was haunted. In 1990 new owners hired a psychic to free the harmless spirit.

(The house is a private residence in Blind Bay on Shaw Island. www.sanjuanguide.com/shaw.html) **173**

DUWAMISH BEND This housing project was terrorized by a poltergeist residents named the Voice. A deep, rich, disembodied voice would sing popular tunes such as "Fools Rush In," "Blue Moon," and "Ghost Riders in the Sky." The wailing started in 1949 and continued for several years, but was never explained.

(Duwamish Bend is a housing project outside of Seattle.) **49**

GLENACRES GOLF COURSE The ghost of a naked man performed Indian dances here. He was also seen on the trail leading onto the golf course grounds. The phantom was witnessed by hundreds of people, including police and newsmen. When authorities tried to capture him, he disappeared as they approached. The apparition appeared regularly between 1940 and 1960. Although some have suggested that the golf course lies on top of an Indian burial ground, no evidence to support the claim has ever been found.

(The golf course is bounded by 10th Str. South and South 110th St. Glenacres Golf Course, 1000 South 112th St., Seattle, WA 98168. Phone: 206-244-1720.) **49**

GREEN LAKE In the 1920s a shadowy apparition was blamed for several kidnappings along the shores of this lake. The disappearances are still unsolved.

(Green Lake is a residential section in north Seattle.) **49**

HARVARD EXIT THEATER This cinema, opened in 1968, is haunted. The movie theater is in a three-story brick building constructed in the 1900s. When a second auditorium and screen was constructed on the third floor in the early 1970s, the ghosts of several women dressed in turn-of-the-century clothing began to appear. Most of the sightings were on the third floor and near a fireplace on the first floor. The encounters were accompanied by an assortment of strange phenomena, which continued until 1987. One possible historical explanation for the haunting is the former tenancy of Bertha Landes, founder of the Women's Century Club. The club occupied the building for many years. From 1926 to 1928, Landes served as Seattle's first woman mayor. In 1988, relics of her administration and her personal belongings were displayed at a downtown museum, which reported a number of inexplicable incidents that some thought were manifestations of Landes's spirit.

(The cinema is located in the Capitol Hill area of Seattle. From I-5 north, take the Olive St. exit to Broadway East. Go north to East Roy St. and turn west to the theater. The address of the theater is 807 East Roy St., Seattle, WA 98122. Phone: 206-323-8986.) **66 (6/90), 68, 101, 133, 160**

KINNEAR PARK For many years in the late 1920s, the ghostly sounds of a baby crying permeated this city park.

(Kinnear Park is on top of Queen Anne Hill in Seattle.) **49**

LEWIS STUDIO In 1952, the studio of sculptor Alonzo Victor Lewis became one of the best-documented hauntings in Seattle. A shadowy apparition was seen by dozens of reputable witnesses, although a local television personality failed in his attempt to secure photographic evidence of the haunting.

(The Alonzo Victor Lewis Studio is now a private residence on Eastlake Ave. North, Seattle, WA 98101.) **49**

MOUNT BAKER This quiet residential neighborhood is built on top of a Salish Indian burial ground. Joshua Winfield, who built a cabin on the site in 1874, reported encountering the ghosts of Indians, who tried to scare him off the land. Not long afterward, his body was found lying on the floor of his locked cabin, his eyes bulging open, his mouth frozen in a scream. According to the records Joshua Winfield died of fright.

(The Mount Baker district is in south Seattle.) **173**

PIKE PLACE MARKET The ghost of an American Indian woman loaded down with baskets is seen trekking up and down the underground ramps of this shopping plaza. Since 1982, she has been spotted at three-month intervals in the Craft Emporium, only to disappear before astonished clerks. Her ghost has also been seen in the old Goodwill Store, as well as in the present Sound View Cafe and the former Shakespeare & Company Bookstore. History suggests she is the spirit of Kickisomlo, daughter of Chief Seattle. Her white friends called the woman Angeline, a name that stuck with her until her death in 1896, at the age of sixty-nine. In 1854, Chief Seattle prophesied: "When the memory of my tribe shall become a myth among white men, when your children think themselves alone in the field, the store, the shop—they will not be alone. When you think your streets deserted, they will throng with the returning hosts that once filled and still love this land, for the dead are not powerless." Other ghosts have been reported here too. The phantom of a tall black youth has been observed looking out the window of the Vitium Capitale Restaurant, and strange footsteps have been heard by clerks at Left Bank Books. And the ghost of a three-hundred-pound woman who fell through the floor of a wooden balcony haunts the spot where she died.

(In downtown Seattle, follow First St. to the Pike Place Market on the waterfront. The center is at 1501 Pike Place Market, Seattle, WA 98101. Craft Emporium: 206-622-2219. Sound View Cafe: 206-623-5700. Left Bank Books: 206-622-0195. www.pikeplacemarket.org) **14, 101, 173**

SEATTLE CENTRAL COMMUNITY COLLEGE This building was constructed in 1907, and a few of the former inhabitants, although deceased, are still around. It originally housed Broadway High School. In 1946, the Burnley School of Professional Art moved in and occupied the building until 1986, when it became the South Annex of the Seattle Community College. Over the years, students at the prestigious art school reported encountering several specters, as well as witnessing apports, the materialization of objects from thin air. The owners of the Burnley School invited psychics to investigate. All three mediums brought into the building contacted the spirit of an eighteen-year-old boy who attended the high school in 1913. He was killed in the old third-floor gymnasium during a fight after a basketball game. One of the employees of the Community College is convinced she encountered the ghost while taking inventory in a storeroom in 1987. The staff has nicknamed the presence Burnley.

(Seattle is on I-5 at Puget Sound in western Washington. For general information on the Seattle area, contact the Puget Sound Attractions Council at 206-443-1244. The school is on the corner of Broadway and Pine in the Capitol Hill district. Seattle Central Community College, 1701 Broadway, Seattle, WA 98122. Phone: 206-587-3800. www.seattlecentral.org) **72, 101, 175, 188**

UNIVERSITY OF WASHINGTON A whole floor of the men's dormitory at this metropolitan university is haunted by the ghost of a student who committed suicide in the building in 1958.

(University of Washington, 1400 Northeast Campus Parkway, Seattle, WA 98195. Phone: 206-543-2100. www.washington.edu) **49**

WEST BEACH In 1933 the apparition of an old Indian materialized on the beach here, in front of dozens of amazed witnesses. The ghost calmly walked across the sand and disappeared into nothingness.

(The West Beach area is located along Beach Dr. Southwest in Seattle.) **49**

WHITE EAGLE CAFE AND SALOON Two ghosts haunt this place. One is named Sam, a man who committed suicide in an upstairs room in the 1930s. The other is Rose, a prostitute who lived in a room down the hall from Sam. Some say Sam killed Rose before he shot himself. In any case, Rose's loud sobbing fills the building after hours. At times, Sam's loud voice, shouting obscenities, is also heard.

(White Eagle Cafe and Saloon, Russell Ave. Northwest, Seattle, WA 98107.) **173**

SKAMANIA

BEACON ROCK TRAILER PARK Mrs. Louis Baxter was driving past this mobile home park on August 19, 1970, when she pulled off the road to check a tire low on air. On the opposite side of the road she spotted a large bigfoot creature eating something. The creature was over ten feet tall with a jutted chin, no neck, and a receding forehead. It was covered with shaggy, coconut brown hair.

(Skamania is on the Oregon border near the Beacon Rock State Park. The town is about thirty miles east of Vancouver on Highway 14. Beacon Rock Trailer Park, Skamania, WA 98648.) **139**

TACOMA

LAKE STEILACOOM This placid lake is possessed by an evil female monster known as Whe-atchee. Legends of the creature attacking people go back over a hundred years. To this day, Nisqually Indians will not fish or swim there.

(Tacoma is south of Seattle on I-5. The lake is south of town.) **173**

VANCOUVER

OFFICERS' ROW Several stately Victorian houses have been remodeled into offices here, and the renovations seem to have let loose a few ghosts. Current and former tenants of buildings along Officers' Row have reported mysterious cold spots, disembodied footsteps, invisible hands touching them, and other paranormal effects. Telephones ring when they are not plugged in, freshly brewed coffee disappears before anyone has a chance to drink it, and a fax machine inexplicably broadcasts a religious station on its speaker.

(The town of Vancouver is in extreme southwestern Washington, across the Columbia River from Portland, at the junction of I-5 and Highway 14. Officers' Row (360-693-3103) is located on Evergreen Boulevard in downtown Vancouver. Among the haunted offices are Wendermere Real Estate, Pacific Mortgage Brokers, and Grant House Art Center and Café. Phone: 360-694-5252) **72**

OLD FORT VANCOUVER Strange glowing mists that move about the parade grounds, as well as other paranormal phenomena, have been reported here for several years. In 1993, a Native American exorcism ritual was performed to calm the restless spirits. Ghostly visitors never bothered one employee, who said: "Those ghosts are no problem. We work days; they work nights."

(The Fort Vancouver National Historic Site is just east of Vancouver. Phone: 206-696-7655) **72**

YAKIMA

INDIAN RESERVATION Orange or yellow UFOs, which sometimes split apart while bouncing along the ground, have been seen here for many years. Activity was especially intense from 1972 to 1974, when many objects were reported by campers and fire wardens in observation towers. The UFOs are said to cause electrical failure in vehicles that come too close.

(Yakima is in south-central Washington, at the junction of 1-82 and U.S. Highway 12. The reservation is southwest of Yakima. Much of the activity has been reported near Toppenish and White Swan.) **126 (12/74, 12/81, 2/82, 6/83, 5/85, 7/95), 150**

WEST VIRGINIA

FLATWOODS

FLATWOODS MONSTER A hissing, glowing UFO left skid marks and flattened a circle of grass here on September 12, 1952. Eight witnesses from three separate families who ventured to the hilltop when they saw the object land went racing back down the hill after encountering a terrifying creature. They described it as "ten to fifteen feet tall with a bloodred face and glowing greenish-orange eyeballs." During a later investigation, additional witnesses to both the UFO and creature were discovered in the nearby town of Sutton.

(The town is in central West Virginia, off I-79 near Sutton Lake. From Charleston, take I-79 northeast sixty-seven miles. The incident took place on a ridge off U.S. Highway 19 between Flatwoods and Sutton.) **34, 53 (1/53), 72, 139**

GREENBRIAR

SHUE HOUSE The case of the Greenbriar Ghost is the only known instance where a spirit's testimony helped convict a murderer. The ghost was that of Zona Heaster Shue, who lived in the town of Greenbriar in the late 1890s with her husband, blacksmith Edward Shue. When the woman's body was found on the kitchen floor of their house on January 23, 1897, a local physician said she died of an "everlasting faint." But Zona's ghost appeared four times to her mother Mary Jane Heaster and claimed that her husband had beaten

her for having no meat for supper. Zona's mother demanded a police investigation, and the body was exhumed. An autopsy revealed her daughter had died from a crushed windpipe and broken first vertebra. Edward was arrested and sentenced to life in prison. Had the defense not brought up the subject of the mother's ghostly encounter in an effort to discredit her testimony, the words of Zona's ghost would not have been admissible. After fighting off a lynch mob, Edward was taken off to prison, where he died three years later.

(Greenbriar is located along the Greenbriar River in south-central West Virginia, off I-64 near White Sulphur Springs. A highway marker just outside town commemorates Zona's ghost. The house is now a private residence in Greenbriar. www.prairieghosts.com/shue.html) **68, 72**

HARPERS FERRY

HARPERS FERRY NATIONAL PARK The white-haired ghost of John Brown walks alongside a black dog down the street here. They stroll past the store fronts to the door of the fire engine house, where they disappear. Brown's ghost is so real that some tourists have asked him to pose for pictures. The Kansas abolitionist brought his band of followers to Harpers Ferry to capture the U.S. Army arsenal and arm the slaves. He took hostages and held them in the arsenal's fire house, but ninety marines under General Robert E. Lee broke into the building and overcame Brown and his followers. John Brown was hanged on December 2, 1859, a little over a year before the start of the Civil War. Hog Alley, also part of Harpers Ferry National Park, is haunted by one of Brown's men who was mutilated and left for the hogs. And at St. Peter's Catholic Church, the ghost of a priest disappears through a wall, and the stone steps leading into the church are haunted by the cries of a baby who was killed by a mortar shell there during the Civil War.

(Harpers Ferry National Park is located in Harpers Ferry at the far-eastern tip of West Virginia. The site is located off U.S. Highway 340, near the confluence of the Potomac and Shenandoah Rivers. Harper's Ferry National Park, P.O. Box 65, Harper's Ferry, WV 25425. For information on private ghost tours of the park, call 304-535-6298. www.nps.gov/hafe) **72, 162, 163, 229**

MIDDLEWAY

LIVINGSTON WIZARD A notorious poltergeist plagued this rural community for many months in the late eighteenth century. The mysterious presence came to be known as the Wizard. The events started in 1797 at the Adam Livingston home, when burning logs jumped from the fireplace. The next day an invisible rope barred carriages from passing on the road in front of their house, until the rope was "cut" with a knife. Then the incessant sound of clipping scissors was heard inside the house, an invisible shears cut holes in all their clothes and linens. Hundreds of curious people descended on the town, which soon came to be known as Cliptown, or Wizard Clip. The Livingstons were convinced the Wizard was the ghost of a young man who had sought shelter in their house after his wagon threw a wheel. The fellow woke in the middle of the night and asked the family to fetch a priest, because he was dying. They refused, thinking the man was delirious. The next morning they found the stranger's lifeless body. After a priest consecrated the man's grave behind their house, the Wizard stopped his harassment. But sometimes, on autumn nights, the specter of a man wearing a black cape is seen disappearing into the Catholic Chapel on the old Livingston property. Tourists visiting the site have reported camera straps, purses, clothing, and other items mysteriously cut to pieces.

(Middleway is a tiny community in Berkeley County in the extreme eastern tip of West Virginia. The old Livingston farm was along the Opequon River, half a mile west of the old Baltimore-Kentucky Trail, now U.S. Highway 11, which runs through the center of Middleway. A thirty-four-acre parcel of land, part of the Livingston farm, was deeded to the Catholic Church in appreciation for getting rid of the demon. In 1978, the Priest Field Pastoral Center was established. www.prairieghosts.com/wizard.html) **5, 166, 172, 175, 201**

MOOREFIELD

COLE MOUNTAIN The orange-red light seen on Cole Mountain has mystified people since the middle of the nineteenth century. The ball of light bobs up and down over the mountainside. No one has gotten close to the luminous ball, and most sightings take place from the road at the base of the mountain. Legend says the light is from the lantern of an old slave who worked on the Charles Jones plantation. The loyal slave disappeared on the side of the mountain during a racoon hunt and was never seen again. Nobody accused the slave of escaping. Most thought he just got lost in the woods.

(Moorefield is located at the junction of Highway 55 and U.S. Highway 220 in the eastern tip of West Virginia. Cole Mountain is located south of town. The best viewing area is from Highway 55.) **132**

PETERSBURG

VAN METER'S FARM The headless phantom of George Van Meter searches the ruins of his farm for the missing part of his body. George was decapitated during an Indian attack in the early 1800s. His mutilated body was buried on the property, but his head was not discovered until several days after the funeral. The Indians had hidden their trophy in a large cooking pot outside the local meeting house.

(Petersburg is in the eastern part of West Virginia, at the junction of Highway 42 and U.S. Highway 220. Van Meter's Farm is in Dorcas Hollow, five miles south of town on Highway 28. Two chimneys sticking out of the ruins of the farmhouse can be seen from U.S. Highway 220. www.prairieghosts.com/vmeter.html) **132**

POINT PLEASANT

MOTHMAN The haunting of Point Pleasant is one of the strangest cases in the history of Fortean phenomena. For thirteen months from 1966 to 1967, this town was haunted by a bizarre creature known as Mothman.

The fuzzy monster had blazing red eyes, huge batlike wings, and the arms and legs of a man. Thousands of people saw the creature, as well as other demonic beings. Homes were plagued with ghostly manifestations, while mysterious UFOs traveled silently through skies. One of the UFOs pursued a Red Cross bloodmobile filled with fresh blood for several miles along a darkened highway. Automobiles stalled and electronic appliances ran amok. Researcher John Keel spent a year at the site and concluded that the Mothman sightings and the collapse of the seven-hundred-foot high Silver Bridge at Point Pleasant were connected to a race of "ultraterrestrials," who would do anything—even kill—to remain anonymous. Scores of people were injured, and thirty-eight died in the December 15, 1967, disaster. See Washington, Texas. The movie *The Mothman Prophecies* (2002) was based on this incident.

(Point Pleasant is on the Ohio River in northwest Mason County. From Charleston, follow Highway 35 north sixty miles. www.prairieghosts.com/moth.html) **34, 53 (11/92), 72, 103, 104**

TALCOTT

BIG BEND TUNNEL The ghost of a dead laborer haunts this traffic tunnel. Big John Henry died from a stroke after an exhausting contest with a machine. In 1870, the two-hundred-pound black man took on a Burleigh steam-powered drill to see who could drill more holes. Big John won but paid with his life. The sound of his hammering is still heard in the tunnel.

(The mile-long tunnel cuts through Big Bend Mountain in Summers County near Talcott, which is on Highway 12. The area is located approximately eleven miles east of Hinton in the southern part of the state.) **166**

WISCONSIN

AMERY

LUTHERAN CHURCH This old Norwegian church dates from 1870, and many parishioners believe it is haunted. Hushed voices are traced to the inside of walls, conversations are heard coming from the empty pews, and the church bell has a way of ringing when no one is around. The bell ringing started in June 1981, when Reverend Elizabeth Robinson heard the bell from the parsonage across the street. She found no one in the church when she investigated. Since then, the bell has rung by itself on several occasions. Some investigators have suggested that a phantom congregation from long ago has returned to this simple country church.

(Amery is in Polk County in the northwestern corner of Wisconsin, at the junction of Highway 46 and County Road J. The church is on a hill, a few miles outside of the town.) **176**

AZTALAN STATE PARK

AZTALAN STATE PARK AND MUSEUM This place has been called one of the most spiritually charged sacred centers in the world. The site consists of three earthen pyramids, burial grounds, a crematorium, and other earthworks that date from A.D. 1000. The city was built by the mysterious Temple Mound Builders and was probably home to over three thousand people. Two opposing religious factions, those who worshiped lunar energies and those who worshiped solar energies, engaged in a continuing battle here for two centuries. The male-dominated sun worshipers prevailed, and the site became desecrated with the bodies of human sacrifices to the sun and scenes of ritual cannibalism. Today, the area seems charged with a powerful sexual energy. Many couples have been wed on the Pyramid of the Sun, which has also been the scene of animal sacrifices by modern satanists. The bodies of seven shamans have been found at the Pyramid of the Moon, which is said to exude a seductive female energy. Nearby Rock Lake conceals an underwater necropolis of pyramid-shaped burial chambers that is still being excavated.

The Pyramid of the Sun is a sacred site charged with sexual energy. See Aztalan State Park and Museum, Aztalan State Park and Museum, Aztalan State Park, Wisconsin (HEATH TORSTVEIT)

According to Indian legends, the lake is a sacred vortex of psychic energy in which time itself is bent. Many unpleasant paranormal experiences have been reported by sensitive individuals in boats about five hundred feet off-shore.

(The site is 50 miles due west of Milwaukee. Follow I-94 to the Lake Mills south exit. Aztalan Mound Park is three miles east of Lake Mills on County Rd. Q. For information, contact Aztalan Mound Park, 2405 Door Creek Road, Stoughton, WI 53589. Phone: 608-873-9695.) **32, 53 (10/89, 10/91, 7/94), 98, 99, 144**

DELAFIELD

ST. JOHN'S MILITARY ACADEMY A fourteen-room house near this campus is haunted by a presence from another house that stood on the same spot. The current building was the home of Dr. Sidney Thomas Smythe, one of the presidents of St. John's Military Academy. He called it Rosslyne Manse, after his uncle's home in Scotland. On the land where he built his mansion, there was once another house, the home of a man named Ashby, who suffered from chronic tuberculosis. In 1905, when the Smythes started seeing the pale revenant of a man in their living room, they had no idea who it was. They only knew they shared their home with a ghost.

(Delafield is sixteen miles west of Milwaukee on I-94. The dilapidated mansion was deliberately burned down by firemen in October 1981. The haunted area is now part of the parade field of the military academy, St. John's Military Academy, 1101 N. Genesee St., Delafield, WI 53018. Phone: 414-646-3311. www.sjnma. org) **176**

EAGLE RIVER

DOG MEADOW LIGHTS A strange light here, described as a "golden bull's-eye" or "moving train headlight," has been reported since 1966. The light usually appears on the northwest horizon and moves northeast. Sometimes it changes color from white to red; at other times it divides into a two smaller lights. Investigators have yet to find an explanation for the phenomenon.

(The town of Eagle River is in Vilas County in extreme northern Wisconsin, at the junction of U.S. Highway 45 and Highway 70. The site is five miles north of Waters-meet, Michigan, thirty miles north of Eagle River. The lights are seen in Dog Meadow, a marshy area off Military Rd., and along the Robbins Pond Rd.) **66 (10/85), 177**

ELMWOOD

BLACK BEAR INN Guests staying at this inn find themselves at the heart of the nation's dairyland, and also smack in the middle of the self-declared "UFO Capital of the World." So many UFO sightings have taken place here in recent years that residents have seriously considered building a flying saucer landing strip. It is common for guests at the inn to share stories of their evening sightings over breakfast the next morning. One famous case involved Elmwood police officer George Wheeler, who was knocked unconscious when a blue beam from a UFO hit his squad car in 1976. The thirty-year police veteran said the experience "made a believer out of me."

(Elmwood is in northwestern Wisconsin, fifty miles west of Eau Claire. Take I-94 west to Highway 25 south and turn west on Highway 72. Black Bear Inn 109 N. Main St., Elmwood, WI 54740. Phone: 715-639-5646.) **72, 126 (4/91)**

EVANSVILLE

EAST SIDE STEAK HOUSE For many years, this former boarding house, constructed in 1834, was haunted by phantom footsteps marching up and down the hallways. Some say the ghost was a man who strangled his young mistress in one of the rooms. He died trying to escape, when he fell under the wheels of a passing train.

(Evansville is in Rock County, sixteen miles northwest of Janesville at the junction of U.S. Highway 14 and Highway 213. East Side Steak House, Evansville, WI 53536.) **101, 177**

GREEN BAY

GREEN BAY HARBOR The phantom ship *Griffin* lurks in the fog off this pleasant lakeside community. The ship belonged to Robert Cavelier de La Salle, the famous French explorer. At the time it was the largest vessel to sail the Great Lakes, and Indians believed the sixty-foot-long ship was an affront to the Great Spirit.

Metiomek, an Iroquois prophet, placed a curse on the *Griffin*. On August 7, 1679, La Salle docked the ship on Washington Island in Green Bay Harbor and embarked on a canoe trip down the St. Joseph River to search for a water link to the Mississippi River. His ship headed back to Niagara without him on September 18 and was never seen again, except as a ghostly outline in the fog. Legend says the *Griffin* "sailed through a crack in the ice," fulfilling the Indian curse.

(The town of Green Bay is in northeast Wisconsin, at the junction of I-43 and U.S. Highway 41. The ghost ship sailed from Detroit Harbor on Washington Island, off Door Peninsula on the northeastern tip of Wisconsin.) **5, 42, 44, 68, 161, 176**

HUDSON

PASCHAL ALDICH HOME The ghost of Dr. Paschal Aldich haunts the home he built in 1840. After he died in October 1860, neighbors often reported his ghost wandering the house at night, as if he were keeping watch over his family.

(Hudson is a small town at the confluence of the Mississippi and St. Croix rivers, just east of St. Paul, Minnesota. The house is a private residence on Coulee Rd., just off I-94.) **177**

LA CROSSE

BODEGA BREW PUB The ghost of a former pool-room owner haunts this building. Paul Malin operated the Malin Pool and Sample Room in the 1890s. After his death in 1901, his ghost started to appear regularly to new owners. No one knew why the building changed hands so many times in the five years after Malin died, but the truth surfaced in 1907, when A. J. "Skimmer" Hine, a popular German immigrant, confided to friends that he was giving up his Union Saloon in the building because it was haunted by Malin's ghost. Hine said the ghost appeared to him each night and kept him from sleeping, by running amok and making strange noises.

(La Crosse is on the Mississippi River in southwest Wisconsin at the junction of U.S. Highway 53 and I-90. A man named George Ritter purchased the Union Saloon from Hine, but he also could not make a go of it. The saloon was later replaced by the Bodega Restaurant. Currently it is known as the Bodega Brew Pub. The two-story

brick building is at South 4th St., La Crosse, WI 54601. Phone: 608-782-0677.) **45**

FIRST EVANGELICAL LUTHERAN CHURCH John Barlow came to this area in 1848 and bought a tract of land now bounded by West Avenue from Market Street to State Street. The haughty Englishman made a poor farmer, and before long his holdings were reduced to a small tract of land on what is now the southwest corner of Cameron and West avenues. Then Barlow's father died in England, and a few months later a messenger arrived from England with ten thousand pounds in inheritance. Just one week later, the bludgeoned bodies of John Barlow and the messenger were found in his modest hut. The money was never found. Later tenants reported seeing the specter of John Barlow walking the property. As the city grew, people reported the ghost walking down Cameron Avenue at around 10:00 P.M. The apparition would cross the street at the corner of West Avenue and make a series of odd-sounding noises before disappearing into oblivion. For fifty years the sightings continued. Groups were formed in an attempt to catch the ghost but none succeeded. Finally, in 1905, after a cornerstone was laid in a new church on the haunted corner, the ghost of John Barlow gave up his strange ritual.

(First Evangelical Lutheran Church, 400 West Ave. S, La Crosse, WI 54601. Phone: 608-784-3867.) **45**

HYDRITE CHEMICAL COMPANY At the old factory building that used to occupy this property, a strange and powerful poltergeist terrorized employees for several years at the turn of the century. The approach of the wrathful spirit was signaled by the sound of a great wind far off in the distance. The sound would grow deafening and suddenly abate, leaving the unseen presence behind. Witnesses heard a wild laugh, and next, objects started flying through the air in a supernatural frenzy. Usually, the presence was heard moving through a wall where there was once a door and up a stairway to an abandoned area above the offices, where an employee was said to have committed suicide in the 1890s. The poltergeist spirit was witnessed by several watchmen, employees, and managers at the site. Three different companies who set up operations in the building experienced poltergeist activity. In 1903, plant owner George Pierce died mysteriously while sleeping overnight in his office. The activity ceased only when the building was razed and a new factory built on the site.

(The original building was occupied by the George Pierce Sash and Door Factory, the Packer's Package Company, and the Vought-Berger Plant. The property is currently occupied by the Hydrite Chemical Company, 701 Summer St., La Crosse, WI 54603. Phone: 608-784-0024.) **45**

OLD HOLMBO RESIDENCE On August 1, 1904, Nicolai Holmbo committed suicide by hanging himself in the front room of his house. The house sat deserted for many years afterward—except for Nicolai's ghost. Many evenings, neighbors reported seeing a blinding flash of light come from the front of the old Holmbo residence. Afterward a white apparition could be seen just behind the windows. Mournful cries were heard as the specter swung its arms wildly and made grotesque gestures. Though police were called several times, the white light and the phantom disappeared as soon as they opened the front gate. No one was ever found inside the house.

(The address of the Holmbo home was 1419 Logan St. in the 1900s. In 1930, it was changed to 1319 Logan St. The house, which still stands, is a private residence.) **45**

LAND O'LAKES

SUMMERWIND Wisconsin's most famous haunted house was built in 1916 by Robert Lamont, who later became secretary of commerce under President Hoover. It is said that Lamont once fired two shots at a ghost that appeared in his kitchen. The house had many owners over the years, but only a few realized they were living with ghosts. Arnold and Ginger Hinshaw and their six children moved into the house in 1970. Within a few days of unpacking, they realized the house was possessed by spirits. Shadows moved through the house, mumbling voices were heard, and the apparition of a woman was frequently seen floating through the French doors into the parlor. Other strange things went on in the house. Windows opened by themselves, appliances failed for no reason, and eerie noises echoed through the house at night. Then, while remodeling a closet, the couple found the mummified remains of a human corpse. Their supernatural house soon became too much for the Hinshaws. Arnold started hinting that he was possessed by demons and finally had a nervous breakdown. Ginger attempted sui-

cide. Ginger's father Raymond Bober asked her and the children to come live with him in Granton. He bought the house and started remodeling it into a restaurant. During renovations, Bober encountered the ghost of Jonathan Carver, an eighteenth-century explorer. The ghost told Bober that it did not want anyone living on his property. According to the phantom, the Sioux Indians had deeded him the northern third of Wisconsin when he negotiated a peace between two tribes. The deed was in a black box sealed under the foundation of Summerwind. The box was never found, and Bober never completed renovations, because contractors refused to work at the haunted house. The house was abandoned in the early 1980s and soon fell into ruin. After three investors bought the twenty-room mansion in 1986, it was struck by lightning and burned down in June 1988. Only the foundation and two thirty-foot-high stone chimneys remain.

(Land O'Lakes is northeastern Wisconsin on U.S. Highway 45 at the Michigan border. Summerwind is on private property overlooking West Bay Lake in Vilas County, ten miles west of Land O'Lakes. Take Highway M north out of Boulder Junction. The stone ruins of Summerwind lie abandoned, except for the ghosts.) **72, 79, 102, 176**

LIZARD MOUND

LIZARD MOUND COUNTY PARK This sacred site glorifies the spirits of nature. It contains thirty-one animal-effigy mounds, many used as graves by prehistoric Indians. The dead were buried under the vital organs or wings of the animals depicted by the four-foot-tall mounds. The animals probably represented the vision-quest spirit or personal totem of the person buried there. The area was suddenly abandoned in A.D. 1310 for unknown reasons.

(West Bend is thirty miles northwest of Milwaukee on U.S. 45. The park is located in Washington County on County Road A, four miles northeast of West Bend, off Highway 144. For information, contact the Washington County Land Use and Park Department, P.O. Box 1986, West Bend, WI 53095. Phone: 262-335-4445. www.co.washington.wi.us/landuse/lizard%20mound.html) **99, 144**

MADELINE ISLAND

INDIAN BURIAL GROUND During a famine here, Chippewa Indians are said to have sacrificed young girls and children and ate their flesh. After awhile, the Chippewa realized that the island was haunted by the spirits of those murdered young people and abandoned their settlement, never to return. But the ghosts still linger near the sacrificial altar at the Indian Burial Ground.

(Madeline Island is the largest of the Apostle Islands group in Lake Superior, off Wisconsin's northwestern coast. The fourteen-thousand-acre island is near Ashland in Chequamegan Bay. The burial ground is near the resort lagoon at La Pointe.) **177**

MADISON

MADISON JAIL   A strange glowing ghost has terrified prisoners here since November 1873. The sightings begin with a bright light that fills the cells, then a wailing apparition appears, which can be felt as it brushes against prisoners.

(Madison is in south-central Wisconsin, at the junction of I-90 and I-94. The old jailhouse is in central Madison at 210 Martin Luther King, Jr. Blvd. Phone: 608-266-4517.) **177**

SPRING GREEN   Architect Frank Lloyd Wright built a summer estate and studio here he called Taliesin. In 1914, Wright's mistress Mamah Borthwick Cheney left her husband in Chicago and moved into Taliesin with her two children. Mamah Cheney was a headstrong woman who fired one of the servants, a man from Barbados, for some minor offense. The man took his revenge by pouring gasoline around two dining rooms where Cheney, her children, and some guests were lunching. He set the rooms ablaze and ran in with a hatchet and killed seven out of the nine people present. Firefighters took the dying victims, many of whom were badly burned, to a small cottage on the property called Tan-Y-Deri. It is there the ghost of Mamah Cheney is seen. She is usually dressed in an all-white gown and is sometimes seen washing clothes. Doors and windows in the cottage slam open and shut for no reason.

(The town of Spring Green is thirty miles west of Madison at the junction of U.S. Highway 14 and Highway 23. Taliesin is two miles south of town off Highway 23 Taliesin, 3210 County Hwy BB, Spring Green, WI 53588 Phone: 608-588-7900. www.taliesinpreservation. org. The distraught servant hanged himself in jail two months after the fire.) **72**

GOOD SAMARITAN HOSPITAL   In the early 1800s, an Indian chief placed a curse on this land after his daughter died in childbirth after getting pregnant by a white man. The chief of Squiteo-Eau-Sippi village dedicated the area to the memory of his daughter and promised that the land would never do the white man any good. His curse seemed to work. In 1886, T. B. Scott started construction on a mansion here but died the same year. His widow continued construction, but she died the next year. Every owner for the next twenty years met a violent death, and the house sat unfinished and empty most of the time. In all, seven mysterious deaths were connected with the partially completed mansion. The city of Merrill purchased the old Scott Mansion in 1919. They gave it to the Sisters of Mercy of the Holy Cross, a Swiss Catholic religious order. That seemed to break the curse, and the building was completed in 1926. Today, the property boasts a modern hospital, chapel, and school.

(Merrill is in north-central Wisconsin, sixteen miles north of Wausau on U.S. Highway 51. The hospital is next to Riverside Park in Merrill. Phone: 715-536-5511.) **72**

MILWAUKEE

GIDDINGS BOARDINGHOUSE   The famous Giddings Poltergeist case took place here. Mrs. William Giddings and her fourteen-year-old servant Mary Spiegel were baking pies on August 8, 1974, when the trouble started. A cellar trapdoor in the kitchen opened by itself, then dishes and silverware flew around the room. Chairs floated to the ceiling and food hovered in midair. The frightened women summoned two neighbors, who also witnessed the phenomena. Suddenly logs and water pails flew over the astonished neighbors' fence. People from blocks around rushed to Giddings Boardinghouse to see what was going on. News reporters soon discovered that the activity occurred only when the young servant girl was present. Mrs. Giddings fired the girl, who was severely beaten by her father. The next day, Mary attempted suicide by jumping in the river, but a bystander jumped in to save her. A prominent Chicago physician took on her case. During his investigation, he discovered that Mary suffered from sleep walking and was "neurotic." Every time the doctor took Mary back to the boardinghouse, objects started to levitate through the air.

(Milwaukee is in southeastern Wisconsin, at the junction of I-94 and I-43. The old boardinghouse is a private

residence in south Milwaukee, on the corner of Allis St. and Whitcomb Ave., Milwaukee, WI 53207.) **177**

MODJESKA THEATER This historic theater built in 1910 is now a discount movie house, but its ghost has not deserted it. In fact, some say the ghost was there before the theater was built. Called the Balcony Ghost, the smoky presence looks down from the balcony and watches the audience during movies.

(Modjeska Theater, 1124 West Mitchell St., Milwaukee, WI 53204. Phone: 414-383-9580. For recorded information, call 414-383-1880.) **72**

PFISTER HOTEL The ghost of the founder of this century-old hotel returns to make sure his guests are well taken care of. The portly, smiling figure of Charles Pfister has been seen surveying the lobby from the grand staircase, strolling in the Minstrel's Gallery above the ballroom, and in a storage area on the ninth floor. Witnesses identify the apparition from a portrait of him in the lobby, Pfister's passionate collecting created the world's largest hotel collection of Victorian art.

(Pfister Hotel, 424 East Wisconsin Ave., Milwaukee, WI 53202. Phone: 414-273-8222. For reservations, call 800-558-8222.) **73**

MINERAL POINT

RIDGEWAY PHANTOM A shape-shifting phantom terrorized this area in the middle of the nineteenth century. Named for the old crossroads town of Ridgeway, the ghost took the form of a headless man, an old woman, a young woman, a ball of fire, and any number of animals, including dogs, pigs, and horses. The phantom would pop out of nowhere to attack travelers, then disappear before they knew what happened. Panic gripped the area for over a quarter-century. Armed escorts accompanied travelers along Ridge Road, and nobody dared go out alone at night. Researchers have traced the origin of the Ridgeway Phantom to the murder of two teenage brothers, ages fourteen and fifteen, at McKillip's Saloon in 1840. A group of rowdies tossed one lad into the fireplace, where he burned to death in agonizing torment. The other boy froze to death trying to escape from the town. From those deaths by fire and ice arose the Ridgeway Phantom. During the same period, strange specters also haunted the Messerschmidt Hotel, McKillip's Saloon, Sampson's Saloon,

the Catholic Church, the cemetery, and dozens of private homes. Some say the Ridgeway Phantom departed when the town burned to the ground in 1910, but others believe he is still out there, waiting in the woods near Mineral Point. The well-documented case is one of the scariest on record.

(Mineral point is in Iowa County in the southwestern corner of Wisconsin, at the junction of U.S. Highway 151 and Highway 23. The phantom was seen along Ridge Rd. between Mineral Point and Blue Mounds. The city of Mineral Point puts on an annual Ghost Days celebration.) **177**

This log inn is haunted by a murderer who was hanged in the front yard. See Walker-Grundy House, Mineral Point, Wisconsin (HEATH TORSTVEIT)

WALKER-GRUNDY HOUSE This log inn, built in 1836, is haunted by a murderer who was hanged in front of it. On November 1, 1842, William Caffee was hanged from a scaffold erected in the yard of the inn. Before a crowd of four thousand people, the contemptuous man rode atop his own coffin and, using two beer bottles, drummed a funeral march on the sides of the casket. Afterward, his cantankerous spirit took up residence in Walker House, and over 150 years later his ghost still walks the halls. Employees and guests complain of the scary sounds of heavy breathing, footsteps on the second floor, and a presence that turns doorknobs but never opens doors. Scary voices and poltergeist activity frequently occur in the main dining room and kitchen. In October 1981, owner Walker Calvert saw Caffee's headless ghost sitting on a bench on the back porch. The phantom stayed visible for several minutes. That same month a waitress saw the ghost, this time with a head, walking on the second floor.

Walker-Grundy House is open to the public. It is a historical site just southwest of town. www.prairieghosts. com/walker.html) **101, 176**

OSHKOSH

GRAND OPERA HOUSE This theater and opera house, established in 1883, is haunted by a former stage manager. Percy Keene died in 1965, and his ephemeral likeness returns to look after young actors in the building. Members of the Drama Lab theater group encountered his ghost many times in the 1970s. Other ghosts might also haunt the premises. The shadowy figure of a man in nineteenth-century clothing, carrying a playbill for the 1895 production of *The Bohemian Girl,* was spotted in the dressing-room corridor. In 1985, a ghostly night watchman was seen peering out a side-street window.

(Oshkosh is on Lake Winnebago in eastern Wisconsin. It is fifteen miles south of Appleton on U.S. Highway 41. The opera house is at 100 High Ave., Oshkosh, WI 54901. Phone: 414-424-2350.) **53 (3/84), 101, 135**

PAINE ART CENTER Just as this English Tudor mansion was completed in the mid-1930s, a ghost moved in. Moaning sounds and unexplained footsteps were heard; old journals were disturbed and furniture moved in the attic. The manor house was begun in 1927 by lumber king Nathan Paine, and it is thought that the ghost is either his grandfather Edward or his father George.

(Paine Art Center, 1410 Algoma Blvd., Oshgosh, WI 54901. Phone: 920-235-6903. www.paineartcenter.com) **101, 177**

PLOVER

OLD SHERMAN HOUSE RESTAURANT The William Sowiak family lived in this clapboard house from 1957 to 1982. They witnessed a variety of ghostly manifestations but were reluctant to talk with anyone about their experiences. In 1982, Tim and Louise Mulderink bought the 125-year-old house and decided to turn it into a restaurant. After extensive renovations, they realized they had stirred up something other than dust. Glasses began flying off the bar, exploding in front of customers. The massive front door would open and close by itself, and a mantel clock chimed thirteen times at midnight. Employees reported an invisible presence that brushed past them in the rooms. The owners did a little research and are now convinced that a man named James Pierce was their ghost. He lived in the house from 1903 to 1945 and was, incidentally, a teetotaler. The ghost finally drove the Mulderinks away. They closed their restaurant after only a few years in business.

(Plover is in Portage County in central Wisconsin, at the junction of U.S. Highways 10 and 51.) **101, 176**

POY SIPPI

DELFOSSE RESIDENCE Mrs. Florence Delfrosse was awakened in the middle of the night by a ghostly presence tugging at the quilt on her bed. "Give me my Christmas quilt!" she heard a disembodied voice insist. She struggled with the entity for over three hours before it relented. The next day, she gave the quilt to her daughter's boyfriend, who offered to take the haunted object to see what would happen if he slept with it. Around midnight, he felt a tugging at the quilt. Within a few minutes, he heard knocking at the front door and went downstairs to see who it was. When he opened the door, he encountered a faceless man, who suddenly turned away and disappeared. Mrs. Delfrosse's mother had found the quilt in an old box when she moved into the house in 1972. Nobody, except perhaps the ghost, knows to whom it once belonged.

(Poy Sippi is in Waushara County in central Wisconsin, on Highway 49 near Lake Poygan. The house is a private residence in town.) **51**

RIVER FALLS

PARKER MANSION Former tenants have told of sensing a strange presence and witnessing poltergeist phenomena in this house. Objects moved by themselves and an icy presence moved through the house. In 1972, a psychic was called in and contacted two entities. One was the original owner, Colonel Charles Parker. The other was a "negative presence," about which nothing more could be discerned.

(River Falls is in Pierce County in extreme western Wisconsin. It is located southeast of St. Paul, Minnesota, at the junction of Highway 69 and Highway 29/35. The

pink wood-frame mansion is a private residence on Maple St., River Falls, WI 54022.) **101, 177**

SUPERIOR

FAIRLAWN MANSION This forty-two-room Victorian museum is haunted by a ghost who helps visitors find their way around. She is usually mistaken for a museum guide who dresses in authentic costumes of the 1890s. Sometimes she even helps visitors find specific displays and then disappears from sight. Her presence is often presaged by a strange damp chill in the air. The ghost is thought to be a servant girl who worked for the Martin Pattison family. They moved into the home in 1891 and lived there until 1918. Pattison sponsored Scandinavian immigrants by paying their way to America. In return they agreed to work in his home for a certain length of time. Pattison was a kind man who treated his servants like members of the family. This particular servant girl is said to have been murdered by her new husband after she left Fairlawn. Perhaps she is returning to the only place where she found real happiness while alive.

(Superior is in Douglas County in extreme northwestern Wisconsin. It is directly across from Duluth, Minnesota. Fairlawn Mansion and Museum, 906 East 2nd St., Superior, WI 54880. Phone: 715-394-5712.) **72**

WAUSAU

FISCHER HOUSE During the 1970s, a modern house here was the site of considerable poltergeist activity. Harry and Jackie Fischer moved into their spilt-level home in 1972. Almost immediately, they noticed a ringing sound, like a tiny bell, that drifted through the house. Their pots and pans seemed to move by themselves, even inside the cupboards, and small objects floated in the air. In 1973, they started hearing footsteps scurrying through the halls, and later the sounds of tribal drumming filled the house. By 1975, the unbelievable activity had increased to the point that knives and straight razors were being hurled at the family. They finally decided to share their experiences with their pastor, who blessed the house. When that did not work, they sold the house to Jim and Mary Strasser. The Strassers thought the ghost stories the Fischers told them were just figments of the couple's imagination until they, too, became the targets of the unfriendly presence. One night Jim Strasser had a terrible nightmare about an old Indian wrapped in a blanket and suffocating. Investigators later discovered that the house was built directly on top of an old Indian burial ground.

(Wausau is in Marathon County in north-central Wisconsin, at the junction of U.S. Highway 51 and Highway 29. The house is a private residence in a subdivision near Wausau.) **176**

WISCONSIN DELLS

DELL HOUSE This old tavern inn was built in 1837 and burned down in 1910. But campers on the property still report the sounds of laughter, cursing, and breaking glass coming from the site where it once stood.

(The Wisconsin Dells are in central Wisconsin, fifty miles northwest of Madison, on I-90/94. Dell House stood in a sandy glen at the Narrows. Today, the ruins are covered by forest. For information, contact the chamber of commerce at 800-94-DELLS. www.dells-delton.com) **177**

WYOMING

The Bighorn Medicine Wheel is an ancient place of worship attributed by Shoshone Indians to a race of Little People over twelve thousand years ago. See Bighorn Medicine Wheel, Bighorn Mountains, Wyoming
(B. A. SCHFFENBERGER)

BIGHORN MOUNTAINS

BIGHORN MEDICINE WHEEL One of North America's most sacred places is located here, but no one knows who constructed it. The eighty-foot-diameter medicine wheel has been used as a site of worship for hundreds of years. Crow Indians say it was built "before light came." Shoshone legends say it is at least twelve thousand years old and attribute it to a race of Little People (see Pedro Mountains, Wyoming; and Pryor Mountains, Montana). The state of Wyoming calls it their most baffling unsolved mystery. The wheel is made up of hundreds of limestone slabs and boulders laid out in a circle with twenty-eight spokes, which is the number of ribs in a buffalo and the number of days in the lunar cycle. Buffalo skulls on the projecting slabs face the rising sun. Five holy cairns that once stood over six feet tall and are said to reach down to bedrock mark the center and four directions of the wheel. A sixth cairn located just outside the circle is intended for sacred ceremonies and rituals. Indians from throughout North America made the pilgrimage here, and all tribes had equal access. They fasted for vision quests and left offerings of meat and jewelry. Today the wire fence surrounding the wheel is littered with scraps of brightly colored cloth and offerings of tobacco and other personal objects that carry the prayers of the Indians who placed them there. Spirits are said to appear to those who fast for four days near the circle.

(The Bighorn Mountains are west of Sheridan in extreme north-central Wyoming. The Medicine Wheel National Historic Site, at an elevation of 9,956 feet, is thirty miles east of the town of Lovell on U.S. Highway 14A. The site is a 1.5 mile hike from the Ranger Station. For information, contact the Bighorn National Forest, 604 East Main St., Lovell, WY 82431. Phone: 307-548-6541, www.fs.fed.us/r2/bighorn) **33, 53 (5/84), 72, 122, 144, 200**

HOT SPRINGS STATE PARK Shoshone Indians believe these springs are sacred and contain supernatural healing powers. Before a battle, it was believed that the first warrior to bathe here would have the most endurance. Sometimes babies were dipped into the springs to ensure a long life, and the sick traveled to the springs seeking cures.

(The Medicine Lodge State Archeological Site is east of Hyattville, off Highway 31 in Big Horn County. Phone: 307-864-2176. http://spacr.state.wy.us/hot1.htm) **33**

BYRON

ROCKY MOUNTAIN HIGH SCHOOL This combination elementary and high school building has been haunted by an unidentified presence since 1952. Custodians, students, teachers; and even superintendents have reported strange happenings near the former library, which was located where the weight and wrestling room is today. Putrefying odors, intense cold spots, moving mists, disembodied footsteps, lights turning off and on, and appliances working even when they are not plugged in are just a few of the unexplainable events. The superintendent at the time, Harold Hopkinson, remembers hearing and feeling an invisible presence walk past him in the hall and head up the short stairway to the old library. Then he heard the door open and close. No one can remember a tragedy occurring at the school, and the manifestations remain unexplained.

(The town of Byron is in Big Horn County in extreme northern Wyoming, fourteen miles east of Powell on U.S. Alternate Highway 14. Rocky Mountain High School, 30 E. Main St., Byron, WY 82412. Phone: 307-548-2723.) **72, 129**

CASPER

RATTLESNAKE RANGE The ghost of a white stallion that once protected herds of wild mustangs by attacking cowboys trying to rope them still roams the deserted prairies here. Called White Devil by ranchers, the horse used to bite and kick anyone attempting to round up the wild horses.

(Casper is in east central Wyoming, at the junction of I-25 and U.S. Highway 20/26. The Rattlesnake Range is southwest of Casper in Natrona County.) **72, 115**

SALT CREEK OIL FIELD Ghost lights have been seen hovering over this land since 1900. The Salt Creek Light is said to be the spirit of an Irishman named O'Rourke, who used to farm here. The light is from a spectral lantern just like the one he carried late at night when he crossed his fields. The phenomenon occurs most often on cool, clear nights.

(The private oil field is thirty miles north of Casper, between Salt Creek and Dugout Creek. The lights can be viewed from the Shepperson Ranch Rd., ten miles west of the oil field.) **129**

CHEYENNE

F. E. WARREN AIR FORCE BASE In the last fifty years there have been over a hundred supernatural incidents reported here. The modern military installation was originally a cavalry outpost established in 1867, and the ghosts of those soldiers haunt the base to this day. The apparitions have been encountered in the quaint brick houses of the Officers Quarters, one of which is called Ghost House, because of the frequency of sightings there. The strictly business Security Police Building is home to a cavalryman ghost who is apt to respond with "Howdy" if you say hello to him. The building once served as the base hospital and is believed to be home to the spirit of a doctor who worked there in the 1960s. A phantom soldier can sometimes be seen standing at attention in front of the Old Russell Guardhouse, and the ghost of an Indian woman haunts the White Crow Creek, where she was raped and murdered by a group of soldiers in the 1890s.

(Cheyenne is in the southeastern corner of Wyoming, at the junction of I-80 and I-25. The base, originally called Fort D. A. Russell, is west of Cheyenne. The main gate is at the junction of I-25 and Highway 85, which is Central Avenue. Francis E. Warren Air Force Base, Cheyenne, WY 82009. Phone: 307-775-1110. www. warren.af.mil) **129**

ST. MARK'S EPISCOPAL CHURCH There is a special room in the bell tower here built for the exclusive use of a ghost. The church was built in 1868, and work on a large bell tower addition was begun in 1886. However, the two Swedish stonemasons working on the project mysteriously disappeared, and work on the tower was not continued until 1926. At that time, construction was halted several times by the appearance of a ghostly figure that frightened workers away. The pragmatic construction crews asked for permission to build an isolated room in the tower for the sole use of the ghost, so that it might be placated and leave the workers alone. The Reverend Charles Bennett agreed. The hidden room is only accessible from the basement by an eighty-five-foot spiral staircase. In 1966, one of the Swedish stonemasons confessed that his partner had fallen to his death while working on the bell tower. His friend panicked, thinking he would be accused of murder, and placed the body in an open part of the foundation. There the corpse lies to this day, encased in a four-foot-wide section of concrete. Of course, the Swede's ghost also has a private suite in the tower.

(The ghost room is surrounded by Gothic windows, just below the carillon bells. St. Mark's Episcopal Church, 19th St. and Central Ave. 1908 Central Ave., Cheyenne, WY 82001. Phone: 307-634-7709.) **129, 175**

DEVILS TOWER

DEVILS TOWER NATIONAL MONUMENT The name Devil's Tower was given to this geologic wonder by white men in 1875. It was declared America's first national monument by Teddy Roosevelt in 1906. To Native Americans, it is God's tower, a sacred site shared by all tribes. A variety of ghostly spirits are said to inhabit the top of the 865-foot column. Sioux call it "Mateo Tipi," or Lodge of the Great Bear, and say that the giant Thunderbird beats its drums from the summit. Chief Sitting Bull came here to gather supernatural power. Kiowa legends relate how the Pleiades star cluster was formed when seven young girls climbed to the top of the rock and were whisked into the heavens by superior beings. Oddly, only six of the stars in the cluster are visible to the naked eye. Perhaps the role played by the mysterious mountain in *Close Encounters of the Third Kind* (1977) was closer to fact than fiction.

(Devil's Tower is located in Crook County in the extreme northeast corner of Wyoming. Follow U.S. Highway 14 north from I-90 to Highway 24, which leads into the park. Devils Tower rises abruptly from the landscape to a height of 1,280 feet, overlooking the Belle Fourche River. For information, contact the Devil's Tower National Monument, Devil's Tower, WY 82714. Phone: 307-467-5283. www.newyoming.com/DevilsTower) **33, 144**

FORT BRIDGER

FORT BRIDGER CEMETERY The apparition of a tall, elderly man wearing a white cowboy hat first appeared here in June 1987. The ghost followed caretaker Ramon Arthur around the grounds and even seemed to help him on a few occasions. Arthur finally

recognized the man, whose widow still lived in Fort Bridger. The ghost vanished forever in May 1988, the same month the man's widow died. The caretaker believed that the lonely spirit was simply biding its time until his loved one joined him.

(Fort Bridger is in Uinta County in the extreme southwest corner of Wyoming, fifty miles west of Evanston on I-80. The cemetery is in the Fort Bridger State Historic Site south of town. Phone: 307-782-3842. http://wyoparks.state.wy.us/bridger1.htm) **129**

GREEN RIVER

SWEETWATER COUNTY LIBRARY Parapsychological phenomena have occurred in this building almost from the day it opened in 1980. Lights and electrical appliances go on and off for no reason, and unexplainable voices and strange flapping sounds reverberate through the building at night. Library director Patricia LeFaivre says her staff has seen balls of light dancing around in the closed art gallery room. At least two typewriters have been observed typing on their own, and once, a spring-steel gate at the entrance to the library started spinning wildly with no one near it. Maintenance workers have reported a ghost sitting in the Multipurpose Room late at night. One night, one of them looked directly at the ghost, and the phantom shot into the air and made a loud popping sound when it hit the ceiling. The library was built on top of a cemetery that dates from the 1860s. The graves were moved in the 1920s, but unearthed bodies started turning up on the property in the 1940s. In 1983, three more unrecorded graves were discovered during the construction of a retaining wall. In 1985, during work on the foundation, the coffin of a small child was found. How many more corpses remain hidden in the ground is anyone's guess.

(Green River is ten miles west of Rock Springs on I-80 in southwest Wyoming. The city is just north of the Flaming Gorge National Recreation Area. The glass and brick library building is downtown. Sweetwater County Library, 300 North First St. East, Green River, WY 82935. Phone: 307-875-3615.) **72, 129, 134**

GREYBULL

OLD NAZARENE CHURCH This former church, dating from the early 1900s, became one of the largest homes in Greybull. During renovations in the 1960s many ghostly phenomena manifested. The persistent sounds of organ music, often accompanied by the sounds of a crying baby, were heard throughout the building at all hours of the day and night. The owners even tore up the old stage to see if the noises were coming from under the boxed-in area. Family members felt as if they were being watched by an unseen presence, and an old wooden rocker left at the site would rock back and forth with no one sitting in it. The effects seemed to lessen as the renovations were completed.

(Greybull is in Big Horn County in north central Wyoming. The town is located at the junction of U.S. Highways 14 and 16/20. The old church is now an apartment building off Main St. in Greybull.) **129**

LAKE DE SMET

MOANING MAN Crow Indians stay away from this lake, which they believe is inhabited by an evil monster that rises from the mist. Settlers also reported seeing the slimy creature, whose presence was sensed by their dogs and horses. The creature's moaning sounds can be heard at night along the lake shore, and Moaning Man is still blamed for pulling people under the water.

(Lake De Smet is named for the first white man to settle in the area. It is located in the northeast corner of Wyoming.) **33**

LARAMIE

BARNES HOUSE This old stone house is haunted by the friendly spirit of a cavalry officer. The slender, bearded ghost appears to be about twenty-five years old and wears a dark blue uniform. Carol and Cynthia Barnes have lived with the phantom, whom they call Luther, since 1983. The house stands on the site of old Fort Sanders, a military outpost abandoned in the 1880s.

(Laramie is fifty miles west of Cheyenne on I-80. The Barnes House is a private residence, located at 808 Park St., Laramie, WY 82070.) **129**

FORT LARAMIE This fort was active from 1834 to 1890 and served as a key stopover point in America's westward expansion. Today, the preserved fort is haunted by a number of ghosts seen by visitors, watchmen, and guides at the facility. The captain's quarters, Quarters A, has been the site of many strange events, such as doors opening by themselves and eerie foot-

steps. The presence has been nicknamed George by employees. The apparition of a cavalry officer walks the halls of another building, known as Old Bedlam, and admonishes people to "Be quiet!" The sounds of heavy boots can sometimes be heard treading over the boardwalk in front of the two-story cavalry barracks, as ghostly troops answer reveille in the early morning hours.

(Fort Laramie National Historic Site is in southeast Wyoming, three miles southwest of U.S. Highway 26. It lies near the Nebraska border between the towns of Douglas and Torrington. Phone: 307-837-2221. www.nps. gov/fola/laramie.htm) **15, 129, 131**

HERONDON HOMES Wyoming's most famous ancestral ghost was encountered in houses lived in by Herondon family members. The family ghost, known as the Lady in Gray, followed descendants from England to America three hundred years ago. She is thought to be young Catherine, niece of Lord Herondon, and is said to appear to every other generation of the family. Dr. Catherine Wiegand and her family were visited by the "Herondon Heritage" when she lived in Laramie in the 1960s. Other family members in Iowa and Texas reported seeing the ghost during the same period.

(The Wiegands encountered their ghost when they lived at 816 Mitchell St., and later, at 1417 Bonneville St., Laramie, WY 82070.) **129**

OREGON TRAIL The ghost of a girl dressed in green velvet, riding a black horse, is seen at regular intervals galloping eastward on this old trail. Every seven years since the early 1800s, she has been spotted wearing a feathered hat on a black stallion, which she urges on with a jeweled whip. In 1871, a cavalry lieutenant from Fort Laramie tried to chase her down, but he was never able to catch up with the phantom. Legend says she is the spirit of a fur trader's daughter, who got lost on horseback in the area in 1790. Despite the warnings of her father, the headstrong girl went galloping out of the stockade to explore the countryside. The army bought the fur trading outpost in the 1840s. Since then, homesteaders, soldiers, cowboys, and Oglala Indians have all reported seeing the girl's apparition.

(The Galloping Ghost of Laramie is next scheduled to make an appearance in 2004. She usually appears

between Fort Laramie and Torrington near the old Oregon Trail, now U.S. Highway 26.) **5, 15, 131**

LOVELL

SHOSHONE BAR This sixty-year-old tavern is one of the most haunted places in Wyoming. Employees and patrons have reported a bewildering variety of strange voices, loud banging sounds, weird electrical problems, floating money, and ghostly forms. Sometimes the apparitions of former owners are seen, accompanied by sounds such as footsteps outside the office, a key being inserted into an unlocked door, or the spinning of the tumblers on the combination safe. One of the more famous ghosts here is Ted Louie, a cigarette and candy salesman who was the subject of a nationwide manhunt in the 1940s. The Shoshone Bar was where he spent his last night on earth. He had complained of feeling a little strange, and the bartender dropped him off in front of his hotel around midnight. But he never spent the night there. In fact, he was never seen again. Search parties combed the highways, prairies, and rivers for miles around, and the FBI questioned everyone in town. No trace of the man was ever found, at least not until his ghost started appearing at the bar. For some reason, people continue to sense his presence in the basement.

(Lovell is in Big Horn County in extreme north-central Wyoming; twenty-two miles east of Powell on U.S. Highway 14. Shoshone Bar, 159 East Main St., Lovell, WY 82431 Phone: 307-548-2675.) **129**

PEDRO MOUNTAIN

PEDRO MOUNTAIN MUMMY The mummified body of a seventeen-inch-tall adult was discovered sitting cross-legged in a cave here. The mummy was found on a ledge by two prospectors blasting for gold. After its discovery in 1932, the body toured with a circus sideshow but eventually was purchased by the American Museum of Natural History in New York. A respected Harvard anthropologist declared the remains to be genuine, and X-ray studies determined the little man to be about sixty-five years old at the time of his death. Unfortunately the mummy was stolen or lost in the 1960s. Some say it provided evidence of the existence of the Little People spoken of in Crow, Shoshone, and Arapaho legends. See Bighorn Mountains, Wyoming; and Pryor Mountains, Montana.

(Pedro Mountain is in central Wyoming near Pathfinder Reservoir, about sixty miles southwest of Casper, off Highway 220 www.geocities.com/TheTropics/Lagoon/1345/pedro.html) **72, 131, 139**

PLATTE RIVER

SHIP OF DEATH A phantom ship that rises out of a strange mist on the Platte River is a harbinger of death. The old sailing vessel emerges from a gigantic rolling ball of fog, with its sails and masts covered with frost. A ghostly crew is seen huddled around a corpse lying on a canvas sheet on deck. Everyone is covered with frost. Slowly the crew steps back to reveal the identity of the corpse. It is always a person known by the witness, someone who will die that same day. In 1862, trapper Leon Weber saw the form of his fiancée on the ship. In 1887, cattleman Gene Wilson saw the body of his wife laid out on the canvas. In 1903, Victor Heibe was chopping down a tree on his riverfront property when he saw the ship. On deck he saw the body of a close friend. In all cases, the person seen on the deck of the phantom ship died that same day, and all the encounters took place in late autumn.

(The Cheyenne Bureau of Psychological Research tracks the sightings. The Platte River runs from Torrington to Alcova in southeast Wyoming. Encounters with the ghost ship have occurred six miles southeast of the town of Guernsey, near the city of Casper, and at Bessemer Bend.) **15, 50, 53 (9/48)**

POWELL

NORTHWEST COMMUNITY COLLEGE Strange things have been reported in the auditorium of this college since the 1970s. Mysterious cold spots hover in the middle of the stage, and during performances an invisible presence occupies a front-row seat (third from the left in the middle section). During one rehearsal, a sinister black cloud formed over seats in the left-rear auditorium. Odd noises, objects moving by themselves, and lighting controls overridden by ghosts are just a few of the weird things that go on. Once, a student writing jokes on the blackboard in the greenroom, turned around to see the apparition of a woman smiling at him. That ghost apparently had a sense of humor.

(Powell is Park County in extreme northern Wyoming, at the junction of U.S. Alternate Highway 14 and High-

way 295. Northwest Community College, 231 W. 6th St., Powell, WY 82435. Phone: 307-754-6000. www.nwc.cc. wy.us) **129**

RAWLINS

DEAN/SUMMER HOUSE This innocent-looking duplex was the scene of a terrifying haunting in the 1970s. The families of Lois Dean and Diantha Summer first noticed odd scratching sounds coming from outside the house. When lights started going on and off randomly they had the whole house rewired, but that did not solve the problem. Both families living in the house started sensing a sinister presence at the back of the building near the garage. Once, fourteen-year-old Mike Summer was picked up and thrown five feet by the Garage Witch, as they came to call it. When Lois and Diantha cornered a dark female shape inside the garage, "something black and cold started coming out of it, like strands or ribbons." The strange tentacles grabbed Diantha and paralyzed her, until Lois pushed her free. The families tried to bless the house, which seemed to lessen the attacks, although they still felt the overpowering presence of the witch. Research uncovered some unusual facts about the house. In the early 1900s, a small church graveyard was on the property. Most of the corpses were exhumed and moved to Rawlins Cemetery, but two were unaccounted for and are presumed still buried in the area under the garage.

(Rawlins is in south-central Wyoming at the junction of I-80 and U.S. Highway 287. The two-story duplex is a private residence on Spruce St., Rawlins, WY 82301.) **129**

FERRIS MANSION The ghost of a woman is seen watering nonexistent plants here, and the ghosts of two little boys are said to while away the hours in an old playroom. The house was built by copper magnate George Ferris, but before it was completed in 1903 he was thrown from a carriage and died instantly. A worker fell from the roof to his death during construction, and in 1904, nine-year-old Cecil Ferris was playing with a loaded gun when it went off and killed him. In all, Julia Ferris lost four out of her seven children in freak accidents.

(The mansion is now a bed-and-breakfast inn. Ferris Mansion, 607 West Maple, Rawlins, WY 82301. Phone: 307-324-3961.) **129**

RAWLINS MIDDLE SCHOOL Some employees of this school believe it is haunted by a lady in white. Custodians have seen her floating near the windows in the science room, walking into the boy's locker room, and standing in a corner in the music room. A policeman investigating disturbances at the school shined his flashlight on the ghost, only to see her fade before his eyes. One janitor quit his job rather than work nights in the haunted building. Rumors suggest the area around the school was a pioneer graveyard, but no physical evidence has been found to confirm this.

(Rawlins Middle School, Rawlins, WY 82301. Phone: 307-328-9205.) **129**

SHERIDAN

SHERIDAN INN This inn is haunted by the spirit of Miss Kate Arnold, a housekeeper who lived here for sixty-five years. The inn opened in 1893 and was once owned by Buffalo Bill Cody. Miss Kate's presence is felt most strongly in her former room on the third floor, near the front downstairs windows, or in the ballroom. Sometimes, she is detected as a moving cold spot; at other times only her soft footsteps are heard. The owners have preserved her room just as she left it and interred her ashes in the wall above her favorite chair.

(The town of Sheridan is in northern Wyoming, at the junction of I-90 and U.S. Highway 14. Sheridan Inn, 856 Broadway, Sheridan, WY 82801. Phone: 307-674-5440. www.sheridaninn.com) **101, 131**

WHEATLAND

ELOXITE COMPANY This wholesale jewelry supplier was plagued by a noisy poltergeist during the 1980s. Loud banging sounds and other strange noises coming from the basement were traced to an old Indian skull the company had received from a trader in Iowa. The skull was stored in the basement after being displayed for some time in a small museum the company maintained on the premises. When objects started flying off the shelves in the basement, the owners decided to contact a mortuary in Iowa to see if they would bury the skull in the Woodland Indian burial grounds near Council Bluffs. The mortuary agreed, and in 1984 the skull was shipped to Iowa for burial. The poltergeist activity immediately halted.

(Wheatland is located in southeastern Wyoming, forty-three miles north of Cheyenne on I-25. Eloxite Company,

806 10th St., Wheatland, WY 82201. Phone: 307-322-3050.) **129**

YELLOWSTONE

Y<small>ELLOWSTONE</small> N<small>ATIONAL</small> P<small>ARK</small> Crow Indians considered the mud pots and geysers around Yellowstone Lake to be possessed by evil spirits. They heard the voices of malevolent earth energies being released from the hissing water and stayed away. The Crow believed the mountains at the head of this river to be the edge of the world. If they climbed up and looked over the mountains, they could see into the next world. When white settlers came, soldiers massacred many of the Indians and drove them back to the great canyon of the Yellowstone River. Rather than be slaughtered by the white man's rifles, a band of surviving Crow built a giant raft and floated over the Lower Falls to their death. Just as they went over the edge, the defiant band turned to face their pursuers and chanted a mournful dirge. It is said that their death chant can still be heard rising up from the mists and white foam below the falls.

The death chant of Crow Indians can be heard rising from the mists of the Lower Falls where they sailed to their doom. See Yellowstone National Park, Yellowstone, Wyoming (B. A. S<small>CHAFFENBERGER</small>)

(Yellowstone National Park is in the northwest corner of Wyoming. U.S. Highways 14 and 89/287 lead into the park. The Lower Falls on the Yellowstone River are 328 feet high. Phone: 307-344-7381. www.yellowstone.net) **33**

BIBLIOGRAPHY

Boldface numbers at the end of each entry refer to the numbered list of sources below.

1. Abelard, Commander X. *Underground Alien Bases.* New Brunswick, NJ.: Inner Light Publications, 1990.

2. Adams, Charles. *Ghost Stories of Berks County.* Reiffton, Pa.: Adams Publishing, 1982.

3. Adams, Charles, and Seibold, David. *Ghost Stories of the Lehigh Valley.* Reading, Pa.: Exeter House, 1993.

4. Alexander, John. *Ghosts: Washington's Most Famous Ghost Stories.* Washington, D.C.: Washington Books, 1975.

5. Anderson, Jean. *The Haunting of America.* Boston, Mass.: Houghton Mifflin Co., 1973.

6. Balliett, Blue. *The Ghosts of Nantuckett: 23 True Accounts.* Camden, Maine: Down East Books, 1984.

7. Bannister, Paul. *Strange Happenings.* New York, N.Y.: Grosset & Dunlap, 1978.

8. Bardens, Dennis. *Ghosts & Hauntings.* New York, N.Y.: Taplinger Publishing Co., 1968.

9. Barlow, Bernyce. Sacred Site Seminars, 1232 Jedburgh St., Glendora, Calif. 91740.

10. Bayless, Raymond. *The Enigma of the Poltergeist.* West Nyack, N.Y.: Parker Publishing, 1967.

11. Beckett, John. *World's Weirdest True Ghost Stories.* New York, N.Y.: Sterling Publishing, 1992.

12. Bell, Charles, and Miller, Harriett. *The Bell Witch of Tennessee.* Nashville, Tenn.: Charles Elder Publishing, 1972.

13. Bergheim, Laura. *Weird Wonderful America.* New York, N.Y.: Collier/MacMillan, 1988.

14. Bingham, Joan, and Riccio, Dolores. *Haunted Houses USA.* New York, N.Y.: Pocket Books, 1989.

15. ———. *More Haunted Houses.* New York, N.Y.: Pocket Books, 1991.

16. Bord, Janet, and Bord, Colin. *Unexplained Mysteries of the 20th Century.* Chicago, Ill.: Contemporary Books, 1989.

17. Boye, Alan. *Guide to the Ghosts of Lincoln.* St. Johnsbury, Vt.: Saltillo Press, 1987.

18. Bradley, Nancy, and Gaddis, Vincent. *Gold Rush Ghosts.* Garberville, Calif.: Borderland Sciences, 1990.

19. Broman, Mickey. *Nevada Ghost Town Trails.* Pico Rivera, Calif.: Gem Guides Book Co., 1984.

20. Brookesmith, Peter, ed. *Great Hauntings.* London, England. MacDonald & Co., 1988.

21. Campbell, Glenn. *Area 51 Viewer's Guide.* Viewers Guides Series, HCR Box 38, Rachel, NV 89001, 1994.

22. Carlson, Bruce, *Ghosts of Des Moines County, Iowa.* Fort Madison, Iowa: Quixote Press, 1986.

23. ———. *Ghosts of the Iowa Great Lakes.* Sioux City, Iowa: Quixote Press, 1989.

24. ———. *Ghosts of the Mississippi River: Dubuque to Keokuk.* Fort Madison, Iowa: Quixote Press, 1988.

25. ———. *Ghosts of the Mississippi River: Keokuk to St. Louis.* Fort Madison, Iowa: Quixote Press, 1988.

26. ———. *Ghosts of Rock Island County, Illinois.* Fort Madison, Iowa: Quixote Press, 1987.

27. ———. *Ghosts of Scott County, Iowa.* Fort Madison, Iowa: Quixote Press, 1987.

28. Carlson, Bruce, and Erickson, Lori. *Ghosts of Johnson County, Iowa.* Fort Madison, Iowa: Quixote Press, 1987.

29. ———. *Ghosts of Linn County, Iowa.* Fort Madison, Iowa: Quixote Press, 1987.

30. Carter, William. *Ghost Towns of the West.* Menlo Park, Calif.: Lane Publishing, 1981.

31. Cavendish, Richard. *World of Ghosts & the Supernatural.* New York, N.Y.: Facts on File, 1994.

32. Childress, David H. *Lost Cities of North & Central America.* Stelle, Ill.: Adventures Unlimited Press, 1992.

33. Clark, Ella. *Indian Legends from the Northern Rockies*. Norman, Okla.: University of Oklahoma Press, 1966.

34. Clark, Jerome. *Unexplained!* Detroit, Mich.: Visible Ink, 1993.

35. Clifton, Chas. *Ghost Stories of Cripple Creek*. Colorado Springs, Colo.: Little London Press, 1993. (Pamphlet.)

36. Clyne, Patricia Edwards. *Ghostly Animals of America*. New York, N.Y.: Dodd, Mead & Co., 1977.

37. Cohen, Daniel. *The Encyclopedia of Ghosts*. New York, N.Y.: Dorset Press, 1984.

38. ———. *Ghostly Tales of Love & Revenge*. New York, N.Y.: G. P. Putnam's Sons, 1992.

39. ———. *The Ghosts of War*. New York, N.Y.: G. P. Putnam's Sons, 1990.

40. ———. *In Search of Ghosts*. New York, N.Y.: Dodd, Mead & Co., 1972.

41. ———. *Phone Call from a Ghost: Tales from Modern America*. New York, N.Y.: G. P. Putnam's Sons, 1989.

42. ———. *The World's Most Famous Ghosts*. New York, N.Y.: Dodd, Mead & Co., 1980.

43. ———. *Young Ghosts*. New York, N.Y.: E. P. Dutton, 1978.

44. Colombo, John. *Mysterious Canada*. Toronto, Canada: Doubleday Ltd., 1988.

45. Connell, Douglas. *True Tales of La Crosse*. La Crosse History Works, POB 2372, La Crosse, WI 54602, 1994.

46. Curran, D. F. *True Hauntings in Montana*. Curran Productions, POB 7067, Missoula, MT 59807, 1986. (Pamphlet.)

47. Curran, Robert. *The Haunted: One Family's Nightmare*. New York, N.Y.: St. Martin's Press, 1988.

48. Daniels, Jonathan. *The Devil's Backbone: The Story of the Natchez Trace*. New York, N.Y.: McGraw-Hill Book Co., 1962.

49. Downer, Deborah. *Classic American Ghost Stories*. Little Rock, Ark.: August House, 1991.

50. Eberhart, George M. *A Geo-Bibliography of Anomalies*. Westport, Conn.: Greenwood Press, 1980.

51. Eldin, Peter. *Amazing Ghosts & Other Mysteries*. New York, N.Y.: Sterling Publishing Co., 1988.

52. Erickson, Lori. *Ghosts of the Amana Colonies*. Fort Madison, Iowa: Quixote Press, 1988.

53. *Fate*. Llewellyn Worldwide, 84 South Wabasha, St. Paul, MN 55107. Carl Llewellyn Weschcke, publisher.

54. Florin, Lambert. *Western Ghost Towns*. Seattle, Wash.: Superior Publishing, 1961.

55. Floyd, E. Randall. *Ghost Lights & Other Encounters*. Little Rock, Ark.: August House, 1993.

56. ———. *Great American Mysteries*. Little Rock, Ark.: August House, 1990.

57. ———. *Great Southern Mysteries*. Little Rock, Ark.: August House, 1989.

58. ———. *More Great Southern Mysteries*. Little Rock, Ark.: August House, 1990.

59. Fowler, Zinita. *Ghost Stories of Old Texas*. Austin, Tex.: Eakin Press, 1983.

60. Fuller, Elizabeth. *My Search for the Ghost of Flight 401*. New York, N.Y.: Berkley Books, 1978.

61. Fuller, John. *Incident at Exeter*. New York, N.Y.: Berkley Publishing, 1974.

62. Gaddis, Vincent. *American Indian Myths & Legends*. New York, N.Y.: Indian Head Books, 1992.

63. Gallagher, Trish. *Ghosts & Haunted Houses of Maryland*. Centreville, Md.: Tidewater Publishers, 1988.

64. Garcez, Antonio. *Adobe Angels: The Ghosts of Albuquerque*. Santa Fe, N. Mex.: Red Rabbit Press, 1994.

65. ———. *Adobe Angels: The Ghosts of Santa Fe*. Santa Fe, N. Mex.: Red Rabbit Press, 1993.

66. *Ghost Trackers Newsletter*. Ghost Research Society, POB 205, Oaklawn, IL 60454.

67. *Ghosts of Washington, D.C.* International Fortean Society, POB 367, Arlington, VA 23185. (Pamphlet.)

68. Guiley, Rosemary. *The Encyclopedia of Ghosts & Spirits*. New York, N.Y.: Facts On File, 1992.

69. Haining, Peter. *A Dictionary of Ghosts*. New York, N.Y.: Dorset Press, 1993.

70. Harden, John. *The Devil's Tramping Ground*. Chapel Hill, N.C.: University of North Carolina Press, 1980.

71. Hart, Herbert. *Tour Guide to Old Western Forts*. Boulder, Colo.: Pruett Publishing Co., 1980.

72. Hauck, Dennis William. Personal investigations, files, and correspondence with author.

73. *Haunting Visits to Historic Hotels*. Washington, D.C.: National Trust for Historic Preservation, 1994.

74. Hein, Ruth. *Ghostly Tales of Minnesota*. Cambridge, Minn.: Adventure Publications, 1992.

75. ———. *Ghostly Tales of Southwest Minnesota*. Fort Madison, Iowa: Quixote Press, 1989.

76. Hein, Ruth, and Hinsenbrock, Vicky. *Ghostly Tales of Northeast Iowa*. Fort Madison, Iowa: Quixote Press, 1988.

77. Helm, Mike. *Oregon's Ghosts & Monsters*. Eugene, Oreg.: Rainy Day Press, 1983.

78. Hoffman, Elizabeth. *Here a Ghost, There a Ghost*. New York, N.Y.: Simon & Schuster, 1978.

79. Hollatz, Tom. *Campfire Ghost Stories*. Wautoma, Wis.: Angel Press, 1990.

80. Holzer, Hans. *Best True Ghost Stories*. Englewood Cliffs, N.J.: Prentice-Hall, 1983.

81. ———. *Elvis Speaks from the Beyond & Other Celebrity Ghost Stories*. New York, N.Y.: Dorset Press, 1993.

82. ———. *Ghosts I've Met*. Indianapolis, Ind.: Bobbs-Merrill Co., 1965.

83. ———. *Ghosts of the Golden West*. New York, New York: Ace Books, 1968.

84. ———. *The Ghosts That Haunt Washington*. Garden City, N.Y.: Doubleday & Co., 1971.

85. ———. *Gothic Ghosts*. New York, N.Y.: Bobbs-Merrill Co., 1970.

86. ———. *Great American Ghost Stories*. New York, N.Y.: Dorset Press, 1990.

87. ———. *Haunted America*. New York, N.Y.: Barnes & Noble Books, 1993.

88. ———. *Haunted Hollywood*. Indianapolis, Ind.: Bobbs-Merrill Co., 1974.

89. ———. *Haunted House Album*. New York, N.Y.: Dorset Press, 1992.

90. ———. *The Phantoms of Dixie*. Indianapolis, Ind.: Bobbs-Merrill Co., 1971.

91. ———. *Real Hauntings*. New York, N.Y.: Barnes & Noble Books, 1995.

92. ———. *Where the Ghosts Are*. West Nyack, N.Y.: Parker Publishing, 1984.

93. Hubbard, Sylvia Booth. *Ghosts! Personal Accounts of Modern Mississippi*. Brandon, Miss.: QRP Books, 1992.

94. Hugget, Richard. *Supernatural on Stage: Ghosts of the Theatre*. New York, N.Y.: Taplinger Publishing Co., 1975.

95. Hutchinson, Duane. *A Storyteller's Ghost Stories: Nebraska & Iowa*. Lincoln, Nebr.: Foundation Books, 1989.

96. Jackson, Robert. *Great Mysteries: Ghosts*. New York, N.Y.: Smithmark Publishers, 1992.

97. Jeffrey, Adi-Kent Thomas. *Ghosts in the Valley: Delaware Valley*. Hampton, Pa.: Hampton Publishing, 1971.

98. Joseph, Frank. *Atlantis in Wisconsin*. St. Paul, Minn.: Galde Press, 1995.

99. ———. *Sacred Sites: A Guidebook to Sacred Centers*. St. Paul, Minn.: Llewellyn Publications, 1992.

100. *Journal of Parapsychology*. Parapsychology Press, POB 6847, College Station, Durham, NC 27708.

101. Kaczmarek, Dale. *National Register of Haunted Places*. Ghost Research Society, POB 205, Oaklawn, IL 60454. (Pamphlet.)

102. Kaye, Marvin. *Haunted America*. New York, N.Y.: Barnes & Noble, 1990.

103. Keel, John. *The Mothman Prophecies*. New York, N.Y.: E. P. Dutton & Co., 1975. New York, N.Y.: Signet, 1976.

104. ———. *Our Haunted Planet*. Greenwich, Conn.: Fawcett Publications, 1971.

105. Kettelkamp, Larry. *Haunted Houses*. New York, N.Y.: William Morrow & Co., 1969.

106. Kimball, Joe. *Secrets of the Congdon Mansion*. Minneapolis, Minn.: Jaykay Publishing, 1985.

107. Knight, David. *Best True Ghost Stories of the 20th Century*. Englewood Cliffs, N.J.: Prentice-Hall, Inc., 1984.

108. ———. *The Moving Coffins: Hauntings Around the World*. New York, N.Y.: Prentice-Hall, Inc., 1983.

109. ———. *Poltergeists: Hauntings & the Haunted*. New York, N.Y.: J. P. Lippincott Co., 1972.

110. Krantz, Grover. *Big Footprints: A Scientific Inquiry into Sasquatch*. Boulder, Colo.: Johnson Books, 1992.

111. Kuclo, Marion. *Michigan Haunts & Hauntings*. Lansing, Mich.: Thunder Bay Press, 1992.

112. L'Aloge, Bob. *Ghosts & Mysteries of the Old West*. Las Cruces, N. Mex.: Yucca Tree Press, 1991.

113. Mackal, Roy. *Searching for Hidden Animals*. Garden City, N.Y.: Doubleday, 1980.

114. Macklin, John. *World's Strangest True Ghost Stories*. New York, N.Y.: Sterling Publishing, 1991.

115. Maple, Eric, and Myring, Lynn. *Haunted Houses, Ghosts & Spectres*. London, England: Usborne Publishing Ltd., 1979.

116. Marinacci, Mike. *Mysterious California*. Los Angeles, Calif.: Panpipes Press, 1988.

117. Martin, Margaret Rhett. *Charleston Ghosts*. Columbia, S.C.: University of South Carolina Press, 1992.

118. Martin, MaryJoy. *Twilight Dwellers: Ghosts, Ghouls, & Goblins of Colorado*. Boulder, Colo.: Pruett Co., 1985.

119. May, Antionnette. *Haunted Houses of California*. San Carlos, Calif.: Wide World Publishing, 1990.

120. McElhaney, Judy. *Ghost Stories of Woodlawn Plantation*. McLean, Va.: EPM Publications, 1992.

121. McNeil, W. K. *Ghost Stories from the American South*. Little Rock, Ark.: August House, 1985.

122. Milne, Courtney. *Sacred Places in North America*. New York, N.Y.: Stewart, Tabori, & Chang, 1994.

123. Montandon, Pat. *The Intruders*. Greenwich, Conn.: Fawcett Publications, 1976.

124. Montell, William. *Ghosts Along the Cumberland*. Knoxville, Tenn.: University of Tennessee Press, 1975.

125. Morgan, Fred. *Ghost Tales of the Uwharries*. Winston-Salem, N.C.: John F. Blair, 1968.

126. *MUFON UFO Journal*. Mutual UFO Network, 103 Oldtowne Road, Seguin, TX 78155.

127. Munn, Debra. *Big Sky Ghosts: Eerie True Tales of Montana*. Boulder, Colo.: Pruett Publishing, 1993.

128. ———. *Big Sky Ghosts: Eerie True Tales of Montana*. Vol. 2. Boulder, Colo.: Pruett Publishing, 1994.

129. ———. *Ghosts on the Range: Eerie Tales of Wyoming*. Boulder, Colo.: Pruett Publishing, 1989.

130. Murbarger, Nell. *Ghosts of the Glory Trail*. Las Vegas, Nev.: Nevada Publications, 1981.

131. Murray, Earl. *Ghosts of the Old West*. New York, N.Y.: Dorset Press, 1988.

132. Musick, Ruth A. *Coffin Hollow & Other Ghost Tales*. Lexington, Ky.: University Press, 1977.

133. Myers, Arthur. *A Ghosthunter's Guide to Haunted Public Places*. Chicago, Ill.: Contemporary Books, 1993.

134. ———. *The Ghostly Gazetteer*. Chicago, Ill.: Contemporary Books, 1990.

135. ———. *The Ghostly Register*. Chicago, Ill.: Contemporary Books, 1986.

136. ———. *Ghosts of the Rich & Famous*. Chicago, Ill.: Contemporary Books, 1988.

137. *Mysteries of Mind, Space, & Time*. 26 vols. Westport, Conn.: H. S. Stuttman, 1992.

138. *Mysteries of the Unexplained*. Pleasantville, N.Y.: Reader's Digest, 1985.

139. *Mysteries of the Unknown*. 20 vols. New York, N.Y.: Time-Life Books, 1989.

140. Nadeau, Remi. *Ghost Towns & Mining Camps of California*. Santa Barbara, Calif.: Crest Publishers, 1965.

141. Nesbitt, Mark. *The Ghosts of Gettysburg*. Gettysburg, Pa.: Thomas Publications, 1991.

142. O'Donnell, Elliott, In *Casebook of Ghosts*, edited by Harry Ludlam. Secaucus, N.J.: Castle Books, 1989.

143. Oesterreich, Traugott. *Possession & Exorcism*. New York, N.Y.: Causeway Books, 1974.

144. Peterson, Natasha. *Sacred Sites: A Traveler's Guide*. Chicago, Ill.: Contemporary Books, 1988.

145. Polonsky, Jane, and Drum, Joan. *A Galaxy of Ghosts*. Hampton, Va.: Polyndrum Publications, 1992.

146. ———. *The Ghosts of Fort Monroe*. Fort Monroe, Va.: 1972. (Pamphlet.)

147. Price, Charles E. *Haints, Witches, & Boogers: Tennessee*. Winston-Salem, N.C.: John F. Blair, 1992.

148. *Quest for the Unknown*. Pleasantville, N.Y.: Reader's Digest, 1992.

149. Randles, Jenny. *Strange & Unexplained Mysteries*. New York, N.Y.: Sterling Publishing Co., 1994.

150. ———. *UFOs and How to See Them*. New York, N.Y.: Sterling Publishing Co., 1992.

151. Reinstedt, Randall. *Ghost Notes: Haunted Monterey Peninsula*. Carmel, Calif.: Ghost Town Publications, 1991.

152. ———. *Ghostly Tales of Old Monterey*. Carmel, Calif.: Ghost Town Publications, 1991.

153. ———. *Ghosts, Bandits, & Legends of Old Monterey*. Carmel, Calif.: Ghost Town Publications, 1972.

154. ———. *Incredible Ghosts of the Big Sur Coast*. Carmel, Calif.: Ghost Town Publications, 1981.

155. ———. *Incredible Ghosts of the Hotel Del Monte*. Carmel, Calif.: Ghost Town Publications, 1981.

156. ———. *Strange Ghosts of the Stevenson House*. Carmel, Calif.: Ghost Town Publications, 1988.

157. Reynolds, James. *Gallery of Ghosts*. New York, N.Y.: Grosset & Dunlap, 1965.

158. ———. *Ghosts in American Houses*. New York, N.Y.: Bonanza Books, 1955.

159. Rhyne, Nancy. *Coastal Ghosts*. Orangeburg, S.C.: Sandlapper Publishing, 1989.

160. ———. *More Tales from the South Carolina Low Country*. Orangeburg, S.C.: Sandlapper Publishing, 1984.

161. Rider, Geri. *The Ghosts of Door County, Wisconsin*. Sioux City, Iowa: Quixote Press, 1992.

162. Roberts, Nancy. *America's Most Haunted Places*. Orangeburg, S.C.: Sandlapper Publishing Co., 1987.

163. ———. *Civil War Ghosts Stories & Legends*. Columbia, S.C.: University of South Carolina Press, 1992.

164. ———. *Ghosts & Specters of the Old South*. Orangeburg, S.C.: Sandlapper Publishing Co., 1984.

165. ———. *Ghosts of the Carolinas*. Columbia, S.C.: University of South Carolina Press, 1992.

166. ———. *Ghosts of the Southern Mountains & Appalachia*. Columbia, S.C.: University of South Carolina Press, 1993.

167. ———. *The Gold Seekers: Gold, Ghosts & Legends*. Columbia, S.C.: University of South Carolina Press, 1989.

168. ———. *Haunted Houses: Tales from 30 American Homes*. Chester, Conn.: Globe Pequot Press, 1988.

169. ———. *Illustrated Guide to Ghosts in the North State*. Asheville, N.C.: Bright Mountain Books, 1985.

170. ———. *South Carolina Ghosts: From the Coast to the Mountains*. Columbia, S.C.: University of South Carolina Press, 1984.

171. ———. *Southern Ghosts*. Orangeburg, S.C.: Sandlapper Publishing, 1979.

172. ———. *This Haunted Southland: Where Ghosts Still Roam*. Columbia, S.C.: University of South Carolina Press, 1992.

173. Salmonson, Jessica. *The Mysterious Doom: Tales of Pacific Northwest*. Seattle, Wash.: Sasquatch Books, 1992.

174. Schulte, Carol Olivieri. *Ghosts on the Coast of Maine*. Fort Madison, Iowa: Quixote Press, 1989.

175. Scott, Beth, and Norman, Michael. *Haunted America*. New York, N.Y.: Tom Doherty Associates, 1994.

176. ———. *Haunted Heartland*. New York, N.Y.: Dorset Press, 1985.

177. ———. *Haunted Wisconsin*. Minocqua, Wis.: NorthWord Inc., 1988.

178. Seibold, David, and Adams, Charles. *Cape May Ghost Stories*. Reading, Pa.: Exeter House, 1988.

179. ———. *Ghost Stories of the Delaware Coast*. Reading, Pa.: Exeter House, 1990.

180. ———. *Pocono Ghosts, Legends, & Lore*. Reading, Pa.: Exeter House, 1991.

181. Senate, Richard. *Ghosts of the Haunted Coast: California*. Ventura, Calif.: Pathfinder Publishing, 1986.

182. ———. *Haunted Ventura*. Ventura, Calif.: Charon Press, 1992.

183. Simon, Seymour. *Ghosts*. New York, N.Y.: J. B. Lippincott Co., 1976.

184. Smith, Helene, and Swetnam, George. *Guidebook to Historic Western Pennsylvania*. Pittsburgh, Pa.: University of Pittsburgh, 1991.

185. Smith, Susy. *Adventures in the Supernormal*. New York, N.Y.: Pyramid Books, 1968.

186. ———. *Ghosts Around the House*. Cleveland, Ohio: World Publishing Co., 1970.

187. ———. *Haunted Houses for the Millions*. Los Angeles, Calif.: Sherbourne Press, 1967.

188. ———. *Prominent American Ghosts*. Cleveland, Ohio: World Publishing, 1967; New York, N.Y.: Dell Books, 1969.

189. Somerlott, Roger. *Here, Mr. Splitfoot: Modern Occultism*. New York, N.Y.: Viking Press, 1972.

190. Spencer, John. *World Atlas of UFOs*. New York, N.Y.: Smithmark Publishers, 1991.

191. Stanford, Ray. *Soccoro Saucer in a Pentagon Pantry*. Austin, Tex.: Blueapple Books, 1976.

192. Starkey, Marion. *The Devil in Massachusetts: Witch Trials*. New York, N.Y.: Bantam Doubleday Dell, 1989.

193. Steiger, Brad, and Steiger, Sherry. *Hollywood & the Supernatural*. New York, N.Y.: St. Martin's Press, 1990.

194. ———. *Montezuma's Serpent*. New York, N.Y.: Paragon House, 1992.

195. Steiger, Brad. *Mysteries of Time & Space*. Englewood Cliffs, NJ.: Prentice-Hall, 1974.

196. Stern, Jane, and Stern, Michael. *Amazing America*. New York, N.Y.: Random House, 1978.

197. Stone, Margaret. *Supernatural Hawaii*. Honolulu, Hawaii: Aloha Graphics, 1979.

198. *Strange Magazine*. Strange Magazine, POB 2246, Rockville, MD 20847.

199. *Strange Stories, Amazing Facts*. Pleasantville, N.Y.: Reader's Digest, 1990.

200. Swan, James A. *Sacred Places*. Santa Fe, N. Mex.: Bear & Co., 1990.

201. Swetnam, George. *Devils, Ghosts, & Witches: Upper Ohio Valley*. Greensburg, Pa.: McDonald/Sward, 1988.

202. Syers, Ed. *Ghost Stories of Texas*. Waco, Tex.: Texian Press, 1991.

203. Szasz, Ferenc. *Great Mysteries of the West*. Boulder, Colo.: Fulcrum Publishing, 1993.

204. Tackaberry, Andrew. *Famous Ghosts, Phantoms, & Poltergeists For the Millions*. New York, N.Y.: Bell Publishing, 1967.

205. Taylor, L. B. Jr., *The Ghosts of Charlottesville & Lynchburg*. Williamsburg, Va.: Progress Printing Co., 1992.

206. ———. *The Ghosts of Fredericksburg*. Williamsburg, Va.: Progress Printing Co., 1991.

207. ———. *The Ghosts of Richmond*. Williamsburg, Va.: Progress Printing Co., 1985.

208. ———. *The Ghosts of Tidewater*. Williamsburg, Va.: Progress Printing Co., 1990.

209. ———. *The Ghosts of Williamsburg*. Williamsburg, Va.: Progress Printing Co., 1983.

210. Taylor, Troy. *Haunted Decatur*. Forsyth, Ill.: Taylor Publishing, 1995.

211. Underwood, Peter. *Ghosts & How to See Them*. London, England: Anaya Publishers, 1993.

212. Walker, Danton. *Spooks Deluxe*. New York, N.Y.: Franklin Watts Inc., 1956.

213. Walters, Ed, and Walters, Frances. *The Gulf Breeze Sightings*. New York, N.Y.: William Morrow & Co., 1990.

214. Warren, Ed, and Warren, Lorraine. *Ghost Hunters*. New York, N.Y.: St. Martin's Press, 1989.

215. ———. *Graveyard*. New York, N.Y.: St. Martin's Press, 1992.

216. ———. *In a Dark Place*. New York, N.Y.: Villard Books, 1992.

217. Webb, Richard. *Great Ghosts of the West*. Los Angeles, Calif.: Nash Publishing, 1971.

218. Weinberg, Alyce. *Spirits of Frederick*. Braddock Heights, Md.: Weinberg Publishing, 1992.

219. Welch, Tom. *Ghosts of Polk County, Iowa*. Fort Madison, Iowa: Quixote Press, 1988.

220. Whedbee, Charles. *The Flaming Ship of Ocracoke*. Winston-Salem, N.C.: John Blair, 1992.

221. William, Ben, and William, Jean. *The Black Hope Horror*. New York, N.Y.: William Morrow & Co., 1991.

222. Wilson, Colin. *Poltergeist: A Study in Destructive Haunting*. New York, N.Y.: Putnam Perigee, 1983.

223. Windham, Kathryn Tucker. *Jeffrey Introduces Thirteen More Southern Ghosts*. Tuscaloosa, Al.: University of Alabama Press, 1987.

224. ———. *Jeffrey's Latest Thirteen: More Alabama Ghosts*. Tuscaloosa, Al.: University of Alabama Press, 1987.

225. ———. *Thirteen Georgia Ghosts & Jeffrey*. Tuscaloosa, Al.: University of Alabama Press, 1987.

226. ———. *Thirteen Mississippi Ghosts & Jeffrey*. Tuscaloosa, Al.: University of Alabama Press, 1987.

227. ———. *Thirteen Tennessee Ghosts & Jeffrey*. Tuscaloosa, Al.: University of Alabama Press, 1987.

228. Windham, Kathryn Tucker, and Figh, Margaret G. *Thirteen Alabama Ghosts & Jeffrey*. Tuscaloosa, Al.: University of Alabama Press, 1987.

229. Woodyard, Chris. *Haunted Ohio*. Beavercreek, Ohio: Kestrel Publications, 1993.

230. ———. *Haunted Ohio II*. Beavercreek, Ohio: Kestrel Publications, 1992.

231. Young, Richard, and Young, Judy. *Ghost Stories from the American Southwest*. Little Rock, Ark.: August House, 1991.

232. Zaunder, Phyllis. *Lake Tahoe*. Sonoma, Calif.: Zanel Publications, 1982.

233. ———. *Virginia City: Its History, Its Ghosts*. Sonoma, Calif.: Zanel Publications, 1984.

INDEX